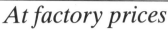

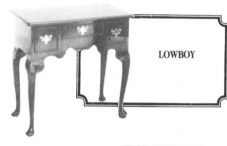

3

MILLER'S

ANTIQUES
PRICE GUIDE

1992
(Volume XIII)

Compiled and Edited by

Judith and Martin Miller

MILLERS PUBLICATIONS

MILLER'S ANTIQUES PRICE GUIDE 1992

Created and designed by
Millers Publications
Sissinghurst Court, Sissinghurst
Cranbrook, Kent TN17 2JA
Telephone: (0580) 713890

Compiled and edited by
Judith & Martin Miller

General Editor: Jo Davis
Editorial and Production Co-ordinator: Sue Boyd
Editorial Assistants: Marion Rickman, Sue Woodhouse
Production Assistants: Gillian Charles, Darren Manser
Advertising Executive: Elizabeth Smith
Advertising Assistants: Trudi Hinkley, Liz Warwick
Index compiled by: DD Editorial Services, Beccles
Design: Tim Arundel, Stephen Parry, Jody Taylor
Additional photography by Ian Booth and Robin Saker

A CIP catalogue record for this book is
available from the British Library

ISBN 0-905879-66-X

Typeset by Mainline Typesetters Ltd., St. Leonards-on-Sea
Illustrations by G.H. Graphics, St. Leonards-on-Sea
Colour origination by Scantrans, Singapore.
Printed and bound in England by William Clowes Ltd.,
Beccles and London

8

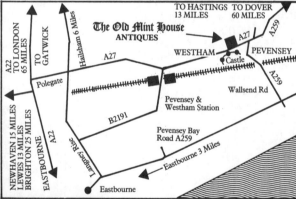

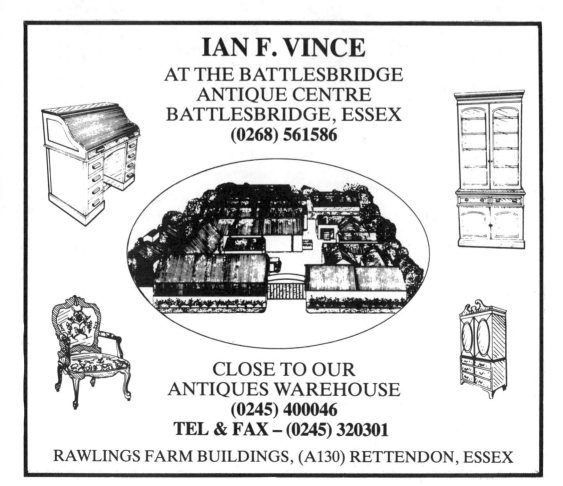

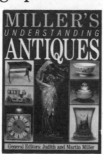

14

15

Robert Bailey
Quality Vetted Datelined Antiques Fairs
1992
SUBJECT TO CONTRACT

JAN 3–5	The Tatton Park Decorative Interiors & Antiques Fair, Knutsford, Cheshire.
FEB 5–9	The Harrogate Antiques Fair, Royal Baths, Assembly Rooms.
FEB 14–16	The Peckforton Castle Antiques Fair, Nr. Chester, Cheshire.
FEB 21–23	The Newcastle-upon-Tyne Antiques Fair, Holiday Inn Hotel.
MAR 2–7	The City of Bath Antiques Fair, The Pavilion, Bath.
MAR 11–15	The Tatton Park Antiques Fair, Knutsford, Cheshire.
MAR 20–22	The Hoghton Tower Antiques Fair, Nr. Preston, Lancashire.
MAR 25–28	The Cotswolds Antiques Fair, Pittville Pump Rooms, Cheltenham.
APR 3–5	The Petworth Antiques Fair, Seaford College, West Sussex.
APR 15–20	The Stowe School Antiques Fair, Buckinghamshire.
MAY 1–4	The Beaumanor Hall Antiques Fair, Leicestershire.
MAY 13–16	The Bath Decorative and Antiques Fair, The Pavilion, Bath.
MAY 22–25	The Harlaxton Manor Antiques Fair, Grantham, Lincolnshire.
JULY 10–12	The Tatton Park Fine Art Fair, Knutsford, Cheshire.
JULY 17-19	The Stowe School Decorative Interiors & Antiques Fair, Buckinghamshire.
JULY 24–26	The Harrogate Antiques Fair, The Granby Hotel
AUG 7–9	The Petworth Antiques Fair, Seaford College, West Sussex.
AUG 14–16	The Charterhouse Antiques Fair, Godalming, Surrey.
AUG 28–31	The Ilkley Antiques Fair, Kings Hall & Winter Gardens, West Yorkshire.
SEPT 4–6	The Hatfield House Antiques Fair, Hertfordshire.
SEPT 9–13	The Tatton Park Antiques Fair, Knutsford, Cheshire.
SEPT 23–26	The City of Bath Antiques Fair, The Pavilion, Bath.
OCT 2–4	The Harlaxton Manor Antiques Fair, Grantham, Lincolnshire.
OCT 23–25	The Lancing College Antiques Fair, Nr. Worthing, West Sussex.
OCT 28–31	The Cotswolds Antiques Fair, The Pittville Pump Rooms, Cheltenham.
NOV 6–8	The Peckforton Castle Antiques Fair, Nr. Chester, Cheshire.
NOV 13–15	The Holker Hall Antiques Fair, Nr. Grange-over-Sands, Cumbria.
NOV 20–22	The Hoghton Tower Antiques Fair, Nr. Preston, Lancashire.
NOV 25–29	The Castle Howard Antiques Fair, York.
DEC 4–6	The Ilkley Christmas Antiques Fair, Kings Hall and Wintergardens, West Yorkshire.

To confirm dates and times

please telephone

TEL: (0277) 362662

PO BOX 1110
ONGAR
ESSEX
CM5 9LU

Additional locations may be added to this list. They will be included in our new 1992 brochure.

INDEX TO ADVERTISERS

Albany Antiques 12
Alfies Antique Market 705
M Allen – Watch and Clock
    Maker 487
Anderson & Garland 771
Anthemion 273
Antique Bulletin 28
Antique Desks 353
Antiques Trade Gazette ..... Inserts
Apollo Antiques 265
A S Antiques 575
Ascent Auctions 766
Ashburton Marbles 411
Atlantic Centres 619
Bacchus Antiques 557
Robert Bailey 16
Beehive Antiques
    (Janice Paull) 53
Bell Antiques 743
Bexhill Antique Centre 8
Bexhill Antique Exporters 8
Bonhams .... Back Cover
Andrew Spencer Bottomley 759
Boulton & Cooper 770
Michael J Bowman 766
Breck Antiques 109
British Antique Exporters 3
William H Brown 769
F G Bruschweiler 7
James Buckingham 2
Roy W. Bunn 43
Burstow & Hewett 764
Gerard Campbell 485
Canterbury Auction
    Galleries 767
Chancellors 764
H C Chapman 770
Chapel House Antiques 750
Peter Cheney 762
City Clocks 433
The Clock Clinic 444
The Clock Shop 437
The Clock Shop (Samuel
    Orr) 439
The Collector (Tom Power) 585
Collins Antiques 371
Cooper Hirst 766
Coppelia Antiques 449
Crested China Company 167
Cultural Exhibitions 10, 12
Cumbria Auction Rooms 771
Cunningham Hart 4
Andrew Dando 41
Julian Dawson 765
Denhams 767
Delvin Farm Galleries 744
Dorking Desks 355
Dowell Lloyd & Co 766
Drummonds of Bramley 419
Dycheling Antiques 283
Robin Elliott
    (Chancellors) 763
Featherstone Shipping 8

For Pine 747
G A (Romsey) 763
Thos W M Gaze & Son 768
George Clocks 453
Gilding's 768
Ray & Diane Ginns 59
Gorringes Auction
    Galleries 762
Goss & Crested China 165, 169
Grays Antiques Market 705
Halifax Fine Art 764
Halifax Antiques Centre 17
Hampstead Antique
    Emporium 361
David Harriman 457
Andrew Hartley Fine Arts 770
John Hartley 385
Harwood Tate 405
Haworth Antiques 435
Giles Haywood 768
Hedleys Humpers 13
Hertford Saleroom 762
Heyford Antiques 57
Muir Hewitt 613
Robert I Heyes 770
Hobbs Parker 762
Paul Hopwell 233
Jonathan Horne 45
Valerie Howard 97
Hubbard Antiques 15
Ibbett Mosely 765
Its About Time 451
John Ives 12
Arthur Johnson & Sons 768
Desmond Judd 764
G A Key 768
Key Antiques 567
Richard Kimbell 331
Kingsbridge Auction 766
Lakeside Ltd. 798, 799
Lambert & Foster 764
Garnet Langton Auctions 766
Lawrences 762
David Lay 762
Ann Lingard 749
Lions Den 583
Lithgow Sons & Partners 771
Brian Loomes 443
Lowe of Loughborough 279
Martel Maides & Le Pelley 763
Jamie Maxtone Graham 681
May & Son 764
McBains 11
McCartneys 768
Meek Antiques Ltd 10
Miller's Antiques
    Checklists 14
Miller's Collectors Cars 23
Miller's Antiques Price
    Guides 24
Miller's Collectables 25
Geoffrey Mole 15
Morgan Evans & Co 770

Nationwide 765
D M Nesbitt & Co 764
B J Norris 763
The Old Cinema 285
The Old Clock Shop 455
Old Court Pine 748
Old Mint House 9
Jacqueline Oosthuizen 39
Oxford Antique Trading Co 17
P A Oxley 445, 495
Pantiles Spa Antiques 335
J R Parkinson Son & Hamer ... 771
Janice Paull (Beehive Antiques) 53
Phillips 631
Piano Export 669
Pieces of Time 489
Pine Finds 740
Plowden & Smith 271
Preston Antique Centre 339
Graham Price 329
Retro Products 10
Rich Designs 593
Riddetts 763
Ripley Antiques 385
Derek Roberts 463
Rochester Fine Arts 465
Roderick Antique Clocks 441
Rogers de Rin 93
Russell Baldwin & Bright 768
Scotts 63
Securikey 737
Shiners 427
Oswald Simpson 243
Allan Smith Clocks 447
Smith & Smith Designs 746
Somervale Antiques 207
Somerville Antiques 748
Spencer-Thomas & Woolland . 763
Henry Spencer & Sons 770
Storm Software 12
Strawsons 755
Sussex Auction Galleries 767
S W Antiques 749
G E Sworder & Sons 762
Christopher Sykes 555
Teddy Bears of Witney 659
Tennants 771
Thesaurus 26
Traditional Pine Furniture . 745
Utopia 747
Jacques Van der Tol BV .. 739, 741
T Vennet-Smith 733
Ian F Vince 13
Peter Wain 17
Walker Barnett & Mill 769
Islwyn Watkins 31
Thos Watson 770
Chris Watts Antiques 379
West Street Antiques 761
Philip Whyte 491
A J Williams (Shipping) 8
Peter Williams 764
Worthing Auction Galleries 767
Wright Manley 771

Acknowledgements

The publishers would like to acknowledge the great assistance given by our consultant editors:

POTTERY:	**Jonathan Horne,** *66b and c Kensington Church Street, London W8.*
	Ron Beech, *Victorian Staffordshire Figures and Pot Lids, No. 1 Brambledean Road, Portslade, Sussex BN41 1LP.*
POTTERY & PORCELAIN:	**Peter Wain,** *7 Nantwich Road, Woore, Shropshire.*
PORCELAIN:	**Nicholas Long,** *Studio Antiques, Bourton-on-the-Water, Glos.*
WORCESTER:	**Henry Sandon,** *11 Perrywood Close, Worcester.*
GOSS & CRESTED WARE:	**Nicholas Pine,** *Goss & Crested China Ltd, 62 Murray Road, Horndean, Hants.*
FURNITURE:	**John Bly,** *50 High Street, Tring, Herts. & 27 Bury Street, St. James's, London, SW1.*
	Richard Davidson, *Richard Davidson Antiques, Lombard Street, Petworth, Sussex.*
OAK:	**Victor Chinnery,** *Bennetts, Oare, Nr Marlborough, Wilts.*
LONGCASE CLOCKS:	**Brian Loomes,** *Calf Haugh, Pateley Bridge, N Yorks.*
VIENNESE REGULATORS:	**Gerard Campbell,** *Maple House, Market Place, Lechdale, Glos.*
CLOCKS:	**Derek Roberts,** *24-25 Shipbourne Road, Tonbridge, Kent.*
GLASS:	**Wing Cdr R G Thomas,** *Somervale Antiques, 6 Radstock Road, Midsomer Norton, Bath, Avon.*
ART NOUVEAU & ART DECO:	**Eric Knowles,** *Bonhams, Montpelier Galleries, Montpelier Street, Knightsbridge, London SW7.*
	Audrey Sternshine, *26 Broad Street, Salford, Manchester.*
LALIQUE:	**Russell Varney,** *Bonhams, Montpelier Galleries, Montpelier Street, Knightsbridge, London SW7.*
CARPETS & TEXTILES:	**Robert Bailey,** *P.O. Box 1110, Ongar, Essex.*
TOYS:	**Stuart Cropper,** *Grays Mews, 1-7 Davies Mews, London W1.*
ARMS & ARMOUR:	**Roy Butler,** *Wallis & Wallis, West Street Auction Galleries, Lewes, Sussex.*
PINE FURNITURE:	**Ann Lingard,** *Rope Walk Antiques, Rye, Sussex.*
JEWELLERY:	**Valerie Howkins,** *Peter Howkins, 39-40 and 135 King Street, Great Yarmouth, Norfolk.*
FISHING:	**Jamie Maxtone Graham,** *Lyne Haugh, Lyne Station, Peebles, Scotland.*
EPHEMERA	**Trevor Vennett-Smith, FRICS, FSVA, CAAV,** *11 Nottingham Road, Gotham, Nottinghamshire.*

An Egyptian bronze figure of a fish (oxyrynchus), wearing the Isis crown of cow horns surmounted by a sun disc with uraeus, c600 B.C., 4in (10cm).
£2,500-3,500 *S*

Key to Illustrations

Each illustration and descriptive caption is accompanied by a letter-code. By reference to the following list of Auctioneers (denoted by *) and Dealers (●), the source of any item may be immediately determined. In no way does this constitute or imply a contract or binding offer on the part of any of our contributors to supply or sell the goods illustrated, or similar articles, at the prices stated. Advertisers in this year's directory are denoted by †.

ABS ● Abstract, 58/60 Kensington Church Street, London, W8. Tel: 071-376 2652.

AC ● Academy Antiques, No. 5 Camphill Industrial Estate, West Byfleet, Surrey. Tel: (0932) 352067.

AG †* Anderson & Garland, Marlborough House, Marlborough Crescent, Newcastle-upon-Tyne. Tel: 091-232 6278.

AH * Andrew Hartley, Victoria Hall, Little Lane, Ilkley, West Yorkshire. Tel: (0943) 816363.

AK * Alder King, The Old Malthouse, Comfortable Place, Upper Bristol Road, Bath. Tel: (0225) 447933.

AL †● Ann Lingard, Ropewalk Antiques, Ropewalk, Rye, Sussex. Tel: (0797) 223486.

ALL * Allen & Harris, Bristol Auction Rooms, St. Johns Place, Apsley Road, Clifton, Bristol, Tel: (0272) 737201.

ARC ● Architectural Antiques, West Ley, Alswear Old Road, South Molton, Devon. Tel: (07695) 3342.

ART ● Artemesia Antiques, 16 West Street, Alresford, Hants. Tel: (0962) 732862.

ASA †● AS Antiques, 26 Broad Street, Pendleton, Salford 6, Lancashire. Tel: 061-737 5938/736 6014.

ASB †● Andrew Spencer Bottomley, The Coach House, 173A Huddersfield Road, Thongsbridge, Holmfirth, Huddersfield. Tel: (0484) 685234.

ASc ● Ascott Antiques, Narborough, Leicestershire. Tel: (0533) 863190.

ASH †● Ashburton Marbles, Grate Hall, North Street, Ashburton, Devon. Tel: (0364) 53189.

AT ● Andy Thornton, Architectural Antiques, Ainleys Industrial Estate, Elland, West Yorkshire. Tel: (0422) 375595.

B * Boardman, Station Road Corner, Haverhill, Suffolk. Tel: (0440) 703784.

BAL ● Sharon Ball, Unit 41, Stratford-upon-Avon Antique Centre, Ely Street, Warwickshire. Tel: (0789) 204180.

Bea * Bearnes, Rainbow, Avenue Road, Torquay, Devon. Tel: (0803) 296277.

BEE †● Beehive House, Janice Paull, 125 Warwick Road, Kenilworth, Warwickshire. Tel: (0926) 55253.

BEL †● Bell Antiques, 68 Harold Street, Grimsby, South Humberside. Tel: (0472) 695110.

BEV ● Beverley, 30 Church Street, London, NW8. Tel: 071-262 1576.

BH ● Bob Hoare Pine Antiques, Unit Q, Phoenix Place, North Street, Lewes, East Sussex. Tel: (0273) 480557.

BHA ● Beaubush House Antiques, 95 Sandgate High Street, Folkestone, Kent. Tel: (0303) 49099/51121.

BLO ● Bloomsbury Antiques, 58/60 Kensington Church Street, London, W8. Tel: 071-376 2810.

BL †● Brian Loomes, Calf Haugh, Pateley Bridge, North Yorks. Tel: Harrogate (0423) 711163.

Bon †* Bonhams, Montpelier Galleries, Montpelier Street, Knightsbridge, London, SW7. Tel: 071-584 9161.

BOW ● Simon Bowler, Smith Street Antique Centre, Warwick. Tel: (0926) 400554/021-783 8930.

BRK †● Breck Antiques, 762 Mansfield Road, Nottingham. Tel: (0602) 605263.

C * Christie's, Manson & Woods Ltd, 8 King Street, St. James's, London, SW1. Tel: 071-839 9060.

CA ● Crafers Antiques, The Hill, Wickham Market, Woodbridge, Suffolk. Tel: (0728) 747347.

CAC ● Cranbrook Antique Centre, High Street, Cranbrook, Kent. Tel: (0580) 712173.

CAG †* Canterbury Auction Galleries, 40 Station Road West, Canterbury, Kent. Tel: (0227) 763337.

CAm * Christie's Amsterdam, Cornelis Schuystraat 5717071 JG, Amsterdam, Holland. Tel: (020) 64 20 11.

Ced ● Cedar Antiques, Stamford Antiques Centre, Broad Street, Stamford, Lincs.

CG * Christie's (International) SA, 8 Place de la Taconnerie, 1204 Geneva, Switzerland. Tel: (022) 28 25 44.

CHa ● Carol Hammond, Unit 8, Kensington Church Street Antiques Centre, 58/60 Kensington Church Street, London W8. Tel: 071-938 4405.

CHA †● Chapel House Antiques, Pendre, Cardigan, Dyfed, and 32 Pentood Industrial Estate, Cardigan, Dyfed. Tel: (0239) 614868 and 613268.

CLC †● The Clock Clinic Ltd, 85 Lower Richmond Road, Putney, London, SW15. Tel: 081-788 1407.

CLG *● Clarke Gammon, 45 High Street, Guildford, Surrey. Tel: (0483) 572266.

CLH ● Clem Harwood, The Old Bakery, Keevil, Trowbridge, Wilts. Tel: (0380) 870463.

CNY * Christie, Manson & Woods, International Inc, 502 Park Avenue, New York NY 10022 USA. Tel: (212) 546 1000 (incuding Christie's East).

COB ● Cobwebs (P. A. Boyd-Smith), 78 Northam Road, Southampton. Tel: (0703) 227458.

CoH †* Cooper Hirst, Goldlay House, Parkway, Chelmsford, Essex. Tel: (0245) 260535.

CS †● Christopher Sykes Antiques, The Old Parsonage, Woburn, Milton Keynes, Bucks. Tel: (0525) 290259/290467.

C(S) * Christie's Scotland Ltd, 164-166 Bath Street, Glasgow. Tel: 041-332 8134/7.

CSK * Christie's (South Kensington), 85 Old Brompton Road, London, SW7. Tel: 071-581 7611.

DA * Dee & Atkinson, The Exchange Saleroom, Driffield, East Yorks. Tel: (0377) 43151.

DDM * Dickinson, Davy & Markham, Wrawby Street, Brigg, South Humberside. Tel: (0652) 53666.

DDS †● Dorking Desk Shop, 41 West Street, Dorking, Surrey. Tel: (0306) 883327/880535.

DEN †* Denham's & Associates, Horsham Auction Galleries, Horsham, Sussex. Tel: (0403) 55699/53837.

DGA ● David Graham Antiques, 104 Islington High Street, Campden Passage, Islington, London N1.

DID ● Didier Antiques, 58/60 Kensington Church Street, London, W8. Tel: 071-938 2537/(0836) 232634.

DM * Diamond, Mills & Co., 117 Hamilton Road, Felixstowe, Suffolk. Tel: (0394) 282281.

DN * Dreweatt Neate, Donnington Priory, Donnington, Newbury, Berks. Tel: (0635) 31234.

DY	†● Dycheling Antiques, 34 High Street, Ditchling, Hassocks, West Sussex. Tel: (0273) 842929.
E	* Ewbank Fine Art, Welbeck House, High Street, Guildford, Surrey. Tel: (0483) 232134.
EHA	● Gloria Gibson, 2 Beaufort West, Bath, Avon. Tel: (0225) 446646.
FP	†● For Pine, 340 Berkhamsted Road, Chesham, Bucks. Tel: (0494) 776119.
FR	* Fryer's Auction Galleries, Terminus Road, Bexhill-on-Sea, E. Sussex. Tel: (0424) 212994.
GA(D)	see DA
GAK	†* GA Key, Aylsham Saleroom, off Palmers Lane, Aylsham, Norfolk Tel: (0263) 733195.
GA(W)	see Canterbury Auction Galleries – GAC.
GC	* Geering & Colyer, Highgate, Hawkhurst, Kent. Tel: (0580) 753181/753463.
G&CC	†● Goss & Crested China Ltd, Nicholas J. Pine, 62 Murray Road, Horndean, Hants. Tel: (0705) 597440.
GeC	†● Gerard Campbell, Maple House, Market Place, Lechlade-on-Thames, Glos. Tel: (0367) 52267.
GH	†* Giles Haywood, The Auction House, St. John's Road, Stourbridge, West Midlands. Tel: (0384) 370891.
GIL	†* Gilding's, Roman Way, Market Harborough, Leicester. Tel: (0858) 410414.
GIN	†● Ray and Diane Ginns, P.O. Box 129, East Grinstead, West Sussex. Tel: (0860) 294789.
GM	* George Mealy & Sons, The Square, Castlecomer, Co. Kilkenny, Ireland. Tel: (010 353 56) 41229.
GRa	● Geoffrey Robinson Alfies, Alfies Antique Market, 13-25 Church Street, London NW8.
GSP	* Graves, Son & Pilcher, 71 Church Road, Hove, East Sussex. Tel: (0273) 735 266.
HAE	†● Hampstead Antique Emporium, 12 Heath Street, London NW3. Tel: 071-794 3297.
HCH	†* Hobbs & Chambers, 'At The Sign of the Bell', Market Place, Cirencester, Glos. Tel: (0285) 4736. Also: 15 Royal Crescent, Cheltenham, Glos. Tel: (0242) 513722.
HEY	†● Heyford Antiques, 7 Church Street, Nether Heyford, Northampton. Tel: (0327) 40749.
HOW	● Howards Antiques, 10 Alexandra Road, Aberystwyth, Dyfed. Tel: (0970) 624973.
HP	● H. Perovetz Ltd, 50/52 Chancery Lane, London WC2.
HPS	†* Halifax Property Services, 15 Cattle Market, Sandwich, Kent. Tel: (0304) 614369/611044.
HSS	†* Henry Spencer & Sons, 20 The Square, Retford, Notts. Tel: (0777) 708633.
HUN	● Huntercombe Manor Barn, Nr. Henley-on-Thames, Oxon. Tel: (0491) 641349.
IM	†* Ibbett Mosely, 125 High Street, Sevenoaks, Kent. Tel: (0732) 452246.
JH	* Jacobs & Hunt, Lavant Street, Petersfield, Hants. Tel: (0730) 62744.
JHo	†● Jonathan Horne (Antiques) Ltd, 66B & C, Kensington Church Street, London, W8. Tel: 071-221 5658.
JMG	†● Jamie Maxtone Graham, Lyne Haugh, Lyne Station, Peebles, Scotland. Tel: (07214) 304.
KEY	†● Key Antiques, 11 Horse Fair, Chipping Norton, Oxon. Tel: (0608) 64377.
KOT	● Kotobuki (Stephen Joseph), Unit F100, Alfie's Antique Market, 13/25 Church Street, London, NW8. Tel: 071-402 0723.
LAY	* David Lay, ASVA, Penzance Auction House, Alverton, Penzance, Cornwall. Tel: (0736) 61414.
LB	● The Lace Basket, 1a East Cross, Tenterden, Kent. Tel: (05806) 3923.
LF	†* Lambert & Foster, 102 High Street, Tenterden, Kent (previously County Group). Tel: (05806) 3233.
LRG	* Lots Road Chelsea Auction Galleries, 71 Lots Road, London, SW10. Tel: 071-351 7771.
LT	* Louis Taylor, Percy Street, Hanley, Stoke-on-Trent, Staffs. Tel: (0782) 260222.
M	* Morphets of Harrogate, 4-6 Albert Street, Harrogate, North Yorks. Tel: (0423) 502282.
MAT	● Christopher Matthews, Heathcote House, Forest Lane Head, Harrogate, North Yorks. Tel: (0423) 887296/883215/885732.
MAW	†● M. Allen, Watch and Clock Maker, 76a Walsall Road, Four Oaks, Sutton Coldfield. Tel: 021-308 6117.
MCA	● Millers of Chelsea Antiques Ltd, Netherbrook House, 86 Christchurch Road, Ringwood, Hants. Tel: (0425) 472062.
McC	†* McCartney's Portcullis Salerooms, Ludlow, Shropshire. Tel: (0584) 2636.
MGM	* Michael G. Matthews, ASVA, ARVA, The Devon Fine Art Auction House, Dowell Street, Honiton, Devon (now Bonhams West Country). Tel: (0404) 41872 and 3137.
MJB	†* Michael J. Bowman, 6 Haccombe House, Netherton, Newton Abbot, Devon. Tel: (0626) 872890.
MN	* Michael Newman, The Central Auction Rooms, Kinterbury House, St. Andrew's Cross, Plymouth, Devon. Tel: (0752) 669298.
MSh	● Manfred Schotten, The Crypt Antiques, 109 High Street, Burford, Oxon. Tel: (099382) 2302.
N	* Neales of Nottingham, The Nottingham Salerooms, 192 Mansfield Road, Nottingham. Tel: (0602) 624141.
NA	* Amersham Auction Rooms, 125 Station Road, Amersham, Bucks. Tel: (0494) 729292 and Wotton Auction Rooms, Tabernacle Road, Wotton-under-Edge, Glos. Tel: (0453) 844733.
NCA	● New Century at Alfie's, 2nd Floor (S002), 13-25 Church Street, London NW8.
NES	* D.M. Nesbit & Co, 7 Clarendon Road, Southsea, Hants. Tel: (0705) 864321.
NH	● Nicholas Harris, 564 Kings Road, London SW6.
OD	● Offas Dyke Antique Centre, 4 High Street, Knighton, Powys, Wales. Tel: (0547) 528634.
OL	* Outhwaite & Litherland, Kingsway Galleries, Fontenoy Street, Liverpool. Tel: 051-236 6561.
ONS	* Onslows, Metrostore, Townmead Road, London, SW6. Tel: 071-793 0240.
OS	†● Oswald Simpson, Hall Street, Long Melford, Suffolk. Tel: (0787) 77523.
OLD	● Old Flame, Architectural Antiques, 133/139 Church Street, Stoke-on-Trent, Staffs. Tel: (0782) 744985.
P	†* Phillips, Blenstock House, 101 New Bond Street, London, W1. Tel: 071-629 6602.
PAO	†● P.A. Oxley, The Old Rectory, Cherhill, Calne, Wilts. Tel: (0249) 816227.
PC	Private Collection.
PCh	†* Peter Cheney, Western Road Auction Rooms, Western Road, Littlehampton, West Sussex. Tel: (0903) 722264/713418.
PH	● Pennard House Antiques, Piccadilly, Bath, Avon. Tel: (074986) 266.
PHA	†● Paul Hopwell Antiques, 30 High Street, West Haddon, Northamptonshire. Tel: (078 887) 636.
P(M)	* Phillips, Trinity House, 114 Northenden Road, Sale, Manchester. Tel: 061-962 9237.
P(S)	* Phillips, 49 London Road, Sevenoaks, Kent. Tel: (0732) 740310.
PSA	†● Pantiles Spa Antiques, 6 Union House, Eridge Road, Tunbridge Wells. Tel: (0892) 541377.
P(Sc)	* Phillips Scotland, 65 George Street, Edinburgh. Tel: 031-225 2266.
PSG	● Patrick & Susan Gould, Stand L17, Grays Mews, 1-7 Davies Mews, London, W1. Tel: 071-408 0129 or 081-993 5879 (home).
PT	†● Pieces of Time, Grays Mews, 1-7 Davies Street, London, W1. Tel: 071-629 2422.

PVH ● Peter & Valerie Howkins, 39, 40 and 135 King Street, Great Yarmouth, Norfolk. Tel: (0493) 844639.

P(W) * Phillips of Winchester, The Red House, Hyde Street, Winchester, Hants. Tel: (0962) 62515.

RBB †* Russell, Baldwin & Bright, Inc Campbell & Edwards, Fine Art Salerooms, Ryelands Road, Leominster, Hereford. Tel: (0568) 611166.

RdeR †● Rogers de Rin, 76 Hospital Road, Paradise Walk, London, SW3. Tel: 071-352 9007.

RFA †● Rochester Fine Arts, 86 High Street, Rochester, Kent. Tel: (0634) 814129.

RGA ● Richard Gibson Alfie's, Alfie's Antique Market, 13-25 Church Street, London NW8.

RID †* Riddetts of Bournemouth, 26 Richmond Hill, Bournemouth. Tel: (0202) 555686.

RK †● Richard Kimbell, Riverside, Market Harborough, Leicestershire. Tel: (0858) 433444.

RO ● Roswith, Stand F103, Alfie's Antique Market, 13-25 Church Street, London, NW8.

RP ● Robert Pugh, 2 Beaufort Mews, St. Saviour's Road, Larkhall, Bath, Avon. Tel: (0225) 314713.

RWB †● Roy W. Bunn Antiques, 34/36 Church Street, Barnoldswick, Colne, Lancashire. Tel: (0282) 813703.

ROW ● Rowena Blackford at Penny Lampard's Antique Centre, 31-33 High Street, Headcorn, Kent. Tel: (0622) 890682/861360.

SAn ● Somerville Antiques & Country Furniture Ltd, Killanley, Ballina, Co Mayo, Ireland. Tel: (096) 36275.

SBA ● South Bar Antiques, Digbeth Street, Stow-on-the-Wold, Gloucestershire. Tel: (0451) 30236.

SCO ● Scot Hay House Antiques, 7 Nantwich Road, Woore, Shropshire. Tel: 063-081 7118.

SH †● Shiners Architectural Reclamation Ltd, 123 Jesmond Road, Newcastle-upon-Tyne. Tel: 091-281 6474.

Sim * Simmons & Sons, 32 Bell Street, Henley-on-Thames, Oxfordshire. Tel: (0491) 591111.

SM ● Stephen Maitland, Now & Then Telephones, 7-9 West Crosscauseway, Edinburgh. Tel: (0592) 890235 and 031-668 2927.

S * Sotheby's, 34-35 New Bond Street, London W1. Tel: 071-493 8080.

S(Am) * Sotheby's, Rokin 102, 1012 KZ Amsterdam. Tel: (020) 6275656.

S(C) * Sotheby's, Booth Mansion, 28 Watergate Street, Chester. Tel: (0244) 315531.

S(NY) * Sotheby's, 1334 York Avenue, New York, NY 10021. Tel: 212 606 7000.

S(S) * Sotheby's, Summers Place, Billingshurst, West Sussex. Tel: (0403) 783933.

SO †● Samuel Orr, The Clock Shop, 36 High Street, Hurstpierpoint, West Sussex. Tel: (0273) 832081.

Som †● Somervale Antiques, 6 Radstock Road, Midsomer Norton, Bath. Tel: (0761) 412686.

SPX ● Smallridge Bros Piano Export, 51 Grove Road, Fishponds, Bristol. Tel: (0272) 658622/650003.

SSD †● Smith & Smith Designs, 58a Middle Street North, Driffield, E. Yorkshire. Tel: (0377) 46321.

Sto ● Stockspring, 114 Kensington Church Street, London, W8. Tel: 071-727 7995.

STR †● Strawsons Antiques, 39-41 The Pantiles, Tunbridge Wells, Kent Tel: (0892) 30607.

SWN ● Swan Antiques, Stone Street, Cranbrook, Kent. Tel: (0580) 712720.

SWO †* Sworders, G. E. Sworder and Sons, 15 Northgate End, Bishops Stortford. Tel: (0279) 651388.

TBC ● The Bramah Collection, P.O. Box 79, Eastleigh, Hants. SO5 5YW.

TG ● Thames Gallery, Thameside, Henley-on-Thames, Oxon. Tel: (0491) 572449.

TPF †● Traditional Pine Furniture, 248 Seabrook Road, Seabrook, Hythe, Kent. Tel: (0303) 239931.

TP †● Tom Power, The Collector, Alfie's Antique Market, 13/25 Church Street, London, NW8. Tel: 071-883 0024.

UC †● Up Country, The Old Corn Stores, 68 St John's Road, Tunbridge Wells, Kent. Tel: (0892) 23341.

VB ● Variety Box, 16 Chapel Place, Tunbridge Wells, Kent. Tel: (0892) 31868.

VH †● Valerie Howard, 131e Kensington Church Street, London, W8. Tel: 071-792 9702.

VS †* T. Vennett-Smith, 11 Nottingham Road, Gotham, Nottinghamshire. Tel: (0602) 830541.

Wai †● Wain Antiques, Peter Wain, 7 Nantwich Road, Woore, Shropshire CW3 9SA. Tel: (063 081) 7118.

WHB * William H. Brown, Fine Art Auctioneers & Valuers, Olivers Rooms, Burkitt's Lane, Sudbury, Suffolk. Tel: (0787) 880305.

WIL * Peter Wilson, Victoria Gallery, Market Street, Nantwich, Cheshire. Tel: (0270) 623878.

WM ● Ward & Morris, Stuart House, 18 Gloucester Road, Ross-on-Wye, Herefordshire. Tel: (0989) 768320.

WW * Woolley & Wallis, The Castle Auction Mart, Castle Street, Salisbury. Tel: (0722) 21711.

A Chinese porcelain wine vessel, with pierced body and decorated panel.
£500-550 *HCH*

A pair of mahogany fauteuils, the backed and bowed seats upholstered in blue distressed brocade, the scrolled arms above lappet carved scrolled legs, one chair with reduced legs, c1825.
£2,200-2,600 *S(S)*

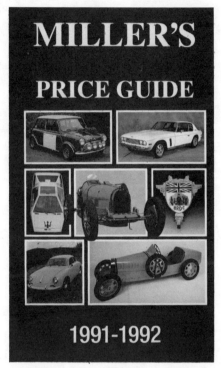

 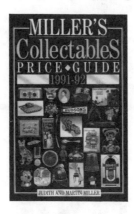 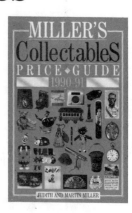
25

THE WAY YOU BUY ANTIQUES IS COSTING YOU TOO MUCH MONEY.

Now there is a way to know precisely what is coming up at auction, within your field

of interest, at over 400 salerooms in the U.K. – from as little as £350 a year.

To find what you are looking for, telephone Thesaurus on 0983 299252 or write to us at

Thesaurus Group Ltd., FREEPOST 6 (WD4 359), London W1E 1JZ.

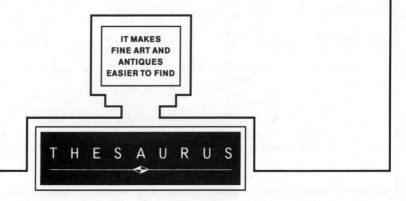

**IT MAKES
FINE ART AND
ANTIQUES
EASIER TO FIND**

THESAURUS

CONTENTS

Index to Advertisers	18
Pottery	29
Porcelain	101
Goss & Crested China	162
Oriental Pottery & Porcelain	170
Glass	202
Oak & Country Furniture .	231
Furniture	252
Architectural Antiques . . .	408
Clocks	430
Barometers	493
Scientific Instruments	496
Silver	506
Silver Plate	530
Tea & Coffee	532
Wine Antiques	554
Metalware	558
Arts & Crafts	568
Art Nouveau	571
Doulton/Royal Doulton . . .	584
Art Deco	587
Ivory	601
Marble	602
Terracotta/Stone	604
Woodcarvings	605
Antiquities	607
Sewing	609
Textiles	611
Fans	643
Dolls	645
Toys	658
Models	665
Games	666
Musical	668
Boxes	671
Electrical	676
Transport	677
Leather & Luggage	678
Sport	680
Lighting	685
Tribal Art	690
Oriental	692
Islamic Art	725
Ephemera	728
Crafts	735
Papier Mâché	736
Jewellery	737
Pine Furniture	738
Kitchenalia	751
Walking Sticks & Canes . .	754
Tunbridge Ware	756
Arms & Armour	758
Directory of Specialists . . .	772
Directory of Auctioneers . .	785
Index	790

A pair of Royal Worcester porcelain New Large Grecian Water Carriers, one decorated in shades of russet and pale green, the other in green, raised upon gilt decorated waisted bases, printed mark in puce and numbered 2 over 125, date cipher 1915 and 1916, 20in (51cm) high. **£1,500-2,000** *HSS*

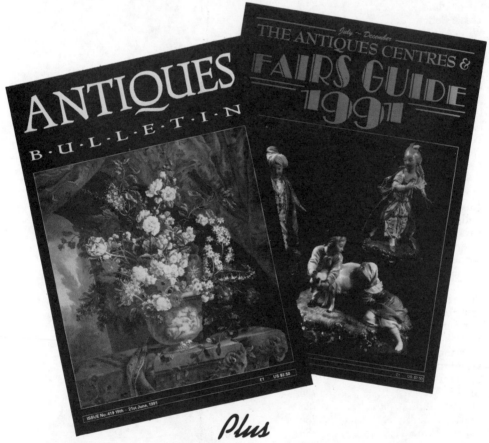

POTTERY

There have been no great surprises in the pottery market this year. Sales at the lower end of the market have been very slow with a definite drop in price on previous years. Some dealers and auction houses have been slow to recognise this with the result that many of them are still looking at last year's stock or having difficulty obtaining high reserve prices. The middle ground of good quality, but not too rare, 18thC pottery has more or less maintained its price level but more as a result of shortage of supply rather than a maintenance of demand level. It would appear that potential sellers are holding back their goods until a more vibrant market comes again. At the top end of the market, good and rare pieces still attract very high prices but are not reaching the dizzy heights of three years ago. There are some relative bargains to be picked up by those who are prepared to invest in these pieces, such as the Whieldon creamware arbour group sold at Bearne's, Torquay, for £32,000 + premium. It would have fetched much more three years ago.

The same market trends apply to the 19th and early 20thC collectors pottery fields of Wedgwood, Wemyss, Mason's, Moorcroft et al. Up to 50% of the more mundane pieces are being bought in at auction whereas the rare and unusual pieces are still fetching very high prices and are maintaining their value. A fine early Moorcroft vase sold at Neales, Nottingham, for £6,600 against an estimate of £2,000-3,000, and a Wedgwood Fairyland lustre vase of the Ghostly Wood pattern reached £8,500 at Bearne's.

Bottles

A Staffordshire saltglazed bottle, c1755, 9½in (24cm).
£630-670 *JHo*

Four South Staffordshire opaque white cruet bottles, named within branches of green foliage, the rims with puce 'feuilles-de-choux', with pierced and turned wood domed covers with knob finials, some damage, c1760, 7 and 6in (18 and 15cm).
£750-1,000 *C*

A Persian polychrome bottle, c1850, 6½in (16cm).
£90-110 *KOT*

Bowls

An English delft 'birdcage' bowl, painted in blue with birds and foliage behind vertical bars, probably Liverpool, damaged and repaired, c1770, 10in (25.5cm).
£150-200 *HSS*

A Bristol tin glazed bowl, c1765, 9in (23cm) diam.
£1,000-1,200 *JHo*

An English delftware butter dish and cover, the cover with blue sponged tree decoration, the glazed interior with a conical spur, probably Bristol, c1740, 5in (12.5cm).
£4,200-4,600 *Bon*

A Staffordshire slipware three-handled tyg, by Robart Pool, the rim inscribed in dark brown with cream dots on a cream ground with the inscription ROBART: POOL:MADE:THIS:CVP:WITH: A:CVP:POSET:FIL, the lower part in dark brown with cream stylised tulips and with 3 small loop handles flanked by rudimentary handles, extensively damaged and repaired, early 18thC, 7½in (18.5cm).
£4,500-6,000 *C*

A London delft dated blue and white bleeding bowl, the centre inscribed A.H.1673, extensively damaged and repaired, 7½in (19cm) wide.
£3,000-3,500 *C*

A creamware char dish, probably Yorkshire, the exterior painted in green, ochre and brown enamels, minor chip to foot, 8½in (22cm).
£250-300 *Bea*

A slipware flared bucket shaped bleeding bowl, with pierced foliate handle, the interior striated with dark brown, light brown and cream slip marbling, the exterior covered in cream slip, cracked and repaired, early 18thC, 6in (15cm) wide.
£1,700-2,000 *C*

A slipware bowl, with small loop handle and central conical spike, the dark brown ground decorated in cream slip with the initials IC and the date 1702, the overturned top rim with cream slip dots, rim chip and minor flaking, restoration to rim and handle, 1702, 8½in (21cm) wide.
£1,200-1,800 *C*

A salt glazed punch bowl, mid-18thC, 9in (23cm).
£600-650 *DN*

A slipware two-handled porringer, decorated in brown slip with cream slip stylised foliage and wavy lines, minor cracks and chips to rim, slight chip and chip to handle, early 18thC, 6½in (17cm) wide.
£1,400-1,600 *C*

Boxes

A large Italian majolica bowl, probably Savona, late 17thC, 13in (33cm).
£500-550 *DN*

An extremely rare Wedgwood & Bentley paint box, damaged, paint pots missing, 18thC, 6in (15cm) wide.
£800-900 *Wai*

A creamware box and cover, the upper surface of the screw top cover moulded in relief with a titled portrait of John Wilkes, within a framework of flowers and scrolls, beadwork rims, c1770, 3½in (8cm).
£2,400-3,000 *S*

A slipware money box, c1760, 5in (12cm).
£500-600 *JHo*

Commemorative

A pearlware and copper lustre small 'Green Bag' jug, printed in puce with a bust portrait of Queen Caroline, captioned 'God Save Queen Caroline', the reverse printed with the 'Green Bag Crew' rhyme in a puce cartouche with the names of her supporters, some damage, early 19thC, 5in (13cm) high.
£150-200 *HSS*

A Staffordshire pearlware lobed commemorative jug, printed in puce with portrait medallions of the promoters of reform, the reverse inscribed 'Royal Assent to the Reform Bill 7th June 1832', possibly Baker, Bevens and Irwin, lip chipped, staining and crazing, 7½in (19cm).
£100-130 *CSK*

A commemorative mug made to commemorate the wedding of H.R.H. the Prince of Wales to H.R.H. Princess Alexandra, 1863, glaze chips, 4in (10cm), and a transfer printed plate to commemorate the same occasion, and a printed plate commemorating the death of Caroline.
£400-450 *S(S)*

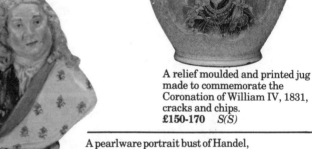

A relief moulded and printed jug made to commemorate the Coronation of William IV, 1831, cracks and chips.
£150-170 *S(S)*

A pearlware portrait bust of Handel, in the manner of Ralph Wood, wearing a floral gown with orange trim over and red and brown jacket, raised on a marbled waisted base, c1800, 9in (23cm).
£500-600 *S*

Busts

A Copeland parian bust, modelled as The Veiled Bride, impressed 'Monte 1860' to reverse, the socle impressed in capitals 'Crystal Palace Art Union', impressed Copeland, c1860, 14½in (37cm).
£800-1,000 *Bon*

A French coloured biscuit bust of a young woman, after the original by Carrier Belleuse, with flesh tints, pale mauve straw hat caught by 2 blue bows, on a spreading socle enriched with gilding and square gilt base, some restoration to base of bust, incised Carrier Belleuse on one shoulder, c1865, 28in (71cm).
£750-850 *C*

Cottages & Pastille Burners

A Staffordshire pottery money box, modelled as a cottage, c1860, 4in (10cm).
£100-110 *RWB*

A Mexborough rock pottery cottage money box, moulded upon 'The Wesleyan Chapel, Bank Street, Mexborough', inscribed 'Sarah Ducker Fendall, Bourne 20 August 1846', mid-19thC.
£850-870 *WHB*

A Staffordshire pottery money box, modelled as a house and decorated in Pratt colours, c1820, 4in (10cm).
£280-300 *RWB*

Cow Creamers

A Staffordshire pottery model of a house, c1860, 6in (16cm).
£90-100 *RWB*

A Pratt-Yorkshire church, c1820, 10in (24cm).
£600-700 *JHo*

A Staffordshire cow creamer, c1775, 4½in (12cm).
£1,000-1,400 *JHo*

An English creamware cow creamer, its coat splashed with large brown patches, on a green base, c1810, 7in (18cm) long.
£200-300 *CSK*

A Staffordshire pink lustre cow creamer, c1830.
£300-350 *RP*

A Staffordshire pearlware cow creamer milking group, the cow sponged in grey, the milkmaid in blue blouse and pleated skirt, cover lacking, horns, ear and base with repairs and restorations, c1780, 7in (18cm) long.
£400-500 *C*

A creamware cow creamer milking group of conventional type, the cow sponged in tones of brown, a milkmaid seated on a stool, on a green washed base, cover lacking, horn chipped, tail restored, chips to base, c1780, 6½in (16cm) long.
£600-800 *C*

Cups

A London delft dated fuddling cup, formed as 3 globular bottles with entwined handles, one with the initials 'I S' above a flourish, another with the date '1633', the initialled vase with rim repair and repair to glaze patches, all with chips to feet and rims, and with glaze flaking to handles, 1633, 3½in (8.5cm).
£7,000-7,500   *C*

A fuddling cup is an earthenware vessel of several cups linked in such a way that anyone challenged to empty one of the cups was in fact forced to drain them all!

A London delft dated armorial caudle cup of squat baluster form with loop handle, painted with the Arms of the Watermen's and Lightermen's Company and with the initials 'D/I A' and the date '1682', extensively damaged and repaired, 1682, 3½in (9cm).
£10,000-11,000   *C*

Caudle: Spiced gruel laced with wine.

A Liverpool delft inscribed and dated blue and white cup with loop handle, inscribed 'A. Wigglesworth 1767' within a scroll and foliage cartouche surmounted by a winged cherub's head and flanked by grapes, beneath an ochre line rim, slight rim chips and 2 cracks, 1767, 2½in (6.5cm).
£2,000-2,200   *C*

A Staffordshire salt glazed cup and saucer, c1745, cup 2½in (6cm), saucer 4½in (11cm) diam.
£800-1,000   *JHo*

Ewers

A Minton majolica ewer, impressed marks and date code for 1867, 14½in (37cm).
£680-720   *CSK*

Figures – Animals

A Hall pearlware group of a ewe and lamb, their coats splashed in iron red, on green glazed base, repair to branch of bocage, impressed mark at back, c1820, 6½in (15.5cm).
£400-500   *C*

A Newport pottery model of an owl wearing a suit, signed M. Epworth, 7½in (18.5cm).
£100-130   *Bea*

A pair of Staffordshire pen holders modelled as recumbent whippets, c1860, 5in (12cm).
£180-200   *RWB*

A Staffordshire pearlware model of a swan, with manganese beak and incised wing and tail feathers, on green mound base, c1790, 4in (10cm).
£1,000-1,300   *C*

A pair of Prattware type figures of
birds, 3½in (9cm).
£700-750   *DN*

A rare Staffordshire group, early
19thC, 8in (21cm).
£2,500-3,000   *JHo*

A Prattware figure of a lion,
probably Staffordshire, c1800, 5½in
(14cm).
£1,500-1,800   *JHo*

A Staffordshire pearlware figure of
a lion, his paw raised upon a yellow
ball, his coat predominantly salmon
pink with a brown glazed mane and
facial details picked out in black,
restored hair crack to base, c1800,
8in (20cm).
£1,500-2,000   *S*

A Staffordshire figure of a cockerel,
the cream coloured bird lightly
sponged in brown and yellow, on a
green glazed base, minor
restoration, c1800, 8½in (21.5cm).
£1,000-1,500   *S*

A pair of Staffordshire models of a
milkboy and milkmaid with cows,
c1860, 6½in (16cm).
£380-400   *RWB*

A rare Staffordshire rabbit, c1865.
£900-1,100   *RP*

A pair of Staffordshire creamware
spaniels, with incised brown coats
and light brown collars, on oval
green-glazed foliage moulded bases,
c1800, 4in (9.5cm).
£1,000-1,500   *C*

A Staffordshire spill vase, modelled
as an eagle over a sleeping child,
c1860, 8½in (21cm).
£100-110   *RWB*

A pearlware model of a recumbent ram,
with yellow horns, his fleece sponged in
yellow, blue and brown, on green
mound base, c1790, 5½in (14cm) long.
£700-800   *C*

A Staffordshire pen holder modelled
as spaniels and pup, c1860, 6½in
(16cm).
£160-180   *RWB*

A pair of Staffordshire figures of spaniels, with both front legs separate, restored, c1850, 8in (20cm).
£250-280 *RWB*

A Staffordshire spill vase, modelled as a hound, c1870.
£280-300 *RP*

A Staffordshire figure of an elephant, c1870.
£350-450 *RP*

A pair of Staffordshire spill holders, modelled as a ram and ewe, c1860, 6in (15cm).
£280-300 *RWB*

A Staffordshire spill vase with coloured glaze, by the Wood family c1780.
£1,800-2,200 *JHo*

A Staffordshire standing hound spill vase, c1870.
£200-240 *RP*

A pair of Staffordshire greyhounds, c1870.
£250-350 *RP*

A Staffordshire group of 2 seated spaniels, one chained to a barrel, with iron red fur markings, on a shaped oval base, 9½in (24cm).
£200-250 *CSK*

A creamware model of a fox of Ralph Wood type, naturally modelled with brown coat, a bird beneath his right forepaw, on a shaped mound base streaked in grey, green and yellow, slight cracks, chip to base, crack to right forepaw, c1780, 4in (10cm).
£1,600-2,000 *C*

A pair of Staffordshire models of greyhounds, one with a hare in its mouth, the other with a hare at its feet, each on a green mound base, one with firing crack, 10½in (26.5cm).
£400-450 *Bea*

A Staffordshire spill group of
a boy with a donkey,
decorated in colours.
£160-200 *RP*

A pair of Staffordshire spill
holders, modelled as cows and
calves, c1875,
10½in (26cm).
£400-420 *RWB*

A pair of Staffordshire pearlware
spaniels, with iron red fur
markings, chains and collars in
gilding, enamels flaked, 12½in
(32cm).
£350-400 *CSK*

A sponged glaze pottery figure of a
cat.
£150-175 *DM*

A pair of Staffordshire greyhounds,
one holding a hare in its mouth, the
other with a hare at its feet, both
with black ears and curled forelocks
and black patched fur markings, on
rockwork applied with foliage and
gilt lined bases, one hind leg
damaged and one body cracked,
10½in (26cm).
£950-1,100 *CSK*

A pearlware group in sponged red,
blue, black and ochre, Staffordshire
or Yorkshire, restoration to horns,
leg and base, 5½in (14cm).
£750-800 *CSK*

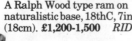

A Ralph Wood type ram on
naturalistic base, 18thC, 7in
(18cm). **£1,200-1,500** *RID*

A pair of Yorkshire buff pottery
groups of cows with attendant
figures, one with a youth in blue
jacket, yellow sash and striped
trousers, the other with a woman
holding a basket, in black hat, light
brown apron and her dress
decorated in blue and light brown,
the animals and oval bases splashed
in black, the woman with repaired
chip to hat and one ear of cow, the
man's head, horns of cow and small
chip to base repaired, c1800, 7½ and
6½in (18.5 and 17cm) wide.
£1,400-1,700 *C*

A pair of Staffordshire spaniels,
their fur with gilt markings and
with painted facial details, slight
wear, 14in (36cm).
£200-250 *CSK*

A salt glazed 'solid agate' figure of a
seated cat, the marbled body on
brown and grey, picked out with
patches of watery blue glaze, minor
restoration, c1745, 5in (12.5cm).
£1,000-1,500 *S*

A creamware model of a lion of
Whieldon type, with incised mane,
the body streaked in dark brown
glazes, his muzzle and mane with
traces of gilding, on a shaped
rectangular base, the base partly
lacking, one tooth lacking, c1760,
7½in (19cm) long.
£6,500-7,000 *C*

A pair of Staffordshire pottery spill holders, each in the form of a fierce leopard by a tree, set on a rococo moulded base, slight damage, 6½in (16.5cm).
£900-1,200 *Bea*

l. A creamware model of a seated spaniel with brown ears, eyes, eyebrows and tail, his coat covered in brown and light brown dots, on moulded base, minor chips to base, c1780, 3in (8cm).
£220-250
front c. A creamware model of a seated bear, with a brown collar, sponged in tones of brown, on green edged base, extensively repaired, c1780, 3in (8cm) wide.
£170-200
r. A creamware model of a recumbent lion, with moulded mane, splashed and sponged in tones of brown, c1780, 3½in (9cm) wide.
£260-300
back c. A buffware model of a seated faun, with incised fur and splashed in brown and black, on black sponged base, crack and repaired chip to base, perhaps Yorkshire, c1800, 5in (12.5cm).
£500-550 *C*

A pair of penholder figures of parrots with brightly coloured plumage, c1860, 4½ and 5in (11.5 and 12.5cm).
£400-450 *CSK*

A pearlware model of a lion with a human face, surrounded by an incised brown mane, on an oval base splashed in green, ochre and brown, c1790, 4½in (11cm) long.
£600-700 *C*

A pearlware figure of a billy goat, with white coat and dark brown horns, on rockwork base covered in green, yellow and brown glazes, one ear lacking and other chipped, perhaps Scottish, c1800, 8½in (21cm).
£650-1,000 *C*

An Obadiah Sherratt group of Polito's Menagerie of conventional type, the yellow stage inscribed POLITOS MENAGERIE OF THE WONDERFUL BURDS AND BEASTS FROM MOST PARTS OF THE WORLD, LION & C, the lower part with 5 musicians and a monkey seated on an organ, on a rectangular scroll and claw footed base, the front with a flight of steps applied with 4 figures, extensive damage, c1830, 12in (30.5cm) wide.
£7,500-8,500 *C*

A pearlware model of a bird, with incised plumage, splashed with brown, ochre and yellow dashes, perched astride a pale green tree stump, tree stump chipped and repaired, chip to beak and tail, c1790, 3in (8cm).
£160-200 *C*

Figures – People

A Poole pottery figure of Buster Boy, modelled by Phoebe Stabler, naturalistically painted, impressed CSA mark, 7in (18cm).
£170-200   *CSK*

A matched pair of Staffordshire figures of cricketers, c1870.
£1,400-1,600   *RP*

A pair of Staffordshire pearlware figures of Apollo and Diana, of Ralph Wood type, the god draped in a green lined pale mauve robe, the goddess wearing a green and grey dress, her neck and right arm repaired, part of quiver and head-dress lacking, his lyre chipped, both with chips to the bases, c1775, 9in (22cm).
£1,800-2,200   *C*

A Staffordshire pottery group in the Walton manner, slight damage, 5in (12.5cm).
£350-400   *Bea*

A Staffordshire pottery group of 2 drunken men, The Night Watchmen, set on an oval mound and octagonal base, 10in (25cm).
£300-500   *Bea*

A Staffordshire pearlware figure of a gardener of Ralph Wood type, wearing black hat, white open-neck shirt, green jacket, blue sash and light brown breeches, left arm and spade restored and restored through legs, pedestal and base, flower pot lacking, c1785, 8in (19.5cm).
£350-500   *C*

A Staffordshire pearlware figure of a bagpiper of Ralph Wood type, wearing black hat, green jacket and brown breeches, his manganese pipes under his arm, very slight chipping to base, c1785, 7½in (19cm).
£900-1,200   *C*

A pair of Robinson and Leadbeater coloured parian figures of a gypsy and his companion, he wearing a red and gold braid tunic with a broad cummerbund holding a violin, she with a red headscarf, pale blue bodice holding a lute, both on coloured rockwork bases, impressed marks, restoration to the violin, lute and her hand, 16½in (42cm).
£170-220   *CSK*

Three flat back Staffordshire figures, 19thC:
l. Red Riding Hood, 9½in (24cm).
c. Garrick as Richard III, 10in (25cm).
r. Two figures at the Well, 9½in (24cm).
£100-150
PCh

A Staffordshire pearlware circus group of Savoyard and his dancing bear, the trainer wearing a brightly coloured costume, minor chips and restoration, early 19thC, 9in (22.5cm).
£1,600-2,000   *S*

A pair of Staffordshire figures, The Fisherman and The Fisherwoman, painted in yellows and rust, 19thC, 13in (33cm).
£120-170   *MN*

A Staffordshire figure of a Flemish musician, decorated in overglaze and underglaze colours, c1810, 9in (23cm).
£240-260   *RWB*

A Staffordshire figure, c1800, 6in (15cm).
£300-350   *JHo*

A Staffordshire pearlware figure of a musician of Ralph Wood type, wearing a black hat, olive green jacket, green waistcoat and yellow breeches, end of horn lacking, stick lacking, chips and restoration to base, c1785.
£1,500-2,000   *C*

A Staffordshire pearlware figure of a Dutch girl of Ralph Wood type, wearing white bonnet, green bodice, yellow sash and manganese skirt, restored through neck, ankles and tree stump, c1790, 6½in (16.5cm).
£400-600   *C*

A pair of Staffordshire figures of a hunter and huntress, c1810, 7 and 7½in (18 and 19cm).
£500-550   *JHo*

39

A Staffordshire group depicting Charity, decorated in Pratt colours, c1820, 8½in (21cm).
£250-270   *RWB*

A Staffordshire group of Persuasion, she wearing a yellow hat, puce blouse and long floral skirt, her suitor sporting a black hat, green coat and cream breeches, offering her a ring, minor chips and restoration, c1820, 7in (17.5cm).
£2,000-2,500   *S*

A Staffordshire figure depicting Hope, c1820, 9in (23cm).
£160-180   *RWB*

A pair of Staffordshire figures of Molyneux and Cribb, c1820.
£2,500-3,000   *JHo*

A Staffordshire rural group of musicians, bocage missing, c1820, 9in (23cm).
£300-340   *RWB*

A pair of Staffordshire groups of Flight and Return, on green rockwork bases applied with moss and flowers, Infant Jesus's head, one tail and tip of one ear lacking, damages and repairs to extremities and foliage, slight glaze flaking, perhaps Walton, c1820, 9in (23cm).
£2,800-3,200   *C*

A Staffordshire group of the Proposal, c1830, 7½in (19cm).
£3,000-4,000   *GIN*

A pair of Staffordshire pearlware groups of The Flight to Egypt and Return from Egypt, on rockwork bases applied with flowers and foliage, perhaps Walton, some damage and repairs, c1820, 11 and 10in (28 and 25cm).
£1,700-2,200   *C*

A Staffordshire model of a cavalier and his female companion, on gilt lined base, c1850, 16in (41cm).
£150-200   *Bon*

A Staffordshire group of The New Marriage Act, typically modelled with a priest, the couple and a young boy all within an arched interior, picked out in bright enamels, the stepped base in blue and iron red, inscribed label restored, c1835, 6½in (16cm).
£1,000-1,400   *S*

A pair of Staffordshire porcellaneous coloured and well modelled figures of gardeners, c1840, 8½in (21cm).
£320-350 *RWB*

A Staffordshire figure of an unidentified dancer, c1850, 8½in (21cm).
£135-150 *RWB*

A pair of Staffordshire figures of children on goats, possibly portraying the Royal children, c1845, 6in (15cm).
£140-150 *RWB*

A Staffordshire pearlware figure of a gentleman of Ralph Wood type, wearing a black hat, grey lined pale green cloak tied with ribbon, pale brown waistcoat and pale yellow breeches, right hand restuck, one of dog's ears lacking and chip to base, c1785, 10in (25cm).
£1,500-2,000 *C*

A Staffordshire pottery figure of Thomas Dartmouth Rice, the American vaudeville performer in his role as Jim Crow, 6½in (16.5cm).
£350-400 *Bea*

A Staffordshire figure depicting Justice, restored, c1820. 8in (20cm).
£160-180 *RWB*

A pair of Staffordshire figures of cricketers, both on gilt lined bases, one restored, c1865, 14in (36cm).
£1,600-2,000 *Bon*

A Staffordshire figure depicting Hygeia, restored, c1820, 8in (20cm).
£140-150 *RWB*

A pair of Staffordshire figures of Queen Victoria and Prince Albert, c1845, 11in (28cm).
£280-300 *RWB*

A pair of Staffordshire pottery
figures of a young man and woman,
he with a monkey, she with a
tambourine, 7in (18cm).
£100-150 *Bea*

A Staffordshire figure, St. George
and the dragon, the dragon painted
green, slightly damaged, 19thC,
10in (25cm).
£80-100 *MN*

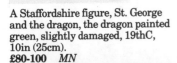

A pair of Staffordshire square based
pottery figures of children, each
carrying a bird, painted in Pratt
enamels, 5in (12.5cm).
£200-230 *Bea*

A pair of Staffordshire pottery
groups, each in the form of a cow by
a stream with a farmer or a
milkmaid, 8½in (21cm).
£250-300 *Bea*

An early Staffordshire pottery
group of a shepherd playing a flute,
his companion standing at his side,
a dog, lamb and goat at their feet,
some damage, 10in (25cm).
£350-500 *Bea*

A pair of creamware figures of
Ralph Wood type, each modelled as
a youth in translucent blue, yellow
and manganese clothes, both bases
with some restoration, c1780, 5in
(12.5cm).
£400-600 *C*

A German pottery figure of a
barefoot boy, draped in a shawl,
playing a mandolin, minor damage,
late 19thC, 23½in (61cm).
£250-300 *Bea*

A figure of Apollo covered in
coloured glazes, by the Wood family,
9in (22.5cm).
£1,000-1,100 *JHo*

Three creamware figures emblematic of Faith, Hope and
Charity, of Pratt type, wearing ochre, dark blue and
brown robes, on bases moulded with ochre and green
stiff leaves, Faith's right arm restored, perhaps
Yorkshire, c1790, 8½ and 9½in (21.5 and 23.5cm).
£650-1,000 *C*

Staffordshire Figures of Victorian Era

A rare Staffordshire figure, probably portraying Lord Melbourne, c1840, 8½in (21cm), (B,1/3).
£600-650   *RWB*

A Staffordshire figure of Napoleon Bonaparte, c1845, 7½in (19cm), (C,18/55).
£140-155   *RWB*

A pair of Staffordshire figures of the Prince of Wales and Princess Royal, c1845, 6in (15cm), (A,47/135 and 136).
£240-260   *RWB*

A very rare Staffordshire group depicting the Allied Powers of the Crimean War, c1854, 12in (31cm), (C,32/74).
£800-900   *RWB*

A rare Staffordshire group depicting the Death of Nelson, c1845, 8in (21cm), (C,9/8).
£450-500   *RWB*

STAFFORDSHIRE FIGURES

The letters and figures in brackets refer to the book *Staffordshire Portrait Figures* by P. D. Gordon Pugh

---

A Staffordshire figure of the Hungarian patriot, Louis Kossuth, c1851, 11in (28cm), (B,19/61).
£200-225   *RWB*

A rare titled Staffordshire figure of William Charles Macrady as James V of Scotland, c1846, 8in (20cm), (E,7/20).
£550-600   *RWB*

A Staffordshire figure of Malakoff, an outwork of Sebastopol, in salmon colour, c1854, 7in (17cm), (C,69/180).
£480-500 *RWB*

A Staffordshire group portraying the prize fight between John Heenan and Tom Sayers, c1860, 10in (24cm), (F,7/15).
£500-550 *RWB*

A Staffordshire figure portraying Ellen Bright, 'Death of the Lion Queen', c1850, 15in (38cm), (E,80/154).
£700-800 *RWB*

A Staffordshire figure of Stanfield Hall, c1849, 8in (20cm), (G,20/46).
£280-320 *RWB*

A Staffordshire figure of John Liston as Swam Swipes, in a green jacket, white apron and brown breeches, standing before a marbled square column, printed 'Lo am I a Gentleman? Upon Your Soul Tho Mother', enamels flaked, restoration to feet, 6½in (16.5cm), (E, 48/85).
£200-250 *CSK*

A pair of titled Staffordshire figures modelled as Moody and Sankey, each wearing a black frock coat, waistcoat and trousers, resting a hand on a book surmounted pedestal, both titled in black raised script, on oval gilt lined bases, c1873, 11in (28cm), (D,4/8/9).
£500-700 *Bon*

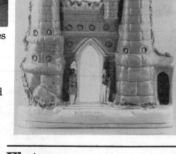

A Staffordshire figure of the Russian fortress of Sebastopol, in salmon colour, c1854, 10in (25cm), (C,69/181).
£420-480 *RWB*

Flatware

A Staffordshire flatback figure entitled Miss Nightingale on base, Miss Nightingale standing beside a seated wounded soldier, in polychrome colours to the front and rear, c1860, (C,55/143).
£480-520 *P(M)*

Two similar Bristol delft plates, 9in (22cm) diam. **£600-650** *DN*

An unusual Bristol charger showing Adam and Eve, c1690, 13½in (34cm) diam.
£3,500-4,000 *JHo*

A London delft inscribed and dated plate, the centre with the inscription 'Weilcom.my.Freinds' with the date 1661 with flourishes below, crack to rim before 7-o-clock towards the centre, slight rim flaking, 1661, 7½in (19cm) wide.
£10,500-12,000 *C*

An English delft blue and white dated plate, painted with Oriental vases of flowers above the inscription 'Sarah Pearson Born 17th Ag.ust 1734', reserved on a blue ground with scrolls and flowers, slight rim chips, perhaps Liverpool, 1734, 9in (23cm) diam.
£3,000-3,500 *C*

A Bristol delft blue dash tulip charger, the centre painted with a stylised blue and yellow tulip flanked by 2 iron red-centred flowers and green and yellow grasses within a concentric blue line cartouche, the border with green and yellow leaves, striped yellow fruits and blue foliage within a blue dash rim, cracks and chips, c1730, 13in (33cm) diam.
£800-1,000 *C*

A Bristol Adam and Eve charger, with blue black glaze, some damage, 13½in (34cm) diam.
£1,200-1,400 *JHo*

An English delft powdered manganese ground plate, the centre painted in underglaze blue within an octagonal cartouche, the border with diamond shaped medallions of flowers divided by stylised carnations, rim chips, Bristol or Wincanton, c1740, 8½in (22cm) diam.
£700-900 *C*

A London delft blue and white Act of Union plate, painted with a thistle and rose beneath the Royal crown, flanked by the initials A R, within a concentric blue line and band rim, c1707, 9in (22.5cm) diam.
£1,300-1,800 *C*

A Llanelly pottery cockerel plate, with a border of continuous blue sponged flowerheads within red lines, the centre with typical cockerel and foliage in blue, red, green, brown enamel, unmarked, 9½in (24cm) diam.
£250-300 *HSS*

A large Irish delftware tureen stand by the Delamain factory, with underglaze blue floral decoration on white ground, mid-18thC, 22in (56cm) wide.
£650-700 *AH*

A rare English delft stand dish, c1740, 10in (25cm) diam.
£1,200-1,700 *DN*

A pair of English delft lobed plates, 6½in (16cm).
£600-650 *DN*

A Bristol delft tulip charger, painted with a blue and yellow striped tulip flanked by iron red-centred flowers and green and yellow foliage, within a concentric blue line cartouche, the border with green and yellow leaves alternating with striped yellow fruits and blue fronds within a powdered blue rim, glaze flaking to rim, c1740, 13in (33cm) diam.
£2,000-2,500 *C*

An English delft powdered manganese ground plate, with the initial A/HT and the date 1740 in an hexagonal cartouche at the top, chip to well, minor rim chips, Bristol or Wincanton, c1740, 8½in (22cm) diam.
£1,700-2,200 *C*

A Lambeth delft Merryman plate, c1734, 7½in (18cm).
£300-350 *DN*

A pair of English delftware leaf dishes, 4in (10cm) wide.
£700-800 *JHo*

A pair of English delft dated plates, with a cartouche reserved on a ground of plants and stylised flowerheads and dot pattern, one with slight rim chip, the other cracked across and repaired, Bristol or London, 1709, 8½in (21.5cm) diam.
£500-600 *C*

A Dillwyn & Co. pottery plate, the shaped rim moulded with roses and other garden flowers, painted in bright enamel colours, the centre printed in black with the seated figure of the young Queen Victoria, 8in (20cm).
£300-350 *Bea*

A pair of Mason's leaf dessert dishes, decorated with the Pagoda Tree pattern, c1835.
£450-500 *BEE*

A Dutch Delft lobed dish, painted in yellow, blue and green, foot pierced, minute rim chips, c1700, 13½in (34.5cm).
£400-600 *C*

A Mason's Ironstone shell dessert dish, decorated with the Japan pattern, c1820, 11in (28cm) long.
£200-250 *BEE*

A Liverpool tin glazed blue and white plate, c1760, 8½in (22cm) diam.
£140-160 *JHo*

A Mason's Ironstone drainer, decoration with the Japan pattern, c1820, 6in (15cm) diam.
£150-180 *BEE*

A Lambeth tin glazed plate, c1780, 9in (23cm) diam.
£180-200 *JHo*

A set of 4 Ironstone plates, Royal Mail, 9½in (24cm) diam.
£30-50 *RFA*

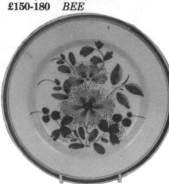

An English polychrome plate, 9in (23cm) diam.
£400-450 *JHo*

A pair of Staffordshire leaf dishes, c1765, 10 by 9in (25 by 23.5cm).
£1,500-1,800 *JHo*

A pair of early English pottery dishes, with scroll side handles, painted with red and green fruiting vine borders, gilt highlights, 11in (28cm) wide.
£75-100   *HCH*

A majolica bread dish, 'Where Reason Rules, the Appetite Obeys', 13in (33cm) wide.
£70-80   *OD*

A Wedgwood creamware armorial and crested dish, the centre bat-printed in black and painted in iron red and enriched in gilding with a coat-of-arms above the motto 'Main-Tien le Droit', the border with iron red flower sprays, small chip to underside of rim, c1768, 11in (28.5cm) wide.
£450-650   *C*

The arms are those of James Brydges, Marquis of Caernarvon (1731-89), who in 1753 married Margaret Nicol (d.1768) whose arms are shown on an escutcheon of pretence. Caernarvon succeeded his father as third Duke of Chandos in 1771.

A pair of Dutch Delft dated blue and white plates, cartouche outlined in black, enclosing the initials WWM and the date 1705, one cracked, rims chipped, c1705, 8½in (21cm) diam.
£500-600   *CSK*

A pair of Dutch Delft lobed dishes, 18thC, 13½in (34cm).
£250-300   *DN*

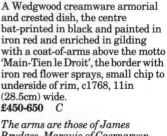

An Hispano Moresque saucer dish, early 18thC, 7½in (19cm) diam.
£250-300   *Wai*

A Spode meat dish and pierced drainer, printed with the Tiber pattern, printed mark, 19in (48cm) wide.
£600-700   *CSK*

A small Hispano Moresque saucer dish, 16thC, 8in (20cm).
£300-400   *DN*

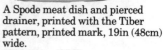

A Bologna deep dish decorated in 'sgraffito' with an enormous fish with ochre body and manganese head and fins, surrounded by flowerheads on a splashed green ground, within a flat rim with cable and line pattern, extensively damaged and repaired, 2 rim chips, 16thC, 16½in (42cm) diam.
£1,400-1,600   *C*

A Frankfurt faience dish, decorated in the Wanli style, c1700, 15in (39cm).
£500-600   *DN*

An Italian majolica dish in the Castelli style, 18thC, 12½in (32cm) diam.
£700-800 *Wai*

A Staffordshire meat dish, printed with the Rural Scenery pattern, within a border of flowers and scrolling foliage, the reverse with a named panel, 19in (49cm).
£300-400 *CSK*

Jardinières

A pair of Wedgwood jardinières, c1872, 9½in (24cm).
£1,200-1,500 *BHA*

A pair of Minton turquoise jardinières, with ram's head handles, the blue ground reserved with cherubs on 3 scrolling legs and ribbed base, impressed marks, 12½in (32cm).
£500-600 *CSK*

A pair of George Jones majolica jardinières, moulded in relief and picked out in strong colours over the navy blue ground, all beneath a yellow rim, pale blue interior, minor restoration, impressed G.J. monogram, black painted pattern No. 3326/D(2), c1865, 15in (38cm).
£2,200-2,600 *S(S)*

Jars

A London delft blue and white drug jar, c1690, 9½in (24cm).
£1,200-1,500 *JHo*

A pair of Dutch Delft blue and white jardinières, blue painted mark for the Greek 'A' pottery, mid-18thC, 8in (20cm).
£2,500-3,000 *Bon*

Two London delft blue and white wet drug jars for S:DE:SPIN:CER and S:E:RUB:IDAEIS with cartouches, surmounted by 2 songbirds among foliage flanking a basket of fruit and with a winged cherub's head suspending swags of fruit and tassels below, one with crack to body, chips to rim and footrim, the other with chip and repair to rim and crack to footrim, both with glaze flaking, c1700, 8in (20cm).
£600-800 *C*

A wet drug jar, probably London, late 17thC, 6½in (16cm).
£450-500 *JHo*

An English delft cylindrical drug jar, probably London, c1760.
£200-250   *DN*

A London delft blue and white wet drug jar named for O.EXCESTREN:, crack to foot, rims chipped, c1720, 7in (17.5cm).
£350-450   *C*

A Bristol delft blue and white wet drug jar, named in manganese for MEL:ROSACEUM, chips to footrim and glaze flaking to rim and spout, manganese 'eye' mark to base, c1740, 8in (20cm).**£350-550**   *C*

An English delftware dry drug jar, inscribed in blue E.LENITIV within a central cartouche between a scallop shell and a winged cherub's mask, flanked by 2 cherubs holding floral sprays and a pair of floral swags, minor rim chips, early 18thC, 10½in (26cm).
£700-800   *S*

A pair of Lambeth delft blue and white baluster drug jars for P:THEBAICAE and P:PACIFICAE, rim chips and cracks, c1770, 3½in (9cm).
£1,000-1,500   *C*

A Dutch Delft ovoid tobacco jar, with brass cover, 18thC, 13in (33cm).
£750-850   *DN*

A Dutch Delft ovoid tobacco jar, with brass cover, 18thC, 11in (28cm).
£600-700   *DN*

A Savona blue and white wet drug jar, named for OI:ANETHI on a ribbon cartouche, pharmacy mark F.R at the base of the handle, rim and spout chipped, blue watchtower mark, late 17thC, 8½in (21cm).
£1,500-2,000   *C*

An Hispano Moresque ovoid jar, 16thC, 12in (31cm).
£3,000-3,500   *DN*

An English delft drug jar, named in manganese for OPII:PURIFICAT: on a strapwork cartouche with a shell and winged cherubs above and flowers and tassels below, rim chips, Bristol or London, c1760, 3½in (9cm).
£600-700 *C*

A London delft blue and white drug jar named for U.NEAPOLIT, minor crack to rim, rim chips, c1720, 7in (17.5cm).
£350-450 *C*

Three Dutch Delft blue and white oviform tobacco jars, each painted with a Red Indian smoking a pipe, seated beneath a tree beside a jar named with the type of tobacco, St. Omer with slight rim chips, contemporary brass covers, 2 with blue 3 bells mark and one with B?P in blue, c1740, 9 and 10½in (23 and 27.5cm).
£3,000-3,500 *C*

An English delft drug jar, named in manganese for EX:GENISTAE: on a blue strapwork cartouche, with a shell flanked by winged cherubs above and a winged cherub's head and flowerheads below, Bristol or London, c1760, 3½in (9cm).
£450-550 *C*

A French faience wet drug jar, with short straight spout and loop handle, named in manganese for S.BERBERIS within a blue berried foliage cartouche, on a circular foot, late 18thC, 8½in (20.5cm).
£200-250 *C*

Jugs

A Dutch Delft oviform jar, painted in tones of blue and outlined in manganese with Orientals in an extensive rocky wooded river landscape, between bands of radiating stiff leaves and scrolling foliage, slight rim chips and glaze flaking, c1700, 9½in (24cm).
£900-1,200 *C*

A Hicks & Meigh jug and bowl set, decorated in polychrome colours, c1825, jug 8in (20cm), bowl 9in (23cm) diam.
£250-300 *BEE*

A London delft blue and white drug jar named on a ribbon, with a winged angel's head above and fluttering pennants below, minute crack to rim, c1680, 3½in (9cm).
£900-1.200 *C*

A Copeland parianware jug, with relief cherub figures picking grapes, late 19thC, 9in (23cm).
£90-120 *PCh*

A Leeds creamware jug with reeded body, mask-head spout and pierced rim, painted with underglaze green streaks, late 18thC, 3in (7.5cm).
£700-800 *Bea*

A Leeds creamware baluster jug, boldly painted with a portrait of the Princess of Orange, reserve within a foliate cartouche, slight restoration, late 18thC, 5½in (14cm).
£120-180 *Bea*

An early Mason's Ironstone jug, with strap handles, painted in polychrome enamels, unmarked, c1815, 11in (29cm).
£550-600 *VH*

A Liverpool delft blue and white puzzle jug of conventional type, with hollow rim and handle with 3 spouts, the neck pierced with hearts and ovals, the body inscribed with a four-line verse 'Here Gentle-men Come Try Your Skill . . .', glaze flaking to handle, rim and spouts, c1760, 6½in (17cm).
£800-1,200 *C*

An early Mason's jug and bowl set, impressed mark, c1815, 7½in (19cm).
£1,100-1,150 *VH*

A Mason's Ironstone jug, decorated with the Heron pattern, No. 311 on base, c1830, 8in (20cm).
£300-350 *BEE*

A Mason's Ironstone jug with strap handle, c1820, 6½in (16cm).
£250-300 *BEE*

An English delft blue and white puzzle jug, c1760, 7in (17.5cm).
£1,000-1,200 *JHo*

A Mason's Ironstone blue ground octagonal jug, with a snake moulded handle enriched in gilding, painted with butterflies and dragonflies in gilding, gilding rubbed, 8½in (21cm).
£100-200 *CSK*

A Minton majolica jug, lip and base repaired, impressed mark, date code for 1864, 12in (31cm).
£400-500 *CSK*

A pearlware pink lustre jug printed and coloured with a view of the Sunderland Bridge, stained, 4½in (11cm).
£150-200 *CSK*

A Staffordshire transfer decorated jug with good colours, c1830.
£70-90 *RP*

A Mason's Ironstone jug with dragon handle, c1840, 7in (17.5cm).
£300-350 *BEE*

Again, this interesting handle is reflected in the price.

An English delft puzzle jug, the body inscribed in blue with a drinking verse, the pierced decoration outlined in blue, neck restored, glaze chips, c1760, 7½in (19cm).
£400-600   *CSK*

A Mason's Ironstone jug, decorated with the Red Scale pattern, c1835, 6½in (18cm).
£250-300   *BEE*

The fact that this piece has a rare and desirable twig handle increases the price.

An early Mason's Ironstone footbath and jug, in Vase and Table pattern with printed crown mark, restored, c1825.
£2,750-3,000   *VH*

A large Mason's Ironstone jug, with traditional Oriental decoration of snake handle, early 19thC, 11in (29cm).
£200-220   *GAK*

A Mason's Ironstone jug and basin set, jug 8½in (21cm) high, bowl 13in (33cm) diam.
£750-800   *SBA*

A Mason's Ironstone jug, God Cermoccus, c1830, 8½in (21cm).
£360-400   *BEE*

A Mason's Ironstone jug, c1820.
£120-240   *BEE*

A Mason's Ironstone jug with Stag Hunt pattern, c1830, 8in (20cm).
£350-400   *BEE*

A Minton majolica jester jug, with impressed marks for 1870, 13in (33cm).
£350-400 *DN*

A Minton grey stone Drunken Silenus jug, base cracked, impressed No. 16 on a scroll, 9in (23cm).
£100-130 *CSK*

A Staffordshire buff stoneware Tam O'Shanter and Souter Johnnie jug, neck and lip cracked, 9½in (24cm).
£70-120 *CSK*

A Wedgwood pearlware jug, with an orange ground border reserved with flowering prunus within bands of gilding, cracked and enamels slightly worn, 6½in (16cm).
£100-130 *CSK*

A Sunderland Bridge pink lustre ground pearlware jug, printed and coloured with a view of Sunderland Bridge flanked by 2 mottos within flower and floral cartouches, crack to the rim and base of handle, 9in (23cm).
£200-300 *CSK*

A Staffordshire saltglazed white pecten shell-moulded baluster cream jug, with reeded scroll handle and on 3 paw feet, moulded with shell ornament and with snails to each side of the lip, small crack to rim, c1755, 3½in (8.5cm).
£800-1,000 *C*

A W. Ridgway & Co. green stoneware Tam O'Shanter and Souter Johnnie jug, impressed mark, 8in (20cm).
£70-100 *CSK*

A fine quality creamware jug, c1775, 7in (18cm).
£2,200-2,600 *JHo*

A Sunderland pink lustre jug with a loop handle, printed in black with a view of the cast iron bridge over the River Weir, flanked by a verse and by a three-masted sailing ship, Northumberland 7, 8in (20cm).
£200-300 *CSK*

A Staffordshire saltglazed white pecten shell moulded baluster cream jug, with reeded loop handle, on 3 mask and paw feet, moulded with shell ornament and with trailing foliage, crack to base of handle, c1755, 3½in (9cm).
£500-600 *C*

A Minton dark green stoneware Drunken Silenus jug, damage and restoration to rim, impressed No. 19 on a scroll, 8½in (21cm).
£120-180   CSK

A Staffordshire jug with coloured, raised hunting scene and leaf decoration, cracked, 19thC, 5in (13cm).
£100-120   P

A creamware jug printed in black, on one side a couple in a blacksmith's shop, entitled 'Gretna Green' or the 'Red Hot Marriage', and on the other an inn interior with a verse, 8½in (21cm).
£250-350   Bea

A German blue and white faience jug, painted with stylised flowers, the handle with blue scrolls, perhaps Hanau, 5½in (14cm).
£300-400   CSK

A Sunderland Bridge pink lustre pearlware jug, printed and coloured with a view of Sunderland Bridge, the reverse with a Seaman's Verse within a flower and floral cartouche, the rims enriched in pink lustre, the top of the handle and base cracked, 8½in (21cm).
£140-180   CSK

A Don pottery jug with loop handle and a grip, printed with the 'Italian Residence of Solinenes, near Vesuvius', below a border of putti amongst flowers and foliage, slight chips, printed marks, 11½in (30cm).
£1,500-2,000   CSK

Toby Jugs

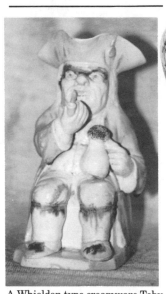

A Staffordshire pearlware oviform jug, printed and coloured with farmer's emblems and trophies and inscribed 'A N' in gilding, enamels and gilding slightly worn, 6in (15.5cm).
£200-250   CSK

A Ralph Wood long-faced Toby jug, with creamware body, unglazed bottom of base, decorated in green and manganese translucent glazes, c1770, 10in (25cm).
£4,000-5,000   HEY

A rare and particularly well modelled example.

A Whieldon type creamware Toby jug with step base, decorated with translucent green glazed coat and manganese to face, hose and shoes, c1760, 9½in (24cm).
£2,500-3,000   HEY

A small Staffordshire Coachman
Toby jug, c1830, 6in (14cm).
£800-1,200   *GIN*

A Walton impressed Toby jug,
c1820, 11½in (29cm).
£900-1,200   *GIN*

A pearlware Toby jug and cover,
probably Yorkshire, painted in blue,
green, ochre and brown enamels,
minor damage, 10½in (26.5cm).
£650-950   *Bea*

Three miniature Toby jugs, c1820-40.   **£110-130**   *GIN*

A Prattware Martha Gunn Toby
jug, c1800, 10½in (26cm).
£2,000-3,000   *GIN*

A creamware Toby jug on Georgian
base, decorated in translucent glazes,
with green waistcoat and blue
taupe patterned coat, c1790, 10in (25cm).
£650-850   *HEY*

A French version of the Toby jug
from the Porquier factory, 19thC,
11½in (29cm).
£900-1,000   *SBA*

A Victorian Toby jug in overglaze
enamels, with brown coat, lime
waistcoat and yellow breeches,
small sparrow beak jug, decorated
with rust flower, c1870, 10in (25cm).
£150-200   *HEY*

A squat Toby jug with painted face
and unusual pink swirled coat,
green vest and chair, c1800, 8½in
(21.5cm).
£200-250   *HEY*

A Toby jug in underglaze mauve coat, turquoise waistcoat and fawn breeches, c1800, 10in (25cm).
£650-800   *HEY*

A monkey band Toby jug, c1835, 10in (26cm).
£400-450   *GIN*

A rare Martha Gunn Toby jug, dressed in red and green sprigged dress with ochre bodice, on red chair and green base, c1840, 10in (25cm).
£2,000-3,000   *HEY*

A Neale & Co. Toby jug complete with measure, decorated in overglaze enamels, brown coat, breeches and hat, red waistcoat and blue hose, on pebbled base, restoration to hat, c1800, 10in (25cm).   **£700-850**   *HEY*

A pearlware Toby jug in running glazes, with blue coat, brown waistcoat, small jug, hose and shoes, with blue delft type decorations to hat, handle and chairback, pipe unusually by left knee, c1790, 10in (25cm).
£900-1,000   *HEY*

A Neale & Co. Toby jug complete with measure, in overglaze enamels, turquoise coat, blue hose, brown jug and waistcoat on pebbled base, restoration to hat, c1800, 10in (25cm).
£750-900   *HEY*

A Wilkinson Toby jug, modelled as Admiral Beatty, by Francis Carruthers Gould in a limited edition of 350, c1918, 11in (28cm).
£350-400   *HEY*

A Toby jug, The Large American Sailor, decorated in blue and grey enamels, the grey chest impressed 'Dollars', impressed 'W' to rear, 'Success to our wooden walls' printed on small mug, restoration to pipe and bocage, c1810, 11in (28cm).
£2,500-3,000   *HEY*

A Yorkshire thin man Toby jug, c1780, 8½in (21cm).
£3,500-4,500 *GIN*

A Ralph Wood traditional model Toby jug, c1780.
£800-1,600 *GIN*

A Staffordshire stepped base Toby jug, c1780, 10in (25cm).
£1,000-1,800 *GIN*

A large impressed Hollins Toby jug, c1805, 9½in (24cm).
£1,500-2,500 *GIN*

A Staffordshire Toby jug of Mr. Punch seated on 3 volumes in a red hat and red striped suit, enriched in gilding, gilding slightly rubbed, 10in (25cm).
£150-200 *CSK*

A Martha Gunn Toby jug by Ralph Wood, c1780, 11in (28cm).
£2,500-3,500 *GIN*

A Ralph Wood type Toby jug, with measure, c1780, 9in (23cm).
£1,200-1,600 *GIN*

A Ralph Wood longface Toby jug, c1780, 10in (25cm).
£1,500-2,500 *GIN*

A Prattware Toby jug, c1800, 10in (25cm).
£350-650 *GIN*

A Staffordshire Collier Toby jug, c1780.
£1,500-2,500 *GIN*

A Ralph Wood Toby jug, c1780.
£1,200-1,600 *GIN*

A Ralph Wood raised cup Toby jug,
c1780, 11in (29cm).
£800-1,600   *GIN*

A Prattware Toby jug, c1800, 9½in
(24cm).
£800-1,000   *GIN*

A Rodney's Sailor pearlware Toby
jug, c1780, 11½in (29cm).
£2,500-4,000   *GIN*

A Staffordshire Toby jug of The
Squire, c1780, 10in (25cm).
£3,500-5,000   *GIN*

An Enoch Wood traditional Toby
jug, c1800, 11½in (29cm).
£450-650   *GIN*

A Yorkshire Toby jug, c1780, 7in
(18cm).
£700-900   *GIN*

A Prattware Hearty
Good Fellow Toby jug,
c1800, 11in (28cm).
£1,000-1,400   *GIN*

A Prattware Toby jug,
c1800, 10in (25cm).
£650-950   *GIN*

59

A Wilkinson Toby jug, modelled as George V by Francis Carruthers Gould in a limited edition of 1,000, sparsely coloured, mainly in underglaze blue, c1919, 12in (30cm).
£400-500 *HEY*

A Hearty Good Fellow Toby jug, in underglaze colours, with overglaze turquoise coat, restoration to hat, c1815, 11in (28cm).
£600-800 *HEY*

Wilkinson Limited First World War Toby Jugs, designed by Sir F. Carruthers Gould, all with printer's marks and facsimile signature, from left:
President Wilson dressed as Uncle Sam with a bi-plane between his legs, 10½in (26cm).
£200-300

Admiral Beatty dressed in naval uniform, supporting a shell entitled 'Dreadnought' between his legs, slight damage to the right hand, 10½in (26.5cm).
£200-300
King George V dressed as an Admiral, 12in (30cm).
£500-550

Lloyd George dressed as Admiral of the Fleet, supporting a shell between his legs, 10in (25cm).
£200-300
Marshall Foch dressed as an Infantry Officer toasting to The Devil, The Kaiser, 12in (30cm).
£250-300 *P(M)*

Mugs

A Nottingham salt glazed stoneware bulbous mug, the neck applied with a silver metal mount and flanked by a grooved strap handle, the silver mount engraved N.R.E, hair crack to neck, late 17thC, 3½in (9cm).
£2,000-2,700 *S*

A Mason's Ironstone cider mug with flared base, c1820, 4in (10cm).
£300-350 *BEE*

A Staffordshire slipware mug, c1700, 3in (7cm).
£2,000-2,200 *JHo*

A creamware cylindrical veilleuse of Whieldon type, with moulded female masks with pendant plaits of hair, the front with an ogee arch to take a burner, slight crack and chip to top rim, c1760, 7in (17.5cm).
£600-1,000 *C*

A Staffordshire redware baluster mug with grooved loop handle, the brown ground with a cream slip band with a 'sgraffito' bird flanked by trailing flowers and the initials 'g B' beneath a cream slip rim, crack to one side, chip to rim, handle repaired, perhaps Newcastle-Under-Lyme, c1745, 6in (15cm).
£2,000-2,500 *C*

A Staffordshire creamware mug, c1775.
£600-700 *JHo*

An English creamware mug printed in black, chipped, c1790, 4½in (11cm).
£175-225 *CSK*

A child's beaker, c1840.
£60-80   *RP*

A Staffordshire tapering cylindrical agate-glazed mug, the interior with an applied frog, chipped and cracked, 6in (15.5cm).
£200-250   *CSK*

A blue and white mug, probably Liverpool, c1740, 4in (9cm).
£400-500   *JHo*

Plaques

A glazed and polychrome earthenware domed panel of the Virgin and Child in a niche, within a fruiting border, in the manner of Della Robbia, 27in (68cm).
£500-600   *CSK*

A Prattware plaque, Liverpool Volunteers, 5in (13cm) square.
£700-800   *JHo*

A Cistercian black glazed mug, restored lip, c1600, 4½in (11cm).
£300-350   *Sto*

The mug was excavated from a pavement in Finsbury.

A pottery plaque, moulded and painted with the bust of Queen Caroline wearing a plumed hat, a crown and the initials 'Q.C.' above, framed in a copper and purple lustre border, 5½in (13.5cm).
£500-600   *Bea*

A Wedgwood & Bentley blue and white jasper portrait medallion of Voltaire, the solid blue ground applied with his portrait, impressed lower case mark, contemporary gilt metal frame with beaded border, c1775, 3½in (8.5cm) high.
£1,500-2,000   *C*

A Toby Phillpot plaque, c1830, 9in (23cm) diam.
£400-800   *GIN*

A pair of creamware plaques, moulded and coloured in blue and brown with The Dipping of Achilles, within brown reeded and leaf moulded rectangular frames, pierced for hanging, both with slight crack to rim, c1800, 3½ by 3in (8.5 by 7.5cm).
£350-500   *C*

Pots

An English delft polychrome baluster posset pot and cover, with blue dash ornament, painted in iron red, blue and green, hair crack to pot and chips and glaze flaking to rim and rim of cover, London or Bristol, c1710, 8in (19cm).
£4,500-5,500   *C*

A Staffordshire redware flower pot,
c1765, 5in (13cm).
£1,200-1,500   *JHo*

A Wedgwood caneware bough pot,
painted on a blue ground, within an
oval gilt line cartouche and painted
in a bright blue palette, crack to one
angle at back, c1790, 8in (20cm).
£600-700   *C*

Pot Lids

Yardley's Tooth Paste, London
and Paris, B.162, coloured square
lid, together with 13 other assorted
monochrome pot lids, including:
Army & Navy Almond Shaving
Cream, D.I. green, Army & Navy
Cold Cream of Roses, Army & Navy
Areca Nut Tooth Paste, 2 square
Tooth Paste lids and various Cold
Cream, Tooth Paste and other lids.
£200-250   *S*

A Staffordshire redware cylindrical
mustard pot and cover, with loop
handle, applied in cream relief with
2 cockerels, a flowerhead and
foliage, the cover extensively
restored, some chipping to relief,
c1745, 3½in (9cm).
£400-600   *C*

Sauceboats

A Staffordshire salt glazed
sauceboat, c1765, 3in (8cm).
£1,200-1,500   *JHo*

A Pratt pottery sauceboat moulded
in the form of a dolphin, painted in
green, brown and ochre enamels,
6½in (16cm) long.
£300-400   *Bea*

A Staffordshire creamware shell
shaped sauceboat, with double
entwined reeded handle, the rim
moulded with feathered scrolls on a
spreading foot, chipped and stained,
6½in (16cm).
£100-150   *CSK*

Services

A Leeds pottery white glazed part
dessert service, moulded in the form
of leaves with twig handles,
comprising: a comport and
19 dishes in 5 sizes, minor chips,
impressed mark Leeds Pottery,
19thC, largest dishes 13in (33cm)
wide.
£750-800   *S(S)*

A Mason's Ironstone part dessert
service, transfer printed and
coloured with flowers within an
elaborate diaper and whorl pattern
border, reserved with pink
flowerheads and blue foliage,
comprising: 2 oval two-handled
sauce tureens, covers and stands,
12 dishes and 22 plates, printed
mark, c1820.
£2,600-3,000   *C*

> ### Did you know
> *MILLER'S Antiques Price
> Guide builds up year by
> year to form the most
> comprehensive photo-
> reference system
> available*

A Copeland & Garrett new faience
137 piece dinner service, transfer
printed on brown trellis ground,
pattern No. 445, mid-19thC.
£2,500-3,000   *WHB*

A Wedgwood creamware breakfast
set, designed by Rex Whistler,
decorated with monochrome
transfer printed vignettes and floral
sprays, comprising: a teapot, cream
jug, sugar bowl, 2 cups and saucers,
and a plate, printed Rex Whistler
Design, with impressed and printed
marks Wedgwood made in England,
teapot 4½in (11.5cm) high.
£250-400   *C*

**Miller's is a price
GUIDE not a price
LIST**

A Wedgwood 67 piece dinner
service, c1880.
£900-1,200   *HSS*

A tea and coffee service attributed to
Ralph and James Clews, pattern
No. 423, c1823.
£1,500-2,000   *DN*

A Spode pearlware part dinner
service, decorated in pattern
No. 3154 in polychrome with pink
flowers, comprising: 2 platters,
9 plates, 4 soup bowls, and a
vegetable dish, impressed Spode
and a digit, printed Spode in brown,
early 19thC.
£200-250   *MN*

A Staffordshire part dinner service,
printed with the Family and Mule
pattern, comprising: 3 shaped oval
meat dishes, a square dish and
10 dinner plates, some damage.
£600-700   *CSK*

63

Tiles

A London delft tin glazed tile, c1740, 5½in (13.5cm). **£80-90** *JHo*

A Bristol tile depicting Jonah and the Whale, c1750, 5in (13cm) square. **£75-100** *JHo*

A Liverpool black transfer ware tile, c1765, 5in (13cm) square. **£120-150** *JHo*

A London delft blue and white tile, c1770, 5in (13cm) square. **£55-70** *JHo*

A London delft tile, c1740, 5in (12cm). **£125-160** *JHo*

A Liverpool black transfer ware tile, restored, c1765, 5in (13cm) square. **£50-60** *JHo*

A Liverpool black transfer printed tile, c1770. **£120-150** *JHo*

Tureens

An early Mason's Ironstone china covered sauce tureen, painted in Imari style, early impressed mark, c1820. **£250-300** *MN*

A Staffordshire sauce tureen and stand, with rosebud finial lid, early 19thC, 6in (15cm) high. **£200-240** *BEE*

A George Jones majolica sardine box and cover, covered in a brown glaze with turquoise interior, small chip inside cover, impressed registration diamond, black painted numerals 3541/111, c1865, 9in (23cm). **£500-600** *S(S)*

A Mason's Ironstone dessert tureen, richly gilded, c1820, 7½in (18.5cm). **£400-500** *BEE*

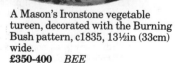

A Mason's Ironstone vegetable tureen, decorated with the Burning Bush pattern, c1835, 13½in (33cm) wide. **£350-400** *BEE*

A Staffordshire hen on nest, c1880.
£180-220   *RP*

A Hicks, Meigh & Johnson vegetable tureen, c1830, 15in (38cm) wide.
£350-450   *BEE*

A John Rogers & Son tureen and cover, decorated with blue floral transfers, lid surmounted by a lion head and with 2 lion masks handles, impressed factory mark to base, early 19thC, 8in (20cm).
£270-300   *HSS*

A Staffordshire soup tureen and cover, with a rose finial, printed with the Bridge of Lucano, the base with a named ribbon, one handle damaged and restuck, 12½in (32cm).
£300-400   *CSK*

A rare salt glazed butter tub and cover, moulded with a seeded diaper ground beneath a single band of small ovolos, the domed cover divided into 4 segments, each pierced with 3 square holes, and surmounted by a recumbent bull, c1760, 4½in (11cm).
£1,200-1,600   *S*

Vases

A Minton majolica two-handled game pie tureen, cover and liner, covered in a brown glaze encrusted and entwined with green oak leaves and acorns, the cover surmounted by a dead hare, duck and jackdaw lying on ferns and leaves, restoration, impressed marks and date cypher, 1878, 13½in (34cm) wide.
£700-800   *S(S)*

A pair of Mason's Ironstone hall vases, with applied rich floral decoration, elaborate dragon handles and matching covers with dragon finials, slight damage to covers, c1820, 26in (66cm).
£4,500-5,000   *GH*

A Liverpool vase, painted with buildings beside a willow tree issuing from rockwork, a figure crossing a bridge and 2 figures in a landscape, with birds above, crack to body and 2 cracks to rim, incised 6 mark, Pennington's factory, c1770, 9in (22.5cm).
£800-1,000   *C*

A Mason's Ironstone vase with centurion handles, with lustre decoration, c1820, 6in (15cm).
£180-240   *BEE*

A Bristol delft boldly painted baluster vase, extensive glaze flaking to body, foot chipped, c1730, 12in (31cm).
£1,200-1,500   *C*

A large Mason's Ironstone two-handled vase on hexagonal foot, with cover, painted with a frieze of classical figures, above and below a band of Greek key, on iron red body, with dragon moulded handles and fish entwined knop, 19thC, 25.5in (65cm).
£650-700 *Bon*

A Mason's Ironstone large vase and cover, with mythical beast lug handles, the cover with entwined dolphin knop, decorated in shades of blue and orange, with printed and impressed marks, some damage and repair, c1840, 25in (63cm) high.
£600-650 *HSS*

A Mason's Ironstone lidded vase, with Dog of Fo finial and Chinese seal mark, lid restored, c1830, 10½in (26cm).
£300-350 *BEE*

A Mason's Ironstone alcove vase, with lion handle, c1835, 17½in (44cm).
£400-500 *BEE*

A pair of Mason's Ironstone vases and covers.
£550-650 *DM*

A Minton vase by Christopher Dresser, shape No. 2693, c1885.
£250-300 *Ced*

A pottery treacle-glazed stoneware vase with gilt-metal mounts, painted all over in gilding with scrolling foliage and flowers, on a spreading foot with engine-turned metal rims and base, the base with an incised mark, gilding slightly rubbed, 10½in (26cm).
£300-500 *CSK*

A salt glazed baluster vase, covered in a Littler's blue glaze, glaze fault to shoulder, slight crack to rim, c1760, 7in (17.5cm).
£2,000-2,500 *C*

William Littler and Aaron Wedgwood shared a pot bank at Brownhills 1745-63. Littler moved to Longton Hall to concentrate on porcelain production leaving Wedgwood on his own. In the sales account book of Thomas and John Wedgwood they refer to their cousin's wares as 'Aaron's Blue'.

A Dutch Delft fluted globular vase, with tapering garlic neck, painted in manganese and blue, slight chips to rim, manganese 8 mark, c1700, 12in (31cm).
£1,000-1,500   C

Three Dutch Delft blue and white vases and covers, painted with a river landscape within a scroll cartouche flanked by trailing flowers, between shaped fluted and panelled borders with flowers, the covers with hound and shield finials, minor rim restorations to vases and covers, slight flaking, 2 finials restored, c1740, 18in (46cm).
£2,500-3,500   C

Wemyss

A Dresden oviform vase and domed cover, with moulded female mask handles, painted within richly gilt scroll, foliage, 'gitterwerk' and strapwork cartouches, cracks to shoulder and body, one handle repaired, imitation blue AR mark, c1890, 17½in (44cm).
£450-650   C

l. A large Wemyss pottery model of a pig, with black patch markings, the ears, snout and mouth coloured in pink wash, one ear restuck, impressed Wemyss Ware, 17½in (45cm) long.
£1,500-2,000
r. A small Wemyss pottery model of a pig, with black patch markings, the face and trotters detailed in pink, inscribed Wemyss, printed Made in England, 6½in (16cm).
£400-600   Bea

A Wemyss jug and basin, painted with fruiting cherries within a blue/green rim, impressed and painted marks, T. Goode & Co. retailer's marks, jug 6in (15cm) high, bowl 11½in (29cm) diam.
£350-500   CSK

A Wemyss pommade pot, painted with roses, 3½in (8cm) diam.
£200-300   RdeR

A Scottish Wemyss ware pottery pig, painted with pink roses and foliage, early 20thC, 16½in (42cm).
£3,500-4,000   CLG

A Wemyss chocolate pot, painted with brown cockerels, 5½in (14cm) high.
£200-300   RdeR

In the Ceramics section if there is only one measurement it usually refers to the height of the piece

A Wemyss dog bowl, with impressed mark, 7in (17cm) diam.
£350-400   DN

A Wemyss 'violet' plaque, with hair cracks, 5½ by 3½in   **£200-300   RdeR**

A Wemyss square honey pot, stand and cover, with thistle finial, painted in colours within a dark green dentil border, inscribed marks, 7in (18cm) wide.
£500-700 *CSK*

A Wemyss ware sugar bowl, cream jug and baluster shaped cream jug, inscribed Bon Jour to side, sugar bowl 2in (5cm) high, impressed retailer's mark Goode & Co, cream jug 2½in (6cm) high, printed retailer's mark Goode & Co, slight rubbing to spout, baluster jug 4in (10cm) high, small hole to the body, rubbing to spout and handle, early impressed mark.
£170-220 *MN*

A Wemyss pig painted with clover, 6½in (16cm) long.
£500-700 *RdeR*

A pair of Wemyss candlesticks with rose design, 12in (30.5cm).
£700-900 *RdeR*

A Wemyss jug and basin set, including a sponge bowl and soap dish, jug 10in (25cm) high.
£1,500-2,500 *RdeR*

A Wemyss bowl painted with buttercups, 6½in (16cm) diam.
£400-500 *RdeR*

A Wemyss plate with wisteria, 5in (13cm) diam.
£200-400 *RdeR*

A Wemyss black and white pig, 6in (15cm) long.
£300-500 *RdeR*

A Wemyss thistle vase, 5½in (14cm) high.
£150-200 *RdeR*

A pair of Wemyss cats with pink bows, 12½in (32cm) high.
£3,000-4,000 each *RdeR*

A Wemyss biscuit pot, painted with apples, 4in (10cm).
£300-500 *RdeR*

A Wemyss goose, 8in (20cm) high.
£600-900 *RdeR*

A pearlware bear-baiting group, Staffordshire or Yorkshire, crack to bear's left flank, c1790, 12½in (31.5cm) wide. **£10,000-12,000** *C*

A Staffordshire creamware equestrian group of Hudibras of Ralph Wood type, some damage and restoration, c1785, 12in (30cm). **£15,000-18,000** *C*

A London delft armorial wine bottle, chipped and restored, c1650, 8in (20cm). **£18,000-22,000** *C*

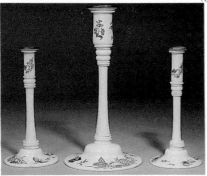

An opaque white candlestick with enamel drip pan, and a similar pair, South Staffordshire, damage, c1760, 10in (25cm) and 7in (18cm). l.&r. **£7,000-8,000** c. **3,000-5,000** *C*

A London delft candlestick with wide drip pan, cracks and glaze flaking, 1653, 10in (25.5cm). **£155,000-160,000** *C*

A saltglaze moulded candlestick, c1760, 8in (20cm). **£6,500-10,000** *C*

A small London delft royal portrait wine bottle with loop handle, inscribed ChARL^S THE 2^D, chipped and cracked, c1660, 6½in (16cm). **£155,000-160,000** *C*

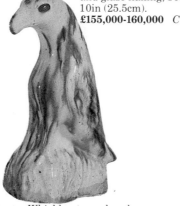

A rare Whieldon-type glazed slipware figure of a hawk, chips to base, late 18thC, 7in (17.5cm). **£5,000-7,000** *S*

A Mason's Ironstone punch bowl, decorated with the table and flower pot pattern, c1820, 13in (33cm) diam. **£1,200-1,300** *BEE*

An English delft inscribed and dated punch bowl, the underside with the initials K/WA and the date 1740, perhaps Bristol, some damage, 12½in (32cm). **£32,000-38,000** *C*

A Staffordshire saltglaze two-handled cup, incised with the initials H:N above the date 1756, with three cracks to the rim, 12in (30.5cm) wide. **£13,000-15,000** *C*

A pair of very rare Staffordshire figures of the royal children, Edward and Victoria, by Thomas Parr, 1850, 10in (25.5cm) high. **£1,400-1,800** *FS*

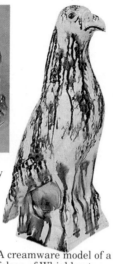

A creamware model of a falcon of Whieldon type, with moulded and incised plumage, c1770, 12in (30cm) high. **£10,000-12,000** *C*

A previously unrecorded Staffordshire group of Jesus and the Woman of Samaria, decorated in enamel colours, c1820, 8in (20cm). **£2,500-3,000** *JHo*

A Staffordshire watch holder modelled as whippets chasing a hare, watch missing, c1860, 8½in (21.5cm) high. **£250-280** *RWB*

A saltglaze model of an owl, with deeply moulded and incised plumage, eyes and short beak, on triangular mound base, some minute glaze fritting, c1750, 8in (20cm) high. **£72,000-75,000** *C*

A creamware model of a parrot of Whieldon type, with incised wing feathers and eyes, streaked in grey and brown glazes, perched astride a conical tree stump, c1760, 7in (17cm) high. **£15,000-18,000** *C*

A Mason's Ironstone cider mug, decorated with chinoiserie panels, c1820, 5in (13cm) high. **£450-500** *BEE*

A pair of Staffordshire pottery poodles with flower baskets in their mouths, c1860, 3½in (18cm) high. **£150-180** *RWB*

A creamware model of a squirrel of Whieldon type, ears restored, c1765, 7½in (19cm) high. **£9,000-12,000** *C*

A Staffordshire figure, probably of Lablache as Falstaff, c1845, 6in (15cm). **£150-170** *RWB*

A pair of Staffordshire figures portraying the Turkish general, Omar Pasha, on horseback, c1854, 4½in (11.5cm) high.
£450-500 *RWB*

A rare Staffordshire figure of Daniel O'Connell, c1845, 15½in (39cm).
£800-900 *RWB*

A Staffordshire figure of the Duke of Wellington, c1850, 12in (30cm) high.
£500-600 *RWB*

A rare Staffordshire figure of Admiral Sir Charles Napier, c1854, 12½in (32cm).
£750-800 *RWB*

A rare Staffordshire penholder depicting Lambton, c1845, 4in (10cm).
£90-100 *RWB*

An unrecorded English delft-ware blue-dash charger, decorated with a shepherd playing the bagpipes, probably London, c1700, 12½in (32.5cm).
£20,000-25,000 *JHo*

A Staffordshire group portraying standing Miss Florence Nightingale and a seated wounded officer, c1854, 10in (25.5cm). high. **£600-650** *RWB*

A Southwark delft poly-chrome La Fécondité dish of conventional type, marked with initials R over N.A and with the date 1659, 18½in (46.5cm) wide.
£25,000-30,000 *C*

A Savona figure of Winter, with minor chips and slight restoration, the underside incised with date 1779, 13½in (33.5cm) high.
£2,500-4,000 *C*

A creamware arbour group of Whieldon type, with two women in crinolines in a garden shelter with a dove roosting on the roof, cracked, 6in (14.5cm).
£33,000-35,000 *Bea*

A creamware figure of a mounted officer of Astbury/Whieldon type, saddle cloth with the initials GR, on fluted base, restoration to his left arm and tail of horse, minute chipping, c1760, 10½in (25.5cm) high.
£20,000-25,000 *C*

COLOUR REVIEW

A Lodi tray with Moses striking the rock, slight chipping, c1720, 19in (48cm) wide.
£6,500-7,500 *C*

A German faience armorial dish, damaged and restored, early 18thC, 20in (50cm). **£4,000-6,000** *C*

A Folch and Sons polychrome plate, c1820, 10in (26cm) diam.
£150-200 *BEE*

A Faenza blue and white crespina, the underside moulded with shells and painted with San Bernardino rays, slight cracks, c1650, 12in (30.5cm).
£1,500-2,000 *C*

A pair of marked dishes by Folch, c1820, 9½in (24cm) wide. **£450-550** *BEE*

An Urbino Piatto di Pompa from the Guidobaldo II service, chipped, c1566, 16½in (42cm). **£30,000-33,000** *C*

A Castelli Tondino painted by Niccoló Tommaso Grue, with 6 figures beside a classical ruin in a sunset wooded landscape, c1755, 6½in (16.5cm) diam.
£2,000-3,000 *C*

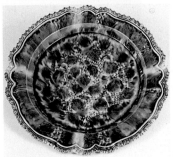

A large Whieldon plate, mid-18thC.
£1,500-2,500 *GIN*

An Hispano Moresque armorial dish, damaged and repairs, late 15thC, 19in (48cm). **£9,000-11,000** *C*

A pair of Mason's Ironstone dessert plates, c1820, 9in (23cm) diam.
£350-400 *BEE*

72

A very rare dated and inscribed delftware puzzle jug, probably Bristol, 1771, 8½in (21.5cm) high. **£4,000-4,500** *JHo*

A saltglaze polychrome jug, cracked, restorations, cross mark, c1760, 13½in (34.5cm). high. **£22,000-25,000** *C*

Two Faenza waisted albarelli, decorated in the workshop of Virgiliotto Calamelli, some damage, c1525, 10½in (27cm) high. **£23,000-25,000** *C*

A Staffordshire slipware dated and inscribed bragget-pot, some damage and restored, 1709, 10½in (27cm) high. **£10,000-12,000** *C*

A creamware jug with unusual handle, probably Greatbatch, Staffordshire, 9in (23cm). **£3,000-3,500** *JHo*

A Davenport Toby jug of Drunken Sal, c1840, 13in (33cm). **£1,000-1,500** *GIN*

A matched pair of majolica jardinières and stands, probably Minton, each moulded and painted with ferns, foxgloves and convolvulus, with matching stands, some damage, c1865. **£1,500-2,000** *Bea*

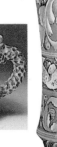

A Dutch Delft 'bleu persan' pewter mounted jug, makers marks, c1720, 9½in (24cm) high. **£6,000-7,000** *CAm*

A pair of faience jardinières, probably Nevers, bases drilled, some damage, c1680, 5½in (13.5cm). **£4,000-5,000** *C*

A Castel Durante albarello, rim chipped, c1555, 12in (30.5cm) high. **£5,500-6,500** *S*

A creamware coffee pot of Whieldon type, c1765, 9½in (24.5cm). **£5,000-8,000** *C*

A Wedgwood blue and white jasper 'Ruined Column' vase, impressed mark, c1795, 8½in (21cm) wide. **£6,000-10,000** *C*

A pottery barrel decorated in prattware colours, c1810.
£250-300 *RP*

A Mintons pâte-sur-pâte vase by M. L.Solon, marked, c1894, 22in (56cm) high.
£9,000-11,000 *C*

A creamware dovecote of Whieldon type, stem, foot and top with extensive restoration, some other restoration, c1760, 10½in (26.5cm). **£42,000-46,000** *C*

An Isle of Man majolica three-legged teapot, late 19thC, 9in (23cm) high.
£350-550 *GIN*

A Prattware figure of seated Toby jug wearing striped breeches,c1800.
£700-900 *GIN*

A pair of Staffordshire garden seats in the Mason's Ironstone mould, early 19thC.
£3,500-4,000 *BEE*

A saltglaze teapot, slight damage, c1760, 6½in (16.5cm). **£22,000-25,000** *C*

A Yorkshire figure of a Toby jug holding a goblet and a jug, impressed crown mark, c1810,
£1,200-1,600 *GIN*

Two Worcester bottles and a Worcester jug, c1753, bottles 4½in (11.5cm), jug 3½in (8cm). l.**£4,000-5,000** c.**£8,000-9,000** r.**£3,500-6,500** *C*

A London delft pill tile, pierced for hanging, with wood stand, cracked and repaired, chips, c1750, 13½in (34.5cm) high. **£15,000-17,000** *C*

A pair of part glazed architectural reliefs, slight damage, 19thC. **£6,500-7,000** *C*

A Worcester fable-decorated bowl, painted in the atelier of James Giles, chip to inside of footrim, c1765, 9½in (23.5cm) diam. **£16,000-18,000** *C*

A pair of Bow globular bottles, painted in the Kakiemon palette with flowering shrubs, c1755, 8in (20.5cm) and 8½in (21cm) high. **£12,000-15,000** *C*

A Meissen silver-gilt mounted squat bottle and cover, c1725, 6in (15cm). **£15,000-18,000** *CG*

A Chelsea cabbage leaf moulded bowl, red anchor mark, c1755, 5½in (16cm) high. **£5,000-6,000** *C*

A pair of Longton Hall leaf-moulded bowls and stands, chips and some restorations, c1755, the bowls 5in (12.5cm). **£6,500-7,500** *C*

A London delft dated salt modelled as a youth, brightly painted, the underside with a blue dragonfly, repairs, chipping, c1676, 7½in (19.5cm). **£178,000-182,000** *C*

Six Meissen coffee cups and saucers and a coffee pot and cover, damaged, marked, c1750. **£5,500-7,000** *S*

A Worcester coffee cup, teacup and saucer and bowl, c1768, cups and saucer. **£5,000-6,000** bowl.**£5,000-6,000** *C*

An English porcelain bust of George II on later socle, damage, c1755, 13½in (34cm). **£37,000-40,000** *C*

A gilt-metal mounted box of 'Girl in a Swing' type, modelled as a recumbent pug dog and pups, cover chipped and cracked, c1750, 2in (5cm) wide. **£3,500-5,000** *CNY*

An early Derby figure of a Florentine boar, on oval mound base, damaged **£2,500-3,500** *DM*

A pair of Böttger beakers and saucers, slight damage, gilders numerals 17, c1725. **£8,000-10,000** *CG*

A Chelsea model of a little hawk owl astride a tree stump, restored, minor chips to foliage, red anchor mark, c1752, 7½in (18cm) high. **£11,000-13,000** *C*

A Meissen gilt metal mounted snuff box, slight rubbing, c1750, 3in (7.5cm). **£6,000-7,000** *C*

A Meissen gold-mounted snuff box, with contemporary vari-coloured gold mounts, c1755, 3½in (8cm) high. **£15,000-18,000** *C*

A Chantilly cartouche shaped Kakiemon snuff box and cover, with contemporary silver mounts, c1740, 3in (7cm) wide. **£9,000-10,000** *CG*

A pair of English porcelain models of dogs, perhaps Coalport, c1810. **£7,500-8,500** *C*

A Staffordshire porcelain pastille burner modelled as a church, c1835, 5½in (14cm) high. **£700-750** *RWB*

A Chelsea white figure of a sphinx, her lioness's body with shaped tasselled cloth, tip of tail missing, chip to base, c1750, 5½in (14.5cm). **£5,000-6,000** *C*

A Kloster Veilsdorf figure of Pierrot by Wenzel Neu, restored, marked, c1765, 5½in (16cm) high. **£10,000-12,000** *CG*

A Liverpool group of La Nourrice, Richard Chaffer's factory, cracks, glaze flaking, c1760, 6in (15.5cm). **£3,000-4,000** *C*

A pair of Fulda figures of a Turk and companion, restored, marked, c1770, 6in & 6¼in (15 & 15.5cm). **£33,000-35,000** *CG*

A Bow figure of The Doctor, his left hand raised and his right hand on his hip, colourfully clothed, on shaped painted base, restoration to brim of hat and left arm at shoulder, slight chip to jacket, c1755, 6½in (16cm) high. **£3,200-4,000** *C*

A Chelsea group of La Nourrice modelled by Joseph Willems, cracked, c1756, 7½in (19cm). **£9,000-10,000** *C*

A pair of Frankenthal figures of a gallant and companion in winter clothes, by J F Lück, both slightly chipped, makers marks, c1760. **£8,000-9,000** *CG*

A pair of Bow sphinxes by the Muses modeller, on rococo scroll-moulded bases, both chipped, c1750, 4½in (12cm) long. **£3,500-4,500** *C*

A Capodimonte group of a youth riding a mastiff by Guiseppi Gricci, some damage, c1755, 6½in (17cm). **£4,500-5,500** *C*

A pair of Bow white figures of Kitty Clive and Henry Woodward, both restored, c1750, 10in (25cm).
£35,000-38,000 *C*

A Bow pierced basket, painted within a waved brown line rim, crack to base and footrim, c1760, 11½in (30cm) diam. **£15,000-18,000** *C*

A Kloster Veilsdorf figure of Harlequin, c1765, 5½in (14.5cm). **£10,000-12,000** *CG*

A Nymphenburg figure of a mushroom-seller by Bustelli, hat restored, impressed marks, c1755, 8in (20cm).
£38,000-40,000 *CG*

A Ludwigsburg group of Bacchus and a Bacchante, chips, marked, c1765, 9½in (24cm). **£3,000-4,000** *C*

A pair of colourful Strasbourg figures of gardeners, heads and one arm re-stuck, one hand and spade missing, c1750, 7½in (19cm) high.
£3,500-4,500 *C*

A Meissen group of The Hand Kiss, by JJ Kändler, restored, chipped, marked, c1740, 7in (18cm).
£4,500-5,500 *C*

A rare Vincennes figure of a water nymph, probably by Fournier, c1750, 8in (20.5cm).
£11,000-13,000 *S*

A Kloster Veilsdorf figure of Gobiel, modelled by Wenzel Neu, in green striped snood, cloak, tunic and trousers, standing on tip-toe before a tree trunk on a mound base, left hand restored replacement, blue CV mark, incised EZ over a script B, c1765, 6½in (16cm).
£18,000-20,000 *CG*

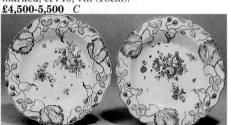

A pair of Longton Hall strawberry leaf moulded soup plates, each with one minute rim chip, c1755, 9½in (23.5cm). **£7,000-8,000** *C*

A Meissen group of satyrs supporting a shell, c1734, 11in (28cm). **£2,500-3,500** *CG*

A pair of Meissen blue and white plates, blue crossed swords marks, Pressnummern 20, c1735, 10in (25.5cm).
£9,000-10,000 *C*

A 'Girl in a Swing' cream jug, some chipping, c1750, 3½in (8.5cm) high.
£15,000-17,000 *C*

A Worcester Flight, Barr and Barr platter, small rim chips, slight wear to paint and gilding, marked, c1820, 22½in (57cm).
£7,000-8,000 *CNY*

A Worcester cabbage leaf moulded jug with double scroll handle, c1768, 10½in (27cm) high. **£5,000-6,000** *C*

Three Worcester fable-decorated plates, painted in the manner of Jefferyes Hammett O'Neale, c1768, 7½in (19cm). **£8,000-9,000** *C*

A Chelsea fluted cream jug, two small rim chips, firing crack to handle, marked, c1745, 5in (12cm). **£9,000-10,000** *CG*

Three Worcester fable-plates, c1768, 7½in (19cm).
l. **£8,000-9,000** c.&r. **£4,500-5,500 each** *C*

A framed English plaque, painted, signed and dated by Bessie Gilson, 1882, 20½in (51.5cm) high. **£2,000-3,000** *C*

A Chelsea beaker, spirally moulded with coloured teaplants, minor chipping to rim and some staining to foot, c1745, 3in (7.5cm) high. **£3,000-4,000** *C*

A Meissen cream jug and cover, supported on three paw feet, painted in 'famille verte' style with an exotic bird perched on a branch, the cover with brown-edged rim, crossed swords in underglaze blue, c1730, 4½in (11.5cm). **£4,500-5,500** *S*

A framed Berlin plaque, painted with a young girl in satin dress, some surface pitting, c1880, 9in (23cm) high. **£3,000-5,000** *S*

A Meissen 'famille verte' dish, painted in underglaze blue within an overglaze enamel band of zig-zag panels, blue crossed swords mark, blue K to rim for Kretschmar, and Dreher's 4 to foot, c1730, 15in (38cm) diam. **£17,000-20,000** *C*

A Berlin plaque, painted with a gypsy girl, in velvet mount and giltwood frame, signed C.S., impressed marks, c1880, 9½in (23.5cm) high. **£3,000-4,000** *C*

A Nymphenburg plate, probably painted by J Zächenberger, with a bouquet and insects beneath the gilt rococo scroll and blue line border, the rim further enriched with gilding, chip to one scroll, minor rubbing on rim, impressed shield mark and 4PM, c1760, 10in (25.5cm). **£12,500-14,000** *S*

A Chelsea white teapot on 6 pad feet, the tip of spout with silver attachment disguising damage, marked, c1745, 4in (9.5cm). **£8,000-9,000** *C*

A Chelsea asparagus tureen, one asparagus curled to form the finial, repaired, marked, c1755, 7½in (18.5cm) wide. **£3,500-4,500** *C*

Three Worcester teapots and covers, c1765, l. **£4,000-5,000** c. **£5,000-6,000**, r. **£1,000-2,000** *C*

A Meissen chinoiserie teapot, chipped and repaired, blue K.P.M. and crossed swords mark, gilder's numeral, c1723, 6in (15.5cm). **£9,000-10,000** *CG*

A Paris gold ground coffee pot and cover, finial repaired, incised 8, c1800, 7½in (18.5cm) high. **£2,000-3,000** *C*

A framed Meissen plaque, crossed swords in underglaze blue, slight bevelling of edges, late 19thC, 7½in (19cm) high. **£3,000-4,000** *S*

A Bristol armorial baluster coffee pot and cover from the Ludlow of Campden Service, Richard Champion's factory, with entwined branch handle, painted with loose bouquets and scattered flower sprays, the domed cover with bud finial and with gilt dentil rim, c1775, 9½in (24cm) high. **£9,000-11,000** *C*

A Venice (Vezzi) teapot and contemporary cover with fruit finial, short crack to rim, cover chipped, incised Z mark, c1725, 6½in (16.5cm) wide. **£12,000-14,000** *C*

A part armorial dinner service, perhaps H&R Daniel, with gilt line and leaf motifs, c1835. **£900-1,000** *WW*

81

Part of the Sèvres Louis Philippe hunting service, with LP monograms, comprising 85 pieces, some damage, various marks, date codes for 1838-48. **£12,000-15,000**　*C*

A Meissen (Marcolini) composite dessert service comprising 89 pieces, some damage, various marks, c1790. **£22,000-25,000**　*C*

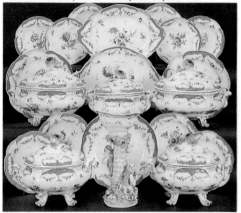

A Meissen dinner service, comprising 169 pieces, some Berlin replacements, minor damage, makers marks, c1755　**£36,000-38,000**　*S*

A Meissen composite pierced part dessert service comprising 12 pieces, some damage, various marks, c1880. **£4,000-5,000**　*C*

A Meissen tea service, comprising 36 pieces, with gilt edged rims, restored, minor rubbing, makers marks, c1750. **£8,000-9,000**　*S*

A Meissen (Marcolini) tête-a-tête, painted in colours, comprising 13 pieces, slight wear to gilding, blue crossed swords and other marks, c1775, **£4,500-5,500**　*CNY*

A Sèvres later decorated 'bleu celeste' part dessert service, comprising 59 pieces, slight chips, marks, 18thC. **£6,500-7,500**　*C*

A Meissen JAGD part coffee service, 11 pieces, some damage, various Pressnummern and marks, c1745. **£5,000-6,000**　*C*

A Meissen (Marcolini) part dinner service comprising 181 pieces, some damage, minor rubbing to gilt rims, blue crossed swords and other marks, c1790. **£34,000-37,000**　*C*

Six Naples coffee cans and saucers, damaged and repaired, incised marks, c1800. **£40,000-45,000**　*C*

A Worcester blue and white tureen and cover, with moulded dolphin finial, chips to finial, c1756, 16in (40.5cm) wide. **£29,000-32,000** *C*

A Meissen écuelle, cover and stand from the St Andrew The First Called Service, restored, blue crossed swords mark and pressnummer 6, c1745, 7in (18cm). **£6,000-7,000** *CNY*

A Worcester hexagonal vase and domed cover, c1770, 11½in (29cm). **£15,000-18,000** *C*

A Worcester garniture of vases, painted in the atelier of James Giles, restorations and replacements, c1770, tallest 12in (30cm). **£18,000-20,000** *C*

A Worcester beaker vase, slight damage, c1754, 6in (15cm) high. **£12,000-14,000** *C*

A Meissen Augustus Rex beaker vase, chipped, blue AR mark, c1730, 15½in (39cm). **£29,000-31,000** *C*

A Chelsea lobed baluster vase, slight damage, c1750, 5in (13cm) high. **£5,500-6,500** *C*

A pair of Meissen Imari tureens, damage, marks, c1735, 13½in (34cm). **£36,000-38,000** *C*

A Worcester baluster vase and a pair of Worcester oviform vases, the pair slightly damaged, c1756, 5in (12.5cm) and 6½in (16cm). **£8,500-9,500** and **£9,000-10,000 the pair** *C*

A Chelsea baluster vase and a pair of Chelsea oviform vases, baluster vase slightly damaged, all with red anchor marks, c1756, **£2,500-3,500** and **£5,500-6,500** the pair. *C*

A pair of Worcester sauce tureens, covers and stands, minor chips to flowers, c1765, 8in (21cm) wide. **£7,500-8,500** *S*

A pair of Berlin armorial tureens, damaged, marks, c1820. **£22,000-26,000** *C*

A Derby elongated campana vase, decorated on both sides, 10½in (26cm) high. **£2,300-2,600** *C*

An ormolu-mounted English porcelain and kingwood encrier, lacking inkwells, pen tray inlaid à quatre faces.
£4,000-5,000 *C*

A Wucai fish bowl, extensively restored, Wanli marks, 19in (48.5cm) diam.
£10,000-12,000 *CAm*

An Imari deep bowl, slight chip to rim restored, late 17thC, 10in (25cm) diam.
£5,000-6,000 *C*

A pair of 'famille rose' vases, iron red Qianlong seal marks, 19thC, 23in (59cm). **£11,000-13,000** *C*

A rare Chinese Imari armorial ribbed basin, one handle restored, c1720, 11½in (29cm) wide. **£6,500-7,500** *C*

A Ko-Imari globular ewer, pierced hole for silver mount, slight damage, late 17thC, 9in (22cm).
£17,000-19,000 *C*

A blue and white bottle vase, the slender handle modelled as a dragon head, Kangxi period, 11in (27cm).
£3,000-4,000 *C*

A Meissen clock case, damaged and repaired, marked, c1745, 16in (41cm) high. **£4,500-5,500** *C*

A Kakiemon bowl, decorated in enamels and gilt, slight crack, c1680, 9½in (23.5cm) high.
£61,000-63,000 *C*

A Derby crayfish sauceboat, Andrew Planché's period, minor chips to applied shells and rim, crayfish lacking front pincers, c1750.
£7,000-8,000 *C*

A Chelsea crayfish salt, some damage, c1745, 5in (12cm) wide.
£11,000-13,000 *C*

A Sèvres porcelain vase, designed by Decoeur, decorated by Gaucher, printed marks, 20in (50cm).
£6,500-7,500 *C*

A pair of 'famille verte' Buddhistic lions and detachable stands, two paws and ball restored, 18th/19thC, 21in (53cm). **£9,000-11,000** *C*

A pair of exportware dishes, of European silver form, depicting a lady adorning her hair before a mirror on a table in the garden, with 7 ladies in waiting, Qianlong, 17in (43cm). **£3,000-4,000** *S(S)*

A pair of 'famille verte' helmet-shaped ewers, one foot restored, rim frits, chips, Kangxi period, 11in (28.5cm) high. **£12,000-15,000** *C*

A pair of turquoise and yellow glazed temple figures, each on a base decorated on each side with stylised clouds on a green ground, some damage to one dragon mouth, Ming Dynasty, 29in (74cm). **£10,000-12,000** *C*

A pair of 'famille rose' models of pheasants, crests chipped, enamels flaked, base cracks, Qianlong, 12in (30.5cm) high. **£23,000-25,000** *C*

An erotic 'famille rose' plate, decorated within eight foliate cartouches, early Qianlong, 8½in (21.5cm). **£3,000-4,000** *C*

A late Ming blue and white 'Kraak porselein' dish, the well with eight lappets alternately painted with auspicious emblems and fruiting foliage, some rim frits, Wanli period, 20in (50.5cm). **£5,500-6,500** *C*

A pair of export figures of cranes, modelled in mirror image, with 'lingzhi' extremities chipped and slightly restored, early 19thC, 18½in (47cm) high. **£18,000-20,000** *C*

A 'famille verte' biscuit wine ewer, Kangxi, 17½in (44.5cm) high. **£7,500-8,500** *C*

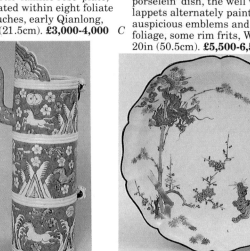

A Kakiemon moulded foliate rimmed dish, decorated with a tiger prowling beneath a dragon coiled in branches of bamboo amongst plum blossom, slight firing crack, c1680, 7in (18cm) diam. **£25,000-28,000** *C*

A 'famille verte' tureen and cover, surmounted by a cockerel finial, minor frits, Kangxi, 10½in (25cm). **£9,000-10,000** *C*

An Imari dish, decorated in iron red enamel and gilt on underglaze blue, late 17th/18thC, 12½in (31.5cm). **£9,000-10,000** *C*

An Imari jar and cover, cover cracked and 'karashishi' tail damaged, c1700, 23½in (60cm) high. **£7,000-8,000** *C*

An Arita blue and white jar, slight chip to neck, cover missing, late 17thC, 24½in (62cm) high. **£7,000-8,000** *C*

A large Imari dish, the reverse painted with 'ho-ho' birds signed Dai Nihon Hichozan Shinpo zo, 19thC. **£12,000-14,000** *C*

A Kakiemon style blue and white tureen and cover, decorated with a continuous band of pavilions beneath pine trees, the domed cover similarly decorated and surmounted by a gilt metal finial, finial later replacement, c1680, 10½in (27cm) high. **£7,000-8,000** *C*

An Arita blue and white ship's tureen with large finial, decorated with peony and plum blossom, late 17thC, 11½in (29cm). **£4,000-5,000** *C*

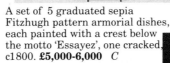

A set of 5 graduated sepia Fitzhugh pattern armorial dishes, each painted with a crest below the motto 'Essayez', one cracked, c1800. **£5,000-6,000** *C*

An Arita blue and white jar, decorated in the Kakiemon manner, c1680, 16in (40cm) high. **£40,000-43,000** *C*

A 'famille rose' Masonic armorial dish, the initials MJD on two sides, Qianlong, 15½in (39.5cm). **£4,000-5,000** *C*

A 'famille rose' eggshell dish, the reverse painted with 3 simple flower sprays, chips, early Qianlong, 8½in (21cm), fitted box. **£4,000-5,000** *C*

A Transitional brush pot, 'bidong', painted with two bearded scholars playing 'weigi', two travellers and a 'qui'-bearing attendant, hallmarked, c1645, 8in (19.5cm). **£5,500-7,000** *C*

A pair of 'famille verte' baluster vases, both cracked and chipped, Kangxi period, 23in (58cm). **£6,000-9,000** *C*

A large porcelain garden lantern in seven sections, restored, signed Nihon Seto Kato Keisa sei, late 19thC, 69in (175cm). **£16,000-18,000** *C*

A pair of 'famille rose' garden seats, one with foot chips, small areas of enamel flaking, 19thC, 19in (48cm) high. **£6,000-7,000** *C*

A rare early Ming blue and white bottle vase, 'yuhuch-unping', Yongle period, 10½in (26cm) high. **£380,000-400,000** *C*

An Imari tureen, decorated in enamels and gilt on underglaze blue, a peony spray on the interior of the tureen and cover, c1700, 10in (25cm). **£30,000-34,000** *CAm*

A large Imari vase, decorated in various coloured enamels, 19thC, 34½in (88cm) high. **£9,000-10,000** *C*

A pair of 'famille rose' vases and covers, minute restorations, Qianlong period, 18½in (46.5cm) high. **£13,000-15,000** *C*

A pair of 'famille rose' tureens and covers, one finial restored, Qianlong, 14in (36cm) wide. **£8,000-10,000** *C*

An Imari tureen and cover, the cover with large knop finial, cover restored, c1700, 15½in (39cm) high. **£6,000-7,000** *C*

A Korean Punc'hong ware vase, decorated in 'hakeme-e' style, restored, 15th/16thC, 11in (28cm). **£90,000-95,000** *C*

A set of 6 green wine glasses,
with conical bowls, bladed knop stems and
plain conical feet, c1830, 5in (13cm) high.
£370-450 *Som*

An amethyst cream jug with loop handle, c1820,
4in (9.5cm) high, and a smaller pale amethyst
cream jug with folded rim, c1820,
4in (9.5cm) high. **£150-250 each** *Som*

Two 'onion' shaped carafes, c1840,
8in (20cm). **£180-220 each.** *Som*

A set of 6 green wine glasses with
round funnel bowls and plain stems, c1840,
5in (12cm) high. **£220-270** *Som*

A pair of wrythen spirit bottles,
c1830. **£450-500.** An amber spirit
bottle, c1845. **£100-150** *Som*

A pair of blue spirit bottles,
c1830. **£350-450** and an amber
spirit bottle with cork/metal
stopper, c1850. **£150-200** *Som*

A pair of green spirit
decanters of ovoid shape, with
bevelled lozenge stoppers,
c1790, 6½in (16cm)
high **£550-600** *Som*

A pair of magnum wine bottles,
with raised seals, inscribed
J Mason, 13in (33cm).
£200-400 *GAK*

A very rare beer jug, with strap
handle and ribbed rim, c1780,
7½in (19.5cm). **£750-850** *Som*

A cream jug and sugar basin with cold
enamelled floral decoration, c1800, 4½in
(12cm). **£500-600** *Som*

An export type wine
glass, the double ogee
bowl on plain stem with
domed foot, c1760, 6in
(15cm). **£800-1,000** *Som*

A wine glass on wrythen knopped stem, with plain conical foot, c1760, 5½in (13.5cm). **£750-850** *Som*

A 'Façon de Venise' flute, on folded foot, 17thC, 10½in (26.5cm). **£8,000-9,000** *C*

A peacock green wine glass, the cup bowl on a wrythen knopped stem and plain conical foot, c1760, 5½in (14cm). **£750-850** *Som*

A Hall-in-Tyrol 'Façon de Venise' goblet, perhaps from the workshop of Sebastian Höchstelter, 16thC, 10½in (26cm). **£17,000-19,000** *C*

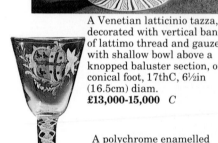

A German green tinted puzzle goblet, with a central column supporting a detachable stag, slight damage, 17thC, 14in (35.5cm). **£6,500-7,500** *C*

A Netherlandish roemer, on a high trailed conical foot and with a kick-in base, mid-17thC, 10½in (26cm). **£6,000-7,000** *C*

A Venetian latticinio tazza, decorated with vertical bands of lattimo thread and gauze, with shallow bowl above a knopped baluster section, on conical foot, 17thC, 6½in (16.5cm) diam. **£13,000-15,000** *C*

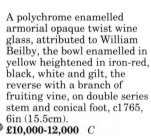

A polychrome enamelled armorial opaque twist wine glass, attributed to William Beilby, the bowl enamelled in yellow heightened in iron-red, black, white and gilt, the reverse with a branch of fruiting vine, on double series stem and conical foot, c1765, 6in (15.5cm). **£10,000-12,000** *C*

A rare blue wrythen ale glass, with everted rim, knopped stem on plain foot, c1810, 4½in (11cm). **£380-450** *Som*

A wine glass with incurved ogee bowl on stem with a multiple spiral air twist, c1760, 6½in (16cm). **£4,000-5,000** *Som*

A set of 10 amber wine glasses, with flute cut trumpet bowls, the stems with collars and cushion knops, on plain conical feet, c1845, 5in (13cm) high. **£650-750** *Som*

A French scent with silver mount, c1780, **£300-350,** an amethyst scent with gilt decoration, **£300-350** and a blue scent with embossed silver mount, **£170-250** *Som*

A blue scent with later mount, c1800, **£260-320** an 'Oxford Lavender' type scent, c1850, **£100-150** and a blue scent with gilt decoration & silver mount, c1780, **£450-550** *Som*

A St Louis concentric millefiori mushroom weight, mid-19thC, 3in (7cm). **£3,000-4,000** *C*

A German enamelled Humpen or Pasglas, 8in (20.5cm) high. **£2,700-3,500** *C*

A German amethyst flask and screw stopper, the foot with silver stiff leaf mount, slight damage, 17thC, 11in (28cm). **£2,000-3,000** *C*

A St Louis cruciform millefiori carpet-ground weight, very small chip, mid-19thC, 3in (7cm). **£5,000-6,000** *C*

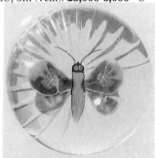

A Baccarat butterfly weight, the insect with translucent mauve body, multi-coloured wings, on a star cut base, mid-19thC, 3in (7cm). **£2,000-3,000** *C*

A blue overlay scent with embossed silver mount, and a similar red one, c1860, 5in (12.5cm) **£170-220 each** and a red scent with silver gilt mount and vinaigrette compartment at base, c1878, 4in (9.5cm). **£550-620** *Som*

Four scent bottles, all with embossed silver mounts, c1870. **£100-300 each** *Som*

A St Louis faceted panelled carpet-ground weight, with closely packed brightly coloured canes, slight chips, mid-19thC, 3in (7cm). **£6,500-7,500** *C*

A red satin scent with darker stripes and silver mount, c1896. **£200-300** and a blue scent with silver mount, c1900. **£50-100** *Som*

l. A red vinaigrette/scent, with cut decoration, 1in (3cm) c. A double ended scent with chased gilt mounts, 5in (12cm) r. A clear scent with opaque overlay, 3in (7.5cm) c1870. **£200-500 each** *Som*

Three cut glass scent bottles, with silver mounts, c1860, 3in (7cm). **£170-250 each** *Som*

A rare Zwischen goldglas scent, c1850, 3½in (9cm). **£1,200-1,600,** an overlay scent with gilt decoration, c1860, 4½in (11cm). **£750-850,** and a rectangular overlay scent with embossed silver mount, c1860. **£250-300** *Som*

An oval clear scent bottle, with enamelled decoration, c1880, 4in (10.5cm). **£170-200** *Som*

l. A prism cut scent with silver mount, c. A horn scent with silver gilt mounts and r. A cut scent with siver mount c1870. **£100-350 each** *Som*

Three red glass scent bottles with silver gilt mounts, l & r hallmarked Samson & Mordan London 1878, 3½in (9cm) high. **£300-600 each** *Som*

Four glass scent bottles, all with silver gilt mounts, 1850-1892, 4in to 6in (10.5cm to 15cm) long. **£150-450 each** *Som*

A Wemyss mug, painted with drakes, 5½in (14cm).
£1,200-1,500   *RdeR*

A Wemyss early three-handled mug, painted with cockerels, 5½in (14cm).
£400-500   *RdeR*

A Wemyss two-handled mug, painted with daffodils, 5½in (14cm).
£500-700   *RdeR*

A Wemyss matching pot and plate, painted with cherries, 7in (18cm).
£300-400   *RdeR*

A Wemyss preserve pot, with painted brambles, 2½in (6cm).
£200-300   *RdeR*

A Wemyss preserve pot, painted with strawberries, 2½in (6cm).
£300-400   *RdeR*

A Wemyss Stuart pot, painted with plums, 5in (13cm).
£300-400   *RdeR*

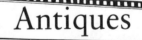

A Wemyss heart-shaped tray, painted with brown cockerels, c1890, 11½in (29cm) long.
£500-700   *RdeR*

A Wemyss porridge bowl, stained, 6in (15cm) diam.
£300-400   *RdeR*

A Wemyss Japan vase, painted with herons, 8in (20cm) high.
£600-700   *RdeR*

A Wemyss beaker vase, painted with sand martins, 11½in (29cm) high.
£1,500-2,000   *RdeR*

A Wemyss teapot, painted with brown cockerels, 4½in (11cm) high.
£250-300   *RdeR*

A Wemyss pin tray, painted with violets, 5½ by 3in (14 by 7cm).
£100-200   *RdeR*

A Wemyss quaiche with handles, painted with plums, 7½in (19cm) diam.
£300-450
RdeR

A Wemyss brush vase, painted with mallard ducks, 4½in (11cm).
£300-400   *RdeR*

Miscellaneous

A rare salt glazed model of a shoe, finely tooled over the upper surface and around the welt and sole, washed in a chocolate brown ferruginous dip, probably Nottingham, c1700, 4½in (12cm).
£900-1,200   *S*

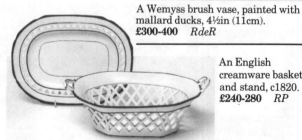

An English creamware basket and stand, c1820.
£240-280   *RP*

A pair of blue and white flower bricks, possibly Liverpool, 4½in (11cm) wide.
£850-950   *JHo*

An English earthenware blue and white footbath, printed with a river landscape and trailing rose border, old restoration to one handle, early 19thC, 18½in (47cm) wide.
£750-850 *P(S)*

A treacle glazed egg stand, formed as 7 receptacles for eggs, covered in streaked brown glazes divided by ropetwist, on a spreading partially glazed foot, minor rim chips, perhaps Sussex, late 18thC, 4½in (11.5cm).
£600-700 *C*

A large Continental painted table centre figure group, some minor chips and restoration, mid-19thC, 18in (46cm) high.
£250-350 *S(S)*

A Davenport two-handled foot bath, printed with the Mosque and Fisherman pattern, within a border of roses and diaper panels, slight glaze cracks, impressed mark.
£1,800-2,500 *CSK*

A creamware flask, painted in the manner of David Rhodes in iron red and black, the reverse with a butterfly and loose bouquets, within circular moulded bead cartouches, with short cylindrical neck, perhaps Wedgwood, c1775, 4½in (11.5cm).
£550-700 *C*

A Staffordshire inkstand, possibly made by John Forster, c1820, 5½in (14cm). **£350-450** *BHA*

A Staffordshire polychrome drainer, 19thC, 12in (31cm) wide.
£150-200 *BEE*

A pepper pot and a vinegar bottle, by Samson and Smith, with gold anchor mark, 5in (12cm).
£40-80 *GIN*

A Prattware pipe, c1800, 10½in (26cm).
£500-600 *JHo*

A pair of Mason's Ironstone letter racks in the Japan pattern, impressed mark, c1815, 3½in (8.5cm) high.
£850-900 each *VH*

A blue and white supper set, each piece printed with a Chinese landscape, with 4 crescent dishes and 2 covers, each with a lion's head knop, probably by Ralph Wedgwood, some damage, complete with mahogany tray, 23½in (60cm) wide.
£450-700 *Bea*

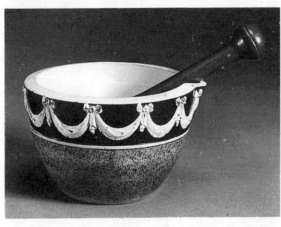

A rare Wedgwood stoneware pestle and mortar, the exterior decorated in white over a chocolate brown ground above a speckled green glazed ground, the plain white glazed pestle mounted on a turned wooden handle, small chip to spout, impressed Wedgwood 3 on the mortar and Wedgwood 4 on the bowl, c1800, bowl 5½in (14cm) diam.
£1,200-1,500 *S*

It is probable that this pestle and mortar formed part of a set produced by Wedgwood for someone of some note, probably as a luxury item for domestic use, although there would appear to be no record of who may have ordered the set in the Wedgwood archives.

QUIMPER

Pottery had been made at Quimper in Brittany since Roman times, but the characteristic style of the 'Petit Breton' peasant figure surrounded by floral garlands in the 'a la touche' techniques (single brush stroke) and concentric blue and yellow borders emerged only about 1870 when interest focused on Brittany with the building of the railways.

Trading on the Quimper success, similar wares were produced at Malicoine in the Sarthe region from about 1870 in a softer, more fluid style in a matt pink glaze on a reddish body. At the same time from Desvres in the Pas de Calais came a large variety of decorative forms in the Rouen manner, boldly painted in primary colours upon rococo shapes. Proximity to England resulted in a considerable quantity reaching these shores.

The two main faience factories were the Grande Maison de la Hubaudiere and the former Dumaine Stoneware pottery acquired by Jean-Baptiste Tanquerey whose grandson Jules Henriot gave the establishment its main impetus when he took over in 1884. Their marks were HB and HR respectively until 1922 when a legal suit obliged Henriot to use his full name.

A pair of Quimper plates, c1893, 9in (23cm).
£180-210 *VH*

If they were c1920 they would be half the price.

A pair of Malicoine pottery bells, c1880.
£90-120 each *VH*

A pair of Quimper plates, c1890, 9½in (24cm).
£300-350 *VH*

A pair of Quimper dishes, c1890,
13in (33cm) wide.
£300-350 *VH*

An early Quimper scallop dish,
c1880, 4½in (11cm) long.
£70-80 *VH*

An unusual Quimper vase,
decorated against a blue
background, c1890, 7in (18cm) high.
£80-100 *VH*

A Quimper cake plate, c1910, 9in
(23cm) diam.
£160-180 *VH*

A Quimper vase in the shape of a
sledge, c1880, 12½in (31cm) wide.
£280-300 *VH*

A pair of early Quimper knife rests,
c1870, 3in (8cm) long.
£20-30 *VH*

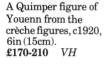

A Desvres teapot, c1880, 4in (10cm)
high.
£130-150 *VH*

A Quimper figure of
Youenn from the
crèche figures, c1920,
6in (15cm).
£170-210 *VH*

A Malicoine egg dish, c1875, 11in
(28cm) high.
£200-250 *VH*

A Quimper vase, c1880, 4in (10cm).
£170-200   *VH*

A Quimper match striker, c1890, 3in (8cm) high.
£100-120   *VH*

A Quimper menu, c1890, 6½in (16cm) high.
£270-300   *VH*

A French spill vase, c1900, possibly Malicoine, 7in (18cm) high.
£100-130   *VH*

An early Quimper bénitier, c1890, 9½in (24cm) long.
£200-250   *VH*

A Desvres Pas de Calais plate, c1892, 10in (25cm).
£195-210   *VH*

'Justice is on the side of the strongest' was the title of the original watercolour from which this subject derives, hence the see-saw and in this plate the tables are turned and the citizen/peasant is winning.

A Quimper inkstand, 7in (18cm) wide.
£350-400   *VH*

A Quimper bowl, some rim chips, c1890, 3½in (9cm) diam.   **£15-25**   *VH*

A Quimper bonbonnière, c1895, 4½in (11cm) diam.
£130-150 *VH*

An early Quimper shoe, signed, c1880, 6½in (16cm) long.
£60-90 *VH*

A Desvres figure Fourmaintraux Frères, c1890, 7½in (19cm).
£70-100 *VH*

A Desvres Pas de Calais plate, centenary of the revolution, c1893, 10in (25cm).
£200-220 *VH*

A Desvres egg cup Fourmaintraux Frères, c1900, 3in (8cm) high.
£20-40 *VH*

A Desvres Pas de Calais plate, commemorating the centenary of the revolution, with inscription, c1891, 9in (23cm).
£170-220 *VH*

A Malicoine pin tray, c1880, 4½in (11cm) long.
£30-40 *VH*

A Quimper vase, c1890, 5in (13cm).
£120-150 *VH*

A Quimper cornucopia, possible Adolphe Porquier, c1880, 4½in (11cm) high.
£150-170 *VH*

A Devres snuff flask, Fourmaintraux Frères pottery, c1880, 3½in (8cm).
£100-120 *VH*

An early Quimper plate, c1875, 9in (23cm).
£100-120 *VH*

A Quimper jug, restored crack, c1890, 9in (23cm) high.
£230-260 *VH*

An early Quimper dish, c1880, 10½in (26cm).
£170-210 *VH*

A Desvres plate, centenary of the revolution, c1893, 9in (23cm) diam.
£190-210 *VH*

A Quimper mug, 6in (15cm) high.
£140-160 *VH*

A Quimper mug with damaged handle, c1925, 5½in (14cm) high.
£70-100 *VH*

A Quimper bowl, some damage and restoration, c1880, 10in (25cm) diam.
£200-300 *VH*

A Malicoine flask with stopper, c1875, 7½in (19cm) high.
£200-225 *VH*

Make the Most of Miller's

In Miller's we do NOT just reprint saleroom estimates. We work from realised prices either from an auction room or a dealer. Our consultants then work out a realistic price range for a similar piece. This is to try to avoid repeating freak results – either low or high

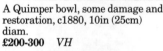

A Malicoine plate, c1890, 7½in (19cm).
£70-100 *VH*

A Quimper pot with lid, c1920, 6in (15cm) diam.
£140-160 *VH*

A Quimper bud vase, c1890, 5in (13cm) high.
£130-150 *VH*

PORCELAIN

As with the pottery market, last year's trends have continued with no real surprises. Quality and rarity still count! It was noticeable at the summer specialist ceramic fairs that the rarities had their red sold dots attached within a few minutes of opening but that the good but not too rare pieces were still available at the end of the show. The traditionally much sought after factories are still bid to high prices as was evident at Lawrence's sale in December when Lund's Bristol coffee cans were sold up to £1,750 each. Figure studies have maintained a stable price and unless of high quality and condition have not readily found a buyer. Good 19thC porcelain has been much in demand, particularly if painted and signed by the top ceramic artists. There has been a considerable upsurge in the demand for porcelain plaques with prices beginning to push £10,000 for the better pieces. These plaques have long been undervalued for the fine works of art that they undoubtedly are. Good, preferably complete, well painted services are still in demand. An Albert Gregory painted Royal Crown Derby dessert service realised £7,200 at Bearne's, Torquay. Porcelain from the Royal Worcester factory is still much in demand for the best signed pieces even though the year has seen a diminishing interest from Japanese buyers.

EUROPEAN PORCELAIN

Good early Meissen continues to be the international currency of the ceramics world and you do not have to sell it in Geneva to realise its potential. A 12-piece part Meissen breakfast service painted in the Herold style and dating from the 1730s fetched £24,000 at Riddetts auction rooms, Bournemouth. Although collectors are still chasing the rarest 18thC figurines the 19thC Meissen figures still represent very good value at £200-300, particularly if compared to some of the bizarre prices being paid for 20thC Staffordshire pieces of questionable quality. Large, attractive Continental figures still find a ready market in the decorative field with good pieces being attained for Sevres biscuit wares if in good condition. The market for Berlin plaques has stabilised with subject matter becoming more important; pretty ladies being the most desirable!

Baskets

A Caughley pierced two-handled basket in the Worcester style, transfer printed with The Pine Cone and Foliage pattern, blue C and raised T mark, c1785, 9in (22.5cm) wide. **£500-600**   *C*

An English porcelain basket, probably Coalbrookdale, applied and painted with flowers, some damage, 10½in (27.5cm) wide. **£250-350**   *Bea*

A Rockingham flower encrusted basket, the flowers and foliage picked out in gilding, all beneath an entwined twig handle, also picked out in gilding, minor chips to foliage, puce printed griffin mark, red painted title, c1835, 9in (23cm). **£900-1,200**   *S*

A Derby chestnut basket and pierced cover, the interior painted with an Oriental building on an island, finial damaged and restuck, inscribed inside the cover August 1762, Wm. Duesbury & Co. 1762, 7in (18cm) diam. **£1,500-2,000**   *C*

A Worcester blue and white pierced basket, transfer printed with The Pine Cone and Foliage pattern, blue crescent mark, c1770, 4½in (11.5cm).
£600-700 *C*

A pair of Meissen sweetmeat figural baskets, modelled as a young lady and gentleman wearing colourful floral attire, the baskets painted on the interior with scattered sprays of flowers, all between gilt rims, minor chips, crossed swords in underglaze blue and incised numerals 2863 and 2858, c1890, 11½in (30cm).
£1,000-1,500 *S*

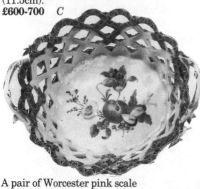

A pair of Worcester pink scale pierced basket, painted in the atelier of James Giles, with puce scale pattern within shaped gilt lines, the exteriors applied with blue-centred puce flowers and the branch handles with flower terminals, one lacking 2 flower terminals, the remaining terminals damaged, handles repaired, one with hair crack to base, some rim restoration, c1770, 9in (23cm) wide.
£6,500-7,000 *C*

A pair of Paris flared baskets on 3 paw feet, enriched in gilding, both cracked, printed vendor's mark, 9in (23cm) diam.
£300-350 *CSK*

A Sitzendorf basket painted in colours, supported by 4 scantily clad putti, blue cross mark, 6in (15cm).
£250-300 *CSK*

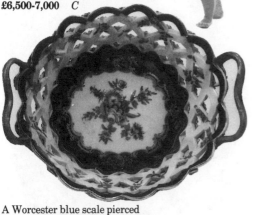

A Worcester blue scale pierced two-handled basket, painted with a loose bouquet within a gilt scroll cartouche reserved on a blue scale ground, the exterior applied with pink flowers and the branch handles with pear terminals, restorations to handles and to the rim, blue square seal mark, c1770, 13½in (33.5cm) wide.
£450-550 *C*

An English porcelain blue ground basket with a loop handle, the centre painted within a surround of meandering gilt foliage, the rim and upper handle moulded with yellow and gilt scrolls, on a spreading foot, handle restored, 11in (29cm) diam.
£80-120 *CSK*

A Worcester pierced basket, painted
over a white ground, the exterior
with yellow and green flowerheads
at the angles, and painted on the
interior with smaller scattered
sprays of flowers, applied hand
written paper label to base and
remains of a collection label, c1760,
6½in (17cm) diam.
£1,200-1,700 *S*

A Worcester blue and white basket,
transfer printed with The Pine Cone
and Foliage pattern, the exterior
with flowerheads at the
intersections, blue crescent mark,
c1770, 6in (15cm) diam.
£500-600 *C*

Bottles

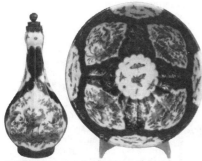

A Worcester powdered blue ground
faceted bottle and a basin, painted
within shaped gilt scroll cartouches
reserved on powdered blue grounds
gilt with flowersprays, the bottle
with later giltmetal mount and
giltmetal-mounted cork stopper
with chain attachment, with repair
to rim of neck, c1765, the bottle
10½in (27cm) high, the basin 11in
(28cm) diam.
£7,000-8,000 *C*

A Worcester blue and white pear
shaped bottle, transfer printed with
The Pine Cone and Foliage pattern,
blue crescent mark, c1775, 11½in (29cm).
£600-800 *C*

Bowls

A Chelsea white sugar bowl, the
exterior moulded in relief in the
Fujian style with branches of
flowering prunus, slight damage to
rim, c1750, 4in (9.5cm) diam.
£800-850 *C*

A Bow baluster finger bowl with
shaped rim, painted in an Imari
palette with pierced blue rockwork,
the interior rim with loop pattern
and pendant foliage, incised R
mark, c1750, 3in (7.5cm).
£800-900 *C*

A Bow baluster finger bowl, the
interior rim with iron red and gilt
flowerheads suspended from blue
foliage, cracks to base, slight rim
chips and staining, incised line
mark, c1750, 2½in (7cm).
£350-450 *C*

A pair of Caughley seaux, painted in
the Chantilly style, with blue line
rims, one with crack to body, blue
S mark, c1785, 6in (16cm).
£400-600   *C*

A Liverpool fluted bowl, 6in (15cm)
deep.
£180-220   *BRK*

A Liverpool Penningtons teabowl.
£70-90   *BRK*

A Liverpool Penningtons teabowl
and saucer, saucer 5in (13cm) diam.
£140-160   *BRK*

A Plymouth patty pan, the flared
sides painted with trees and shrubs
in a fenced garden, hair cracks and
minute rim chip, 2/– mark, Wm.
Cookworthy's factory, c1770, 4in
(9.5cm) diam.
£550-600   *C*

A Caughley seau or finger bowl, 3in
(7.5cm).
£120-150   *BRK*

A Fairyland Lustre bowl, with
hairline crack.
£900-1,000   *LT*

A Worcester baluster finger bowl
and stand, transfer printed after
Robert Hancock, within a black line
rim, minute rim flake to stand and
crack to centre, c1760, bowl 4in
(10cm) diam, stand 6½in (16.5cm)
diam.
£1,000-1,500   *C*

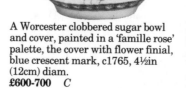

A Spode blue ground cupboard
custard pail and pierced cover,
painted on dark blue grounds
enriched with gilt scale pattern, the
waved gilt rim with loop handles
and the cover with gilt finial,
pattern No. 1166, c1820, 3in (8cm)
diam.
£900-1,200   *C*

A Worcester clobbered sugar bowl
and cover, painted in a 'famille rose'
palette, the cover with flower finial,
blue crescent mark, c1765, 4½in
(12cm) diam.
£600-700   *C*

A Worcester blue scale bowl,
painted within gilt vase and
mirror-shaped cartouches reserved
on a well defined blue scale ground,
blue square seal mark, c1768, 6in
(15.5cm) diam.
£800-900   *C*

A pair of Worcester blue and white patty pans, with flared sides and flat rims, transfer printed with trailing loose bouquets, blue crescent marks, c1770, 4½in (12cm) diam.
£350-450   *C*

A Royal Worcester bowl, decorated by Chivers, signed, printed marks for 1902.
£950-1,100   *DN*

PORCELAIN

★ porcelain can be sub-divided into hard and soft paste. The best way to distinguish between the two is to obtain a damaged example of each type and study the difference

★ **hard paste:** fired at a higher temperature than soft paste; cold feel to the touch; chip is flint- or glass-like; hard, glittery glaze which is fused to the paste

★ **soft paste:** a file will cut easily into soft paste (not a test to be recommended!); chip is granular; warmer feeling to the touch; less stable in the kiln – figures in particular were difficult to fire (*note:* no English soft paste figures can compare with Meissen and other German factories); the glaze was soft as it tended not to fuse into the body as much as glaze on hard paste and was liable both to pooling and crazing; early soft paste was prone to discolouration

A pair of Sèvres pattern ormolu mounted bowls, painted in a bright palette, the interiors similarly painted within the 'bleu nouveau' borders, on ormolu four-footed bases, both with restoration to sides and bases, imitation blue interlaced L marks, both with incised number 25, mid-19thC, 10½in (27.5cm) diam.
£3,500-4,000   *C*

A Meissen, Marcolini, bowl and a cover with flower finial, painted on a ground of gilt diaper enclosing flowerheads, the bowl with blue crossed swords and star mark, and impressed numbers, worn and small chips to extremities, late 18thC, 7½in (19cm) wide.
£950-1,100   *CSK*

Boxes

A Royal Worcester lobed and fluted bowl in blush ivory, with gilt scroll handles, initialled B.T. and marked in green on base, 8in (21cm) diam.   **£350-450**   *P(M)*

A Meissen gilt metal mounted snuff box and cover, painted in colours within a gilt floral scroll border, the base finely decorated with a 'Kauffahrtei' scene in purple 'camaieu', gilt interior, cover cracked, c1740, 3in (7.5cm), the chased metal mounts 19thC.
£3,500-4,000   *S*

The initials M.S. could possibly refer to Marc Solon who, after retiring from Mintons in 1904, worked independently decorating blanks.

A pair of Berlin boxes and covers, each cover decorated in 'pâte-sur-pâte' over a pale green ground, signed M.S., within a gilt rim, the sides in pale pastel shades picked out in gilding with panels and foliate scrollwork, sceptre mark in underglaze blue, feint K.P.M. and orb mark and impressed marks, late 19thC, 3½in (8.5cm) diam.
£700-800   *S(S)*

Please refer to index for other sections on boxes.

A Furstenberg snuff box, moulded with scales and gilt scrolls, painted in colours, the inside cover with flowers tumbling from an upturned gilt basket on a marble plinth, with gilt metal mount, c1770, 4in (10cm) long.   **£700-800**   *C*

A Meissen box and cover, painted in puce, enriched in gilding within gilt lined rims, blue crossed swords mark, 3in (7cm) diam, and a Meissen rectangular box, similarly decorated in yellow monochrome within gilt lined firms, blue crossed swords mark, 3in (7cm) wide.
£50-100 *CSK*

A Mennecy white snuff box, moulded with radiating flutes and sprigs of flowers, crack to back and base, contemporary silver mounts with décharge mark for Julien Berthe, c1740, 3in (8cm) wide.
£550-800 *C*

A Mennecy snuff box as a seated man wearing a blue night-cap and yellow flowered robe, the interior painted with a flowerspray, cracked, yellow enamel rubbed, contemporary silver mounts with décharge mark for Julien Berthe, c1750, 2½in (5.5cm).
£600-800 *C*

Caskets

A Paris, Jacob Petit, gilt metal mounted casket, the cover with a porcelain panel painted on a shaded ground within an oval gilt dot cartouche and reserved on a richly gilt green ground, the gilt metal mounts elaborately chased and moulded with foliage scrolls and with a standing putto playing the pipes at each angle, c1830, 9½in (24cm) wide.
£2,800-3,200 *C*

A French porcelain and ormolu mounted casket, heightened in gilt, on caryatid putti supports, 19thC, 8in (20cm) wide. **£900-1,200** *CSK*

Centrepieces

A pair of Sèvres pattern turquoise ground and ormolu mounted centre dishes, the flared bowls painted on turquoise grounds gilt with swags and floral foliage, the ormolu mounts to the rims applied with Bacchus masks with elaborate pineapple, foliage scroll and snake terminals, the ormolu supports modelled as 4 paws above fluted cylindrical and laurel wreath stems, the bases with a canted section inset with porcelain plaques painted with flowers, one bowl broken in two, the other cracked, c1865, 16in (41cm).
£4,500-5,000 *C*

A Royal Dux centre bowl, modelled as 2 nymphs scantily clad and seated on the side of a conch shell, shell cracked, slight wear, pink triangle mark and impressed number 1066.
£250-300 *CSK*

A Bevington centrepiece, set on a rococo foliate moulded base, some damage, 18in (45cm). **£650-750** *Bea*

A pair of English porcelain two-handled pierced tazzas, enriched in gilding and supported by 2 children in loosely draped robes, on rockwork bases, gilding rubbed and damage to extremities of the tazzas, 11in (29cm).
£200-300   *CSK*

A Carl Thieme Potschapel pierced centrepiece, applied with flowers, painted in colours and enriched in gilding, some damage, blue mark, 12½in (31cm).
£400-450   *CSK*

A Meissen centrepiece, with 2 cherubs on a scroll and flower encrusted base, the flared column supporting a pierced scroll basket, minor chips, crossed swords in underglaze blue and incised M141, c1880, 11in (28cm).
£1,700-2,500   *S*

A Sèvres pattern and gilt metal mounted centre bowl, the blue ground reserved with 18thC lovers in a garden with a raised gilt scroll and flower cartouche, on a socle stem with square metal mount cast with a laurel wreath and with Vitruvian scrolls, mid-19thC, 13in (33cm).
£2,000-3,000   *CSK*

A Sèvres porcelain comport, signed F. Roper in gilt borders, with deep blue background and floral interior, on raised foot with moulded ormolu base, 15in (38cm) wide.
£600-700   *AH*

Clocks

A French clock set, comprising a clock case and 2 nine-light candelabra, on gilt marbled bases, edged with blue beading, the clock case fitted with an 8-day striking movement with an enamel dial, each candelabra with one branch damaged, the top-most nozzle a replacement, minor chipping to all pieces, imitation blue crossed swords and x marks, c1880, candelabra 27in (69cm) high, clock case 18½in (47cm) wide.
£3,500-5,000   *C*

A Meissen mantel clock, the rectangular plinth base with a broken front, painted with gilt panels of birds perched amongst branches, minor chips and restoration, crossed swords mark in underglaze blue and incised numerals, c1880, 16in (40cm).
£1,700-2,100   *S*

A Rudolstadt-Volkstedt porcelain cased mantel timepiece.
£750-850   *HSS*

A French three
-piece clock garniture in the manner of Jacob Petit, the clock with white enamel dial and 8-day bell striking movement by Henri Marc, small faults, 19thC, 16 and 17½in (41 and 44cm). **£800-1,000** *P(S)*

A Sèvres pattern garniture-du- cheminée, the dial set into a gilt metal surround above a porcelain plaque, with turquoise ground pillars at the angles, flanked by 2 gilt metal figures of Cupid, the upper part surmounted by a gilt metal and porcelain vase held by 2 putti, the 2 flanking vases with turquoise ground porcelain bodies, c1900, clock with gilt wood and plush shaped stand, vases 15in (39cm), clock 20½in (52cm). **£1,000-1,500** *C*

Cottages & Pastille Burners

A Staffordshire porcelain pastille burner, modelled as an octagonal cottage with bun feet and detachable roof, c1835, 5in (12cm) high. **£280-300** *RWB*

A Staffordshire porcelain pastille burner, modelled as a house, c1835, 5in (12cm) high. **£260-300** *RWB*

l. A pastille burner in the form of a yellow gazebo with an integral base and a fluted roof, 5in (13cm).
c. A pastille burner in the form of a cottage, applied with green clay chips and flowerheads, 4in (10cm). All with damages.
£450-550 *CSK*
r. A Staffordshire porcelain pastille burner in the form of a church with a tower and arched windows, applied with coloured clay chips, 5in (13cm).

An English cottage pastille burner, applied with foliage and enriched with colours and gilt, 5in (13cm). **£250-300** *CSK*

A Staffordshire porcelain pastille burner with applied foliage, enriched in yellow and gilding, 6in (15cm), together with 2 others, similarly decorated, one with chimney restored. **£200-250** *CSK*

A pastille burner in the form of a pale yellow octagonal cottage with 'parasol' roof, applied with flowers and mosses, slight damage, 8in (20cm). **£270-320** *Bea*

Cups

A First Period Worcester teabowl, hand painted in blue, underglazed blue painted W to base, 3in (8cm) diam.
£100-120   MN

A Chelsea/Derby cup and saucer, c1770.
£180-200   BRK

A Worcester blue and white cup with loop handle, painted with a pavilion and a tree on a rocky island, with a sailing boat before an island, c1752, 3½in (8.5cm).
£4,000-4,500   C

A Chelsea/Derby teabowl and saucer.
£300-350   BRK

The Chelsea and Derby factories amalgamated in 1785.

A Caughley trio comprising a saucer, a teabowl and a coffee cup, in the full Nanking pattern.
£250-280   BRK

A Chelsea teabowl and trembleuse saucer, painted within chocolate brown rims, saucer with minute chipping, red anchor marks, c1755.
£2,500-3,000   C

A Derby inscribed and dated teabowl and saucer, transfer printed with The Fisherman pattern, the footrim to the teabowl and the underside of the saucer inscribed 'Mary Frances 1782', Wm. Duesbury & Co., 1782.
£800-900   C

A Bow white libation cup after a Fujian original, moulded with prunus and resting on a pierced oval foot, minor staining to rim, c1755, 4in (9.5cm) wide.
£1,200-1,500 *C*

A Worcester fluted teabowl and saucer, painted with green diaper panels edged with gilt scrolls alternating with puce floral swags, c1765.
£500-700 *C*

An early Worcester coffee cup, painted in a 'famille verte' palette with flowering Oriental shrubs alternating with insects, applied paper label for D.M. & P. Manheim, c1753, 2½in (6cm).
£1,000-1,500 *S*

l. A Worcester coffee can and saucer, painted in the 'famille rose' palette, minute rim chips to underside of saucer, c1758.
£2,700-3,200
c. A Worcester moulded saucer dish, the centre painted in a 'famille rose' palette, the border with moulded scrolling foliage within a puce scroll rim, c1758, 8in (20cm) diam.
£3,500-4,000
r. A Worcester pleated teabowl and saucer, painted in a 'famille rose' palette, within moulded foliage scroll cartouches, the borders with puce C-scrolls and stylised pendant foliage, minute glaze flake to rim of teabowl, c1758.
£2,300-2,600 *C*

A Worcester teacup and saucer, painted in puce with sprigs and sprays of flowers within a gold line rim, hair crack to handle, crossed swords and numeral mark in underglaze blue, c1760.
£250-350 *Bea*

A Bow cup, applied with prunus pattern decoration, 2½in (6cm).
£120-150 *BRK*

A pair of Doccia teabowls and saucers, painted 'alla Sassonia' in landscapes within gilt 'Laub-und-Bandelwerk' cartouches with iron red scrolls and purple panels within gilt line rims, one saucer with very slight rubbing, c1770.
£1,700-2,200 *C*

A Chelsea teabowl and trembleuse saucer, with chocolate brown rims, red anchor marks, c1755.
£2,500-3,000 *C*

A Worcester teacup and saucer, c1770, saucer 5in (13cm) diam.
£170-190 *Wai*

A Worcester faceted coffee cup and saucer, painted in a 'famille rose' palette and in underglaze blue, within gilt scroll cartouches reserved on an iron red scale pattern ground, c1765.
£2,200-2,600   *C*

A Worcester baluster coffee cup and saucer, painted in the Kakiemon palette with The Quail pattern, within a border of iron red scrolling foliage, red crescent marks, c1765.
£1,500-2,000   *C*

A Worcester teabowl and saucer, painted in a 'famille rose' palette with figures at discussion in a fenced garden, flanked by boulders and grasses, c1765.
£400-500   *C*

A Worcester powdered blue ground coffee cup and saucer, painted within gilt circular and fan-shaped cartouches flanked by gilt foliage, red anchor and crescent mark, c1765.
£400-500   *C*

A Worcester teacup and saucer, painted in the atelier of James Giles, in green monochrome and gilt with a chrysanthemum spray, the rims gilt, slight chip to footrim of cup, blue crossed swords and 9 mark, c1770.
£250-350   *C*

A Worcester apple green cup and saucer, painted with fruit over a white ground enclosed by a gilt rococo scroll border and apple green ground rim, crossed swords and the numeral 9 in underglaze blue, c1770.
£800-1,200   *S*

A Worcester coffee cup, the lobed sides with spiralling green leaves enriched with gilt veining, the entwined handle with leaf terminals, beneath a chocolate brown rim, c1767.
£600-700   *C*

A Worcester powdered blue ground matched trio, painted within gilt fan and circular cartouches, reserved on a powdered blue ground gilt with trailing foliage, the rims gilt, the saucer with a red anchor mark, c1770.
£450-700   *C*

A Worcester blue scale teacup and saucer, painted 'en grisaille' perhaps in the atelier of James Giles, with coloured flowers within gilt vase and mirror-shaped cartouches edged with scrolls, the entwined handle with foliage terminals and enriched with gilding, with gilt rims, blue square seal mark, c1770.
£500-800   *C*

A Worcester, Flight & Barr, beaker painted with a band of scrolling red-centred green and yellow feathery flowers and green and gilt foliage, between pink bands edged with gilt lines, the rim gilt, incised B mark, c1800, 4in (10cm).
£450-550   *C*

A Worcester baluster custard cup and cover, painted in the atelier of James Giles, with loose bouquets, the cover with flower finial and gilt line rim, minute chips to finial, c1770, 4in (9.5cm).
£1,700-2,200   *C*

A Worcester faceted coffee cup and saucer, painted in the atelier of James Giles, with gilt floral swags pendant from the rim on alternate turquoise and puce striped grounds edged with gilding, with gilt dentil rims, saucer with small chip to underside, blue square seal marks, c1770.
£700-800   *C*

A pair of Pinxton yellow ground two-handled cups and covers, painted with flowers and a view, on a canary yellow ground, each domed cover with a plain yellow ground enclosed by a gilt foliate band and rim and surmounted by a gilt button knop, minor chips and restoration to covers, c1800, 4in (10.5cm).
£3,000-3,500   *S*

A Barr, Flight & Barr, cabinet cup and stand, the body raised on 3 gilt paw feet and painted over a cream ground within gilt borders, small chip to rim of stand, brown printed circular Royal Warrant mark, c1810.
£900-1,200   *S*

A Chamberlain's Worcester documentary blue ground cylindrical cup and saucer, painted by Humphrey Chamberlain with 'Penelopel (sic) weeping over the Bow of Ulyfses', within a gilt band cartouche, reserved on a dark blue ground gilt with stylised ornament above a black band, with gilt interior, the saucer with a central gilt medallion, with gilt dentil rims, small star crack to base, signed H. Chamberlain pinxt. on a shell cartouche beneath The Prince of Wales feathers in iron red and with script marks, c1815.
£2,000-2,500   C

A Royal Worcester coffee cup, the exterior painted by Harry Davis with a misty view of Venice, the interior painted in gold, printed mark and date code for 1926.
£220-260   Bea

A Royal Worcester cup and saucer, pierced in the manner of George Owen, with honeycomb decoration heightened in turquoise and with equally spaced iron red and gilt medallions, the borders of rose pink with white and turquoise jewelled ribbon decoration, compressed year mark for 1877.
£750-800   Bon

A Worcester faceted coffee cup and saucer, painted in the atelier of James Giles with alternate blue panels and bands of gilt trailing foliage on a white ground, the centre of the saucer with a gilt bouquet, the cup with a bouquet in green 'camaieu', blue square seal mark.
£450-550   C

A Worcester teabowl and saucer, with The Three Flowers pattern, 4½in (11cm).
£175-200   BRK

A Berlin K.P.M. cabinet cup and saucer, with central panel painted with a portrait of Frederick the Great in military uniform, enriched in gilt, the interior with a wide band of gilt, c1847, 4in (11cm) high.
£170-210   Bon

A Böttger two-handled chinoiserie slender beaker and saucer, painted in the manner of J. G. Höroldt with figures at various pursuits, within gilt 'Laub-und-Bandelwerk' cartouches with panels of 'Böttgerluster' and iron red scrolls, the underside of the saucer moulded with 3 gilt chrysanthemum branches, beaker with restored crack, 2 rim chips and a footrim chip to saucer, c1725.
£1,500-2,000   C

A Chamberlain's Worcester cup and saucer.
£180-220   DN

A Worcester, Barr, Flight & Barr, cup, cover and stand, painted with brightly coloured feathers within a rectangular gilt line cartouche, with richly gilt angular handles and loop finial, finial restored, chip to rim of cover, puce script marks to cup, incised B marks to cup and stand, c1810.
£1,000-1,500 *C*

A Meissen turquoise ground teabowl and saucer, painted within elaborate gilt and brown borders, very slight rubbing, crossed swords in underglaze blue, gilder's numeral 80, impressed Drehermarke xx, c1740.
£1,800-2,500 *S*

A Meissen, Marcolini, blue ground coffee can and saucer, painted within a gilt tooled band reserve, the rims enriched with gilt egg-and-dart ornament, the base inscribed 'd'apres l'original de Raphael dans la Gallerie de Sa Majesté le Roi de Saxe', blue crossed swords and star marks, Pressnummer 23 and B9 to can, c1800.
£500-800 *C*

A Fürstenberg teacup and saucer, decorated with monkeys smoking, marks in blue.
£1,200-1,600 *DN*

A Staffordshire porcelain hound's head stirrup cup, the white body with black patches and muzzle details, black whiskers and yellow and black eyes, wearing a gilt bordered collar with central gilt oval tag, hair crack to rim, early 19thC, 4in (10.5cm).
£450-650 *S*

A Derby trout's head stirrup cup, painted in shades of green puce and pale pink, the rim inscribed in gilt 'The Angler's Delight', between gilt lines, Robt. Bloor & Co., c1825, 5½in (13.5cm).
£1,500-2,000 *C*

A Worcester blue and white teabowl and saucer, in Rock Warbler pattern, c1760, 4½in (11cm).
£700-800 *BRK*

Ewers

An English miniature blue ground ewer and basin, perhaps Coalport, 4½in (11cm).
£270-320 *CSK*

A Paris powder blue ground ewer and basin, painted in colours with richly gilt rims, c1830, ewer 10½in (26cm) high, basin 16½in (42cm) wide.
£500-600 *C*

A German gold ground ewer in the form of a rhyton, the short foot with a band of false gadroons, some damage and restoration, mid-19thC, 9in (23cm).
£550-700 *CSK*

A Royal Worcester ewer with leaf and flower decorated scrolled handle, painted by Harry Stinton with highlight landscape and cattle, 11½in (29cm).
£1,500-2,000 *AH*

Figures – Animals

An English white model of a finch, naturally modelled with incised and moulded plumage, on an oval base, chipping to leaves, probably Chelsea, c1750, 8in (19cm).
£9,000-12,000 *C*

A pair of 'Sèvres' gilt-bronze ewers, the bodies painted between white beaded borders, the reverse with a landscape scene, reserved on a turquoise, gilt and 'jewelled' ground, some glaze flaking, c1870.
£850-1,000 *S*

Two Meissen models of hoopoe birds, naturalistically modelled with feathered crests and with shaded black, cream and brown plumage, damage to extremities, blue crossed swords marks, incised and painted numbers, c1860, 12in (31cm).
£550-750 *CSK*

A Chamberlain's Worcester white model of a kingfisher, with moulded and lightly incised plumage, on a base applied with waterweeds, moss and a fish, some minute chipping to flowers, c1795, 4½in (11.5cm).
£1,500-2,000 *C*

A Derby group of a cow and calf with iron red markings, the cow before a tree stump applied with pale yellow flowers, the base applied with white flowers, damage to tree stump and flowers, chip to one horn and tip of calf's tail, Wm. Duesbury & Co., c1770, 5in (12.5cm).
£300-400 *C*

A Royal Worcester model of a Suffolk stallion, after a model by Doris Linder, 10in (25cm) high, complete with wood base.
£150-250 *Bea*

A Meissen bird nesting group of a pair of canaries, restored, crossed swords in blue, c1780, 3½in (9cm).
£450-700 *S*

A Royal Worcester model of a Brahman Bull, after a model by Doris Linder, on a wood base, No. 390 of an edition limited to 500, complete with certificate, 8½in (21.5cm) high overall.
£250-350 *Bea*

An unusual white glazed porcelain model of a lion, probably English, chipped, c1765, 8in (19.5cm).
£850-1,200 *S(S)*

A Meissen group of Europa and the Bull draped in pink and white, gilt and blue flowered robes and garlanding the white bull with flowers, on a base moulded with gilt scrolls, restoration to bull's tail, extremities and Europa's finger and toe, blue crossed swords mark, various Pressnummern and incised numerals, c1880, 9½in (24cm).
£550-850 *C*

An English dated model of a white pug on a tasselled cushion, the underside with the incised date '1750', slight chips and repair to tail, tassels lacking, probably Derby, 2½in (5.5cm) wide.
£2,000-2,500 *C*

A Meissen group of 3 dogs, modelled as a pug wearing a blue and gilt collar, a brown and white spaniel and a black and white spaniel scratching its face, slight chip to one ear, blue crossed swords and incised numeral marks, c1880, 8in (20cm) wide.
£1,700-2,200   *C*

A large Meissen elephant and rider group, the rider wearing a richly embroidered and colourful robe holding a sceptre and a censer, on grey elephant with a tasselled saddle cloth, minor chips and repairs, c1870, 16½in (42cm).
£3,800-4,200   *S*

A Meissen group of a pug bitch suckling its puppy, its brown coat with dark extremities, slight chips to claws, blue crossed swords and incised numeral marks, c1880, 9in (22.5cm).
£1,400-1,700   *C*

Two Meissen models of parrots with long tail feathers and brightly coloured plumage, on rockwork bases enriched in gilding, one with tail feathers broken, one beak and leaves chipped, blue crossed swords marks and impressed and incised numbers, c1880, 8in (20cm).
£850-1,000   *CSK*

A Samson 'famille rose' model of a horse, with tasselled saddle cloth, enamels worn, 13½in (34cm).
£400-600   *CSK*

A Meissen model of a turkey, beak repaired, blue crossed swords mark and incised and impressed numbers, c1890, 4in (10cm).
£150-200   *CSK*

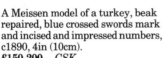

Two Meissen figures of bullfinches with brightly coloured plumage, blue crossed swords and impressed and incised numbers, c1900, 6in (15.5cm).
£850-950   *CSK*

A large Meissen model of a monkey snuff taker, seated on a tree stump, realistically enamelled, damage to one foot, 20thC, 19in (48cm).
£2,000-3,000   *Bon*

A group of 8 Meissen and one Berlin mute swans, mostly with wings outstretched in various poses, the Berlin example with wings folded, all with white feathers and faces with red and black markings, minor chips, crossed swords in underglaze blue, incised and impressed marks, printed K.P.M. orb and sceptre marks, late 19thC, tallest figure 11in (28cm).
£4,000-5,000   *S*

A Meissen figure of a cockerel, naturally modelled with brightly coloured plumage in shades of yellow, brown, iron red, mauve, green and black, damage to comb and damage and restoration to tail feathers, blue crossed swords and impressed marks, late 19thC, 12in (31cm) wide.
£900-1,200   *C*

Figures – People

A Bow white glazed figure of a seated nun wearing a voluminous habit and reading the Divine Office, minor chips and damage to base, c1755, 6in (15cm).
£400-600   *S*

A Bow white glazed figure of a seated nun wearing a voluminous habit and reading her breviary, minor chips, c1755, 6in (15cm).
£450-600   *S*

A pair of Bow figures, a gallant and his companion, on rococo turquoise and gilt scroll bases, minor damage, red enamelled sword and anchor marks, 18thC, 8in (20cm).
£1,200-1,500   *LAY*

A Bow figure of Harlequin, wearing yellow hat, chequered jacket and trousers and yellow shoes, enriched in turquoise and puce, damage to hat, slap-stick and his right hand, chips to flowers, c1765, 7in (18cm).
£1,200-1,800   *C*

A Chelsea Derby group of Venus by a rocky outcrop, Cupid at her feet with his bow and quiver of arrows, minor damage, late 18thC, 8in (20cm).
£500-600   *Bea*

A Bow figure of a nun, reading from an iron red bound book, wearing a mauve veil, the sleeves to her white robe edged in mauve and with mauve shoes, with an iron red and gilt rosary, book and left hand repaired and chipped, chips to edge of veil, sleeves and base, c1765, 6½in (16.5cm).
£650-750   *C*

A Bow figure of a rustic piper, wearing a puce hat, floral jacket and yellow knee breeches, minor chips, c1755, 6in (15cm).
£1,700-2,200 *S*

A Duesbury Derby figure of a highlander in feathered cap, flowered waistcoat, standing on a circular base, iron red, crown and batten mark, hand restored, 4½in (11.5cm).
£350-450 *WW*

A Chelsea figure group, after Boucher, wearing colourful costume, on scroll moulded base picked out in turquoise and gilding, minor chips and some restoration, gold anchor mark, c1760, 10in (25cm).
£1,000-1,500 *S*

A Bow figure of a girl, wearing pale blue bodice and yellow skirt and blue and iron red flowers, restoration to waist, apron, basket and extremities, incised AF mark to base, c1758, 6in (15.5cm).
£600-700 *C*

A pair of Derby 'dry-edge' figures, wearing floral 18thC court costumes on circular scroll moulded and flower encrusted bases, picked out in puce, minor chips, c1755, 6½in (17cm).
£2,500-3,000 *S*

A Copeland parian figure of Wellington wearing full uniform, impressed mark.
£300-400 *HSS*

A Chelsea figure of a shepherd, wearing pink hat, green jacket and his breeches painted in blue, iron red and gilt, the base enriched with gilding, parts of tree stump lacking and chips to his fingers and to flowers, foliage and extremities, gold anchor mark at back and incised R to base, c1765, 8½in (21cm).
£950-1,200 *C*

A pair of Derby figures of children, representing Spring and Summer, minor chips, c1760, 4½in (11.5cm).
£1,800-2,400 *S*

A Chelsea figure of a shepherdess, wearing pale lilac hat, pink-lined yellow jacket and a striped green-spotted reserved and gilt with flowerheads, her apron filled with brightly coloured flowers, on shell moulded base enriched in pink and gilt, chips to her right hand and to flowers, damage to tree trunk, gold anchor mark at back, c1765, 10in (24cm). **£1,500-1,800** *C*

Four Derby hand painted allegorical figures representing the Four Seasons, 18thC.
£2,800-3,200 *DM*

A Chelsea porcelain group, emblematic of Spring, 9in (22.5cm). **£750-950** *Bea*

A Derby porcelain figure of a piper, modelled after a Meissen figure by J. J. Kändler, wearing a black hat, puce overcoat, pale yellow waistcoat and colourful breeches, minor chips, c1760, 7in (17.5cm).
£400-600 *S(S)*

A pair of Derby figures of Haymakers, each wearing colourful attire, on elaborate scroll bases picked out in turquoise, green and gilding, minor chips and restoration, c1770, 10½in (27cm).
£900-1,200 *S*

A Derby figure of Milton, c1770-75, 11½in (29cm).
£500-600 *DN*

A pair of Derby arbour musicians, wearing feathered head-dresses and pink, turquoise and flowered clothes, seated in arbours, enriched in puce and encrusted with coloured flowers, the bases enriched in turquoise, green and with gilding, some chipping to flowers and foliage, Wm. Duesbury & Co, c1775, 14in (35.5cm).
£6,500-7,000 *C*

A rare Derby porcelain figure of The Parson, a separate individual from the Tithe Pig Group, wearing a long black gown and black hat, minor restoration, c1765, 7in (17.5cm).
£350-450 *S(S)*

A pair of Derby porcelain figures emblematic of Spring and Summer, late 18thC, 6in (15cm).
£1,000-1,200 *Bea*

A Derby group of a dancing couple, their white clothes edged in gilding, on a base enriched in pale green, turquoise and with gilding, minor chips, Wm. Duesbury & Co, c1775, 6½in (17cm).
£1,500-2,000 *C*

Two Derby figures of Sight and
Smell, from a set of the Senses,
restored, incised No. 59, late 18thC,
6½in (17cm).
£650-700 *S(S)*

A Derby figure of David Garrick as
Richard III, c1790, 11½in (29cm).
£500-600 *DN*

A Derby porcelain figure of The
Farmer, wearing a jacket and
black hat, russet yellow breeches,
standing on a flower encrusted pad
base, minor restoration, c1765, 7in
(17.5cm). **£400-450** *S(S)*

A Derby figure of Shakespeare,
c1770-75, 11½in (29cm).
£800-900 *DN*

A Derby figure of John Wilkes,
c1770-75, 13in (33cm).
£500-600 *DN*

A Derby figure of a gardener,
restored, late 18thC, 7½in (18cm).
£300-350 *S(S)*

A Royal Worcester figure of a Cairo
water carrier, in a gold decorated
dress, slight damage, shape
No. 1250, printed mark and date
code for 1899, 10in (25cm).
£250-350 *Bea*

A Derby figure of a Lady Musician,
her hair tied back with a pale blue
ribbon, minor chips, incised model
No. 311, c1775, 8½in (21cm).
£750-850 *S*

*According to Haslem's list of Derby
figures, model No. 311 is for a pair of
musicians, the male figure playing
an end flute and the female figure
playing a tambourine.*

A pair of Derby figures of a youth
and companion, he wearing a white
nightshirt and yellow-lined
turquoise jacket, his companion
wearing pink-lined pale yellow
dress, her underskirt painted in
purple and gilt with flowers, he on a
washed green base, his chair back
restored, minor chipping, incised
No. 71, Wm. Duesbury & Co, c1775,
6in (15cm).
£950-1,200 *C*

A Derby figure of Britannia, wearing yellow-lined pink drapery, gilt scale cuirass and her dress painted with purple and gilt flowers, the base enriched in turquoise and with gilding, chip to hat, tip of flag-pole lacking, chips to foliage, incised 3 mark, Wm. Duesbury & Co, c1770, 10½in (27cm).
£450-550 *C*

A Royal Dux bisque porcelain figure group.
£500-600 *HSS*

A Derby figure of a young boy, late 18thC, 6in (15.5cm).
£200-300 *Bea*

A Derby figure of Fame, her dress painted and gilt with pink flowing drapery, base enriched in turquoise and with gilding, trumpet lacking and minor chipping to foliage, Wm. Duesbury & Co, c1770, 10in (25.5cm).
£500-800 *C*

A pair of Royal Worcester figures modelled by James Hadley in the Kate Greenaway style, painted in muted enamel colours, printed mark, c1895, 10in (25.5cm).
£900-1,200 *Bea*

A Royal Worcester figure of a female water carrier, with a floral dress, shape No. 637, printed mark and date code for 1912, 6in (14cm).
£300-400 *Bea*

A Royal Worcester figure, The Parakeet, modelled by F. G. Doughty, printed mark in black, 7in (17cm).
£200-250 *HSS*

A rare and previously unrecorded Plymouth figure of The French Shepherd, in white jacket lined in pale puce with similar striped waistcoat and breeches decorated with iron red flower sprigs, his feet with red buckled shoes, a small puppy with forepaws on his chest, some damage, c1770, 5½in (14cm).
£1,500-2,000 *Bon*

A pair of Worcester figures modelled as the Cairo Water Carriers by James Hadley, in tones of blush ivory, marked in puce, date code for 1919, 20in (51cm).
£1,000-1,500 *P(M)*

Three Frankenthal figures of Chinamen, modelled by K. G. Lück, one wearing yellow, white, puce and iron red, another wearing pink, green and iron red, and the other wearing white, puce, blue and yellow, all standing on scroll-edged gilt and green moulded bases, chips and restoration, part of musician's triangle missing, all with crowned CT mark, one with 77, in underglaze blue, c1777, 5in (12.5cm).
£1,700-2,200   *S*

A pair of Royal Worcester figures of cherub musicians, impressed marks, c1880, 6in (15.5cm).
£480-550   *Bea*

A Royal Worcester bronzed new large Grecian Water Carrier, class 2/125, c1916, 15in (38cm). **£550-650**
PCh

A pair of Royal Worcester 'Kate Greenaway' figures by James Hadley, shape No. 893, printed mark and date code for 1886, 9in (22.5cm).
£850-900   *Bea*

A Longton Hall figure of Harlequin wearing a black mask, yellow jacket and chequered trousers, repaired through tree stump, c1753, 5in (12.5cm).   **£2,000-2,500**   *C*

A Royal Worcester 'Ivory' group of 2 children after the model by James Hadley, the boy holding a gilt jug to the lips of his companion, their features and hair naturalistically painted and enriched in gilding, his right cuff with minute chip, impressed Hadley on the back, the base with green printed marks and No. 813, date code for 1898, 7in (17.5cm).
£400-600   *C*

A pair of Meissen figures emblematic of Summer and Autumn, from a set of the Seasons, Summer as a scantily draped woman, Autumn with grapes in his hair, painted in colours and enriched in gilding, on high mound bases moulded with white and gilt scrolls, Summer with one hand restored, slight chipping, blue crossed swords and incised marks, c1900, 9in (22.5cm).
£450-550   *C*

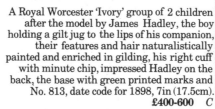

Locate the source

The source of each illustration in Miller's can be found by checking the code letters below each caption with the list of contributors

A Royal Worcester figurine on circular plinth, The Violinist, by Thomas Brock, with green gilded jacket, breeches and shoes, pattern No. 1487, puce mark 1919, 20in (51cm).
£1,800-2,200   *GH*

A Meissen group depicting a gentleman writing a letter, with green and brown gilt line moulded base, minor chips, crossed swords in underglaze blue and incised N.179, c1865, 5½in (14cm).
£800-900   *S*

A Royal Worcester figure of a woman on a swing, entitled 'Alice', from the series of Victorian figures by Ronald Van Ruyckevelt, No. 102 of an edition limited to 500, complete with certificate and fitted box.
£250-300   *Bea*

A Royal Dux figure of a young girl with a lute, dressed in shades of putty and green, pink triangle mark and impressed model No. 1707, 22½in (58cm).
£800-900   *WHB*

A Meissen group of a putto with a leopard, modelled by J. J. Kändler, possibly representing Autumn, in a puce lined cloak patterned with 'indianische Blumen', one arm, one leg and toes restored, chips, crossed swords in underglaze blue, c1760, 4in (10cm).
£1,000-1,200   *S*

A Meissen figure group emblematic of Earth, conceived as a goddess on the back of a recumbent lion, all on a naturalistic domed base with gilt rim, minor restoration, crossed swords in underglaze blue and incised numerals, c1880, 9½in (24cm).
£3,000-4,000   *S*

A Royal Dux group of a goat boy playing pipes and a girl with a tambourine, pink triangle mark and impressed No. 170, 15in (38cm).
£700-800   *WHB*

A set of 5 Meissen figures emblematic of the Senses, each modelled as a lady in 18thC dress, painted in colours and enriched in gilding, the shaped rectangular bases moulded with pink flutes with gilded details, mirror, one table leg and area of clavichord restored, crossed swords in underglaze blue, 2 incised E.4 and E.5, c1880, 4½ to 6in (12 to 15cm).   **£4,000-5,000**   *S*

A pair of Meissen figures of a fisherman and fishwife, the man wearing a black hat, a lilac smock and purple, green and yellow striped breeches, his companion wearing a lilac dress edged in yellow and a white apron with yellow, iron red and purple stripes, each standing on rococo scroll bases applied with flowers, the girl's fishing net restored and her hat repaired, the man's fishing net restored and rim of hat restored, feint crossed swords mark and impressed numerals 3 and 1, c1760, 6in (15.5cm).
£2,000-2,500 *S*

A pair of Royal Dux figures of a shepherd boy playing pipes, wearing green classical dress and sheepskin robe, and his companion similarly attired, pink triangle mark and impressed Nos. 579 and 580, 17in (43cm).
£850-950 *WHB*

Two Limbach figures of the Continents, Europe as a king in armour, wearing an ermine-lined purple cloak, Asia as an Oriental wearing a turban, on scroll moulded bases, outlined in purple, 2 hands restored and minor chipping and restoration, crossed swords in purple, c1775, 7½in (19cm).
£2,600-3,200 *S*

A large Meissen pastoral group, after a model by Acier and Schönheit, picked out in bright enamel colours and gilding, minor chips and repairs, crossed swords in underglaze blue, incised D.46 and with impressed and script numerals, c1880, 18½in (47cm).
£3,500-4,500 *S*

A Meissen group of Neptune, seated in a chariot and dressed in a red flowing robe, coloured in bright enamels and enriched in gilding, crossed swords in underglaze blue and incised 2189, c1880, 6½in (16cm).
£900-1,300 *S*

A Meissen figure of Schindler modelled by J. J. Kändler, wearing a buff hat with a fur brim, buff jacket and trousers with gilt frogging, purple belt and red boots, holding a goat formed as bagpipes, a black and white dog at his feet, on gild edged base, damaged, c1740, 6½in (17cm).
£3,000-5,000 *C*

A Meissen group of a gallant and companion, he in frock coat, blue sash, striped waistcoat, black breeches and shoes, holding a snuff box, she in a flowered crinoline dress and lilac underskirt, holding a fan, on a brown base, minute chip to back of dress, nosegay and ribbon, blue crossed swords mark and incised 556, c1880, 8½in (21.5cm).
£600-1,000 *C*

A pair of Meissen figures of a Turk and his companion, 7in (17.5cm).
£1,500-2,000 *LAY*

A Meissen group of School for Love after a model by Acier, picked out in bright enamel colours on a green and brown rockwork base, area of the base restored, crossed swords in underglaze blue, c1880, 11½in (29cm).
£1,500-2,500 *S*

A Meissen figure of Sight, from a set of the Five Senses, modelled as a young woman seated at a dressing table admiring herself in a mirror, very minor chips, crossed swords in underglaze blue, incised E.3 and impressed 127, late 19thC, 5½in (14cm).
£900-1,200 *S*

A pair of Meissen figures of a youth and a girl, their clothes painted in colours and enriched in gilding, on rockwork bases enriched with gilt lines, minor chipping to flowers, blue crossed swords and incised numeral marks, c1880, 6½in (16.5cm).
£1,200-1,600 *C*

A Berlin figure of a classical maiden, allegorical of Spring from a set of the Seasons, the low drum shaped base raised on a separate waisted socle, moulded in relief with gilt scrollwork panels painted with colourful flowers, minor chips to extremities, cancelled sceptre mark in underglaze blue and impressed numerals, c1880, 19in (49cm).
£1,000-1,500 *S*

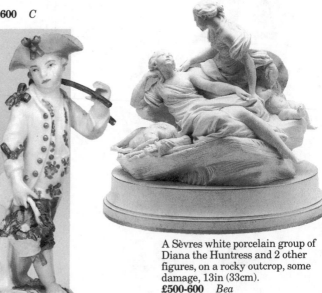

A Sèvres white porcelain group of Diana the Huntress and 2 other figures, on a rocky outcrop, some damage, 13in (33cm).
£500-600 *Bea*

A Meissen group of the Seasons, each putto with flowers or a sheaf of corn or seated on a barrel holding a wine goblet, base of goblet restored and minor chips, crossed swords in underglaze blue and incised 1068, c1880, 6in (15cm).
£1,500-2,000 *S*

A Meissen figure of a boy as a gardener carrying a hoe and a basket of flowers, wearing a pink hat and turquoise and yellow clothes, chips to flowers and leaves, blue crossed swords mark and incised 14, c1750, 5½in (13.5cm).
£700-900 *C*

Did you know
MILLER'S Antiques Price Guide builds up year by year to form the most comprehensive photo-reference system available

A pair of Meissen groups of Bacchic putti, representing the Four Seasons, on rocky bases with scroll moulded rims picked out in gilding, minor chips, crossed swords in underglaze blue, incised numerals 1230 and 1236, c1860, 8½in (22cm).
£2,000-2,500   *S*

A Meissen group of a Domestic Incident, the whole group in bright colours and gilding, some minor restoration, crossed swords in underglaze blue and incised D.64, c1875, 8in (20cm).
£900-1,200   *S*

A Meissen group depicting Venus and Cupid riding in a large clam shell, minor restoration, crossed swords in underglaze blue and incised 127, c1880, 13½in (34cm).
£2,500-3,000   *S*

A pair of Meissen 'Bouquetier' figures after models by J. J. Kändler, the woman in black, white and gilt, and an apron decorated with 'indianische Blumen', her companion in green and white, with yellow shoes, some damage, crossed swords mark in underglaze blue, mid-18thC, 7½in (19cm).
£2,500-3,500   *S(S)*

A Meissen group of 2 semi-naked children, chip to base, impressed H.88, cancelled crossed swords mark, 6in (15cm).
£400-450   *Bea*

A Royal Worcester figure from The Countries of the World series by James Hadley, in the form of a Scotsman, minor damage under base, shape No. 913, printed mark and date code for 1899, 6in (15cm).
£250-300   *Bea*

A Meissen group of the Druken Silenus, painted in colours, on an oval rockwork base moulded with white and gilt scrolls, tip of donkey's ear and tail lacking, slight damage to basket and foliage, chip to footrim, blue crossed swords and incised numeral mark, c1880, 8½in (21cm).
£500-700   *C*

A Meissen figure, after a model by Jüchtzer and based on the marble by Bernini, depicting a naked Daphne changing into a tree and pursued by Apollo who wears a green robe, gilt lined base, crossed swords in underglaze blue and incised J.9, c1875, 14in (36cm).
£1,200-1,500   *S*

A Meissen group after a model by Acier and Schönheit, with grinning marble muse of Music overlooking the proceedings, all in bright polychrome enamels, crossed swords in underglaze blue and incised G.32, c1880, 10½in (27cm).
£2,000-3,000   *S*

A Meissen apple-picking group, minor chips, c1865, 11in (29cm).
£2,000-2,500 *S*

A pair of Dresden figures of a lady and gentleman in 18thC dress, she with yellow overskirt full of flowers, he with yellow floral breeches and purple frock coat, 17in (43cm).
£750-850 *P(M)*

A Meissen figure group of Count Bruhl's Tailor, after a model by J. J. Kändler, the bewigged gentleman wearing a pale pink floral decorated coat and black hat, some minor restoration, crossed swords in underglaze blue and incised No. 177, c1880, 9in (23cm).
£900-1,200 *S*

A brightly coloured Staffordshire porcelain figure of Nelson in dress uniform, 6½in (16.5cm).
£90-120 *Bea*

A pair of Meissen Malabar figures, the man playing a guitar and his female companion with a hurdy-gurdy, wearing colourful robes, some restoration, crossed swords in underglaze blue and incised numerals 1576 and 1569, c1880, 7in (18cm).
£1,000-1,500 *S*

A pair of Samson figures of a gentleman in a gold ground jacket, painted with flowers, and his companion in a pink jacket and floral dress, on rock moulded bases, slight damage to extremities, 9in (23cm).
£250-350 *CSK*

A Longton Hall figure of Columbine after a Meissen model by J. J. Kändler, seated playing the hurdy-gurdy, in pink cap, pink and puce bodice, yellow dress and white apron painted with cards and flowers, her yellow shoes with pink bows, some minute chipping to extremities, c1758, 5in (13cm).
£2,700-3,200 *C*

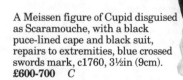

A Meissen group of the Ravishment of Proserpina, after a model by J. J. Kändler, on gilded scroll base, minor restoration on foliage, crossed swords in underglaze blue, c1885, 7in (18cm).
£400-600 *S*

A Meissen figure of Cupid disguised as Scaramouche, with a black puce-lined cape and black suit, repairs to extremities, blue crossed swords mark, c1760, 3½in (9cm).
£600-700 *C*

A Meissen figure of a goddess, wearing a flowered dress and purple robe dotted with gilt stars, on a stepped base moulded with pink drapery, damaged, blue crossed swords mark and impressed and incised numbers, c1860, 19½in (49cm).

£1,000-1,500   CSK

Two white glazed Meissen porcelain figures, both probably after Meyer, one allegorical of Fire modelled as a scantily clad bearded male, the other of a young woman in flowing robes, minor chips, crossed swords and star in blue, respective numerals 34 and 1394, late 18thC, 5½ and 6½in (14 and 16cm).

£300-400   S(S)

A pair of Royal Dux bisque porcelain figures of a shepherd and shepherdess wearing rustic garb, picked out in typical muted colours, patch mark, 30 and 32in (76 and 81cm).

£2,500-3,000   HSS

A German crinoline group of 2 ladies on a green settee, and a young gentleman in a yellow jacket and breeches kneeling pointing a sword, the base inscribed 'L'eroica' on a scroll moulded base enriched in gilding, damaged, 8in (20cm).

£200-250   CSK

Two Samson figures of Dancing Courtiers, 8in (20cm).

£220-260   GAK

A Meissen group of child musicians, damage and repair to several extremities, blue crossed swords mark, c1760, 6½in (16cm).

£1,000-1,500   C

A Frankenthal figure of a Chinese musician, modelled by K. G. Lück, with large hat lined in yellow, and wearing a green and yellow striped jacket with pink bib and white sleeves, his white trousers striped in green with a sash similarly decorated, end of guitar missing, crowned CT mark 76 in underglaze blue, c1776, 6in (15cm).

£1,000-1,200   S

A pair of Meissen groups emblematic of America and Africa, from a set of the Continents after the original models by J. J. Kändler, America as a woman seated on an alligator wearing feathered headdress, cloak and skirt, Africa as a Negro wearing elephant's head headdress, pink cloak edged with jewelling, feathered bodice and leggings and with blue drapery over his knees, some damage and restorations, blue crossed swords, impressed and incised numeral marks, early 20thC, 10in (25cm) wide.

£3,500-4,000   C

A Meissen figure of a gallant, in a waistcoat and long overcoat holding a flower, crossed swords in underglaze blue and incised A.58, c1870, 8in (20cm).

£850-950   S

129

A Meissen apple-picking group, decorated in bright enamel colours on a scroll moulded gilt lined base, minor restorations, crossed swords in underglaze blue and incised 2229, c1870, 10½in (26cm).
£1,200-1,500 *S*

A pair of Meissen musician figures, on scroll moulded gilt lined bases, minor repairs, crossed swords in underglaze blue and incised 1351, c1875, 13in (33cm).
£1,400-1,800 *S*

A Meissen group of 'Das Verlobnis' or 'The Betrothal', after an 18thC original by J. J. Kändler, the man wearing a red jacket picked out in gilding, the lady wearing a mauve-lined dress painted with colourful sprays of flowers on a white ground edged in gilding, and a white cap with a pale blue ribbon on her head, minor chips to foliage, c1880, 7½in (19cm).
£1,200-1,500 *S*

A Meissen figure group of a lady with a spinning wheel, 'Leserin am Spinnrocken', modelled in the 18thC taste, she holds a gilt bound book, all on a rococo base with relief moulded gilt scroll rim, minor chips and restoration, crossed swords in underglaze blue, incised numerals 2685 and impressed numerals 127, c1880, 6½in (16cm). **£1,700-2,200** *S*

A Nymphenburg figure of an egg-seller, 'Eiergretel', modelled by Franz Anton Bustelli, wearing a black neckerchief, green bodice, a yellow skirt and holding her white puce-spotted apron, on a flat base washed in grey, base restored, incised 43, c1755, 5½in (14.5cm).
£1,000-1,500 *S*

A Samson figure of a young woman seated in a sleigh with a swan support, painted with flowers and moulded and pierced with gilt scrolls, the lady wearing a tricorn hat, grey flowered skirt and a feather muff, blue marks, 6½in (16cm).
£400-450 *CSK*

A pair of Samson figures of musicians in the Chelsea style, on rococo scroll moulded bases enriched in puce and gilding, chips to extremities, 9½in (24cm).
£400-500 *CSK*

A pair of Royal Dux figures of classical maidens, wearing long pink robes picked out in gilding, pink triangles, impressed numerals 2018/2019, early 20thC, 18½in (47cm).
£1,500-2,000 *S(S)*

A pair of Continental coloured bisque figures, probably French, he about to lose his tricorn hat, she with her parasol blown inside out and about to lose her bonnet, minor restoration, incised A.M. in scroll frame, mid-19thC, 15in (38cm).
£400-450 *S(S)*

A Royal Dux figure of a shepherdess, and a smaller pair of figures of a farmer and his companion, shepherdess 12in (31cm), smaller figures 8½in (21cm).
£300-350 *Bea*

A Sitzendorf porcelain musical group of 'The six-year old Mozart playing the piano at the Court of the Empress Maria Theresa of Austria', narrow stress crack to base, crowned S in underglaze blue, 20thC, 22in (56cm) wide, separate title panel.
£850-900 *S(S)*

A pair of Continental figures of a young man in colourful 18thC costume, his hat under one arm, offering a string of beads to his companion, 17in (43cm).
£600-700 *Bea*

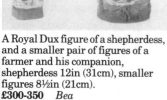

A pair of Samson figures of a drummer, in turquoise and red jacket and chocolate breeches, his companion playing a flute, in turquoise and floral jacket and yellow floral skirt, damage to extremities, 12½in (32cm).
£450-550 *CSK*

A German porcelain group of the Marriage Contract, modelled as a gentleman and companion standing either side of a seated lawyer, painted in colours and enriched in gilding, slight damage to extremities, 10½in (26cm).
£500-600 *CSK*

A pair of German figures of Cupid-like figures, each with a bow and quiver, standing on a foliate base, 14½in (37.5cm).
£250-350 *Bea*

A Meissen porcelain nodding figure of a sage, after an 18thC original, wearing a pale pink robe decorated with flowers in blue, green and puce picked out in gilding, minor restoration, crossed swords in underglaze blue, incised 2187, c1880, 8in (20cm).
£450-550 *S(S)*

A pair of Continental coloured bisque figures of a gypsy and companion in a pink jacket and pale blue cape, she with a duck egg blue headdress, pale blue bodice and floral dress, both on rocky mound bases, enriched in gilding, both with damage to hands, her headdress damaged, bases chipped, 20in (51cm).
£700-750 *CSK*

131

Flatware

A Bow patty pan, the exterior to the flared sides with stylised flowers, small hair crack, painter's numeral 28, c1758, 4in (10.5cm) diam.
£350-450   *C*

A Bow dish, the white body painted with a colourful spray of flowers, fruit and foliage, within a border moulded in relief with fruiting vines picked out in puce, green and yellow, all within a shaped wavy rim with gilt edge, restored chips, red painted anchor and dagger mark, c1765, 10½in (26cm).
£1,200-1,800   *S*

A Bow dish, 10½in (26cm) wide.
£380-420   *BRK*

A Caughley plate decorated with the full Nanking pattern, 8in (20cm).
£160-180   *BRK*

A Caughley powdered blue ground dish, painted with flowering plants within a circular cartouche, the powdered blue border reserved with shaped panels enclosing stylised flowers, utensils and zig-zag ornament, blue C mark, c1775, 10in (24.5cm) wide.
£400-450   *C*

A Caughley dish, 7½in (19cm).
£250-270   *BRK*

A Chelsea leaf-moulded dish, the centre painted in the manner of Jeffereys Hammett O'Neale with 2 cows with black and pale brown markings, standing and recumbent in a landscape vignette, wear to decoration, small rim crack, red anchor mark, c1758, 8½in (21cm).
£1,700-2,200   *C*

A Caughley spoon tray, 6in (15cm) wide.
£170-200   *BRK*

A pair of Coalport shell shaped dishes, early 19thC, 9½in (24cm).
£300-400   *DN*

Two Worcester Blind Earl pattern plates, painted in the atelier of James Giles, in brown, green and puce over the white ground, all within a gilt fluted rim, one restored, c1765, 7½in (19cm).
£1,200-1,600   *S*

A Coalport plate, painted and signed by Fred Sutton, c1850, 9in (23cm).
£130-150   *Wai*

Two Sèvres pattern yellow ground plates, painted in the Japanese taste in a bright palette, with lobed gilt rims, imitation interlaced L marks, c1880, 9½in (24cm).
£550-650   *C*

A Caughley lozenge dish, decorated with the Fisherman pattern, c1770, 10½in (26cm) wide.
£200-250 *BRK*

A Chelsea red anchor miniature dish, with twig handles, the centre painted with exotic birds, the pierced rim applied with flowerheads, slight discolouration, mid-18thC, 4½in (11cm).
£550-650 *Bea*

A pair of Chelsea plates, crazed, brown anchor marks, c1758, 9in (22.5cm) diam.
£500-800 *C*

top. A Chelsea dish boldly painted within a brown and green feather-moulded rim, minute rim chip, slight rubbing, crazed, brown anchor mark, c1758, 11in (28cm) wide.
£350-450
below. A Chelsea dish, painted in a light palette, brown anchor mark, c1758, 10in (24.5cm) wide.
£500-600 *C*

A Chelsea plate, painted with a tight bouquet of flowers and fruit within a border of asparagus, flowers, nuts and insects, within a gilt and turquoise scroll and feather-moulded rim, paint worn, gold anchor mark, 8in (20cm) diam.
£200-300 *CSK*

A Caughley patty pan, decorated with the Fisherman pattern, 10in (25cm) wide.
£250-300 *BRK*

A Worcester dish painted in the 'famille verte' palette with Chinese figures in a garden, the rim painted with a flowerhead and diaper design, mid-18thC, 10½in (26cm).
£700-800 *Bea*

A pair of Copeland & Garrett plates, with named views, c1840, 9½in (24cm).
£220-240 *Wai*

A Chamberlain's Worcester 'Aesop's Fables' dessert plate, the centre painted in dark brown enamel with a scene from the hare and the tortoise story, the lightly fluted rim decorated in gold on a blue band, late 18thC, 8½in (21.5cm).
£400-500 *Bea*

A Chamberlain's Worcester Japan pattern dish, painted in iron red, blue, green, turquoise and gilt with flowers and foliage issuing from rockwork, beneath demi-fans and divided by iron red panels gilt with diaper and trellis pattern, the rim gilt, c1800, 8½in (21cm).
£450-550   *C*

top. Four Coalport/Chamberlain's Worcester square dishes, early 19thC, 8in (20cm).
£1,000-1,500
below. Twelve Coalport/Flight/ Chamberlain plates, early 19thC.
£1,200-1,700   *P(S)*

A Worcester, Flight, Barr & Barr plate, the centre painted with St. Bernards Well, Water of Leith, named on the reverse, the border gilt with seaweed pendant from a gilt shaped gadrooned rim, printed marks, c1820, 9in (22.5cm).
£250-350   *C*

A Coalport 'trompe l'oeil' plate, painted all over a gilt ground with a border of S-scrolls in pale pink and gilding, minor wear to rim, c1808, 9in (23cm).
£1,300-1,700   *S*

Twelve Meissen pierced plates, the centres painted within pierced borders of radiating panels of blue and yellow flowerheads, blue crossed swords marks and various Pressnummern, c1870, 10in (25cm).
£4,500-5,000   *C*

A Derby dish, painted in a pale palette within turquoise 'feuilles-de-choux' rims, the shell thumbpieces enriched in puce, rubbing to enamels, slight rim chip, Wm. Duesbury & Co, c1758, 9½in (24cm).
£380-450   *C*

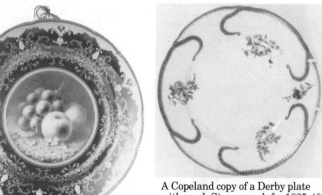

A Coalport plate, painted and signed by F. H. Chivers, with still life of fruit enclosed by raised gilt flowers and scrolling foliage on a 'gros bleau' ground, printed mark in green, c1900, 12in (31cm) diam.
£450-550   *P(M)*

A Copeland copy of a Derby plate with mock Sèvres mark for 1825-48, plate made for T. Goode, c1891-1910.
£48-50   *Wai*

A Worcester pickle dish, transfer printed after Robert Hancock with Winter, the pencilled diaper pattern border reserved with foliage, slight rim chip, c1755, 4in (10cm) wide.
£1,200-1,500   C

A Chelsea dish, painted with flowers over the white ground, within a shaped brown rim, minor chip to rim, red anchor mark, c1765, 15in (38cm).
£1,400-1,700   S

A Paris blue ground plate, painted within a circular cartouche with oval cartouches of flowers and flowerheads, the border with sprigs of flowers within diamond cartouches on a gold ground, the base inscribed in gilt, gilding slightly rubbed, printed retailer's mark, 8½in (21cm).
£450-500   CSK

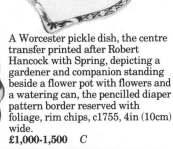

A Vienna dish, the centre painted with Venus, Cupid and Minerva, the border with maroon coloured panels painted in white and gilt, signed F. Koller, 9½in (23.5cm).
£250-300   P(S)

A Worcester pickle dish, the centre transfer printed after Robert Hancock with Spring, depicting a gardener and companion standing beside a flower pot with flowers and a watering can, the pencilled diaper pattern border reserved with foliage, rim chips, c1755, 4in (10cm) wide.
£1,000-1,500   C

A pair of Vienna plates, inscribed to rear 'Marie Mancini' and 'Montesson', 19thC, 10in (25cm).
£1,700-2,200   P(M)

A Worcester blue scale plate, painted within gilt vase and mirror shaped cartouches, reserved on a well defined blue scale ground, minute rim chip, blue square seal mark, c1770, 8in (20cm).
£150-200   C

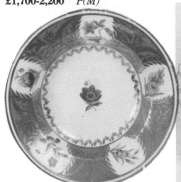

A Worcester fable-decorated deep plate, painted within a gilt band and turquoise husk cartouche reserved with foliate ornament and edged in gilding, the well painted with 3 sprays of fruit and 3 exotic birds, the fluted border with a bright blue band edged with gilt scrolls and 'feuilles-de-choux', within a waved gilt dentil rim, slight wear to gilding, blue crescent mark, c1775, 8½in (22cm).
£3,000-3,500   C

A pair of Derby plates, some restoration, c1800, 10in (25cm).
£450-500   Wai

A set of 4 Berlin porcelain plates, c1760, 10in (25cm).
£900-1,200   SBA

A set of 12 Royal Worcester dessert plates, after originals by Dorothy Doughty, each moulded and painted on a cream ground within a gold painted wavy rim, 9½in (23.5cm).
£350-550   *Bea*

A Royal Worcester plate with pierced rim, painted by Charles Henry Clifford Baldwyn, with white swans flying amongst reeds, the moulded border painted in gold, printed mark and date code for 1905, 8½in (21.5cm).
£1,500-2,000   *Bea*

A Worcester dish, the border with a bright blue band edged with gilt scrolls, within a gilt dentil rim, gilding to rim slightly worn, blue crescent mark, c1775, 10in (25cm).
£400-500   *C*

A Worcester pink scale fluted soup plate, painted in the atelier of James Giles, with a central loose bouquet and with trailing flowers pendant from a cornucopia-shaped puce scale border edged with gilt scrolls, within a waved gilt rim, c1770, 10in (25cm).
£3,000-3,500   *C*

A Böttger chinoiserie saucer, painted within a gilt quatrefoil cartouche with Böttger lustre panels, iron red and puce scrolls within a band of gilt interlocking scrolls, gilt line rim, slight rubbing, gilder's numeral 34, c1725. **£600-700**   *C*

A set of 6 Sèvres soup plates, each painted in colours with sprays of flowers, gilt dashed blue line borders, gilt and shaped rims, interlaced L marks and date letters in blue and black, painter's marks in blue and black, various incised marks, c1773.
£500-770   *P(S)*

A Worcester shell dish, decorated with the 2 peony, rock and bird pattern, 5in (13cm) diam.
£380-420   *BRK*

A Derby deep plate, painted in a 'famille verte' palette after a Chinese original, with false gadroon bands and a waved gilt rim, crown, crossed baton and D mark in carmine, Duesbury & Kean, c1800, 10in (25cm).
£800-900   *C*

A large Sèvres portrait charger, the centre painted with a titled portrait of Louis XVI, surrounded by 8 titled medallion portraits, each within a gilt ribbon border flanked by gilt scrolls, pendants and 'fleur-de-lys' motifs reserved on a pale pink ground, minor wear to gilding, interlaced L's in blue and incised numerals, black painted titles for portraits, c1880, 19in (48.5cm).
£600-800   *S*

A Meissen 'pâte-sur-pâte' plate, decorated with a classical female wearing a diaphanous white robe, all reserved on a pink ground, the pierced border gilt with interlinking ovals centred by tiny florets in relief, crossed swords in underglaze blue, c1880, 9½in (24cm).
£1,700-2,000   *S*

A Worcester spoon tray of scroll outline, painted in a 'famille rose' palette with Putai and 2 attendants on a lightly moulded pleated ground edged with scrolls, within a gilt rim, rubbing to enamels and slight rim chip, c1760, 5½in (14cm) wide.
£1,700-2,200   *C*

A Sèvres armorial two-handled tray, later decorated, the centre painted within a gilt dentil quatrefoil cartouche reserved on a 'bleu celeste' ground enriched with gilding, the border reserved with a coat-of-arms and a mirror monogram within oval cartouches, the rim gilt, gilding slightly rubbed, imitation interlaced L marks, c1875, 12in (31cm) wide.
£600-800   *C*

A gilt metal mounted Paris porcelain tray, with scroll ends, Egyptian masks and winged lion masks on the gilt underside, finely painted in the centre, within a tooled gilt border, fitted into a later gilt metal frame of fruiting vines and raised on 4 short lappet feet, c1830, 18in (46cm).
£2,200-2,600   *S*

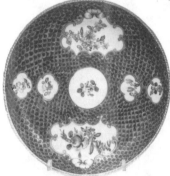

A Liverpool blue scale saucer dish, slight rim chip, Philip Christian's factory, c1770, 6½in (16cm) diam.
£200-300   *C*

A Worcester, Flight, Barr & Barr dish, the centre painted with a pink rose within a gilt band cartouche, the border with a band of pink roses beneath a gilt shaped gadrooned rim, impressed mark, c1815, 9½in (23.5cm).
£450-550   *C*

A set of 6 Vienna plates painted in Imari style on alternating underglaze blue and white grounds, shield marks and 8 in underglaze blue, painter's numerals in iron red, impressed and incised numerals, c1750, 8½in (21.5cm).
£2,000-2,500   *S*

A Worcester, Flight, Barr & Barr plate, painted by Simon Astles with a gilt band well, the border with gilt stylised anthemion beneath a shaped gilt gadrooned rim, script marks, c1820, 10in (25cm).
£2,500-3,000   *C*

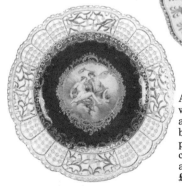

A Meissen cabinet plate, painted with a titled scene of 'Der Frühling', after Watteau', between a gilt scroll border on a blue ground, the rim pierced with floral designs, rim chip, crossed swords in underglaze blue and script title, c1870, 10in (25cm).
£700-800   *S*

A Vienna plate by Hav.(?) Sartory, signed, painted after Ch. du Jardin with a rural scene, one flake, shield mark in underglaze blue, impressed date code and numeral, inscribed in black enamel 'L' original 'peint par Charles du Jardin, se trouve dans la galerie de Mr = le Comte Ant:de Lamberg à Vienne, cop:par Hav:Satory 1815', dated 1815, 9½in (24.5cm).
£1,700-2,200   *S*

An English topographical tray, the centre enamelled with a view of a country house, within a moulded floral and foliage border enriched with gilding, repaired, c1820, 9in (23cm).
£170-220 *Bon*

A Liverpool plate, painted with 2 figures on a bridge and with a house and pavilion among trees on river islands, within a diaper pattern well and rim, Richard Chaffer's factory, c1765, 8in (20cm) wide.
£850-1,000 *C*

A Worcester plate, painted in the atelier of James Giles, in green monochrome with a loose bouquet and with scattered flowers, the fluted border with a waved gilt line rim, slightly rubbed, c1768, 8½in (21cm).
£350-450 *C*

A 'Vienna' deep dish, the central square panel painted with a classical scene, within a gilt key pattern border on a puce ground decorated with classical silhouettes, imitation blue beehive mark, gold plush mount and rectangular carved giltwood frame, 17in (43.5cm).
£1,700-2,200 *C*

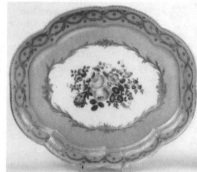

A Sèvres pink ground shaped tray, later decorated, painted within a gilt floral foliage cartouche reserved on a pink ground enriched with bands of entwined gilt foliage and husks beneath a dentil rim, imitation interlaced L marks, the decoration 19thC, 11in (28cm) wide.
£500-800 *C*

A Sèvres pattern portrait charger, the turquoise ground reserved and painted with a central portrait of Louis XV surrounded by 6 portraits of Court Beauties, each within a gilt band, imitation blue interlaced L marks, c1875, 18in (45.5cm).
£1,200-1,500 *C*

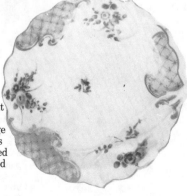

A Paris plate, painted within a blue square cartouche enriched in gilding with flowerheads, the well painted within a green border enriched in gilding with foliage, line and dots, gilding slightly rubbed, 8½in (21cm).
£450-550 *CSK*

A Worcester Blind Earl sweetmeat dish, the branch handle with rose bud terminal, moulded with foliage and painted with scattered flowers with alternating cornucopia-shaped panels of pink diaper pattern edged with gilt C-scrolls, c1770, 6½in (16cm).
£1,700-2,000 *C*

A Worcester pickle dish, transfer printed after Robert Hancock with Autumn from the Four Seasons, depicting a harvester and companion cutting corn, within a black pencilled diaper pattern border reserved with foliage, rim chip, c1755, 4in (11cm) wide.
£1,000-1,500   *C*

A Lowestoft pickle tray, 4in (10cm) wide.
£220-250   *BRK*

A Copenhagen tray, painted with a purple bow flanked by medallions painted in sepia, enclosed by gilt bead bands and border, the underside painted with a bouquet of flowers in green and black, blue wave mark, c1780, 16½in (42.5cm).
£1,600-2,000   *C*

A pair of Coalport yellow ground two-handled topographical trays, the centres painted in enamels within a gilt cartouche, the borders with moulded feather and vine reserves enriched in gilding, both views in red script, one bearing the name Apley Park, Salop, the other Milley Park, Salop, one tray with repaired handles, c1820, 16in (41cm).
£2,500-3,500   *Bon*

A Worcester leaf dish, painted with an exotic bird before foliage and with scattered butterflies and insects, the moulded overlapping leaves with puce veining and with gilt rim, red anchor mark, c1768, 10½in (26cm).
£850-950   *C*

A pair of Flight, Barr & Barr square dishes, decorated within a blue ground border containing floral panels, and a gilt gadrooned rim, impressed marks, c1820, 9½in (24cm).
£1,000-1,200   *S*

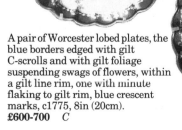

A pair of Worcester lobed plates, the blue borders edged with gilt C-scrolls and with gilt foliage suspending swags of flowers, within a gilt line rim, one with minute flaking to gilt rim, blue crescent marks, c1775, 8in (20cm).
£600-700   *C*

Make the Most of Miller's

Every care has been taken to ensure the accuracy of descriptions and estimated valuations. Price ranges in this book reflect what one should expect to pay for a similar example. When selling one can obviously expect a figure below. This will fluctuate according to a dealer's stock, saleability at a particular time, etc. It is always advisable to approach a reputable specialist dealer or an auction house which has specialist sales

Inkwells

A Staffordshire porcelain inkwell modelled as a gazebo, c1835, 4in (10cm).
£225-250 *RWB*

An English inkwell, with lion mask terminals and 4 paw feet, painted in colours, the lid with finial, painted with flowers, 3in (7cm).
£120-200 *CSK*

A Marseilles inkstand, wing restored, c1790, 7½in (18cm) wide.
£350-400 *BRK*

Factory closed in 1793.

A late Meissen blue ground inkstand, reserved with cherubs amongst clouds and with flowers within gilt scroll cartouches, the tray fitted with 2 inkwells and covers, blue crossed swords mark, 8½in (21cm) wide.
£200-300 *CSK*

A Fürstenberg square section inkwell and matching sander, 4in (9cm).
£270-320 *DN*

A Worcester, Barr, Flight & Barr pale blue ground inkwell and cover, painted with a white and tan spaniel within a gilt line cartouche, enriched with gilt 'vermicule', the gilt scroll handle with male mask terminal flanked by 2 containers for sand, slight rim chip and gilding rubbed, printed marks, c1810, 5½in (13.5cm).
£800-900 *C*

Jardinières

A Worcester blue and white jardinière, chip to footrim and warped in firing, blue crescent mark, c1770, 10in (24cm).
£3,500-4,000 *C*

A Royal Worcester 'Gloire de Dijon' moulded jardinière in Hadley style, painted by Harry Martin, the body with 3 panels of red, pink and yellow roses on a shaded ivory ground and with gilded base, signed H. Martin, shape No. 1295, subject No. 1275, date mark 1911, 9½in (23.5cm).
£1,400-1,600 *HSS*

A Royal Worcester jardinière, painted by Harry Stinton.
£3,500-4,000 *HSS*

A pair of Sèvres-pattern turquoise ground ormolu mounted jardinières, each on 4 cast foliage feet, one extensively damaged, imitation blue interlaced L marks, c1880, 12in (30cm).
£1,700-2,200 *C*

Make the most of Miller's

Unless otherwise stated, any description which refers to 'a set' or 'a pair' includes a valuation for the entire set or the pair, even though the illustration may show only a single item

A Royal Worcester biscuit ground blush ivory jardinière, with weave body with leaf decoration including 3 folding leaves extending to outer rim forming side handles, shape No. 1947, puce mark 1918, 14in (36cm) diam.
£600-700 *GH*

Jugs

A Caughley cream jug, with the Temple pattern, 3in (7.5cm).
£220-250   *BRK*

A Derby blue and white creamer, 3in (7.5cm).
£750-850   *BRK*

A Worcester blue and white cabbage leaf moulded jug, the rim moulded with a band of stiff leaves, painter's mark, c1758, 8½in (21cm).
£700-800   *C*

A Caughley cabbage leaf moulded mask jug, painted in the Chantilly style with scattered flowersprays, the spout moulded with a bearded mask and with double scroll handle, blue S mark, c1790, 9in (23cm).
£460-520   *C*

A Caughley claret ground pear-shaped milk jug and cover, the shaped claret borders gilt with flowersprays and edged in gilding, the domed cover with gilt knob finial, c1785, decoration later, 5in (12.5cm).
£1,600-2,000   *C*

A Caughley inscribed and dated cabbage leaf moulded mask jug, inscribed 'Griffin Beaufoy White' and with the date 1791, the spout with a bearded mask and with double scroll handle, cracked, blue S mark, 1791, 9in (23cm).
£600-700   *C*

A Worcester herringbone moulded baluster cream jug, painted with blue flowers and with traces of gilding, with scroll handle, small chip and haircrack to rim, painter's mark, c1758, 3½in (9cm).
£350-450   *C*

A Pinxton creamer, c1800, 4½in (11cm) wide.
£225-280   *BRK*

A Caughley cabbage leaf moulded mask jug, transfer printed with the Fisherman pattern, with a bearded male mask beneath the spout, blue Sx mark, c1785, 8½in (22cm).
£400-450   *C*

A Liverpool baluster jug, with scroll handle and cornucopia moulded spout, decorated in light relief with fruiting vine, painted with a European landscape vignette, some damage, c1762, Richard Chaffer's factory, 8½in (22cm) high.
£1,600-2,000   *C*

A Liverpool baluster mask jug with elaborate scroll handle, transfer printed, the spout moulded with a female mask, Penningtons factory, c1775, 7in (18cm) high.
£550-650   *C*

A Worcester yellow ground cabbage leaf moulded mask jug, the body transfer printed and coloured after Robert Hancock with Milk Maids, within puce scroll cartouches, the handle enriched in puce and with a bearded mask beneath the spout, with brown line rim, chips to spout and small chip to rim, c1765, 7in (17.5cm).
£3,500-4,000   *C*

A Worcester blue and white cabbage leaf moulded mask jug, transfer printed with flowers, small chip to spout, blue script W mark, c1775, 8½in (22cm).
£270-320   *C*

A Worcester blue and white herringbone moulded cream jug, painted with trailing flowersprays and an insect on a crisply moulded ground, with scroll handle, painter's mark, c1758, 3½in (9cm).
£700-800   *C*

A Worcester blue and white baluster mask jug, transfer printed with loose bouquets and scattered butterflies, with a bearded mask beneath the spout, minute chip to spout, crescent mark, c1770, 7½in (18.5cm).
£450-550   *C*

A Worcester sparrow beak jug, c1775.
£170-200   *BRK*

A Liverpool cabbage leaf moulded mask jug, with scroll handle, painted with loose bouquets beneath a border moulded with dot and stiff leaf ornament, the spout moulded with a female mask, some damage and restoration, Philip Christian's factory, c1770, 9½in (24cm) high.
£500-800   *C*

A Liverpool baluster jug with scroll handle, painted with peony and a willow tree beside a fence, some damage, Richard Chaffer's factory, c1765, 7½in (19cm) high.
£1,000-1,200   *C*

A Worcester clobbered baluster cream jug with grooved loop handle, painted in underglaze blue, decorated in overglaze enamels, the top rim inscribed in iron red 'Desire the sincere milk of the world.i Peter', the lip restored, blue crescent mark, c1770, the overglaze decoration slightly later, 3½in (9.5cm).
£250-350 *C*

A Worcester baluster cream jug, painted within an iron red and gilt line cartouche, the reverse painted in puce monochrome with an Oriental in a sampan, reserved on a gilt foliate scroll ground, tiny chip to spout, c1770, 3½in (9cm).
£600-700 *C*

A Liverpool cream jug, 4in (10cm) wide.
£175-200 *BRK*

A Worcester Imari pattern baluster jug, cover and deep basin, painted with The Kempthorne pattern, the radiating flowering shrubs within an elaborate flowerhead and diaper pattern border, c1770, jug 10in (25cm), basin 11in (28.5cm) diam.
£4,500-5,000 *C*

Mugs

A Derby baluster mug, transfer printed with The Boy on a Buffalo pattern, with ribbed loop handle, minute rim chip, Wm. Duesbury & Co, c1770, 5in (12.5cm).
£450-500 *C*

A Liverpool mug with scroll handle, painted beneath a diaper border, on a grooved circular foot, some damage, c1765, 6in (15cm) high.
£700-800 *C*

A Liverpool mug with scroll handle, painted with bamboo beside a fence flanked by rockwork, Richard Chaffer's factory, c1765, 5in (12cm) high.
£1,500-2,000 *C*

A Derby mug, painted in a bright palette in the Oriental style, with scroll handle, cracked, Wm. Duesbury & Co, c1765, 4in (10cm).
£350-400 *C*

A Derby mug, painted in a soft palette in the manner of the Cotton Stem painter, with a large spray of flowers on either side, flanked by smaller sprigs all beneath the brown line rim, applied paper label for the Cottam Collection, c1760, 3½in (9cm).
£1,000-1,500 *S*

A Liverpool baluster mug with scroll handle, some damage, Philip Christian's factory, c1768, 7in (17cm) high.
£470-520 *C*

A Worcester blue and white mug, with ribbed loop handle, haircrack round top of handle, c1765, 3½in (9cm).
£400-600 *C*

A rare early Meissen fluted beaker, painted in Kakiemon style and gilding, crossed swords mark in blue enamel, incised Johanneum mark N = 362/W and //, c1725.
£2,000-2,500 *S*

A Chamberlain's Worcester mug, painted with a portrait of the Duke of Wellington within an oval gilt line and foliate wreath cartouche, the ground with scattered gilt leaves and with the monogram IP, named in black script on the base, slight wear to gilding, c1828, 3in (8cm).
£500-600 *CSK*

A Worcester blue and white baluster mug, transfer printed with loose bouquets and scattered flowers, blue crescent mark, c1770, 6in (15cm).
£400-450 *C*

A Plymouth mug with grooved loop handle, painted in an inky blue, tiny rim chip, base cracked, blue 24 mark, Wm. Cookworthy's factory, c1770, 5½in (13.5cm).
£1,000-1,500 *C*

A Worcester blue and white baluster mug, crescent mark, c1768, 6in (15cm).
£530-570 *C*

A Worcester mug in 'La Peche' pattern, c1770, 3½in (9cm) diam.
£350-400 *Wai*

A Chamberlain's Worcester beaker, finely painted with a colourful arrangement within a broad gilt border, the reverse with a plain pale yellow panel framed by a narrower gilt line border, all between gilt line rims, script Chamberlains Worcester in orange, c1800, 3½in (9cm).
£780-900 *S*

Plaques

An English plaque, by F. N. Sutton, signed, c1880, 11 by 7½in (28 by 18.5cm).
£1,000-1,500 *McC*

F. N. Sutton worked at the Royal Worcester factory during the 1880s.

A Berlin plaque, painted with a Vestal Virgin after Angelica Kaufmann, wearing filmy white robes with a blue sash, signed with the initials F St, impressed K.P.M. and sceptre marks, c1880, claret plush mount and carved giltwood frame, 10½ by 9in (26.5 by 22cm).
£2,200-2,600 *C*

A Berlin plaque, painted with a portrait of a saint wearing dark red drapery, seated in a rocky landscape reading from a book, impressed K.P.M. and sceptre marks, c1880, 12½ by 10in (32 by 25.5cm).
£800-1,200 *C*

A Berlin dated plaque, painted by E. Böhm with Jupiter and Antiope after Corregio, chips to edge on reverse, impressed K.P.M. and sceptre marks, signed and dated Paris 1863, carved giltwood frame, 13½ by 9½in (34 by 23.5cm).
£4,000-5,000 *C*

A Meissen plaque after Corregio, depicting The Repentant Magdalene, lying in a forest landscape and reading from the Scriptures, crossed swords in underglaze blue, c1870, 8 by 11½in (21 by 29cm).
£1,600-2,500 *S*

A Berlin plaque, painted with a portrait of the bearded old man, his eyes raised heavenwards and his hands resting on the hilt of a sword, impressed K.P.M. and sceptre marks, c1880, 12½ by 10in (32 by 25.5cm).
£800-1,200 *C*

A Berlin plaque, painted after Boucher with a pastoral scene, impressed K.P.M. and sceptre marks, c1880, 14in (35.5cm).
£800-1,000 *Bon*

A Berlin plaque of rococo inspiration, painted all within an elaborate border of scrolling cartouches picked out in gilding and painted with scattered sprays of flowers and insects, minor chips and restoration, sceptre mark in underglaze blue, printed K.P.M. Orb mark in red and impressed numerals, late 19thC, 22in (55cm).
£1,200-1,800 *S*

A Berlin plaque, impressed K.P.M. sceptre and H marks, c1880, giltwood frame, 9½ by 6½in (23.5 by 16cm).
£4,000-4,500 *C*

A Limoges plaque, later painted with a south view of Christchurch from the meadows by Turner, signed in the bottom left hand corner 'Leighton', the view named on the reverse, 20thC, 13½in (34cm), in ornate gilded frame.
£700-900 *Bon*

A Berlin K.P.M. plaque, in original frame, signed and dated 1884, 11in (29cm) high.
£1,200-1,400 *Wai*

A Meissen plaque after Raphael, painted with the Virgin Mary wearing a blue robe and red and gold skirt, with the infant Christ by her knee and St. John kneeling at her side, the front inscribed in gilding C. Raphalo, crossed swords in underglaze blue, c1865, 11 by 8in (28 by 20cm), framed.
£4,500-5,000 *S*

The original painting of La Belle Jardinière after Raphael hangs in the Louvre.

A Continental porcelain plaque painted with 'Murillo's Children', the 2 children with a basket of grapes, 19thC, 6 by 4½in (15 by 11cm), framed.
£500-600 *CLG*

Pots

A pair of 'Vienna' plaques, painted with three-quarter length portraits of a girl wearing a puce, yellow and white dress and with long hair, and with a girl wearing a blue dress seated beside a ledge leaning on her elbow, signed with 'CR' monogram, late 19thC, 9in (22cm), plush and giltwood frame.
£2,000-2,500 *C*

A Worcester mustard pot and cover, cracked cover.
£450-500 *BRK*

A Berlin plaque, painted with a mother and child, impressed K.P.M., Sceptre, 111, Z, 19thC, 7 by 5in (17 by 13cm), framed.
£800-1,000 *CLG*

A Worcester baluster dry mustard pot, outline-printed and coloured with The Red Ox pattern, the interior with a brown line to the rim c1758, 3in (7.5cm).
£1,200-1,700 *C*

A Worcester blue and white sauceboat, minute glaze blemish to rim, minute crack to handle, painter's mark to base of handle, c1756, 6in (15cm) wide.
£900-1,200   *C*

A Worcester inverted baluster wet mustard pot and a cover, printed and coloured with Oriental figures and a youth at various pursuits, the cover with insects and green and iron red knob finial, small restoration to rim of pot and crack near top of handle, c1760, 3in (7.5cm).
£2,000-2,500   *C*

A small Derby sauceboat, painted with a landscape vignette and lightly moulded with C-scrolls, Wm. Duesbury & Co, c1765, 6in (14.5cm) wide.
£550-600   *C*

Sauceboats

A small Derby sauceboat, moulded with fruit and painted with stylised flowersprays, Wm. Duesbury & Co, c1765, 6in (15cm) wide.
£450-500   *C*

A Liverpool sauceboat in the Worcester style, painted with an Oriental lady and a boy with a bird on a pole, Richard Chaffer's factory, c1765, 8½in (20cm) long.
£1,700-2,000   *C*

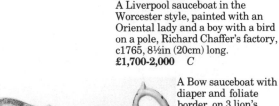

A Bow sauceboat with diaper and foliate border, on 3 lion's mask and paw feet, c1752, 8½in (21cm) long.
£600-700   *C*

A sauceboat with scroll handle in the manner of Worcester, in underglaze blue, damaged handle.
£250-350   *P(M)*

A Worcester blue and white sauceboat of compressed form, painted with The Plantation pattern, crack to rim and round foot, c1756, 8in (20cm) long.
£250-350   *C*

A Longton Hall sauceboat, painted with foliage within relief moulded cartouches of flowersprays tied with ribbon, with waved rim, chip to rim and firecrack, c1755, 7in (18cm) wide.
£400-450   *C*

A First Period Worcester sauceboat of cos lettuce form, branch loop handle, painted with insects, flowerheads and leaves, on stem foot, c1756, 9½in (24cm) wide.
£800-850   *WW*

A Longton Hall sauceboat, painted in the Oriental style, crack to base of handle, c1755, 8in (20cm) wide.
£300-500 *C*

A Lowestoft creamer, 6½in (16cm) wide.
£250-300 *BRK*

A Derby leaf moulded butter boat, the interior painted with flowers beneath a shaped blue dentil rim, Wm. Duesbury & Co, c1765, 3½in (9cm) wide.
£450-500 *C*

A Derby blue and white sauceboat, 8in (20cm) long.
£320-350 *BRK*

Services

A Coalport dinner service, each piece decorated with an emerald green band dispersed with pale yellow panels and leaves, all highlighted in gilt and on a white ground, comprising 96 items, pattern No. S.1931, c1820.
£2,000-2,500 *HSS*

A Copeland topographical part dessert service, each piece painted with a named view within a cerise band and gilt reticulated border, comprising: 16 plates, 2 damaged, 3 dishes, 4 circular tazza on three-footed bases, one with damage, c1850.
£850-950 *Bon*

An English dessert service, possibly John Ridgway, painted within cobalt blue borders reserved with a scrolling foliate or lobed orange and gilt designs, comprising: 18 plates and 8 dishes, 2 plates cracked, pattern number in red 6/2767, c1835, plates 9½in (23.5cm).
£5,000-5,500 *S*

A Royal Crown Derby dessert service, each piece enamelled by W. E. J. Dean, with fishing scenes within cobalt blue borders with raised gilt scroll and foliage decoration, comprising: 12 plates and 5 dishes, c1900.
£2,500-3,500 *Bon*

A Minton dessert service, with central monogram E.M.B, impressed date code for 1858.
£350-400 *DN*

A Royal Crown Derby part tea service, printed in iron red, enriched in underglaze blue with scrolls and foliage in gilding, comprising: a tray, a teapot and cover, a milk jug, a two-handled sugar bowl, a slop bowl, 10 side plates, 13 cups and 14 saucers, some damage and gilding slightly rubbed.
£800-900   *CSK*

An English dessert service, probably Minton, painted over a white ground within a 'malachite' border and shaped gilt rim, comprising: one tall pierced two-handled comport, 3 dishes and 12 dessert plates, minor hair cracks, red painted pattern No. 2311/1, c1830.
£1,000-1,500   *S(S)*

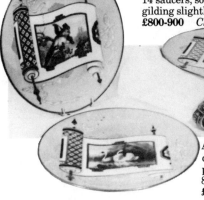

A Minton dessert set, decorated with fine picture panels, comprising 8 pieces, dated 1888.
£650-700   *HSS*

A composite Royal Derby tea service.
£600-650   *DN*

A Coalport part dessert service painted in the studio of Thomas Baxter, the centres with loose bouquets within gilt line cartouches reserved on iron red grounds gilt with dots and stars, the borders with flowersprays alternating with yellow ground lozenge shaped and diamond shaped panels of pink roses edged in gilding, the rims gilt, comprising: a two-handled centre dish, an oval tureen stand, 10 dishes, 14 plates, gilding rubbed and some rubbing and flaking to enamels, some damage, c1805.
£2,700-3,500   *C*

A Derby part tea service, printed in iron red and underglaze blue, enriched in gilding, comprising: a bread plate, 12 side plates, a slop bowl, 9 cups and 10 saucers, some damage, gilding rubbed.
£350-400   *CSK*

A Davenport part dessert service, painted within a gilt foliate hexafoil cartouche suspending salmon pink medallions, beneath border of pink roses and gilt C-scrolls, comprising: 2 sauce tureens and covers with gilt bud finials, slight damage to one finial, 7 dishes, c1820.
£2,600-3,000   *C*

An English dinner service, painted in green, blue, pink and gilt, comprising 123 pieces, probably Coalport, early 19thC.
£1,700-2,000   *P(S)*

A Meissen coffee set, painted with colourful sprays of flowers on a white ground, all within shaped gilt rims, comprising: a baluster coffee pot and cover, a sucrier and cover, a baluster cream jug, 6 cups and saucers and 6 plates, crossed swords in underglaze blue, painted and impressed numerals, c1900, coffee pot 10in (25.5cm).
£1,000-1,500 *S*

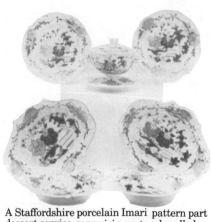

A Staffordshire porcelain Imari pattern part dessert service, comprising: a two-handled dish, 12in (31cm) wide, a sauce tureen, cover and stand, 6½in (16cm) high, 8 dishes and 16 plates, some damage.
£400-500 *CSK*

A comprehensive Meissen 'Streublumen' dinner service, each piece decorated with sprigs of colourful summer flowers, comprising: 12 soup plates, 53 plates, 2 serving dishes, 3 tureens and covers, 2 two-handled sauceboats on stands, one two-handled oval tray, 3 oval meat dishes, 4 cruet frames and 2 ladles, minor chips, crossed swords in underglaze blue and impressed numerals, late 19thC, tray 19½in (49cm) wide.
£5,000-6,000 *S*

A porcelain dessert service, possibly Worcester, each piece bearing pattern No. 3998, comprising: 24 dessert plates, two-handled comport, 2 lidded sauce tureens and stands, 4 plates and 8 dishes, c1830.
£3,000-3,500 *HSS*

A Chamberlain's Worcester crested dessert service, painted over a white ground within a gilt frame and deep blue ground border with 4 gilt edged shell panels, minor chips, impressed mark, c1850, dessert plate 8½in (22cm).
£1,500-2,000 *S*

A Worcester porcelain part dessert service, decorated within a gilt lined scalloped border, comprising: 12 plates, 2 sauce tureens and covers, 2 dishes with open moulded borders, and 5 dishes, some damage, some pieces underfired.
£2,300-2,700 *Bon*

A Meissen tête-à-tête, each piece painted with colourful sprays of flowers over a white ground within a shaped gilt rim, minor chips, one cup restored, crossed swords in underglaze blue and incised mark No. 8, late 19thC, tray 17½in (44cm) wide.
£1,500-2,000 *S*

A Meissen coffee service, each piece painted with trailing green ivy between gilded borders, comprising: 14 cups, 14 saucers, 14 dessert dishes, a coffee pot and cover, a teapot and cover, 2 cream jugs, a sucrier and cover, some minor chips and rubbing, crossed swords in underglaze blue and script numerals, c1885, coffee pot 10½in (27cm).
£3,000-4,000 *S*

An English part dessert service, comprising: 2 comports, 4 low stands and 12 plates, each painted with a spray of flowers within a lobed rim, in green enamel and gold, some damage.
£460-520 *Bea*

An English part dessert service, each piece painted in the centre with a floral bouquet, enclosed by an elaborate gilt and pea green border, comprising: 12 plates, 4 dishes and one medium tazza, c1820.
£800-1,000 *Bon*

A Coalport tea and coffee service, painted in a bright palette and gilt beneath gilt dentil rims, comprising: a teapot, cover and stand, a sugar bowl and cover, a milk jug, a slop bowl, small star crack to base, 2 bread and butter plates, 24 cups and 12 saucers, one with star crack, one cracked, gilding slightly rubbed, pattern No. 830, c1825.
£1,700-2,200 *C*

A Staffordshire porcelain part dessert service, painted in colours on an apple green ground within beaded rims, comprising: 2 tall comports with dolphin supports, 4 similar shallow comports and 12 plates, some damage and repairs, pattern No. 1797, 19thC.
£1,000-1,500 *HSS*

A Royal Worcester dessert service, with impressed marks and registration No. 198236, printed marks for 1898.
£3,000-3,500 *DN*

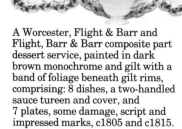

A Worcester, Flight & Barr and Flight, Barr & Barr composite part dessert service, painted in dark brown monochrome and gilt with a band of foliage beneath gilt rims, comprising: 8 dishes, a two-handled sauce tureen and cover, and 7 plates, some damage, script and impressed marks, c1805 and c1815.
£1,000-1,500 *C*

A Rockingham part tea service, with leaf and scroll moulded rim, painted in grey with grapes and foliage, all enriched in gilding, comprising: a teapot and cover, a two-handled sugar bowl and cover, a milk jug, a slop bowl, 3 bread plates, 11 teacups and 12 saucers, pattern No. 12/61, and another teacup, some damages and gilding rubbed.
£900-1,000 *CSK*

A Berlin cabaret set, painted with bouquets and sprays of flowers within gilt cartouches, including an oval tray with scroll moulded handles, blue sceptre and iron red K.P.M. and globe marks, various impressed and painted numerals, c1880, the tray 16½in (42cm) wide.
£4,000-5,000 *C*

A Nantgarw part dessert service, possibly decorated by Thomas Pardoe, painted over a white ground within a 'bleu celeste' border, framed by gilt foliage, all within a shaped gilt dentil rim, comprising: 2 dishes and 3 dessert plates, one dish restored, impressed marks, c1820, dessert plates 8½in (22cm).
£1,600-2,000 *S*

Tankards

A Worcester tankard, printed in blue with The Plantation pattern, c1765, 5½in (14cm).
£300-350 *GAK*

An early Worcester tankard, painted in blue with a palm and a fir tree before a pagoda, the reverse painted with a fishing boat beside a shrine, all under a diaper border, 2 chips to foot rim, 4½in (11cm).
£300-350 *MN*

Tureens & Butter Tubs

A Worcester blue and white butter tub and cover, on 4 scroll feet, with bud finial, stalk to finial lacking, blue crescent mark, c1760, 5½in (14cm) wide.
£1,500-2,000 *C*

A Berlin tureen and cover, painted with panels of 18thC gentlemen engaged in scenes of revelry and festivity, the domed cover surmounted by a Bacchic cherub knop, minor chip to cherub, sceptre mark in blue, late 19thC, 14in (36cm).
£800-1,200 *S(S)*

A Worcester white partridge tureen and cover with incised plumage, the edge of the cover with stylised entwined straw and feathers, the basket weave moulded base with feathers and corn, c1765, 6½in (16cm) long.
£1,800-2,200 *C*

A Meissen hen and chick tureen and cover, the hen picked out in black and brown, the base with 6 chicks and the cover surmounted with a single chick, cover restored, crossed swords in underglaze blue and incised D,9, c1870, 7½in (19cm).
£600-800 *S*

A pair of Worcester quatrefoil tureens, covers and stands, painted in underglaze blue and gilt within blue borders, gilt with foliage and entwined ribbon and edged with C-scrolls, with gilt dentil rims, blue crescent marks to the stands, c1780, stands 10½in (26cm) wide.
£4,000-5,000 *C*

A Barr, Flight & Barr two-handled sauce tureen, cover and stand, raised on a pedestal base with radiating gilt lines, finely painted with a chinoiserie pattern of flowers and 'mon' in iron red, green, pink and gilding, brown printed and impressed marks, c1810, 7in (18cm).
£650-750 *S*

A pair of Chamberlain's Worcester pedestal sauce tureens and covers, painted with the Dejeuney pattern on a gold decorated rich blue band, bearing the crest and motto of Sir James Yeo, one cover with some restoration, 8in (20cm).
£1,500-2,000 *Bea*

A pearlware shaped dish and cover, printed and coloured with scrolling foliage and flowers enriched in gilding, slight rubbing and flaking, damage to one corner, 9½in (24cm) diam.
£100-150 *CSK*

A Derby blue and white tureen and cover, 5in (13cm).
£800-900 *BRK*

Vases

A Chelsea pot pourri vase and cover, enriched in pale puce and with gilding, the pierced domed cover with flower finial, restoration to vase, her right arm and drapery and to hound, cover restored, gold anchor mark, c1765, 16½in (42.5cm).
£900-1,200 *C*

A pair of Bow baluster frill vases of conventional type, with female mask and flower handles, the shoulders pierced and with blue and yellow flowerheads at the intersections, both with chips to flowers and handles, one with cracked neck, c1765, 8in (19.5cm).
£1,000-1,500 *C*

A Derby type porcelain tulip vase, with yellow petals enriched in orange and puce, on sinuous green stems and surrounded by green foliage, all on a naturalistic base applied with smaller coloured flowers, minor chips, restoration to bud, c1800, 6in (15.5cm).
£1,000-1,500 *S*

An early Derby pedestal vase, c1810.
£800-1,200 *GIL*

A pair of Derby bottle vases and stoppers, early 19thC.
£550-650   *HSS*

A pair of Derby flower encrusted vases, moulded with scrollwork picked out in shades of green and puce, minor chips, c1765, 9in (23.5cm).
£2,000-2,500   *S*

A pair of Coalport baluster two-handled vases and covers in the Chelsea style, enamelled in colours within gilt reserves and on a blue scale ground, florid ribbon and leaf scroll handles and finials, one finial and one scroll on handle repaired, unmarked, 14½in (37cm).
£1,200-1,600   *GA(W)*

A Meissen vase, finely painted with various birds perched on a dead tree covered in ivy, gilt scroll border, rim restored, crossed swords in underglaze blue, c1755, 6in (15cm).
£2,000-2,500   *S*

A pair of Derby spill vases, 4in (10cm).
£900-950   *BRK*

A small Spode blue ground two-handled vase of Warwick shape, reserved on a dark blue ground gilt with scale pattern, the looped snake handles and rims gilt, marked in red and pattern No. 1166, c1820, 4in (10cm) wide.
£850-950   *C*

A pair of Staffordshire porcelain urn shaped vases, the blue scale ground reserved with bouquets of flowers within gilt scroll cartouches, with flared necks and on socle stems and square bases, 11in (29cm).
£300-350   *CSK*

A Minton Gothic vase, by T. Steel, c1840, 9in (22cm).
£550-600   *SBA*

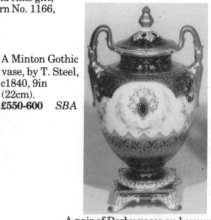

A pair of Mintons turquoise ground tapering vases and covers, painted in colours, signed 'Dean', printed globe mark, 8in (19cm).
£120-200   *CSK*

A pair of Derby vases and covers, with polychrome floral on gilt decorated white reserves with blue ground, 9in (24cm).
£1,500-1,800   *AH*

A Derby blue ground two-handled campana shaped vase, painted in colours within a cartouche and gilding, cracked, chipped and worn, iron red mark, 7in (18cm).
£100-150   *CSK*

> In the Ceramics section if there is only one measurement it usually refers to the height of the piece

A pair of English porcelain lobed campana-shaped pierced vases, with applied flowers enriched in colours on a turquoise ground with gilt rims and bases, perhaps Minton, some damage and restorations, 13½in (34cm).
£1,200-1,700 *CSK*

A pair of Derby two-handled spill vases of tapering baluster form, the handles in the form of ewes heads, the body decorated with a line of roses and symmetrical embellishments, early 19thC, 5½in (14cm).
£400-450 *HSS*

A Royal Worcester porcelain two-handled slender necked vase, painted with floral sprays on a cream ground, with gilt edges, date code for 1895, 9in (23cm).
£250-300 *GC*

A Royal Worcester tusk shaped vase, with antler shaped handle, date code for 1899, 6in (15.5cm).
£160-220 *GC*

A Royal Worcester Hadley ware pot pourri vase and cover, painted by A. Shuck.
£750-850 *HSS*

A Worcester, Flight, Barr & Barr claret ground two-handled vase of Warwick shape, painted with views of Flesk Bridge, Lake of Killarney, Ireland, and Mucrafs Abbey, Killarney, Ireland, named on the base, reserved on shaped claret grounds edged with gilt scrolls, minute chip to footrim, impressed and script marks, c1825, 10in (25.5cm).
£3,500-4,500 *C*

A Worcester, Flight & Barr flared flower pot and stand, with gilt fixed-ring handles, painted 'en grisaille' perhaps in the studio of Thomas Baxter, within a rectangular gilt line cartouche, inscribed on the base St. Luke Ch.XXII.V62, the reverse and waisted circular stand gilt with scrolling floral foliage, the rims gilt, incised B and puce script marks, c1805, 6in (15cm).
£1,200-1,600 *C*

A pair of Barr, Flight & Barr period Worcester two-handled vases, inscribed 'Julius Caesar' and 'As You Like It', one handle restored, red script and impressed marks, together with a relevant verse also in red script, c1810, 6½in (17cm).
£1,800-2,200 *S*

A Worcester white oviform pierced pot pourri vase and domed cover, the shoulder applied with 3 female masks, the cover decorated with flowers and with bird finial, on a knopped stem and domed foot, fire crack to foot and to top rim, some minor chipping and restoration to finial, c1770, 16½in (42cm).
£7,000-7,500 *C*

A pair of Worcester vases, signed and painted by Harry Stinton, shape No. 2471, marked in puce and retailer's mark Townsend and Company, Newcastle on Tyne, date code for 1914, 6in (14.5cm).
£1,500-2,000 *P(M)*

l. & r. A pair of Worcester vases and covers, signed and painted by Harry Stinton, in shades of green and coral with highland cattle watering and grazing by a stream, slight damage to covers, marked in green, date code for 1909, shape No. H 247, 10in (25.5cm).
£2,500-3,000

c. A Worcester vase, signed and painted by Harry Davis, in tones of blush ivory, with a recumbent ram lying amongst heather and grass, marked in green, date mark for 1907, shape No. G 1040, 5½in (13.5cm).
£1,000-1,500 *P(M)*

A Worcester oviform pot pourri vase and pierced hexagonal cover, transfer printed in black after Robert Hancock, within a gadrooned rim, part of cover lacking, c1765, 11in (29cm).
£2,600-3,000 *C*

A Grainger's Worcester reticulated bottle vase.
£400-500 *GIL*

A Royal Worcester vase and cover, the ivory and gilt body painted with cattle by John Stinton, signed, printed mark and date code for 1907, shape No. 1572, 11in (28cm).
£2,000-2,500 *WHB*

A Worcester vase by Harry Stinton, in green and gilt, slight crack on reverse, marked in green, date code for 1901 and shape No. G.32, 8½in (22cm).
£800-1,200 *P(M)*

A Royal Worcester vase and cover, painted and signed by John Stinton, shape No. 151, printed marks, rd. No. 168915, 8in (21cm).
£2,000-2,500 *P(S)*

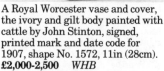

A small Royal Worcester vase, painted by Harry Stinton with cattle in a highland landscape, printed mark and date code for 1911, shape No. G.923, 4½in (11.5cm).
£450-500 *Bea*

A late Victorian Royal Worcester vase and cover, painted by C. H. C. Baldwyn.
£4,500-5,000 *HSS*

A Royal Worcester two-handled vase and lid, painted and signed by Harry Davis, pattern No. 2453, damage to lid, dated 1913, 12in (31cm).
£1,500-2,000   *PCh*

A Royal Worcester vase, with scroll feet and pierced rim, decorated by Raymond Rushton with a thatched cottage in a country landscape entitled 'Ripple', shape No. G.42, printed mark and date code for 1929, 8½in (22cm).
£500-550   *Bea*

A large Dresden flower encrusted vase and a cover of rococo inspiration, with a pair of nymph head handles picked out in pale green and gilt, minor chips to flowers, cancelled mark, late 19thC, 26in (67cm).
£3,000-3,500   *S*

A pair of English blue ground faceted vases, painted in bright colours, enriched with gilt flower, leaf and scale patterns, one repaired at foot, both with wear to gilding, 8in (21cm).
£550-650   *CSK*

A pair of Royal Worcester vases with 4 loop handles, the blush ivory ground painted with flowers and gilt, shape No. 991, printed mark and date code for 1904 and 1907, 3in (8cm).
£250-300

A Royal Worcester blush ivory bottle shape vase, painted with flowers, shape No. 2491, printed mark and date code for 1912, 5½in (14cm).
£75-100   *WHB*

A pair of Worcester vases and covers, signed and painted by Harry Stinton in shades of green and gold, marked in puce, date mark for 1911, 4½in (11.5cm).
£3,500-4,000   *P(M)*

A pair of Worcester bottle vases, decorated on pale blue ground with gilt banding, 15in (39cm).
£800-850   *AH*

A pair of Berlin pot pourri urns and cover, raised on square gilt plinths with a central band painted on either side, flanked by 2 ram mask handles above vine leaves and branches tied by pale blue ribbons, all over a puce scale ground gilt with stars, each pierced cover similarly decorated and surmounted by a gilt artichoke knop, minor chips, one knop restored, sceptre mark in underglaze blue, c1880, 14in (35cm).
£1,500-2,000   *S*

157

A pair of 'Sèvres' vases, painted by L. Malpass, signed, the trumpet neck and flared foot in light blue with gilded flowers, one foot repaired, interlaced L's in underglaze blue, c1880, 21½in (55cm).
£600-900   S

Two Royal Worcester baluster shaped vases, on ivory ground, one decorated with highland cattle, signed H. Stinton, the other with black faced sheep, signed A. Davies, shape No. 294H, date code 1911, 8in (20cm).
£1,500-2,000   HSS

A pair of Meissen may-blossom campana shaped vases, each applied with a woodpecker and a bullfinch perched on trailing flowering branches, one woodpecker's beak damaged, minor chipping, blue crossed swords marks, c1880, 14in (35cm).
£2,500-3,000   C

A Meissen baluster vase and lid, the lid with a horn-blowing Triton decorated with 'deutsche Blumen' and realistically moulded flowers, the body similarly decorated, painted mark, 19thC, 15in (38cm).
£300-350   MN

A pair of 'Sèvres' gilt bronze mounted vases and covers, painted by Bernier, the domed covers reserved with floral panels on a blue ground, the covers with printed marks and interlaced L's on blue, c1880, 13in (33cm).
£1,500-2,000   S

A large pair of 'Sèvres' gilt metal mounted vases, the bodies painted with battle scenes, the reverse painted with buildings in a wooded landscape, gilded borders reserved on a dark blue ground, typical wear on gilding, c1870, 34½in (87cm).
£13,000-15,000   S

A pair of Pirkenhammer porcelain vases and covers, each decorated in gold with birds on boughs of blossom, a band of insects and foliage around the neck and foot on a deep blue ground, 17in (43.5cm).
£750-800   Bea

A pair of Royal Worcester porcelain flower vases, decorated by E. J. Raby, with hand painted floral picture panels with insects, initialled, highlighted in gilt, all on an ivory ground, shape No. 1556, slight damage, puce transfer mark to base, c1896, 9½in (24cm).
£800-850   HSS

The damage is reflected in this price.

A pair of Paris porcelain vases, painted on a malachite green ground highlighted in gilt, some rubbing, early 19thC, 12in (30cm).
£450-500   HSS

A garniture of 3 English vases, with foliate and goat head handles, each painted with a basket of flowers on a puce ground, early 19thC, 6½ and 7½in (16.5 and 18.5cm).
£250-350   *Bea*

A Sèvres covered vase, the base with swagged tied drapery, the ground colour in 'bleu de roi', decorated 'oeil de perdrix' mounted with chased and chiselled classical ormolu, lacks chains, interlaced 'A' mark, the ormolu with Fondeurs mark, 18thC, 13in (33cm).
£250-300   *MN*

A pair of Royal Worcester peach ground two-handled vases, each with hand painted picture panels of long horned highland cattle, signed H. Stinton, shape No. 2425, date code 1911, 8in (20cm).
£1,500-2,000   *HSS*

A Vienna vase, the handles, foot and plinth gilt, chipped, shield mark in underglaze blue, c1830, 25in (64cm).
£5,500-6,000   *S*

A pair of Sèvres pattern gilt metal mounted blue ground oviform vases and covers, with cast rope-twist, scroll and mask handles, painted by L. Bertion, the waisted necks and spreading feet enriched with gilding, gilt metal mounts to feet and rims, imitation blue interlaced L and F marks, c1900, 20½in (51.5cm).
£1,700-2,000   *C*

A German porcelain blue ground urn shaped vase and cover, moulded with mythological dancing figures between moulded gilt swags, leaves and gadroons, the fretwork handles, berried finial and rims enriched with gilding, perhaps Fürstenberg, chips to stem, chip to base and underside of cover, c1790, 16in (41cm).
£4,000-4,500   *C*

A 'Vienna' vase, painted by Kray, signed, reserved on a pale green ground with complex gilded and coloured panels, painted shield mark and script title 'Wasser trägerin', c1890, 12½in (32cm).
£1,000-1,200   *S*

A pair of Helena Wolfsohn vases and covers, painted in colours with alternate panels of 18thC lovers in landscapes and sprays of summer flowers on a black ground within gilt scroll borders, 12in (30cm).
£650-700   *HSS*

Miscellaneous

A Worcester blue and white spittoon, transfer printed with loose bouquets, scattered flowers and insects, blue W mark, c1775, 4½in (11.5cm).
£500-600 *C*

Four Worcester blue and white asparagus servers, painted beneath a cell pattern border, the pierced upright sides edged with a foliate border, one with a small extended firing crack, c1765, 3in (7.5cm).
£1,300-1,700 *C*

A 'Vienna' vase, indistinctly signed, painted with a forest setting, reserved on a lustrous purple and blue ground brightly painted and enriched with gilding, shield mark and script title, c1885, and a 'Vienna' stand, en suite, in burnished gilt with a scroll border, 10in (25cm).
£4,000-4,500 *S*

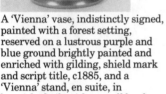

A pair of Bow white pistol-shaped knife and fork handles, mounted with a steel blade and a two-pronged fork, c1753, 3½ and 4in (9 and 10cm).
£100-150 *C*

A large 'Sèvres' gilt metal mounted vase, painted with a continuous scene of Venus, Cupid, maidens and cherubs at play in a woodland setting, reserved on a light blue and gilt ground, some gilding rubbed, interlaced L's in blue, c1860, 36in (91cm), giltwood foot.
£3,000-5,000 *S*

> In the Ceramics section if there is only one measurement it usually refers to the height of the piece

A Bristol salt spoon, the fluted bowl painted with bouquets within a gilt line rim, the handle moulded with gilt foliage and painted with a pink Martagon Lily, the reverse with an iron red flower, Richard Champion's factory, c1775, 4½in (11cm).
£1,800-2,200 *C*

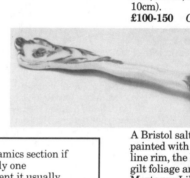

A Worcester ladle, the bowl painted in an Imari palette with The Old Mosaik pattern, slight rim chips, c1768, 6½in (17cm) long.
£500-550 *C*

A Worcester ladle, the bowl gilt with a loose bouquet within a scroll cartouche reserved on a blue ground, the top of the curved handle with gilt ornament on a similar ground, c1780, 6½in (16.5cm) long.
£300-350 *C*

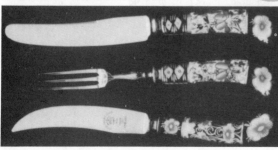

Six Royal Crown Derby Imari pattern cake knife handles, painted in underglaze blue and iron red and enriched in gilding, with steel blades, in a plush lined box, 6 cake forks in a plush lined box en suite and 6 fruit knives in a plush lined box en suite, gilding very slightly rubbed.
£400-500 *CSK*

A Worcester mustard spoon, the shell moulded bowl painted with a flowerspray within a gilt rim, the handle enriched with puce, c1768, 3½in (9cm) long.
£3,000-3,500 *C*

A Worcester white salt spoon, the handle moulded with scrolling foliage, tiny chip to rim of bowl, c1765, 4in (10cm).
£250-350 *C*

A rare Chelsea shell salt, painted in the London workshop of William Duesbury, in orange and green, with a winkle shell centred by fronds of coral and seaweed, raised on a colourful base of sea shells, coral and seaweed, minor rim chips, feint incised triangle mark, c1745, 3in (7.5cm).
£3,700-4,200 *S*

An English porcelain pod of peas, probably Coalport, the naturalistic green painted pod with one seam split to reveal the pale cream coloured peas inside, minor chips at either end, c1830, 3½in (9cm).
£350-500 *S*

Twelve St. Cloud blue and white knife handles, painted with bands of lambrequin and scrolls, the rounded ends with false gadroons, 9 cracked, contemporary silver ferrules, finials and steel blades with cutler's mark of a crowned I, c1715, handles 3½in (8cm) long.
£750-800 *C*

Jars

Five Royal Worcester candle snuffers:
l. to r.
A Royal Worcester candle snuffer modelled as Granny Snow, wearing a pink dress and yellow bonnet, marked in puce, date code for 1930, 3in (7.5cm).
£100-200
A Royal Worcester candle snuffer modelled as a French nun, wearing a black and white habit and carrying a bible under her arm, no mark, 4in (10cm).
£100-200
A Royal Worcester candle snuffer modelled as the head and shoulders of Mr. Caulder from Punch, wearing a nightcap and a blanket wrapped around him, marked in puce, date code for 1920, 3in (7.5cm).
£100-200
A Royal Worcester candle snuffer modelled as a monk wearing a brown habit and reading from the bible, marked in puce, date code for 1922, 5in (12.5cm).
£100-200
A Royal Worcester candle snuffer modelled as a French cook, marked in puce, date code indistinct, 2½in (7cm).
£100-200 *P(M)*

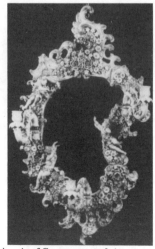

A pair of German porcelain kidney-shaped girandoles with elaborate moulded rococo scrolls enriched in pink, pale blue and gilding, applied all over with flowers and putti, the branches with leaf moulded sconces, some damage, 30in (76cm) high.
£1,500-2,000 *CSK*

A Royal Worcester lobed jar and cover, with long horned cattle in highland setting, signed John Stinton, marked in green on the base, date code for 1912, 7½in (18.5cm).
£2,000-2,500 *P(M)*

161

GOSS CHINA

Between 1890 and 1915, collecting Goss and crested china was a craze which swept the country.

The originator of these small, white models and shapes decorated with coats-of-arms of towns was William Henry Goss, a potter in Stoke-on-Trent.

Goss commenced in 1858 making busts and figurines out of parian ware. This is termed the First Period, and the Second is when his son, Adolphus, introduced the idea of placing the coat-of-arms of a town on a model of an ancient British, Roman or Greek shape, normally to be found in a museum local to where the piece would be sold. Some 90% of all

Goss porcelain is Second Period and this continued until after the First War when the factory changed hands and was bought by J. A. Robinson Ltd whose main trademark was Arcadian. This period from 1930-39 is termed the Third Period and products made then normally have the word England added to the normal Gosshawk mark and tend to be of heavier porcelain with thicker glazing. By 1914, some 1,600 outlets (called agencies) were in operation in the UK and over 2,500 different shapes were available bearing no less than 8,000 different coats-of-arms.

For further information collectors are recommended to read *The Concise Encyclopaedia and Price Guide to Goss China* and *The Price Guide to Arms and Decorations on Goss China* both by Nicholas Pine available from Milestone Publications, 62 Murray Road, Horndean, Hants. For those who wish to learn about the history of the factory and the family who produced Goss china, the definitive biography: *William Henry Goss, The Story of The Staffordshire Family of Potters Who Invented Heraldic Porcelain* by Lynda and Nicholas Pine is also available from Milestone Publications and is a fascinating vignette on the craze of crested china collecting which is now enjoying a renaissance.

First Period Goss figurines, Leda and the swan, and lady and the kid, coloured.
£1,500 each *G&CC*

A Beccles ringers jug, rare.
£500 *G&CC*

St Nicholas Chapel, Ilfracombe.
£190 *G&CC*

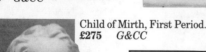

Manx cottage.
Small **£125**
Night-light **£165** *G&CC*

l. Newquay look-out house. **£145**
r. Thomas Hardy's cottage.
£350 *G&CC*

First Period basket with acanthus leaves.
£300 *G&CC*

Dr Samuel Johnson's house, Lichfield.
£175 *G&CC*

Child of Mirth, First Period.
£275 *G&CC*

Use the Index!

Because certain items might fit easily into any of a number of categories, the quickest and surest method of locating any entry is by reference to the index at the back of the book.
This has been fully cross-referenced for absolute simplicity

Brown Kirk Braddon Cross.
£85 *G&CC*

Goss St Ives Cross, white, unglazed.
£200   *G&CC*

Three versions of Shakespeare's house. **£90-150**   *G&CC*

Assorted Goss models. **£10-45 each**   *G&CC*

Globe vase with thistle sprays.
£80   *G&CC*

Lincoln Delights, Goss and other factories.
£20-150 each
G&CC

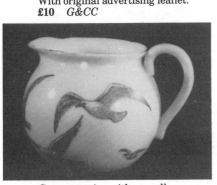

A pair of Queen Victoria's first shoes.
£30 each
With original advertising leaflet.
£10   *G&CC*

Goss cream jug with seagull transfers.
£25   *G&CC*

A selection of Goss pin trays.
£10-25   *G&CC*

Flower Girl Lady Betty.
£250 *G&CC*

A New Forest pony.
£220 *G&CC*

Various Goss shapes, all bearing
Bournemouth arms.
£10-40 each *G&CC*

CRESTED CHINA

Some 20 major and up to a
hundred minor factories,
mainly in Stoke-on-Trent,
produced crested china. Small,
white models and shapes all
bearing coats-of-arms for the
souvenir market which grew up
in late Victorian and Edwardian
times.

Major factories who produced
their own large ranges of
crested china include Arcadian,
Carlton, Grafton, Shelley and
Willow Art who produced a total
of some 10,000 shapes bearing
over 4,000 coats-of-arms.

Whereas Goss china tended to
be sold at the best china shop in
the town, products from other
manufacturers were sold at
bazaars, tea rooms, lending
libraries, at the end of the pier,
indeed anywhere that a suitable
outlet could be found.

Not to be left out, German and
Czechoslovakian manufacturers
also produced crested china in
hard paste porcelain and
enthusiastically exported these
wares into the UK, undercutting
the prices of UK manufacturers,
much to their consternation.

The ranges made tended to be
more amusing than those made
by Goss. For example, large
ranges of animals, buildings,
comic/novelty items, traditional/
national souvenirs, and a
sizeable range of domestic ware
was produced. During and after
the First World War, a range of
some 500 different World War I
shapes were made and these
proved popular until the early
1920s.

The quality of most crested
china does not match that of the
Goss factory as, with a few
exceptions, earthenware was
used as opposed to the parian
ware favoured by the Goss
factory.

For further information,
collectors are recommended to
*The Price Guide To Crested
China* by Nicholas Pine, which
contains a full list of all pieces
made, factory marks, over 1,000
illustrations and an up-to-date
list of retail prices.

Full details from Milestone
Publications, 62 Murray Road,
Horndean, Hants.

Grafton photograph frame.
£350 *G&CC*

Isle of Man selection, Goss and other
factories.
£10-45 each *G&CC*

164

Pillar boxes, policemen, charabanc and open tourer.
£10-25 each   *G&CC*

Carlton map of Blighty.
£45   *G&CC*

Florentine Tower Bridge.
£25   *G&CC*

Third Period Goss, assorted shapes.
£35-100 each   *G&CC*

Arcadian giant tank.
£450
Carlton Vickers tank.
£250
Arcadian small tank.
£20   *G&CC*

Assorted buildings.   **£20-75 each**   *G&CC*

Arcadian Tommy and his
machine
£30   *G&CC*

Unmarked lady tortoise
pin box and lid.
£12   *G&CC*

Leisure selection.
£10-80 each
G&CC

Arcadian boy and girl on log.
£50   *G&CC*

Boots and shoes. **£10-20 each**   *G&CC*

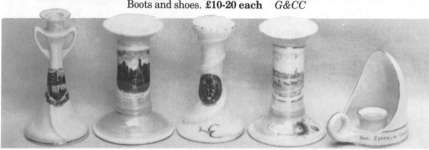

Candlesticks. **£10-40**   *G&CC*

Arcadian Alfred the Great
Monument.
£30   *G&CC*

Grafton monkey.
£20   *G&CC*

World War I models. **£15-50 each**   *G&CC*

Crested personalities. **£15-30 each**   *G&CC*

General Booth.
£40   *G&CC*

Willow doll
with real hair and
painted eyes.
£150   *G&CC*

Carlton dustpan and Shelley handbag.
£10 and 12   *G&CC*

Donkey and well, Carisbrooke Castle.
£40   *G&CC*

World War I models. **£20-250 each**   *G&CC*

Warships.
£20   *G&CC*

Arcadian Peeping Tom.
£17   *G&CC*

Boy leaning on globe, foreign. **£15**   *G&CC*

Willow Art conduit, Uttoxeter Market.
£40   *G&CC*

Bottles of cheer. **£5-20 each**   *G&CC*

167

Chairs.
£6-20 each
G&CC

Grandfather clocks.
£15 each   *G&CC*

Bears and pigs. **£10-30 each**   *G&CC*

Grimwades wall plaque
with Old Bill cartoon.
£50   *G&CC*

Countryside assortment.
£10-30 each   *G&CC*

Miller's is a price Guide not a price List

The price ranges given reflect the average price a purchaser should pay for similar items. Condition, rarity of design or pattern, size, colour, provenance, restoration and many other factors must be taken into account when assessing values.
When buying or selling, it must always be remembered that prices can be greatly affected by the condition of any piece. Unless otherwise stated, all goods shown in Miller's are of good merchantable quality, and the valuations given reflect this fact. Pieces offered for sale in exceptionally fine condition or in poor condition may reasonably be expected to be priced considerably higher or lower respectively than the estimates given herein

Grafton mouse, Florentine elephant and Cyclone toad.
£15 each *G&CC*

Willow Art Souter Johnny.
£30
And monk with lantern.
£15 *G&CC*

Seaside selection.
£10-90 each
G&CC

Shelley lifeboatman.
£80
And Carlton Yorkshireman.
£30 *G&CC*

Crested dogs.
£15-20 each *G&CC*

Kitchen ranges.
£15 each *G&CC*

Oriental Pottery & Porcelain

The year has seen great variance in demand and prices with the best fetching the expected high prices and the run of the mill hard to sell. The Oriental porcelain market is one of the most fickle, depending to a large extent on the buying fashions of a few very wealthy Far East buyers. The recent upsurge in demand for Qing mark and period pieces would appear to have levelled as supply has met demand and many Oriental dealers are well stocked. There has been renewed interest in Korean ceramics, particularly from Korea itself, which has pushed up the prices of the better pieces. At Christie's a small Yi Dynasty blue and white tortoise shaped

kendi with underglaze blue and copper red decoration fetched £52,000 and a superb early 15/16thC brown on white Korean bottle vase sold for £80,000.

Exceptional pieces of Ming and Yuan blue and white are still contested to high prices but Dingyao and other Song ceramics are in the main ignored. There will never be a better time to buy early Chinese pieces with many desirable objects being available for a few hundred pounds.

Isnik pottery continues to be in

great demand. Prices have continued to soar for high quality, perfect pieces. The end of the year saw £50,000 being paid in Phillips for a 16thC blue Isnik dish painted in imitation of the 15thC Ming original. Japanese ceramics still maintain a buoyant market for the better pieces of any period. Good 17thC Imari is still in demand although collectors are being more selective with condition and pattern playing a more important role. A well decorated, signed Meiji period Makuzu vase sold at Sotheby's Sussex for £12,000.

Bottles

A Japanese celadon glazed bottle, carved with sprays of leaves below a band of key pattern at the shoulder, glaze cracks and staining, 17thC, 13in (33cm).
£1,500-2,000   *CSK*

A pair of Hirado blue and white oviform bottles, painted with wooded landscapes, each with 3 indentations, modelled in relief with a chrysanthemum head and leaves, 6½in (16cm).
£900-1,200   *C*

An Imari bottle, painted in underglaze blue, slight colours, enamels and gilt with a sparse river landscape, with iron red and gilt scrolling foliage, c1700, 9in (23cm).
£350-550   *C*

Bowls

An Imari deep bowl, painted in iron red, yellow and aubergine enamels, underglaze blue and gilt, base crack, c1700, 6in (15cm) diam.
£350-550   *CSK*

A pair of blue and white decanters, each painted in deep blue tones, one with rim chips, Kangxi, 9in (23cm).
£2,000-2,500   *C*

A Japanese Cha-Wan bowl, Ko-Imari Edo, repaired, 17thC, 3½in (8.5cm) diam.
£120-140   *Wai*

A Sancai moulded pottery bowl, the exterior decorated overall in relief with four-petalled blooms on a granular ground, coloured in spotted green, cream and chestnut glazes, restored break, Tang Dynasty, 4in (10cm).
£850-950   *S*

A small Arita bowl with foliate rim, painted in the interior in iron red, green and aubergine enamels, underglaze blue and gilt, the exterior with iron red and underglaze blue emblems, early 18thC, 5½in (14cm) diam.
£400-500 CSK

An Arita polychrome wucai style deep dish, with everted rim painted with the Eight Immortals around a central dragon and wave medallion, the rim with flowersprays, flaking to enamels, early 18thC, 8½in (21cm) diam.
£200-300 C

A Koryo incised celadon bowl on a short foot, incised on the interior with waves within a line border, covered overall in a bright pale blue-green glaze crackled in places, firing adhesions on the foot, rim chip, 12thC, 4in (10cm).
£7,000-8,000 S

A Japanese Cha-Wan bowl, E-Karatsu, 18thC, 4in (10cm) diam.
£400-500 Wai

A pair of Transitional dated blue and white bowls, freely painted with an abstract band around the interior rim, inscribed with a regnal date Tianqi qinian, Tianqi 7th year, corresponding to AD 1628, and of the period, 4½in (11cm) diam.
£1,000-1,500 C

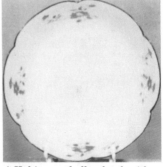

A Kakiemon shallow bowl, with chocolate brown hexafoil rim, painted in the interior with 4 groups of flowering shrubs, rubbed, c1700, 10½in (26cm) diam.
£1,400-1,800 CSK

A Cantonese bowl made for the export market, 18thC, 2½in (6cm) high.
£150-200 KOT

A Chinese tea bowl and saucer, with eggshell finish, Yongzheng, c1730, saucer 4½in (11cm) diam.
£180-200 Wai

A Japanese Arita bowl, early 18thC, 4½in (11cm) diam. **£400-500 Wai**

Chinese dynasties and marks

Earlier Dynasties

Shang Yin, c.1532-1027 B.C.
Western Zhou (Chou) 1027-770 B.C.
Spring and Autumn Annals 770-480 B.C.
Warring States 484-221 B.C.
Qin (Ch'in) 221-206 B.C.
Western Han 206 BC-24 AD
Eastern Han 25-220
Three Kingdoms 221-265
Six Dynasties 265-589
Wei 386-557

Sui 589-617
Tang (T'ang) 618-906
Five Dynasties 907-960
Liao 907-1125
Sung 900-1280
Chin 1115-1260
Yüan 1280-1368

Ming Dynasty

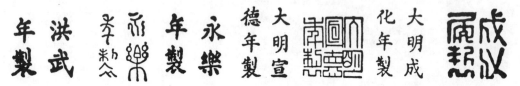

Hongwu (Hung Wu)
1368-1398

Yongle (Yung Lo)
1403-1424

Xuande (Hsüan Té)
1426-1435

Chenghua (Ch'éng Hua)
1465-1487

Hongzhi
(Hung Chih)
1488-1505)

Zhengde
(Chéng Té)
1506-1521

Jiajing
(Chia Ching)
1522-1566

Longqing
(Lung Ching)
1567-1572

Wanli (Wan Li)
1573-1620

Tianqi
(Tien Chi)
1621-1627

Chongzhen
(Ch'ung Chêng)
1628-1644

Qing (Ch'ing) Dynasty

Shunzhi
(Shun Chih)
1644-1661

Kangxi (K'ang Hsi)
1662-1722

Yongzheng (Yung Chêng)
1723-1735

Qianlong (Ch'ien Lung)
1736-1795'

Jiaqing (Chia Ch'ing)
1796-1820

Daoguang (Tao Kuang)
1821-1850

Xianfeng (Hsien Féng)
1851-1861

Tongzhi (T'ung Chih)
1862-1874

Guangxu (Kuang Hsu)
1875-1908

Xuantong
(Hsuan T'ung)
1909-1911

Hongxian
(Hung Hsien)
1916

172

A large Cantonese punch bowl, painted within gold key pattern surrounds divided by butterflies, birds, flowers and emblems, restored, Daoguang, 23in (59cm) diam.
£3,000-4,000   *CSK*

A large 'famille rose' punch bowl, painted on the exterior with bands of pink lotus petals and iron red and gilt scrolling foliage, restored, Qianlong, 16in (40cm).
£1,500-2,000   *CSK*

An Annamese blue and white bowl, the centre painted with a fish, the exterior with 2 dragons between lappet and diaper borders, late 16th/early 17thC, 6in (15cm) diam.
£350-450   *Bea*

POTTERY AND PORCELAIN

★ the Chinese discovered the art of making porcelain in the Tang Dynasty (618-906)
★ by the end of the 17thC it had become a European obsession to discover the secret, since Chinese porcelain was being exported to Europe in ever increasing quantities
★ Johann Böttger at Meissen discovered the formula for *hard paste* porcelain in the early years of the 18thC
★ by 1770 the secret had spread to Vienna, Strasbourg, Frankenthal and Nymphenburg
★ in France, Vincennes and Sèvres first produced *soft paste* porcelain in 1745-72
★ soft paste porcelain was produced at most of the 18thC English and Welsh factories. Only Plymouth, Bristol and Newhall used hard paste

A wucai bowl, the exterior painted with dragons in green enamel and iron red, hair crack and rim chipped, Qianlong mark and period, 5½in (13cm).
£300-400   *Bea*

A blue and white Immortals bowl, painted in underglaze blue with the Eight Immortals, the interior with a medallion of Three Immortals seated in a garden under a pine tree within a double line repeated at the rim, seal mark and period of Daoguang, 6in (15cm).
£1,200-1,800   *S*

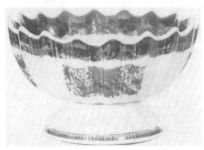

A Chinese blue and white Fitzhugh pattern fluted bowl, with serrated rim and spreading foot, after a silver rose bowl original, painted with groups of flowers and emblems around a central medallion below trellis pattern, flowers and key pattern, minor restoration to rim, c1800, 11½in (30cm).
£800-900   *CSK*

A set of 4 Chinese porcelain dishes with shaped sides, 19thC, 8in (21cm) wide.
£350-400   *HCH*

A 'famille rose' export punch bowl, painted with green and gilt roundels of iron red baskets of flowers below pink, green and gilt bands at the borders, late Qianlong, 14in (36cm) diam.
£1,000-1,500   *CSK*

A 'famille rose' bowl with shaped rim, painted with 2 panels of figures at leisure in fenced pavilion gardens, divided by panels of flowers, all on a puce trellis pattern ground, Qianlong, 11½in (29cm) wide.
£550-650 *CSK*

A set of 6 Chinese iron red decorated bowls, painted on the exterior with bats and groups of pomegranate, the interiors with further pomegranate, iron red Xuantong six-character marks and of the period, 5½in (14cm) diam.
£950-1,200 *CSK*

A Korean celadon parrot bowl, standing on a short foot and incised on the interior with a long-tailed parrot in flight, covered overall in a crackled translucent grey-green celadon glaze pooling in the recesses, warped, slightly ground rim, stained crackle, early 12thC, 7in (17.5cm).
£1,500-2,000 *S*

A 'famille rose' armorial shaped deep dish, painted to the centre of the interior with a rococo shell coat-of-arms above the motto 'Laedere conantor' amidst loose flowersprays, the exterior with a continuous band of bamboo and flowersprays, rim chips, Qianlong, 11½in (30cm) wide.
£1,600-2,000 *C*

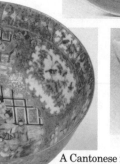

A Koryo moulded celadon bowl, decorated on the interior within a band of foliate scroll below the rim, covered overall with a bubbled grey-green glaze shading to olive green on one side, the glaze extending over the low footrim and base punctuated with 3 spur marks, 12thC, 7½in (18.5cm).
£1,200-1,500 *S*

A Cantonese footed bowl, richly decorated and gilded internally and externally, 19thC, 13in (33cm) diam.
£600-700 *GH*

An Arita polychrome ogee-shaped bowl and domed cover, with foliate rim, painted in iron red, yellow, green and aubergine enamels around the exterior and cover, with flowering shrubs between bands of peony and 'shobu', minor flaking, c1700, 7½in (18.5cm) diam.
£1,400-1,800 *CSK*

A large blue and white cylindrical basin, pierced for drainage, late 18thC, 25½in (65cm) diam.
£3,500-4,500 *C*

A large late Ming blue and white kraak bowl, fritted, Wanli, 14½in (38cm) diam.
£1,400-1,700 *CSK*

A blue and white 'poem' tea bowl, inscribed around the exterior with a poem running in a band around the bowl, with the seals of the Emperor Jiaqing and dated to the spring of the year 'dingsi' (1797), between a 'ruyi' border reserved in white on blue above and below, seal mark and period of Jiaqing, 4in (10.5cm).
£4,000-5,000   *S*

A Junyao deep bowl under a streaked pale lavender glaze, turning to pale brown at the rim, the interior with one purple splash, the glaze finishing irregularly above the foot, Song Dynasty, 8in (20cm) diam.
£1,000-1,500   *CSK*

A pair of copper red decorated phoenix medallion bowls, decorated around the exterior with 5 roundels of phoenix, with wings displayed and long tails curled underneath, small chip to one, seal marks and period of Daoguang, 6in (14.5cm).
£1,600-2,000   *S*

A Tao-Kung Chinese porcelain bowl, with 'famille verte' dragon decoration, c1850, 13in (33cm).
£300-500   *GAK*

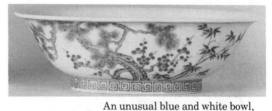

An unusual blue and white bowl, painted in underglaze blue of slightly pale tone with a design of the 'sanyou', 'Three Friends', of pine, prunus and bamboo on either side, above a continuous square scroll band around the foot, the interior white, seal mark and period of Daoguang, 10in (26cm).
£3,500-4,500   *S*

It is rare to find a bowl of this type of oval section, with flared sides, although the design is well known on smaller rounded bowls.

A large Cantonese bowl, 19thC, 20in (51cm) diam.
£2,400-2,800   *DN*

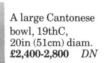

A pair of Chinese blue and white dishes, painted with pagodas in wooded rocky river landscapes within borders of scrolls, stylised flowers and butterflies, one with rim chip and associated hairline, the other with body crack, Qianlong, 21½in (54cm) wide.
£1,000-1,200   *C*

In the Ceramics section if there is only one measurement it usually refers to the height of the piece

A 'famille rose' bowl, the exterior painted with 3 poppy blooms, one striated pink, one shaded white and one in iron red, all borne upon slender hairy stems with leaves in shaded tones of bluish-green and yellowish-green, the interior with 3 fallen blossoms in pink and white, restored, mark and period of Yongzheng, 3½in (9cm).
£5,500-7,500   *S*

A pair of 'famille rose' ruby ground bowls, painted to the exterior with chrysanthemum issuing from leafy stems, the interiors plain, ruby enamelled Kangxi 'yuzhi' marks, 19thC, 4½in (11.5cm), wood stands, box.
£1,200-1,700   *C*

Two 'famille rose' bowls, with rounded sides rising to flaring rims with plain interiors, painted to the exterior with flowersprays, both with iron red Guangxu six-character marks and of the period, 6½in (17cm) diam.
£2,500-3,500   *C*

A 'famille rose' yellow ground bowl, painted with a bird below blossoms among flowers and bearing the mark of the Empress Dowager, 5in (12.5cm) diam.
£450-550   *CSK*

A rare Korean blue and white bowl, with stoutly potted steep rounded sides standing on a straight foot, the exterior with 2 sprays of fruiting finger-citron and a stylised flowerhead within a double line medallion in the centre, Yi Dynasty, 19thC, 10in (26cm).
£40,000-45,000   *S*

A fragment with a similar cobalt blue design, excavated from the Punwonli kiln site at Namchong-myon, Kwangju-gun Kyonggi-do is now in the National Museum of Korea, Seoul.

A large Cantonese punch bowl, painted with panels of figures on terraces and birds and butterflies among flowers on a green scroll gold ground, base cracked, 16in (41cm) diam.
£1,000-1,500   *C*

An Imari monteith, decorated in typical coloured enamels and gilt on underglaze blue, late 19thC, 12½in (31.5cm) diam.
£2,500-3,000   *C*

A Cha-Wan bowl with documentary inscription, c1906, 5in (13cm) diam.
£300-400   *Wai*

Awarded as 1st school prize.

A large Kaga ware deep bowl, decorated in iron red and green enamels and gilt, late Kutani, late 19thC, 12in (30.5cm).
£2,500-3,000   *C*

A pottery deep dish, the coarse pale grey body burnt to a brick red and glazed in Ki-Seto style, with patches left unglazed and pooling in the well, gold lacquer 'naoshi' in the rim, signed 'to', 12in (31cm) diam.
£1,800-2,200   *C*

A Cantonese bowl, painted inside and out with panels containing figures in conversation, the rim painted with a wide band of birds, insects and flowers, 16in (41cm) diam, with damaged wood stand.
£2,000-2,500 *Bea*

A Bencharong bowl, 7in (17.5cm) diam.
£100-120 *KOT*

A Chinese 'famille rose' bowl, Tongzha mark and of period, 7in (17.5cm).
£1,000-1,200 *Wai*

Cups

A 'famille rose' wine cup, painted around the exterior in enamels with a peony plant bearing one pink bloom, growing beside a chrysanthemum bush bearing 3 yellow blooms, the reverse with a purple butterfly, the interior white, Yongzheng mark and of period, 2½in (6cm).
£3,000-3,500 *S*

A 'famille rose' European Subject teacup and saucer, enamelled with 'The Ascension', Christ in Majesty above a group of 9 adoring, standing and kneeling Apostles, all on a plain grassy terrace, Yongzheng.
£1,800-2,500 *C*

An Imari tankard decorated in iron red, green, yellow, aubergine and black enamels and gilt on underglaze blue, the loop handle with scrolling foliage and flowerheads, body crack and chip to rim, late 17thC, 8in (20cm).
£1,400-1,700 *C*

A matching pair of 'blanc de chine' libation cups of rhinoceros horn form, moulded in relief, 18thC, 3in (8cm).
£500-550 *P(S)*

A Chinese yellow ground trio, Guangxu mark and period, plate 6in (15cm) diam.
£400-500 *Wai*

A pair of Imari beakers and saucers, decorated in iron red enamel and gilt on underglaze blue, and 6 Imari beakers and 3 saucers of similar design, one beaker and one saucer with a hairline crack, c1700, beakers 3½in (9cm) high, saucers 6in (15.5cm) diam.
£1,700-2,200 *C*

Ewers

An Imari ewer, decorated in iron red enamel and gilt on underglaze blue with sprays of chrysanthemum and wild pinks surrounding a roundel containing the letter 'O' (olieum), loop handle, slight chips to neck, c1700, 7in (17.5cm).
£700-800   *C*

Figures – Animal

A painted pottery figure of a camel, with traces of pigment overall, Wei Dynasty, 9in (23cm).
£17,000-20,000   *S*

A turquoise glazed figure of a water buffalo, c1800, 14in (35.5cm) wide. **£600-900**   *C*

An Arita polychrome group of a cockerel flanked by half grown chicks, the plumage painted in iron red and black with green and aubergine enamels heightened in gilt, the rockwork base predominantly black, green and white, heightened in iron red, comb restored, late 17thC, 6in (15cm).
£3,500-4,500   *CSK*

An Imari model of 2 'Oshidori' decorated in iron red, green, brown and black enamels and gilt, one beak restored, 19thC, 9½in (23.5cm).
£1,200-1,700   *C*

A large Japanese porcelain figure of a sleeping cat with gilt fur markings, an iron red and green decorated bow around its neck, 12in (30cm) long.
£800-850   *CSK*

Figures – People

A pair of turquoise glazed parrots, their wing feathers naturalistically moulded, chipped, c1850, 14½in (36.5cm).
£2,000-2,500   *C*

A turquoise and mustard glazed roof tile, modelled as a standing scholar, with a wise expression and wearing long loose robes, chip to finger, slightly degraded, Ming Dynasty or later, 17in (43cm).
£1,200-1,500   *C*

A pair of painted pottery figures of ladies, with features picked out in black, with detailing in red pigment on an ivory ground, Han Dynasty, 12in (30cm).
£3,500-4,500   *S*

A 'blanc de chine' seated figure of Guanyin, her flowing robes forming the base, 17th/18thC, 8½in (21cm). **£950-1,200** *CSK*

An Imari model of a bijin decorated in iron red, green and black enamels and gilt on underglaze blue, old damage to her hair, some old cracks, c1700, 15in (39cm). **£3,000-4,000** *C*

A black, green and mustard glazed equestrian roof tile, modelled as an official on a horse with an elaborate saddle cloth, Ming Dynasty or later, 13in (33cm). **£1,400-1,700** *C*

A large Imari model of a bijin decorated in iron red, green, aubergine and black enamels and gilt on underglaze blue, late 17thC, 20in (50cm). **£3,500-4,500** *C*

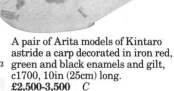

A pair of Satsuma figures, each in colourful floral dress, holding a fan and a cone, slight damage, 6½in (16cm). **£150-250** *Bea*

A pair of Arita models of Kintaro astride a carp decorated in iron red, green and black enamels and gilt, c1700, 10in (25cm) long. **£2,500-3,500** *C*

An Imari figure of a woman, her kimono painted with small birds in flight among hanging wisteria and fences, chips, 11in (27cm). **£300-400** *CSK*

A pair of Imari bijin, decorated in iron red, green and aubergine enamels and gilt on underglaze blue, the kimono with peony sprays and cloud scrolls, minor damage and cracks, c1700, 10½in (26.5cm). **£1,700-2,200** *C*

A Dehua 'blanc de chine' figure of Guanyin wearing long flowing robes and a high cowl on her knotted hair, late Qing Dynasty, 15in (37.5cm). **£1,000-1,500** *C*

An export figure of a lady, holding an underglaze blue and white jar and wearing a gown over a long yellow ground robe, painted in underglaze blue, turquoise, yellow, blue, iron red, green and gilt, base possibly not original, head cracked, hands and base of robe restored, base chipped, Qianlong, 12in (31cm). **£2,000-2,500** *C*

179

Flasks

A pair of Satsuma flasks, painted in colours and gilt, the short cylindrical necks with key pattern, one foot repaired, 5in (12cm).
£1,500-2,000 *CSK*

A large blue and white saucer dish, painted in underglaze blue, extensively restored, early Ming Dynasty, 16in (41cm).
£4,000-5,000 *S*

A Chinese blue and white 'Rotterdam Riot' plate, painted with a scene representing the demolished house of Jacob van Zuylen, 2 small rim chips, Chenghua six-character mark, Kangxi, 8in (20cm).
£1,200-1,600 *CSK*

Flatware

A late Ming blue and white blue ground lobed dish, painted with a central roundel of waves with cranes among lotus, rim frits, Chenghua six-character mark, Tianqi/Chongzheng, 8½in (21cm).
£400-500 *CSK*

A Chinese blue and white plate, painted with 2 ladies, within a trellis pattern border reserved with 4 panels of fruit, Kangxi six-character mark within a double circle and of the period, 8in (20cm).
£700-800 *CSK*

A Chinese yellow ground underglaze blue decorated saucer dish, painted with 3 phoenix amongst clouds, the reverse with 2 further phoenix and flowers, small rim cracks, Chenghua six-character mark, Kangxi, 6in (15cm).
£400-500 *CSK*

A pair of 'famille verte' plates, painted to the centre of the interior with auspicious emblems and scholars' objects, the exterior with 6 loose ribboned emblems, the base painted in underglaze blue with a 'lingzhi' spray, rim chip restored, rim chips, Kangxi, 8½in (22cm).
£900-1,200 *C*

A late Ming blue and white saucer dish, Tianqi four-character mark within a double circle and of the period, 6½in (16cm).
£500-600 *CSK*

A Ming blue and white deep saucer dish painted within a double circle, the border with stylised trailing flowers and the reverse with 6 cranes in flight divided by stylised clouds, 16thC, 17in (43cm).
£2,000-2,500 *CSK*

A dish in the form of a peach with short lipped upright sides, painted in underglaze blue heightened in copper red, the base unglazed, cracked from firing fault in rim, Kangxi, 10in (25cm).
£1,500-2,000   *S*

Fifteen Chinese blue and white plates, each painted with a central flowerspray medallion within a dense panel of flowers and foliage, the rims with sprays of chrysanthemum and daisies, 5 cracked, most with small chips or frits, Kangxi, 10in (24cm).
£800-1,100   *CSK*

A 'famille verte' dish painted within a seeded green border reserved with 6 panels of vessels, rim frit, Kangxi, 14in (36cm).
£1,000-1,500   *C*

A large 'famille verte' dish, painted with a central roundel of a small bird among flowers and rockwork within 2 phoenix, the border with 4 panels of sea creatures and with moulded iron red and gilt rim, restored, Kangxi, 15in (37cm).
£400-600   *CSK*

A pair of 'famille verte' plates, each painted at the centre with a boy on a terrace, within a band of floral roundels and scholars' utensils beneath cash emblems at the rim, Kangxi, 9in (22.5cm).
£2,400-2,700   *C*

A 'famille verte' dish painted at the centre, the piecrust rim decorated in iron red and gilt, fritted, rim chip and associated short crack, Kangxi, 14in (35.5cm).
£1,500-2,000   *S*

An Imari deep dish, painted to the centre with a roundel of a jardinière of pine and plum on a wooden terrace, the border with 3 panels of flowering chrysanthemum and gilt quail below grasses, divided by dark blue ground panels of flowers and leaves, crack, late 17thC, 19in (48cm).
£2,500-3,000   *CSK*

A Chinese blue and white dish, with scroll border, early 17thC, 8in (20cm).
£400-450   *WW*

A set of 4 Arita blue and white kraak style deep dishes, painted to the centre with a deer below pine and overhanging rockwork within panels of flowersprays, the everted rims with masks, c1700, 7in (17.5cm).
£1,200-1,500   *CSK*

A pair of 'famille verte' plates, each painted at the centre with a bird perched above dense prunus and tree chrysanthemum, the seeded border reserved with bird and butterfly cartouches, one cracked, Kangxi, 8½in (24cm). **£1,000-1,200**   *C*

A large Arita blue and white dish, painted within a broad border of boldly scrolling lotus and leaves, star crack, late 17thC, 24in (61cm).
£2,000-2,500   *CSK*

An Arita blue and white deep dish, painted with a central jardinière of flowers on a terrace within 4 panels of peony divided by stylised foliage, stained, late 17thC, 12½in (32cm).
£300-400   *CSK*

A Chinese blue and white saucer dish, with Chenghua mark, Kangxi, 6in (16cm).
£160-180   *Wai*

A blue and white deep dish, painted at the centre, reserved on a key pattern ground in the well and at the foliate border, fritted, encircled Kangxi six-character mark and of the period, 13½in (34cm).
£1,700-2,200   *C*

A Kakiemon type shallow dish, decorated in iron red, green, blue and black enamels on underglaze blue, late 17thC, 9in (23cm).
£2,500-3,000   *C*

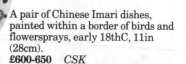

A pair of Chinese Imari dishes, painted within a border of birds and flowersprays, early 18thC, 11in (28cm).
£600-650   *CSK*

A large Chinese blue and white charger painted with plum trees, bamboo and 'lingzhi' fungus issuing from rockwork, cracked and rim ground, Kangxi, 22in (55cm).
£900-1,400   *CSK*

A set of 9 Arita foliate dishes, each painted with the Hall of the Hundred Boys, 3 with rim repairs, 18thC, 4in (11cm).
£600-700   *CSK*

TRANSITIONAL WARES

★ these wares are readily identifiable both by their form and by their style of decoration

★ forms: sleeve vases, oviform jars with domed lids, cylindrical brushpots and bottle vases are particularly common

★ the cobalt used is a brilliant purplish blue, rarely misfired

★ the ground colour is of a definite bluish tone, probably because the glaze is slightly thicker than that of the wares produced in the subsequent reigns of Kangxi and Yongzheng

★ the decoration is executed in a rather formal academic style, often with scholars and sages with attendants in idyllic cloud-lapped mountain landscapes

★ other characteristics include the horizontal 'contoured' clouds, banana plantain used to interrupt scenes, and the method of drawing grass by means of short 'V' shaped brush strokes

★ in addition, borders are decorated with narrow bands of scrolling foliage, so lightly incised as to be almost invisible or secret (anhua)

★ these pieces were rarely marked although they sometimes copied earlier Ming marks

A 'famille verte' Pomegranate saucer dish, painted in aubergine, yellow and shades of green with fruiting peach and pomegranate, outlined in black over a lightly incised design of five-clawed dragons, the exterior similarly decorated, riveted, cracked, encircled Kangxi six-character mark and of the period, 10in (25cm), wood stand.
£1,200-1,700   *C*

A Japanese Arita blue and white plate, late 17thC, 8½in (21cm).
£300-400   *Wai*

A Hausmaler decorated Chinese porcelain dish, painted in 'Schwarzlot' and gilding by Ignaz Preissler, in iron red, turquoise, blue and gilt, small chips, c1715, 8½in (21cm).
£2,800-3,500   *S*

A 'famille rose' deep dish, painted with 4 figures in conversation, the everted cell pattern rim reserved with 4 river landscape panels divided by flowers, one area of rim restored, early Qianlong, 15½in (39cm) diam.
£700-800   *CSK*

A Kakiemon blue and white foliate rimmed dish, decorated with a lakeside landscape, the reverse with scrolling 'karakusa', small silver lacquer repair, late 17thC, 7½in (18cm).
£700-800   *C*

A large Chinese blue and white shallow dish, the centre painted with deer in a landscape, the rim with a band of insects, flowers and foliage, 2 hair cracks, minor glaze chipping to rim, Transitional, 17½in (44cm).
£250-350   *Bea*

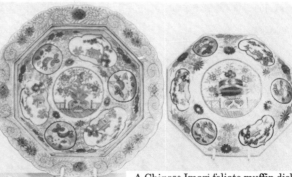

A Chinese Imari foliate muffin dish and domed cover, rim repairs, early 18thC, 11in (29cm).
£1,400-1,700   *CSK*

A large blue and white deep dish, painted at the centre below a band of trellis pattern at the border, the exterior with 3 flowersprays, Qianlong, 17in (43.5cm).
£1,200-1,700   *C*

A pair of Chinese export 'famille rose' plates, Qianlong, 8½in (22cm).
£400-500   *DN*

A pair of Chinese Imari armorial plates, fritted, one repaired, c1720, 12in (30.5cm).
£2,000-3,000   *C*

A set of 10 Chinese deep dishes, brightly painted in 'famille rose' enamels with crabs, lilies and a spray of peonies, 4 cracked, the rest with minor glaze damage, Qianlong, 9in (23cm). **£750-850**   *Bea*

A pair of 'famille rose' plates, painted within a band of iron red and gilt spearheads, the border with 3 branches of peony and fruit, chipped, one with hairline crack, Qianlong, 12in (30.5cm).
£1,000-1,500   *C*

A 'famille rose' dish, painted within an iron red and gilt spearhead well and rim, the border with trailing flowers, fritted, Qianlong, 14in (36cm).
£1,000-1,500   *CSK*

A 'famille rose' dish, painted in a pierced iron red and gilt border, Qianlong, 14in (36cm).
£1,400-1,700   *C*

A 'famille rose' plate, painted with a traveller and attendant, Qianlong, 9in (23cm).
£200-300   *CSK*

A Chinese 'famille rose' quatrefoil dish, with Mandarin pattern, c1770, 8in (20cm) wide.
£350-400   *Wai*

A set of 3 Chinese export 'famille rose' plates, Qianlong, 9in (23cm).
£600-700   *DN*

A Chinese blue and white charger, painted within a border of stylised pomegranates and floral designs, Qianlong, 21½in (54cm).
£1,000-1,400   *CSK*

A 'famille rose' pseudo tobacco leaf meat dish, painted with large overlapping serrated leaves and flowerheads, 2 rim chips, Qianlong, 18½in (47cm) wide.
£2,700-3,200　*CSK*

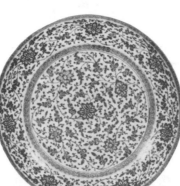

A set of 3 'famille rose' plates, the rims with iron red and gilt bands, one with hairline crack and chip, Qianlong, 9in (23cm).
£600-700　*CSK*

A Chinese blue and white thickly potted saucer dish, densely painted with Ming-style scrolling flowers and leaves divided by bands of whorl pattern, the exterior similar, small rim crack, rim chip restored, Qianlong, 14½in (37cm).
£900-1,500　*CSK*

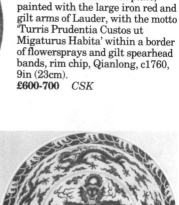

A 'famille rose' armorial plate, painted with the large iron red and gilt arms of Lauder, with the motto 'Turris Prudentia Custos ut Migaturus Habita' within a border of flowersprays and gilt spearhead bands, rim chip, Qianlong, c1760, 9in (23cm).
£600-700　*CSK*

A blue and white dragon dish, painted in the centre in deep underglaze blue with a large leaping dragon enclosing a 'shou' character, chip on rim, seal mark and period of Qianlong, 17½in (45cm).
£5,000-6,000　*S*

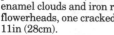

A pair of 'famille rose' plates, painted with sprays of peony, chrysanthemum and daisy, within borders of flower and fruit sprays within iron red and gilt whorl pattern surrounds, divided by blue enamel clouds and iron red half flowerheads, one cracked, Qianlong, 11in (28cm).
£1,000-1,500　*CSK*

A pair of Chinese export 'famille rose' meat dishes, Qianlong, 15in (38cm) wide.
£1,700-2,000　*DN*

A pair of Chinese blue and white warming dishes, each painted with a pagoda in a riverside garden, Qianlong, 11in (29cm).
£300-400　*Bea*

A pair of Japanese Kakiemon fluted saucer dishes, late 18thC, 6in (15cm) diam.
£1,000-1,200　*Wai*

A Chinese porcelain blue and white saucer, Qianlong.
£90-120　*ART*

A popular item of salvage from the Nanking Cargo.

A dragon dish, later enamelled in green and iron red, the centre painted in underglaze blue, seal mark and period of Qianlong, 17½in (45cm).
£7,000-8,000   *S*

A pair of Chinese 'famille rose' dishes, late 18thC, 10in (25cm) wide.
£800-1,000   *Wai*

A pair of 'famille rose' armorial plates, each painted to the centre with an elaborate coat-of-arms, small rim chips, Qianlong, 9in (23cm).
£850-900   *CSK*

The Arms are those of Carr, c1765-70.

A set of 10 Chinese blue and white plates with foliate rims, minor damages and rubbing, Qianlong, 9½in (24cm).
£2,000-2,500   *CSK*

A blue and white dragon saucer dish, painted in the centre with a leaping scaly dragon chasing a flaming pearl, the reverse similarly painted with a frieze of 2 dragons, all between line borders, seal mark and period of Daoguang, 6½in (16cm).
£800-900   *S*

A large iron red and gilt dragon dish, the centre of the interior enamelled with 2 five-clawed dragons pursuing a flaming pearl, with similar exterior, rim crack, iron red Guangxu six-character mark and of the period, 20½in (51.5cm).
£2,000-2,500   *C*

A blue and white saucer dish, the interior decorated within a double line border repeated around the rim, the underside with similar phoenix and clouds, mark and period of Xianfeng, 6½in (16.5cm).
£1,700-2,200   *S*

A late Ming blue and white kraak dish, painted within alternate panels of flowers and emblems, repaired, Wanli, 20in (51cm).
£600-800   *CSK*

A 'famille rose' export deep dish for the Danish market, painted with a central pink ground portrait medallion, with white brickwork and green enamel and gilt rim, late Qianlong, 6½in (15.5cm) wide.
£350-450   *CSK*

Fourteen Arita style blue and white dishes, painted with a butterfly hovering above flowers issuing from pierced rockwork, four-character mark, early 19thC, 8in (20cm).
£300-400   *CSK*

A Chinese blue and white plate, decorated in underglaze blue, the central panel depicting a fisherman and a young child walking alongside a river bank with trees in the background, mid-19thC, 13in (33cm).
£170-220   *HSS*

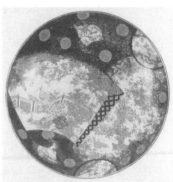

An Arita soup plate, decorated in iron red enamel and gilt, the centre with 2 entwined 'ho-o' birds, the wide rim with 2 dragons divided by sacred pearls, wax inventory marks, late 19thC, 10in (25cm). **£1,500-2,000** *C*

A pair of large Chinese export plates painted in 'famille rose' enamels, in orange and black, rims within black lines, slight glaze damage, Qianlong, 13½in (35cm). **£600-800** *Bea*

An Imari dish, painted on a blue gilt ground reserved with scrolling foliage, 24in (61cm). **£1,200-1,500** *CSK*

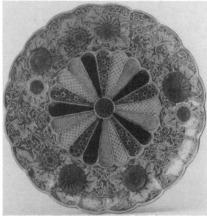

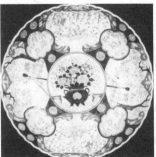

A pair of Imari fluted dishes, printed and painted with central roundels of jardinières of flowers on terraces, within panels of 'ho-o' among flowers, 18½in (47cm). **£950-1,200** *CSK*

An Imari foliate rimmed shallow dish, decorated in various coloured enamels and gilt, signed in underglaze blue 'Dai Nihon Bizen Arita..sei', late 19thC, 12in (30.5cm). **£1,500-2,000** *C*

A set of 6 Imari fluted dishes, painted with central iron red and gilt floral medallions within radiating panels of 'ho-o', stylised foliage, scrolling flowers and swastikas, 8½in (22cm). **£700-900** *CSK*

A Ming blue and yellow dish painted in an underglaze blue, all on Imperial mustard yellow ground within double line borders repeated at the foot, restored, encircled Hongzhi six-character mark and of the period, 10½in (26.5cm). **£3,000-4,000** *C*

A pair of Japanese chargers, with scalloped edges and decorated in the Imari style with a central panel of a ginger tree, 18in (46cm) diam. **£1,000-1,200** *P(M)*

A pair of Chinese dark blue glazed meat dishes, decorated in gilt with figures within a border of butterflies and further foliage, rubbing, Qianlong, 13½in (35cm). **£800-1,000** *CSK*

Twenty-one 'famille rose' plates with shaped rims, 5 damaged, Qianlong, 9in (23cm). **£3,000-3,500** *CSK*

An Imari deep dish, painted with 2 bijin among pine in a landscape beside dense flowering shrubs reserved with panels of 'ho-o' and foliage, the everted rim with gilt cranes among blue clouds and dragons behind blue lattice-work, 20½in (52cm).
£2,300-2,600 *CSK*

A Cantonese plaque, the centre painted with a basket of flowers reserved on a ground of insects, fruit and foliage, 14½in (37cm).
£360-420 *Bea*

A pair of 'famille verte' dishes, each painted with a pair of peacocks among flowering shrubs issuing from pierced iron red rockwork, 16in (41cm).
£300-400 *CSK*

A pair of Chinese blue and white meat dishes, painted with peacocks before flowers, 10½in (26cm) wide.
£300-400 *CSK*

A Satsuma saucer the cavetto dish, painted with warriors on the banks of a river, within a rim painted with a band of stylised flowerheads, 10in (25cm).
£400-450 *Bea*

A pair of Imari dishes, decorated in ochre, underglaze blue and gilt, c1800, 14in (36cm).
£1,200-1,700 *P(S)*

A set of 7 Satsuma plates, decorated with scenes progressing through the seasons, 8½in (21cm).
£1,800-2,200 *P(M)*

A Satsuma shallow dish, 12in (30.5cm).
£750-800 *Bea*

A Satsuma fluted dish, painted with panels containing figures in conversation, reserved on a brocade ground, 10in (25cm).
£450-500 *Bea*

A Japanese earthenware galleried tray, painted in enamels, on a deep blue ground gilded with stylised blooms, painted and impressed seal mark of Kinkozan, 5½in (14.5cm) wide.
£550-650 *HSS*

Jardinières

A Satsuma thickly potted fluted saucer dish, painted in coloured enamels and richly gilt, 13in (33cm).
£700-1,000   *CSK*

A wucai jardinière, painted on the exterior with 3 yellow Buddhistic lions among dense scrolling iron red peony and green leaves, fritted, Transitional, 9½in (24cm) wide.
£1,500-1,800   *CSK*

A 'famille rose' jardinière, painted on the exterior with 4 panels of baskets of flowers, on a yellow ground reserved with dense scrolling flowers and leaves, below a trellis pattern band at the rim, 18in (46cm) diam.
£1,500-2,000   *CSK*

A large Ming blue and white jardinière, firing crack, chipped and scratched, Jiajing six-character mark and of the period, 16½in (42.5cm) diam.
£4,500-5,500   *C*

An Imari porcelain jardinière, with fluted body, 12in (30cm).
£500-550   *GAK*

Jars

A Chinese jar and cover, Han Dynasty, 8in (20cm) high.
£450-550   *KOT*

A green glazed pottery jar with lipped mouth, applied with a minutely crackled olive green glaze falling in an uneven line revealing the buff ware below, Tang Dynasty, 6½in (16.5cm).
£1,500-2,000   *S*

A late Ming blue and white jar and domed cover, painted with 2 Buddhistic lions among scrolling flowers and leaves below a band of lappets at the shoulder, the cover with 4 flowersprays, Wanli, 6in (16cm).
£300-400   *CSK*

A wucai baluster jar and a domed cover, fritted, c1650, 15in (38.5cm).
£3,000-4,000   *C*

Locate the source
The source of each illustration in Miller's can be found by checking the code letters below each caption with the list of contributors

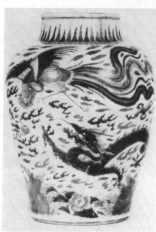

Two Chinese blue and white broad oviform jars, each painted with 3 shaped panels of 'qilin' on a cracked ice pattern ground, reserved with sprays of prunus, Kangxi, 8in (21cm), with pierced wood covers.
£1,000-1,500 *CSK*

A wucai broad baluster jar, painted below iron red scale pattern and floral lappets at the shoulder, rim restoration, Transitional, 10½in (26cm).
£450-550 *CSK*

A Transitional blue and white jar and cover, decorated beneath a band of descending leaves on the cylindrical neck, the cover decorated with 3 figures on a terrace, cover restored, vase cracked, c1650, 12in (30.5cm).
£2,000-2,500 *C*

A wucai baluster jar, painted with dragons and phoenix amongst cloud scrolls and above foaming waves crashing on the rocks, the neck with stiff leaves, damaged, Transitional, 12½in (31cm).
£900-1,200 *CSK*

A Korean blue and white jar, painted in underglaze blue, cracks and chips, Yi Dynasty, 19thC, 5in (12.5cm).
£1,200-1,500 *S*

A pair of blue and white jars and shallow domed covers, decorated on the exterior with 4 foliate panels of scholars' utensils divided by lotus and peony sprays, the covers similarly decorated, one foot rim chipped, 19thC, 13in (33cm).
£1,800-2,200 *C*

A blue and white oviform jar, painted with 4 panels alternately depicting figures in mountainous riverscapes and archaistic vessels amongst precious emblems, all reserved on a trellis pattern ground between 'ruyi' lappets at the foot and on the shoulder, Kangxi, 12½in (32cm), wood cover.
£3,000-3,500 *C*

A Satsuma moulded jar and cover, decorated in various coloured enamels and gilt on a brocade ground, signed 'Nihon Bijitsuto Satsuma yaki Shuko', late 19thC, 8in (20cm), wood stand.
£4,000-4,500 *C*

A Korean blue and white faceted jar, with a band of 8 facets around the middle, decorated in underglaze blue with a line around the low foot, 4 scroll motifs around the middle and on the angled shoulders with 3 'shou' characters interspersed with foliate sprays centred with a bloom, chip to inside of foot, Yi Dynasty, 19thC, 5in (12cm).
£1,700-2,200 *S*

A pair of Imari jars and covers, each painted with a figure standing outside a house by a river, reserved on a foliate decorated orange and blue ground, one cover chipped, 13in (33cm).
£1,400-1,800   *Bea*

A pair of late Kutani squat pear-shaped jars and domed covers, painted in green, yellow, blue enamels and iron red, one cover repaired, 11½in (29.5cm).
£450-550   *CSK*

A pair of Imari jars, each with inner and outer covers, each facet painted with a jardinière of chrysanthemum or peonies within a gold decorated deep blue border, 10in (24.5cm).
£1,000-1,500   *Bea*

Tureens

A pair of Imari oviform jars and high domed covers, with 'shi-shi' finials, densely painted in gold ground panels, some repairs, 21in (53cm).
£4,000-4,500   *CSK*

A Chinese blue and white tureen and domed cover, with fruit finial and lion mask handles, painted with sprays of flowering shrubs, finial chipped, 10½in (26cm) wide.   **£800-1,000**
CSK

A Chinese export tureen and cover, with animal head handles, each piece boldly painted with scrolls, flowers and insects in the tobacco-leaf palette, Qianlong, 13½in (34.5cm).
£6,000-6,500   *Bea*

A Chinese clobbered blue and white tureen stand, later ormolu mounted on 4 rams head feet and with flowerspray handles, the porcelain 18thC, 20in (50cm) wide.
£800-1,000   *CSK*

A Chinese blue and white soup tureen and domed cover with boars' head handles, painted with pagodas and bridges in river landscapes within trellis pattern bands, c1800, 12½in (32cm) wide.
£900-1,200   *CSK*

A Chinese blue and white soup tureen, cover and shaped stand, with lion mask handles and Buddhistic lion finial, painted with scattered flowersprays within borders of further flowers, trellis pattern and cell pattern, Qianlong, stand 15in (38cm) wide.
£1,500-2,000   *CSK*

A pair of Cantonese 'famille rose' oval vegetable tureens and covers with gilt berry finials, and a matching rectangular tureen and cover with bamboo handle, one rim chip, gilt slightly rubbed, 19thC, oval tureens 10½in (26.5cm) wide, rectangular tureen 9½in (24cm) wide.
£1,000-1,500   C

A Chinese porcelain covered bowl with tab handles, painted in 'famille rose' colours with peonies, 19thC, 9in (23cm). **£500-600   HCH**

Vases

A Sancai glazed vase, the body liberally splashed overall in chestnut and green on a straw-coloured ground, the glaze falling in an uneven line around the base, showing the pale buff ware of the low flat-bottomed foot, 2 restored rim chips, Tang Dynasty, 4½in (11cm).
£1,000-1,200   S

A pair of late Ming blue and white 'kraak porselein' double gourd vases, moulded and decorated on the exterior, one neck cracked and chipped, Wanli, 12in (30.5cm).
£3,500-4,000   C

A Cantonese vegetable tureen and domed cover, painted on a green scroll gold ground, 9½in (24cm) wide.
£400-500   C

A Transitional polychrome baluster vase, of characteristic tall shouldered form with a flared neck, painted in different shades of underglaze blue and bright polychrome enamels, damage to rim, 20in (50cm).
£1,500-2,000   S

A Dehua 'blanc de chine' slender pear shaped vase, with flared neck modelled in relief with a coiled dragon, chips to extremities, 17thC, 14in (36cm).
£300-350   C

A Transitional blue and white sleeve vase, decorated in underglaze blue, the base unglazed, slight wear, 19in (48cm).
£3,000-3,500   S

Two Transitional blue and white bottle vases, the tall flaring neck painted with flowersprays, one with 2 insects in flight, c1640, 13½in (34cm).
£2,500-3,000   C

An unusual pear shaped vase, decorated with a pair of undulating green dragons pursuing flaming pearls amid cloud scrolls, all reserved on a white ground with details in 'an hua', the base with a Hongzhi six-character mark, Kangxi, 16in (41cm).
£1,700-2,000   *C*

A pair of Imari vases, the exteriors with an allover deep cobalt underglaze blue and decorated in gilt, the inside of the rims decorated in iron red enamel and gilt on underglaze blue with sprays of peony, one with some restoration to the rim, c1700, 12½in (32cm).
£1,200-1,500   *C*

A blue and white globular bottle vase with garlic neck, Kangxi, 17½in (45cm).
£2,200-2,700   *C*

A 'famille verte' rouleau vase, the neck with bamboo sprays, encircled Xuande six-character mark, Kangxi, 7in (18cm).
£1,000-1,500   *C*

A large 'famille verte' vase with rounded shoulder and short flared neck, painted with 2 panels of equestrian figures before buildings and among clouds divided by panels of scrolling leaves, restored, Kangxi, 20in (51cm).
£1,000-1,200   *CSK*

A blue and white gu-shaped beaker vase, foot chip restored, rim with one small chip, encircled Chenghua six-character mark, Kangxi, 18½in (47cm).
£1,500-2,000   *C*

A 'famille verte' rouleau vase, base repaired, Kangxi, 17½in (44.5cm).
£2,000-2,500   *C*

An Arita 'Tokkuri', decorated in iron red, green, aubergine and black enamels and gilt on underglaze blue, chip to neck, c1700, 7½in (18.5cm).
£1,000-1,500   *C*

Two blue and white square vases, painted on each side with an audience scene below birds amongst lotus scroll on the sloping shoulder and precious emblems on the slightly waisted shoulders, one chip restored, fritted, impressed Xuande four-character marks, Kangxi, 11½in (29cm), wood stands.
£2,700-3,200   *C*

A 'famille rose' Mandarin pattern three-piece garniture, all reserved on a white raised-dot ground embellished with flowersprays and iron red and gilt bats, one foot rim chipped, one small rim chip re-stuck, Qianlong, 10in (25cm).
£2,200-2,800 *C*

An Imari polychrome bottle vase, painted in typical enamel colours and gold, minor glaze chip to rim, late 17thC, 12in (30.5cm).
£1,500-2,000 *Bea*

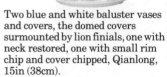

A pair of 'famille rose' vases and covers, each painted beneath a band of turquoise lappets embellished with flowers at the shoulder, the covers similarly decorated and surmounted by knop finials, necks with hairline cracks, covers chipped, one repaired, Qianlong, 14in (36cm).
£1,500-2,000 *C*

A 'famille verte' vase, painted with flowers issuing from rockwork between ascending and descending lappets, the shoulder with a band of half flowerheads on a green ground, Kangxi, 9in (22.5cm), wood cover.
£1,000-1,400 *C*

Two blue and white baluster vases and covers, the domed covers surmounted by lion finials, one with neck restored, one with small rim chip and cover chipped, Qianlong, 15in (38cm).
£1,200-1,600 *C*

A blue and white bottle vase, reserved on a dark blue ground, late Qianlong/Jiaqing, 17in (43.5cm).
£900-1,200 *C*

A Chinese 'famille rose' vase, Qianlong mark, Jiaqing, 10in (25cm).
£600-800 *Wai*

A rare copper red and blue and white dragon bottle vase, on a slightly splayed foot, boldly painted in copper red and underglaze cobalt blue, restored neck, cracked, seal mark and period of Qianlong, 20½in (52cm).
£4,500-5,500 *S*

A 'famille rose' baluster vase, painted with a pheasant perched on rockwork amongst peony and prunus and beside a magnolia tree extending up the tall cylindrical neck, 19thC, 20½in (52cm).
£2,500-3,000   *C*

A pair of Cantonese porcelain vases, the shoulder of each with lion mask ring handles, 19thC, 14in (36cm).
£850-950   *LAY*

A Chinese vase with flared neck, covered in a thick streaked semi-translucent 'sang-de-boeuf' glaze, paling at the neck and pooling around the foot, c1800, 16in (41cm), wood stand.
£900-1,200   *CSK*

A pair of Imari beaker vases with splayed rims, each painted in typical enamel colours and gold with panels of flowers on a blue scrolling foliate ground, early 18thC, 12in (30cm).
£800-1,200   *Bea*

A large Imari porcelain floor vase, 18thC.
£16,000-20,000   *DM*

A 'famille rose' vase with flaring neck, the base unglazed, 19thC, 17in (43cm).
£800-1,000   *C*

A blue and white vase, painted with large flying phoenix amongst rising peony on a ground of scale pattern, 18thC, 13½in (34.5cm).
£1,000-1,500   *C*

A Ming blue and white pear shaped vase, 'yuhuchun', painted with flowerheads, the rim with silver gilt mount, the neck possibly reduced, Jiajing four-character mark and of the period, 13in (33cm).
£3,300-3,700   *C*

A Chinese baluster vase, painted with simulated bamboo decorated bands, on a raised circular base, 19thC, 18in (46cm), on hardwood stand.
£400-500   *CLG*

195

A moulded Satsuma vase, decorated in various coloured enamels and gilt, neck restored, signed 'Dai Nihon Satsuma yaki Meigyokudo', late 19thC, 10in (25cm).
£1,700-2,200 *C*

A large Satsuma vase, decorated in various coloured underglaze enamels and gilt, base restored, unsigned, late 19thC, 19½in (49cm).
£3,000-3,500 *C*

An Arita polychrome vase decorated in the late Ming style, horizontal Wanli six-character mark at the rim, 19thC, 24in (61cm).
£4,000-4,500 *C*

A pair of Cantonese vases, with handles in the form of standing figures, applied at the shoulders with dragons, reserved within a diaper border on a ground painted with flowers and insects, each with an interior hair crack, 25in (63cm).
£800-1,200 *Bea*

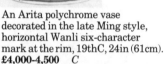

A pair of Satsuma vases, decorated in various coloured enamels and gilt, signed 'Gyokushu' with impressed seal 'Taizan', late 19thC, 5in (12.5cm).
£3,000-4,000 *C*

A Cantonese vase with flared neck and scalloped collared shoulder, with gilt elephant head handles, painted with Immortals divided by precious objects and flowers, 24in (61cm).
£1,000-1,500 *CSK*

A pair of Cantonese vases with wavy rims, gilt Buddhistic lion cub handles and 'guei' dragons to the shoulders, painted on green gold scroll grounds, 18in (46cm)
£600-700 *CSK*

A Satsuma vase with everted rim, the blue ground finely gilded, chip to underneath rim, late 19thC, 8in (21cm).
£300-350 *MN*

A pair of Satsuma oviform vases, decorated in various coloured enamels and gilt, with gilt rims, signed 'Dai Nihon Taizan sei', late 19thC, 12in (30cm).
£1,600-2,000 *C*

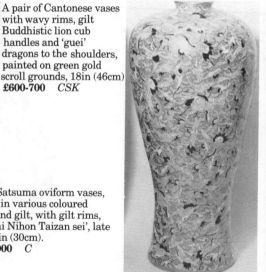

A pair of large Satsuma vases, decorated in enamels and gilt with a multitude of Manchurian cranes in flight, 20thC, 31½in (80cm).
£1,500-2,000 *Bon*

An Imari bottle vase, painted on a ground of flowering shrubs and 'ho-o', the neck with 2 dragon roundels on a ground of dense flowers, Fukugawa mark, 16in (40cm).
£1,000-1,500   CSK

A pair of Cantonese vases, with slender rounded cylindrical bodies and slightly flared necks, painted within gold key pattern surrounds divided by smaller similar panels and roundels, on grounds of butterflies, flowers and emblems, 15½in (39cm).
£1,500-2,000   CSK

A pair of Imari flattened flask-shaped oviform vases with flared rims, 9½in (24cm).
£700-800   CSK

A Satsuma vase of slender ovoid form and short neck, 9in (23cm) high.
£1,200-1,700   P(M)

A Satsuma porcelain vase, with flared rim, gilt dragon handles and allover polychrome figure decoration on patterned gilt ground, 10in (25cm).
£650-700   AH

A pair of Cantonese 'famille verte' vases, the handles modelled as standing Immortals, painted allover with groups of vessels, furniture and emblems among flowers, below green key pattern bands at the rims, one neck repaired, 24in (61cm).
£850-1,000   C

A pair of Satsuma vases, each painted on one side with warriors in a mountain landscape and on the other with a panel of flowers and birds, 6in (15cm).
£170-250   Bea

A pair of Japanese Satsuma heart-shaped vases, decorated within shaped cartouches with floral strewn borders, having square necks and pedestal bases, late 19thC, 3½in (8.5cm).
£1,700-2,000   WW

A pair of Imari hexagonal waisted beaker vases with bulbous feet, 14in (36cm).
£1,500-2,000   CSK

A pair of Satsuma vases, painted with panels of geese, fish beneath wisteria, river landscapes and ladies before flowers, all on a dark blue gilt ground, signed, 7in (18cm).
£900-1,200 *CSK*

A Satsuma slender oviform vase, painted in colours and gilt on one side, the shoulder within iron red ground band of emblems, 6½in (17cm).
£3,500-4,500 *CSK*

A Satsuma vase with rounded shoulder and foot, painted in colours and richly gilt with 2 rectangular panels of 'bijin', signed Seizan, 10in (25cm).
£1,700-2,000 *CSK*

A large Imari vase, decorated in typical palette, foot damaged, piece missing, Meiji period, 42½in (108cm).
£1,700-2,000 *Bon*

A pair of Satsuma vases, painted and heavily gilt with panels of Immortals in river landscapes, and ladies and attendants in gardens on a ground of stylised flowerheads, signed, 15in (38cm).
£1,500-2,000 *CSK*

A Satsuma square vase with floral decoration, 5in (13cm).
£70-100 *PCh*

A pair of Japanese Satsuma vases, highlighted in gilt, 7in (18cm).
£350-400 *GC*

A pair of small Japanese Satsuma ovoid two-handled vases, signed, 2½in (6cm).
£120-160 *DN*

An Arita blue and white vase, painted with floral medallions on a cracked ice and prunus ground, applied with 2 confronting dragons in high relief, Meiji period, 17in (44cm).
£650-850 *Bon*

A pair of Satsuma vases, painted in colours and richly gilt, 7½in (18.5cm).
£850-950 *CSK*

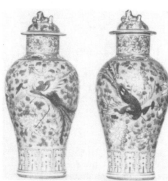

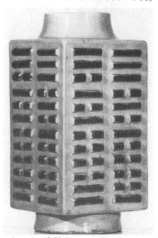

A pair of Imari vases of ovoid form, decorated in typical palette with birds amongst pine trees and flowering peony between formal borders, both with rim restoration, Meiji period, 18in (46cm).
£700-900 *Bon*

A Japanese Kutani vase, decorated with extensive crowd scenes amidst orange and gilt highlighted clouds, Daini Pon Kutani mark on a yellow enamel rectangular panel, Meiji, 12in (30cm).
£1,000-1,500 *WW*

A Japanese Satsuma vase of tapering square section, the shoulders and foot allover decorated with gilt diaper patterns, each face with numerous figures, Meiji, 8½in (21cm).
£400-450 *WW*

A Satsuma vase and stand, with long cylindrical neck, decorated in enamels and gilt, raised on a stand with 5 mask-head feet, stand chipped and tassel chipped, Meiji period, 34½in (87cm).
£500-800 *Bon*

A Kinkozan pottery vase of globular form, painted with an encircling band of women in conversation under sprays of wisteria, the foot and neck painted with flowers, 5in (12.5cm).
£950-1,200 *Bea*

A Japanese porcelain vase, decorated on an iron red ground, Meiji period, 11½in (29cm).
£400-500 *P(S)*

A pair of 'famille rose' turquoise ground vases and domed covers, the yellow ground necks with scrolling foliage, the covers with pink everted rims, 14in (36cm).
£500-600 *CSK*

A pair of Kyo-Satsuma vases with waisted rims and feet, each painted in colours and gilt with a band of 'karako' among furniture on a ground of 4 birds among bamboo, 7in (18cm).
£750-1,000 *CSK*

A pair of Chinese yellow ground Cong-shaped vases, painted in blue, green and aubergine and modelled in relief on each side with 8 trigrams, 9½in (24cm), wood stands.
£200-250 *CSK*

A 'famille rose' garniture, restoration to 2 cover rims, the necks of the vases and the rim of one beaker, early Qianlong, 6½ and 7in (16 and 18cm).
£2,200-2,700   *CSK*

A Chinese underglaze blue and copper red decorated vase, with angled shoulder and flared neck with pierced handles, Qianlong, 19in (48cm).
£1,500-2,000   *CSK*

A pair of Kutani vases, each decorated with a continuous landscape with figures and buildings, Meiji period, 18in (46cm).
£4,000-4,500   *N*

A Chinese monochrome vase, with incised decoration, mid-19thC, 9in (23cm).
£180-220   *Wai*

A pair of important documentary Yixing vases, with superb calligraphy, signed and dated 1926, 12in (31cm).
£600-800   *Wai*

A pair of crackled celadon glazed pear-shaped vases, ormolu mounted as lamps, 24in (61cm) overall.
£2,000-2,500   *CSK*

A Fukagawa vase, decorated in various coloured enamels and gilt on underglaze blue and brown, signed in underglaze blue 'Dai Nihon Arita-cho Fukagawa sei', late 19thC, 15in (38cm).
£3,000-3,500   *C*

A Chinese blue and white garniture, comprising: 3 slender baluster vases and domed covers and a pair of gu-shaped beaker vases, small restorations to cover rims and one beaker rim, small hairline to one rim, Kangxi, 9½ and 11½in (24 and 29cm).
£5,000-6,000   *CSK*

Miscellaneous

A 'famille rose' shell-shaped cup stand, painted with sprays of flowers on the moulded dish, below a pierced holder, rim chips, Qianlong, 9in (23cm) wide.
£500-600 *CSK*

A pair of 'famille rose' Sèvres-style ice pails, each decorated with flowersprays below a floral garland, divided by gilt shell-shaped handles, chipped, one restored, Qianlong, 10in (25cm) wide.
£2,500-3,000 *C*

Two 'blanc de chine' joss stick holders, modelled as seated Buddhistic lions with brocade balls, one holder restored, 18thC, 10½in (26cm).
£650-750 *CSK*

A Chinese green glazed brush rest, modelled as a five-peak group of craggy rocks, one peak repaired, 18thC, 6in (16cm) wide, wood stand.
£350-450 *CSK*

A Chinese underglaze blue and iron red decorated compressed brush washer, painted with scrolling lotus below a band of trailing foliage and above stylised linked leaves near the foot, Qianlong, 4in (9cm).
£1,500-2,000 *CSK*

An Imari spitoon, painted in iron red, underglaze blue and gilt with pine branches and flowering shrubs, the globular body with a flowerspray on each side, c1700, 7in (17.5cm) diam.
£800-1,000 *CSK*

A 'famille rose' brush pot, painted around the exterior in bright enamels, the base and interior glazed turquoise and the rim gilded, seal mark and period of Jiaqing, 5½in (12.5cm).
£2,000-2,500 *S*

A Canton 'famille rose' bough pot and a cover, with 2 gilt rope-twist handles, all reserved on a relief-decorated squirrel and vine ground, 19thC, 8½in (21.5cm).
£1,700-2,000 *C*

GLASS – PRICE TRENDS

Unlike most areas of the antiques field where a general depression exists, and where some salerooms are either shedding staff or closing down, glass has held its own and has advanced in varying degrees in many specialisations. The reason for this bucking of the trend is probably because of the general shortage on the market, an increasing interest and the often expressed statement that glass has for a long time been under-valued.

There is little point in quoting increased prices for particular glasses because in the following pages readers can compare for themselves the broad spread of prices obtained. Having said that, I give some examples of English and Continental glass that is either of interest, not in the limelight, or is not easy to obtain because of rarity and/or high price.

For instance, at a well publicised Hampshire house sale there was a broad spread of good glass and high prices were obtained from the large number of dealers and collectors present. Some good cut glass,

always difficult to find, remains in my mind; £2,200 for a pair of 'Irish' oval turnover bowls (5¾in), c1800, and £1,320 each for two larger similar bowls, £440 for a good Irish cut cream jug and £1,760 for a pair of cut 'honey jars' (comports with covers), c1800.

Of lesser value, but not of lesser interest, a large collection of 19thC coloured hyacinth bulb glasses which made about £25-35 each, and a large collection of 19/20thC witches' balls, sold in lots of five or six, which made over £100 each (a very good price).

Back to 18thC drinking glasses, Beilbys go 'marching on' and a Beilby in pristine condition with the usual enamelled fruiting vine can now easily fetch over £1,000, whereas damaged (chipped) or restored examples can still be had for £600 upwards. The moral is obvious and any 18thC decanter with good engraving, particularly those with the beverage engraved within a cartouche of scroll, will easily fetch over £500.

A large and varied collection, including about 60 glasses, tumblers, beakers and decanters

came onto the market late last year, instead of going into a museum as had been hoped. However, looking back at what I paid for rummers and decanters in 1981, the prices realised for similar examples in this sale showed no, or very small, increases in what I paid then. For example, two dram firing glasses with opaque twist stems with white enamelled symbols (often mistakenly attributed to the Beilby workshop) made £1,540 and £1,100 compared with £990 I paid for a plain stem example in a London saleroom in 1981.

In conclusion, although glass is in a rising market, which I think will continue while so little is available, prices can be unpredictable. I have always counselled that it is better to save one's money and buy one good example instead of two or three mediocre items, and if one sees a very good specimen that is needed to fill a particular gap in one's collection, then forget about price trends, guides and saleroom estimates and buy it, as in later years invariably one will not be disappointed with the purchase.

R. G. Thomas (January 1991)

Beakers

An engraved beaker, monogrammed CW, c1810, 3½in (9.4cm) high.
£80-120   *Som*

A South Netherlands beaker, the lower part of the cylindrical body moulded with 'nipt diamond waies' and with kick-in base, on 3 flattened bun feet, crack to base, 17thC, 5½in (14.5cm) high.
£800-1,200   *C*

A Venetian latticinio beaker in vetro a reticello, supported on 3 bun feet, early 18thC, 4in (10cm) high.
£3,500-4,500   *C*

Bottles

A set of 3 blue cruet bottles, with gilt labels 'Soy', 'Ketchup' and 'Kyan', in a leather covered iron stand, c1800.
£700-900   *Som*

A 'Façon de Venise' beaker, the lower part applied with 2 rows of small curled bosses enriched with gilding beneath a milled band similarly enriched, the conical foot with applied trailed ornament, perhaps Italian or Spanish, early 17thC, 6½in (15.5cm) high.
£2,000-2,500   *C*

A pair of barrel shaped spirit bottles with flute cutting and bands of diamonds, and cut ball stoppers, c1820, 6½in (17cm) high.
£170-200   *Som*

A novelty duck amber glass sauce bottle, with silver head spout, with hinged cover, set glass eyes, by Akers & Co., Birmingham, c1919, 6½in (16cm).
£400-450 *WW*

Three square spirit bottles with vertically fluted bodies and cut ball shaped stoppers, in a silver plated trefoil frame, c1820, 7in (18cm) high.
£450-550 *Som*

An enamelled bottle and stopper, inscribed in white 'Betty Hodgon AP 1767' within a C-scroll and 'feuilles-de-choux' cartouche, with teared flattened knob stopper, slightly damaged, perhaps Scottish, 7½in (18.5cm) high.
£600-800 *C*

An 'onion' olive green tint serving bottle with kick-in base, the applied scroll handle with pincered thumbpiece, c1725, 6½in (16.5cm) high.
£850-1,000 *C*

A set of 3 blue club shape cruet bottles, with gilt labels and gilt lozenge stoppers, c1800, 4in (10cm) high.
£550-650 *Som*

Bowls

A fruit bowl with turned over rim, diamond, serrated and geometric cut body, on a knopped stem and lemon squeezer foot, c1800, 8in (20cm) high, 10½in (27cm) diam.
£1,500-2,000 *Som*

A Venetian enamelled deep bowl with everted folded rim, gilt with a wide band of scale ornament embellished with enamelled dots in white, iron red, green and blue, with upturned folded blue rim, slight damage to rim, c1500, 9½in (24cm) diam.
£3,000-5,000 *C*

A Venetian footed bowl, the body with gadrooned underside and with 2 applied blue filigree threads to the folded rim, the spreading vertically ribbed foot with an upturned folded blue rim, 16thC, 10½in (27cm) diam.
£1,700-2,200 *C*

A Venetian enamelled bowl, with everted folded rim and gadrooned lower part, decorated with a gilt band embellished with blue dots and edged with pink and white dots above an applied trailed blue thread, the kick-in base with an applied footring, mid-16thC, 6in (14.5cm) diam.
£2,000-2,500 *C*

A Venetian diamond engraved armorial tazza, with a coat-of-arms and a circle of turquoise chain ornament between milled bands, the waisted spreading foot applied with a trailed collar and folded rim, c1600, 13in (33.5cm) diam.
£8,500-9,000 *C*

The arms are those of the Vangelisti family of Verona.

A tazza, the flat platform on a stem with moulded Silesian decoration on domed folded foot, c1750, 10in (25cm) diam. **£250-350** *Som*

Decanters

A Venetian tazza, the tray with upturned rim decoration on the underside with applied turquoise chain ornament between clear milled bands, supported on a waisted spreading stem with a trailed collar and folded foot, early 17thC, 11in (27.5cm) diam.
£1,500-2,000   *C*

A pair of Webb rock crystal shallow dishes, engraved by W. Fritsche in an intaglio technique with swags of fruit including pineapples and pears encircling oval bosses enclosed within berried foliage, one signed, c1890, 6½in (15.5cm) diam. **£1,000-1,500**   *C*

A tapered spirit decanter with fluted base and facet cut neck, lunar cut lozenge stopper, c1790, 8in (20cm) high.
£170-220   *Som*

A tapered spirit decanter with fluted base and looped band of engraved stars, printies and lunar, cut lozenge stopper, c1780, 8½in (21cm).
£200-250   *Som*

An engraved ale decanter, the reverse inscribed Mathew Tankey Harble Down Kent, c1775, the inscription perhaps later, 10½in (26.5cm) high.
£400-500   *C*

A pair of clear spirit decanters with a gilt band of fruiting vine and labelled 'Brandy' and 'Rum', with gilt lozenge stoppers, c1790, 8in (20cm) high.
£420-450   *Som*

A pair of glass decanters and stoppers, each painted in gold with an encircling band of scrolling foliage above a flute cut base, the shoulder cut with a diamond and fan design below a faceted triple ring neck, slight damage to one stopper, 19thC, 9½in (24.5cm).
£200-250   *Bea*

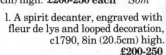

Four blue decanters with gilt cartouches and gilt lozenge stoppers, c1800, 7 to 7½in (18 to 19.5cm) high. **£200-250 each**   *Som*

A Cork mallet shaped engraved glass decanter and a stopper, with three applied rings to the neck, the engraved shoulders above a fluted body, impressed mark, c1810, 10½in (26cm) high.
£600-700   *CSK*

l. A spirit decanter, engraved with fleur de lys and looped decoration, c1790, 8in (20.5cm) high.
£200-250

r. A decanter with cut star and looped decoration, lunar cut stopper, c1780, 9½in (24cm) high.
£420-450   *Som*

l. An ovoid decanter with flute cut base and shoulder, three plain neck rings and with target stopper, c1810, 8in (20cm) high.
£170-220
c. A cylindrical spirit decanter with flute, prism and diamond cutting and prism cut neck, with mushroom stopper, c1825, 7½in (19cm) high.
£80-120
r. An ovoid decanter with cut neck rings and mushroom stopper, c1820, 9in (22.5cm) high.
£170-200 *Som*

l. & r. A pair of blue spirit decanters with three neck rings and plain lozenge stoppers, c1800, 8in (19.5cm) high.
£550-600
c. A blue spirit bottle with everted rim, c1820, 9½in (24cm) high.
£150-220 *Som*

Two 'Bristol' blue decanters with gilt labels for 'Hollands', and gilt stoppers, c1790, 7in (18cm) high.
£200-250 each *Som*

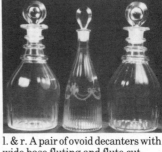

l. & r. A pair of plain ovoid spirit decanters with three bladed neck rings and target stoppers, c1810, 7in (18cm) high.
£240-300
c. An ovoid spirit decanter with flute cut tapered body, spiral neck ring and diamond cut, with lozenge stopper, c1800, 7½in (19cm) high.
£180-240 *Som*

l. An ovoid spirit decanter with three cut neck rings and mushroom stopper, c1810, 7in (18cm) high.
£120-150
r. An ovoid decanter with three plain neck rings and target stopper, c1810, 8½in (21.5cm) high.
£200-250 *Som*

l. A flute cut ovoid decanter with annulated neck rings, and target stopper, c1810, 9in (23cm) high. **£150-250**
r. A straight sided decanter with plain neck rings and cut mushroom stopper, c1810, 8½in (21cm) high.
£150-200 *Som*

l. & r. A pair of ovoid decanters with wide base fluting and flute cut necks, with target stoppers, c1810, 8½in (21cm) high.
£550-650
c. A tapered decanter engraved with looped ribbon, bows and Prince of Wales' feathers, flute cut base and neck, lozenge stopper, c1780, 8in (20cm) high.
£150-220 *Som*

l. An ovoid decanter with flute cut base and neck, and cut mushroom stopper, c1810, 8in (20cm) high.
£120-160
c. A spirit decanter with a band of small cut diamonds, c1810, 7½in (19cm) high.
£120-160
r. An ovoid spirit decanter with flute cut neck and base, cut mushroom stopper, c1810, 7in (18cm) high.
£80-120 *Som*

l. & r. A pair of round spirit decanters, with base flute cutting and a band of diamonds, prism cut necks and cut mushroom stoppers, c1815, 6½in (16.5cm) high.
£250-320
c. A barrel shaped spirit decanter with moulded prism bands, pouring neck and cut ball stopper, c1825, 6in (15.5cm) high.
£80-220 *Som*

An Irish decanter, the Prussian shaped body with base fluting, engraved with stars and cut vesical pattern with two annulated neck rings and moulded target stopper, c1815, 8½in (21.5cm) high.
£500-550 *Som*

A pair of Prussian shaped decanters, with flute cut bases and a band of small diamonds, annulated neck rings and target stoppers, with monogram 'E.R.R.', c1820.
£550-650 *Som*

l. A spirit decanter with cut mushroom stopper, c1825, 7½in (19cm) high.
£80-120
c. A decanter, with overall small diamond and prism cutting, three diamond cut neck rings, c1825, 9in (22cm) high.
£170-220
r. A spirit decanter with 2 cut and one annulated neck rings, c1825, 7½in (19cm) high.
£80-120 *Som*

A decanter cut with small diamonds and prisms, three cut neck rings and cut mushroom stopper, c1820, 9in (22cm) high.
£200-250 *Som*

l. A decanter with band of broad fluting at base and band of strawberry cut diamonds, two annulated neck rings, and cut mushroom stopper, c1825, 9in (22.5cm) high.
£150-220
r. A cut decanter with three neck rings, c1825, 7in (18cm) high.
£150-220 *Som*

l. An ovoid spirit decanter with bands of flute, strawberry cutting and alternate panels of small diamonds, cut mushroom stopper, c1825, 7in (17cm) high.
£100-150
r. A barrel shaped spirit decanter with flute and diamond cutting, annulated neck ring and cut mushroom stopper, c1820, 6½in (16cm) high.
£60-100 *Som*

A pair of ovoid shaped decanters, with flute bodies and 3 neck rings, cut mushroom stoppers, c1825, 8½in (21.5cm) high.
£550-650 *Som*

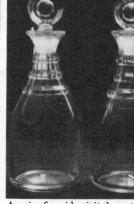

A pair of ovoid spirit decanters with flute cut necks and cut neck rings, with target stoppers, c1820, 7½in (19cm) high.
£300-350 *Som*

l. A plain ovoid decanter with flute cut base and neck, three cut neck rings and lozenge stopper, c1810, 9in (22.5cm) high.
£180-220
r. A flute and diamond cut decanter with two cut and one plain neck ring, cut mushroom stopper, c1810, 8in (20.5cm) high.
£180-220 *Som*

A pair of cut oviform decanters with bull's-eye stoppers, with 3 applied rings to the necks, faceted shoulders with a band of cross-hatch diamonds, the lower parts faceted, slight damage, c1825, 10in (25cm) high.
£250-350 *CSK*

l. An early Victorian flute cut decanter with egg-and-tulip engraving, crest on body and stopper, probably French, c1830, 10in (25cm) high.
£180-250
c. A 'Nelson' type decanter with flute cut body, single annulated neck ring and cut mushroom stopper, c1840, 8½in (22cm) high.
£80-120
r. A flute cut decanter with cut neck rings and cut mushroom stopper, c1845, 9½in (24cm) high.
£70-100 *Som*

A pair of cut decanters, the bodies cut with alternate panels of pillar moulding and small diamonds, with 3 neck rings and diamond cut ovoid stoppers, c1825, 8½in (21cm) high.
£600-700 *Som*

A pair of plain glass spirit decanters, overlaid with silver and coloured stones, with faceted stoppers, 9in (23cm) high.
£100-150 *PCh*

A pair of carafes, with prism flute and diamond cutting, prism cut necks, c1830, 9in (22cm) high.
£450-550 *Som*

A decanter with flute cut base, three annulated neck rings and cut mushroom stopper, c1820, 9in (23cm) high.
£200-300 *Som*

l. & r. A pair of Prussian shaped spirit decanters, with broad cut flutes and 3 neck rings, target stoppers, c1830, 7in (18cm) high.
£200-300
c. A flute cut spirit decanter with target stopper, c1810, 7½in (19cm) high.
£80-100 *Som*

l. A pair of flute and diamond cut decanters, with cut neck rings and flat topped mushroom stoppers, c1830, 9in (22cm) high.
£450-550
r. A pair of decanters with ovoid bodies, flute, diamond and prism cutting, cut mushroom stoppers, c1830, 7½in (19cm) high.
£600-700 *Som*

l. & r. A pair of square spirit decanters, with prism and strawberry diamond cutting, cut ball stoppers, c1825, 7in (17cm) high.
£200-300
c. A pair of round spirit decanters, with flute and diamond cutting, annulated neck rings, cut mushroom stoppers, c1820, 7in (17cm) high.
£250-320 *Som*

l. A cylindrical shaped decanter with flute and diamond cutting, diamond cut neck rings and cut mushroom stopper, c1825, 9in (23cm) high.
£180-220
c. A plain ovoid decanter with flute cut base and shoulder, plain neck rings, engraved with the initials 'MG', target stopper, c1810, 9in (22.5cm) high.
£200-250
r. A decanter with plain neck rings, c1825, 9in (23cm) high.
£180-220 *Som*

A pair of cut glass ship's decanters, with cut triple neck rings and mushroom stoppers, c1880, 9½in (24cm) high.
£450-500 *BAL*

A set of 3 spirit decanters with prism, small diamond and printy cutting, 2 neck rings and cut mushroom stoppers, c1825, 8in (19.5cm) high.
£450-550 *Som*

A set of 4 cut glass cordial decanters without stoppers, with knopped and faceted necks above sloping faceted shoulders, the sides with a central engraved medallion bearing the titles 'Shrub', 'Mint', 'Raspberry' and 'Lovage' respectively, within an engraved grapevine garland, on star cut bases, 19thC, 11in (28cm) high.
£400-500 *Bon*

Drinking Glasses

A set of 10 dwarf ale glasses, with conical bowls wrythen moulded at their bases, on plain conical feet, c1810, 5in (13cm).
£450-550
A tazza with hollow Silesian stem, domed folded foot, c1760, 8½in (21cm) diam.
£250-300 *Som*

An ale glass, with engraved deep funnel bowl, on a stem with a double series opaque twist stem, plain conical foot, c1760, 8in (19.5cm).
£500-550 *Som*

A slender ale glass, the trumpet bowl engraved with a Jacobite rose and bud, the reverse with hops and barley, on a drawn stem with air twist cable on folded conical foot, c1750, 8in (19.5cm).
£1,800-2,200 *Som*

GLASS

DRINKING GLASSES

l. A dwarf ale glass, with engraved conical bowl on an unusual stem and plain conical foot, c1790, 6in (15cm).
£40-60
c. A fluted wine glass, on a drawn stem with centre knop and plain conical foot, c1830, 5in (13cm).
£20-50
r. A pair of Wellington flutes, the conical bowls flute cut at the bases, collared and bladed knop stems and plain feet, c1825, 7in (17cm).
£60-100 *Som*

An unusual ale glass, the trumpet bowl engraved with fruiting vine, on a plain drawn stem with air tear, folded conical foot, c1750, 7½in (18.5cm).
£350-450 *Som*

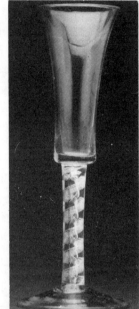

l. A dwarf ale glass, engraved with hops and barley on plain drawn stem and folded conical foot, c1790, 6in (15cm) high.
£40-60
r. A dwarf ale glass, the plain conical bowl on a short knopped stem and folded conical foot, c1790, 5in (13cm) high.
£30-50 *Som*

An ale flute, with flared waisted bowl on air twist stem enclosing central spiral column, 18thC, 8½in (21cm).
£500-550 *RBB*

An ale glass, with round funnel bowl set on a double series opaque twist stem and plain conical foot, 7in (17cm).
£130-180 *Bea*

Two dwarf ale glasses, with engraved conical bowls on plain drawn stems with folded conical feet, 5½ and 6in (14 and 15cm).
£50-80 each *Som*

A set of 4 dwarf ale glasses, with engraved conical bowls on plain conical feet below plain drawn stems, 6in (15cm).
£50-80 each *Som*

A composite stemmed wine flute of drawn form with a slender bell bowl, the stem filled with air-twist spirals and set into a beaded inverted baluster knop, on a domed foot, c1750, 8½in (21cm).
£850-950 *C*

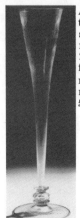

A 'Façon de Venise' flute, the slender funnel bowl supported on a flattened ribbed knop set between 2 mereses, on a conical foot with thinly folded rim, The Netherlands, mid-17thC, 11in (28cm).
£2,000-3,000 *C*

A dwarf ale glass, the conical bowl on a stem with a collar and bladed knop, plain conical foot, c1825, 6in (14.5cm).
£30-60 *Som*

209

A champagne flute, with honeycomb moulded lower part supported on a shoulder knopped stem above a conical foot, mid-18thC, 8in (20cm).
£200-250 *C*

A baluster goblet, the stem with an angular knop above a true baluster section, on a conical foot, c1730, 8½in (21.5cm).
£700-900 *C*

A cordial glass, with engraved funnel bowl on a double series air-twist stem and plain conical foot, c1745, 7in (17cm).
£500-550 *Som*

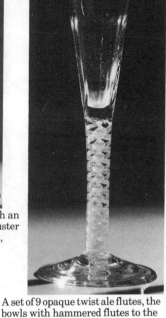

A set of 9 opaque twist ale flutes, the bowls with hammered flutes to the lower parts, the stems with gauze corkscrew cores within ten-ply spirals, on conical feet, 4 with chips, c1765, 7in (17cm).
£1,500-2,000 *C*

A Williamite opaque twist cordial glass, the funnel bowl inscribed 'Our Glorious & Immortal King William III', the stem with two entwined corkscrew spirals, on a conical foot, c1770, 7in (17cm).
£1,200-1,500 *C*

A set of 10 opaque twist ale flutes, the funnel bowls with hammered flutes to the lower parts, the stems with gauze corkscrew cores entwined by ten-ply spirals, on conical feet, 4 with chips, c1765, 7in (18cm).
£1,700-2,000 *C*

A Williamite cordial glass, the funnel bowl inscribed below the rim 'The glorious memory of King Will III', above a band of foliate ornament, supported on a plain stem above a domed foot, small chip to footrim, c1750, 7in (17cm).
£1,500-2,000 *C*

A cordial glass, the round funnel bowl on a double series opaque twist stem and plain conical foot, c1760, 6½in (16.5cm).
£450-550 *Som*

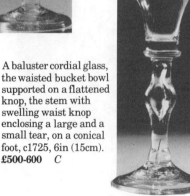

A baluster cordial glass, the waisted bucket bowl supported on a flattened knop, the stem with swelling waist knop enclosing a large and a small tear, on a conical foot, c1725, 6in (15cm).
£500-600 *C*

A baluster goblet, supported on a ball knop terminating in a basal knop and enclosing 2 small tears, on a folded conical foot, c1700, 6½in (16cm).
£1,000-1,300 *C*

A goblet with trumpet bowl, on a drawn plain stem with small air tear, plain conical foot, c1745, 9in (22cm).
£200-300   *Som*

A pair of goblets, with trumpet bowls and drawn plain stems with air tears, folded conical feet, c1730.
£550-650   *Som*

A cordial glass with engraved ogee bowl, on a stem with a double series opaque twist stem, and plain conical foot, c1760, 5½in (14cm).
£450-550   *Som*

GLASS APPENDIX

Drinking glasses

STEM FORMATIONS

 ball knop

 collar

 annular knop

 annulated knop

 true baluster

 swelling knop

 flattened knop

 cushioned knop

 inverted baluster

 the knop proper

 cone knop

 angular knop

 acorn knop

 drop knop

 cylinder knop

 wide angular knop

 shoulder knop

 mushroom knop

 true baluster ridged

BOWL FORMS

 lipped bucket

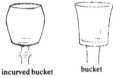 incurved bucket

bucket

 conical

bell, with solid base

waisted, with solid base

waisted, with solid base

round funnel

 cup

 waisted ogee

 waisted bucket

 hexagonal

 thistle

 trumpet

 waisted

 bell

 lipped

 pan-topped

 bucket-topped

 pointed

 ogee

 trumpet

 waisted

 saucer-topped

FOOT FORMS

 folded

 firing

 solid conical

 plain conical

 pedestal

 stepped square foot

 domed square foot

 flanged

 terrace-domed solid square foot

 domed and folded

211

A champagne or ale glass, the very deep bowl fluted at base on double series opaque twist stem and plain conical foot, c1760, 10in (25cm).
£350-450 *Som*

A pair of Richardson's 'Waterlily' goblets, painted with a continuous frieze of flowering waterlilies, marked Richardson's Vitrified and with registry mark for 1848, 6½in (16.5cm).
£1,200-1,600 *C*

A baluster goblet, the funnel bowl supported on an inverted baluster stem above a folded conical foot, c1705, 7in (17cm).
£600-650 *C*

An engraved air-twist goblet of Jacobite significance, with double knopped stem filled with spiral threads, on a domed foot, c1750, 8in (20cm).
£700-800 *C*

A light baluster armorial goblet, in the manner of Jacob Sang, the funnel bowl engraved with the crowned arms of Willem V of Orange and Nassau within the Garter, above the motto 'Je Maintiendrai', on an angular knop, above a beaded inverted baluster stem and base knop, on a domed conical foot, c1760, 8in (19.5cm).
£600-800 *CAm*

A Nuremburg engraved goblet, attributed to Herman Schwinger, supported on hollow cushion and inverted baluster knops divided by plain sections and sets of mereses, base of stem and foot damaged, c1680, 13in (33cm).
£3,500-4,000 *C*

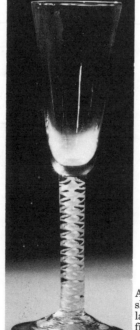

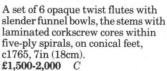

A cordial glass, with drawn trumpet bowl and multiple series air-twist stem, small chip to foot rim, 18thC, 7in (17cm) high.
£350-450 *RBB*

A goblet, with engraved bowl, the air-twist stem with swelling waist knop and filled with spiral threads, on a conical foot, c1750, 9in (22cm).
£500-600 *C*

A set of 6 opaque twist flutes with slender funnel bowls, the stems with laminated corkscrew cores within five-ply spirals, on conical feet, c1765, 7in (18cm).
£1,500-2,000 *C*

A large glass wheel engraved goblet, on inverted baluster stem and raised foot, 10½in (26cm).
£600-1,000 *P*

A large goblet, the bucket bowl engraved with the Sunderland Bridge and inscription under, hollow ball stem and plain conical foot, c1825, 9½in (24cm).
£550-650 *Som*

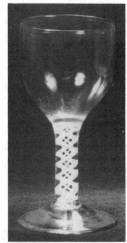

A goblet, with ogee bowl on a double series opaque twist stem and plain conical foot, c1760, 6½in (16cm).
£320-370 *Som*

A Newcastle type goblet, the funnel bowl engraved with the arms of the Province of Zeeland, on a stem with air beaded inverted baluster knop, base knop and plain conical foot, c1750, 7½in (18cm).
£2,000-2,500 *Som*

The engraving is important to the price of this goblet.

A tall 'Façon de Venise' goblet, with a shallow flared bowl, the stem formed as 3 hollow pear shaped knops divided by mereses and short plain sections, on a folded conical foot, Liège, 17thC, 10in (25cm).
£3,500-4,000 *C*

A Williamite double portrait goblet, engraved with a bust portrait of King William III and Queen Mary, inscribed above 'The glorious & immortal memory of King William III & His Queen Mary', the stem with a tear above a folded conical foot, some restoration, late 18thC, 7½in (18.5cm).
£1,800-2,200 *C*

A composite stemmed goblet, engraved by Jacob Sang, the reverse inscribed 'de milde goedheyd van den heer, daal, op dees, blijde iaar dahg neer en schenke, uw, soveel heyl en zeegan als ooyt van imand is verkreegen', supported on a beaded dumb-bell section above an inverted baluster stem with base knop, the conical foot inscribed, Amsterdam, 1760, 7in (18cm).
£8,000-8,500 *CAm*

Two ovoid bowl rummers, with collars, square domed lemon squeezer feet, c1800, 5in (13cm).
£65-85 each *Som*

A baluster goblet, with straight sided funnel bowl, supported on an inverted baluster stem enclosing a large tear and basal knop, on a folded conical foot, c1700, 8in (20cm).
£850-950 *C*

A Venetian goblet, the funnel bowl moulded with vertical ribs and supported on a merese over a barley sugar twist stem and conical foot, early 17thC, 8in (20cm).
£2,500-3,000 *C*

A Sunderland Bridge rummer with engraved bucket bowl, on bladed knopped stem and plain conical foot, c1820, 5½in (14cm).
£350-450 *Som*

A Sunderland rummer, with engraved bowl, inscribed 'Sunderland Bridge' in diamond point with cut tasselled drapery below, the reverse inscribed 'C.F. Barber Golden Inn Boston' and with a rampant lion, flanked by sprays of rose, thistle and shamrock, on a short knopped stem and circular foot, c1825, 9in (22cm).
£750-800 *C*

l. A round funnel bowl wine glass, engraved with fruiting vine, and plain conical foot, c1750, 6in (15cm).
£200-270
c. A trumpet bowl wine glass, on drawn stem and folded conical foot, c1745, 7½in (19cm).
£150-220
r. A trumpet bowl wine glass, with solid section double knop stem and plain domed foot, c1745.
£270-340 *Som*

A baluster wine glass, the bell bowl supported on a slender inverted baluster stem enclosing a large tear and terminating in a basal knop, on a folded conical foot, c1715, 7in (17cm).
£450-500 *C*

l. & r. A pair of bucket bowl rummers, with flute cutting on bladed knop stems and plain feet, c1825, 5½in (14cm).
£100-150
c. A bucket bowl rummer, c1825, 5in (13cm).
£50-80 *Som*

A pair of wine glasses, with waisted trumpet bowls on stems with multiple spiral air-twists, with central vermicular collars and plain conical feet, c1745, 7in (17cm).
£350-450 each *Som*

Three ovoid rummers, with collars, square domed lemon squeezer feet, c1800, 5 and 5½in (13 and 13.5cm).
£65-85 each *Som*

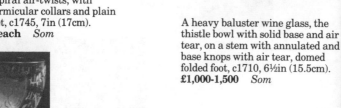

A heavy baluster wine glass, the thistle bowl with solid base and air tear, on a stem with annulated and base knops with air tear, domed folded foot, c1710, 6½in (15.5cm).
£1,000-1,500 *Som*

A Nelson ovoid rummer, the bowl engraved 'Trafalgar may his memory never be forgotten October 21st 1805', with an anchor in a shield, reverse shield with monogram, square lemon squeezer foot, c1805, 5½in (14cm).
£650-700 *Som*

A Bohemian blue overlay cut goblet
and cover with oviform hexagonal
finial, gilding rubbed and foot
chipped, 13in (33cm).
£900-1,200   *CSK*

A small rummer, the flared bucket
bowl inscribed 'Wellington for Ever'
above a naked sword, the reverse
with a bird in flight with a twig in its
beak, early 19thC, 4½in (11cm).
£150-200   *C*

A wine glass, with trumpet bowl on
a drawn stem with multiple spiral
air-twist and plain conical foot,
c1745, 6½in (16.5cm).
£150-250   *Som*

A baluster wine glass, the bell bowl
with a tear to the solid lower part,
supported on an annulated knop
above a plain section enclosing an
elongated tear and basal knop, on a
folded conical foot, c1725, 6in
(15cm).
£375-450   *C*

Two similar ovoid rummers with
capstan stems and plain feet, c1825,
4½ and 5in (12 and 13cm).
£50-70 each   *Som*

A heavy baluster wine glass, the
conical bowl with deep solid section
and air tear, on a stem with an
inverted baluster and base knop,
folded conical foot, c1710, 7in
(17cm).
£1,200-1,500   *Som*

A balustroid wine glass of 'Kit Kat'
type and drawn trumpet shape, the
stem with a slender tear, set on an
inverted baluster section above a
folded conical foot, c1740, 7in
(17cm).
£350-400   *C*

A large Victorian rummer, the
upper part wheel engraved with a
boxing scene, the lower part
diamond cut, 7in (17cm).
£170-200   *P*

A Jacobite wine glass, the trumpet
bowl engraved with the Jacobite
rose, 2 buds, oak leaf and star, a
drawn multiple spiral air-twist
stem and folded conical foot, c1745,
6in (15cm).
£1,600-2,000   *Som*

A wine glass with bell bowl, on a
stem with an inverted baluster and
base knop, folded conical foot, c1715,
6in (15cm).
£350-450   *Som*

A trumpet bowl wine glass, on a
stem with multiple spiral air-twist,
and plain conical foot, c1745, 7½in
(19cm).
£300-400 *Som*

l. A double ogee bowl rummer, with
capstan stem and plain foot, c1830,
5in (12.5cm).
£60-70
c. A rummer with round bowl and
capstan stem, on domed plain foot,
c1810, 5½in (13.5cm).
£65-80
r. A rummer with ovoid bowl,
capstan stem and plain conical foot,
c1810, 5in (13cm).
£65-80 *Som*

A wine glass with the trumpet bowl,
on a drawn stem with multiple
spiral air-twist, folded conical foot,
c1750, 6in (15cm).
£150-250 *Som*

Four small wine glasses, one with
engraved rim, two with engraved
bowls and one plain, 1750-1810.
£30-45 each *Som*

A bobbin knopped wine glass with
an ogee bowl, the stem formed as
8 cushion knops above a domed and
folded foot, mid-18thC, 6½in
(16.5cm).
£700-800 *C*

A wine glass, with ogee bowl on a
stem with angular central knop, on
folded conical foot, c1750, 6in
(15cm).
£200-250 *Som*

A wine glass, with trumpet bowl on
a drawn stem with multiple spiral
air-twist and vermicular collar,
plain conical foot, c1750, 6½in
(16.5cm).
£420-480 *Som*

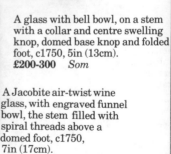

l. A plain stem wine glass, with
trumpet bowl on folded conical foot,
c1750, 5in (13cm).
£150-200
c. A plain stem wine glass on folded
conical foot, c1750, 7½in (18cm).
£150-200
r. A wine glass with round funnel
bowl, rim engraved with a band of
hatched curtain decoration, plain
stem, on plain conical foot, c1750,
5in (13cm).
£150-200 *Som*

A glass with bell bowl, on a stem
with a collar and centre swelling
knop, domed base knop and folded
foot, c1750, 5in (13cm).
£200-300 *Som*

A Jacobite air-twist wine
glass, with engraved funnel
bowl, the stem filled with
spiral threads above a
domed foot, c1750,
7in (17cm).
£900-1,200 *C*

Three air-twist wine glasses:
l. With trumpet bowl on drawn
multiple spiral air-twist stem and
folded conical foot, c1745, 6½in
(16cm).
£200-250
c. With round funnel bowl with
single series air-twist cable stem, on
plain conical foot, c1745, 6in
(15.5cm).
£300-350
r. With bell bowl and multiple spiral
air-twist stem with shoulder knop,
on plain conical foot, c1750, 6in
(15.5cm).
£150-200   *Som*

A 'Newcastle' wine glass, the round
funnel bowl engraved with a band of
cross hatching and stars with a
floral meander below, angular and
air-beaded inverted baluster and
base knops, on plain conical foot,
c1750, 7½in (18cm).
£1,000-1,500   *Som*

A wine glass, the round funnel bowl
on a stem with double series
air-twist, plain conical foot, c1750,
6in (15cm).
£250-320   *Som*

A Williamite plain stemmed wine
glass of drawn shape, the bell bowl
inscribed 'The Glorious Memory of
King William III', on a conical foot,
mid-18thC, 6½in (16cm).
£800-1,200   *C*

A pair of wine glasses, with round
funnel bowls on stems with shoulder
cushion knop and multiple spiral
air-twist stems, and plain conical
feet, c1750, 7in (18cm).
£500-700   *Som*

A wine glass, the round funnel bowl
on a stem with multiple spiral
air-twist, on plain conical foot,
c1750, 7in (18cm).
£250-350   *Som*

A wine glass, the bowl on a stem
with multiple spiral air-twist with
swelling knop, plain conical foot,
c1750, 6in (15.5cm).
£500-550   *Som*

A wine glass, the
trumpet bowl on a
drawn plain stem,
plain conical foot,
c1750, 6in (15.5cm).
£160-210   *Som*

A Jacobite air-twist wine glass of
drawn trumpet shape, with
engraved bowl, c1750, 6½in (16cm).
£1,000-1,500   *C*

l. A wine glass, the moulded
round funnel bowl on a stem with a
double series opaque twist, plain
conical foot, c1750, 6in (15cm).
£200-240
r. A cordial glass, the small round
funnel bowl on a stem with a double
series opaque twist, plain conical
foot, c1760, 6in (15cm).
£450-500   *Som*

l. A plain stem wine glass, the trumpet bowl with air tear at base, on folded conical foot, c1750, 6in (14.5cm).
£120-160
c. A wine glass, with engraved ogee bowl, plain stem, on folded conical foot, c1750, 5½in (14cm).
£160-200
r. A wine glass, the round funnel bowl on plain stem with folded conical foot, c1750, 5½in (14cm).
£100-140 *Som*

JACOBITE GLASSES
Jacobite glasses, which began to be engraved c1730, have commanded much attention and popularity among collectors. The dating and the significance of the various motifs on these glasses is still the subject of debate and disagreement, but considered opinion is that few of them can be dated to before Culloden in 1746. Jacobite engraved glasses continued to be produced through the various stem formations (plain, air-twist, opaque and faceted) until the death of Prince Charles Edward Stuart in 1788. Countless numbers of old glasses have been later engraved. There were also the counter Jacobite glasses supporting the Loyalists but these are considerably fewer in number.

Three wine glasses with multiple spiral air-twist stems, on plain conical feet:
l. With bell bowl and shoulder knop, c1750, 6½in (16cm).
£170-200
c. With trumpet bowl and plain stem, c1750, 5½in (14cm).
£180-240
r. With round funnel bowl and shoulder knop, c1750, 6½in (16cm).
£260-300 *Som*

A balustroid wine glass, the bell bowl on a stem with angular knop above a true baluster knop, and plain conical foot, c1745, 7in (18cm).
£500-570 *Som*

A wine glass, the ogee bowl engraved with a hatched rose and floral spray, double series opaque twist stem, on plain conical foot, c1760, 6in (15cm).
£150-220 *Som*

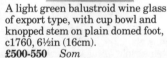

A light green balustroid wine glass of export type, with cup bowl and knopped stem on plain domed foot, c1760, 6½in (16cm).
£500-550 *Som*

A wine glass, the ovoid body engraved with a band of hatched decoration and rosebud spray, single series opaque twist, on plain conical foot, c1760, 5½in (13cm).
£150-250 *Som*

Three opaque twist wine glasses with double series twists and plain conical feet, c1760, 5½ to 6in (14.5 to 15.5cm).
£160-200 each *Som*

A wine glass, the trumpet bowl with honeycomb moulded, incised twist stem, on plain conical foot, c1750, 6½in (16cm).
£350-450 *Som*

A Jacobite light baluster wine glass, with engraved bowl, on conical foot, c1750, 6½in (16cm).
£1,500-2,000 *C*

l. A 'Newcastle' wine glass, the trumpet bowl with air beaded, knopped stem, on folded conical foot, c1750, 7½in (18cm).
£800-850
c. A cordial glass, the moulded round funnel bowl on a double series opaque twist stem, on plain conical foot, c1760, 6½in (17cm).
£800-850
r. A wine glass, the trumpet bowl on a drawn plain stem, with air tear, on plain conical foot, c1750, 6½in (16cm).
£120-170 *Som*

A Jacobite air-twist wine glass, with engraved bowl, the stem with a swelling waist knop and filled with spiral threads, on a conical foot, c1750, 6in (15cm).
£500-600 *C*

An engraved quadruple knopped opaque twist wine glass, the bell bowl with a border of beehives and bees, the stem with a gauze core entwined by 2 spiral threads, on a conical foot, c1765, 7in (17cm).
£800-900 *C*

A Williamite wine glass of drawn shape, the bell bowl engraved and inscribed 'The Glorious Memory of King William III', the rim with hatched ornament, the plain stem enclosing an elongated tear and on a conical foot, mid-18thC, 7in (17cm).
£1,000-1,400 *C*

A Jacobite wine glass, the round funnel bowl engraved with rose and a bud, on a multiple spiral air-twist stem, on plain conical foot, c1750, 6½in (16cm).
£750-850 *Som*

A Lynn wine glass, the round funnel bowl with horizontally ribbed bands, with a double series opaque twist stem, on plain conical foot, c1760, 6in (15cm).
£750-820 *Som*

A wine glass, the ovoid bowl engraved with stars and printies on a drawn stem, diamond facet cut with centre knop and plain conical foot, c1770, 5in (13cm).
£170-200 *Som*

l. A wine glass, with pan top bowl on a stem with a multiple spiral air-twist, on folded conical foot, c1750, 7in (17cm).
£400-460
r. A wine glass, the bell bowl on a drawn stem with multiple spiral air-twist, on plain conical foot, c1750, 7½in (18cm).
£300-400 *Som*

l. A set of 3 green wine glasses, with cup shaped, honeycomb moulded bowls, on facet cut baluster stems, with plain conical feet, c1850, 5½in (13cm).
£70-90 each
r. A set of 4 amber, rib moulded bowl wine glasses, with plain stems, and plain feet, c1840, 5in (12cm).
£50-70 each   *Som*

l. A green wine glass with cup shaped bowl, ball knopped stem and plain conical foot, c1770, 5in (12cm).
£150-250
r. A green wine glass, with conical bowl, ball knopped stem and plain conical foot, c1820, 5½in (13cm).
£50-70   *Som*

A set of 4 unusual emerald green wine glasses, with cup shaped bowls and everted rims, bladed knop stems and plain conical feet, c1830, 4in (10cm).
£350-450   *Som*

A composite stemmed wine glass, the funnel bowl supported on an annulated knop above an opaque twist shoulder knopped stem with a gauze core enclosed within 2 spiral threads, on a conical foot, c1765, 6½in (16cm).
£500-600   *C*

A set of 10 green wine glasses, with bladed knop stems, on plain conical feet, c1830, 5in (13cm).
£550-650   *Som*

A round funnel bowl wine glass, on single series opaque twist stem, on conical foot, 6in (15cm).
£70-100   *CSK*

l. A pair of wines, with bucket bowls, band of engraving, knopped stems and plain feet, c1870, 4½in (11cm).
£25-50
r. A pair of wines, with conical bowls, star and printy engraving, drawn stems and folded conical feet, c1820, 5in (12cm).
£20-50   *Som*

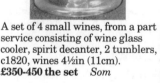

A set of 4 small wines, from a part service consisting of wine glass cooler, spirit decanter, 2 tumblers, c1820, wines 4½in (11cm).
£350-450 the set   *Som*

A wine glass, the ogee bowl engraved with an entwined Jacobite rose and a thistle, set on a double series opaque twist stem and conical foot, 6in (15cm).
£350-450   *Bea*

Four wine glasses, 2 with drawn stems, c1825, 3½ and 4in (9 and 10cm).
£30-50 each   *Som*

A set of 6 green wine glasses, with conical bowls and bladed knop stems, on plain conical feet, c1825, 5½in (13cm).
£220-260 *Som*

l. A pair of wine glasses with engraved bowls, on plain drawn stems, with plain conical feet, c1820, 4in (10cm).
£60-100
r. A pair of wine glasses cut with stars, c1820, 4in (10cm).
£60-100 *Som*

An ogee bowl wine glass with multi-spiral opaque twist stem, on conical foot, chips to foot, 5in (12.5cm).
£120-150 *CSK*

A pair of wine glasses with bell bowls, on multi-spiral opaque twist stems, chips to foot, 5in (12.5cm).
£170-200 *CSK*

A wine glass with bell bowl, on multi-spiral opaque twist stem and conical foot, 6½in (16cm).
£60-80 *CSK*

A round funnel bowl wine glass, on multi-spiral opaque twist stem, and conical foot, 7½in (19cm).
£90-120 *CSK*

A trumpet drawn wine glass, the stem with tear inclusion on domed and folded foot, 6½in (16cm).
£100-120 *CSK*

Three plain stem wine glasses, the trumpet bowls on drawn stems with air tears, c1750.
l. 5½in (14cm). **£120-160**
c. 6½in (16cm). **£120-160**
r. 7in (17cm). **£140-180** *Som*

An armorial opaque twist wine glass, the bowl engraved with a coat-of-arms surmounted by a crest within scroll mantling, on a double series stem and conical foot, chip to footrim, c1765, 6in (15cm).
£200-250 *C*

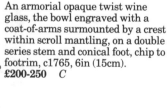

A pair of round funnel bowl wine glasses, on triple knopped stems and conical folded feet, chips to rim, 6½in (16cm).
£200-250 *CSK*

An engraved wine glass with bell bowl, with fruiting vine on a multi-spiral opaque twist stem and conical foot, chips to foot, 6½in (16cm).
£100-130 *CSK*

A wine glass, the ogee bowl set on a double series opaque twist stem and plain conical foot, 5½in (14cm).
£100-150 *Bea*

A pan topped bowl wine glass, with double series opaque twist stem and conical foot, chips to foot, 6in (15cm).
£60-90 *CSK*

A pair of ogee bowl wine glasses, on double series opaque twist stems and spreading feet, chips to foot, 5in (12cm).
£250-300 *CSK*

A panel moulded ogee bowl wine glass, on multi-spiral opaque twist stem and conical foot, 6½in (16cm).
£140-170 *CSK*

An engraved water glass, with engraved bell bowl, on a spreading conical foot with folded rim, c1740, 4½in (11cm).
£240-280 *C*

An engraved water glass of Jacobite significance, the bell bowl engraved with a sunflower and a moth, c1870, 3in (7cm).
£520-580 *C*

A dated, engraved barrel shaped tumbler, one side with a view of Yarmouth Church, named above, the reverse with the initials 'JRP' above the date '1798', and inscribed above and below 'Plenty to a Generous Mind/Success to Farming', the lower part cut with flutes, 5in (12cm).
£900-1,200 *C*

A dated engraved tumbler inscribed 'Mary Moody 1766', within a shaped scrolling foliage cartouche, 4½in (11cm).
£350-400 *C*

Four trumpet drawn wine glasses, on multi air-twist stems and conical feet.
£300-350 *CSK*

A Jacobite wine glass, with bucket bowl engraved with flower and moth, on air-twist stem, with double knop, 6in (15cm).
£420-460 *RBB*

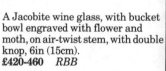

A firing glass, the ovoid bowl fluted at base, on a drawn stem with a conical undersewn foot, c1780, 3½in (9cm).
£130-170 *Som*

Three dram glasses with ogee bowls and plain drawn stems, c1780.
l. 3½in (9cm). **£30-50**
c. With rare undersewn foot, and moulded bowl, 4in (10cm).
£140-170
r. 4in (10cm). **£30-50** *Som*

A crested shipping tumbler, inscribed 'Suc^s to the Bee' beneath a sailing ship, flanked by ears of barley, the reverse with the initials 'RG' beneath a crest with a bird to the left, late 18thC, 5in (13cm).
£350-400   *C*

l. A barrel shaped tumbler with band of hatched decoration, c1800, 4½in (11cm).
£80-100
r. A tapered beaker engraved with band of hatched roses and inscription 'George and Mary Owen 1835', 4in (10cm).
£90-120   *Som*

An engraved cylindrical tumbler decorated with a continuous scene, with facet cut footrim and the base with 'LLH' monogram, c1800, 4½in (11cm).
£400-450   *C*

l. A dwarf ale glass, the conical bowl engraved with hops and barley, plain drawn stem, on conical foot, c1790, 6in (15cm).
£120-150
c. A port glass, with engraved band, plain stem, c1830, 5½in (14cm).
£25-40
r. A wine glass, the ovoid bowl with band of looped star and printy cutting and engraving, on plain conical foot, c1790, 5in (12cm).
£50-80   *Som*

A firing/dram glass, the ogee bowl on a short plain stem and terraced conical foot, c1760, 3½in (9cm).
£130-170   *Som*

A panel moulded ogee bowl wine glass, on double series opaque twist stem and conical foot, chips to foot, 6in (15cm).
£120-170   *CSK*

Jugs

A two-handled baluster mug, with lightly ribbed everted rim and on a circular foot, mid-18thC, 5in (12cm).
£360-400   *C*

A green glass claret jug and stopper, of faceted form with ribbed neck, early 19thC, 11in (28cm).
£350-400   *Bea*

Four Nailsea jugs, with olive green bodies and opaque white marvered splashes, c1810, 4½ to 7½in (11 to 19cm).
£250-500 each   *Som*

A pair of Continental cut glass claret jugs, with bracket handles and domed hinged covers with artichoke finials, the mounts die stamped with rococo flowers and foliage incorporating vacant cartouches, 11½in (29cm).
£900-1,400 *CSK*

A claret jug, the globular body with broad cut fluting, 2 neck rings, and cut spout, applied strap handle similarly cut and mushroom stopper, c1840, 10½in (26.5cm).
£350-400 *Som*

A Georgian ale jug, with engraved hops, barley and monogram, with pinched loop handle, 7in (18cm).
£350-400 *RBB*

Paperweights

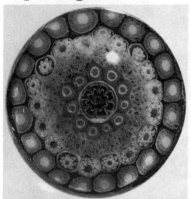

An oviform cut jug, with an applied opaque panel painted in colours within a cartouche of scrolls and foliage in gilding, on an octagonal knopped stem and foot, handle damaged and repaired, gilding rubbed, 13½in (34cm) and a pair of goblets.
£500-550 *CSK*

A Bacchus close concentric millefiori weight, in shades of pink, blue, white and yellow about a central red and white lobed cane and with a circle of green lined hollow crimped tubes at the periphery, mid-19thC, 3½in (8.5cm) diam.
£700-750 *C*

An Islington Glass Co., close concentric millefiori mantel ornament, in shades of pink, white and dark blue, supported on a facet cut knop and fluted inverted baluster stem, above an hexagonal foot, late 19thC, 5½in (14cm) high.
£950-1,200 *C*

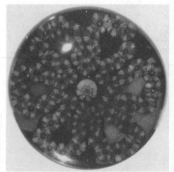

A Clichy blue ground patterned millefiori weight, the central pale blue and white cane enclosed by a hexafoil looped garland of green centred pink and white canes, set on a translucent dark blue ground, mid-19thC, 3in (7.5cm) diam.
£700-800 *C*

A Paul Stankard spray weight, with pink flowers and buds with green leaves and brown stalk, the underside of the spray with a cane inscribed 'S', 1970s, 2½in (7cm) diam.
£450-550 *C*

A Baccarat flower paperweight, with millefiori flowers on a bed of 5 leaves within a border of star and pastry mould canes on an amber ground, cut with 6 side printies, chipped, mid-19thC, 3in (8cm) diam.
£300-400 *CSK*

> **Did you know**
> *MILLER'S Antiques Price Guide builds up year by year to form the most comprehensive photo-reference system available*

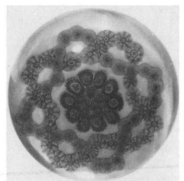

A Clichy 'Sodden Snow' patterned millefiori weight, in pale green, red, blue and pink, on an opaque white ground, mid-19thC, 3in (8cm) diam.
£450-500   *C*

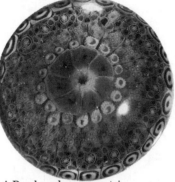

A small clear glass paperweight, enclosing a single pink clematis flower flanked by 2 buds and 5 leaves, with star cut base, probably Baccarat, 2in (4.5cm) diam.
£430-480   *HSS*

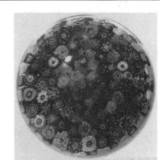

A Clichy close millefiori weight, with pink, green and white staves, slight bruising, mid-19thC, 2½in (6.5cm) diam.
£1,500-2,000   *C*

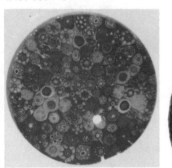

A Clichy close millefiori weight, with pink, dark blue, pale blue, white and green staves, mid-19thC, 3in (7cm) diam.
£600-650   *C*

A Bacchus close concentric millefiori weight, in shades of red, blue, pink, white and pale mauve, mid-19thC, 3½in (8.5cm) diam.
£600-650   *C*

A Clichy swirl weight, the alternate turquoise and white staves radiating from a large red, white and blue cane with a yellow stamen centre, mid-19thC, 3in (8cm) diam.
£700-800   *C*

Vases

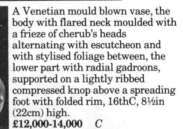

A Venetian mould blown vase, the body with flared neck moulded with a frieze of cherub's heads alternating with escutcheon and with stylised foliage between, the lower part with radial gadroons, supported on a lightly ribbed compressed knop above a spreading foot with folded rim, 16thC, 8½in (22cm) high.
£12,000-14,000   *C*

A Bohemian glass vase, the body painted with cows wading in a stream before a house, enclosed by gilt medallion, the reverse painted with a floral bouquet also enclosed by gilt medallion, interspaced by a white fluted lozenge shaped panel above acanthus leaf lappet, on scrolling gilt ivy leaf and tendril on clear glass, 19thC, 16½in (42cm) high.
£700-1,000   *Bon*

A small opaque white vase, with enamelled floral and bird decoration, London or South Staffordshire, c1765, 5in (12cm) high.
£900-1,200   *Som*

A decalomania vase and cover, transfer printed with religious subjects, and including the Sacred Monogram, the domed cover with birds, butterflies and loose bouquets within a floral band and with knob finial, minor damage, mid-19thC, 21½in (55cm) high.
£700-1,000   *C*

A Federzcichnung style cased air-trap glass vase, with cylinder neck, being clear glass over brown with air-trap decoration, external gilded body decoration, pattern No. on base 9159, c1890, 11in (28cm) high.
£1,700-2,000 *GH*

A Stourbridge three overlay cameo bulbous vase, with tapering cylinder neck, with latticed satin opal over ruby over citrine, c1880, 15½in (39cm) high.
£200-250 *GH*

A pair of blue overlay tulip shaped vases with castellated rims, the Persian style blue panels decorated with scrolls in gilding, on knopped stems and hollow bases, 11in (28cm) high.
£300-400 *CSK*

A pair of Bohemian white overlay green glass lustre vases, decorated with alternate panels of foliage and diamond designs on a ground painted in gold with scrolling foliage, hung with clear glass prism drops, minor chip to foot rim, mid-19thC, 11in (28cm) high.
£800-1,200 *Bea*

Miscellaneous

A Stourbridge glass inkwell and stopper, the base and domed cover decorated with concentric bands of coloured canes, c1850, 6in (15cm) high.
£150-250 *Bea*

A 'Façon de Venise' latticinio two-handled vase, in vetro a retorti, decorated with bands of white gauze cable, the clear scroll handles with lion's mask terminals, Low Countries or Venice, early 17thC, 6in (14.5cm) wide.
£1,200-1,700 *C*

A set of 6 trumpet jelly glasses, with flute moulded bodies and plain conical feet, c1810, 4in (10cm).
£220-260 *Som*

Two trumpet bowl jelly glasses, with vertical ribbing on plain feet, c1780.
£35-50 each *Som*

A sweetmeat, the double ogee bowl with flute cutting over cut with ladder cutting, the knopped stem similarly cut, with domed scallop cut foot and crenellated rim, c1770, 6½in (17cm).
£360-400 *Som*

A sweetmeat glass with double ogee bowl with dentil rim, knopped opaque twist stem on radially moulded foot, c1760, 4in (10cm) high.
£300-350 *RBB*

A pair of bonnet glasses, with diamond cut double ogee bowls, with square domed lemon squeezer feet, c1820, 3½in (9cm).
£80-140 *Som*

A 'coin' tankard, with trailed rim, central trailed band and base gadrooning on hollow conical foot, with applied strap handle, the base containing a silver George II coin, c1757, 6½in (17cm) high.
£550-650 *Som*

A baluster 'coin' tankard and cover, the base set with a George III silver threepence dated 1762, the domed cover with acorn knop finial, some damage, c1765, 7½in (19cm) high.
£460-520 *C*

Scent Bottles

Three oval blue scent bottles with cut decoration.
l. Blue with gilt decoration, c1780, 4½in (11cm).
£450-550
c. Blue with embossed silver mount, c1780, 4½in (11cm).
£250-300
r. Blue with copper gilt mount, c1780, 4½in (11cm).
£200-250 *Som*

A Fürstenberg scent bottle and gilt metal stopper, after a Chelsea model, in a simulated wicker basket, a gilt chain moulded about the shoulders, with a label inscribed 'Eau de Senteur', the neck with sprigs of flowers, blue script F mark, gilt metal mount and stopper with broken chain, c1770, 3½in (9cm).
£1,500-2,000 *C*

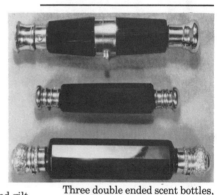

Three double ended scent bottles, with gilt brass mounts.
top. Blue opera glass type, c1870, 5½in (14cm).
£160-200
c. Red, c1880, 4in (10cm).
£60-100
bottom. Red, with embossed mounts, c1880, 5½in (14cm).
£130-150 *Som*

A Venetian scent bottle, attributed to Franchini, the multi-coloured scrambled glass with aventurine inclusions set with 2 portrait canes and silhouette of a gondola, with hinged gilt metal cover and chain, repaired, 2½in (6cm).
£30-70 *GH*

A clear glass double travelling perfume flask, with lozenge and diamond decoration, each end with silver gilt mounts and covers, stamped London hallmarks for 1874, 6½in (16cm).
£150-250 *Bon*

A Venetian scent bottle, attributed to Franchini, the multi-coloured scrambled glass with aventurine inclusions set with 5 portrait canes and panel 'Venise', with silver screw top, 3½in (9cm).
£350-400 *GH*

A Venetian scent bottle, attributed to Franchini, the multi-coloured scrambled glass with aventurine inclusions set with 4 portrait canes, with hinged gilt metal cover and chain, 3in (8cm).
£250-300 *GH*

A deep blue stained scent bottle for Worth, the spherical body moulded with stars, the disc stopper with 'dans la nuit', moulded R. Lalique, 4in (10cm).
£450-550 *Bon*

A clear glass double travelling perfume flask, cut with a zigzag design, with gilt metal mounts and chased screw tops, 5in (12cm).
£100-120 *Bon*

A clear and blue stained scent bottle for Forvil, chipped stopper, moulded R. Lalique Paris France, 4½in (11cm).
£350-450 *Bon*

A frosted grey stained perfume pendant, moulded on 2 sides with curved spear shaped leaves, pierced at the shoulders for suspension cord and with matching mushroom stopper, moulded Lalique, 2in (4.5cm).
£3,200-3,600 *Bon*

A Venetian scent bottle attributed to Franchini, of flattened and tapering ovoid shape, the multi-coloured scrambled glass with aventurine inclusions set with 5 portrait canes, the hinged gilt metal cover with inset green cut 'jewel' finial, 3in (8cm).
£300-350 *GH*

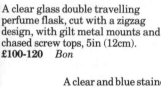

A clear and frosted scent bottle, enclosing a plaque moulded in intaglio with 2 nude female figures amongst flowering branches, the stopper moulded as 2 nude female figures holding up a garland of flowers, small chip, engraved R. Lalique France, 5½in (14cm) high.
£7,200-8,000 *Bon*

'Vers le Jour', an amber frosted and clear scent bottle for Worth, moulded with a repeating triangular design and Worth in the bottle, with matching stopper, moulded R. Lalique, France, 5½in (14cm).
£2,000-2,500 *Bon*

'Ramses', a crystal bottle for Ramses Inc., with chamfered shoulders, the ribbed lotus flower stopper suspending a nude female figure dipper, 8in (20cm).
£250-300 *Bon*

A Baccarat bottle, intaglio moulded with a figure teasing a woodpecker, the stopper moulded as a large woodpecker, 6½in (16cm).
£300-350 *Bon*

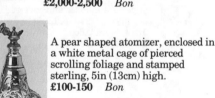

A pear shaped atomizer, enclosed in a white metal cage of pierced scrolling foliage and stamped sterling, 5in (13cm) high.
£100-150 *Bon*

A clear green scent bottle for Worth, flattened circular, with Worth moulded in the bottle, and stepped disc stopper, moulded R. Lalique France, 3in (8cm).
£450-550 *Bon*

A frosted and clear glass bottle, flanked by 2 female nude figures seated at the base, with shallow conical moulded foliate stopper, heightened with green and amethyst staining, 5in (13cm).
£150-180 *Bon*

'L' Amour dans le Coeur', a clear scent bottle for Arys, one side moulded with Cupid within a heart, with moulded flower stopper, heightened with sienna staining, minute chip, moulded R. Lalique, 4in (10cm).
£300-400 *Bon*

A clear green scent bottle for Worth, cylindrical with stepped disc stopper, on original square metal/wood base, some chips, impressed Worth, moulded R. Lalique, stopper and bottle with engraved No. 102, 4½in (11cm).
£500-700 *Bon*

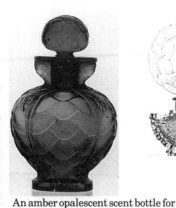

An amber opalescent scent bottle for Morabito, moulded with 4 turtles, the spherical stopper with turtle shell markings, base moulded in intaglio Morabito No. 7 Paris, etched Lalique France, 5½in (14cm).
£4,500-5,500 *Bon*

A cut glass scent bottle of inverted fan shape, the frosted stopper pierced and moulded with a courting couple within a garland of roses, 8in (20cm).
£150-200 *Bon*

An ornate fan shaped bottle, moulded at the base with frosted flowers, beneath vertical ribbing, the stopper moulded as a large orchid, 9in (22cm).
£150-200 *Bon*

A set of 3 clear and blue shaded bottles, with white metal collars and diamond cut glass stoppers, encased in a pierced cylindrical white metal mount, 5in (12cm).
£200-250 *Bon*

An ornate pierced and cut glass bottle, modelled as a crown with orb stopper, 6½in (16cm).
£150-250 *Bon*

A Cartier amber lozenge shaped scent bottle, with ornate pierced gilt mount at the base, inset with simulated lapis lazuli cabochons and other coloured stones, the angular stopper intaglio moulded with a kneeling female figure, small chip, inscribed Cartier Paris, 5in (13cm).
£150-200 *Bon*

A cobalt blue and white overlay perfume flask, of slender tapering form, with chased gilt metal cover, 4½in (11cm) high.
£120-150 *Bon*

'Jolanda', a large amphora shaped clear bottle on gilt pedestal, with gilt metal mount at the shoulders, cast with roses, square stopper and label, 10in (25cm).
£70-120 *Bon*

An opalescent glass 'pedestal' bottle, the stepped base rimmed with malachite glass segments, the 'pedestal' stopper moulded in green glass as a bust of Pan, 9in (23cm) high.
£300-350 *Bon*

A blue tinted scent bottle, decorated on a frosted ground, with polished and frosted berried tiara stopper, 12in (31cm).
£250-300 *Bon*

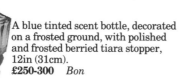

A clear and sepia stained bottle, with graduated base, on hexagonal foot, moulded with stylised flowers, with matching spire stopper, 7in (18cm).
£300-350 *Bon*

An Art Deco black enamelled scent bottle, with faceted tubular stopper, 6in (15cm).
£120-170 *Bon*

A frosted and clear perfume counter tester for D'Orsay, each of the 5 testers with flowerhead dipper, the body moulded with brambles and the word 'D'Orsay', 9in (22cm) long.
£1,500-2,000 *Bon*

A ruby glass and gilt double scent and vinaigrette flask, with foliate chased mounts and covers, 4in (10cm).
£250-300 *Bon*

A Meissen scent bottle and 2 stoppers, modelled as the Provender of the Monastery, wearing a brown habit, carrying a dead pigeon, a young lady hidden in a wheatsheaf with cornflowers on his back, the pink ground base with indianische Blumen, restored, blue crossed swords mark under base decoration, c1770, 3in (8cm) high.
£1,000-1,200 *C*

'Iris', a clear scent bottle for Houbigant, the front moulded with interlaced strapwork, with matching stopper, heightened with blue staining, moulded Lalique, 3in (8cm).
£200-250 *Bon*

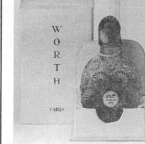

A clear scent bottle for Worth, moulded with an allover design of flowerheads with gilt label at the centre, with matching flowerhead stopper, moulded R. Lalique, in original case, 3½in (8cm).
£300-400 *Bon*

A clear glass perfume pendant, enclosed in an ornate scrolling white metal and gilt mount and with filigree metal 'crown' stopper, on suspension chain, 3in (7cm).
£150-200 *Bon*

A Baccarat bottle for Christian Dior, with gilt decoration, in red velvet coffret lined with red satin, chipped stopper, 9in (23cm).
£800-900 *Bon*

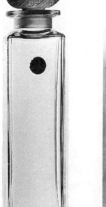

'Tentacion', a novelty bottle for Parera, the stopper moulded as the half length figure of a woman, the bottle as her long skirt, with paper label, 7½in (19cm).
£100-150 *Bon*

A clear scent bottle for Worth, with scalloped edging stained in blue, the flat topped tapering stopper moulded with the letter W, moulded Lalique France, 3in (7cm).
£300-450 *Bon*

A clear glass double travelling perfume flask, cut with a lozenge design, with chased gilt metal mounts and covers, 5in (13cm).
£120-150 *Bon*

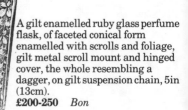

A gilt enamelled ruby glass perfume flask, of faceted conical form enamelled with scrolls and foliage, gilt metal scroll mount and hinged cover, the whole resembling a dagger, on gilt suspension chain, 5in (13cm).
£200-250 *Bon*

A clear and frosted glass cologne flask, etched on one side with a wild rose spray, and with matching gilt metal top, 5½in (14cm) long.
£200-250 *Bon*

'L'Origan', a clear display bottle for Coty, the cushion shaped frosted and sienna stained round stopper moulded with entwined branches, applied gilt label, moulded Coty France, 11in (28cm).
£300-500 *Bon*

'Tulipes', a clear and green stained scent bottle for Jay-Thorpe, the compressed globular body moulded with tulip blooms, and with flowerbud stopper, one bud moulded Jaytho, with crack, moulded R. Lalique France, 3in (8cm).
£150-250 *Bon*

OAK & COUNTRY FURNITURE

Beds

An oak bed, with arched plank ends, one with faceted ball finials, joined by plain rails, the rails lengthened, lacking bolts and slats, 17thC, 82½in (209cm) long.
£1,760-2,500 *C*

MONARCH CHRONOLOGY		
Dates	**Monarchs**	**Period**
1558-1603	Elizabeth I	Elizabethan
1603-1625	James I	Jacobean
1625-1649	Charles I	Carolean
1649-1660	Commonwealth	Cromwellian
1660-1685	Charles II	Restoration
1685-1689	James II	Restoration
1689-1694	William & Mary	William & Mary
1694-1702	William III	William III
1702-1714	Anne	Queen Anne
1714-1727	George I	Early Georgian
1727-1760	George II	Georgian
1760-1812	George III	Late Georgian
1812-1820	George III	Regency
1820-1830	George IV	Late Regency
1830-1837	William IV	William IV
1837-1860	Victoria	Early Victorian
1860-1901	Victoria	Late Victorian
1901-1910	Edward VII	Edwardian

An oak tester bed, the panelled canopy with a flute carved frieze, the back with deep moulded panels with baluster turned front posts, plain panelled footboard, 17thC and later, 84in (213cm) long.
£3,500-4,500 *P(S)*

This bed has been made up using old parts.

A heavily carved oak tester bedstead, part 17thC, 83in (210cm) long.
£9,500-11,000 *CSK*

Bureaux

A small early oak bureau, with interior drawers, c1780, 32in (81cm).
£1,800-2,000 *DDS*

An oak bureau, with reading ledge and fitted interior, on bracket feet, lock missing and replacement handles, 18thC, 35½in (90cm).
£2,000-2,500 *CSK*

Use the Index!
Because certain items might fit easily into any of a number of categories, the quickest and surest method of locating any entry is by reference to the index at the back of the book.
This has been fully cross-referenced for absolute simplicity

A George I oak bureau bookcase with stepped interior, well and secret drawers, original brasses, c1725.   **£8,000-12,000** *PHA*

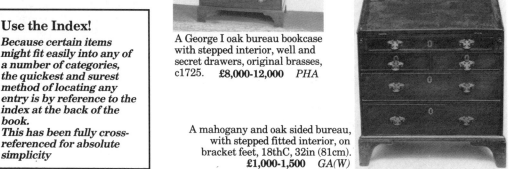

A mahogany and oak sided bureau, with stepped fitted interior, on bracket feet, 18thC, 32in (81cm).
£1,000-1,500 *GA(W)*

A mid George III oak bureau, with a later sloping fall enclosing a fitted interior, on bracket feet, minor restoration, 36in (92cm). **£800-1,000** *CSK*

The later fall will have affected the price.

A George III provincial oak bureau, the fall enclosing a fitted interior of a small door flanked by drawers and pigeonholes. **£1,000-1,200** *Bon*

A George III oak bureau, the fall revealing stationery compartments, on bracket feet, restored, c1770, 35½in (90cm). **£1,500-2,000** *Bon*

Cabinets

A French Provincial oak cabinet, with brass barrel hinges and pierced keyhole plates, shaped aprons and scrolled feet, 55in (139.5cm). **£1,800-2,500** *P(S)*

An oak cabinet on stand in the Gothic style, with moulded cornice, burr veneered, fitted pair of arch panelled doors enclosing 12 small drawers around a recess, 19thC, 50in (127cm). **£1,000-1,500** *RBB*

An oak cabinet with geometrically panelled doors enclosing 14 drawers, the sides with carrying handles, on later bun feet, adapted, mid-17thC, 30½in (77.5cm). **£2,000-3,000** *CSK*

Chairs

A set of 8 ash spindle back chairs, English, in first class condition, early 19thC. **£5,000-7,000** *PHA*

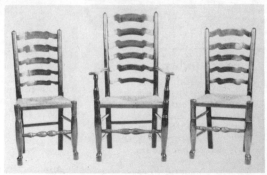

A set of 8 Yorkshire elm dining chairs, with wavy ladder backs, rush seats, turned supports terminating in pad and block feet, late 18thC. **£2,700-3,000** *HSS*

232

Paul Hopwell Antiques

Early English Oak

A set of six 19th Century ash spindle back chairs.
English c1840

A small mid 18th Century oak
dresser and rack with spoon slots.
Excellent colour and patination.
N. Wales c1750

A mid 18th Century oak Cabriole legged dresser base.
Original brasses. Excellent colour and patination.
English c1750

30 High Street, West Haddon, Northamptonshire NN6 7AP
Tel: (0788) 510636

A Charles I carved oak armchair, the solid seat above a chevron inlaid apron and bobbin turned legs joined by stretchers, c1640.
£1,200-1,700   *S(S)*

An oak and walnut panel back open armchair with scroll cresting, the solid seat and rail with a scrolling apron, on baluster legs joined by stretchers, late 17thC.
£7,000-8,000   *CSK*

A Charles I oak panel back armchair, the arms with plain turned cap and cover supports, on similarly turned legs, Salisbury, lacking finials.
£800-1,000   *Bon*

A North Cheshire oak panel back open armchair with a blind parapet toprail, the panel carved with stylised foliage with solid seat, on ring turned baluster legs joined by stretchers, late 17thC.
£6,600-7,200   *CSK*

A well proportioned chair in original condition and good contemporary carving.

An oak open armchair with carved panelled back, the arms carved with conforming decoration, with panelled seat on spirally twisted and rectangular legs joined by conforming stretchers, 17thC and later.   **£850-1,200**   *C*

An oak panel back open armchair, the solid seat on ring turned baluster legs joined by stretchers, late 17thC.   **£4,600-5,200**   *CSK*

A pair of William and Mary oak side chairs with carved rails and panelled backs, English, c1695.
£1,500-2,000   *PHA*

A set of 8 Charles II style carved walnut and beech chairs, including a pair of armchairs, with oval cane splats and cane seats with cushions, c1870.
£3,000-3,500   *S(S)*

A late George III yew and elm Windsor armchair, the bowed railed back above a saddle seat, on turned tapering splayed legs joined by a crinoline stretcher. **£600-700**   *CSK*

A Derbyshire ash and fruitwood lambing chair, 18thC.
£800-1,200   *B*

The fact that this piece has been heavily restored is reflected in the price.

An early Georgian lambing chair in elm with original paint.
£7,000-7,500   *SWN*

An oak open armchair, the panelled back with pyramid finials, with slightly spreading arms on turned supports with plank seat, on turned legs with block feet joined by square stretchers, South Lancashire/North Cheshire, seat possibly replaced, second half 17thC.
£1,000-1,500   *C*

Pyramid finials are a characteristic feature of chairs made in South Lancashire and North Cheshire from the mid-17thC.

A yew and elm wheelback Windsor chair, with a pierced solid splat above a solid seat tied by spindle turned stretchers, 19thC.
£250-300   *Bon*

A George III ash comb back Windsor chair, c1800.
£1,500-2,500   *PHA*

A George III oak wing back armchair, the panel back above a webbed seat and an enclosed base with a lateral frieze drawer, on stile feet, Lancashire/Yorkshire Dales, late 18thC.
£3,000-3,500   *S(S)*

An oak chair, 18in (46cm) wide.
£350-400   *PH*

A yew and elm broad arm Windsor chair, 19thC.
£1,500-2,000   *MJB*

Being yew will boost the price.

A pair of richly carved oak wainscot
chairs, with pierced scalloped
cresting rail, with solid seats, raised
upon bobbin turned and block
carved front supports and plain
stretchers, dated 1629.
£600-800   *HSS*

A Charles II oak nursing chair,
English, c1680.
£500-1,000   *PHA*

A North Cheshire oak chair, the
panelled back with a pierced
parapet cresting initialled S.E., the
solid seat on baluster legs joined on
stretchers, some restoration to
toprail, late 17thC.
£2,700-3,000   *CSK*

A yew and elm wheelback
Windsor armchair, some
restorations, 19thC.
£170-250   *Bon*

A set of 8 oak and ash spindle
back chairs, including a pair of
armchairs with rush seats, on
turned tapering legs with pad
and ball feet, late 18th/early
19thC. **£3,500-4,000**   *S(S)*

A matched set of 6 ash
ladder back chairs, with rush
seats, on turned legs with pad
and ball feet, Lancashire/Cheshire,
requiring re-seating and joints
tightening, late 18th/early 19thC.
£1,700-1,800   *S(S)*

A set of 3 William and Mary oak and
beech chairs, with scroll cresting
rail, with conforming stretchers, on
scroll legs, some variations.
£600-700   *S(S)*

A William and
Mary oak side
chair, with carved
rail, English, c1695.
£500-1,000   *PHA*

A Derbyshire oak chair with spindle
filled back beneath an eared arch
cresting with pierced finialled
roundel, the solid seat on baluster
turned legs joined by a bobbin
turned front stretcher, late 17thC.
£1,500-2,000   *CSK*

A pair of North Cheshire oak
chairs, decorated with stylised foliage and
initials G.B., on ring turned baluster legs joined
by stretchers, late 17thC.   **£6,000-7,000**   *CSK*

*A single chair would probably only command a
quarter of this price – pairs are at a premium.*

A later carved North German ash turner's chair with chip carved toprail and triangular solid seat, on turned legs joined by turned stretchers, basically 18thC.
£400-600   *CSK*

An oak corner chair, the elevated canopied panelled back above a solid seat and base drawer, basically 17thC.
£2,700-3,200   *CSK*

A set of 6 Lancashire dining chairs, with slightly dipped cresting rails, 2 sets of spindle splats, rush seats and on turned and tapering front supports terminating in pad and block feet, with baluster turned seat rails and turned stretchers, 18thC.
£1,500-2,000   *HSS*

A child's painted chair, 11in (28cm) wide.
£150-200   *PH*

A Bavarian stained oak seat in the form of a bear with outstretched arms, late 19thC, 51in (129cm) high.
£1,500-2,000   *CSK*

A Victorian child's oak framed Orkney chair, the enclosed curved back in bound rush, open flat scroll arms and woven sea-grass seat.
£400-500   *GA(W)*

Reputed to be made from the oak of St. Magnus Cathedral.

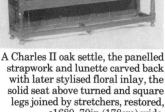

A Charles II oak settle, the panelled strapwork and lunette carved back with later stylised floral inlay, the solid seat above turned and square legs joined by stretchers, restored, c1680, 70in (178cm) wide.
£900-1,200   *S(S)*

An oak panelled and carved settle, English, excellent colour and patina, late 17thC.
£2,000-3,000   *PHA*

A fruitwood and mahogany child's high chair, the finialled back with a marquetry panel, the panelled arms and tasselled seat on square chamfered legs joined by a foot-rest and turned stretchers, early 19thC.
£750-900   *CSK*

A carved oak settle, the scrolled cresting above a grape vine frieze with the date 1651, the hinged box seat with a panelled front, 48in (122cm) wide.
£800-1,000   *S(S)*

An oak settle, the box seat half hinged, with steel H hinges, and with panelled fascia, on fluted extended stile supports, some later additions, hence price, 18thC, 67in (171cm). **£700-800** *HSS*

The later additions are reflected in the price.

A William and Mary oak chest in two parts, with mitred and bobbin turned mouldings, the drawers with walnut veneered panels, inlaid with mother of pearl and bone floral scrolls, including the date and initials Anno 1568, E.B.:J.B., on stile feet, 40½in (102cm). **£2,000-2,500** *S(S)*

A Charles II oak chest of 4 drawers, decorated with geometric moulding and split balusters, on original bun feet, English, c1670. **£6,000-8,000** *PHA*

Rare to find original feet these days.

Chests

An oak geometrically moulded chest of drawers with lifting lid top section, English late 17thC. **£2,000-3,000** *PHA*

A George II oak chest of drawers with walnut veneer, excellent colour and patina with original brasses, English, c1730. **£2,000-3,000** *PHA*

An early George III oak small chest with mahogany crossbanded drawers, 34in (86cm). **£1,200-1,700** *Bon*

A George III oak chest, the top above a brushing slide and 4 drawers, on bracket feet. **£400-600** *Bon*

An oak 6 drawer chest, c1870, 42in (106.5cm). **£450-550** *SSD*

An oak chest with panelled drawers, on stile feet, late 17thC, 38½in (98cm). **£1,800-2,200** *CSK*

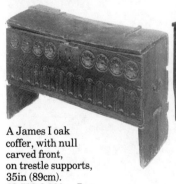

A James I oak coffer, with null carved front, on trestle supports, 35in (89cm). **£2,700-3,000** *Bon*

An oak coffer with hinged top above a front carved with guilloche and inlaid with stars, on stile feet, early 17thC, 42in (106.5cm). **£1,500-2,000** *CSK*

An oak chest with moulded top and 3 geometrically panelled drawers, on stile feet, late 17thC, 31½in (80cm). **£2,000-2,500** *CSK*

238

An oak coffer with later carving and pierced and shaped apron flanked by stile feet, 62in (157cm).
£1,000-2,000   *S(S)*

An oak carved panelled coffer, Lake District, c1695.
£1,000-1,500
PHA

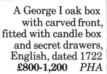

An oak coffer, the hinged top with a gouge carved edge above a triple arched panelled front with nulled frieze between moulded stile uprights, mid-17thC, 51in (130cm).
£1,800-2,200   *CSK*

A George I miniature oak coffer, the front carved with roses and tulips, the lid inscribed with and bearing the initials I.T. in a cartouche, the date 1717 11in (28cm).
£700-750   *CSK*

A George I oak box with carved front, fitted with candle box and secret drawers, English, dated 1722
£800-1,200   *PHA*

A small Charles II oak panelled coffer, excellent colour and patina, English, c1670.
£1,500-2,000   *PHA*

An oak panelled and carved coffer, excellent colour and patina, English 17thC.
£2,000-3,000   *PHA*

A Welsh oak coffer bach, Carmarthen, c1790.
£1,000-1,300   *RP*

A Charles II oak carved coffer, excellent colour and patina, English, dated 1684.
£2,000-3,000   *PHA*

A small dark oak plank coffer, with original iron lock and hinges, simple but in original condition, 18thC.
£250-300   *FR*

An oak carved plank coffer, English, 17thC.
£1,000-1,500   *PHA*

A Charles I carved oak boarded coffer, the hinged cover with hasp, the front with incised twin lozenge carving and palmettes, together with an iron escutcheon, c1620, 48in (122cm).
£900-1,200 *S(S)*

A Charles I oak boarded coffer, the front with twin stylised quatrefoils and punchwork, c1630, 42½in (107cm).
£600-900 *S(S)*

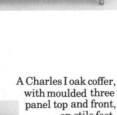

A Charles I oak coffer, with moulded three panel top and front, on stile feet, some damage, c1640, 50½in (128cm).
£700-900 *S(S)*

A Commonwealth oak coffer, the moulded hinged top above a twin panel front, on stile feet, c1650, 37½in (95cm).
£900-1,200 *S(S)*

A Charles II oak boarded coffer, the front with iron escutcheon and nailed border, c1680, 53½in (136cm).
£400-600 *S(S)*

A Charles II oak boarded coffer, the cover with iron hasps, the front with iron escutcheon and gouge borders, c1680, 65in (165cm).
£800-900 *S(S)*

A Charles II oak coffer, c1680, 43in (109cm).
£700-1,000 *S(S)*

A panelled top would be more valuable.

A French oak clamp front chest with hinged moulded top above a front carved with geometric roundels, on standard feet, 16thC, 58½in (148cm).
£4,700-5,500 *CSK*

Fine example of the carver's art.

Cupboards

A German oak cupboard, with egg and dart carved cornice above a shaped panel cupboard, on sledge feet.
£700-1,000 *Bon*

A Louis XV Provincial oak buffet, with cartouche shaped mouldings and roundels, the 3 frieze drawers above a pair of fielded panel doors, on later bun feet, raised back now missing, c1750, 63in (160cm). **£2,000-2,500** *S(S)*
Less valuable than an English dresser base.

An oak corner cupboard, with fitted interior. **£400-500** *LF*

A George III hanging press, with brass knob handles throughout, bracket feet missing, 53in (134.5cm). **£1,500-2,000** *HSS*

An oak press cupboard, the ogee moulded cornice above a pair of arched fielded panel cupboard doors, the lower section with an arrangement of 5 short drawers, on square section feet, mid-18thC, 53in (134.5cm). **£1,700-2,200** *Bon*

An oak barrel back corner cupboard, with restorations, late 18thC. **£700-900** *Bon*

An oak double corner cupboard, 18thC. **£1,700-2,300** *B*

A Charles II panelled and carved fitted cupboard, English, c1680. **£1,000-1,500** *PHA*

A George II oak press cupboard, the base with 3 dummy drawers and 2 real drawers, on ogee bracket feet, c1750, 65in (165cm). **£1,000-1,500** *S(S)*

A Louis XV carved oak armoire, the cornice above a pair of arched later glazed panelled doors, enclosing 3 drawers and a shelf, on stile feet, c1770, 67in (170cm). **£2,000-2,500** *S(S)*

An oak court cupboard, the canopied superstructure with moulded frieze, the lower part with a pair of moulded doors, with iron butterfly hinges throughout, the feet being continuations of the stiles, and with shaped brackets, late 17thC, 57in (144.5cm). **£4,000-5,000** *HSS*

A carved oak court cupboard, with 2 recessed doors, 2 panelled doors below and a further pair of drawers, on block feet, dated 1685 and initialled H.I.K., 64½in (163cm). **£2,000-3,000** *CSK*

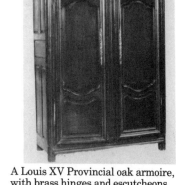

A Louis XV Provincial oak armoire, with brass hinges and escutcheons, the interior with hanging space, on stile feet, c1740, 64in (162.5cm). **£1,400-1,800** *S(S)*

An oak credence cupboard, on ring turned baluster legs joined by square moulded stretcher, the top and door later, 39in (99cm).
£3,500-4,500 *CSK*

An original would be worth considerably more.

A French Provincial brass mounted chestnut armoire, with arched moulded cresting above 2 doors enclosing shelves, with waved apron on scrolled feet, minor restorations, late 18thC, 61in (155cm).
£1,500-1,800 *CSK*

A Charles I oak cupboard, with square and turned supports with platform undertier, restored, c1640, 36in (92cm).
£1,800-2,500 *S(S)*

Dressers

An oak dresser, with brass knobs and escutcheons and 3 tier fitted back, 18thC, 63in (160cm).
£3,000-3,500 *GH*

An oak Welsh dresser, with delft rack, the projecting base crossbanded in fruitwood, over a deep scalloped apron, raised upon cabriole front supports with pointed pad feet, and square back supports on block feet, 18thC, 80in (203cm).
£4,500-5,500 *HSS*

A Charles II carved oak livery cupboard, the plank top above a pair of perforated panel doors enclosing a shelf, on tall stile supports, c1680, 43½in (110cm).
£1,000-1,500 *S(S)*

An oak cupboard with rectangular moulded top above 2 doors, each with a carved panel between fluted uprights headed by lions' masks (formerly a linen press), 30in (76cm).
£800-1,200 *CSK*

An oak dresser, 18thC, 65in (165cm).
£2,500-3,000 *DM*

A mid-Georgian oak dresser, with 3 mahogany banded frieze drawers and an arcaded apron, on cabriole legs and pad feet, the 2 parts associated, restorations, 80½in (204.5cm).
£2,000-3,000 *Bon*

A George III oak dresser and rack, English, c1795.
£6,000-8,000 *PHA*

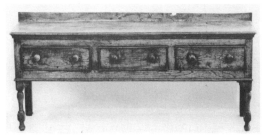

An elm dresser base with moulded edges to top, on turned front supports, 18thC, 78in (198cm).
£1,500-2,000   *GA(W)*

A small oak dresser, 18thC.
£3,700-4,000   *B*

A 3 drawer dresser, supported on shaped tapering legs, the crossbanded drawers with brass swan neck handles with pierced backplates and matching escutcheons, early 18thC, 72in (182.5cm).
£2,000-2,500   *GH*

A George II oak dresser, the raised open shelf back with a cavetto cornice, above a shaped apron and square legs, joined by a platform stretcher, c1750, 62in (157cm).
£3,000-4,000   *S(S)*

An oak dresser with shaped apron supported on square legs, 3 drawers with swan neck brass handles, early 18thC, 72in (182.5cm).
£1,300-1,700   *GH*

An oak dresser base on cabriole legs, inlaid with mahogany, English, c1750.
£4,500-6,000   *PHA*

An oak dresser base, English, c1750. **£6,000-8,000** *PHA*

A George III oak pot board dresser, excellent colour and patination, South Wales, c1780.
£6,000-8,000   *PHA*

A George II oak dresser base with cabriole legs and moulded shaped apron, part original brasses, of rare form, English, c1740.
£12,000-15,000 *PHA*

A George III oak dresser and rack with applewood quartered pillars, crossbanded with mahogany, Yorkshire, c1760.
£10,000-12,000 *PHA*

A George III oak dresser, the planked top above an arcaded frieze fitted with 3 drawers on baluster column supports and pierced slatted pot board, adapted, 51½in (132cm).
£2,000-2,500 *CSK*

A small George III oak cupboard dresser and rack with spoon slots, excellent colour and patina, N. Wales, c1760.
£8,000-10,000 *PHA*

An oak dresser with a moulded cornice above open shelves and geometrically moulded cupboard doors above 2 similar frieze drawers, between turned mouldings on turned legs joined by stretchers, a 19thC reproduction, 55in (139cm).
£1,200-1,500 *CSK*

An oak dresser with moulded cornice, an arrangement of 5 drawers around the arched underframe and on simple turned supports joined by an undertier, 71in (180cm). **£3,000-4,000** *Bea*

An oak inlaid dresser with fitted shelves with ¾ cupboard and drawer on either side, with brass swan neck handles and escutcheons, on shaped apron, supported on shaped legs, 69in (175cm).
£2,000-3,000 *GH*

An oak and crossbanded mahogany dresser, the 2 side cupboards with marquetry shell inlay, the base with 2 diamond inlaid panelled doors, all with brass drop handles and escutcheons, shaped apron and square cabriole legs, 70in (177cm).
£2,000-2,500 *AH*

A Flemish oak sideboard carved with lion masks, flowersprays and strapwork, the inverted boxed canopy top on baluster column supports above 3 frieze drawers and central arcaded panelled door, flanked by recesses on platform and turned bun feet, 19thC, 69in (175cm).
£600-800 *CSK*

A carved oak Gothic-style sideboard, with pierced tracery and linen fold panels above a pair of frieze drawers and tracery panelled doors with brass mounts, on cluster column supports with an undertier, late 18thC, 42½in (107cm).
£1,200-1,600 *S(S)*

A Dutch oak low dresser, profusely carved with urns, roundels, strapwork and guilloche, the planked top above 3 frieze drawers and a pair of fielded panelled doors on bracket feet, 19thC, 62in (157cm). £800-1,200 *CSK*

An earlier piece that has been modified later in the 19thC.

An oak box stool with hinged, moulded top above a cabled frieze, on baluster turned legs joined by stretchers, mid-17thC, 20½in (52cm). £4,000-5,000 *CSK*

Stools

An oak joint stool with moulded top and frieze, on ring turned slightly splayed baluster legs joined by stretchers, late 17thC, one stretcher replaced, 19in (48cm). £700-800 *CSK*

Replaced stretcher will reduce the price.

A Charles II oak joint stool, the plain frieze with a scroll apron, the scroll and baluster turned legs joined by peripheral stretchers, c1680, 16in (41cm). £800-1,200 *S(S)*

An oak joint stool, the moulded top and rail with a separate profile-shaped apron, on complex baluster turned legs joined by stretchers, late 16thC, 19in (48cm). £4,500-5,000 *CSK*

Early joint stools in original condition are rare today.

Tables

A William and Mary oak gateleg table, with a drawer, on baluster turned legs joined by stretchers, c1690, 42in (107cm) extended. £1,000-1,500 *S(S)*

Did you know

MILLER'S Antiques Price Guide builds up year by year to form the most comprehensive photo-reference system available

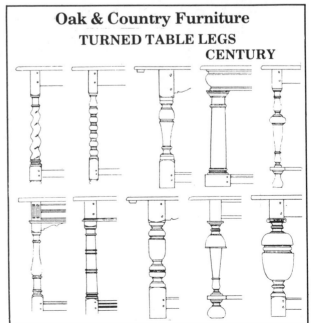

Oak & Country Furniture
TURNED TABLE LEGS
CENTURY

A Charles II style oak centre table, made-up, the carved frieze with 2 end drawers, the spiral twist legs above square feet joined by square stretchers, 51½in (130cm).
£400-500   *S(S)*

'Made-up' is a trade term used to describe a piece which has been constructed from old materials but which is not genuine.

An oak gateleg dining table, on moulded frieze with single drawer, on baluster turned legs joined by stretchers, minor restorations, late 17thC, 55in (139cm).
£3,500-4,500   *CSK*

An oak counter table, the sliding top above a triple parchment panelled front, on moulded stile feet joined by a stretcher, the sliding mechanism replaced, the apron later, the toes replaced, mid -16thC, 47in (119cm).
£2,500-3,500   *CSK*

An oak 8-seater bobbin turned gateleg table, English, excellent condition, colour and patina, c1695.
£6,000-8,000   *PHA*

Large gateleg dining tables now fetch a premium price.

A William and Mary chestnut and beechwood gateleg table, on baluster turned and square legs, joined by stretchers, c1700, 54½in (138cm).
£850-1,200   *S(S)*

A walnut gateleg table, including later timber, the moulded top above spiral twist and square legs, joined by stretchers, late 17thC, formerly with a frieze drawer, 59in (150cm).
£1,500-2,000   *S(S)*

The missing drawer will lower the price.

A small Queen Anne oak gateleg table, good colour and patina, English, c1710.
£1,500-2,500   *PHA*

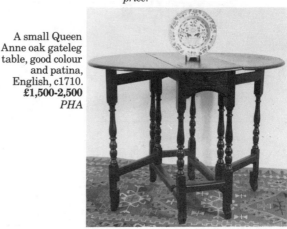

A Jacobean style drawer leaf table, the planked top above a moulded frieze on bulbous baluster legs, joined by cross stretcher, 116in (294cm), extended.   **£3,500-4,500**   *CSK*

PATINA
Surface colour of genuinely old wood resulting from the layers of grease, dirt and polish built up over the years, and the handling the piece of furniture has received in that time. It differs from wood to wood, and is difficult to fake.

A red walnut gateleg table, the moulded single flap top and frieze drawer on ring turned baluster legs joined by a square stretcher, on Spanish scroll feet, mid-18thC, 34in (86cm).
£1,000-1,500   *CSK*

An oak gateleg table, the demi-lune foldover top on baluster column supports joined by stretchers, 37½in (95cm).
£1,500-2,000   *CSK*

An oak gateleg dining table, on turned baluster supports with plain stretchers, with inset quadrant outer corners, 51in (129cm).
£900-1,200
HCH

An oak side table with crossbanded full width drawer with cockbeading and brass swan neck handle, supported on tapering circular legs with pad feet, mid-18thC, 32in (81cm).
£700-900   *GH*

The oak refectory table was the only type until gateleg tables and side tables appeared in the early 17thC. From the turn of the 18thC tables were increasingly designed to serve a specific purpose.

An oak refectory table with a planked top above a lunette carved frieze on baluster turned legs joined by stretchers, parts late 17thC, top and frieze later, 121in (307cm).
£4,000-5,000   *C*

A Charles I oak refectory table, the guilloche and paterae carved frieze above bulbous turned supports joined by peripheral stretchers, one support bears the initials R.D. and the date 1637, top bears indistinct branded initials, including restorations, surfaces distressed, 114in (290cm).
£4,500-5,500   *S(S)*

A William and Mary oak X-stretchered side table, on original bun feet, excellent colour and patina, English, c1695.
£1,500-2,500   *PHA*

A Charles II oak side table, the frieze drawer above square and bobbin turned legs joined by peripheral stretchers, c1680, 29in (74cm).
£1,000-1,500   *S(S)*

A single flap oak side table with drawer, excellent colour and patina, c1710.
£1,400-2,000
PHA

A William and Mary ash side table with platform X-stretcher, on baluster and bobbin turned legs, excellent colour and patina, English, c1695.
£3,000-4,000   *PHA*

A Queen Anne oak stretchered side table on baluster turned legs, with original bun feet and finial, English, c1710.
£4,000-5,000   *PHA*

A late George II oak lowboy, the crossbanded top above one shallow and 2 deeper drawers, on square section cabriole legs with pointed pad feet, drawers re-lined and drawer fronts replaced, 25½in (65cm).
£600-800   *Bon*

A George II oak side table, on slender turned and square legs, joined by stretchers, c1730, 37in (94cm).
£750-950   *S(S)*

A small Queen Anne side table, excellent colour and patina, English, c1710.
£1,500-2,000   *PHA*

A George II oak side table, with 3 drawers and a shaped apron with re-entrant corners, on cabriole legs and pad feet, c1740, 32½in (83cm).
£1,500-2,000   *S(S)*

A George II oak lowboy, crossbanded with walnut, good colour and patina, English, c1740.
£2,500-3,500   *PHA*

A George I walnut small side table, on baluster turned legs, joined by stretchers, c1720, 18½in (47cm).
£1,000-1,500   *S(S)*

A George II fruitwood side table, the moulded top above a frieze drawer and a shaped apron, the turned tapering legs on spade feet, c1740, 30in (76cm).
£500-800   *S(S)*

A rare George II oak side table on tapered, octagonal legs and turned toes, English, c1740.
£1,500-2,000   *PHA*

An oak and red walnut lowboy, the coffered top above a frieze fitted with drawers on cabriole legs with pad feet, basically 18thC, 30in (76cm).
£2,500-3,000   *CSK*

A George III oak lowboy, crossbanded with mahogany, original brass handles, English, c1760.
£4,000-5,000   *PHA*

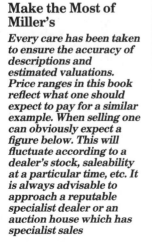

A George III pollard oak side table, the quarter veneered top with moulded rim, on square chamfered supports headed by pierced brackets, 33in (84cm).
£1,200-1,600   *Bon*

A George III oak lowboy, crossbanded with mahogany, with original brass handles, good colour and patina, English, c1760.
£2,500-3,500   *PHA*

A George III burr elm tripod table, good colour and patina, English, c1790.
£2,500-3,000   *PHA*

The burr top will boost the price.

Make the Most of Miller's

Every care has been taken to ensure the accuracy of descriptions and estimated valuations. Price ranges in this book reflect what one should expect to pay for a similar example. When selling one can obviously expect a figure below. This will fluctuate according to a dealer's stock, saleability at a particular time, etc. It is always advisable to approach a reputable specialist dealer or an auction house which has specialist sales

A Spanish chestnut side table, the projecting top above a frieze carved with stylised flowerheads, including a pair of drawers, on square legs, joined by stretchers, 76½in (194cm). **£1,000-1,500**   *S(S)*

A Dutch oak side table with planked top above a long frieze drawer on bobbin baluster legs, joined by stretchers, late 17thC, 36in (92cm). **£1,000-1,300**   *CSK*

A George III oak candlestand, with one-piece top, excellent colour and patina, English, c1790. **£1,200-1,800**   *PHA*

A George III oak 2-tier cricket table, the triple splayed supports with an undertier, c1800, 23½in (60cm) diam. **£700-1,000**   *S(S)*

A rare tiny William and Mary oak tripod table, English, c1695. **£6,000-8,000**   *PHA*

A small George III applewood tripod table, English, c1795. **£800-1,200**   *PHA*

An oak lowboy with brass swan neck drop handles with backplates, shaped apron beneath, supported on circular tapering legs with pad feet, mid-18thC, 33in (84cm). **£1,500-2,000**   *GH*

A George III elm tripod table with tilt top, one piece, well figured top, English, c1820. **£700-1,200**   *PHA*

A Georgian burr yew tripod table, excellent colour and patina, English, c1820. **£2,000-3,000**   *PHA* *Yew is always highly collectable.*

A cherry wood dining table, 63in (160cm). **£1,000-1,300**   *PH*

Miscellaneous

A French fruitwood table, 71in
(180cm).
£1,000-1,400 *PH*

A fruitwood table, 68in (172cm).
£875-975 *PH*

A small 16thC oak plank coffer,
English.
£3,000-4,000 *PHA*

Pieces of this early date are now rare.

An oak box, the hinged lid above a
carved panelled front, the end
boards extending to form feet, 20in
(51cm).
£400-600 *CSK*

An oak desk box, the hinged
rectangular slope with a
gouge-carved edge above front and
sides carved with scrolling dragons,
late 17thC, 27½in (70cm).
£400-600 *CSK*

A rare oak box on cabriole legs,
English, c1760.
£2,000-3,000 *PHA*

An oak desk box, the moulded slope
with a book ledge, on an associated
stand fitted with a frieze drawer, on
baluster turned legs joined by
square stretchers, some restoration,
17thC, 27in (69cm).
£1,500-2,000 *CSK*

FURNITURE

Beds

A William and Mary carved walnut and cane day bed, made up, the hinged end panel with spiral twist supports and coronet cresting rail, with square and spiral twist legs, 72in (183cm) long. **£1,000-1,500** *S(S)*

An early Victorian mahogany full tester bed, with moulded cornice, carved acanthus capitals and bases, 54in (137cm) wide, 102in (259cm) high, 84in (213cm) long. **£4,000-5,000** *P(M)*

This bed was formerly the property of the Watt family of Abney Hall, Cheadle, Nr. Stockport, Cheshire. Agatha Christie was a frequent house guest at Abney Hall as her sister married James Watt and during her visits would always sleep in this bed. Such visits influenced the 'Adventures of the Christmas Pudding' which was dedicated to the memory of Abney Hall and in which there is mention of a 'big four poster bed'.

DAY BEDS
Early versions reflect contemporary chair styles. Later, under French Empire influence, they became increasingly elaborate with rich upholstery, gilding, paint and exotic motifs.

A Victorian brass and black painted iron bedstead, with brass label R.W. Winfield & Son Pattentees and Manufacturers, London & Birmingham, with registry mark for 1856, lacking slats and mattress, 54½in (138cm) wide, 78½in (99cm) long. **£1,700-2,100** *C*

The firm of R. W. Winfield were manufacturers of metal furniture and appear in Pigot's Directory in 1839. Among the large variety of goods which they made in iron and brass were metallic military bedsteads for which they claimed to be 'Proprietor of the English Patent'. They exhibited beds of various styles at the 1851 Great Exhibition and were patronised by Queen Victoria.

A mid-Victorian brass half tester bedstead, with railed headrest and footboard, centred by a pierced roundel with paterae between finialled uprights, 76in (193cm). **£6,500-7,500** *C*

A Victorian brass and iron bedstead, the foot and headboard with scrolling toprail cast with simulated bamboo on column supports cast with foliate mouldings, on porcelain casters, no slats or mattress, 81½in (207cm) long. **£3,000-3,500** *C*

A Victorian mahogany bed, the headboard with moulded frame inset with a pleated cream panel, the footboard with a moulded panel complete with base, c1860, 63in (160cm). **£1,000-1,200** *S(C)*

A red painted ebonised and parcel-gilt boat shaped day bed, of antique Egyptian style, the dished seat covered in black horsehair, the seat rail painted with a border of anthemia, the prow in the form of a gazelle's head on oar feet and H-shaped base, 76in (193cm) wide. **£1,500-2,000** *CSK*

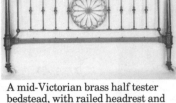

A French Empire mahogany and parcel gilt bed, the panelled ends with sphinx and lantern finials above columnar pilasters with foliate capitals, including side rails and box spring mattress, c1815, 84in (213cm). **£2,000-3,000** *S(S)*

A Regency mahogany campaign bed, with hinged top enclosing hinged side panels and hinged slatted base, on turned tapering legs, labelled Patent, John Durham, London, 42in (106cm) wide.
£3,000-3,500 *C*

John Durham, foreman of Morgan and Sanders, 16 Catherine Street, Strand, took over their patent furniture business in 1820 and specialised in cabinet, camp and field-beds.

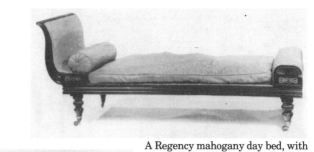

A Regency mahogany day bed, with a scrolled guilloche carved end, on baluster turned legs with lobed collars, headed by gilt metal opposing anthemia, 80in (203cm) wide. **£800-1,000** *Bon*

A mahogany child's rocking cradle, with domed hood, 18thC, 36in (92cm) long.
£150-200 *WHB*

A French mahogany, parquetry and gilt metal mounted bed of Louis XVI design, each end with a pierced laurel floral ribbon-tied cresting above a parquetry panel between fluted uprights headed by paterae on turned legs, bedhead with an incised inscription 8/11/02 No. 9928 Linke, and a pencilled inscription 99287V. VS. 4 Linke, the bedhead 49in (124cm) wide.
£2,000-3,000 *CSK*

Although the famous Czech born Parisian furniture maker François Linke usually signed his pieces in script on the ormolu or with a stencilled stamp in the timber and also worked in a more florid rococo style, the quality of the mounts suggest that this may have originated from his workshops.

A Charles X inlaid bird's-eye maple bed, with solid headboard and solid footrest and one concave side, the other plain side of oak, no box spring or mattress, 76½in (194cm).
£2,000-2,500 *C*

Bonheur du Jour

An Italian giltwood cradle, with ribbed hull and scrolling ends, hung with a blue velvet curtain, the sides with gilt metal railings, the padded interior lined with blue velvet with padded cushion, with scrolling end supports joined by a waved stretcher on scrolling feet carved with acanthus, repaired, mid-19thC, 57in (145cm) long.
£3,500-4,500 *C*

A Regency rosewood bonheur du jour, the superstructure with brass pierced key pattern three quarter gallery, the slightly projecting base with a drawer, opening to reveal a hinged and ratcheted blue morocco writing surface, flanked by wells for pens and ink, over a long drawer with brass knob handles.
£5,500-6,500 *HSS*

A Regency mahogany cradle, with basket covered in faded glazed cotton with slatted base, on turned end supports joined by turned stretchers on downswept legs, some restoration, 41in (104cm) long.
£700-1,000 *C*

> ### Locate the source
> *The source of each illustration in Miller's can be found by checking the code letters below each caption with the list of contributors*

A Louis XV style tulipwood and gilt metal mounted bonheur du jour, with Sèvres style plaques, stationery compartments above a frieze drawer, on cabriole legs, c1870, 24½in (62cm). **£2,500-3,000** *S(S)*

A late Victorian painted satinwood and mahogany bonheur du jour, with overall neo-Classical trailing floral decoration, a pierced three quarter brass gallery above open shelves flanked by doors, with grisaille painted classical figures, on square tapering legs joined by an undershelf, 25in (64cm). **£2,000-2,500** *CSK*

A mahogany and painted bonheur du jour, the galleried superstructure decorated, above a hinged writing slope and fitted drawer, on square tapered legs, part late 18thC, adapted, 24in (61cm). **£1,500-2,000** *CSK*

A Napoleon III ebonised, gilt metal mounted and tortoiseshell and brass inlaid bonheur du jour, with a frieze drawer with writing slide on cabriole legs with female mask headings and gilt sabots, restored, 32in (81cm). **£1,500-2,000** *CSK*

An inlaid rosewood bonheur du jour, with folding baize-lined top and frieze drawer with turned wood knob handles, the superstructure with brass galleried shelf and gilt tubular and spindle supports, cupboards each with an interior 2 side drawer, one with 2 glass ink and sand receivers, on tapered squared supports with fitted casters, early 19thC, 27in (69cm). **£4,500-5,000** *GSP*

An ormolu and porcelain-mounted amaranth bonheur du jour, banded in tulipwood, the fold-out top inlaid with strapwork and lined in green leather, the shaped frieze drawer mounted with tassels on cabriole legs with scroll and rockwork clasps reaching to sabots, late 19thC, 32½in (82cm). **£4,200-5,000** *C*

An Edwardian mahogany lady's bonheur du jour, with inlaid stringing and rosewood banding, the top with tooled leather inset and brass gallery, with 2 front frieze drawers with brass handles, the square tapering legs on casters, 36in (92cm). **£1,000-1,200** *WW*

Breakfront Bookcases

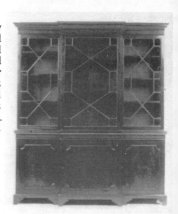

A George III style mahogany breakfront bookcase, the dentil moulded cornice with a blind fretwork frieze, above 3 astragal glazed doors, the lower section with a blind fret frieze above panel cupboard 3 cut corner doors, on bracket feet, late 19thC, 80in (203cm). **£2,500-3,500** *Bon*

A Regency pale mahogany breakfront library bookcase, 140in (355cm). **£16,000-20,000** *McC*

A Regency breakfront secretaire library bookcase, inlaid with radial boxwood lines, on later bracket feet, some restoration, 82in (208cm).
£10,000-12,000 *CSK*

A Regency rosewood small breakfront bookcase, the upper part with 4 grille and glazed doors, enclosing shelves, the base enclosing 9 graduated drawers, the side cupboards with shelves, on plinth base, the lower doors with later panels, 66½in (168cm).
£2,000-3,000 *E*

A mahogany breakfront bookcase, of George III design, the moulded cornice above 8 astragal glazed doors centred by 4 frieze drawers, on plinth base, 92in (234cm).
£3,500-4,000 *CSK*

A William IV rosewood breakfront bookcase, with an arrangement of open adjustable shelves, divided by moulded pilasters, on a plinth base, c1835, 63½in (161cm).
£2,200-2,600 *S(S)*

A mahogany bookcase of mid-Georgian design, the breakfront lower section with central panelled door flanked by 4 astragal glazed doors on plinth base, 19thC, 124in (315cm). **£2,500-3,000** *CSK*

A Victorian burr walnut veneered breakfront library bookcase, the base with mahogany lined frieze drawers above cupboards, fitted shelves, enclosed by domed top panelled doors, the flanking pilasters with scroll scale carved brackets above floral drapes, on a plinth base, 100in (254cm).
£11,000-13,000 *WW*

A Victorian walnut breakfront open bookcase, with leather trimmed open shelves flanked by gilt metal mounted pilasters, on a plinth base.
£1,400-1,700 *Bon*

A Continental satinwood breakfront secrétaire bookcase, the moulded cornice above 4 astragal glazed doors, the lower section with a secrétaire drawer above 2 further drawers, flanked by cupboard doors inlaid with oval fan paterae, on turned tapered legs, probably Scandinavian.
£1,500-2,500 *Bon*

A Victorian mahogany breakfront bookcase, the ogee moulded cornice above 4 arched glazed doors with horizontal astragals, the flanking pilasters with lotus caps, above 4 arched panel cupboard doors, on a plinth base.
£4,500-5,000 *Bon*

> ### Did you know
> *MILLER'S Antiques Price Guide builds up year by year to form the most comprehensive photo-reference system available*

Bureau Bookcases

A banded walnut bureau bookcase of George II design, 'made up', 37in (94cm).
£2,000-3,000 *CSK*

A walnut bureau bookcase inlaid with feather banding, the early Georgian base with flap enclosing a fitted interior above 2 short and 3 graduated long drawers, on bracket feet, top and bottom associated, restorations, 40½in (103cm).
£7,000-8,000 *C*

'Associated' in furniture terms means not an original, but of the same period and style. Losses are often made good with 'associated' parts.

A George III mahogany bureau bookcase, hinged sloping flap with a fitted interior, on later bracket feet, 52in (132cm).
£2,400-2,800 *CSK*

A George III mahogany bureau bookcase, with inlaid sloping fall front, the drawers below with brass loop handles, and shaped back plates, on ogee bracket feet, the whole with chequered and boxwood stringing, 44in (112cm).
£3,000-3,500 *HSS*

A mid George III inlaid mahogany bureau bookcase, with a pierced broken scroll well shaped pediment and dentil moulded cornice above a pair of astragal glazed doors, on moulded bracket feet, associated, 41in (104cm).
£4,600-5,200 *CSK*

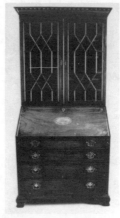

A Victorian walnut bureau bookcase, the superstructure with boss, foliate carved and pierced shaped cresting to the stepped moulded cornice, the panelled front enclosing a fitted interior and green baize writing surface, the base flanked by pierced foliate carved corbels, fluted stiles, on a plinth, 48in (122cm).
£1,500-2,000 *HSS*

A George III mahogany bureau bookcase, the later top with a pair of geometrically glazed astragal doors above sloping flap and 4 graduated long drawers, on bracket feet, 42in (106.5cm).
£1,200-1,700 *CSK*

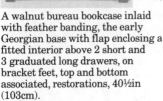

A mahogany bureau bookcase, with a dentilled cavetto cornice and enclosed by a pair of glazed astragal doors above a hinged sloping flap with a fitted interior and 4 graduated long drawers, on bracket feet, late 18thC and later, 41in (104cm).
£3,700-4,200 *CSK*

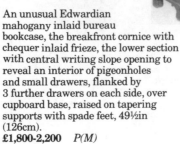

An unusual Edwardian mahogany inlaid bureau bookcase, the breakfront cornice with chequer inlaid frieze, the lower section with central writing slope opening to reveal an interior of pigeonholes and small drawers, flanked by 3 further drawers on each side, over cupboard base, raised on tapering supports with spade feet, 49½in (126cm).
£1,800-2,200 *P(M)*

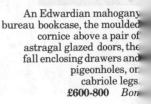

An Edwardian mahogany bureau bookcase, the moulded cornice above a pair of astragal glazed doors, the fall enclosing drawers and pigeonholes, on cabriole legs.
£600-800 *Bon*

A George III mahogany bureau bookcase, with fall front enclosing drawers and pigeonholes over 4 graduated long drawers with brass drop handles, on bracket supports, 45in (114cm).
£2,700-3,200 *AH*

A late George III inlaid mahogany bureau bookcase, with a satinwood fitted interior, on bracket feet, adapted, 43in (109cm).
£3,000-3,500 *CSK*

A late Victorian mahogany bureau bookcase, the upper section with a moulded cornice above a pair of astragal glazed doors, the base with a fall enclosing a fitted interior above 4 long graduated drawers, on bracket feet.
£800-1,200 *Bon*

A Victorian walnut cylinder bureau bookcase, the shutter fall enclosing a sliding leather lined writing panel and fitted interior above a pair of panelled doors, on plinth base, 49½in (126cm).
£2,000-2,500 *CSK*

Dwarf Bookcases

An Edwardian satinwood revolving bookcase, the top inlaid with tulipwood bandings and stringing, the open sides with pierced fret panels, on cabriole legs joined by an undertier, 18in (46cm). **£1,600-2,000** *S(S)*

A late Victorian mahogany satinwood crossbanded square shaped revolving bookcase raised on dwarf cabriole legs with pad feet, 24½in (62cm).
£900-1,200 *AG*

Library Bookcases

A pair of Victorian walnut library bookcases, the lower section of inverted breakfront form with 2 frieze drawers over 2 mirrored doors flanked by carved brackets raised on moulded plinth bases, 49in (124cm).
£10,000-12,000 *P(M)*

A George III mahogany library bookcase, inlaid with satinwood, the base with a slide above a pair of doors enclosing an adjustable shelf with oval segmented veneers and flanked by 8 short drawers, on a plinth base, c1800, 70in (178cm).
£5,500-6,500 *S(S)*

Basically a fine piece requiring sympathetic restoration.

A Georgian mahogany book cabinet.
£4,500-5,000 *DM*

A George IV mahogany and marquetry inlaid bookcase, with moulded cornice and a pair of geometrically glazed doors above 2 drawers and a pair of panelled cupboard doors, on bracket feet, 62in (157cm).
£2,700-3,500 *CSK*

A Regency mahogany bookcase, with an associated moulded cornice above 2 glazed doors, 2 drawers below and doors, on plinth base, possibly a section from a larger bookcase, 40in (101cm).
£1,300-1,700 *CSK*

A late George III mahogany open bookcase on chest, on turned tapered feet, 29in (74cm).
£1,400-1,800 *Bon*

A Colonial padouk cabinet bookcase, the moulded cornice above a pair of arched glazed doors enclosing adjustable shelves, on shaped bracket feet, c1830, 30in (76cm).
£2,000-3,000 *S*

An Edwardian mahogany and satinwood crossbanded cabinet bookcase, on tapered square legs, 42in (106cm).
£700-1,000 *S(S)*

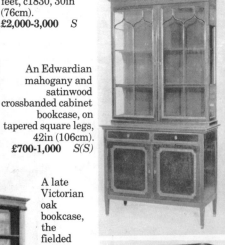

A William IV rosewood bookcase, with moulded cornice above 2 sets of adjustable shelves, the lower part with similar adjustable shelves, on a plinth base, c1835, 70½in (179cm).
£4,000-4,500 *S(C)*

A late Victorian oak bookcase, the fielded panelled doors enclosing drawers and shelves, 90in (228cm).
£650-750 *AG*

An Edwardian mahogany bookcase, the arched pediment inlaid with scrolls and swags in satinwood and stinkwood, the base with drawers above 2 panelled doors inlaid with ribbons, on bracket feet, 49in (124cm).
£3,700-4,200 *CSK*

A Victorian mahogany library bookcase, 102in (259cm).
£4,000-5,000 *CSK*

A Victorian mahogany bookcase with a pair of glazed doors enclosing adjustable shelves above a pair of panel doors enclosing a shelf and a drawer, 35½in (90cm)
£600-900 *S(S*

Secrétaire Bookcases

A Victorian carved oak bookcase in the Gothic style, the raised back with turned finials, below are 3 adjustable shelves and a pair of panel doors, 47½in (120cm).
£650-750   *S(S)*

A Regency mahogany and ebony-strung breakfront secretaire bookcase, with a fitted interior with 2 panels below, flanked by glazed doors with drawers and cupboards below, on plinth base, with later bun feet, 90in (228cm).
£8,000-10,000   *CSK*

A Victorian mahogany secrétaire bookcase, the drawer falling to reveal 6 small drawers with maple fascias, centred by pigeonholes, 50in (127cm).
£1,500-2,000   *HSS*

A late Regency mahogany secrétaire bookcase, with a cavetto moulded cornice and enclosed by a pair of arched lancet astragal doors above a deep drawer with a fitted writing interior and 3 graduated long drawers, on splayed bracket feet, 45in (114cm).
£2,000-3,000   *CSK*

A Victorian mahogany secrétaire bookcase, the lower section with a secrétaire door and fitted interior above a pair of arched panelled doors, on a plinth base.
£1,500-2,000   *Bon*

Buckets

A mahogany secrétaire bookcase, the serpentine scrolling pediment carved with flowerheaded paterae and enclosed by a pair of glazed panelled doors above a writing drawer and 3 graduated drawers, on splayed bracket feet, early 19thC and later, 45in (114cm).
£1,700-2,200   *CSK*

A George IV mahogany secrétaire bookcase, the secrétaire drawer enclosing a satinwood interior of drawers and pigeonholes around a cupboard door concealing secret compartments, and with one of the drawers inscribed on the base, Mr. Baldy, Surgeon, Cornwall Street, Plymouth, on bracket feet, 43in (109cm).
£1,500-2,000   *Bon*

A mahogany brass-bound plate bucket, with pierced sides and brass loop handle, late 18thC, 12in (28cm) high.
£800-1,000   *S(S)*

A George III mahogany and brass-bound pail, with a hinged brass handle, 16½in (42cm) high.
£1,500-2,000 *CSK*

A George III brass-bound mahogany peat bucket, the tapering sides with carrying handles, lacking liner, 16in (41cm) high.
£1,200-1,600 *C*

An Irish Regency brass -bound mahogany peat bucket with brass carrying handle, scrolling hinge, tapering ribbed sides and tin liner, 17in (43cm) high. **£2,800-3,200** *C*

A brass-bound mahogany bucket of navette shape, with brass liner and carrying handle, 19thC, 13in (33cm) high. **£500-800** *C*

Bureaux

A walnut bureau, the fall front enclosing an interior of drawers and pigeonholes above a well, with 2 short and 2 long drawers divided by half round mouldings, on bracket feet.
£1,700-2,200 *Bon*

A walnut and feather banded bureau, with hinged slope and fitted interior with well above 3 graduated drawers, on bun feet, 38in (96cm).
£2,000-2,500 *CSK*

A Queen Anne walnut bureau, the crossbanded top above a hinged slope enclosing a fitted interior and well above 4 drawers, on turned bun feet, adapted, 33in (84cm).
£2,000-3,000 *CSK*

A Queen Anne bureau, on later shaped apron and bracket feet, c1710, possibly Colonial, 35in (89cm).
£1,500-2,000 *S(S)*

A William III figured walnut veneered bureau in 2 sections, the feather banded base with brass handles and raised on later bracket feet, 36½in (93cm).
£4,500-6,500 *WW*

Early bureaux were made in two parts.

An early Georgian figured walnut bureau with feather banding, the flap enclosing a stepped and shaped fitted interior, on later plinth base, 37in (94cm). **£3,500-4,000** *PCh*

A walnut bureau, with flap enclosing a fitted interior above 4 long graduated drawers, on bracket feet, parts 18thC, 36in (92cm).
£1,200-1,800 *CSK*

A burr walnut, inlaid and oyster veneered banded bureau, with fitted interior above 4 graduated long drawers, on bracket feet, early 18thC and later, 31in (79cm). **£2,500-4,000**   *CSK*

A George II mahogany bureau, the fall above 4 long graduated drawers, on shaped bracket feet, c1750, 35½in (90cm). **£1,000-1,500**   *S(S)*

A mid George III mahogany bureau, the hinged slope enclosing a fitted interior, above 4 graduated drawers, on bracket feet, restored, 36in (92cm). **£700-1,000**   *CSK*

A George II crossbanded figured walnut bureau, with fitted interior, the drawers all with brass swan neck handles, on bracket feet, 37in (94cm). **£2,000-2,700**   *HCH*

A George II mahogany bureau, the fall revealing stationery compartments, the 4 long graduated drawers above bracket feet, handles replaced, c1750, 39in (99cm). **£800-1,200**   *S(S)*

A George III mahogany bureau, the fall enclosing a fitted interior, on bracket feet, basically 18thC with restorations. **£1,200-1,700**   *Bon*

A George III mahogany bureau, the fall front enclosing an interior of drawers and pigeonholes around a cupboard door, on later bracket feet, 35½in (91cm). **£1,200-1,700**   *Bon*

A George III mahogany bureau, the hinged sloping flap enclosing a fitted interior, above 4 graduated long drawers, on bracket feet, adapted, 36in (92cm). **£2,000-2,500**   *CSK*

A George III mahogany bureau, the hinged sloping flap enclosing a fitted interior, above 2 short and 2 graduated long drawers, on bracket feet, 36in (92cm). **£1,500-2,000**   *CSK*

A mid George III mahogany bureau, the hinged slope enclosing a fitted interior above 4 graduated drawers, on bracket feet, slight restoration, 39in (99cm). **£1,500-2,000**   *CSK*

A George III mahogany bureau, 37in (94cm).
£3,500-4,000   *DN*

Good features, such as the inlaid star to the fall.

A George III style mahogany miniature bureau, the fall revealing stationery compartments, the graduated drawers above ogee bracket feet, 9½in (24cm).
£650-800   *S(S)*

A George III mahogany bureau, the hinged sloping flap enclosing a fitted interior, above 4 small and 3 graduated long drawers, on bracket feet, 42in (106cm).
£1,000-1,500   *CSK*

A late George III mahogany bureau, the hinged slope enclosing a fitted interior, on bracket feet, restored, 42in (106cm).
£1,000-1,200   *CSK*

A mahogany bureau, the fall flap enclosing a well fitted and inlaid interior, on bracket feet, 36in (92cm).
£1,200-1,700   *DEN*

An Edwardian satinwood and painted bureau in the George III style, decorated throughout with flowers, cornucopiae and urns, the fall depicting a classical scene, the interior with stationery compartments, on bracket feet, c1910, 30in (76cm).
£3,200-3,700   *S(S)*

An early George III mahogany bureau.   **£1,700-2,200**   *DM*

An Edwardian Sheraton style satinwood banded mahogany bureau, decorated with floral marquetry panels incorporating horticultural implements, 30in (76cm).
£600-700   *FR*

A mahogany bureau, crossbanded with satinwood, the fall flap enclosing a fitted interior, on cabriole supports, 1920s, 34in (86cm).
£450-600   *DEN*

A French mahogany and marquetry bureau à cylindre, with gilt metal mounts throughout, the galleried red marble top above a pair of doors the fall revealing stationery compartments and a pull-out writing surface with a frieze drawer on fluted, turned legs joined by a galleried platform stretcher, with turned feet and ceramic casters, one caster off, late 18th/early 19thC, 20in (51cm)
£1,500-2,000   *S(S)*

A Dutch mahogany bureau, the fall revealing a well and shaped stationery compartments centred by a door and brass mounted secret drawers, on ogee-shaped base, above a carved and shaped apron, on claw and ball feet, c1750, 38in (98cm).
£2,000-2,500 *S(S)*

A Victorian Sheraton revival inlaid satinwood cylinder bureau de dame, enclosed by a tambour shutter with a fitted interior and sliding writing panel, on square tapering legs with spade feet, 17in (43cm).
£1,500-2,000 *CSK*

A George III inlaid mahogany cylinder bureau, the crossbanded top with a tambour shutter enclosing a fitted interior above a leather-lined writing slide and long frieze drawer, on square tapering legs, 34in (86cm).
£1,700-2,500 *CSK*

A walnut and feather banded miniature bureau on stand, of early 18thC design, with a hinged slope enclosing a fitted interior with a concave frieze drawer below and shell headed cabriole legs with pad feet, 18in (46cm).
£1,500-2,000 *CSK*

A Dutch walnut bureau, inlaid overall with chequer lines, the top and hinged fall with shell motifs enclosing a fitted interior, on later bracket feet, late 18thC, 41in (104cm).
£2,500-3,500 *CSK*

An Anglo Indian padouk bureau, the hinged sloping flap enclosing a fitted interior, on bracket feet, with later handles and loper stiles, 44½in (113cm).
£1,000-1,500 *CSK*

A George III Irish mahogany bureau, inlaid overall with barber pole stringing, the fall front enclosing fitted interior, with door inlaid with Prince of Wales feathers, above 2 short and 3 long drawers, on bracket feet, bearing a retail label from Millar & Beatty, Grafton Street, 41in (104cm).
£1,700-2,200 *Bon*

A George III mahogany cylinder bureau, the tambour fall revealing stationery compartments and a pull-out ratchet adjusted writing surface, on panelled tapered square legs with spade feet, c1790, 32½in (82cm).
£2,500-3,500 *S(S)*

A Portuguese hardwood bureau, inlaid overall with ivory and ebonised panels of classical design, the sloping front revealing a fitted interior, on ebonised cabriole legs, the knees carved with foliage ending in French-knot feet, 19thC, 28in (71cm).
£1,800-2,500 *C*

A late Regency mahogany and ebony strung cylinder bureau, the top and sliding fall enclosing a fitted interior, above a long frieze drawer and 2 drawers to either side of the kneehole, on turned legs, 44in (111cm).
£3,000-4,000 *CSK*

A Viennese mahogany cylinder bureau, the tambour fall revealing stationery compartments, restored, c1820, 26½in (67cm).
£2,500-3,000 *S(S)*

A William and Mary style walnut bureau, on inverted baluster turned legs.
£350-500 *Bon*

A North Italian figured inlaid walnut bureau of serpentine and bombe shaped outlines, the hinged sloping flap enclosing a fitted interior above 2 long drawers, on cabriole legs with knob feet and foliate carved headings, 43in (109cm).
£2,000-2,500 *CSK*

A German mahogany cylinder bureau, with fitted interior and 3 graduated long drawers, early 19thC, 39½in (100cm).
£1,500-2,000 *CSK*

A George III satinwood tambour cylinder bureau, inlaid throughout with stringing, the fall revealing stationery compartments and a pull-out writing surface, the frieze drawer above tapered square legs with brass casters, 36in (92cm).
£3,000-4,000 *S(S)*

A small Edwardian satinwood cylinder bureau, the cylinder painted with figure and scrolls, 24in (61cm).
£2,000-2,500 *WHB*

A Dutch walnut bureau, with writing slope and fitted interior, profusely inlaid with marquetry flowers and scrolls, on bracket feet, early 18thC, 36in (92cm).
£5,500-7,000 *RID*

Bureau Cabinets

Collectors Cabinets

A George III mahogany and ebony outlined coin collectors cabinet, the hinged door enclosing a quantity of tulipwood faced trays, with brass side carrying handles, 13in (34cm).
£800-1,200 *C*

A George III mahogany collectors cabinet, enclosing on one side 56 and on the other 22 mahogany lined drawers, on bracket feet, 43in (109cm).
£5,000-6,000 *C*

A Venetian blue, cream and floral painted bureau cabinet, with pierced cresting and open shelves above a hinged fall with 3 serpentine drawers below, on bracket feet, 28½in (72cm).
£900-1,200 *CSK*

A mahogany cylinder bureau vitrine cabinet, applied with gilt metal mounts with brass mounted outlines, the elevated mirror lined cabinet back with inset marble galleried canopy, on turned tapering fluted legs with toupie feet joined by C-scrolling stretchers, 36in (92cm).
£2,000-2,500 *CSK*

A Victorian satinwood small collectors cabinet, the drawers lined in green printed paper and with a locking pilaster, on a plinth base with ivory ball feet, c1880, 16in (41cm).
£900-1,200 *S(S)*

Display Cabinets

A Victorian mahogany collectors cabinet, with a pair of arched panelled doors, 40 glazed graduated drawers enclosing a collection of Lepidoptera, on plinth base, labelled J. Thorne, 1 Gernon Road, Esmond Road, Victorian Park, also part of the collection of Egar Greenwood Esq. S.E.S., F.Z.S. presented by Jennifer Greenwood, 1933.
£2,700-3,200 *CSK*

A Dutch walnut display cabinet, the arched moulded cornice with broken pediment centred by a finial, the glazed door with conforming glazing bars, enclosing 4 shelves, formerly the top section of a bureau bookcase, early 18thC, 40in (102cm).
£1,500-2,200 *C*

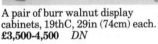

A pair of burr walnut display cabinets, 19thC, 29in (74cm) each.
£3,500-4,500 *DN*

A giltwood display cabinet, in the William and Mary taste, with a central glazed door flanked by glazed panels, enclosing shelves, the whole decorated with floral carving.
£1,000-1,500 *Bon*

A Dutch walnut hanging display cabinet, with moulded serpentine top and central carved cartouche above glazed doors flanked by canted glazed side panels, late 18thC, 46in (116.5cm).
£1,000-1,500 *CSK*

A Queen Anne style mahogany inlaid dome shaped bookcase/display cabinet, the base with fitted cupboards and double opening doors, supported on shaped cabriole legs with shell carved knees, 1920s.
£1,200-1,600 *GH*

A mahogany display cabinet, in the 18thC style, with an elaborately inlaid central door in the manner of Chippendale, flanked by a pair of bevelled glass doors, with shaped and pierced apron and satinwood inlay throughout, early 20thC.
£2,500-3,500 *LRG*

An Edwardian inlaid mahogany display cabinet, with a moulded pediment and cavetto cornice above a pair of astragal glazed doors on square tapering legs, 35in (90cm).
£800-1,200 *CSK*

A brass banded display cabinet, enclosed by 2 side panelled doors with a mirror lined interior and adjustable rectangular shelves mounted on a gilt wood 18thC style stand, 55in (140cm).
£2,000-3,000   CSK

A French mahogany and gilt metal mounted vitrine of Louis XV design, on cabriole legs with gilt paw sabots, signed Albertini, 40in (101.5cm).
£2,600-3,200   CSK

A late Victorian mahogany and marquetry standing display cabinet, with satinwood banded outline, on square tapering legs, 26in (67cm).
£800-1,000   CSK

An Edwardian mahogany display cabinet, with cavetto cornice above the satinwood ribbon tied bellflower swag and astragal glazed door and side panels above, on square section legs tied by a shelf stretcher.
£500-700   Bon

A Georgian style mahogany display cabinet, with carved decoration, on square tapering supports, 34in (86cm).
£400-600   DEN

A mahogany display cabinet, of George II design, on a stand with chamfered square legs with Marlborough block feet and pierced wings, 50½in (128cm).
£1,700-2,500   CSK

An Edwardian inlaid mahogany glazed fronted display cabinet, with 3 internal adjustable shelves lined with silver floral patterned damask, the base with inlaid and crossbanded drawer with brass knobs, on turned tapering legs.
£2,500-3,000   GH

A rosewood mirror backed display cabinet, with pierced galleried surmount, moulded and beaded cornice and base with protruding corners and wrythen supports to the front, on squat bun front feet, 19thC, 48in (122cm).
£3,500-4,500   AH

An early Victorian rosewood display cabinet, 1866, 30in (76cm).
£900-1,200   LAY

An Edwardian mahogany and boxwood strung display cabinet, the frieze inlaid with floral swags above an arched glazed apron, inlaid with an urn and floral scrolls, on square tapered legs with spade feet tied by a shelf stretcher.
£800-1,000   Bon

An early Victorian satinwood and gilt metal mounted display cabinet, with glazed door on bracket feet, 26in (66cm).
£1,200-1,700   CSK

A late Victorian mahogany display cabinet, the serpentine upper section with inlaid dentil cornice above a finely inlaid foliate scroll frieze and plain glazed doors, the conforming lower section with a pair of figured and veneered cupboards, on square tapered legs joined by a platform stretcher, 45in (114cm).
£2,800-3,500 *Bon*

The fine quality of the inlay lifts this above the ordinary.

A Victorian walnut music cabinet, 24in (61cm).
£900-1,200 *DN*

An Edwardian mahogany display cabinet, the moulded cornice above a ribbon tied floral swag inlaid frieze, and a pair of shaped glazed doors, similar inlaid apron on square section splayed tapering legs.
£900-1,200 *Bon*

An Edwardian mahogany and satinwood banded display cabinet, the swan neck cresting above a pair of astragal glazed doors and side panels with concaved platform shelf below on square tapering legs and spade feet.
£1,200-1,600 *CSK*

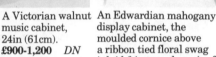

An Edwardian mahogany display cabinet, inlaid with musical instruments and marquetry in rosewood and boxwood line outlines, on fluted turned tapering legs, 49in (124.5cm). **£800-1,200** *CSK*

A late Victorian painted satinwood and rosewood banded display cabinet, on square tapering legs, 26in (66cm).
£2,000-2,500 *Bon*

An Edwardian mahogany serpentine fronted display cabinet. **£1,100-1,600** *S(S)*

An Edwardian mahogany and satinwood crossbanded display cabinet, with glazed panel doors enclosing lined shelves raised on square tapering legs, 43in (109cm).
£1,500-2,000 *AG*

A French second Empire mahogany and gilt metal mounted vitrine, 27in (69cm).
£3,000-3,500 *CSK*

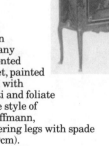

An Edwardian inlaid mahogany serpentine fronted display cabinet, painted and decorated with portraits, putti and foliate festoons in the style of Angelica Kauffmann, on square tapering legs with spade feet, 47in (119cm).
£1,500-2,000 *CSK*

A Dutch marquetry mahogany display cabinet, 19thC.
£2,200-2,700 *GIL*

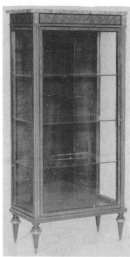

A French ormolu-mounted inlaid kingwood vitrine, with serpentine glazed door and sides with bombe lower parts, painted with Vernis Martin allegorical groups, velvet-lined interior, marble top, 32in (81cm).
£3,600-4,200 *GSP*

A giltwood vitrine of Louis XVI design, with beaded and foliate carved outlines, enclosed by a bevelled glazed door and side panels, on cabriole legs with scroll feet, 33½in (85cm).
£900-1,400 *CSK*

A French beech salon cabinet in the Louis XV -style, with rococo scroll arched cresting over crimson velvet backed glass shelves, raised upon fluted scroll supports terminating in knurl and peg feet, 19thC, 27in (69cm).
£1,000-1,500 *HSS*

A Louis XVI-style rosewood and tulipwood vitrine, with gilt metal mounts, the brèche d'alep marble top above a glazed door enclosing a lined interior with glass shelves, the sides with inlaid fluting, on toupie feet, c1900, 27½in (70cm).
£1,500-2,000 *S(S)*

Cabinets on Stands

A North Italian walnut and marquetry cabinet-on-stand, with ripple moulded banded outlines, the coffered top above drawers flanking a central panelled door enclosing small drawers, 19thC, 30in (76cm), the later stand with a simulated frieze drawer and spiral tapering baluster legs joined by stretchers.
£2,000-2,500 *CSK*

A walnut and feather-banded cabinet on associated stand, of Queen Anne design, with broken pediment above a pair of arched bevelled mirrored doors, fitted with 3 drawers below, above a shaped apron on cabriole legs with pointed pad feet, 39in (99cm).
£1,700-2,200 *CSK*

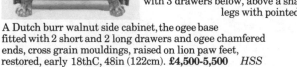

A Dutch burr walnut side cabinet, the ogee base fitted with 2 short and 2 long drawers and ogee chamfered ends, cross grain mouldings, raised on lion paw feet, restored, early 18thC, 48in (122cm). **£4,500-5,500** *HSS*

Side Cabinets

A Victorian mahogany and marquetry cabinet-on-stand, the top with a pierced three-quarter brass gallery fitted with 3 drawers above a rectangular plateau and long frieze drawer, on square tapering legs, 20in (51cm).
£900-1,400 *CSK*

A George IV breakfront cabinet, 48in (122cm).
£2,500-3,000 *DN*

A late George III mahogany side cabinet, the sides with an arrangement of 5 opposing drawers, on turned feet, c1805, 50in (127cm).
£2,500-3,000 *S(S)*

A pair of mahogany tulipwood banded and marquetry bowfront corner cabinets, inlaid with floral scroll motifs on fluted tapering legs joined by a shaped undertier, possibly reconstructed from a Regency sideboard, each 51½in (131cm).
£2,600-3,000 *CSK*

A pair of mid-Victorian gilt metal, walnut and marquetry dwarf side cabinets, with glazed panelled doors between mask mounted pilasters, on plinth bases, 31in (79cm).
£2,200-2,700 *CSK*

A Regency style mahogany breakfront side cabinet, the crossbanded top above a central brass grille door, flanked by fluted pilasters and bowed cupboard doors, on lobed tapered legs.
£600-800 *Bon*

A French kingwood and parquetry side cabinet, the mirror with gilt metal cresting centred by a ribbon tied Sèvres style plaque, the lower section with similar plaques on quatrefoil parquetry reserves, on a plinth base, 72in (183cm).
£4,000-5,000 *Bon*

A Victorian burr walnut and inlaid credenza, with serpentine fronted glazed doors on each side, a central panelled door, gilt metal mounts, 59in (149.5cm).
£1,800-2,200 *P(S)*

A mid-Victorian walnut and marquetry dwarf side cabinet, applied with gilt metal mounts, the ebonised banded top above 2 glazed panelled doors between pilasters, on turned tapering bun feet, 42in (107cm).
£800-1,000 *CSK*

A Victorian walnut and gilt metal mounted side cabinet, inlaid throughout with amboyna bandings and stringing, the serpentine top with a geometric inlaid frieze, the columnar pilasters terminating in a plinth base with turned feet, c1870, 72in (182cm).
£3,000-3,500 *S(S)*

A Victorian burr walnut bowfront dwarf side cabinet, inset with painted decorated oval plaques and applied with gilt metal mounts in tulipwood banded borders, on a shaped plinth with block feet, 47in (119cm).
£2,500-3,500 *CSK*

A Victorian burr walnut serpentine dwarf side cabinet, the eared Carrara marble top above a pair of arched mirror panelled doors, between canted angles applied with foliate carved mouldings, on plinth base, 60½in (154cm).
£1,400-2,000 *CSK*

An ebonised, boulle and gilt metal mounted side cabinet, the eared Carrara marble top above an oval panelled door, between canted angles headed by putti, on plinth base, 36in (92cm).
£900-1,500 *CSK*

FURNITURE   SIDE CABINETS

A pair of Buhl-style cabinets, mid-19thC.
£2,500-3,000   *McC*

A Victorian burr walnut breakfront **credenza**, decorated with inlaid floral scrolls, stringing and crossbanding, the glazed panel **doors** to the ends enclosing lined **shelves**, raised on a plinth base with turned feet, 65in (165cm).
£2,500-3,000   *AG*

A suite of 3 ormolu mounted ebonised pietra dura cabinets comprising a pair of side cabinets, each heavily ormolu-mounted, the doors inlaid with brass lines and flowers, 19thC, 38in (96.5cm), and a similar, but not matching, credenza, 66in (167.5cm).
£6,000-7,000   *GSP*

A Victorian burr walnut breakfront side cabinet, the frieze inlaid with arabesques, above a similarly inlaid panelled cupboard door, flanked by bowed glazed doors, divided by gilt metal espagnolettes, on a plinth base, 68in (172.5cm).
£3,000-3,500   *Bon*

A Victorian burr walnut and marquetry breakfront dwarf side cabinet, the glazed doors flanked by bowed panelled doors, on a bracketed plinth base, 58in (147cm).
£3,000-4,000   *CSK*

An ebonised side cabinet crossbanded in amboyna, 19thC, 60in (152cm).
£1,600-2,000   *HSS*

A French breakfront contra-Buhl **side** cabinet, the ebonised top with **brass** stringing, 62in (157cm).
£6,000-7,000   *WW*

A similar cabinet is in the Wallace Collection.

A Victorian walnut breakfront side cabinet, inlaid overall with boxwood stringing, on ebonised feet, 62½in (159cm).
£2,800-3,200   *Bon*

A Louis Philippe ebony, thujawood banded, marquetry and gilt metal mounted side cabinet, with Carrara eared marble top and gilt foliate border, on plinth base, 33in (84cm).
£1,700-2,200 *CSK*

A Dutch satinwood and marquetry corner cabinet, the crossbanded bowfront above 2 frieze drawers and 2 doors, on square tapering legs with ball feet, damaged, 37in (94cm).
£950-1,200 *CSK*

A Victorian burr walnut and gilt metal mounted side cabinet, inlaid throughout with laburnum bandings and stringing, the panel doors with Sèvres style plaques, the sides enclosed by a pair of bowed glazed doors, on a plinth base with bun feet, c1870, 72½in (184cm).
£3,000-3,500 *S(S)*

A rosewood and brass strung pedestal cabinet, stamped 'Maigret', 19thC.
£1,200-1,600 *DN*

A mid-Victorian burr walnut and marquetry dwarf side cabinet, with amaranth bands and applied with gilt metal mounts, on bracketed plinth base, 33in (84cm).
£2,000-2,500 *CSK*

A German mahogany side cabinet, with a long frieze drawer above a pair of cupboard doors, on a plinth base with block feet, mid-19thC.
£400-600 *Bon*

A boulle and gilt metal side cabinet, with velvet lined shelves and applied mounts in the form of child-like figures and scroll mounts, all on a blind plinth, early 19thC, 64in (162.5cm).
£1,500-2,000 *HSS*

A mid-Victorian inlaid walnut and gilt metal mounted credenza of broken D-shaped outline with inlaid panelled door between column uprights and bowed glazed doors, on plinth base, 70½in (179cm).
£3,200-3,600 *CSK*

Canterburies

A pair of Louis XVI style marble topped and ormolu mounted side cabinets, on turned tapered legs.
£1,500-2,000 *Bon*

An early Victorian rosewood canterbury, the 4 divisioned rectangular top carved with foliage above a base drawer, on turned tapering baluster legs, 21in (53cm).
£700-900 *CSK*

An early Victorian rosewood canterbury, with 4 pierced and shaped divisions joined by turned spindles, with frieze drawer, raised on turned lobed feet with brass cappings and casters, 20in (51cm). **£2,500-3,000** *P(M)*

A William IV rosewood canterbury, with 4 divisions above a single drawer, on turned supports with brass casters, c1835, 20in (51cm). **£1,800-2,200** *S(C)*

A late Regency mahogany canterbury, with bobbin turned column supports and 4 divisions above 2 drawers, on turned tapered legs, some restoration. **£1,200-1,500** *Bon*

A William IV mahogany canterbury, the rectangular top with gadrooned edge, with 3 waved pierced rails supported by C scrolls above a single frieze drawer, on reeded bun feet, drawer with inventory number in white paint C19FRN/2156/A, 27in (69cm). **£5,000-5,500** *C*

An early Victorian mahogany canterbury, the top with 5 rails with turned end supports and pointed finials, with single frieze drawer, on ring turned legs and brass caps, 20in (51cm). **£1,500-1,800** *C*

A Regency mahogany canterbury, the top with 5 curved rails on turned spreading end supports with single frieze drawer, on turned tapering legs and brass caps, some damage, 20in (51cm). **£2,000-2,500** *C*

273

CANTERBURIES

- ★ the first canterburies were made c1700, originally as plateholders to stand by the supper table
- ★ Sheraton attributed the name to the first piece having supposedly been commissioned by an Archbishop of Canterbury
- ★ the earliest canterburies are of mahogany but satinwood examples are known
- ★ the number of divisions varies, though four is common. Tops are square or slightly convex, with a drawer below
- ★ early pieces are pleasingly simple with decoration generally limited to the legs and corner supports, sometimes with stringing. Rare 'colonnaded' examples in which all the supports are carved to resemble pillars are highly desirable
- ★ square legs are an indication of an early date, round tapered and turned legs appeared c1810
- ★ in the 19thC canterburies were used to hold sheet music, and the Victorians' passion for the piano accounts for the large number of such pieces surviving
- ★ 19thC canterburies became increasingly elaborate with barley-twist supports, fretwork side panels and ingeniously shaped racking
- ★ later still it was common to add a superstructure to the racks, so combining the functions of canterbury and étagère, sometimes with a music stand in the top tier
- ★ elegance is the quality most sought after by collectors, and elaborate pieces often do not command such good prices as a simple, well proportioned piece
- ★ high prices are paid for rare shapes, crisp deep carving and canterburies decorated with musical motifs, e.g. lyre sides. Rosewood pieces often achieve better prices than walnut

A Victorian burr walnut canterbury and whatnot, the top with three-quarter gallery over reeded and carved supports, the lower section with spindle divisions and frieze drawer, raised on ribbed bun feet with casters, 24in (61cm).
£1,500-2,000 *P(M)*

A Victorian burr walnut music canterbury, with 4 divisions above a single drawer, resting on turned legs with brass casters, 19½in (50cm).
£1,200-1,700 *RID*

Open Armchairs

A Victorian gentleman's walnut open armchair, the spoon back, arm pads and serpentine seat upholstered in floral machine woven tapestry, the legs terminating in knurl and peg feet and ceramic casters.
£800-1,200 *HSS*

A pair of beechwood armchairs, each with cartouche shaped padded back, armrests and seat upholstered in blue patterned cotton, in a moulded frame, the cresting and seat rail carved with a cabochon and scrolling foliage, on cabriole legs, stamped C. Mellier & Co 50 Margaret Street W, late 19thC.
£2,600-3,000 *C*

A pair of Victorian rosewood armchairs, in the French taste, the carved shell and flowerheaded cresting above upholstered panelled backs, serpentine seats and armpads upholstered in Aubusson tapestry, on cabriole legs with knob feet.
£2,000-2,500 *CSK*

A walnut open armchair, with padded back and seat upholstered in floral material with slightly scrolled arms, on bobbin turned and square legs joined by scrolling stretchers.
£800-1,200 *C*

A Georgian style mahogany open arm children's chair, with drop-in seat upholstered in gold Regency stripe, 20in (51cm) high.
£300-400   *GH*

A George III mahogany open armchair, with waved eared toprail carved with C-scrolls centred by acanthus with confronting C-scrolls with pierced vase-shaped splat, the arms with channelled down scrolling supports, with bowed drop-in seat upholstered in beige floral silk, on square chamfered legs joined by an H-shaped stretcher.
£1,000-1,500   *C*

A mahogany open armchair, the arched toprail carved with paterae, the scrolling arms with channelled downward scrolling supports, with serpentine drop-in seat covered in beige floral damask, on square chamfered legs with H-shaped stretchers.
£1,200-1,500   *C*

An Edwardian satinwood armchair, with caned seat, on turned tapered legs, the whole with floral painted decoration, stamped WBL.
£450-650   *Bon*

A pair of George III style mahogany upholstered armchairs, on ogee bracket feet.
£800-1,200   *Bon*

A Victorian walnut lady's chair, the ribbon cabochon carved cresting above a balloon moulded back and seat upholstered in stamped velvet, on cabriole legs with knob feet.
£350-550   *CSK*

A George III mahogany open armchair, with shield shaped back and pierced splat carved with wheat ears above demi-star, the bowed seat covered in cut floral velvet, on square stop-fluted legs and block feet, later blocks, some restoration.
£1,200-1,700   *C*

A pair of 17thC style beech armchairs, with close nailed serpentine tapestry panelled backs and seats, pierced aprons carved with foliage, on baluster legs with paw feet joined by stretchers.
£1,500-2,000   *CSK*

A pair of Swiss walnut open armchairs, each with caned cartouche shaped back and bowed seat, with moulded arms and seat rails, on stop fluted turned tapering legs, headed by gadrooning and paterae, late 18thC.
£1,700-2,200   *C*

A Hepplewhite style mahogany open elbow desk chair, the arms with reeded supports on turned reeded tapered legs.
£1,200-1,700   *PCh*

A pair of late Regency simulated rosewood open armchairs, with padded drop-in seats covered in white cotton, on sabre legs, restored.
£1,200-1,700   *CSK*

A pair of painted satinwood open armchairs, the bowed cane filled seats with patterned squab cushions, on turned tapering sabre legs.
£3,700-4,200   *C*

These chairs are Sheraton revival and date from the late 19thC, if they were period (late 18thC) the price would be doubled.

A George IV rosewood tub shaped library chair.
£700-900   *DN*

A late Regency painted and decorated armchair, the tablet railed radial moulded back above a cane filled seat, on square tapering legs.
£300-600   *CSK*

A pair of Regency open armchairs, each with curved toprail, and channelled X-shaped splat centred by a patera the channelled arms on baluster supports, the seats covered in yellow striped cotton, on turned tapering legs, some restorations.
£3,000-3,500   *C*

A pair of Regency mahogany open armchairs, each with a bar back, reeded outscrolled uprights and X-framed bar above a padded seat, on reeded tapered legs, restored.
£1,700-2,200   *CSK*

Two George III black painted and parcel gilt open armchairs, one with scrolled cane filled back, the other with back pierced with ovals, each with cane filled seat and squab cushion covered in blue floral damask, on turned tapering legs, re-caned, one partially re-decorated.
£1,500-2,000   *C*

A pair of Regency mahogany open armchairs, each with curved toprail inlaid in ebony with geometric stringing, with drop-in seat covered in striped silk, on moulded sabre legs, some restorations.
£2,000-3,000   *C*

A late Victorian walnut drawing room suite, comprising a chaise longue and a pair of tub armchairs.
£450-650   *CSK*

A pair of Edwardian mahogany and marquetry open armchairs, inlaid with bone, on splayed legs.
£800-1,000 *CSK*

A pair of North Italian giltwood open armchairs, with incised floral decoration and padded serpentine seat, on cabriole legs, late 18thC, decorated later.
£2,000-2,500 *CSK*

A matched set of 6 Regency mahogany rail back chairs, the gadrooned crestings above pierced mid rails, and green dralon upholstered seats, on turned legs, c1820.
£1,500-2,000 *S(S)*

A pair of French green painted fauteuils, of Louis XV design, upholstered in Aubusson tapestry, each on foliate headed cabriole legs, late 19thC.
£1,500-2,000 *CSK*

A Victorian rosewood gentleman's armchair, with acanthus carved crested buttoned upholstered balloon back, serpentine seat and armpads in dralon, on cabriole legs with knob feet and flowerheaded carved headings.
£1,600-2,000 *CSK*

A Victorian walnut armchair, upholstered in green velvet, on cabriole legs with knob feet and foliate carved headings.
£600-800 *CSK*

A mahogany open armchair, with cartouche shaped padded back, arm rests and serpentine seat upholstered in floral silk, on channelled cabriole legs headed by scallop shells, later blocks.
£1,000-1,500 *C*

A George III mahogany armchair, with upholstered drop-in seat, on square chamfered legs, adapted, and a similar side chair.
£700-1,000 *CSK*

A Victorian carved walnut and button upholstered armchair, with a foliate scroll cresting above a balloon shaped back and serpentine sprung seat covered in crimson dralon, on cabriole legs with scroll feet ending in ceramic casters, together with a companion occasional chair, c1855.
£1,700-2,000 *S(S)*

A Louis Philippe mahogany open armchair, the moulded solid toprail carved with flowerheads, scrolled horizontal splat and leather padded seat, on baluster tapering legs.
£800-1,200   *C*

A pair of Charles X mahogany open armchairs, with red and white needlework upholstery, on cabriole legs with scroll feet.
£1,700-2,000   *CSK*

A Louis XIV silvered and cream painted open armchair, lacking upholstery, the scrolling arms carved with foliage and flowerheads, the S-scroll legs with paw feet joined by a foliate carved front stretcher and H-shaped stretchers bearing printed label Fundacao Ricardo Do Espirito Santo Silva Exposicao D Arte Decorativa Inglesa Peca Que Figurou No Catalogo Com O N.36, re-decorated, some restorations.
£1,500-2,000   *C*

The closest parallel to this chair is the giltwood armchair from the collection of the Duke of Buccleuch and Queensbury, Boughton House, now in the Victoria and Albert Museum. It is possible that the Buccleuch armchair, previously thought to be English, formed part of the furnishings of Montagu House and was acquired by Ralph, Duke of Montagu, who was twice ambassador to the French court (1669-72 and 1676-78). Peter Thornton has argued that this chair together with the Dolphin Chairs at Ham House, represents the stage of development of the Parisian fauteuil by about 1675.

A pair of walnut open armchairs, of Louis XV style, covered in olive velvet, the arms with scrolled terminals on downward scrolling channelled supports, with channelled waved seat rail on channelled cabriole legs, later blocks, Italian, one with repairs.
£1,500-2,000   *C*

A pair of Spanish walnut Gothic revival open armchairs, the padded seats covered in white cotton, on turned legs and block feet, later blocks, mid-19thC.
£1,800-2,000   *C*

A mid-George III mahogany and blue upholstered Gainsborough armchair, restored.
£2,500-3,000   *CSK*

A pair of Italian throne chairs, with acanthus finials, above flat arms with baluster turned supports and deep box seat, on short turned legs and sled feet with paws, late 17thC.
£900-1,200   *RBB*

A pair of late Victorian mahogany open armchairs, the casters stamped Hamptons & Sons, Pall Mall.
£2,000-2,700   *C*

Upholstered Armchairs

A walnut bergère suite, with carved decoration, the backs and sides with caned panels, upholstered seats and raised on turned melon supports, early 20thC.
£1,000-1,500   *DEN*

A Regency mahogany Uxbridge bergère, with cane filled curved back, arms and seat, the padded arms and squab seat covered in green leather, the arms pierced with holes for a reading slope, on turned supports, and tapering legs, some damage.
£1,800-2,200   *C*

A George IV mahogany bergère library armchair, with cane filled bowed back and seat, on crenellated lappeted turned tapering legs.
£700-900   *CSK*

A mahogany bergère suite, carved with anthemions and stiff leaves, comprising a 2 seater sofa and 2 armchairs, upholstered in figured damask with loose cushions.
£1,700-2,000   *CSK*

An Edwardian mahogany and satinwood banded bergère, on square tapered legs.
£500-700   *Bon*

A pair of French Second Empire gilt gesso bergères, upholstered in Aubusson floral tapestry. **£2,500-3,000**   *CSK*

A pair of giltwood fauteuils à oreilles, the ribbon foliate carved frames with close nailed figured brocade upholstered panels and detachable canopies, the cane filled backs with central monogrammed flowerheaded carved splats, on turned tapering fluted legs with paterae headings.**£1,600-2,000**   *CSK*

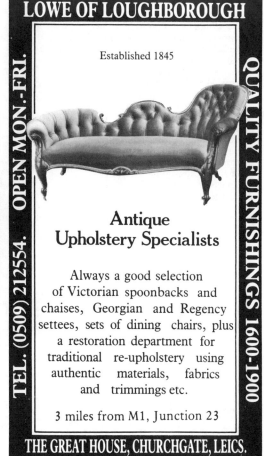
279

ANTIQUE UPHOLSTERY

★ Condition is all-important.
An early piece with
sagging seat but with
original or early
needlework which is still
largely intact will attract
a higher value for its
originality, but generally
speaking an authentically
re-upholstered item in
good condition is clearly
more valuable than an
item requiring attention.
Quality re-upholstery
work is not cheap

★ Re-upholstery is
acceptable provided it has
been restored
authentically with hand
sewn hair borders, and
hair padding, to the
original contours of the
design. Test the upholstery
by prodding with one
finger. Hair will crackle.
Cotton flock and foam will
not!

★ Pre-Regency furniture
was not sprung, but was
webbed on top of the seat
rails and the upholstered
pad invariably had a firm
hair roll at the outer edge,
and all hair stuffing. Later
sprung upholstery is
webbed beneath the seat
rails to accommodate the
springs

★ Originality of the cover
fabric is immediately
questionable if it is out of
period. Textiles is a wide
field but a study of fabric
history and types,
damasks, chintzes,
crested, turkey-work,
hand tapestry, brocades,
etc, is well worthwhile to
date an item

★ The use of dralon modern
acrylic velvets will
devalue an item in the
same way as foam fillings,
or similar low-grade
upholstery work

★ The general quality of
upholstery work is
another pointer to value

A William IV library armchair,
with brown upholstery, the waisted
back, padded seat, reeded scroll
arms and seat rail on reeded
tapering legs.
£900-1,200   CSK

A Victorian walnut gentleman's
armchair, with buttoned spooned
back, serpentine seat and side
panels upholstered in green velvet,
on cabriole legs with scroll knob feet.
£650-750   CSK

A mid-Georgian mahogany wing
armchair, covered in bargello
patterned material, on square
chamfered legs joined by an
H-shaped stretcher, and cushion.
£1,500-2,000   C

A mahogany wing armchair, of
Queen Anne design, upholstered in
figured pink damask, on cabriole
legs with shell headings joined by
stretchers.
£1,000-1,200   CSK

A Regency mahogany bergère
armchair, with reeded surround
above padded arms with spiral
turned uprights and a loose red
leather cushion, on turned legs and
splayed back legs.
£2,000-2,500   CSK

A mahogany armchair, of George III
design, the eared back, seat and
scrolling arms upholstered in
tapestry, on cabriole legs with ball
and claw feet, with acanthus carved
headings, and a similar armchair.
£1,000-1,400   CSK

A George IV library chair, on fluted mahogany front legs, back legs restored. **£3,000-3,500** *WW*

A 6 piece walnut drawing room suite, of Louis XV design, comprising a pair of canapés en cabriolet carved with flowerheads and acanthus C-scrolls, 2 armchairs and 2 side chairs, upholstered in printed linen, on cabriole legs with knob feet.
£1,500-2,000 *CSK*

A Regency simulated rosewood and cane bergère, the seat with a buttoned velvet cushion, the turned and reeded legs ending in brass cappings and casters, bearing the label of Gill & Ryegate Ltd., Oxford Street, London, seat rail stamped G.R. 35P107, cane brittle.
£1,200-1,600 *S(S)*

A walnut wing armchair, with a bowed seat and scrolling side panels, upholstered in tapestry, on pad feet, early 18thC and later.
£1,500-2,500 *CSK*

A Victorian walnut armchair, the shell cresting above a buttoned ballooned back, seat and scrolling arms upholstered in orange velvet, on cabriole legs with ribbon carved headings and knob feet.
£600-800 *CSK*

Corner Chairs

A mahogany corner chair, with curved toprail and twin vase shaped splat, with drop-in seat covered in red velvet, on square chamfered legs joined by an X-shaped stretcher.
£900-1,200 *C*

An inlaid rosewood splat back corner chair, on turned legs and stretcher frame with stuff over tapestry upholstered seat, late 19thC.
£250-300 *PCh*

These chairs fetch more if they have cabriole legs.

A George IV mahogany tub shaped library chair, upholstered in pale brown leather, on reeded tapering legs.
£2,000-2,500 *CSK*

A pair of George II style walnut corner chairs, with drop-in seats, on carved front cabriole legs with claw and ball feet, c1900.
£1,200-1,600 *S(S)*

Locate the source

The source of each illustration in Miller's can be found by checking the code letters below each caption with the list of contributors

Dining Chairs

A set of 12 Carolean style walnut dining chairs, the cane filled seats above a scrolling arcaded carved apron on inverted baluster column supports with Spanish scroll feet joined by stretchers, early 20thC.
£1,400-1,800   *CSK*

A set of Chippendale period mahogany dining chairs, comprising 6 side chairs and 2 armchairs.
£9,000-12,000   *P(M)*

A set of 8 mahogany dining chairs, including 2 carvers, each with an eared shaped toprail and pierced ladder back carved with stiff leaves, above a padded drop-in seat, on cabriole legs with cabochon headings and claw and ball feet.
£1,200-1,700   *CSK*

A George I walnut dining chair, the cresting rail with compressed centre panel, over a solid vase splat, drop-in seat raised upon cabriole front supports terminating in pad feet and turned and block carved back supports tied by baluster turned and block carved stretchers.
£370-500   *HSS*

A set of 6 late Victorian mahogany dining chairs, of George III design, including an armchair, each with a serpentine and foliate carved toprail above a pierced scrolling splat, with leatherette drop-in seats below, on cabriole legs with claw and ball feet and scroll headings.
£1,200-1,700   *CSK*

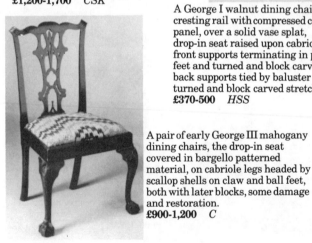

A pair of early George III mahogany dining chairs, the drop-in seat covered in bargello patterned material, on cabriole legs headed by scallop shells on claw and ball feet, both with later blocks, some damage and restoration.
£900-1,200   *C*

A pair of mahogany George III Chippendale style chairs, with raised scrolling bead moulded front legs, loose seats, c1780.
£550-650   *HSS*

A set of 4 single and 2 arm mahogany dining chairs, in George II style, with drop-in seats above the gadrooned apron raised on heavy cabriole legs with claw and ball feet.
£1,000-1,500   *AG*

A set of 8 mahogany dining chairs, of George III design, each with serpentine cresting and carved pierced foliate splat above an upholstered drop-in seat, on carved cabriole legs with claw and ball feet and acanthus headings.
£2,200-2,600   *CSK*

A set of 14 George III style mahogany ladder back dining chairs, with pierced waved horizontal splats headed by anthemions, on moulded square chamfered legs.
£1,800-2,200   *Bon*

A set of 12 George III style mahogany dining chairs, including 2 armchairs, with pierced interlaced tracery splats, on cabriole legs and claw and ball feet.
£3,500-4,500   *Bon*

A set of 6 Regency period mahogany sabre leg dining chairs, the backs with a carved scallop shell central to the horizontal bars, turned and rope twist cresting rails, the seats caned, some restoration.
£3,500-4,500   *WW*

A set of 8 mahogany dining chairs, of George III design, including 2 armchairs, with upholstered drop-in seats.
£1,700-2,000   *CSK*

If period, (c1760), the price of these chairs would be more like £6,000-8,000.

Six George III style hardwood dining chairs, with drop-in seats in tapestry, on square supports.
£350-450   *HCH*

A set of 8 mahogany dining chairs, of George III design, including 2 armchairs, with gadrooned banded aprons, on cabriole legs with claw and ball feet with shell headings.
£3,200-3,600   *CSK*

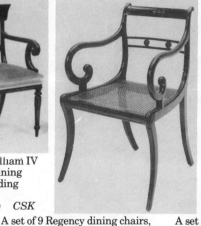

A set of 8 William IV mahogany dining chairs, including 2 armchairs.
£2,200-2,700   *CSK*

A beechwood and painted dining chair, the shield shaped back with vase shaped splat with Prince-of-Wales feathers, with padded seat covered in apricot repp, on slightly splayed legs headed by husks, some restoration, later blocks.
£200-300   *C*

A set of 9 Regency dining chairs, with stained beech frames and brass inlay, caned seats and sabre legs, comprising 7 side and 2 elbow chairs.
£4,500-5,000   *WW*

A set of 7 George III mahogany dining chairs, the tapestry upholstered seats on moulded tapered square legs with H-shaped stretchers and spade feet, some damage and restoration.
£2,500-3,500   *S(S)*

A set of 8 Hepplewhite style mahogany dining chairs, the pierced splat backs with ribbon tied motifs, the moulded frames with serpentine crests carved in a leaf spray, the leather drop-in seats on front square chamfered legs with H stretchers.
£2,000-2,500   *WW*

A set of 6 William IV mahogany railback dining chairs, with foliate carved mid bars and figured gold velvet upholstered drop-in seats, on reeded turned legs, c1830.
£1,400-1,800   *S(S)*

A set of 6 William IV mahogany railback dining chairs, including a pair of armchairs, with carved mid rails and red dralon upholstered drop-in seats, on lobed baluster turned legs, c1835.
£1,600-2,000   *S(S)*

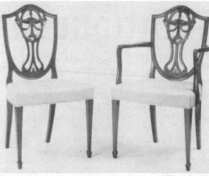

A set of 8 mahogany dining chairs, of Hepplewhite design, each with a shield shaped back, pierced vase and swag splat above a padded seat, on square tapering legs with spade feet, including 2 armchairs.
£2,500-3,500   *CSK*

A set of 6 William IV mahogany dining chairs, the acanthus carved lappeted scrolling semi-balloon backs above upholstered seats, on reeded turned tapering legs.
£2,000-3,000   *CSK*

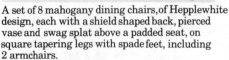

A set of 5 Regency mahogany dining chairs, including an armchair.
£900-1,200   *CSK*

A set of 6 William IV rosewood dining chairs, each with an acanthus scroll, berry and foliate carved top, centre rail and reeded waisted uprights above a drop-in seat on acanthus headed reeded tapering legs, 2 seats missing.
£1,400-1,700   *CSK*

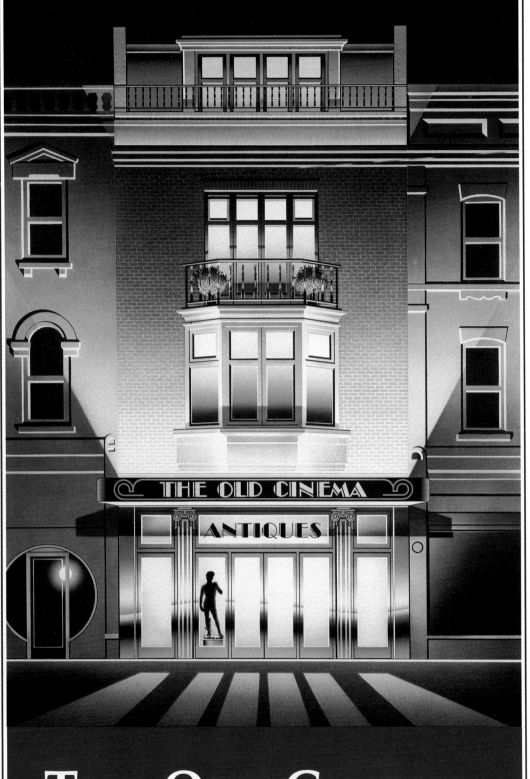

A matched set of 6 Charles II carved oak Yorkshire chairs, now with figured seat cushions and loose covers, c1680. **£6,000-7,000** *S(S)*

A Charles I oak coffer with moulded top above a fluted frieze, the three-panelled front carved with stylised flowerheads and the initials AW flanked by foliate strapwork and stile supports, Somerset, c1640, 42in (106cm) wide. **£1,500-2,500** *S(S)*

A mahogany Windsor chair, one arm repaired, mid-19thC. **£2,500-3,500** *C*

An oak bench with padded seat covered in close-nailed brown leather, on turned legs and square channelled stretchers, basically 17thC, 60in (152.5cm) wide. **£2,700-4,000** *C*

A Charles II oak bench with solid seat, the plain frieze with channels, on four baluster legs joined by stretchers, one stretcher replaced, 67in (170cm) wide. **£2,500-3,500** *C*

An ebonised oak and fruitwood chest, inlaid with ivory and mother-of-pearl in two sections, the panelled drawer inlaid with the date 1652, 19thC. **£3,000-5,000** *C*

A primitive Welsh chair, dry scraped down to it's original paint finish. **£1,000-1,500** *SWN*

A Queen Anne oak bureau bookcase, with associated top, the featherbanded fall revealing stepped interior, on later bun feet, c1710, 79in (199cm) high. **£2,500-3,500** *S(S)*

A William and Mary burr yew chest inlaid with geometric lines, on later bun feet with later veneer. **£6,000-7,000** *C*

An oak bureau, the fall front revealing a fitted interior, with two short and three long drawers, on bracket feet, early 19thC, 36in (92cm) wide. **£1,500- 2,500** *GAK*

A George II mahogany side table, with moulded top above waved apron, on cabriole legs headed by acanthus on claw-and-ball feet, small repair. **£6,000-8,000** *C*

A George I oak lowboy, with crossbanded top, on pad feet, c1715. **£10,000-12,000** *S(NY)*

A William and Mary burr yew wood and yew wood side table, the legs joined by wavy double Y stretchers, on later inverted cup feet. **£8,000-10,000** *C*

A pot board dresser, with plate racks over three drawers, with original fretwork, South Wales, c1785. **£5,000-6,000** *PHA*

A Charles II oak side table, the plank top enclosing a well, the front with two simulated drawers, on bun feet, back feet replaced, restorations. **£5,000-6,000** *C*

A George III oak cupboard dresser with a rare three cupboard formation, North Wales, c1780. **£9,000-12,000** *PHA*

A French Provincial walnut buffet, on later beechwood ball feet, mid-18thC. **£2,500-3,500** *C*

A George III oak dresser, the raised back with moulded cornice, the base flanked by reeded quarter turned pilasters, on stile feet, c1790. **£3,000-5,000** *S(S)*

A George III oak and pine dresser, with associated back, on stile feet, base c1780, top early 19thC. **£2,500-4,000** *S(S)*

A pair of Regency oak and ebonised daybeds, covered in blue striped repp, on hairy monopodia with paw feet, inscribed in ink underneath 5244, repair to seat rail. **£16,000-19,000** *C*

A George III mahogany and painted four-poster bed, the arched tester painted with flowers on a cream ground, the reeded end posts carved with wheat ears and with reeded lower parts, with box-spring and mattress, 1790. **£12,000-15,000** *S*

A black and gilt japanned four-poster bed, on turned feet, late 19thC. **£3,500-4,500** *C*

A walnut and parcel-gilt lit en bateau, the curtain edged with original bobbin tassels, early 19thC. **£18,000-22,000** *C*

An Empire mahogany bed, each end faced by a free-standing column, c1810, 60in (152.5cm) wide, 83in (210.5cm) long. **£10,000-12,000** *S*

A blue and grey painted lit à la polonaise, with dome hanging canopy, on scroll feet joined by a waved rail carved and decorated on one side only, one rail later. **£8,000-10,000** *C*

A mahogany tester bed, with two George III front posts, made up and requires restoration. **£2,000-3,000** *C*

A Louis XVI painted and parcel-gilt bed, with guilloche-carved frame, the arched upholstered back surmounted by a swagged urn, with over-scrolled padded ends and fluted tapering legs, with later oval corona, circa 1785, 76in (193cm) wide. **£12,000-15,000** *S*

A George III mahogany breakfront bookcase with some alterations. **£10,000-12,000** *S(NY)*

A Regency mahogany and ebony bookcase, on bun feet, restorations to one back foot. **£9,000-11,000** *C*

A George III mahogany breakfront bookcase cabinet in two parts, 3rd qtr.18thC. **£30,000-40,000** *S(NY)*

A George III mahogany bookcase in three sections, 88in (224cm) wide. **£8,000-9,000** *C*

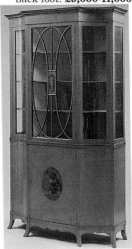

An Edwardian satinwood and painted display cabinet, 78in (198cm) high. **£5,000-7,000** *C*

A Louis XV ormolu mounted tulipwood, kingwood and marquetry secrétaire à abattant, with 'arc-en-arbalette' breccia marble top. **£27,000-37,000** *C*

pair of Regency mahogany, rcel-gilt bookcases, adapted. 9,000-22,000 *C*

A George II mahogany breakfront bookcase in the manner of Thomas Chippendale, on shaped bracket feet. **£85,000-90,000** *C*

A George II mahogany breakfront bookcase, the broken architectural pediment above 4 glazed doors, on plinth base, originally fitted in an alcove. **£6,500-7,500** *Bon*

A George I small walnut bureau cabinet, with moulded swan neck cornice, c1720.
£37,000-45,000 *S*

A George III satinwood secrétaire cabinet crossbanded in amarillo, the cornice surmounted by four later urn-shaped finials, the base with fall flap and mahogany lined drawers.
£27,000-32,000 *C*

A George I figured walnut bureau cabinet, the broken scroll pediment with 3 later urn finials above a pair of later bracket feet, restorations.
£25,000-30,000 *C*

A George I figured walnut bureau cabinet, the base in t parts, inlaid with featherban the flap enclosing a fitted interior, on later bun feet.
£10,000-15,000 *C*

A Biedermeier birch secrétaire à abattant, on block feet, restorations.
£3,000-5,000 *C*

A George II mahogany bureau bookcase, 77in (196cm) high.
£5,000-7,000 *CNY*

A Louis XVI kingwood and marquetry secrétaire à abattant, with grey fossil marble top, the interior of the fall lined with leather, 56½in (143.5cm) high.
£13,000-16,000 *C*

A George II walnut bure bookcase, with 4 long cockbeaded drawers, on later bracket feet, c1750
£13,000-18,000 *S(NY)*

A Queen Anne walnut escritoire, formerly on bun feet. **£11,000-14,000** *C*

A Queen Anne burr walnut bureau cabinet in three sections, on later bun feet, the sides with carrying handles, some restorations, 76½in (194cm) high.
£16,000-20,000 *C*

A George I figured walnut bureau cabinet, with fitted interior and well, on later bun feet.
£21,000-25,000 *C*

A Venetian yellow painted lacquer pover bureau cabinet, with fitted interior, on cabriole legs and paw feet. **£7,500-9,000** *C*

A George I walnut bureau, inlaid overall with featherbanding, on bracket feet, 43in (110cm) high. **£10,000-12,000** *C*

A pair of ormolu mounted open bookcases with inset Basque Jaspe marble tops. **£6,000-8,000** *C*

A Victorian ormolu mounted amboyna display cabinet, one putto mount lacking, 26¹/₂in (67cm). **£2,000-3,000** *C*

A Queen Anne walnut bureau with featherbanding, the flap lined with green baize, 30in (76cm). **£4,000-5,000** *C*

A George III mahogany corner cabinet, the triangular pediment with dentilled border, on moulded plinth, 91¹/₂in (233cm) high. **£4,500-6,000** *CNY*

A George I inlaid walnut bureau, with herringbone crossbanding, on bracket feet, restorations, 36in (92cm). **£11,000-13,000** *S(NY)*

A Victorian walnut display cabinet, with ormolu mounts, 30in (76cm). **£600-800** *GAK*

A Queen Anne walnut bureau, inlaid overall with boxwood stringing above a flap enclosing fitted interior, restorations, 31in (79cm). **£6,000-8,000** *C*

A boulle, ebony and brass side cabinet, the doors inlaid with foliate strapwork, 40¹/₂in (103cm) wide. **£2,000-3,000** *C*

A Portuguese carved rosewood bureau, the sloping front enclosing a fitted interior with small drawers, pigeonholes and a central cupboard, the serpentine lower part with four graduated long drawers flanked by carved canted corners, mid-18thC 43in (110cm) high. **£22,000-30,000** *S*

291

A Louis XV marquetry bureau, with pull-out leather lined writing slide, on cabriole legs, all inlaid with naive marquetry, 39¹/₂in (100cm). **£40,000-50,000** *S*

A George III mahogany bonheur du jour, banded in satinwood and inlaid overall with boxwood stringing, on brass paw feet, 36in (92cm). **£9,000-11,000** *C*

A Regency kingwood and tulipwood cylinder bureau, inlaid with boxwood and ebony lines. 30in (76cm). **£6,000-8,000** *C*

A Regency amaranth, satinwood and ebony cabinet-on-stand, on beaded turned tapering legs with lotus leaf capitals with concave-fronted undertier, feet damaged, 50in (127cm) wide. **£5,000-8,000** *C*

A Portuguese brass mounted rosewood, ebonised and tortoiseshell cabinet-on-stand, with trade label, with brass finials, on bun feet, 19thC. 48in (122cm). **£12,000-15,000** *C*

A figured walnut cabinet-on-stand, inlaid overall with featherbands, the stand with a frieze drawer, on multi-baluster legs and bun feet, 22in (56cm). **£5,000-7,000** *C*

A Louis XIV marquetry bureau marazin, with two drawers in the frieze, a recessed cupboard with four further drawers, the whole inlaid with floral marquetry on an ebony ground, late 17thC, 44¹/₂in (113cm). **£17,000-20,000** *S*

A Flemish silver-mounted parcel gilt, tortoiseshell, ebony, rosewood and marquetry cabinet-on-stand, the sides inlaid with vases of flowers, 76¹/₂in (193cm). **£75,000-100,000** *C*

A Charles II japanned cabinet on a silvered wood stand, the stand with rich foliate scrollwork, the decoration re-painted, c1680, 42¹/₂in (108cm). **£9,000-11,000** *S*

A pair of mid-Victorian ormolu mounted, amboyna and walnut side cabinets, 51in (129.5cm). **£17,000-20,000** C

A pair of ormolu mounted kingwood and parquetry side cabinets c1875. **£7,000-9,000** C

A William IV amboyna and parcel gilt side cabinet, the doors enclosing purple velvet-lined shelves, on plinth base, 72in (182.5cm). **£5,000-6,000** C

A lacquer and kingwood parquetry side cabinet with portor marble top, stamped P. Garnier, part c1780, altered, 88in (224cm). **£25,000-35,000** S

An early Victorian ormolu mounted and brass inlaid calamander side cabinet with marble top, 80½in (204cm). **£5,000-7,000** C

A George IV mahogany folio cabinet with twin reading stand, each end with door enclosing two vertical dividers, 39in (99cm). **£3,000-5,000** C

An Edwardian satinwood and painted side cabinet, 48in (122cm). **£4,000-5,000** C

A pair of late Victorian amboyna cabinets by Gillow & Co. **£6,000-8,000** C

A German walnut and marquetry cabinet, with cast iron handles, 17th/18thC. **£7,000-9,000** C

An Italian ebony and white metal inlaid cabinet, early 18thC with later back, 34in (86cm). **£9,000-12,000** C

A George III mahogany collector's cabinet-on-stand, with 20 small drawers, and contents list in French, stamped. **£15,000-20,000** C

An Indian rosewood and ivory inlaid cabinet, with chequered band to the base, restorations, 21in (53cm). **£5,000-6,000** C

An Italian bone and ebony cabinet with later stand, restorations, the cabinet 17thC. **£20,000-25,000** C

A Louis XV painted desk armchair, mid-18thC.
£6,500-8,000 *S*

A matched pair of Louis XV giltwood bergères, re-gilded, stamped. **£15,000-20,000** *C*

An early George III mahogany wing armchair.
£12,000-15,000 *S(NY)*

A Louis XV walnut large bergère, cabriole legs, mid-18thC.
£18,000-20,000 *S*

A George III mahogany library armchair.
£3,000-4,000 *C*

A Queen Anne walnut armchair on later blocks.
£7,000-9,000 *C*

Two giltwood bergères of Louis XV style on scrolling cabriole legs.
£3,000-4,000 *C*

A pair of Louis XV walnut bergères, arched stuffed backs, padded arms, loose cushioned seats and cabriole legs, mid- 18th C.
£8,000-10,000 *S*

A George II walnut wing armchair on cabriole legs and pad feet, later blocks, minor restorations. **£8,000-9,000** *C*

A William and Mary elmwood wing armchair, on pad feet. c1700. **£6,000-8,000** *S(NY)*

A George III mahogany armchair, with waved padded back, arms and seat upholstered with floral needlework, on cabriole legs carved with acanthus and flowerheads, claw-and-ball feet, seat rail reconstructed, restored, **£9,000-11,000** *C*

A George II walnut wing armchair, on cabriole legs, minor restorations.
£9,000-11,000 *C*

A Queen Anne beechwood wing armchair, restorations to front legs, later blocks, some replacements. **£8,000-10,000** *C*

A pair of walnut bergères, arched padded backs, sides and cushions covered in moiré silk, on short cabriole legs with scroll toes, restorations. **£7,000-8,000** *C*

A George III mahogany wing armchair, minor restorations.
£4,000-6,000 *C*

A William and Mary beechwood and fruitwood armchair, one later stretcher. **£8,000-10,000** *C*

A pair of George III gilt metal mounted ebonised open armchairs, on turned tapering fluted legs headed by anthemia, redecorated, the gilt metal added in 19thC. **£5,000-6,000** *C*

A George II mahogany open armchair, with later upholstery and blocks. **£25,000-30,000** *C*

A George II red japanned caned armchair, attributed to G. Grendy. **£5,000-7,000** *S*

A Russian ormolu mounted mahogany bergère, on sabre legs, early 19thC. **£38,000-45,000** *C*

A pair of George III mahogany library armchairs, on square fluted tapering legs, c1775. **£20,000-25,000** *S(NY)*

A Chippendale walnut armchair. **£16,000-20,000** *CNY*

A George I burr walnut armchair, restorations. **£40,000-50,000** *C*

A George I walnut open armchairs, formerly with stretchers, restorations. **£14,000-16,000** *C*

A set of 6 Dutch walnut open armchairs, on scrolled pad feet. **£4,000-5,000** *C*

A pair of George III mahogany chairs, restorations. **£10,000-15,000** *C*

A pair of George II japanned chairs. **£8,000-12,000** *S*

A George III mahogany desk chair, with pierced splat, on chamfered legs joined by stretchers, later blocks. **£4,000-5,000** *C*

295

An ormolu mounted mahogany revolving desk chair, restorations. **£2,000-3,000** *C*

A Regency mahogany library bergère, with cane filled back, arms and seat, lacking part of one arm support. **£2,000-3,000** *C*

A Regency mahogany tub chair, with cane filled arched back and seat and squab cushion, stamped S. **£2,000-2,500** *C*

A giltwood open armchair, with arched padded panel back, early 19thC. **£5,000-6,000** *C*

A pair of modern ebonised and parcel gilt open armchairs. **£3,000-5,000** *C*

A George III mahogany bergère, numbered in ink no.397, indistinct inscription. **£1,500-2,500** *C*

A George III mahogany tub armchair, upholstered in close nailed leather. **£5,000-6,000** *C*

A pair of George III mahogany open armchairs. **£9,500-10,500** *C*

A Regency mahogany bergère, partially re-railed, and another matching chair. **£3,000-4,000** *C*

Two French open armchairs, one walnut, one elm, late 17thC. **£3,500-4,500** *C*

A pair of George III beechwood open armchairs, restorations. **£2,000-3,000** *C*

A pair of George III mahogany open armchairs, restorations. **£6,500-8,000** *C*

Two Flemish open armchairs, late 17thC. **£5,500-6,000** *C*

A Pair of George III giltwood open chairs. **£20,000-22,000** *C*

A pair of George III giltwood open armchairs, re-gilded, minor variations in size. **£4,000-5,000** *C*

A George III giltwood open armchair. **£2,000-3,000** *C*

A Napoleon III rosewood prayer seat, with hinged back, covered in needlework, **£700-900** *C*

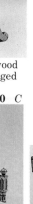

A Regency rosewood library open armchair, lacking reading stand. **£2,200-2,500** *C*

A pair of Louis XVI carved giltwood armchairs, c1780. **£11,000-13,000** *S*

A pair of Italian walnut and parcel gilt open armchairs, basically 17thC. **£2,200-2,500** *C*

A Victorian parcel gilt and polychrome painted Gothic suite, comprising a sofa and 2 open armchairs. **£3,500-4,500** *C*

A North Italian simulated rosewood and parcel gilt Klismos armchair, c1820. **£7,000-8,000** *C*

A pair of Empire white painted and parcel gilt fauteuils, stamped Cressent. **£16,000-20,000** *C*

A rare Empire mahogany Campaign chair, stamped J D c1805. **£6,000-7,000** *S*

A pair of Empire mahogany fauteuils, plain frame and armrests. **£4,000-6,000** *C*

A pair mahogany armchairs, the arm rests with ball finials and baluster supports c1800. **£10,000-12,000** *S*

A pair of Louis XVI painted armchairs, stamped Jacob, c1785. **£5,000-6,000** *S*

A Restauration rosewood armchair, c1830. **£8,000-10,000** *S*

A set of 4 North Italian parcel gilt and grained open armchairs. **£9,000-10,000** *C*

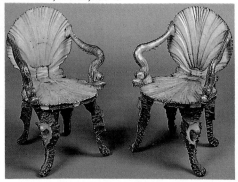

A harlequin pair of Venetian silvered grotto chairs, with scallop backs and seats, dolphin arm supports and shaped legs carved with rockwork and scrolls. **£8,000-10,000** *C*

A pair of Louis XVI fauteuils, stamped G. Jacob, restored. **£5,500-6,500** *C*

A pair of Empire chairs, later blocks. **£1,200-1,500** *C*

A set of 6 Regency mahogany dining chairs, and 2 others of later date, one with Norman Adams label. **£5,200-6,000** *C*

A set of 4 George IV mahogany hall chairs, by Gillows, slight variations in carving, repaired. **£3,500-4,500** *C*

An Empire mahogany chair, perhaps Jacob Desmalter, c1810. **£2,500-3,500** *S*

A set of 10 Regency dining chairs, stamped Ford, damage. **£12,000-14,000** *C*

A set of 12 Regency mahogany dining chairs, minor restorations. **£40,000-45,000** *C*

A set of 4 Piedmontese painted chairs, 2 repaired, redecorated, traces of old gilding, late 18thC. **£5,000-7,000** *C*

A set of 12 WilliamIV rosewood dining chairs, with variously upholstered seats above cane filled seats, one lacking splat, one re-railed. **£8,000-9,000** *C*

A set of 12 Regency mahogany dining chairs, restored. **£20,000-22,000** *C*

A set of 4 satinwood dining chairs, each with pierced shield shaped back painted with an oval. **£2,500-3,500** *C*

A set of 12 Regency parcel gilt simulated rosewood dining chairs, by Gee. **£26,000-30,000** *C*

A set of 4 Regency gilt metal mounted ebonised chairs, on X-frame supports, stamped IW, minor restorations, decorations retouched. **£4,500-5,500** *C*

A George I walnut tallboy, inlaid with featherbands, on later bracket feet, 41in (104cm). **£6,000-8,000** *C*

A George III walnut tallboy, with fluted quadrant columns and brass mounts, c1765, 44in (112cm). **£6,000-8,000** *S*

A Queen Anne walnut tallboy, Pennsylvania, c1750, 41½in (105cm). **£9,000-11,000** *CNY*

A mid-Georgian mahogany bachelor's chest, with hinged top, 33in (84cm). **£14,000-16,000** *C*

A mid-Georgian mahogany tallboy, 41in (104cm). **£8,000-10,000** *C*

A walnut oyster veneered chest, inlaid and crossbanded with fruitwood, part early 18thC. **£2,000-3,000** *C*

A Chippendale mahogany chest of drawers, c1780, 41in (104cm). **£4,500-6,000** *CNY*

A George II mahogany tallboy, with dentil cornice and broken dentil triangular pediment, c1755, 48in (122cm). **£5,500-6,500** *S*

A Queen Anne figured maple tallboy, in 2 sections, New England, c1750, 40½in (102cm). **£8,000-10,000** *CNY*

A Chippendale carved mahogany block front chest of drawers, Massachusetts, 37½in (95cm). **£12,500-14,000** *CNY*

A George III mahogany secrétaire tallboy, with moulded broken swan neck pediment centred by scrolling acanthus above a band of blind fretwork, the secrétaire drawer with fitted interior, 46½in (116.5cm). **£10,000-12,000** *C*

299

A George III mahogany chest, inlaid with chevron bands, 42½in (107cm). **£10,000-12,000** *C*

A North Italian walnut bombé commode, 38in (96.5cm). **£8,000-10,000** *C*

A Regency mahogany chest, inlaid with fruitwood, 42in (106cm). **£3,000-4,000** *C*

A George III mahogany dressing chest, the top drawer with a slide, previously fitted, 43½in (110cm). **£8,000-10,000** *C*

A George III mahogany dressing commode. **£7,000-9,000** *C*

A late Victorian satinwood and marquetry commode, by Edwards & Roberts, banded and inlaid with kingwood and harewood, 60in (152cm). **£10,000-12,000** *C*

A George III mahogany chest, inlaid with ebonised lines, with slide above 2 short and 4 graduated mahogany lined drawers, on angled bracket feet and later blocks, 40in (102cm).**£5,500-6,500** *C*

A George III mahogany and marquetry chest, inlaid with fruitwood lines, the top with an oval medallion with an urn, 41½in (105cm). **£4,000-5,000** *C*

A George III parquetry commode, the doo. with central medallions frame. by parquetry, enclosing slides, 66in (168cm). **£55,000-75,000**

A George III satinwood commode, crossbanded with amaranth and inlaid with boxwood and ebonised lines, restorations, 39½in (100cm). **£17,000-20,000** *C*

A German walnut parquetry commode, inlaid with simple parquetry, c1740, 46in (117cm). **£8,000-10,000** *S*

A bird's-eye maple chest with slide, early 19thC, with restorations, 30in (76cm). **£2,000-3,000** *C*

A Louis XIV boulle commode, inlaid partly in coloured shell on a brass and tortoiseshell ground, 37in (119cm). **£120,000-125,000** *S*

A Louis XVI style kingwood and ormolu commode, by Henry Dasson, dated 1889, the doors inlaid with trellis pattern, 54½in (138cm). **£9,000-11,000** *Bon*

A Dutch black and gilt commode, redecorated, 36½in (93cm). **£4,500-5,500** *C*

A Louis XV Provincial walnut commode, 50in (127cm). **£6,000-8,000** *C*

A Danish walnut and parcel gilt commode, the pierced frieze carved with acanthus, C-scrolls, rockwork and flowerheads, on cabriole legs headed by acanthus with scroll feet, mid-18thC, 37in (94cm). **£20,000-22,000** *C*

An Italian walnut commode, with 3 drawers, on later short cabriole legs, restorations, 47in (119cm). **£6,000-8,000** *C*

A Venetian walnut, olivewood and marquetry commode, heightened with mother-of-pearl and bone, the eared crossbanded top inlaid with Apollo within a scrolling cartouche, the drawers inlaid with a putto and scrolling foliage, the sides inlaid with vases of foliage, early 18thC. 30½in (77cm). **£15,000-18,000** *C*

A Louis XV ormolu mounted kingwood commode, 58in (147cm). **£16,500-18,000** *C*

A South Italian walnut commode, banded overall with tulipwood with moulded quarter veneered top, minor restorations, 3rd quarter 18thC, 50in (127cm). **£18,000-20,000** *C*

A Louis XIV olivewood veneered commode, c1710, 52in (130cm). **£8,000-9,000** *S*

A North Italian walnut, burr beech ebonised and marquetry commode, 18thC, restorations, 56in (143cm). **£9,000-12,000** *C*

A Regency mahogany pedestal desk, outlined with ebony stringing, with leather-lined top, c1805, 61½in (155cm). **£28,000-30,000** *S*

A Louis XV style kingwood, parquetry and ormolu bureau, late 19thC, 50in (127cm). **£7,000-9,000** *Bon*

A George III mahogany tambour desk in Chippendale style, c1780, 50½in (128cm). **£8,000-10,000** *S*

A mahogany kneehole desk, with 4 banks of drawers below slides, handles replaced, c1800, 47in (119cm). **£14,000-16,000** *S*

A satinwood double-sided library desk, now stamped Gillows, part early 19thC, 79in (200cm). **£8,000-10,000** *S*

A George III pedestal partners desk, leather-lined top, by S&H Jewell, 71½in (180cm). **£9,000-10,000** *C*

A George III mahogany double-sided library desk, with leather-lined top, c177 69in (175cm). **£25,000-30,000** *S*

A William IV mahogany Gothic revival pedestal desk with leather-lined top, c1830, 58in (147cm). **£4,000-5,000** *S*

A George III mahogany pedestal partners desk, with leather-lined top, locks stamped Lingham, 61in (155cm). **£11,000-13,000** *C*

A George I walnut dressing chest of drawers, crossbanded throughout, 33in (84cm). **£7,000-9,000** *S(NY)*

An early Georgian walnut kneehole desk, 31in (78.5cm). **£7,000-9,000** *C*

A mid-Victorian walnut and marquetry davenport, 23in (59cm). **£2,500-3,500** *C*

A George III giltwood mirror, with pierced carved frame, re-silvered, 38in (96.5cm). **£7,000-9,000** *C*

A Pair of George III giltwood, églomisé two-light girandoles, 37in (94cm). **£7,500-8,500** *S(NY)*

A George II giltwood mirror, c1740. **£8,000-9,000** *S*

A George II walnut and parcel gilt mirror, 50in (127cm). **£5,000-6,000** *C*

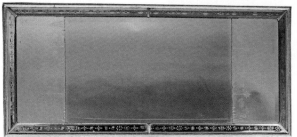

A Queen Anne giltwood overmantel mirror, with triple engraved plates, and moulded frame, 55in (140cm) wide. **£3,500-4,500** *C*

A George III giltwood mirror, c1760, 54in (137cm). **£11,000-13,000** *S(NY)*

A George II mirror, c1730. **£3,500-4,500** *S*

A George II giltwood mirror, re-gilt. **£5,000-6,000** *C*

A George I walnut and parcel gilt mirror, lacking cresting. **£2,000-3,000** *C*

A George II giltwood mirror, embellished, 76in (193cm). **£7,500-8,500** *S(NY)*

A George II giltwood mirror, possibly Irish, c1755. **£5,500-6,500** *S*

A pair of George I gilt gesso mirrors, each two-part bevelled and arched plate within mirror borders c1725, 60in (152cm). **£45,000-50,000** *S(NY)*

A George II giltwood mirror, c1755, 52¹/₂in (133cm). **£5,000-6,000** *S*

A George III giltwood mirror, 69in (175cm). **£11,000-13,000** *S(NY)*

A George III giltwood mirror, the frame with acorns and oak leaves, re-gilt, 34 1/2 in (87cm). **£7,000-9,000** *C*

An Irish George II giltwood grotto mirror, restored, 60in (152cm). **£10,000-12,000** *C*

A George III giltwood mirror, the frame pierced and carved, damage and restored, 48in (122cm). **£12,000-14,000** *C*

A George III giltwood overmantel mirror, restored, 29in (74cm). **£7,000-9,000** *C*

A George III mirror. **£7,000-9,000** *C*

A George III giltwood mirror, with later plate, 49in (124.5cm). **£4,000-6,000** *C*

A pair of George III carton-pierre mirrors, later plate and restored, 92in (234cm). **£15,000-16,000** *C*

An early George III giltwood mirror, 42in (107cm). **£2,000-3,000** *S*

A George III style giltwood mirror. **£5,000-6,000** *C*

A George II wall mirror, some damage, c1750. **£7,000-10,000** *S*

A George III mirror, in John Linnell style, re-gilded, 53in (134.5cm). **£14,000-16,000** *C*

A pair of Regency cobalt and mirrored glass mounted mirrors, slight losses, c1800, 24in (61cm) **£6,000-7,000** *S(NY)*

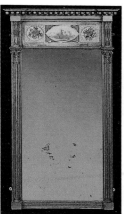

A Regency gilt and composition wall mirror, 52¹/₂in (132cm). **£2,000-3,000** *C*

A Regency giltwood and verre églomisé mirror, restored, 49in (125cm). **£2,000-2,500** *C*

A giltwood mirror, 19thC, 62¹/₂in (158cm). **£1,200-1,500** *C*

A Florentine giltwood mirror, with pierced carved frame, some losses, 64in (163cm). **£4,500-5,500** *C*

A Danish parcel gilt and walnut mirror, mid-18thC, 53in (135cm). **£7,000-9,000** *C*

A Scandinavian giltwood mirror. **£2,000-3,000** *C*

A giltwood mirror, 59in (150cm). **£2,500-3,000** *C*

A giltwood and ebonised mirror, re-gilt. **£2,000-3,000** *C*

A Regency giltwood mirror, with convex plate and ebonised slip, 30in (76cm) diam. **£2,500-3,500** *C*

A giltwood mirror, c1850, 52in (132cm). **£4,000-5,000** *C*

A German verre églomisé mirror, 18thC. **£5,500-6,000** *C*

A Regency giltwood mirror, 41¹/₂in (105cm). **£2,500-3,000** *C*

An early Victorian giltwood and composition 4-light Gothic girandole, 75in (190.5cm). **£3,000-4,000** *C*

A pair of mahogany and parcel gilt mirrors, 19thC, 53in (135cm). **£3,000-4,000** *C*

A kingwood toilet mirror, the frame edged with boxwood, bone finial, restored, 24in (61cm) high. **£3,500-4,500** *C*

A Regency giltwood mirror, restored, 42in (107cm). **£2,000-2,500** *C*

A Dutch six-leaf painted leather screen, with imitation coromandel lacquer, the panelled back painted later, distressed, 18thC, 90in (229cm). **£3,500-4,500** *C*

A painted leather six-leaf screen, late 17thC, borders refreshed, 77¹/₂ (197cm). **£10,000- 12,000** *C*

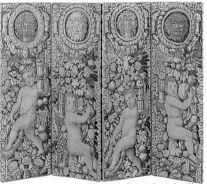

A four-leaf screen with 17thC wool and silk Brussels tapestry, minor restoration, mark of Jean Rals, 61in (155cm). **£5,000-6,000** *C*

A carved giltwood firescreen, stamped G. Jacob, with trestle feet, 40in (101.5cm). **£3,500-4,500** *S*

An Empire ormolu mounted burr maple firescreen, with later gros point floral needlework panel, possibly German, 41in (104cm) high. **£3,000-4,000** *C*

Two Louis XVI giltwood firescreens, by Jean Baptiste-Claude Sené, with Beauvais tapestry panels **£15,000-17,000** *C*

A George III mahogany two-leaf screen, with later painted canvas panels, 45in (114cm) high. **£2,000-3,000** *C*

A Dutch six-leaf painted leather screen, the reverse painted later, restored, 18thC, 96¹/₂in (245cm) high. **£3,500-4,500** *C*

A Regency bronze mounted mahogany firescreen, with pleated silk panel, 55in (140cm) high. **£4,500-5,500** *S(NY)*

A Dutch six-leaf leather screen, painted with chinoiserie scenes, the leather 18thC, frame later, 98in (249cm) high. **£10,500-12,000** *C*

A George III mahogany sideboard, the bowfronted top crossbanded in satinwood and tulipwood, above a central drawer and tambour shutter flanked by a cellaret drawer, on square tapering legs and spade feet, 36in (92cm). **£11,000-13,000** *C*

A Regency mahogany breakfront sideboard, banded with fruitwood and ebonised lines, repair to leg, 75in (191cm). **£2,000-3,000** *C*

A George III mahogany pedestal sideboard, with cellaret drawers, 91in (231cm). **£4,000-5,000** *C*

A George III mahogany bowfront sideboard, leg repaired, 72in (182cm). **£3,000-4,000** *Bon*

A George III mahogany sideboard, with bowfront top, central drawer and 2 cellaret drawers, inlaid with boxwood and ebonised lines and satinwood fan-shaped paterae, restoration to one front foot, 43in (109cm). **£3,000-4,000** *C*

A Regency mahogany sideboard, restorations, one drawer lacking back, 82in (208cm). **£4,500-5,500** *C*

A George III mahogany sideboard, with serpentine front, c1780, 60in (152cm). **£4,000-5,000** *S*

A Federal maple sideboard, with line inlays, probably Massachusetts, legs warped, 77¹/₂in (197cm). **£12,500-14,500** *CNY*

A Federal mahogany and mahogany veneer sideboard, New York, labelled Thomas Burling, c1785, 68in (172.5cm). **£17,000-19,000** *CNY*

A George III mahogany sideboard, banded with tulipwood and inlaid with chequered lines, probably Scottish, 72in (182.5cm). **£9,000-10,000** *C*

A mid-Victorian conversation settee, each end with rotating seat, on turned tapering legs, 68½in (173cm). **£5,000-6,000** *C*

A George III mahogany sofa, upholstered in close nailed wool, restoration, 94in (238cm). **£3,000-4,000** *C*

A George III needlework upholstered mahogany settee, alterations, 68in (173cm). **£3,500-4,500** *S(NY)*

A George IV beechwood two-part sofa, later brackets, partially re-supported, 93in (236cm). **£5,500-6,500** *C*

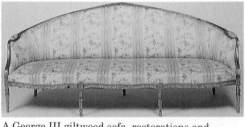

A Louis XV giltwood marquise, stamped Delanois, c1765, 43in (109cm). **£16,000-18,000** *S*

A George III giltwood sofa, restorations and re-gilt, 96in (244cm). **£10,000-12,000** *C*

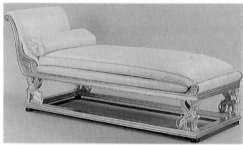

A gilt mahogany chaise longue, covered on close nailed leather, gilding later, 77in (196cm). **£3,000-4,000** *C*

A Regency brass inlaid rosewood sofa, the waved padded back with inlaid tablet, 75in (191cm). **£3,500-4,500** *C*

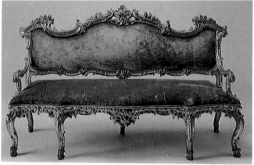

An Italian giltwood canape, upholstered in silk velvet, seat frame partially reinforced, mid-18thC, 77in (196cm). **£7,000-8,000** *C*

A Regency giltwood chaise longue, the moulded frame carved with eagle's head terminals, on eagle's claw-and-ball feet, with interchangeable side, 89in (226cm). **£6,000-7,000** *C*

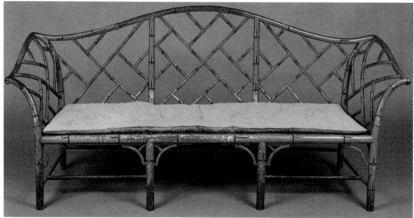

A George III simulated bamboo settee, with hump back and outscrolled arms filled with paling, the drop-in rush seat with squab covered in buttoned linen, on turned legs with pierced angle brackets joined by stretchers, seat distressed, 82$\frac{1}{2}$in (209cm). **£22,000-25,000** *C*

A double spoon ended giltwood settee, early 19thC. **£800-1,200** *GAK*

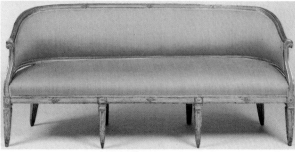

An Italian neo-classical grey painted and parcel gilt canape, redecorated, c1800. **£3,000-4,000** *C*

A Russian Nicholas I parcel gilt mahogany sofa, the padded back and drop-in seat upholstered in printed cloth, with solid scrolling arm supports and shaped legs 74in (188cm). **£3,500-5,000** *C*

A Louis XV beechwood sofa with flower carved moulded frame, arched stuffed back, padded arms, double serpentine fronted seat and cabriole legs, 51$\frac{1}{2}$in (131cm). **£8,000-10,000** *S*

An Italian giltwood sofa, upholstered in leather, the channelled seat rail on turned fluted tapering legs, late 18thC, 104in (264cm). **£12,000-15,000** *C*

A Louis XV beechwood sofa, with carved moulded frame, arched stuffed back, padded arms, loose cushioned seat and cabriole legs, mid-18thC, 77in (196cm). **£10,000-12,000** *S*

A George III mahogany dumb waiter, 59¹/₂in (150cm) high.
£2,500-3,500 *C*

An early George III mahogany urn stand, with pierced fret gallery, c1765, 12in (305cm) wide
£3,000-4,000 *S*

A George II mahogany bowl stand, 29¹/₂in (75cm).
£2,500-3,500 *S*

An early George III mahogany torchère, 49in (122cm) high.
£2,000-3,000 *C*

A pair of George II giltwood torchères, re-gilded, 43in (108cm).
£15,000-17,000 *C*

A George III satinwood whatnot, with cedar lined drawer, 52in (132cm) high.
£12,000-15,000 *C*

A pair of parcel gilt and ebonised pedestals, re-decorated, basically early 19thC, 47¹/₂in (120cm) high.
£15,000-18,000 *C*

A pair of George III mahogany washstands, inlaid with ebony stringing, formerly with mirrors, 19in (48cm) wide.
£2,000-3,000 *C*

A pair of ormolu mounted ebony boulle pedestals, 51in (130cm).
£10,000-12,000 *C*

A pair of mahogany dining room pedestals, each with a cellaret drawer, on later blocks, 36¹/₂in (93cm) high.
£6,000-8,000 *C*

A pair of Italian walnut and parcel gilt stands, each with later verde antico marble top, lacking one mask, previously washstands, 30¹/₂in (77cm) high.
£5,000-6,000 *C*

A Victorian mahogany reeded column, with acanthus leaf decoration, 39in (99cm).
£300-400 *PCh*

An early Victorian mahogany folio stand, by Kendell & Co., 36in (92cm).
£16,000-18,000 *C*

A walnut and parcel gilt stool, the cabriole legs carved with foliage, claw-and-ball feet, 19thC, 27in (69cm). **£2,500-3,500** *C*

A William and Mary walnut dressing stool, the over-upholstered seat raised on gadrooned trumpet legs, c1690, 23in (58cm).
£8,000-10,000 *S(NY)*

A pair of George III mahogany stools, the legs carved with blind fretwork, later cross struts, 19in (48cm). **£8,000-10,000** *C*

A Regency mahogany stool, in the manner of C. H. Tatham, the seat with scroll ends, 20¹/₂in (52cm). **£5,000-6,000** *C*

A George III Gothic cream painted stool, lacking upholstery, 16in (40.5cm). **£1,500-2,000** *C*

A mahogany stool, the padded seat covered in close nailed needlework, on carved cabriole legs headed by lion masks, on paw feet, 19thC, 26¹/₂in (67cm). **£3,500-4,500** *C*

A William and Mary beech and walnut stool, the padded seat covered in 17thC tapestry, formerly decorated.
£3,000-4,000 *C*

A pair of George II mahogany stools, each with rounded rectangular drop-in seat covered in bargello pattern, the waved frieze on cabriole legs and pad feet, 17in (43cm).
£10,000-12,000 *C*

A Regency white painted and parcel gilt stool, the padded seat covered in calico, on X-framed legs carved with flowerheads and cleft feet joined by a baluster stretcher, 20in (51cm). **£2,500-3,500** *C*

A matched pair of Regency mahogany X-frame stools, by Gillows, restored, 20¹/₂in (52cm). **£10,000-12,000** *C*

COLOUR REVIEW

A Regency painted and parcel gilt stool, after a design by Thomas Hope, c1810, 34½in (87cm). **£22,000-25,000** *S(NY)*

A second Empire ormolu footstool, the bowed upholstered top in floral velvet, with foliate 'pied-de-biche', 12½in (32cm). **£1,000-1,500** *C*

A giltwood stool, covered in tapestry, labelled S. Dawes & Sons, early 19thC, 19½in (49cm) **£3,000-4,000** *C*

A Louis XIV style giltwood stool, the X-shaped stretchers carved with conforming acanthus scrolls, 43in (109cm) **£2,000-3,000** *C*

A William IV mahogany bench, the waved frieze carved with acanthus and S-scrolls, 91in (231cm). **£3,000-4,000** *C*

A mahogany stool, with adjustable support and turned baluster legs, c1820, 17in (43cm). **£3,000-4,000** *S*

Two Victorian giltwood simulated bamboo stools, covered in green cotton, on turned sabre legs joined by X-shaped stretchers, 19in (48cm). **£3,500-4,500** *C*

A pair of Regency mahogany footstools, after a design by George Smith, minor restorations, 16in (41cm). **£2,000-3,000** *C*

A Regency beechwood tabouret, the waved seat rail centred with scallop shells and carved with acanthus, 21in (53cm). **£5,500-7,000** *C*

A French giltwood stool, after a design by A. C. M. Fournier, the seat rail, legs and X-shaped stretcher carved in the form of knotted rope, 19in (48cm) diam. **£3,000-4,000** *C*

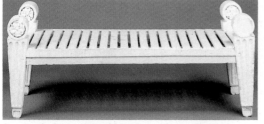

A pair of white painted benches, after a design by C. H. Tatham, slight differences, re-decorated, 57in (144.5cm). **£14,000-16,000** *C*

An ebonised scroll and cane footstool, early 19thC, 16in (41cm). **£150-200** *PCh*

312

A George III satinwood card table, banded in amaranth and inlaid with boxwood and ebonised lines, the top crossbanded in rosewood, restored, 36in (91cm). **£2,000-2,500** *C*

A George I laburnum concertina action card table, inlaid with featherbanding, 35in (88cm). **£8,000-10,000** *C*

A Russian mahogany architect's table, with double ratchet support, c1795, 40¹/₂in (102cm). **£14,000-15,000** *S*

A pair of George III painted and satinwood card tables, crossbanded with rosewood and decorated overall with flowers, foliage and husks, decoration later, gateleg action replaced, 36in (92cm). **£12,000-14,000** *C*

A pair of George III satinwood bedside tables, inlaid with mahogany lines, with hinged tops, restored. **£14,000-15,000** *C*

A mid-Georgian triple leaf tea and card table, the baize lined flap with counter wells above a deep frieze with hinged top, 29¹/₂in (75cm). **£6,000-7,000** *C*

A George III satinwood card table, crossbanded and inlaid with rosewood, decorated with flowers, 36in (91cm). **£9,000-10,000** *C*

A George III mahogany architect's table with pull-out section enclosing a fitted interior, 40in (101.5cm). **£6,000-8,000** *C*

A pair of mahogany card tables, with hinged tops, one later drawer, 36in (92cm). **£7,000-8,000** *C*

A George II mahogany concertina action card table, in the manner of Benjamin Goodison, restored 36in (91cm). **£12,000-15,000** *C*

A George III mahogany card table, banded in satinwood with hinged top, part of gateleg action replaced, 39in (99cm). **£2,000-2,500** *C*

A pair of Federal inlaid mahogany card tables, attributed to Jacob Forster, Massachusetts, c1800, 35in (89cm) diam. **£15,000-17,000** *CNY*

A Dutch walnut and marquetry card table, inlaid with flowers, birds and foliage, the baize lined interior with wells and inlaid with cards, 33¹/₂in (85cm). **£4,000-5,000** *C*

A pair of French ormolu mounted amaranth, burr walnut and marquetry card tables, inlaid with boxwood, 34in (86cm). **£10,000-12,000** *C*

A Regency mahogany, ebony and ebonised card table, inlaid with yew wood, 36in (92cm). **£6,000-7,000** *C*

A George III satinwood card table, inlaid with ebonised and boxwood lines and banded with thuya, with folding top above panelled frieze, 36in (92cm). **£5,000-6,000** *C*

A Regency brass inlaid rosewood card table, inlaid with boxwood and ebonised stringing, the D-shaped top with panelled frieze, on sabre legs headed by anthemia, the back support and part of gateleg replaced, 36in (92cm).
£2,500-3,500 *C*

A George III satinwood and marquetry card table, crossbanded with mahogany, gateleg action later, 44in (112cm). **£10,000-12,000** *C*

A Regency ormolu-mounted brass inlaid rosewood card table, crossbanded in ebony, restorations, 36in (92cm). **£7,000-8,000** *C*

A mahogany centre table, with pierced fretwork gallery top, 28in (71cm).
£4,000-5,000 *C*

A William IV mahogany centre table, crossbanded with maple, parts later and re-supported, 60in (152cm).
£5,000-7,000 *C*

A mid-Victorian walnut and marquetry centre table, top formerly with tilt, 51¹/₂in (131cm). **£7,000-8,000** *C*

A rosewood and parcel gilt centre table, modern, 29¹/₂in (75cm).
£3,500-4,500 *C*

A pair of George I Irish giltwood and lacquer centre tables, the Japanese export tops late 17thC with some English decoration, traces of original 'Nashig' border, 34in (86cm).
£50,000-55,000 *C*

A Dutch marquetry, simulated tortoiseshell, ebonised and parcel gilt centre table, distressed, 42in (107cm).
£7,500-9,000 *C*

A William IV fruitwood centre table, the segmented tilt top banded in rosewood, on turned shaft and concave sided base on bun feet, 48in (122cm). **£2,000-3,000** *C*

A Regency rosewood and parcel gilt centre table, with tilt top, 54in (137cm).
£7,000-8,000 *C*

A William IV giltwood centre table, with Florentine pietra dura top inlaid in marbles and semi-precious stones 29¹/₂in (75cm).
£45,000-50,000 *C*

A mahogany centre table, the apron centred by a bearded mask flanked by acanthus scrolls, on cabriole legs headed by lion ring masks, with claw-and-ball feet, 19thC, 55in (140cm).
£6,000-8,000 *C*

A Swedish neo-classical bronzed and gilt centre table, with later marble top, c1800, 42in (106cm). **£3,000-4,000** *C*

A Louis XV giltwood console table, with marble top, and another matching table, restored and re-gilded, marble 18thC, 52in (132cm). **£11,000-13,000** *C*

A pair of Italian giltwood centre tables, with marble tops, re-gilded, early 19thC, 30¹/₂in (77cm) high. **£15,000-17,000** *C*

A Spanish ormolu mounted mahogany centre table, the top inset with black fossil marble, restored mid-19thC, 47¹/₂in (120cm). **£9,000-12,000** *C*

A George III pine pier table, with bardiglio marble top, the fluted frieze centred by a tablet carved with a patera and husks, 55¹/₂in (141cm). **£8,000-10,000** *C*

An ormolu centre table, the pietra dura top banded with porphyry and malachite, 19thC, 41in (104cm). **£44,000-48,000** *C*

A Flemish ebony and marquetry centre table, inlaid with bone and mother-of-pearl, 19thC, 58¹/₂in (148cm). **£4,000-5,000** *C*

A George III giltwood console table, with Sicilian jasper marble top, inlaid with various marbles, re-gilded, 38in (97cm). **£11,000-13,000** *C*

A Regènce giltwood console table, with veined marble top, restorations, 46in (117cm). **£3,000-4,000** *C*

316

A Pair of Genoese giltwood corner consoles, with mottled marble tops, the pierced friezes carved with foliage and acanthus, one inscribed 'an Boffi', mid-18thC, 30in (76cm).
£7,000-8,000   *C*

A pair of Italian silvered wood tables, with simulated marble tops, mid-18thC, 52in (132cm). **£35,000-40,000**   *C*

A pair of Spanish painted and parcel gilt corner tables, 18thC, 34¹/₂in (87cm).
£3,500-4,500 *S*

A pair of giltwood console tables, with marble top, carved with rockwork, 54in (137cm). **£11,000-13,000**   *C*

A pair of Louis XVI painted console tables, with later marble tops, restored and reduced, 21in (54cm).
£5,000-6,000 *C*

A Restauration rosewood console table, stamped Jacob, with later marble top, c1830, 53in (135cm).
£20,000-25,000 *S*

A pair of Italian giltwood console brackets, 27in (68cm).
£3,000-4,000   *C*

A pair of Italian giltwood corner console tables, c1750, 32in (81cm).
£27,000-30,000   *C*

A Louis XV console table, the frieze with ribbon tied flowers, 48in (122cm).
£18,000-20,000   *S*

A pair of Italian silvered and painted console tables, 41¹/₂in (105cm).
£9,000-10,000   *C*

A North Italian painted and parcel gilt console table, with later simulated scapliola top, late 18thC, 50in (127cm).
£2,500-3,500   *C*

317

COLOUR REVIEW

A George III mahogany gateleg table, the twin flap top on square chamfered legs, 67in (170cm). **£3,500-4,500** *C*

A George III mahogany dining table, crossbanded in satinwood, lacking extra leaf, later section to edge, 70in (178cm). **£10,000-12,000** *C*

A pair of North Italian rosewood and marquetry console tables, Milan, mid-19thC, 65in (165cm). **£5,000-6,000** *C*

A mid-Georgian mahogany concertina-action dining table, restorations, the back legs possibly associated, 66in (168cm). **£4,000-5,000** *C*

A Regency mahogany breakfast table, with tilt top, the quadripartite base with downswept legs and brass caps 63in (106cm). **£5,500-7,500** *C*

A Regency mahogany dining table, the base associated, 4 leaves in a baize lined box, 84in (213cm) extended. **£35,000-40,000** *C*

A Regency mahogany revolving library table, labelled Waring & Gillow, 69½in (176cm). **£5,500-6,500** *C*

An early Victorian oak dining table, with 3 extra leaves, 117in (297cm) extended. **£5,000-7,000** *C*

A late Regency mahogany pedestal dining table, adapted, 223½in (568cm) long. **£18,000-20,000** *C*

A George III mahogany drum table, crossbanded with rosewood, the drawers crossbanded with tulipwood, 24in (61cm). **£9,000-10,000** *C*

318

A Regency brass mounted rosewood games table, restored and adapted, 28in (71cm). **£3,500-4,500** *C*

A French ormolu mounted kingwood gueridon, with brocatelle marble top, 19thC, 21in (53cm). **£2,000-3,000** *C*

A late Louis XV marquetry gueridon table, with later marble top, 29¹/₂in (75cm). **£3,500-4,500** *S*

An ormolu mounted mahogany and marquetry gueridon, by H. Dasson, with spring operated drawer, c1888, 15in (38cm). **£3,500-4,500** *C*

A Regency rosewood and parcel gilt games table, formerly with work basket, 31¹/₂in (80cm). **£6,000-7,000** *C*

An Austrian walnut games table, with parquetry lifting top, 41in (104cm). **£2,500-3,500** *S*

A Regency ormolu mounted mahogany and parcel gilt occasional table, with later leather lined top, restorations, 24in (61cm). **£2,000-2,500** *C*

A Regency kingwood games table, with frieze drawer and silk work box, 31¹/₂in (80cm). **£2,000-2,500** *C*

A William IV figured walnut drum table, one leg spliced, 28in (71cm). **£2,500-3,000** *C*

A Victorian figured mahogany library table, with scrolled carved frieze, fluted and carved dual ends to cross stretchers, 48in (122cm). **£900-1,200** *GAK*

A satinwood occasional table, the panelled frieze fitted with a drawer, 26in (66cm). **£900-1,200** *C*

COLOUR REVIEW

A black and gold japanned pedestal table, the tilt-top with a Chinese lacquer panel, early 19thC, 30in (76cm). **£12,000-13,000** *C*

A George III mahogany supper table, 3 sides filled with gilt chicken wire, 42in (106cm) **£5,000-6,000** *C*

A George III satinwood Pembroke table, crossbanded with rosewood, oval twin flap top with central oval, 33in (84cm). **£4,500-5,500** *C*

A Restauration mahogany reading table, adjustable in height, 30in (76cm). **£3,000-4,000** *S*

A George III mahogany and marquetry Pembroke table, 42in (107cm). **£6,500-7,500** *C*

A Louis XV kingwood table, the serpentine top inlaid with a diamond shaped panel, 14in (36cm). **£3,000-4,000** *C*

A pair of brass gueridon tables, marble tops, 29in (74cm). **£7,000-8,000** *C*

An ormolu mounted kingwood and tulipwood table, 12¹/₂in (32cm). **£2,000-3,000** *C*

A George III harewood, satinwood and marquetry Pembroke table, 36¹/₂in (93cm). **£27,000-30,000** *C*

A George III mahogany Pembroke table, with twin flap banded in rosewood, single frieze drawer, square tapering legs with brass caps, 39in (99cm). **£2,500-3,500** *C*

A George III mahogany serving table, the edge applied with blind fretwork moulding with C-scroll brackets, legs reduced in height, 74in (188cm). **£3,500-4,500** *C*

A George III harewood marquetry and parcel gilt table, 64¹/₂in (163cm). **£120,000-125,000** *C*

A mahogany side table, with the inlaid specimen marble top, 37¹/₂in (95cm). **£7,000-8,000** *C*

A George III white painted and parcel gilt side table, with later simulated marble top, restorations, redecorated, legs spliced, 67¹/₂in (171cm). **£5,500-6,500** *C*

A pair of Irish Regency brass mounted rosewood and parcel gilt side tables, the marble tops supported by winged eagle monopodiae, restorations, 46in (117cm). **£10,500-11,000** *C*

A satinwood side table, with a thuya oval and chequered lines, restorations, 44in (112cm). **£6,000-7,000** *C*

A pair of early Victorian oak side tables, by J. D. Crace, tops cracked and repaired, 66in (168cm). **£35,000-40,000** *C*

A German walnut, burr walnut, ebony and parquetry side table, mid-19thC, 43¹/₂in (110cm). **£2,000-3,000** *C*

A pair of George III satinwood side tables, the tops crossbanded with harewood and rosewood and inlaid with ebonised and boxwood lines, branded BO, 33in (84cm). **£14,000-16,000** *C*

A Regency parcel gilt and brass mounted side table, banded with satinwood, mahogany lined frieze drawers, parts lacking, 36in (92cm). **£3,500-4,500** *C*

A Federal inlaid cherrywood tray top table, attributed to John Dunlap II, Antrim, New Hampshire, c1800, 35in (89cm). **£6,000-7,000** *CNY*

A pair of Italian giltwood side tables, one supported by Bacchus and Flora, 59½in (151cm). **£12,000-15,000** *C*

A mahogany side table, with Italian specimen marble top, 69½in (176cm). **£40,000-45,000** *C*

A Portuguese palisander side table, with eared serpentine moulded top and a frieze drawer, the apron carved with rockwork, on foliate cabriole legs and claw-and-ball feet, partly re-lined, mid-18thC, 42in (107cm). **£10,000-12,000** *C*

A Regency rosewood sofa table, inlaid with fruitwood stringing, banded in burr yew, stretcher possibly replaced, restored, 59in (149cm). **£6,000-7,000** *C*

An ormolu, mahogany and ebony side table, stamped H. Fourdinois, 32½in (82cm). **£15,000-16,000** *C*

A Regency gilt metal mounted rosewood sofa table, the twin flaps banded with maple and ebonised lines, one foot with wooden replacement, restorations, 62in (157cm). **£12,000-15,000** *C*

A Regency mahogany sofa table, banded in satinwood and ebony, restored, 72in (182cm). **£8,000-9,000** *C*

A Regency mahogany sofa table, inlaid with boxwood and ebonised lines, crossbanded in fruitwood and rosewood, 61½in (156cm). **£6,000-8,000** *C*

A Regency brass mounted rosewood sofa table, inlaid with boxwood, restored, 62in (152cm). **£7,000-8,000** *C*

A pair of George III mahogany tea tables, crossbanded with satinwood and tulipwood and inlaid with boxwood lines, restorations, 34in (86cm). **£10,000-12,000** *C*

A mahogany tripod table, the top with spindle gallery, 10in (25.5cm). **£9,000-10,000** *C*

A mahogany tea table, the tilting top on a ball turned pedestal, c1770, 36in (92cm) diam. **£8,000-10,000** *CNY*

A mahogany tripod table, the tilt top with spindle gallery inlaid with brass, restoration to one leg, 30in (75cm). **£17,000-20,000** *C*

An Empire bronze and ormolu gueridon, the marble base on brass casters, 19in (49cm). **£25,000-30,000** *C*

A George II mahogany tripod table, with fret pierced gallery, 26$\frac{1}{2}$in (67cm) diam. **£17,000-19,000** *S*

A George III mahogany tea table, the twin flap top enclosing a well, with plain frieze and waved apron, 30in (76cm). **£4,000-5,000** *C*

A Regency ormolu mounted rosewood and parcel gilt work table, the top with a contemporary English School watercolour, 18in (46cm). **£22,000-25,000** *C*

A Regency mahogany sofa table, inlaid with ebony, with cedar lined drawer, 30$\frac{1}{2}$in (77cm). **£4,000-5,000** *C*

A mahogany tripod table, the top with raised waved rim, 17in (43cm). **£2,500-3,500** *C*

An Austrian mahogany work table, with hinged top enclosing an architectural fitted interior, 37in (94cm) high. **£9,000-12,000** *C*

A Regency brass inlaid rosewood sofa table, with crossbanded twin flap top, restored, 60in (152cm). **£5,000-6,000** *C*

323

COLOUR REVIEW

A Regency rosewood table, with easel reading slope, 29in (75cm). **£17,500-19,000** *C*

A George IV rosewood writing table, with rounded top, 2 panelled frieze drawers, on solid panelled end supports and tapering bun feet, 60in (152cm). **£4,000-5,000** *C*

A Regency rosewood writing table, the scalloped frieze with milled ormolu drops, 40in (102cm). **£20,000-23,000** *C*

A Regency mahogany writing table, with leather lined top and 2 frieze drawers, 45½in (115cm). **£6,000-7,000** *C*

A mahogany writing table, with 2 drawers back and front, adapted, part early 19thC, 59in (150cm). **£5,000-7,000** *C*

An ormolu mounted rosewood amboyna and marquetry writing table, labelled G. Trollope & Sons, 43in (109cm). **£3,000-4,000** *C*

A Louis XV tulipwood parquetry bureau plat, in the manner of Jacques Dubois, mid-18thC, 51in (129cm). **£90,000-100,000** *S*

A Regency rosewood writing table, the frieze with 2 drawers and 2 false drawers, restored, 44in (111cm). **£4,000-5,000** *C*

A mahogany writing table, with leather lined top, restored, 62in (157cm). **£4,000-5,000** *C*

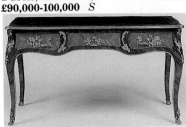

A Louis XV ormolu mounted rosewood and tulipwood bureau plat, 19thC locks, 57½in (146cm). **£30,000-35,000** *C*

A Regency rosewood writing table, with leather lined top, the frieze with 2 mahogany lined drawers, with ormolu paw feet, 45in (115cm). **£8,000-9,000** *C*

A Regency brass inlaid mahogany writing table, inlaid with ebonised lines, some damage and restorations, 54½in (138cm). **£6,500-7,500** *C*

A Louis XV style ormolu mounted kingwood and fruitwood bureau plat, English, mid-19thC, 67in (170cm). **£7,000-9000** *C*

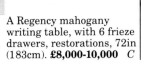

A Regency mahogany writing table, with 6 frieze drawers, restorations, 72in (183cm). **£8,000-10,000** *C*

A Louis XV marquetry writing table, perhaps Strasbourg, c1765, 19½in (49cm). **£32,000-35,000** *S*

A George IV mahogany wine cooler, with later fitted interior, 33in (84cm). **£3,500-4,500** *C*

A French ormolu mounted rosewood, mahogany and burr walnut writing table, mid-19thC, 55in (140cm). **£5,000-6,000** *C*

A Spanish mahogany centre table, c1835, 27in (69cm). **£2,000-3,500** *HUN*

A lacquer, gilt bronze and mahogany writing table, stamped P. A. Foullet, 31½in (80cm). **£35,000-40,000** *S*

A matched pair of George III mahogany hanging shelves, with later mirror and back, 24in (61cm). **£6,000-7,000** *C*

A Transitional kingwood table à écrire, 17½in (45cm). **£9,000-10,000** *C*

A Louis Philippe boulle centre table, with 3 drawers and 3 dummy drawers, c1830, 47in (120cm). **£5,500-6,500** *S*

A Louis XV/XVI Transitional tulipwood parquetry writing table, stamped RVLC, c1775, 19½in (50cm). **£50,000-60,000** *S*

An ormolu mounted tulipwood, kingwood and marquetry table à écrire, restored. **£28,000-30,000** *C*

A Transitional tulipwood and marquetry table à écrire. **£42,000-45,000** *C*

A Louis XV style ormolu mounted painted bureau plat, 75in (190cm). **£11,000-13,000** *C*

A George III mahogany breakfront wardrobe, the cupboard doors enclosing 5 shelves to the centre, 104¹/₂in (265cm). **£4,500-5,500** *C*

A Louis XIV boulle and ebony cabinet en armoire, 57in (154cm). **£105,000-120,000** *C*

An oak and inlaid sideboard, c1890, 80¹/₂in (204cm). **£3,000-4,800** *HUN*

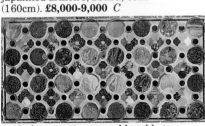

A pair of malachite and Belge-noir table tops, with a sunburst within a Greek border, 24in (61cm) diam. **£9,000-10,000** *C*

A German black and gilt japanned armoire, 18thC, 63in (160cm). **£8,000-9,000** *C*

An Italian specimen marble table top, late 18thC, **£35,000-40,000** *C*

An Italian specimen marble table top, on a modern painted iron stand, 52in (132cm). **£12,000-14,000** *C*

A French Provincial mahogany armoire, 18thC, 66in (168cm). **£3,500-4,500** *C*

A mahogany tambour pedestal desk, inlaid with box and ebony, c1850, 70in (178cm). **£8,000-14,500** *HUN*

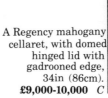

A Regency mahogany cellaret, with domed hinged lid with gadrooned edge, 34in (86cm). **£9,000-10,000** *C*

COLOUR REVIEW

A George III mahogany cellaret, banded in satinwood, one leg repaired, lacking interior, 20in (51cm). **£2,200-2,500** *C*

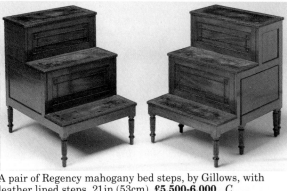

A pair of Regency mahogany bed steps, by Gillows, with leather lined steps, 21in (53cm). **£5,500-6,000** *C*

A George III mahogany inlaid wine cooler, 21in (53cm). **£2,500-3,000** *C*

A George III mahogany cellaret-on-stand, banded and inlaid, 16in (40cm). **£2,000-2,500** *C*

An early George III mahogany wine cooler, with brass and loop handles, restored, 24in (61cm). **£3,000-4,000** *S*

An oak hall letterbox, by A. Rodrigues, 42 Piccadilly, dated 7th May 1872, 17in (43cm) high. **£2,000-3,500** *HUN*

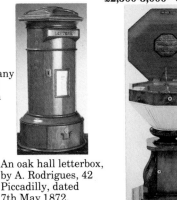

A Biedermeier mahogany teapoy, with hinged lid, inlaid with boxwood and ebonised lines, with fitted interior, restored, 20½in (52cm). **£2,000-2,500** *C*

A George III mahogany cellaret, 16in (41cm). **£2,200-2,500** *C*

A pair of George III giltwood wall brackets, 21in (30.5cm). **£10,000-12,000** *C*

A George III mahogany bottle holder, brass carrying handles, 25in (63cm). **£4,000-5,000** *C*

A George III mahogany wine cooler, with brass bands and loop handles, 27in (69cm). **£3,000-4,000** *S*

A George III brass bound mahogany cellaret-on-stand, with lead lined interior with compartments, 18½in (47cm). **£5,500-7,000** *C*

A mid-Georgian mahogany butler's tray, containing 6 glass decanters, one broken, 21in (53cm). **£2,000-3,000** *C*

327

A pine sideboard, c1850, 96in (244cm). **£600-800** *SAn*

A pitch pine wardrobe, c1870, 48in (122cm). **£450-550** *SSD*

A pine cupboard base, c1800, with later breakfront display plate rack, 60in (152cm). **£600-800** *SSD*

A pine delft rack, c1840, 60 by 42in (152 by 106.5cm). **£300-350** *AL*

A pine dresser base with gallery back, c1860, 66in (168cm). **£650-850** *SSD*

A hazel pine wardrobe, c1890, 39in (99cm). **£400-450** *SSD*

A pine and elm dresser base, c1850, with later plate rack, 72in (182cm). **£1,200-1,500** *SSD*

A pine serpentine front Yorkshire dresser base, c1860, with later plate rack, spice drawers original, 54in (137cm). **£1,000-1,200** *SSD*

A pitch pine dresser base, c1900, with later plate rack, 42in (107cm). **£600-800** *SSD*

A four door pine cupboard, County
Limerick, with shaped interior and
panelled sides, c1780, 72in (182.5cm).
£2,500-3,500 *SAn*

A pine chest of drawers, with
waved gallery, c1820, 39in (99cm).
£350-450 *SSD*

A hazel pine dressing
chest, c1890, 36in (92cm).
£400-500 *SSD*

A pine farmhouse larder
cupboard, with 4 drawers,
c1850, 66in (167.5cm).
£1,000-1,200 *SSD*

A pine glazed display
cabinet, c1880, 39in
(99cm). **£250-350** *SSD*

A pine veterinary medicine chest,
marked 'Restorine Remedies',
c1890, 24in (61cm). **£150-250** *SSD*

A pitch pine and pine glazed
bookcase, c1870, 48in (122cm).
£450-550 *SSD*

A pine mule chest, with 2
short drawers, c1800, 44in
(112cm). **£250-350** *SSD*

A pine mule chest, with long
drawer and brass handles,
c1800, 42 in (107cm).
£250-350 *SSD*

An Empire ormolu and steel fender, the lions on stepped plinths linked by a chain, 40in (101.5cm) closed. **£1,500-2,500** *C*

A Restauration gilt bronze fender, adjustable in width, c1830. **£2,200-2,500** *S*

A Restauration adjustable bronze and gilt bronze fender, c1830. **£3,500-3,800** *S*

A Restauration adjustable gilt bronze fender, c1820. **£1,400-1,600** *S*

A pair of cast iron lion chenets, the confronting roaring beasts with brass rings supporting cartouches on pierced scrolling bases, late 19thC, 19in (49cm) high. **£2,500-3,500** *C*

A mid-Victorian steel and brass fender, stamped No. 178 and with registry mark for 15 March 1858, 61in (155cm). **£1,300-1,800** *C*

An early Victorian steel and ormolu fender, with Registry mark for 1845, the frieze with restoration, 67in (170cm). **£1,400-1,800** *C*

A bronze and gilt bronze fender, adjustable in width, mid-19thC, 56in (142cm). **£5,000-6,000** *S*

A pair of Louis XVI ormolu and bronze chenets, modelled as recumbent lions on draped plinths, 14in (35.5cm) wide. **£4,500-5,000** *C*

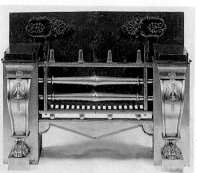

A Regency brass mounted polished steel and cast iron fire grate, in George Bullock style, repaired, 40in (102cm). **£4,000-5,000** *C*

A set of gilt bronze and steel fire irons and stand, each piece with a finely cast dog's head handle, mid-19thC, 29½in (75cm). **£11,000-12,000** *S*

A Regency ormolu mounted steel fire grate, attributed to George Bullock, the railed front with pyramid finals, the U-shaped sides and back on scrolling pilasters with acanthus headings and paw feet with plinth bases, 34in (86cm) **£9,000-10,000** *C*

A statuary marble chimneypiece, the siena marble frieze embellished with scrolling Roman acanthus foliage, 63 by 86in (160 by 219cm). **£20,000-30,000** *C*

A Georgian statuary marble chimneypiece, with engraved steel slip, 60 by 73in (152 by 185cm). **£22,000-25,000** *C*

A set of 6 late George III mahogany dining chairs, including an armchair, the turned and panelled crestings above pierced rail backs, the pale blue moiré fabric drop-in seats on turned legs, c1805.
£3,000-4,000   *S(S)*

A set of 6 George III mahogany dining chairs, the backs with pierced stick splats each inlaid with an oval floral harewood medallion, the bowed nailed hide upholstered seats above tapered square legs, c1790.
£2,500-3,500   *S(S)*

A set of 6 William IV mahogany dining chairs, including 2 armchairs, the rail backs with carved clasps above loose seats, on turned legs.
£2,000-2,700   *S(S)*

A set of 6 George IV mahogany dining chairs.
£1,200-1,600   *DN*

A set of 6 Regency mahogany dining chairs, the scroll bar draped cresting and railed backs above upholstered drop-in seats, on sabre legs.
£2,500-3,500   *CSK*

A set of 4 Regency padouk dining chairs, the rope twist toprails above splats incorporating circular tablets carved with paterae, supported by S scrolls, above caned seats, on sabre legs.
£1,500-2,000   *Bon*

A set of 6 Regency rosewood grained and parcel gilt dining chairs, the bowed upholstered backs with moulded stiles and scroll supports, above caned seats, on moulded sabre legs.
£2,500-3,500   *Bon*

A set of 10 mahogany dining chairs, the brocade upholstered seats on square tapering legs joined by stretchers, parts late 18thC.
£2,600-3,000   *CSK*

A set of 6 Victorian mahogany dining chairs, the arched toprail with a double C-scroll pierced splat above button down spring seats, on turned baluster legs.
£1,200-1,700   *Bon*

A set of 8 Edwardian mahogany dining chairs, including 2 armchairs, outlined in boxwood stringing, the open oval backs with pierced splats, on square tapered legs.
£2,000-2,500   *Bon*

A pair of George III mahogany dining chairs, the spindle splat hung with drapery, the bowed seat covered in pink floral silk, on square tapering legs joined by an H-shaped stretcher, on spade feet, one block replaced.
£850-1,000   *C*

A set of 6 William IV mahogany dining chairs.
£1,500-2,000   *DN*

A set of 10 William IV mahogany dining chairs, upholstered in brown leatherette, raised on formal foliate, sheathed, melon fluted, turned and tapering front supports, terminating in peg feet.
£4,600-5,500   *HSS*

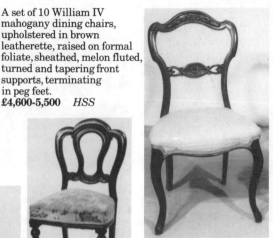

A set of 6 William IV rosewood dining chairs, the foliate carved scrolling semi-balloon backs above serpentine brocade upholstered seats, on turned tapering legs.
£1,500-1,800   *CSK*

A set of 6 early Victorian rosewood dining chairs, with flower carved crest rail.
£2,000-2,500   *AH*

A set of 10 mahogany dining chairs, of Hepplewhite design, including 2 elbow chairs.
£3,000-3,500   *CSK*

A set of 6 Victorian walnut dining chairs, the serpentine cresting and S scrolling balloon backs above upholstered tapestry seats, on turned legs.
£1,200-1,600   *CSK*

A set of 5 Victorian walnut balloon back dining chairs, shaped overstuffed seats and scrolled cabriole front legs with peg feet.
£800-1,200   *AH*

A set of 6 Victorian mahogany dining chairs, on turned baluster legs.
£1,000-1,400   *CSK*

A set of 6 mid-Victorian walnut dining chairs, on cabriole legs with foliate carved feet, one stamped 849.
£2,500-3,000   *CSK*

A set of 9 late Victorian oak dining chairs, with padded seats, on turned supports tied by block stretchers, including one armchair.
£750-1,000   *Bon*

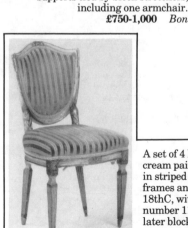

A set of 5 late Victorian oak and leather upholstered dining chairs, of Gothic revival design, and another almost matching, each stamped Gillow & Co., Lancaster, some with maker's stamp W. Bromfitt,NoLL5178, also with various names inscribed in pencil. **£900-1,400**   *CSK*

A set of 4 Italian parcel gilt and cream painted chairs, upholstered in striped gold velvet, with moulded frames and square fluted legs, late 18thC, with painted inventory number 1163, 1164, 1166 and 116?, later blocks, slight damage.
£1,600-2,000   *C*

A set of 8 white painted dining chairs, of Louis XV style, including 2 open armchairs, each upholstered in close nailed yellow cotton, the moulded toprail and waved channelled seat rail carved with an oval flanked by husks on channelled cabriole legs, 2 stencilled C.H.T., redecorated.
£2,000-2,500 *C*

A set of 3 Empire mahogany chairs, each with curved reeded toprail with lotus leaf ends with swan's head terminals and apricot velvet drop-in seats on sabre legs, later blocks, one inscribed Charles No. 9. **£1,000-1,500** *C*

A set of 6 Louis Philippe dining chairs, of Gothic revival design, each with an indistinct oval stencilled inscription C… Tapissier…
£2,000-2,500 *CSK*

A set of 4 French walnut chairs, with pierced dining splats above yellow satin upholstered drop-in seats, on cabriole legs with knob feet, late 18thC, adapted.
£650-900 *CSK*

A set of 8 Victorian mahogany dining chairs.
£1,600-2,000 *CSK*

Hall Chairs

A pair of George III mahogany hall chairs.
£800-1,200   *DN*

A pair of George IV carved mahogany hall chairs, with shell shaped backs and solid seats, on ring turned splayed legs, c1820.
£800-1,000   *S(S)*

A pair of Tuscan walnut high panelled back side chairs, with moulded narrow tapering backs, one roundel cresting carved with the Arms of the Medicis with octagonal seats and spreading square legs carved with rope twist decoration.
£2,200-3,000   *C*

A set of 8 George III mahogany hall chairs, each with vase shaped back, dished bowed seat and vase shaped support to front and back, on splayed feet joined by a waved stretcher, one with repair to seat.
£3,000-4,000   *C*

A Regency mahogany and ebonised hall chair, the back on lotus leaf support, the bowed solid seat on ring turned and tapering fluted legs, with splayed feet, stamped T. Luke, later blocks, minor restorations.
£600-900   *C*

A pair of Victorian mahogany hall seats, with turned toprails above partially pierced fret backs and solid seats, on pierced fret trestle supports joined by turned stretchers, c1850.
£1,200-1,500   *S(S)*

A set of 3 George III mahogany hall chairs, each with solid shield shaped back centred by a painted oval with crests and the motto Constantia et Vigilantia, with dished solid seat, on square tapering legs and spade feet, some restoration.
£2,000-2,500   *C*

Side Chairs

A mid-Victorian brown lacquer and papier-mâché occasional chair, the horseshoe shaped back inlaid with brass and white metal bands above a tapestry upholstered pin cushion seat, on hipped cabriole legs.
£350-450   *CSK*

A pair of William and Mary style walnut and beech chairs, the stuffed seats covered in claret velvet, the scroll legs joined by X shaped stretchers, on gadrooned bun feet, c1900.
£500-700   *S(S)*

A Victorian walnut framed lady's nursing chair.
£400-500   *S(S)*

Chests of Drawers

A William and Mary dwarf chest, the bottom applied with split moulding, on block feet, 31in (79cm).
£2,500-3,000 *CSK*

A rare George II mahogany small chest, with caddy top, 24in (61cm).
£3,000-3,500 *Bon*

The small size is a major factor here.

A William and Mary walnut and crossbanded chest, inlaid throughout with stringing, minor restorations, on later bracket feet, c1700, 37½in (95cm).
£2,500-3,000 *S(S)*

An inlaid walnut and elm chest, with crossbanded top, on bracket feet, basically early 18thC, 37in (94cm).
£2,200-2,700 *CSK*

An inlaid walnut chest, with crossbanded top above 3 frieze drawers and 3 long drawers, on bracket feet, basically 18thC, 37½in (95cm).
£1,000-1,500 *CSK*

An early Georgian walnut, crossbanded and herringbone inlaid chest, of 4 graduated oak lined long drawers, with brass handles and escutcheons, fitted with a brushing slide, on bracket feet, small pieces of veneer missing, 31in (79cm).
£25,000-30,000 *GC*

These early 18thC walnut small chests with figured veneers and in original condition now fetch large sums.

A William and Mary walnut and featherbanded chest, with quarter veneered and crossbanded top, handles replaced, on later bun feet, c1700, 38in (97cm).
£2,500-3,000 *S(S)*

A burr walnut and feather banded bachelor's chest, of George I design, the fold-over top above 2 short and 3 graduated long drawers, on bracket feet, with side carrying handles, 32in (81cm).
£1,400-1,700 *CSK*

A mahogany chest with moulded top edge, brass handles with pierced plates and keyhole plates, on bracket feet, 18thC, 32½in (83cm).
£1,000-1,400 *P(S)*

A George I style burr walnut bachelor's chest, the top with feather banding, on bracket feet.
£1,000-1,400 *Bon*

If period (early 18thC) this chest would be worth £20,000.

A Georgian mahogany chest of drawers, with brass handles, on bracket feet, 27in (69cm).
£4,000-4,500 *IM*

A George III mahogany chest, with 4 long drawers, 34in (86cm).
£1,000-1,500 *DN*

An early George III mahogany chest of drawers, the moulded top with canted angles above 2 short and 3 graduated long drawers, on ogee bracket feet, 33½in (85cm).
£1,700-2,000 *CSK*

A George III mahogany chest, on later ogee bracket feet, c1770, 38in (97cm).
£1,200-1,700 *S(S)*

A George III mahogany chest of drawers, 41in (104cm).
£750-900 *CSK*

A late Georgian mahogany chest, the drawers with cockbead borders and brass loop handles, the top with ogee edge, on shaped bracket feet, 40½in (103cm).
£750-1,000 *HCH*

A George III style mahogany crossbanded chest of drawers, with brushing slide, brass drop handles and escutcheons, supported on bracket feet.
£2,200-2,500 *GH*

A George III mahogany chest of drawers, on bracket feet, 37in (94cm).
£650-850 *CSK*

A mahogany bow fronted chest of drawers, early 19thC, 42in (107cm).
£650-850 *DN*

A George III mahogany chest, with later ogee bracket feet, restorations, 36in (92cm).
£1,400-2,000 *CSK*

A George III mahogany serpentine chest of drawers, with a moulded top above 4 long drawers, on later bracket feet, 44in (111cm).
£3,200-4,000 *CSK*

A mahogany serpentine fronted chest of drawers, 19thC, 34in (86cm).
£1,200-1,500 *DN*

A George III mahogany bowfront chest of drawers, with later turned wood handles, scalloped apron, on French bracket feet, together with glass top, 36in (92cm).
£900-1,200   *HSS*

A George III mahogany secretaire chest, with a secretaire drawer and 3 graduated drawers, on bracket feet.
£2,000-2,500   *Bon*

A Germany mahogany chest of drawers, with 5 wavy drawers flanked by canted corners, on scrolled feet, 19thC.
£500-600   *Bon*

A Dutch chest of drawers, with bird and foliate marquetry in coloured woods, divided by oyster veneered walnut strapwork, late 18thC, 38in (97cm).
£2,500-3,500   *HSS*

A mid-George III mahogany chest, with a moulded top above a later brushing slide and 4 graduated long drawers, on bracket feet, 32in (81cm).
£1,200-1,500   *CSK*

A George III mahogany chest of drawers, with canted top above slide and 4 long a drawers, with fluted column angles, on ogee bracket feet, back feet partly replaced, restorations, 37in (94cm).
£1,500-2,000
C

A mahogany chest of drawers, with original brass drop handles and escutcheons, fluted canted angles, on ogee bracket feet, 18thC, 35½in (91cm).
£1,600-2,000
GSP

A Regency inlaid mahogany bowfront chest of drawers, the crossbanded top above 2 short and 3 graduated long drawers and serpentine apron, on splayed bracket feet,
£650-750 *CSK*

A Regency inlaid mahogany bowfront chest of drawers, with rosewood crossbanded top, on splayed bracket feet, 41in (104cm).
£450-650 *CSK*
The large proportions of this chest restrict the price.

A late George III mahogany, satinwood and tulipwood banded chest of drawers, the later inlaid top above a brushing slide, 2 small and 3 long graduated drawers, on later bracket feet, 30½in (78cm).
£1,200-1,600 *CSK*

A George III mahogany and satinwood crossbanded bowfront chest of drawers, with boxwood and chevron stringing, the drawers above a valanced apron and splayed bracket feet, some damage, c1790, 41½in (106cm).
£600-900 *S*

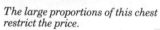

A Dutch walnut and marquetry break bowfront chest of drawers, with later brass loop handles, 30in (76cm).
£4,000-5,000 *HSS*

An early Victorian inlaid mahogany bowfront chest of drawers, fitted with 4 graduated long drawers, on splayed bracket feet, 39in (99cm). **£900-1,200** *CSK*

A Dutch mahogany and brass inlaid chest of drawers, on square tapering legs, late 18thC, 46in (117cm).
£900-1,200 *CSK*

A mahogany dwarf chest, the coffered top above a brushing slide and 4 graduated long drawers, on bracket feet, basically 18thC, 31½in (80cm).
£1,500-2,000 *CSK*

A teak military chest of drawers, in 2 parts, 19thC, 38½in (97cm).
£900-1,000 *DN*

A George IV mahogany bowfront chest of drawers, with gadrooned mouldings, flanked by turned pilasters, on turned feet, c1820, 42i? (107cm).
£900-1,200 *S(S)*

A serpentine fronted black japanned chest of drawers, 18thC, 27in (69cm).
£2,000-2,500 *DN*

A George III mahogany chest of drawers, with moulded top, on ogee bracket feet, 43½in (110cm).
£1,000-1,400 *C*

A Dutch burr walnut and inlaid elm chest of drawers, of bombe outline, on an inverted plinth, on turned bun feet, 18thC, 28½in (73cm). **£4,500-5,500** *CSK*

A mahogany bowfront chest of drawers, 19thC, 42in (107cm).
£700-900 *DN*

A mahogany secretaire tallboy, with rococo gilt metal handles and keyhole plates, bracket feet, 18thC, 42½in (108cm).
£4,000-5,000 *P(S)*
The secretaire drawer is an interesting feature that enhances the value of this piece.

Chests-on-Chests

A walnut and feather banded tallboy of William and Mary design, on a finialled arcaded base, with 6 frieze drawers, on bracket feet, part 18thC, 40in (102cm).
£1,200-1,600 *CSK*

A George I walnut chest-on-chest, inlaid throughout with stringing, on shaped bracket feet, c1725, 40½in (103cm).
£2,500-3,500 *S(S)*

A George III mahogany bowfront chest-on-chest.
£2,500-3,000 *DM*

Bowfronted tallboys are uncommon.

A walnut and feather banded chest-on-chest, with a moulded cornice above 3 short and 6 graduated long drawers, on bracket feet, partially re-veneered, early 18thC, 41½in (105cm).
£3,000-4,000 *CSK*

A George III mahogany chest-on-chest, the upper section with moulded cornice above 5 drawers flanked by fluted canted corners, the lower section with a brushing slide above 3 further drawers, 42in (107cm).
£1,500-2,000 *Bon*

A late George III mahogany
chest-on-chest, the frieze inlaid with
3 oval shell paterae over drawers,
flanked by satinwood banded canted
stiles, on slightly projecting base,
with brass swan neck loop handles,
on bracket feet, 44in (112cm).
£1,000-1,500   *HSS*

A George III mahogany chest-on-
chest, the lower section with a
brushing slide above 3 long
graduated drawers, on bracket feet,
44in (112cm).
£1,200-1,700   *Bon*

A mid-Georgian tallboy, with
moulded cornice between fluted
canted angles, the base with a slide
and 3 long drawers, on bracket feet,
43in (109cm).
£2,500-3,500   *C*

A George III mahogany and blind
fret carved chest-on-chest, with
dentilled cornice, on bracket feet,
c1760, 44in (112cm).
£1,200-1,600   *S(S)*

A late George III mahogany
chest-on-chest, with a brushing
slide and 3 drawers below, on
bracket feet, 44in (112cm).
£2,200-2,700   *CSK*

A late George III mahogany tallboy,
with a cavetto moulded cornice
above 3 short and 6 graduated long
drawers between fluted angles, on
bracket feet, 43in (109cm).
£1,500-2,000   *CSK*

A George III style miniature
mahogany veneered chest-on-chest,
on ogee bracket feet, 15½in (40cm)
high.
£1,500-2,000   *CSK*

A Georgian mahogany tallboy with
a dentil cornice, with fitted moulded
brass handles and lock escutcheons,
the upper section flanked by blind
fret carved corners, raised on
bracket feet, 43in (109cm).
£1,000-1,500   *AG*

A Regency mahogany bowfront
chest-on-chest, the scrolled
pediment above an ebony strung
frieze, on splayed bracket feet.
£800-1,200   *Bon*

Chests-on-Stands

A walnut and feather banded chest-on-stand, with moulded cornice and shaped apron, on cabriole legs with pointed pad feet, 38in (97cm).
£1,200-1,700   *CSK*

A Queen Anne style walnut tallboy, the moulded broken arched cornice above a small drawer with 2 short and 3 long further drawers below, the lower section with a brushing slide, 2 long drawers, on cabriole legs and claw and ball feet.
£2,200-2,600   *Bon*

A walnut chest on later stand, with a moulded cornice, the stand with a shaped apron, on turned legs and feet joined by flattened stretchers, 38in (97cm).
£1,200-1,600   *CSK*
This piece would be worth at least three times the price if the stand was original.

An early Georgian walnut crossbanded chest-on-stand, with brass drop handles and escutcheons, the stand with matching handles, arched shaped apron, supported on shaped legs.
£5,000-6,000   *GH*

A William and Mary walnut and marquetry chest-on-stand, the stand with one long drawer, on later baluster turned oak supports joined by waved stretchers and with bun feet, some moulding missing, c1690, 40in (102cm).
£1,800-2,200   *S(S)*

A Queen Anne style walnut chest-on-stand, fitted with a cushion moulded frieze drawer above 9 drawers, on plain cabriole legs.
£700-800   *Bon*

An American cherrywood chest-on-stand, the stand with waved apron, on club legs and pad feet, Salem, Massachusetts, 40½in (102cm).
£3,500-4,500   *C*

A walnut chest-on-stand, on flat stretchers, early 18thC, 40in (102cm).
£2,800-3,200   *RID*

A George I walnut chest-on-stand, 37in (94cm).
£1,500-2,000   *DN*

A William and Mary walnut and crossbanded chest-on-stand, the quarter veneered top above 2 short and 3 long graduated drawers, the stand with one long drawer, on later turned feet, restored, c1700, 38in (97cm).
£2,500-3,500   *S(S)*

Wellington Chests

A Victorian burr walnut Wellington chest, the top above 6 graduated drawers flanked by hinged locking stiles, with carved acanthus scroll headings, on a plinth base, damaged, 20in (51cm).
£600-700   *CSK*

A Victorian walnut Wellington chest with 8 drawers and locking pilaster, 23½in (60cm).
£1,500-2,000   *DN*

A Queen Anne walnut and crossbanded tallboy, with moulded cornice, the upper stage with 5 drawers, with pierced brass drop handles, the lower stage with 3 drawers, shaped frieze and cabriole legs with pad feet, 39½in (101cm).
£2,500-3,500   *AH*

A small mahogany Wellington Chest of 7 graduated drawers, handles not original.
£600-800   *LF*

A William IV rosewood Wellington secretaire chest with moulded top, leaf carved brackets, one upper drawer, secretaire and fully fitted interior over 4 lower drawers, turned knobs and plinth, 26in (66cm).
£1,600-2,000   *AH*

A walnut chest-on-stand, the upper section with shallow ogee moulded cornice, the projecting base with chamfered edge, with brass baluster pendant handles, circular back plates and pierced shaped lock escutcheons, and crossbanded, raised upon 6 ring turned inverted trumpet shaped supports tied by a wavy flat stretcher, on onion feet, some later additions, early 18thC, 41in (104cm).
£2,000-3,000   *HSS*

Commodes

A George III mahogany tray bedside commode, with satinwood strung front, ceramic liner and cover, c1790, 20in (51cm).
£900-1,200   *S*

A George III mahogany tray top bedside commode, the frieze drawer above a pair of doors and a converted apron drawer, on square legs, c1790, 22in (56cm).
£1,200-1,600   *S*

A George II mahogany commode, with tray top, the waved pierced sides with carrying handles above a hinged flap and sliding front, the sides with brass carrying handles, on club legs and pad feet with later base, 23in (59cm).
£2,600-3,000 *C*

A George III mahogany commode, the top above a tambour shutter and a simulated drawer, on square chamfered legs, 19in (48cm).
£1,200-1,600 *CSK*

A George III mahogany tray top night commode.
£800-1,000 *DN*

Commode Chests

A George III mahogany tray top tambour fronted commode, the apron drawer with ceramic liner, c1790, 21in (54cm).
£1,500-2,000 *S*

A late George III mahogany night commode.
£450-550 *DN*

A Louis XV style marquetry petite commode, with galleried top, understage and 3 drawers inlaid with flowers, birds, trophies and writing motifs, 19½in (50cm).
£2,000-2,500 *GSP*

A George III Hepplewhite concave commode.
£8,500-10,000 *B*

A rosewood, marquetry and gilt metal mounted serpentine commode, with a rouge marble top above 3 drawers between foliate scroll clasps, on splayed legs with gilt sabots, 39in (99cm).
£1,800-2,200 *CSK*

An Italian walnut serpentine commode, with crossbanded top, 2 drawers with original brass drop handles, on carved rococo and floral parcel gilt base and cabriole legs, early 18thC, 34in (86cm).
£6,000-7,000 *GSP*

A Queen Anne style walnut and lacquer commode, the top with radiating veneer with herringbone band above 2 lacquer drawers flanked by 2 doors, on cabriole legs, decorated with chinoiserie scenes.
£700-900 *Bon*

345

An Italian walnut commode, with armorial mask handles and original locks, flanked by caryatids, the moulded base raised on lion's paw supports, 17thC, 58in (147cm).
£13,000-16,000 *P(M)*

A Dutch walnut and floral marquetry commode, of serpentine outline, on angled scroll feet, 34½in (88cm).
£1,900-2,200 *CSK*

A South German marquetry serpentine petite commode with bombé sides, the top and drawers with satinwood and ivory inlaid hunting scenes, the legs and sides with scrolling foliage, 19thC, 30in (76cm).
£2,000-2,500 *GSP*

A South German walnut serpentine fronted commode, the top decorated with a panel of cubed marquetry, 18thC, 47in (119cm).
£3,500-4,000 *P(S)*

A Continental crossbanded walnut commode of small proportions and serpentine form, fitted with 4 long drawers and resting on short cabriole legs, 19thC, 23½in (60cm).
£3,000-3,500 *RID*

A rosewood, kingwood floral marquetry and gilt metal mounted bombé commode, with serpentine rouge marble top above 3 drawers between foliate scroll rocaille clasps, on splayed legs with gilt sabots, labelled C. Sale, Antique Furniture Store, Church Street, Kensington, possibly Spanish, late 19thC, 36in (92cm).
£2,500-3,000 *CSK*

A Swedish marquetry and gilt metal mounted bombé commode, of serpentine outline with a moulded verde antico marble top above 3 drawers between foliate scroll clasps, on splayed legs, 35½in (91cm).
£1,000-1,500 *CSK*

A Dutch bowfront commode, with 2, and 2 false, frieze drawers above a pair of tambour doors, on square tapered feet, the whole inlaid with chequered stringing, restorations, 18thC.
£900-1,300 *Bon*

A French kingwood and tulipwood marquetry commode, the serpentine red marble top above gilt metal mounted sides and 3 gilt metal mounted drawers, on splayed legs, inside loose lock stamped Paris, c1900, 27½in (70cm).
£1,000-1,500 *S(S)*

A Louis XVI walnut commode, with an eared top of brocatelle marble above 3 graduated drawers between fluted uprights, on turned feet, restorations, 53in (135cm).
£3,000-3,500 *CSK*

A Louis XV style rosewood and gilt metal mounted bombé commode, the serpentine white marble top above 2 short and 2 long drawers inlaid with stringing, the splayed bracket feet on later blocks, 53½in (136cm).
£2,200-2,700   *S(S)*

A North German brass mounted mahogany commode, with eared top, one panelled drawer and 2 further drawers between canted angles, on later square tapering legs, c1800, 50½in (128cm).
£5,000-5,500   *C*

This commode is possibly Russian.

A French Provincial walnut commode, with moulded top and 3 long drawers with rounded angles, waved apron and panelled sides, on cabriole feet, mid-18thC, 49in (125cm).
£2,600-3,000   *C*

A Louis XV walnut petite commode, with waved breccia marble top above a slide with reading ledge and 2 drawers, the right hand side with a small drawer, on square tapering cabriole legs with brass caps, stamped MO and ON, formerly with ormolu mounts, reconstructed, 24½in (62cm).
£3,500-4,000   *C*

The stamp does not appear to match that of Francois Mondon, 1694-1770.

A pair of Dutch colonial hardwood serpentine commodes, the moulded tops each above 2 short and one long drawer, the shell flanked by cabriole legs on claw and ball feet, carved aprons late 19thC, 40in (102cm). **£1,500-2,000**   *S(S)*

A Scandinavian yew veneered commode, the single frieze drawer and sides inlaid with sphinxes and scrolling designs above 2 deep drawers, on tapering block feet, early 19thC, probably Swedish, 50in (127cm).
£1,800-2,200   *CSK*

A North Italian ormolu mounted kingwood and mahogany bombé commode, with moulded serpentine top inlaid à quatre faces above 3 conforming graduated drawers between keeled angles, 41½in (106cm).
£1,500-2,000   *C*

A Dutch mahogany breakfront commode, with a later top, with drawers between fluted uprights, on tapering fluted legs, late 18thC, 41½in (106cm).
£2,200-2,700   *CSK*

An Empire mahogany commode, with later white marble top and overhanging frieze drawer flanked by turned columns with panelled sides, on turned tapering front feet, possibly Italian, 50in (127cm).
£3,500-4,500   *C*

Cupboards – Armoires

An Austrian grained armoire with arched scrolling cornice and a pair of panelled cupboard doors painted with vases of flowers, with moulded square base, re-decorated, mid 18thC, 59½in (151cm).
£3,500-4,000   *C*

Corner Cupboards

A George IV mahogany bowfronted hanging corner cupboard, the cavetto cornice above a pair of boxwood strung doors, c1780, 31in (79cm).
£650-800   *S(C)*

A Georgian mahogany corner cupboard.
£500-600   *LF*

A South German painted and grained marriage armoire, with moulded cornice, the frieze inscribed Andre Anna Kech 1850, above 2 doors painted with religious scenes, with central spirally turned pilaster upright, the canted sides with flower festoons on block feet, mid 19thC, 53in (135cm).
£2,600-3,000   *C*

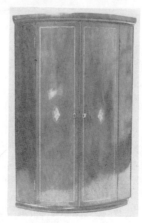

A Victorian mahogany bowfronted corner cupboard on stand, with cornice, brass escutcheon and door plate, central fitted drawer, supported on stand with shaped legs, 36in (92cm).
£400-500   *GH*

A brass-mounted mahogany armoire, the top with finials above a panelled frieze and long mirrored door with bevelled plate enclosing shelves and a drawer between fluted spreading pilasters, above one long drawer with a slide on toupie feet, possibly Russian, 19thC, 44in (111cm).
£2,000-3,000   *C*

An Edwardian mahogany and satinwood inlaid double corner cupboard, the moulded overhanging cornice with sunburst frieze, over a pair of 13 pane astragal glazed doors opening to reveal shelving, the lower section with a pair of 5 pane astragal glazed doors, raised on shaped bracket feet, 35in (89cm).
£2,200-2,700   *P(M)*

A George III mahogany bowfront hanging corner cupboard, inlaid with oval shell paterae, crossbanded in satinwood and strung with ebony and box, 26in (66cm).
£900-1,200   *HSS*

A Regency mahogany linen press, the finialled classical apex pediment above a pair of radial panelled doors and drawers, on splayed bracket feet, 46½in (118cm).
£900-1,200 *CSK*

A George III mahogany hanging corner cupboard, the cavetto cornice above a frieze inlaid with urns, drapes and a vase of flowers, above a pair of doors, 29in (74cm).
£1,000-1,500 *S(C)*

A Dutch mahogany standing bowfront corner cupboard, inlaid with boxwood geometric lines and rosewood bands, 3 short and 4 graduated long drawers, on bracket feet, late 18thC, 31½in (80cm).
£2,500-3,000 *CSK*

Linen Presses

A George III plum pudding mahogany wardrobe inlaid overall with ebonised lines, the top section with moulded rectangular cornice, above 2 panelled doors enclosing 2 later shelves and hanging space, the lower section with 2 short drawers and 2 graduated long drawers, on splayed bracket feet, 51in (129cm).
£1,600-2,000 *C*

A Victorian inlaid satin birch linen press, by Morant & Co., 91 New Bond Street.
£900-1,200 *SWO*

A George III mahogany clothes press, the moulded cornice with key pattern dentils above a frieze inlaid with paterae, and a pair of panelled doors with re-entrant corners and similar paterae, the base with 2 short and one long drawer, on bracket feet, resupported, 51in (130cm).
£4,000-5,000 *C*

This press is in fine condition and of good colour all over; the panels, unlike those of many presses, have not suffered from splitting.

A George III mahogany linen press, the upper section with dentil carved cornice over slides enclosed by a pair of beaded panelled doors, the slightly projecting base set with 2 short and 2 long drawers, with brass swan neck loop handles, on bracket feet, 51in (129cm).
£2,000-2,500 *HSS*

A mahogany linen press, with shelved upper section enclosed by a pair of panelled doors, with lower section with 2 long and 2 short drawers with circular brass handles, on bracket feet, 19thC, 48in (122cm).
£800-1,000 *HCH*

A mahogany linen press with
4 shelves to the upper section
enclosed by a pair of panel doors,
3 long drawers below with wooden
knob handles, turned side columns,
on plinth base, 19thC, 56in (142cm).
£600-800 *HCH*

A late Victorian mahogany
wardrobe of mid Georgian design,
on scroll carved bracket feet, 53in
(134cm).
£1,500-2,000 *CSK*

A late George III inlaid mahogany
gentleman's press, with a broken
scroll pediment inlaid with urns
above a simulated fluted frieze with
a pair of oval panelled doors and
2 short and 2 long drawers, on
bracket feet, 48½in (123cm).
£3,000-4,000 *CSK*

A George II mahogany linen press,
the moulded top above a pair of
fielded panel doors, now enclosing
hanging space, on shaped bracket
feet, c1750, 47½in (120cm).
£1,500-2,500 *S(S)*

A George IV mahogany
dwarf breakfront clothes
press, the 4 sliding trays
enclosed by a pair of
crossbanded beaded
panel doors, between
4 short drawers on
either side, on reeded
bun feet, 74in (188cm).
£2,500-3,000 *WHB*

A George III mahogany clothes
press, the dentil moulded cornice
above a pair of curvilinear fielded
panels with 2 short and one long
graduated drawers, on bracket feet,
54½in (138cm).
£2,000-2,500 *CSK*

A late George III mahogany linen
press, with moulded dentil cornice
above a pair of fielded panelled
doors, with similar doors below,
enclosing 4 drawers, on ogee
bracket feet, 53in (134cm).
£2,000-2,500 *CSK*

Wardrobes

A Dutch mahogany wardrobe with a
dentil cornice, above a pair of fielded
panel doors decorated with applied
swags and paterae, flanked by a pair
of Corinthian pilasters, 2 dummy
and one long drawers below with
moulded handles, raised on square
tapering legs, early 19thC, 61in
(155cm).
£1,500-2,000 *AG*

A reproduction Georgian style mahogany breakfront wardrobe, 97in (246cm).
£600-700   *AG*

A William IV mahogany breakfront wardrobe, with cavetto moulded cornice above 3 fielded panelled doors, enclosing central sliding shelves and 4 graduated drawers, on plinth base, 81in (205cm).
£1,700-2,000   *CSK*

A burr walnut and banded hanging cupboard of William and Mary design, with 2 simulated drawers, with 2 drawers to the apron on faceted turned tapering baluster columns and turned bun feet, joined by scrolling flat stretchers, 38½in (98cm).
£1,700-2,000   *CSK*

An early Victorian mahogany breakfront wardrobe, the moulded cornice above 4 fielded panelled doors flanking 4 central drawers, on plinth base, 109in (276cm).
£1,500-2,000   *CSK*

A Victorian mahogany and satinwood banded wardrobe, inlaid with geometric boxwood lines, the cavetto banded pediment above 2 fielded panelled doors and 2 base drawers, on bracket feet, 49in (124cm).
£700-900   *CSK*

Davenports

A George IV rosewood davenport, the sliding box top with a spindled baluster three-quarter gallery with a leather lined folding flap enclosing fitted interior, above 4 graduated side drawers, on plinth base, 18½in (47cm).
£1,700-2,000   *CSK*

A William IV mahogany davenport, the sliding top with fretwork gallery and hinged slope inset with original tooled leather, opening to reveal a polished, fitted interior, the lower section fitted with slide to each side and 4 drawers to one face, opposed by 4 dummy drawers, all with rosewood handles, on moulded base and ribbed bun feet, with casters, stamped GILLOW, 20in (51cm).
£4,500-5,500   *P(M)*

A late Victorian burr walnut and oak davenport, carved overall with fruiting vine leaves, with a hinged pencil compartment superstructure above a leather lined slope, 18in (46cm).
£1,500-2,000   *CSK*

Did you know

MILLER'S Antiques Price Guide builds up year by year to form the most comprehensive photo-reference system available

A William IV rosewood davenport, with spindle filled three-quarter gallery, tooled leather inset to the flap, hinged pen and ink drawer, above a door enclosing sliding trays, and on lotus headed columnar supports, with bun feet and casters, 23½in (60cm).
£750-950   *Bea*

A William IV rosewood davenport.
£2,000-2,500   *DM*

A late Victorian rosewood veneered davenport, 23in (59cm).
£900-1,200   *S(S)*

An early Victorian rosewood davenport, the inset leather lined sloping flap enclosing a maple lined interior, on an inverted plinth base, 19in (49cm).
£800-1,200   *CSK*

A Victorian ebonised and amboyna davenport, inlaid with geometric boxwood lines, with leather lined hinged sloping flap below a brass galleried lidded stationery compartment, above 4 side drawers, on bar and scroll block feet, 22in (56cm).
£900-1,200   *CSK*

A Regency rosewood davenport with a three-quarter pierced gallery above a lined slope enclosing a fitted interior, on bun feet, 20in (51cm).
£2,700-3,200   *CSK*

A late Victorian walnut and marquetry davenport, with three-quarter galleried top and hinged fall, decorated with figures before a church in a foliate landscape, the marquetry panels probably German, late 18thC, 26in (66cm).
£800-1,200   *CSK*

A late Victorian ebonised davenport, banded in burr walnut, 22in (56cm).
£900-1,200   *DN*

★ davenports are small desks derived from a design ordered by Captain Davenport in 1790
★ qualities adding substantially to the value are fine veneering in figured walnut, bird's-eye amboyna, tulipwood, kingwood, rosewood or speckled veneer; crisp deep carving to the brackets, brass stringing to the writing surface and ingenious fittings such as a rising top and concealed drawers
★ mass produced versions in bleached oak, elm, Virginia walnut or light mahogany are considerably less valuable
★ beware: marriages are commonplace. Check veneer match and colour between desk top and base, back, sides and front
★ look for evidence of replaced desk supports, rising top and drawer knobs. In particular, a plain writing top may have been replaced with a piano top to increase value

Desks

A walnut and feather banded desk, the top with re-entrant corners, above a long frieze drawer and 7 small drawers flanking a central kneehole panelled door, on ogee bracket feet, 18thC and later, 32½in (83cm).
£1,600-2,000   *CSK*

A mahogany kneehole desk, the rounded top above 8 drawers about a single recessed door, on bracket feet, basically 18thC, adapted, 30in (76cm).
£1,700-2,200   *CSK*

A mahogany kneehole desk, the moulded top above 2 frieze drawers above 6 drawers flanking the kneehole cupboard, on bracket feet.
£600-800   *Bon*

A George IV mahogany pedestal desk, the tooled leather inset top with a reeded border above an arrangement of 9 drawers, on plinth bases, restored, c1820, 59in (150cm).
£2,000-3,000   *S(S)*

A George III mahogany kneehole desk, the kneehole with a shaped apron drawer and recessed cupboard door, the sides with fluted chamfered corners, on ogee bracket feet, c1760, 36½in (93cm).
£2,000-2,500   *S(S)*

A mahogany pedestal desk, with red leather lined top, on moulded plinth base, basically 18thC, restorations, 56in (142cm).
£3,500-4,500   *C*

A mahogany pedestal desk, with rexine inset, mid 19thC, 46in (117cm).
£1,500-2,000   *Bea*

An Edwardian mahogany partners' desk, with divided red leather lined top, each end with 3 frieze drawers flanked by 6 pedestal drawers, on a moulded bases, minor restorations, 60½in (154cm).
£3,500-4,000   *C*

A mahogany partners' desk, the inset top with bevelled edge above 6 frieze drawers on pedestals of 3 drawers opposing panelled cupboard doors, with plinth bases, stamped W. Priest 17 & 24 Water St., Blackfriars, early 19thC.
£3,000-3,500   *Bon*

The restoration cost will be a significant extra on this piece.

A Regency mahogany kneehole desk, with red leather lined top and bead and reel moulded frieze, the sides applied with split mouldings, the back with false drawers, on stiff leaf scroll feet, 45in (114cm).
£12,500-14,000   *C*

A mahogany kneehole desk, the rounded top centred by a conch shell motif, with 7 drawers about the kneehole, fitted with a door and secret drawer, on bracket feet, late 18thC, the inlay later, 28½in (72cm).
£2,000-2,500   *CSK*

A partners' mahogany pedestal desk, late 19thC, 60in (152cm).
£1,000-1,300   *DN*

A George III mahogany partners' desk, with green leather lined top, on pedestals each fitted with 3 graduated short drawers opposing another 3 drawers, on plinth bases, fitted with side carrying handles, restored, 64in (162cm).
£6,500-7,500   *CSK*

A Victorian mahogany partners' pedestal desk, the inset leather lined top above 6 drawers and a panelled door, the same to the reverse, on plinth bases, 59½in (151cm).
£2,500-3,000   *CSK*

Locate the source

The source of each illustration in Miller's can be found by checking the code letters below each caption with the list of contributors

A Victorian mahogany partners' desk, with maroon leather lined top, on plinth bases, 72in (183cm).
£3,000-3,500   *CSK*

A William IV mahogany kneehole double pedestal desk, with 4 graduating drawers on either side and a central drawer with turned wooden handles and inset green leather top.
£900-1,400   *GH*

A Victorian mahogany kneehole desk, the inset lined top with 3 frieze drawers and 6 pedestal drawers, 60in (152cm). £1,500-2,000 *CSK*

A mahogany kneehole desk, of recessed outline with a moulded leather lined top, on reeded tapering legs, each lock stamped Gillows, Lancaster, labelled Gillows, 406-414 Oxford Street, London, W. and Lancaster, 60in (152cm). **£1,600-2,200** *CSK*

A Victorian mahogany kneehole desk, the inset leather lined top above 9 drawers to the pedestals, 61in (155cm). **£2,200-2,600** *CSK*

A Victorian walnut collectors' pedestal desk, with leather lined top above 2 frieze drawers and 15 small drawers with locking stiles, and plinth bases, 39in (99cm). **£700-1,000**   *CSK*

A mahogany partners' pedestal kneehole desk, the inset leather lined top with a fluted and roundel banded frieze above 4 graduated drawers and a radial panelled door, the same to the reverse, on plinth bases, basically early 19thC, 67in (170cm). **£4,000-5,000**   *CSK*

A Victorian mahogany kneehole pedestal desk, the inset leather lined coffered rectangular top above 9 drawers, on plinth bases, 56½in (144cm). **£2,000-2,500**   *CSK*

A Victorian mahogany partners' desk, with green leather lined top, on pedestals each with a door opposed by 3 drawers, on plinth bases, 60in (152cm).
£3,000-3,500 *CSK*

A Victorian mahogany partners' desk, with green leather lined top, on pedestals each with a door opposed by 3 drawers, on bracket feet, 60in (152cm).
£1,000-1,500 *CSK*

A partners' mahogany kneehole desk, the inset leather lined rectangular top above 6 drawers and a panelled door, the same to the reverse, on plinth bases, 72in (183cm).
£800-1,200 *CSK*

A mahogany pedestal desk, the top inset with gilt key pattern tooled red leather top, with gadroon carved edge, the 3 drawers to the frieze with foliate carved fascias and brass knob handles, each pedestal set with drawers opposing a cupboard enclosed by panelled door carved with a musical trophy, and flanked by fluted column stiles with acanthus carved capitols, with 2 fielded side panels and on a plinth and casters, late 19thC, 59in (150cm).
£2,000-2,700 *HSS*

A Victorian burr walnut kneehole desk, with coffered and inset leather lined top, on plinth bases, 54in (137cm).
£5,000-6,000 *CSK*

A late Victorian walnut and rosewood banded pedestal desk, the inset leather lined rectangular top above 9 drawers between canted angles, on bracket feet, 51in (130cm).
£1,500-2,000 *CSK*

A mid-Victorian mahogany clerk's desk, with lined top and shelved superstructure incorporating a hinged slope and 8 small drawers, with 9 drawers about the kneehole, on plinth bases, 60in (152cm).
£1,500-2,000 *C*

A Victorian mahogany pedestal desk, on plinth bases and casters, c1850, 47½in (121cm).
£1,200-1,600 *S(S)*

A Second Empire plum pudding mahogany pedestal desk, with inset leather lined top above 9 drawers and reverse panelled door between quadrant angles, on plinth and turned bun feet, 60in (152cm).
£1,500-2,000   *CSK*

A Victorian stained oak twin pedestal desk, stamped Edwards & Roberts, 48in (122cm).
£800-1,200   *HSS*

A mahogany kneehole writing desk, the inset leather lined inverted rectangular top above 7 drawers, on fluted turned tapering legs, 42in (107cm).
£1,000-1,500   *CSK*

A partners' kneehole desk with foliate lunette and gadrooned carved banded borders, with inset leather lined top, basically early 19thC, 60in (152cm).
£2,600-3,200   *CSK*

A Victorian carved oak pedestal partners' desk, the leather inset top with carved edge, the drawers with mask handles, on pedestals of 3 similarly covered drawers opposing panelled cupboard doors covered with lions' masks.
£1,000-1,500   *Bon*

A Chippendale style mahogany pedestal desk, the leather inset top with gadrooned edge above 3 frieze drawers, with acanthus carved cabriole legs and ball and claw feet.
£700-900   *Bon*

A late Victorian mahogany roll top desk, with a tambour fall enclosing drawers and pigeonholes and an adjustable writing slope, on pedestals of 3 drawers, with plinth bases.
£900-1,200   *Bon*

A Victorian mahogany cylinder top desk with original interior, c1870, 48in (122cm).
£1,800-2,200   *DDS*

A Victorian mahogany partners' kneehole desk, with inset leather lined top above 6 drawers and enclosed by a panelled door, the same to the reverse, on plinth bases, 60in (152cm).
£4,000-5,000   *CSK*

A late Victorian mahogany
partners' desk, inlaid throughout
with stringing and narrow
satinwood bandings, with leather
inset top, on shaped bracket feet,
one pedestal now with 2 drawers
converted to a deep drawer, c1900,
54in (137cm).
£4,000-4,500   *S(S)*

A walnut S-shape roll
top desk, with panel
sides and finished
reverse,
c1910, 60in (152cm).
£1,800-2,400   *DDS*

A South German/North Italian
walnut, rosewood and foliate scroll
marquetry kneehole desk, of broken
serpentine outline, the
geometrically inlaid top with
central motif of deer, with 3 drawers
and hinged doors to either side of the
arched kneehole, on turned feet,
reconstructed, the marquetry
possibly 18thC, 47in (119cm).
£4,500-5,500   *CSK*

Dumb Waiters

An early Victorian metamorphic
occasional table/dumb waiter, the
rising circular top with moulded rim
containing 2 further shelves, usable
in any combination, on octagonal
stem and concave platform base.
£800-1,200   *RBB*

A George III mahogany dumb
waiter, the 3 dished circular tiers on
gun-barrel turned columns and
cabriole tripod support, slight
restoration.
£700-1,000   *Bon*

A William IV mahogany dumb
waiter, the 3 graduated tiers with
three quarter galleries, the tapering
square supports surmounted by
anthemion finials, on foliate
moulded platform bases with bun
feet, c1835, 48in (122cm).
£1,000-1,500   *S(S)*

A pair of early Victorian mahogany
dumb waiters, each with 2 galleried
moulded tiers and a baluster shaft
with turned boss, on tripod base
with splayed feet, one leg broken
and repaired, 27in (69cm).
£1,700-2,200   *C*

An early Victorian 3-tier adjustable
dumb waiter, with rounded
rectangular divisions, on dual scroll
carved supports with turned feet,
48in (122cm).
£650-850   *CSK*

A George IV mahogany dumb
waiter, with brass column supports
and embossed mouldings.
£2,500-3,000   *WW*

Mirrors & Frames

A George I carved and gilt gesso wall mirror, the broken arch cresting with a central cartouche above foliate scrolls, the later plate with a shaped shell carved apron mounted with gilt metal candle sconce brackets, c1720, 40 by 24in (102 by 61cm).
£1,200-1,700   *S(S)*

An Adam style gilt gesso wall mirror, with an oval plate surrounded by subsidiary plates, with a jasperware patera crest.
£350-450   *Bon*

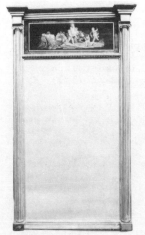

A Regency giltwood mirror, with original plate and moulded frame, 58 by 33in (147 by 84cm).
£3,600-4,200   *P(M)*

A George II wall mirror, the walnut veneered frame with giltwood and gesso borders and pendants, 56 by 28in (142 by 71cm).
£4,500-5,000   *WW*

A pair of George II style gilt gesso mirrors, the scrolled pediments centred by eagles with outspread wings, the friezes decorated with foliage and cherub masks, the shaped aprons centred by scallop shells.
£450-550   *Bon*

A William and Mary white painted overmantel mirror, with bevelled plate and cushion frame, 31 by 41½in (79 by 104cm).
£2,600-3,200   *C*

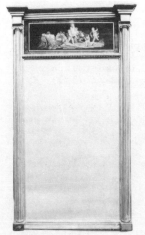

A Regency giltwood and gesso wall mirror.
£750-1,000   *HSS*

A mahogany and parcel gilt mirror, of early Georgian design, the frame with scrolled cresting headed by a basket of flowers flanked by C-scrolls and acanthus leaves, the sides carved with fruit, flowerheads and leaves, 43 by 22in (109 by 56cm).
£2,700-3,000   *CSK*

An early George III mahogany and parcel gilt mirror, 43 by 25in (109 by 64cm).
£4,000-4,500   *DN*

A giltwood mirror, the bevelled plate in a foliate gesso re-entry banded frame below a pierced leafy C-scrolling cabochon cresting and base, 18thC, 36 by 22in (92 by 56cm). **£800-1,200** *CSK*

A Regency mahogany cheval mirror, with swing plate on ring turned column supports and reeded downswept legs, with 2 brass adjustable candle holders, 32½in (83cm) wide. **£3,000-3,500** *C*

A Dutch mahogany and marquetry inlaid toilet mirror, the base inlaid with foliate marquetry and fitted with a single drawer, 19thC, 17in (44cm) wide. **£350-450** *CSK*

A Regency style mahogany and boxwood strung cheval mirror, the plate within a square section frame on outsplayed legs terminating in brass lion's paw feet. **£600-700** *Bon*

A gilt pier mirror, the pronounced leaf and foliate crest above foliate swags, the base support a pair of sconces, 19thC. **£370-470** *Bon*

A Chippendale style mahogany and parcel gilt triple plate overmantel, the plates with gilt inner slips and surmounted by a shaped crest with gilt ho-ho bird finial, 55 by 50½in (140 by 128cm). **£700-800** *Bon*

A Regency green painted and parcel gilt overmantel, the sphere applied cornice above a frieze centred by a scallop shell flanked by floral scrolls above a bevelled mirror plate, flanked by moulded pilasters with leaf carved capitals. **£600-800** *Bon*

A mahogany and parcel gilt mirror, the moulded frame with scrolling cresting centred by a roundel mounted with a ho-ho bird, with scrolling apron, 34½ by 19½in (88 by 50cm). **£800-1,000** *C*

A George III mahogany and parcel gilt toilet mirror, on square spreading supports with brass finials, the base with concave front and 3 drawers, on bracket feet, 25in (64cm) high. **£1,200-1,500** *C*

A Flemish ebonised and tortoiseshell mirror, the cushion frame with ripple moulded border, 38 by 29in (97 by 74cm).
£3,500-4,000   *C*

A late Victorian gilt metal mounted and boulle mirror, of serpentine outline, fitted with grotesque masks, 81in (206cm) wide.
£650-900   *CSK*

A Sheraton period bow fronted toilet mirror, 27 by 26in (69 by 66cm).
£525-570   *PH*

A giltwood mirror, of Queen Anne design, with bevelled divided plate within a cushioned frame carved with flowerheads and acanthus, 22 by 64½in (56 by 164cm).
£900-1,200   *CSK*

If this mirror was early 18thC it would be worth at least 5 times more.

A repoussé gilt metal and ebonised mirror, the bevelled plate with a slip of roses and acanthus leaves, the mirrored cushion frame with angles mounted with S-scrolls, acanthus and roses, the border with acanthus and roses, the arched cresting with conforming decoration, 47 by 32in (119 by 81cm).
£1,200-1,700   *C*

A giltwood pier mirror, with original glass, with arched finial with plasterwork ornate floral swags, sprays and bird decoration, 19thC, 72 by 54in (183 by 137cm).
£2,000-2,500 *GH*

A George III style mahogany overmantel with 3 bevelled mirror glass panels with carved gilded surround, pierced and carved shaped finial with bird and floral gilded decoration, 34in (86cm) high. **£300-400** *GH*

A George III mahogany toilet mirror, the crossbanded and strung plinth with 3 drawers, restored, c1790, 16½in (42cm) wide. **£400-600** *S*

A late Regency giltwood and gesso convex girandole, with foliate cresting piece surmounted by an outstretched eagle, the glass with an ebonised slip and 2 scroll candle branches below, 21in (53cm) diam. **£600-700** *CSK*

The reverse bears the trade label J. F. Barber, Newark. This being composition rather than carved wood is reflected in the low price.

A giltwood and gesso mirror frame, boldly carved with flowerheads, foliage and scrolls, late 18thC, the glass later, 32 by 28in (81 by 71cm). **£600-700** *CSK*

A Regency ornate gilt plasterwork overmantel, with original mirror glass, 60in (152cm) high. **£1,000-1,500** *GH*

A Venetian painted mirror, the plate surmounted by a cartouche and within a carved and moulded frame, painted with flowers and leafy tendrils, 29½ by 18½in (75 by 47cm). **£2,000-2,500** *Bon*

A Regency giltwood mirror, the plate in an ebonised slip and moulded foliate frame, the cresting with an eagle on a tapering plinth between dolphins, with foliate apron, 38 by 22in (97 by 56cm). **£1,000-1,600** *C*

A late Victorian giltwood and red and black painted overmantel mirror, of Gothic revival design, with a cornice of rope mouldings above a bevelled plate between Gothic arched columns with foliate capitals and oak leaf mouldings, on a moulded plinth, 72 by 51½in (183 by 131cm). **£620-900** *CSK*

A French giltwood and grey painted overmantel mirror, above an 18thC style painted panel with figures in a pastoral setting, an arched plate below within a ribbon tied surround flanked by female busts above foliate leaf moulded uprights, 19thC with some later decoration, 95 by 62in (241 by 157cm). **£3,700-5,000** *CSK*

An Edwardian mahogany and satinwood banded cheval mirror, the swan neck pediment flanked by reeded finials, above a plate on outswept supports.
£500-600 *Bon*

A Venetian wall mirror, with pierced scroll surmount, bevelled plate with etched and chamfered margin plates, c1900, 39 by 37in (99 by 94cm).
£1,900-2,500 *S*

An Italian carved giltwood wall mirror, the later plate within a pierced foliate scroll surround interspersed with putti, early 18thC, 24 by 19½in (61 by 50cm).
£800-1,000 *S(S)*

A Regency giltwood and composition mirror, with later plate below a verre eglomisé panel painted with a vase of flowers with inverted breakfront cornice cast· with balls above an acorn frieze, the sides with cluster columns, re-gilt, the cornice later, restorations, 51 by 32in (130 by 81cm).
£1,700-2,000 *C*

A rococo revival giltwood mirror, the shaped plate framed by C-scrolls, rockwork and foliage, incorporating brackets, and surmounted by an open lattice C-scroll, Italian, mid-19thC, 48 by 32in (122 by 82cm).
£800-1,200 *Bon*

A walnut mirror, the sides carved with flowerheads and foliage, with broken pediment cresting centred by rockwork, the waved apron carved with acanthus, 55½ by 32in (141 by 81cm).
£2,500-3,000 *C*

A William IV giltwood overmantel, the plate in a moulded frame with arched cresting with broken pediment centred by acanthus scrolls and flowerheads, stencilled on reverse From W. Froom's Looking Glass Warehouse, 136 Strand, London, 74 by 59in (188 by 150cm).
£2,000-2,500 *C*

William Froom is recorded as a carver, gilder and looking glass manufacturer from 1825 to 1839.

A pair of Victorian gilt gesso girandoles, with pierced cartouche crests and pierced aprons issuing 3 scrolled branches.
£550-600 *Bon*

363

A giltwood mirror, with cartouche shaped plate, the eared frame carved with acanthus, the moulded cresting mounted with martial trophies, the apron centred with a scallop shell, 19thC, 29 by 21in (74 by 53cm).
£400-600   *C*

A mahogany and parcel gilt mirror, with bevelled plate, the moulded frame with scrolling cresting and roundel mounted with a ho-ho bird, with scrolling apron, 18thC and later, and an additional mirror plate, 49 by 24in (125 by 62cm).
£2,000-2,500   *C*

An Italian giltwood mirror, with later bevelled plate, the frame boldly carved with pierced foliate scrolls, the cresting with an oval plate and gadrooned surround surmounted by sunflowers, 17thC, 55 by 35in (140 by 89cm).
£2,000-2,700   *C*

A giltwood wall mirror, of rococo scrolling form, carved with overlapping leaves, and of 2 shaped mirrored panels, late 18thC, 36in (92cm) wide.
£1,700-2,000   *HSS*

A George III style mahogany wall mirror, the bevelled plate within a gilt slip, the pierced scroll crest centred by a ho-ho bird, the scrolled apron centred by an inlaid shell.
£250-300   *Bon*

A George III mahogany and satinwood inlaid swing frame toilet mirror, the serpentine plateau with 3 drawers, on bracket feet, 18in (46cm) wide.
£600-700   *CSK*

A Flemish tortoiseshell and ebonised mirror, with later stepped bevelled plate, the channelled frame with ripple moulded corners and scrolled cresting, 19thC, 33 by 29in (84 by 74cm).
£1,200-1,600   *C*

A late Victorian composition mirror, the bead and stiff leaf frame decorated with berried trailing foliage on a velvet ground, with pierced urn and scroll cresting and conforming apron, 70 by 42in (178 by 107cm).
£2,500-3,000   *CSK*

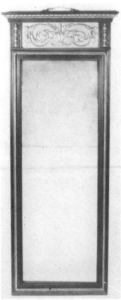

A pair of stained wood and gilt gesso pier mirrors, each with a moulded cornice above a foliate scroll frieze and divided rectangular plate within a rope twist surround, early 19thC, probably Scandinavian, 59 by 24in (150 by 61cm).
£1,500-2,000 *CSK*

A French giltwood cheval firescreen, inset with an Aubusson tapestry panel, on downward scrolling end supports carved with acanthus, the tapestry 18thC, the frame 19thC, 29in (74cm).
£1,500-2,000 *C*

l. A Regency rosewood polescreen, with carved corners and inset with Victorian wool and silk canvaswork flowers, the brass pole on reeded column and concave triangular base.
£200-250

r. A Regency rosewood polescreen, the brass pole of concave triangular form, on reeded column and concave triangular base.
£250-300 *WHB*

Screens

A French four-leaf screen, each leaf painted with rural scenes on leather, 19thC.
£850-950 *DN*

A George II mahogany tripod polescreen, with a silk and woolworked adjustable panel, on a fluted column with shell carved downswept supports and club feet, converted from a tripod table, c1750.
£700-1,000 *S(C)*

This polescreen bears the Nostell Priory inventory mark.

A Victorian walnut fire screen, carved in 17thC style, with 18thC gros and petit point panel.
£400-450 *DN*

A four-leaf painted leather screen, depicting Chinese figures of various pursuits, hunting and entertaining, with panels of blossoming foliage and birds above, within a red leather surround, 19thC, each leaf 28in (71cm).
£1,500-2,000 *CSK*

The condition of the leather is an important factor in assessing the value.

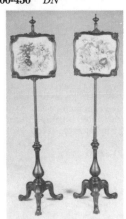

A pair of Victorian rosewood polescreens, with needlework banners.
£500-550 *DN*

An early Victorian rosewood and gilt brass polescreen, the adjustable guard with needlepoint panel, on trefoil base with scroll feet, 55in (140cm) high.
£250-350   *CSK*

A William IV giltwood cheval fire screen, with a needlework panel woven with a basket of flowers and a parrot, the cresting centred by an anthemion, on turned end supports and downswept legs, on bun feet, 29½in (75cm).
£800-1,200   *C*

A mahogany cheval fire screen, with arched needlework panel depicting a parrot and peacock, the moulded frame joined by a turned stretcher, on downswept legs and pad feet, the needlework 18thC.
£400-600   *C*

Settees

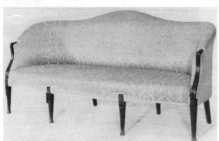

A mahogany sofa, upholstered in yellow floral damask, the curved toprail and waved seat rail carved with gadrooned edge, on cabriole legs headed by foliate scrolls and scrolling feet, 19thC, 80in (203cm).
£4,000-4,500   *C*

A William and Mary style walnut framed two-seater settee, the shaped back and scroll arms raised on scrolling front supports united by stretchers.
£600-700   *P(M)*

A George III beechwood sofa, upholstered in yellow silk, the arms with spirally fluted turned supports, on turned tapering fluted legs, lacking finials, minor restorations, 80in (203cm).
○ **£2,000-3,000**   *C*

A George III carved mahogany sofa, upholstered in green brocade, the moulded arm facings above fluted and stop fluted tapered square legs headed by paterae, c1780, 76½in (194cm).
£2,200-3,000   *S(S)*

A George III sofa, of Chippendale design, 86in (219cm).
£4,500-5,500   *DN*

A pair of George I style mahogany framed two-seater sofas, on shell capped cabriole legs, with brown floral embroidered upholstery.
£1,500-2,000   *Bon*

A Victorian chaise longue, on carved walnut cabriole legs.
£270-320 *FR*

The price reflects the state of the upholstery.

A Regency giltwood framed settee, upholstered in eggshell damask, on lotus carved tapering legs with reeded brass casters, 90in (229cm).
£2,000-2,500 *Bea*

A Regency mahogany sofa, with blue floral upholstery, on reeded splayed legs and 2 similar legs to the centre, legs strengthened, upholstery distressed, 92in (234cm).
£1,500-2,000 *CSK*

A Regency brass inlaid simulated rosewood sofa, upholstered in green corduroy, inlaid with anthemia and foliate scrolls, on short gadrooned cylindrical tapering legs, 84in (213cm).
£1,500-2,000 *C*

A Regency mahogany sofa, with pale green floral upholstery, on turned tapering legs, restored, back legs replaced, 77½in (197cm).
£1,000-1,500 *CSK*

A Regency mahogany sofa, with scrolled serpentine back, outscrolled reeded arm fronts and on conforming splayed legs, 90in (229cm).
£750-950 *Bea*

An Italian walnut three-seater sofa, in Louis XVI style, on fluted turned tapering legs, with loose seat squab, 19thC, 61½in (156cm).
£900-1,200 *CSK*

A Dutch walnut canapé, with waved back rail carved with acanthus, padded back and serpentine seat covered in floral material, on cabriole legs headed by scallop shells and pointed pad feet, 63in (160cm).
£700-1,000 *CSK*

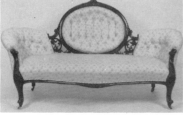

A Victorian walnut, three-seater settee, on cabriole legs with original casters, upholstered in ivory ground floral patterned linen, 78in (198cm).
£2,500-3,000 *GH*

A Louis Philippe rosewood and gilt metal mounted canapé, lacking upholstery, the seat rail applied with gilt foliate mounts, on cabriole legs, 65in (165cm).
£1,000-1,500 *CSK*

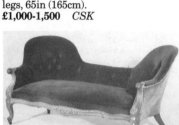

A William and Mary style sofa, 56in (142cm).
£600-700 *DN*

A Victorian sofa, with shaped curved back in buttoned red velvet.
£650-750 *DN*

A mid Victorian walnut chaise longue, buttoned and upholstered in bottle green, on cabriole legs with scroll feet.
£1,200-1,700 *CSK*

A Knole sofa, upholstered in Gothic style gros point tapestry.
£800-1,000 *Bon*

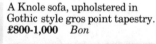

A Regency mahogany sofa, upholstered in cream and crimson striped fabric, on turned reeded legs, replacements, 76in (193cm).
£1,500-2,000 *CSK*

A William IV mahogany chaise longue, with green upholstery and dual foliate carved scroll ends and scroll back, with a moulded seat rail and reeded baluster turned legs, 81in (206cm).
£2,000-2,500 *CSK*

A Victorian walnut framed nine-piece suite, comprising a sofa, a pair of lady's and gentleman's armchairs and 6 side chairs, the backs with imbricated moulding surmounted by acanthus carved crests, the arms with husk carved supports continuing to turned and fluted legs, the sofa 68½in (174cm).
£3,000-5,000 *Bon*

A Victorian mahogany open arm sofa, of George III design, with figured brocade drop-in seat, on cabriole legs with claw and ball feet, 41in (104cm).
£500-800 *CSK*

A North German mahogany sofa, upholstered in yellow moiré silk, on splayed legs and paw feet, 76in (193cm).
£500-700 *CSK*

A pair of giltwood sofas, of Louis XVI design, upholstered in scarlet damask, the channelled frame elaborately carved, the arms terminating in rams' heads, the seat rail with guilloche pattern, on turned stop fluted legs carved with lotus leaves and headed by fleurs de lys, one stamped 2 on seat rail, one stencilled 17, the other 18, 56in (142cm).
£2,000-2,500 *CSK*

A Victorian walnut chaise longue and a lady's salon chair, the cushion moulded cresting rails richly carved, the frames pierced and richly carved, raised upon cabriole supports carved at the knees, terminating in knurl and peg feet and ceramic casters, the whole upholstered in floral machine woven tapestry.
£900-1,200 *HSS*

A late Victorian mahogany and crimson upholstered chaise longue, with a scroll and berry carved back rail and similarly carved single scroll end, on reeded bun feet, 75in (191cm). **£1,500-2,000** *CSK*

A George III painted chair back settee, black and gilt with pierced lattice splats with oval cresting panels of gilt chinoiserie scenes, the scrolling arms to lion's paw and ball supports, the front turned splay legs to brass casters, c1805, 72in (183cm). **£8,000-9,000** *WW*

A Knole style upholstered modern settee, covered in pale green damask, with twin seat cushions, 67in (170cm). **£900-1,200** *S(S)*

A mid Victorian walnut double chair back settee, with beige floral upholstery, on cabriole legs, 67½in (171cm). **£2,500-3,000** *CSK*

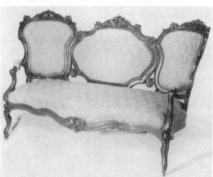

A rosewood sofa, carved with cabochon and acanthus scrolls, upholstered in figured brocade, on cabriole legs, with knob feet, late 19thC, 66in (168cm). **£800-1,200** *CSK*

A William IV satinwood settee, with rounded toprail, covered in green velvet with reeded seat rail, on scrolling paw feet headed by tablets and scrolls, restorations to feet, 99½in (253cm). **£3,000-4,000** *C*

A Victorian mahogany sofa, of early Georgian design, upholstered in pink velvet, with cabriole legs and hairy paw feet, 78in (198cm). **£1,200-1,700** *CSK*

A Victorian walnut chaise longue, the shaped frame with relief and incised carving, the back, sides and serpentine seat upholstered in beige dralon, c1865, 79in (201cm). **£1,500-2,000** *S(S)*

A Victorian four-seater Chesterfield sofa, upholstered in lining, on foliate carved rosewood bun feet, with loose floral cover, 94in (238cm). **£600-900** *CSK*

A walnut three-piece drawing room suite, comprising a two-seater sofa, with a serpentine crested back, on cabriole legs with knob feet, 67in (170cm), and 2 open armchairs upholstered in velvet and leather. **£1,500-2,000** *CSK*

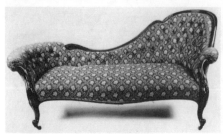

A Victorian rosewood scroll end settee, with scroll arm terminals extending down to cabriole front supports terminating in knurl and peg feet, all carved with scrolling acanthuus leaves, the buttoned back, arms and overstuffed seat upholstered in blue floral brocade.
£1,300-1,700   HSS

A walnut three-piece bergère suite, comprising a three-seater sofa with double caned back and side panels, above a tapestry upholstered seat with pierced scrolling apron on stump feet, 72in (183cm), and 2 armchairs with loose cushions.
£2,000-2,500   CSK

Shelves

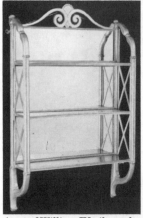

A Biedermeier mahogany scroll end sofa, the serpentine back and seat upholstered in green fabric, the splayed supports headed by paterae, c1840, 79in (201cm).
£1,900-2,400   S(S)

A set of William IV giltwood and simulated rosewood hanging shelves, with later pierced scrolling cresting and 3 shelves with mirrored back, the concave fronted top with pierced X-shaped sides, 34in (86cm) high.
£1,900-2,100   C

A pair of French Provincial cream painted and polychrome corner hanging shelves, with bowed stepped shelves and pierced backs, above tambour shutters painted with floral sprays, 41in (104cm) high.
£2,000-2,500   C

A George III inlaid mahogany bowfront sideboard, the top above a frieze drawer flanked by swivelling cellarette drawers, on square tapering legs and spade feet, adapted, 61in (155cm).
£3,700-4,200   CSK

Sideboards

A George III mahogany sideboard, with a single frieze drawer flanked by 2 further drawers, on square tapering supports with spade feet, c1800, 90in (229cm).
£2,000-3,000   S(C)

A late Regency mahogany sideboard, with eared concave top, on turned tapering reeded legs, top restored, 84½in (215cm).
£1,700-2,200   CSK

A George III mahogany breakfront sideboard, decorated with rosewood crossbanding and boxwood stringing, with octagonal handles, raised on square tapering legs and spade feet, 84in (213cm).
£4,000-4,500   AG

A George IV mahogany breakfront sideboard, 88in (224cm).
£1,800-2,500 *DN*

A George III mahogany sideboard, inlaid overall with boxwood stringing, on square tapering legs, 44in (112cm).
£1,200-1,600 *C*

Sideboards with only two front legs usually fetch less.

A George III mahogany breakfront sideboard, outlined in boxwood and ebony stringing, surmounted by a brass rail, on square tapering legs, 78in (198cm).
£4,500-5,500 *Bon*

A Regency mahogany breakfront sideboard, fitted with a frieze drawer and arched napery drawer flanked by cellaret drawer and fall front cupboard, on ring turned tapered legs, the whole outlined with ebony cockbeadings, 67in (170cm).
£2,600-3,000 *Bon*

A Georgian bowfront mahogany sideboard, with 2 central drawers and 2 deep drawers with string inlay, on 6 ring turned tapered legs, 49in (125cm).
£2,500-3,000 *GSP*

A Victorian inlaid mahogany serpentine sideboard, of George III design, the top above 2 frieze drawers flanked by a panelled door and cellaret drawer, on square tapering legs with spade feet, 60in (152cm).
£500-700 *CSK*

A large Hepplewhite mahogany sideboard, inlaid and bow ended, with wine cupboard and tambour front, on tapered legs.
£1,500-1,800 *FR*

A Regency mahogany inlaid and crossbanded sideboard, the top with raised three-quarter beading, with brass knob handles, on 4 turned and reeded supports, 42½in (107cm).
£1,500-2,000 *AH*

A Victorian inlaid mahogany
sideboard, the rosewood banded top
above an arcaded frieze, fitted with
3 drawers and a simulated cellaret
drawer, on square tapering legs
with spade feet, 58½in (148cm).
£1,200-1,500 *CSK*

An early Victorian mahogany
sideboard, on plinth base, 70½in
(179cm).
£900-1,200 *CSK*

An early Victorian mahogany
sideboard, 66in (168cm).
£2,000-2,500 *P(S)*

A mahogany
bowfronted
sideboard,
early 19thC,
53½in (136cm).
£3,500-4,500
DN

A late George III mahogany and
boxwood strung sideboard, on
square tapering legs and block feet,
restored, 68in (173cm).
£3,500-4,500 *CSK*

*The serpentine shape of this
sideboard is a desirable feature.*

An inlaid mahogany bowfront
sideboard, with cellaret drawer, on
ring turned tapering legs, basically
early 19thC, 35½in (91cm).
£1,500-2,500 *CSK*

A mahogany and marquetry
bowfront sideboard, the satinwood
and rosewood banded top with low
ledge back above 2 central drawers
flanked by a panelled door and
cellaret drawer, on square tapering
legs, basically early 19thC, 46½in
(118cm).
£1,500-2,000 *CSK*

The inlay is a later addition.

A late George III mahogany
sideboad, with brass baluster pillar
uprights with urn finials, the doors
with brass loop handles and
elliptical back plates, raised upon
square tapering supports with collar
divides, the whole crossbanded with
circular and oval double stringing in
box, 76in (193cm).
£2,500-3,000 *HSS*

A late George III mahogany and
ebony strung bowfront sideboard,
with an eared top above a central
frieze drawer with arched apron
drawer flanked by cupboards, on
turned legs, 63½in (161cm).
£2,200-2,700 *CSK*

A George IV mahogany pedestal
sideboard, with brass rail and urn
finials, 76in (193cm).
£900-1,200 *DN*

*For many years this type of
sideboard has been undervalued
but they are now quickly rising
in price.*

An inlaid mahogany serpentine sideboard, the rosewood banded top
above 3 frieze drawers and a cellaret drawer, on square tapering legs
with spade feet, basically early 19thC, 46in (117cm).
£1,700-2,200 *CSK*

A profusely carved Anglo-Indian rosewood sideboard, the doors flanked by a pair of cellarets with ribbed lids, brass lined interior and bottle holders, on turned pedestals, on canted rectangular base and winged scrolled feet, c1830, 94in (238cm).
£1,200-1,700 *C*

A Regency mahogany and ebony string inlaid bowfronted sideboard, the raised back containing shallow cupboard with sliding drawer fronts, on 6 turned and reeded supports, 84½in (215cm).
£1,700-2,200 *AH*

A Regency mahogany pedestal sideboard, inlaid with ebonised stringing, the superstructure with canted, moulded top, above a panelled tablet flanked by sliding doors above a bowfronted centre section, each pedestal with a drawer and a door flanked by monopodia, on a plinth base, each enclosing a single drawer with compartments, later bases, restorations, 84½in (215cm).
£1,500-2,000 *C*

Stands

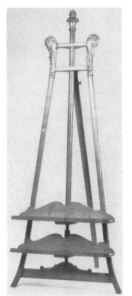

A George IV mahogany folio stand, 45½in (115cm) wide.
£3,000-3,500 *DN*

A Victorian walnut duet stand, with 2 pierced scroll carved panels, each rising on a ratchet, on a turned column, with moulded downswept supports, c1870, 63in (160cm) extended.
£700-900 *S(C)*

An Eastern carved hardwood plant stand, with inset marble top and carved floral decoration.
£200-250 *MGM*

A parcel gilt and satin birch easel, with foliate finial and scrolling shoulders with splayed supports and 2 adjustable shelves, 73in (185cm) high.
£2,000-2,500 *C*

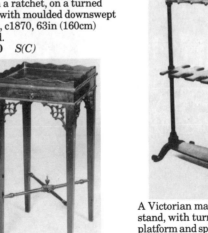

A George III mahogany urn stand, 12in (31cm).
£1,700-2,000 *DN*

A Victorian mahogany riding boot stand, with turned supports, shaped platform and splayed legs, in need of some repair, 40in (101cm) high.
£350-450 *HSS*

A walnut, marquetry and gilt metal mounted candle stand, inlaid with flowering foliage on a pierced spiral twist support, with dished circular base with trailing fruiting vines, 19thC, 12in (30cm) diam.
£500-700 *CSK*

A satinwood duet stand, the back-to-back adjustable ratcheted music stands on turned and knopped stem, united to the single drawer box pattern base by 4 scroll shaped members, decorated throughout with painted scrolls, flowers and oval reserves, 19thC, 48in (122cm) high.
£4,000-4,500 *P(M)*

A Regency mahogany metamorphic library chair, with scroll arms and rope twist back, on sabre supports folding over to form 4 steps.
£4,000-5,000 *LRG*

Steps

A matched pair of Regency mahogany bedsteps, inlaid with ebony stringing, inset with panels of patterned Brussels carpet, the hinged top step enclosing a well, on turned tapering legs, each with label inscribed in ink 'Trader', one with damage to back and top step loose, 22in (56cm) high.
£1,700-2,000 *C*

Pairs are very rare today, and highly sought after as bedside tables.

A set of early Victorian mahogany bed steps, inset with panels of patterned Brussels carpet, the second step enclosing a pull-out commode drawer with porcelain pan, on turned legs, 25½in (65cm) high.
£650-750 *C*

A late Victorian mahogany chair/library steps.
£300-400 *DN*

Stools

A late Regency rosewood stool, the floral woolworked padded top on X-form supports, joined by a turned pole stretcher, c1820.
£1,000-1,500 *S(C)*

A pair of William IV mahogany stools, with needlework tops, on baluster turned legs, 11in (28cm).
£400-500 *CSK*

A pair of George IV walnut X frame stools, 23in (59cm).
£2,000-2,500 *DN*

A Victorian rosewood and button upholstered stool, covered in pink chintz, the carved apron with cabriole legs, on scroll feet, c1850, 39in (99cm).
£1,400-1,700   S(S)

An early Victorian walnut stool with padded seat and waved channelled seat rail centred by flowerheads, the channelled cabriole legs headed by flowerheads, on foliate feet, 20in (51cm).
£900-1,200   C

A William IV rectangular stool, in the manner of Bulloch, 15in (38cm).
£350-450   DN

A George III cream painted and parcel gilt stool, the padded seat covered in close nailed yellow cotton, on cabriole legs headed by flowerheads, redecorated, previously gilt, 19½in (49cm).
£1,500-2,000   C

A George IV round adjustable music stool.
£350-400   DN

A George IV mahogany music stool, the nailed hide button upholstered seat with adjustable revolving action, the turned stem on quadruple scrolled and reeded legs, with ball feet, c1825, 13½in (34cm) diam.
£450-550   S(S)

A pair of Victorian walnut footstools, with upholstered tops, on cabriole legs with scroll feet, 13in (33cm).
£320-400   CSK

A George II walnut stool, the padded drop-in seat on cabriole legs with pad feet, restorations, 17½in (44cm).
£650-850   CSK

A pair of Regency beech framed footstools, 9½in (24cm) square.
£1,200-1,700   DN

A Victorian walnut X framed stool, the tapestry seat on moulded cabriole supports, with bobbin turned stretcher.
£700-800   Bon

A George IV rosewood and cut brass inlaid music seat, with a pierced lyre shaped splat, the hide upholstered revolving seat on a brass mounted turned pillar and gadrooned triform base with scroll feet, c1825.
£1,500-2,000   *S(S)*

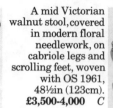

A mid Victorian walnut stool, covered in modern floral needlework, on cabriole legs and scrolling feet, woven with OS 1961, 48½in (123cm).
£3,500-4,000   *C*

A pair of giltwood stools of Louis XV style, each with padded seat upholstered in floral embroidered silk, the waved channelled seat rail carved with S-scrolls, acanthus, C-scrolls and rockwork on channelled cabriole legs headed by rockwork within confronting C-scrolls.
£1,700-2,200   *C*

A George II style mahogany stool, the stuffed seat covered in needlework, the scroll cabriole legs with elongated cabochon motifs and cabochon scroll feet, c1910, 23in (58cm).
£800-1,000   *S*

A Dutch walnut and marquetry window seat, 30in (76cm).
£500-700   *DN*

A George I style walnut stool, with slip-in needlework seat, the hipped cabriole legs with fan and leaf scroll motifs to the knees, on claw and ball feet, 21in (53cm), together with a similar walnut stool, 22in (56cm), both c1920.   **£1,700-2,000**   *S*

A carved walnut stool with floral carved front panel, supported on shaped matching carved cabriole legs, upholstered in sage green floral patterned cut velvet, 19thC, 42in (106cm) long.
£350-450   *GH*

A James II brown painted stool with padded seat, covered in tapestry style material, on cabriole legs headed by foliage and punched trellis work, joined by a waved and H shaped baluster stretcher, 20½in (52cm) wide.
£800-1,200   *C*

A Regency mahogany footstool,
after a design by George Smith, of
lotus carved S-scroll form, with
reeded rails and on bun feet, some
restoration.
£300-500   *Bea*

A Victorian giltwood stool, the
green velvet upholstered seat on
cabriole legs with scroll feet and
cabochon headings, 25in (64cm).
£300-500   *CSK*

TABLES
Breakfast Tables

A Victorian mahogany breakfast
table, the top on a baluster turned
column and 3 carved outswept legs,
terminating in scroll feet.
£1,000-1,400   *Bon*

A Regency rosewood circular
breakfast table, on triform base,
51in (129cm).
£2,000-2,500   *SWO*

A Regency mahogany breakfast
table, with gadrooned tip-up top, on
a reeded turned shaft and
quadripartite platform, with
4 reeded splayed legs, 44in (111cm).
£2,000-3,000   *CSK*

A late George III mahogany
breakfast table, with a
reeded top above a turned
shaft and splayed legs,
48½in (123cm).
£1,400-1,700   *CSK*

*Larger sizes will be
considerably more expensive.*

A William IV mahogany
breakfast table, the tip-up top
above a carved and
lappeted central shaft on a
triform platform base,
with paw feet, 52in (132cm).
£1,700-2,000   *CSK*

A mid Victorian rosewood breakfast
table, the snap-top on octagonal
baluster pillar issuing from concave
square platform, on compressed bun
feet and casters, 51in (129cm).
£1,000-1,500   *HSS*

A Victorian inlaid walnut breakfast
table, the amboyna banded oval
tip-up top on quadruple baluster
columns, with splayed legs and
foliate carved terminals, 48in
(122cm) wide.
£900-1,200   *CSK*

A Victorian walnut
breakfast table, the
moulded top raised on a
bulbous stem, with
downswept supports,
carved with leafage,
stamped 216,
48in (122cm).
£1,700-2,200   *S(C)*

A green painted breakfast table, including 4 extra leaves to add to the outer rim, in a fitted black painted box, modern, 76½in (194cm) extended.
£4,000-5,000   *CSK*

A Victorian rosewood breakfast table.
£1,500-2,000   *GIL*

An early Victorian burr walnut breakfast table, with a quarter veneered circular moulded top on a baluster and gadrooned shaft and 3 splayed scroll carved legs, 50in (127cm).
£1,600-1,800   *CSK*

A Victorian rosewood breakfast table, the tilt-top with a moulded border, on a bulbous leaf cast baluster support, on triple downswept legs profusely carved with flowers, c1845, 54in (137cm).
£2,000-2,500   *S(S)*

A Regency mahogany breakfast table, with rosewood crossbanding, the ring turned pillar on quadruple splayed legs ending in brass cappings and casters, c1810, 54in (137cm).
£1,900-2,200   *S(S)*

An early Victorian mahogany breakfast table, on turned column and tripod base, top and bottom associated, base stamped A Blain, Liverpool.
£1,400-1,800   *CSK*

A mid-Victorian burr walnut breakfast table, the tilt-top on a tripod base, with bulbous fluted shaft, with splayed legs and scroll feet, 52in (132cm).
£2,400-2,800   *CSK*

A George III mahogany pedestal breakfast table, the tip-up top on a tapering shaft and quadruple splayed legs, with brass box terminals, 57in (144cm).
£1,200-1,800   *CSK*

A William IV mahogany tip-up breakfast table, on 4 acanthus carved hipped splayed legs with brass caps and casters, 54½in (138cm).
£1,500-2,000   *Bea*

A Regency rosewood, marquetry and brass inlaid breakfast table, the tip-up top with a trailing floral border, on a faceted tapering shaft and beaded concave platform with foliate carved paw feet, 50in (127cm).
£4,000-4,500   *CSK*

The price of this piece reflects the quality and inlaid decoration.

A William IV mahogany breakfast table, of good colour, on bulbous turned column with moulded outswept legs and lappet carved feet, 56in (142cm).
£900-1,200   *Bon*

A mid-Victorian walnut breakfast table, with a burr veneered tip-up top on a fluted and beaded turned column and 4 splayed foliate and flowerhead carved legs, with scroll feet, the base stamped Lamb, Manchester, 19189, 51in (129cm) wide.
£1,700-2,200   *CSK*

A late George III mahogany breakfast table, with tip-up top, on a baluster turned shaft and 4 moulded splayed legs, 36in (92cm).
£1,500-2,000 *CSK*

A Victorian rosewood tip-up breakfast table, 48in (122cm).
£1,700-2,000 *DN*

Card Tables

A George II walnut card table, 33½in (85cm).
£2,500-3,000 *DN*

A George III satinwood card table, outlined in boxwood and ebony stringing, the purpleheart banded top above a similarly banded frieze, on square tapered legs, 35½in (91cm).
£2,500-3,000 *Bon*

An inlaid walnut card table, the eared and inverted fold-over top above a frieze drawer on a concertina action and club legs, parts 18thC, stamped Gill & Reigate, London, 31in (79cm).
£1,000-1,300 *CSK*

A George III mahogany concertina action card table, the frieze with tongue and groove carved border and acanthus carved angles, raised on fluted chamfered square supports, terminating in block feet, 36in (92cm).
£900-1,200 *HSS*

A pair of George III style demi-lune inlaid satinwood gateleg card tables, with sunburst top with ebony stringing and rosewood scallops, green baize lining, supported on square tapering inlaid legs, 19thC, 29in (74cm).
£5,500-6,000 *GH*

Pairs of card tables are always much sought after.

A George III mahogany and boxwood strung semi-circular card table.
£1,200-1,700 *DN*

A George III mahogany concertina action card table, with a hinged top, above a blind fret frieze, on square chamfered legs, 36in (92cm).
£1,800-2,200 *CSK*

This piece is decorated in typical Chinese Chippendale style.

A George II style mahogany tea/card table, the twin shaped panelled folding top enclosing a baize lined interior, above 2 frieze drawers on blind fret square moulded legs, with pierced wings, 35in (89cm).
£1,500-2,500 *CSK*

A walnut and feather banded card table, the quarter veneered fold-over top enclosing a baize lined interior, 18thC, 29in (74cm).
£3,000-3,500 *CSK*

An Edwardian mahogany and satinwood banded card table, the envelope folding top above a frieze drawer, on square tapering legs, 22in (56cm).
£900-1,200 *CSK*

A Victorian rosewood envelope card table, 21in (53cm).
£400-450 *GAK*

A George III mahogany card table, the top crossbanded in satinwood and rosewood, on square tapered legs inlaid with boxwood stringing, 35½in (91cm).
£1,500-2,000 *Bon*

A Georgian inlaid rosewood folding card table.
£1,700-2,000 *GIL*

A George II mahogany card table, the fold-over top with counter wells, above a concertina action base with cabriole legs, on pad feet, 34in (86cm) wide.
£1,200-1,700 *S(S)*

A mahogany and satinwood crossbanded folding card table, with boxwood and ebony stringing, the frieze similarly inlaid, on square tapering supports, 19thC, 37in (94cm). **£900-1,200** *HCH*

A late George III inlaid mahogany demi-lune card table, the tulipwood banded baize lined top with central fan inlay on square tapering legs, 36in (92cm). **£900-1,200** *CSK*

A Regency satinwood ebonised and brass inlaid card table, with a canted hinged baize lined top, above a reeded frieze on turned uprights, the platform on 4 reeded splayed legs, restored, 36in (92cm).
£2,000-2,500 *CSK*

A Georgian mahogany and ebony strung demi-lune card table, on square tapered legs with spade feet.
£800-1,000 *Bon*

An inlaid satinwood card table, the hinged baize lined top inlaid with fan motifs on square tapering legs, with spade feet, 34in (86cm).
£800-1,000 *CSK*

An Adam style satinwood and mahogany banded serpentine card table, the fan inlaid top above a deep frieze, on square tapered legs inlaid with bellflower chains, late 19thC.
£1,500-2,000 *Bon*

An Edwardian mahogany card table, 34in (86cm).
£1,500-2,000 *HSS*

An early Victorian rosewood crossbanded fold-over card table, on shaped and fluted columns with 4 carved legs.
£1,500-1,800 *FR*

A William IV rosewood pedestal card table, the swivelling fold-over top enclosing a baize lined interior, on a collared tapering shaft and concave sided platform base, 36in (92cm).
£550-800 *CSK*

A Regency rosewood card table in the Empire style, the plain rectangular top and frame raised on cheval base with paired twin pillars, all with gilt brass capitals and bases, on inverted sabre legs, 36in (92cm).
£3,500-4,000 *RBB*

The value of this piece is greatly enhanced by the fact that the legs close up when the top is rotated.

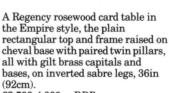

A Regency mahogany card table, the rosewood crossbanded hinged top on a turned column with moulded downswept supports and brass casters, c1810, 36in (92cm).
£600-900 *S(C)*

A George IV rosewood and brass inlaid pedestal card table, with a baize lined interior, on a bulbous tapering column and concave sided platform base and splayed legs, with brass paw feet, 36in (92cm).
£650-900 *CSK*

A Regency rosewood card table, inlaid throughout with cut brass floral motifs, the top above a vase shaped pillar and quadruple splayed legs ending in brass paw feet and casters, c1815, 36in (92cm).
£2,500-3,000 *Bon*

A Sheraton period inlaid mahogany demi-lune card table.
£1,700-2,000 *SWO*

A George IV mahogany pedestal card table, with satinwood banding, the fold-over top above a ring turned pillar, the inlaid quatreform platform on splayed legs, with leaf scrolled feet ending in casters, c1825, 36in (92cm).
£1,000-1,500   *S(S)*

A Victorian rosewood and inlaid envelope card table, fitted with a drawer, on tapered square legs joined by an undertier, 31in (79cm) open.
£750-900   *S(S)*

A Louis Philippe style ormolu mounted burr walnut and marquetry card table inlaid with scrolling foliage and a central urn of flowers on dark ground, protruding corners, baize lined inlaid folding and swivelling top, on ebonised fluted tapered legs, 34in (86cm).
£2,200-2,600   *GSP*

A Dutch marquetry card table, the top inlaid with bands of cattle in landscape, and a chess board inside, the square tapering legs folding flat, allowing the top to be displayed vertically, 19thC, 36in (92cm).
£700-1,000   *RBB*

A boulle and gilt metal mounted card table, the serpentine top centred by putti, the frieze centred by a mask medallion, on cabriole legs with caryatids and sabots, c1860, 36in (92cm).
£1,500-2,000   *S(S)*

A Napoleon III walnut and gilt metal mounted card table, inlaid throughout with tulipwood bandings and stringing, on cabriole legs ending in sabots, c1870, 33in (84cm).
£1,500-2,000   *S(S)*

An ormolu mounted tulipwood and marquetry card table, the folding swivelling baize lined top inlaid with a central bowl of fruit in stained woods and scrolling foliage and banding, on fluted ebonised supports with cross stretchers, 24½in (62cm).
£1,500-2,000   *GSP*

A Louis XV style walnut and gilt metal mounted card table, the serpentine top with narrow tulipwood banding, the cabriole legs ending in sabots, probably English, c1870, 36in (92cm).
£1,300-1,800   *S(S)*

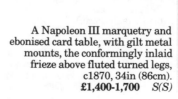

A Napoleon III marquetry and ebonised card table, with gilt metal mounts, the conformingly inlaid frieze above fluted turned legs, c1870, 34in (86cm).
£1,400-1,700   *S(S)*

Centre Tables

A mid Victorian walnut and gilt metal mounted centre table, inlaid with geometric scrolling motifs, the moulded top on 4 turned supports with finialled platform on splayed legs, 47½in (121cm).
£1,200-1,500   *CSK*

A Victorian rosewood and marquetry centre table, the top segmentally veneered, on baluster column and 3 hipped downscrolled legs, 48½in (123cm).
£2,500-3,000   *Bon*

A Regency rosewood centre table, banded with ebony and satinwood, on column end supports joined by a turned stretcher, on downswept legs with brass caps, 49in (125cm).
£3,000-3,500   *C*

A Regency rosewood centre table, with 2 true and 2 false frieze drawers, on end standards with scroll mouldings, joined by a stretcher, on turned feet, 60in (152cm).
£2,200-2,600   *CSK*

A Regency mahogany centre table, crossbanded with rosewood, on end supports and scrolling capitals, inlaid with ebonised lines joined by a high plain stretcher, on downswept legs with brass paw feet, 36in (92cm).
£1,800-2,200   *C*

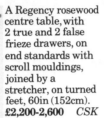

A French tortoiseshell brass inlaid and gilt metal mounted centre table, in the manner of A C Boulle, of broken recessed outline, the top with egg and bellflower border above 2 frieze drawers centred by a female mask, on cabriole legs headed by bearded masks trailing to leaf and paw sabots, distressed, early 19thC, 41in (104cm).
£1,700-2,000   *CSK*

A walnut and red walnut centre table, with claw-and-ball feet with acanthus carved headings, early 18thC and later, 40½in (103cm).
£800-1,200   *CSK*

A Victorian giltwood and composition centre table, with an inset glazed tapestry panelled top, 51in (130cm).
£1,200-1,600   *CSK*

A Victorian walnut centre table, of serpentine outline, the top inlaid with arabesques above a drawer, on gilt metal mounted cabriole legs.
£900-1,200   *Bon*

A late Victorian rosewood and marquetry centre table, with 4 swivelling drawers, on square tapering legs joined by stretchers, 21½in (54cm).
£700-900   *CSK*

An early Victorian rosewood centre table, 40in (102cm).
£900-1,200
HSS

A Victorian burr walnut and carved centre table, the top with stipple ground border, on conjoined quadruple scroll supports and ceramic casters, c1855, 60in (152cm).
£2,000-2,500   *S(S)*

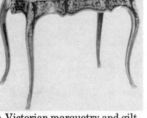

A gilt gesso table, carved in low relief, divided by strapwork within a flowerhead border with plain frieze and shaped apron with shells and foliage, on club legs and pad feet with acanthus trailing husks, 37½in (95cm).
£2,000-2,500   *CSK*

A Regency rosewood centre table, with beaded edged tip-up top, turned leaf carved column with gadrooned collar, with 3 scrolled supports having leaf decorated embossed brass toes and brass casters, 45½in (115cm).
£2,500-3,000   *AH*

An unusual Dieppe bone centre table, with later mirrored top, the whole applied with overlapping leaves incorporating dolphins and mythological figures, c1860, 36in (92cm).
£900-1,200   *Bon*

A Victorian marquetry and gilt metal mounted centre table, in the Louis XV style, inlaid throughout with deities and cherubs within floriated leafy scrolls, the serpentine kingwood banded top above a concealed frieze drawer, the cabriole legs ending in sabots, c1870, 36in (92cm).
£2,200-3,000   *S(S)*

A Biedermeier walnut centre table, with spreading hexagonal and ribbed pedestal on concave sided tripod base, with downward scrolling legs, restorations to top, 42in (107cm).
£2,500-3,000   *C*

A Victorian rosewood centre table, the top above 2 frieze drawers, on end column supports, with platform supports and paw feet.
£800-1,200   *Bon*

A giltwood centre table, of late 17thC design, with mottled marble top and stiff leaf carved border, on carved bun feet joined by flattened stretchers centred by an acorn finial, 39½in (100cm).
£1,500-2,000   *CSK*

A Victorian walnut centre table, the serpentine quarter veneered top with leaf carved baluster supports joined by a pole stretcher, c1850, 48in (122cm).
£1,200-1,500   *S(S)*

An early Victorian mahogany centre table, with scroll brackets, on dual turned feet, 66in (168cm).
£1,200-1,500
CSK

A William IV rosewood centre table, with moulded top above 2 frieze drawers on stiff leaf carved turned end standards, and splayed legs with reeded bun feet, 60in (152cm).
£900-1,200 *CSK*

Console Tables

A Regency parcel gilt rosewood console table, the Siena brocatelle marble top on scrolling foliate supports flanking a mirror plate, on platform base, 49in (125cm).
£1,500-2,000 *CSK*

A French giltwood console table, of serpentine outline with a mottled green marble top, on cabriole legs headed with foliate mouldings and trailing flowerheads and terminating in foliate scroll feet joined by a scroll stretcher, mid-18thC and later, 24½in (62cm).
£1,000-1,500 *CSK*

A cast iron console table, with variegated serpentine marble top, the cast iron support painted in beige, cast and pierced in the Louis XV design, on cabriole legs and cross stretcher, the back legs stamped James Yates, Rotherham, registered March 1842, top cracked, mid-19thC, 59in (150cm).
£7,000-8,000 *C*

Yates' firm at Effingham works, having merged with J. Haywood and Co., received considerable praise for their work at the Great Exhibition of 1851.

A pair of gilt decorated and later blue painted console tables, of Louis XVI design, each with a white marble top, on turned fluted legs joined by a concave stretcher centred by an urn, on turned feet, mid-19thC, 51in (130cm).
£2,500-3,500 *CSK*

A green veined, cream painted console table, of Louis XV design, with moulded eared serpentine grey marble top, cabriole legs joined by a scrolling stretcher on scroll feet, 46½in (118cm).
£1,200-1,600 *CSK*

A pair of early 20thC console tables and a round table en suite, with marble tops.
£1,200-1,500 *DN*

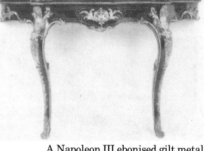

An Anglo-Indian rosewood console table, with scagliola top above a plain frieze, on S-scroll end supports carved with acanthus leaves and paterae, on concave fronted moulded rectangular plinth base, restorations, 19thC, 48in (122cm).
£2,000-2,500 *C*

A Napoleon III ebonised gilt metal mounted and boxwood strung console table, on paw sabots, 55in (140cm).
£1,200-1,700 *CSK*

Dining Tables

A Georgian style mahogany three-pillar dining table, with 2 spare leaves, raised on turned vase shaped stems each with 4 reeded downswept legs and brass paw feet, 149in (379cm).
£1,000-1,200 *AG*

A William IV mahogany D-end extending dining table, the drop-leaf top with telescopic action, on reeded turned legs with brass casters, including 3 leaf insertions, lacking clips, c1830, 88½in (225cm) long extended.
£2,700-3,000 *S(S)*

A William IV mahogany three-pedestal extending dining table, the centre piece in the form of a Pembroke table, 96in (244cm) long.
£5,500-6,000 *HSS*

A mahogany triple pedestal D-end dining table, on later tripod supports, with 2 extra leaves, basically early 19thC.
£2,500-3,000 *CSK*

A mahogany concertina action extending dining table, with moulded edge and 2 drop flaps, raised on melon fluted turned and tapering supports terminating in casters, each end drawing out to incorporate the 3 additional leaves, with a central melon fluted turned support, early 19thC, 104in (264cm) long extended.
£3,000-4,000 *HSS*

A Regency mahogany draw leaf table, with D-shaped end sections and central section with reeded edge and 2 frieze drawers, on turned shaft with downswept reeded legs and brass caps, minor restorations, 60in (152cm).
£3,000-3,500 *C*

An early Victorian mahogany secrétaire dining table, the extending coffered top revealing a frieze writing drawer with a leather lined writing plateau, including an extra leaf, 75in (191cm) long.
£4,000-5,000 *CSK*

A mahogany extending D-end dining table, in 3 sections with a central drop leaf, on square tapering legs, adapted, late 18thC.
£2,500-3,000 *CSK*

A Victorian mahogany extending dining table, the top with telescopic action, the lobed baluster turned legs on brass casters, including 4 leaf insertions, c1850, 148in (376cm) long extended.
£3,000-4,000 *S(S)*

A Victorian mahogany dining table, on turned tapering legs with link cabochon headings, including 3 extra leaves in a grained pine housing unit, 119in (302cm) long extended.
£2,700-3,000 *CSK*

A George IV mahogany extending dining table, with veneered friezes, ribbed panels above turned ribbed tapering legs to onion feet, on brass casters, 106in (269cm) extended.
£5,200-5,600 *WW*

A Regency mahogany dining table, on splayed legs with brass block terminals, including an extra leaf, extending to 67½in (171cm).
£1,800-2,500 *CSK*

An early Victorian mahogany extending dining table, 98in (249cm).
£2,700-3,000 *DN*

A George III mahogany dining table, inlaid with ebonised banding, with 2 extra leaves, on square tapering legs, with gateleg action, restorations, 99in (252cm) long, including leaves.
£1,700-2,200 *C*

A George III mahogany twin pedestal dining table, with spare leaf, supported on twin fluted columns with 4 shaped legs, ornate brass feet and casters, 78in (198cm) long. **£5,000-6,000** *GH*

A George III mahogany drop-leaf dining table, on square tapered legs.
£600-800   *Bon*

A late Georgian mahogany D-end dining table, on square tapering legs with spade feet, including an extra leaf, 68½in (174cm) long.
£2,000-2,500   *CSK*

A Victorian mahogany dining table, on reeded turned tapering legs, including 2 extra leaves, 81in (206cm) long extended.
£1,300-1,600   *CSK*

A Regency mahogany dining table, on reeded turned legs, including a later spare leaf, c1810, 82in (208cm) long extended.
£2,000-2,500   *S(S)*

A mahogany framed dining/snooker table by E. J. Riley.
£1,200-1,600   *S(S)*

An Edwardian Chippendale revival carved mahogany dining table, on cabriole legs with acanthus knees and claw-and-ball feet, including 2 spare leaves and winding key, c1910, 96in (244cm) long extended.
£1,400-1,700   *S(S)*

A Biedermeier bird's-eye maple expanding dining table, with later top, opening to enclose 3 later leaves, on pierced shaped trestle ends joined by a ring turned stretcher and bun feet, including 3 leaves, adapted, 94in (238cm) extended.
£3,500-4,000   *C*

Three-pillar tables that are original now fetch considerable sums.

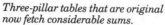

A Regency mahogany three-pillar dining table, 130in (330cm) long.
£40,000-45,000   *McC*

A Regency mahogany twin pedestal dining table, on a platform base and foliate carved downcurved legs, including an extra leaf, 87½in (222cm) long.
£3,500-4,000   *CSK*

Display Tables

An Edwardian satinwood and marquetry vitrine table, inlaid overall with scrolling foliage with glazed hinged top and sides enclosing an interior with green velvet lined base, on square tapering legs joined by an X-shaped stretcher, on spade feet, damage to stretcher, 24in (61cm).
£1,500-2,000   C

Dressing Tables

A mahogany dressing table, inlaid with boxwood stringing, on square tapering legs, one front leg broken and repaired, 37½in (95cm).
£1,700-2,000   C

An Empire mahogany and gilt metal mounted dressing table, the arched swing-plate above a single frieze drawer, on turned column supports with concave platform base, adapted, 32in (81cm).
£2,000-2,400   CSK

A French Second Empire kingwood and gilt metal mounted vitrine table, the glazed top with three-quarter pierced gallery above a shaped apron, on cabriole legs with gilt foliate clasps, 25½in (65cm).
£850-1,000   CSK

A Venetian giltwood and blue and floral painted vitrine table, with a hinged lid, on cabriole legs headed by foliate mouldings and armorial devices with turned feet, 36in (92cm).
£1,700-2,000   CSK

A mahogany tray top dressing table, early 19thC, 38½in (98cm).
£500-600   DN

A French kingwood and ormolu mounted bijouterie table, with shaped bevelled glass top enclosing velvet lined interior, the bombé sides with torch, mask and floral motifs, on cabriole legs, 19thC, 30in (76cm).
£4,200-4,600   GSP

A rosewood and marquetry display table, late 19thC, 24in (61cm).
£900-1,000   DN

A Victorian burr walnut dressing table and matching washstand, 48in (122cm).
£650-800   DN

A black and gilt japanned dressing table, the top with three-quarter gallery with 4 short drawers around a kneehole drawer, on turned tapering legs with brass caps, stamped 1033, early 19thC, 42in (107cm).
£3,000-3,500   C

A George III mahogany dressing table, with hinged top, the interior banded in tulipwood with easel mirror flanked by lidded compartments with chased ormolu handles, on square tapering legs joined by a concave side undertier, 28in (71cm).
£1,600-2,000 *C*

Drop-leaf Tables

A mahogany drop-leaf table, with double gateleg action, on turned tapering supports with pad feet, 63½in (161cm).
£650-750 *S(S)*

A Regency mahogany drop-leaf dining table, with twin flap top, on turned tapering legs and brass caps, previously the centre section of a larger table, some repairs, 64in (163cm).
£2,200-2,600 *C*

Games Tables

A yew wood games table with fold-over top, games board, slide and drawer under, on sabre legs with brass terminals, early 19thC, 19in (48cm). **£650-750** *PCh*

A Biedermeier rosewood dressing table, banded overall with fruitwood lines, the base with grey veined white marble top with single ash lined frieze drawer with compartments, on S-scroll supports joined by double U-shaped stretcher, on downswept legs, 32in (81cm).
£2,000-2,500 *C*

A George II mahogany oval drop-leaf table, with single extension to either side, small fitted drawer, plain cabriole legs having scroll carved knees with pointed pad feet, 45in (114cm).
£1,000-1,500 *GH*

A George II red walnut drop-leaf table, the top supported by turned tapering legs with pad feet, c1740, 55in (139cm).
£1,200-1,600 *S(S)*

A Victorian mahogany duchesse dressing table, of serpentine form, the superstructure with drawers and swing mirror, 48in (122cm).
£550-650 *WHB*

A George II mahogany drop-leaf table, the top on round tapering legs, with plain husk outline mouldings to the knees, on pad feet, some damage, 56in (142cm).
£650-750 *MJB*

Did you know
MILLER'S Antiques Price Guide builds up year by year to form the most comprehensive photo-reference system available

A mahogany games table with an eared hinged top, the baize lined surface with gaming dishes above a dummy frieze drawer, on cabriole legs with pad feet, adapted, mid-18thC, 32in (81cm).
£850-1,200   *CSK*

This table is adapted and this is reflected in the price.

A Dutch mahogany and marquetry games table, the fold-over top enclosing a recess above a frieze drawer, on cabriole legs with claw-and-ball feet, 19thC, 27in (69cm).
£1,900-2,200   *CSK*

A New Zealand thuyawood parquetry games and work table, the hinged top revealing a chessboard and compartments, the hexagonal pillar support on a shaped platform base with bun feet, with original trade label of James Annear, Sydney Street, Wellington, New Zealand, c1840, 27½in (70cm).
£2,500-3,000   *S(S)*

A George III mahogany games table, the rosewood crossbanded top with a slide opening to reveal a backgammon board and inlaid for chess on the reverse, above a single frieze drawer opposed by 2 dummy drawers, on square tapering boxwood strung supports with brass casters, c1800, 44in (112cm).
£6,000-7,000   *S(C)*

A mahogany games table with eared folding top, inset with counter wells and a gaming board, on cabriole legs headed by acanthus and hoof feet, with folding backgammon board, drawer distressed, adapted, 31½in (80cm). **£2,000-2,500**   *C*

A Regency rosewood games table, the top with pierced brass gallery flanking a panel, sliding to reveal a chessboard and a backgammon board, on ring turned legs with splayed feet joined by twin turned stretchers, gallery loose, c1815, 31in (79cm).
£1,200-1,600   *S(S)*

A French kingwood and harewood inlaid tic-tac games table, the rimmed detachable top with a central chessboard and enclosing a backgammon board above 2 side drawers, on cabriole legs, 19thC, 33½in (85cm).
£3,000-3,500   *CSK*

Library Tables

A George III mahogany library table, the top with replacement green hide, 42in (107cm).
£2,600-3,000   *WW*

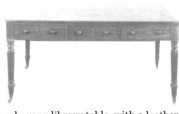

A George III mahogany partners'library table, with inset leather writing surface, with reeded edge, each side fitted with 3 drawers, on turned and finely fluted tapering supports, brass toe caps and casters, 60in (152cm).
£3,200-3,600   *RBB*

A mahogany library table, with a leather lined top above 3 frieze drawers, on square tapering legs, late 18thC and later, 48in (122cm).**£2,500-3,000**   *CSK*

A mid Victorian mahogany library table, with a reeded top above 3 frieze drawers to either side, on turned tapering legs, 54in (137cm).
£1,800-2,200 *CSK*

A William IV rosewood library table, the top with a gadrooned border and a pair of frieze drawers, the reeded and fluted supports on platform bases with gadrooned bun feet, c1830, 45½in (115cm).
£2,000-2,500 *S(S)*

A late Regency rosewood library table, the leather lined top with hinged reading slope, above 3 frieze drawers, on pierced end standards with bun feet, 34in (86cm).
£1,500-2,000 *CSK*

A George IV mahogany library table.
£3,000-3,500 *DM*

A George IV mahogany library table, with 2 frieze drawers to either side, on panelled end supports with scroll brackets, and bun feet, 57in (145cm).
£1,700-2,000 *Bon*

A Georgian style quartetto of mahogany coffee tables, inlaid with fruitwood.
£900-1,200 *GH*

A William IV library table, the top on twin reeded turned end supports, with shaped platform bases and scroll feet, c1835, 50in (127cm).
£800-1,200 *S(S)*

Nests of Tables

A set of George III style mahogany quartetto tables, outlined in boxwood stringing, the rosewood banded tops on twin ring turned column supports, on downswept feet, late 19thC.
£800-900 *Bon*

A set of Regency mahogany quartetto tables, with beaded tops on slender turned legs joined by later stretchers, on splayed feet, smallest table stamped Wilkinson, Ludgate Hill, 11781, c1815, 19in (48cm).
£2,200-2,700 *S(S)*

The firm of William Wilkinson operated from 14 Ludgate Hill from c1808 and continued to stamp products Wilkinson, Ludgate Hill until c1820 when the business traded as William Wilkinson & Sons. After this date furniture was stamped Wilkinson & Sons, 14 Ludgate Hill. The company remained in business at these premises until c1840.

A nest of Victorian mahogany and marquetry quartetto tables, the tops painted within satinwood banded borders, on twin column end standards and splayed feet joined by stretchers, labelled F.W. Greenwood & Sons Ltd., 24 Stonegate, York, 22in (56cm) and smaller.
£1,600-1,900 *CSK*

Occasional Tables

A French ormolu mounted occasional table, fitted with 2 small drawers, 18½in (47cm).
£500-600   *LF*

Pedestal Tables

A Regency mahogany three-tier occasional table, on plinth base.
£450-550   *FR*

A Louis XV style occasional table, 16in (41cm) diam.
£900-1,200   *GSP*

An early Victorian burr elm and amboyna pedestal table, in the manner of Edward Baldock, the marquetry tip-up top with yew banded borders, on a triform stem and scroll block feet, 26in (66cm).
£3,500-4,000   *CSK*

A Regency rosewood library table, in the manner of Thomas Hope, 48in (122cm).
£11,000-13,000   *McC*

A French marquetry occasional table, in the Louis XVI style, the top with paterae at each corner within ormolu border, the top frieze and platform with dotted marquetry trellis on satinwood ground, with frieze drawer, on square tapered mahogany legs encased in ormolu foliage with slender twist turned acanthus sabots, 19thC, 16in (41cm).
£1,500-2,000   *WHB*

A Victorian walnut and floral marquetry pedestal table, inlaid on ebonised grounds within crossbanding, the lobed baluster support on a scrolled tripod base, c1860, 57½in (146cm).
£5,300-6,000   *S(S)*

A mid Victorian gilt metal pedestal table, with octagonal Derbyshire spire and black slate top, on tripod stand with scrolling feet, 20in (51cm).
£1,200-1,700   *CSK*

A Victorian rosewood pedestal table, the tilt-top above a baluster turned pillar, on quadruple scroll carved supports, c1845, 63in (160cm).
£1,500-2,000   *S(S)*

An early Victorian Derbyshire slate pedestal table, the top inset with a band of trailing white flowers in pietra dura on baluster shaft with concave sided canted triangular base, on bun feet, 20in (51cm).
£1,000-1,500   *CSK*

393

A Victorian walnut pedestal table, the quarter veneered tilt-top inlaid with arabesques and stringing, c1870, 51½in (131cm).
£700-1,000   S(S)

A Victorian walnut pedestal table, the tilt-top inlaid with various segmented veneered woods, on a spiral turned shaft with splayed legs and scroll feet with bell flower headings, 16in (41cm).
£700-1,000   CSK

An early Victorian walnut and parquetry pedestal table, on tapering faceted shaft on tripartite platform base, with carved claw feet, 32in (81cm).
£800-900   CSK

A George III mahogany Pembroke table, the folding top with serpentine outlines, with 2 frieze drawers, on square chamfered moulded legs joined by a pierced flat stretcher, 34in (86cm).
£1,700-2,000   CSK

Pembroke Tables

A George III mahogany Pembroke table, outlined in boxwood stringing, the crossbanded top above an end drawer, on square tapering legs headed by oval fan paterae, 29in (74cm).
£2,000-2,500   Bon

A George III mahogany Pembroke table, the twin flap top above a single frieze drawer opposed by a false drawer, on square tapering legs with spade feet, 36in (92cm).
£1,700-2,200   CSK

A George III mahogany Pembroke table, decorated with whitewood stringing, 44in (112cm).
£1,200-1,700   S(S)

A George III mahogany Pembroke table, with moulded twin flap top above 2 cedar lined drawers and 2 simulated drawers inlaid with ebonised stringing, on a turned shaft with quadripartite base with reeded legs and brass caps, the top possibly associated, 35½in (91cm) open.
£1,200-1,500   C

A George III mahogany and rosewood banded Pembroke table, the top with 2 hinged flaps above a bowfront frieze drawer, on square tapering legs, 38in (97cm).
£1,500-2,000   CSK

A George III style satinwood Pembroke table, the kingwood crossbanded top outlined in barber pole stringing, above an end drawer, on similarly inlaid square tapering legs, late 19thC, 36in (92cm).
£1,200-1,600   Bon

A George III satinwood Pembroke table, with painted top, the double crossbanding painted with ribbon and a bay leaf meander, above frieze drawer, on square tapered legs with brass casters, 30½in (78cm).
£2,700-3,200   *WHB*

Although this table is 18thC, it was decorated in the Edwardian period.

A George III inlaid mahogany Pembroke table, the rosewood banded folding top above a frieze drawer, on square tapering legs, 41½in (105cm) extended.
£2,700-3,000   *CSK*

A Sheraton style small mahogany and satinwood inlaid Pembroke table, with small marquetry panel and serpentine top and flaps.
£450-550   *FR*

A William IV mahogany Pembroke table, the reeded top above a single frieze drawer on a vase turned column with beaded downswept supports, with leaf cast brass casters, Scottish, c1835, 29in (74cm).
£1,800-2,400   *S(C)*

Serving Tables

A George III mahogany Pembroke table, 38in (97cm).
£1,000-1,200   *DN*

A George IV mahogany Pembroke table, the top with opposing frieze drawers, the turned pedestal support on quadruple moulded splayed legs ending in brass paw casters, c1825, 44in (112cm) open.
£650-750   *S(S)*

A Victorian mahogany buffet, the 3 tiers supported on turned and reeded columns, on gadrooned feet and casters, 55½in (140cm).
£1,000-1,200   *S(S)*

A late George III mahogany serpentine serving table, on square tapering legs headed by paterae and ribbon tied trailing bellflowers terminating in spade feet, some carving of a later date, 63in (160cm).
£3,000-3,500   *CSK*

A mahogany and marquetry serpentine serving table, the top crossbanded in rosewood, on square tapering legs with block feet, adapted, some repair, late 18thC, 60in (152cm).
£2,000-2,500   *CSK*

A William IV mahogany serving side table, with tongue and dart and beaded carved outlines, on cabriole front column supports with a concave platform base, 66½in (169cm).
£4,000-5,000   *CSK*

The bold designs of this period are now much in vogue.

A sycamore sideboard, 19thC, 83in (210cm).
£1,600-2,000   *PH*

A mahogany serving side table of George III design, the top with gadrooned carved borders above a ribbon banded frieze fitted with 3 drawers, on cabriole legs with claw-and-ball feet with acanthus and bellflower carved headings, 72in (182cm).
£1,200-1,600   *CSK*

Side Tables

A William IV mahogany breakfront serving table with beaded frieze carved with lotus leaves, on turned tapering ribbed legs, each headed by a patera and with a stiff leaf collar, 120in (305cm).
£10,000-12,000   *C*

It is possible that this serving table was provided for the Stone Banqueting Hall. An important piece of its period.

A mid Victorian satinwood and kingwood banded bowfront side table, the quarter veneered top above 2 frieze drawers, on square tapering legs with spade feet, 44in (111cm).
£1,500-2,000   *CSK*

A kingwood, tulipwood and parquetry table a ecrire, inlaid overall with a sycamore leaf pattern, with eared waved sliding top above a drawer, with 2 lidded compartments with waved frieze, on cabriole legs with foliage scroll sabots, 32in (81cm).
£1,700-2,200   *C*

A George III mahogany side table, the veined Carrara marble top above a frieze, on square tapering legs carved with blind fret bands and paterae, raised on later pine column supports, 41in (104cm).
£5,500-6,000   *CSK*

A Victorian walnut side table, on fluted column supports tied by a shelf stretcher, on turned feet carved with floral swags.
£350-400   *Bon*

A South German parcel gilt and cream painted side table, with simulated marble top, on claw-and-ball feet, joined by a later scrolling X-shaped stretcher, centred with a later vase of flowers, 41in (104cm).
£1,700-2,200   *C*

A walnut veneered side table, the top with boxwood outline and crossbanded, the feet restored, early 18thC, 53in (134cm).
£3,500-4,000   *WW*

A George III mahogany serpentine side table, the moulded top above 3 frieze drawers, on square tapering supports, reconstructed, 35in (89cm).
£1,200-1,700   *S(C)*

A George III mahogany and boxwood strung side table, the top above a frieze drawer, on square tapered legs.   **£500-600**   *Bon*

A William IV mahogany side table, with marble top and cushion frieze, on foliate and scroll headed monopodia supports, with hairy paw feet, 40in (101cm).
£1,600-2,000   *CSK*

A Venetian 18thC style green painted side table, the moulded top painted with a floral bouquet, above a similarly decorated wavy frieze containing a drawer, on floral carved moulded cabriole legs.
£900-1,200 *Bon*

An early George III walnut side table, the quarter veneered and crossbanded top above 2 frieze drawers, on square chamfered legs, 32in (81cm).
£1,200-1,800 *Bon*

A George III mahogany side table, the top inlaid with an oval in ebony, the waved frieze, on cabriole legs, 33in (84cm).
£1,700-2,200 *C*

An Irish mahogany side table, surmounted by a moulded verde antico marble top, on foliate and feather carved tapering legs, with paw feet, 71in (180cm).
£3,200-5,000 *CSK*

A walnut side table, on baluster turned legs, joined by a waved X stretcher, centred by a vase, on bun feet, with paper label Messrs. Stair & Andrew Ltd., restorations, part late 17thC, 38in (96cm).
£3,500-4,000 *C*

A William IV rosewood side table, raised on standard carved supports, c1835, 24in (61cm).
£450-550 *S(C)*

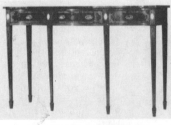

A reproduction mahogany serpentine fronted side table, crossbanded in rosewood with shell inlay, with brass drop handles, on spade feet, bearing the Redman and Hales Limited trade label, 58in (147cm).
£500-600 *AG*

A Georgian style mahogany serpentine front side table, with later raised back, decorated with crossbanding and stringing, the drawers stamped M. Butler, 61in (155cm). **£900-1,200** *AG*

A William and Mary style walnut side table, the top inlaid with 2 panels of arabesque marquetry, the borders similarly inlaid, on slender inverted baluster turned legs joined by wavy stretchers, stamped Gillows, 32in (81cm).
£700-1,000 *Bon*

A George III mahogany kneehole side table, the serpentine top above 5 drawers, on tapered square legs, with spade feet, c1785, 42in (106cm).
£2,000-2,500 *S(S)*

A Portuguese rosewood side table, with the frieze with convex panel and rippled borders, fitted with 3 drawers, on bulbous turned legs joined by spirally twisted stretchers, with bun feet, 19thC, 54in (137cm).
£4,000-4,500 *C*

A Venetian polychrome blackamoor side table, the top draped with an imitation rug supported by a kneeling girl, on stepped base carved with lotus leaves and paw feet, 19thC, 21in (53cm).
£2,500-3,000 *C*

Sofa Tables

A Regency mahogany sofa table, with 2 frieze drawers, on end standards joined by a turned stretcher, on splayed legs, 54in (137cm).
£1,700-2,000 *CSK*

A calamander sofa table, with twin flap top above 2 frieze drawers, on end standard supports, with dual legs joined by a stretcher, early 19thC and later, 58in (147cm).
£3,500-4,500 *CSK*

A mahogany and satinwood banded sofa table, possibly Dutch, lacks casters, early 19thC, 61in (155cm).
£2,000-2,700 *CSK*

A mahogany sofa table, on solid end standards, with fluted splayed legs and brass paw terminals, early 19thC and later, 66in (167cm) extended.
£1,700-2,000 *CSK*

A pair of late Regency mahogany sofa tables, with rosewood banded tops, fitted with 2 drawers with ebony banding and brass lion mask ring handles, on trestle end supports, the swept legs with ebony line brass sabots and casters, 61½in (156cm) extended.
£17,000-20,000 *WW*

A Regency rosewood and banded sofa table, with 2 hinged flaps above 2 frieze drawers, on square tapering end standards with splayed legs and brass terminals, 58in (147cm).
£4,300-4,700 *CSK*

A mahogany sofa table, with 2 frieze drawers, on solid end supports and outsplayed legs, part early 19thC.
£700-1,200 *Bon*

A mahogany and ebony strung sofa table of Regency design, on brass paw terminals, 59in (149cm).
£1,000-1,300 *CSK*

A Regency mahogany sofa table, crossbanded with boxwood stringing, with turned central stretcher and shaped feet with ebony stringing and brass lion paw feet with brass casters, 51in (129cm).
£2,500-3,000 *GH*

A George III mahogany sofa table, inlaid overall with ebony and boxwood stringing, each side with a drawer and a dummy drawer, on downswept legs and brass caps, platform carved with W, 61in (155cm).
£4,000-5,000 *C*

A George IV brass inlaid rosewood sofa table, with inlaid border, the frieze decorated with foliage and scrolls, with single mahogany lined drawer, on square spreading shaft and concave sided rectangular base, on scrolling feet, 59in (150cm).
£5,000-6,000 *C*

A Regency rosewood sofa table, outlined with brass stringing, with 4 hipped splayed legs, brass caps and casters, top and frieze varnished, 55½in (141cm).
£1,700-2,200 *Bea*

A Regency mahogany and satinwood banded sofa table, on end standards joined by a later stretcher, on dual splayed legs with spiral inlay, 63in (160cm).
£4,000-5,000 *CSK*

An inlaid rosewood sofa table, the crossbanded top with 2 frieze drawers, on twin S-scroll end standards and octagonal platform with quadruple splayed legs with brass paw feet, basically early 19thC, 60in (152cm).
£2,700-3,000 *CSK*

A George III style mahogany and painted sofa table of Sheraton design, the frieze with a pair of real and opposing dummy drawers, on rectangular end supports with splayed legs ending in brass paw feet and casters, 61in (155cm), extended.
£2,000-2,500 *S(S)*

A Regency mahogany sofa table, inlaid overall with ebony stringing, the frieze with 2 drawers and 2 false drawers, on vase shaped end supports inlaid with scrolls, on downswept legs with brass caps, restorations, 57½in (146cm).
£2,700-3,000 *C*

A William IV rosewood sofa table, decorated with crossbanding, raised on solid end supports with splay legs and paw feet, 41in (104cm).
£1,600-2,000 *AG*

Sutherland Tables

An early Victorian rosewood Sutherland table, 52in (132cm).
£1,000-1,500 *CSK*

A Victorian burr walnut Sutherland table, with pierced shaped end supports and slender turned tapered legs.
£700-800 *Bon*

A Victorian walnut Sutherland table, on pierced end supports and outswept legs.
£450-550 *Bon*

A Victorian walnut Sutherland table, with baluster turned end supports joined by a conforming stretcher, on flower carved splayed feet with casters, some restoration, 41in (104cm).
£800-1,000 *Bea*

A mid Victorian walnut Sutherland table, with twin flap top, on turned supports and dual scroll feet joined by a stretcher, 36in (92cm).
£350-550 *CSK*

Tea Tables

A Georgian mahogany tea table, with semi-circular fold-over top, on turned tapering supports with pad feet, 27in (69cm).
£600-700 *RBB*

A George III mahogany and fretwork tea table, in the Gothic manner, with pierced gallery above a drawer, supports loose, c1760, 21½in (54cm).
£2,900-3,500 *S(S)*

A George II style concertina action tea table, the rectangular top on carved cabriole legs and claw-and-ball feet. **£500-600** *Bon*

A period example of this table (c1750) would probably be worth five times this price.

A George III mahogany tea table, with hinged top with plain frieze, on square chamfered legs with pierced brackets, 28in (71cm).
£1,500-2,000 *C*

A George III mahogany and satinwood banded tea table, inlaid throughout with stringing, the semi-ellipitcal fan inlaid top above tapered square legs, c1785, 35½in (90cm). **£2,500-3,000** *S(S)*

A pair of late 18thC mahogany D-shaped tea tables, folding to double gate supports, on later legs, 29in (74cm).
£6,500-7,500 *WW*

A Regency mahogany fold-over swivel top tea table, with mahogany crossbanding and 2 rosewood bandings, shaped panel and string inlay, raised on square tapered pillar rectangular platform with coved sides and paterae, 4 sabre legs with scroll tops terminating in pot casters, 35in (89cm).
£1,200-1,700 *HSS*

A late Victorian satinwood and marquetry tea table, inlaid with classical urns and acanthus scrolls, on square tapering legs.
£700-900 *Bon*

A mahogany satinwood inlaid fold-over tea table, with centre drawer, on square tapered legs, mid-19thC, 38in (97cm).
£800-900 *PCh*

A George IV mahogany tea table, the hinged moulded top swivelling to reveal a recess, on a double column stem and platform base, with reeded downswept supports, c1825, 35in (89cm).
£1,200-1,800 *S(C)*

A late Regency rosewood tea table, on a U-shaped scroll support and lobed column, on 4 acanthus carved hipped outswept legs, 36in (92cm).
£750-900 *Bon*

Toilet Tables

A pair of mahogany tea tables, each with rectangular fold-over top above a frieze drawer, on square tapering reeded legs with spade feet, early 19thC, 33½in (85cm).
£700-800 *CSK*

A Regency mahogany tea table, the yew wood crossbanded top inlaid with ebonised stringing, the gilt metal mounted ring turned pillar above quadruple splayed legs ending in chased brass cappings and casters, c1815, 42in (107cm).
£1,500-2,000 *S(S)*

A Georgian mahogany toilet table, on squared sectioned supports with undertier, the top opening to reveal a mirror, 36in (92cm) high.
£1,200-1,500 *LRG*

A George III mahogany pedestal toilet stand, the folding top enclosing bowl apertures above a simulated drawer front enclosed by a pair of panelled doors and base drawer, on square tapering legs, flanking a side bidet with creamware liner, 23in (59cm).
£600-700 *CSK*

Tripod Tables

An early 19thC mahogany round tip-up table, 22in (56cm).
£700-900   *DN*

A George II walnut tripod table, with associated top, formerly with spindle gallery now with hobnail edge, on plain turned shaft with spirally reeded urn, on arched cabriole tripod base and pad feet, 11½in (29cm).
£900-1,200   *C*

A George III mahogany round tip-up table, 33in (84cm).
£600-700   *DN*

A George III mahogany round tip-up table, on turned and spiral fluted column, 30½in (77cm).
£550-650   *DN*

With contemporary carving and a dished top this table would fetch a higher price.

A mid Georgian mahogany tripod table, with tilt-top, now fixed, on a turned pedestal and arched cabriole legs with pointed pad feet, 24in (61cm).
£800-900   *C*

A mahogany table, the top made from a single piece of timber, c1780, 32in (81cm).
£350-400   *S(S)*

Wine/Lamp Tables

A pair of rosewood and satinwood banded lamp tables, each with an octagonal top and faceted shaft, on 3 splayed legs with gilt metal ball feet, modern, 14in (36cm).
£1,500-2,000   *CSK*

If these tables were late 18thC they would be worth in the region of £8,000-£10,000.

A mahogany tripod table, the hinged top with pierced gallery and birdcage support, on a stop fluted spirally twisted spreading shaft, on downswept legs headed by acanthus and rockwork, on claw-and-ball feet, branded TMW, 24½in (62cm).
£900-1,200   *C*

This table is out of period otherwise the price would be considerably higher.

A Victorian walnut wine table, with floral marquetry inlay, raised on a spiral turned column, with cabriole tripod, with retailer's stamp beneath, 22in (56cm).
£550-650   *DEN*

A small lamp/chess table, 28in (71cm) high.   **£400-450**   *PH*

Work Tables

A George IV mahogany Pembroke work table, with 2 real and 2 opposing dummy frieze drawers the pierced lyre shaped supports joined by a turned stretcher, on splayed legs ending in brass cappings and casters, c1820, 29½in (75cm).
£1,500-2,000   *S(S)*

A Regency mahogany work table, with sliding semi-circular box with support, on rectangular platform with coved sides, 4 sabre legs terminating in claw box casters, 24in (61cm).
£1,200-1,700   *HSS*

A late George III mahogany work table, 18in (46cm).
£1,800-2,000   *DN*

A kingwood, tulipwood and end cut marquetry work table, the lifting top inlaid with scrolls, enclosing a divided interior of satinwood and bird's-eye maple, on square cabriole legs mounted with chased ormolu plaques and Joseph pattern angles, bearing trade label of Edwards & Roberts, 20 & 21 Wardour St. and 7 Chapel St. Oxford St., London, mid-19thC, 23in (59cm).
£1,000-1,500   *C*

A George III rosewood and painted work table, banded overall with boxwood and ebonised lines, the top banded with satinwood enclosing a green pleated repp well on square tapering legs headed by anthemia and husks and joined by a later X-shaped stretcher, 16in (41cm) wide.
£1,200-1,500   *C*

A Regency rosewood work table with sliding top with hinged green leather lined reading slope, above 2 mahogany lined drawers, on turned tapering reeded legs and brass caps, stamped Cope Patent, formerly with work basket, with pencil inscription J.V. Barnard, the support for one flap detached, 46in (116cm) extended.
£1,700-2,200   *C*

A. J. Barnard is recorded in the directories as a cabinet maker between 1805 and 1808 at Coleshill Street, Birmingham.

A satinwood and painted work table, the sides each with one drawer, one lacking compartments, with red pleated silk work basket, on square tapering legs headed by husks and joined by an X-shaped stretcher, on spade feet, 18in (46cm).
£1,700-2,000   *C*

A late George III mahogany and part ridgewood work table, the hinged canted and crossbanded top above a simulated frieze fitted with a drawer below, on square tapering legs inlaid with ebony stringing, 18in (46cm).   **£1,200-1,600**   *CSK*

An early Victorian rosewood games/sewing table, the fold-over top enclosing an inlaid chessboard and baize lined top, on lyre shaped end standards with bar and bun feet joined by a turned stretcher, 21in (53cm).   **£500-800**   *CSK*

403

Writing Tables

A Victorian mahogany writing table, 54in (137cm).
£750-850 *DN*

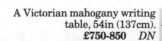

A mid-18thC style mahogany and ebony banded writing table, by Maple & Co., on plain cabriole legs.
£500-700 *Bon*

A Regency mahogany writing table, by Gillows, Lancaster, 31in (79cm).
£4,000-4,500 *McC*

A lady's French kingwood and parquetry writing table, the sliding tray top with parquetry centre enclosed within wide bandings above fitted writing drawer, fitted with leather lined slide, on square tapered legs, with gilt metal sabots,19thC, 16in (41cm).
£1,400-1,800 *GA(W)*

A Louis Philippe ebony, floral marquetry and gilt metal mounted bureau plat, of Louis XV design, on cabriole legs with gilt sabots, 51in (129cm).
£4,000-5,000 *CSK*

A Victorian boulle bureau plat in Louis XV style, the serpentine top inlaid in première partie, fitted with 2 drawers on gilt metal mounted cabriole legs.
£750-850 *Bon*

A French kingwood and gilt metal mounted bureau plat of Louis XV design, with a leather lined top above 3 frieze drawers with shell and foliate scroll mounts, on cabriole legs, 59in (150cm).
£1,500-2,000 *CSK*

A mid Victorian oak writing table, with green leatherette lined top, the panelled apron carved with Gothic tracery, on C-scroll end supports carved with trefoils joined by a square stretcher on foliate scroll feet, 46in (116cm).
£1,800-2,200 *C*

A black lacquer and chinoiserie decorated kneehole writing table, the coffered top above 3 frieze drawers, on square tapering legs, early 19thC and later, 31in (79cm).
£1,200-1,700 *CSK*

An early Victorian rosewood writing table, with leather lined top and three quarter pierced brass gallery above end standards, with scroll mouldings joined by a turned stretcher, on dual reeded bun feet, 43in (109cm).
£2,200-2,700 *CSK*

An Edwardian mahogany writing table of patent design, with purple leatherette writing slope which opens to reveal crimson taffeta lined interior for sewing accessories, raised on 4 square section supports, 20in (51cm).
£200-300 *HSS*

A French ormolu mounted mahogany writing table, the leather lined top with three-quarter pierced gallery and rim cast with drapery swags, on turned fluted legs headed by foliate collars and brass toupie feet, late 19thC, 40in (101cm).
£1,500-2,000 *C*

An early Victorian walnut, kingwood banded and gilt metal mounted bureau plat of Louis XV design, the eared serpentine leather lined top with cabochon rocaille corner mounts and egg-and-dart border, above 3 frieze drawers on cabriole legs with foliate gilt clasps trailing to gilt sabots, 54in (137cm).
£4,000-4,500 *CSK*

A Napoleon III kingwood and gilt metal mounted bureau plat, with a crossbanded serpentine top and leatherette inset, surrounded by stamped brass foliate mouldings above a frieze drawer crossbanded in rosewood with brass mounts on cabriole legs and brass sabots, 42in (106cm).
£1,500-2,000 *CSK*

A parquetry and gilt metal mounted bureau plat of Louis XV design, on cabriole legs with foliate scroll clasps leading to gilt sabots, 59in (150cm).
£1,500-2,000 *CSK*

A Napoleon III ebony, marquetry and gilt metal mounted bureau plat, of Louis XV design, inlaid within a border of scrolling foliage, with gilt cabochon corner mounts and egg and leaf gilt border, on cabriole legs with foliate gilt clasps trailing to gilt sabots, 51in (129cm).
£5,500-6,000 *CSK*

A mahogany bureau plat of Louis XV design, applied with gilt metal mounts, with serpentine leather lined top above a frieze inlaid with trellis work and fitted with 6 drawers, on cabriole legs with foliate headings and sabots, 19thC, 68in (172cm). **£3,500-4,500** *CSK*

A mahogany and marquetry writing table, the leather lined top in rosewood banded borders, early 19thC and later, 47½in (120cm). **£1,000-1,500** *CSK*

405

Washstands

A black lacquered washstand with gold design, 34in (86cm).
£550-700 *PH*

Whatnots

A Victorian burr walnut canterbury whatnot, with a finialled three-quarter fret gallery, the top on spiral supports above a three divisioned box base fitted with a drawer, on turned tapering legs, 24in (61cm).
£1,000-1,500 *CSK*

A Regency mahogany five-tier whatnot, the 3 lower shelves with drawer beneath, on turned supports, 22in (56cm).
£1,500-2,000 *WHB*

A Regency mahogany two-teir corner washstand, the top lacking bowls and 2 false frieze drawers, on splayed square section legs tied by a platform stretcher.
£250-350 *Bon*

A Regency mahogany whatnot, with drawer below the third tier, 13½in (35cm).
£700-900 *CSK*

A Victorian rosewood four-tier corner whatnot, 23in (59cm).
£600-700 *DN*

A Second Empire mahogany washstand, the Carrara marble top below a C-scrolling elevated shelved back above 2 frieze drawers and a panelled door, between quadrant angles, on bracket feet, 27½in (70cm).
£800-1,000 *CSK*

A rosewood tricoteuse, with veneered shelves, early 19thC, 30in (76cm).
£1,600-2,000 *WW*

A George IV mahogany three-tier whatnot, on plain end standards, with scrolling supports, 36in (92cm).
£1,500-2,000 *C*

An early Victorian rosewood serpentine three-tier whatnot, with pointed finials, on brass caps and casters, 18in (46cm).
£850-1,000 *GC*

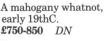

A mahogany whatnot, early 19thC.
£750-850   *DN*

A Regency mahogany four-tier whatnot, each tier with baluster turned column supports, with a frieze drawer to the base, on turned tapered legs.
£1,000-1,200   *Bon*

A Victorian rosewood whatnot, with 3 serpentine tiers between barleytwist columns, with a centre single drawer, on turned supports with brass casters, c1860, 23in (59cm).
£650-950   *S(C)*

A George IV mahogany standing whatnot, with a three-quarter gallery above triple undertiers, on finialled ring turned baluster column supports and casters, shelves adapted, 54in (137cm) high.
£1,200-1,500   *CSK*

Miscellaneous

A mahogany pedestal artist's necessaire, the detachable boxed top with a fitted zinc lined interior and inset brass side carrying handles, above 3 graduated drawers and a concave undertier, on turned tapering legs with casters, basically early 19thC, 18in (46cm).
£700-1,000   *CSK*

A walnut lap desk, by Halstaff and Hannaford, London, with pierced brass mounts, parquetry inlaid fall front, domed lid enclosing fitted interior, with embossed red leather covered light and ink well, stamped Berry's Patent, on moulded base, 14½in (37cm).
£450-550   *AH*

A German iron bound casket with studded hinged lid enclosing a formerly fitted interior, 17thC, 14in (36cm).
£350-450   *C*

A Spanish carved walnut marriage chest, the hinged top revealing a carved giltwood picture frame and a void interior, the front with 3 formal buildings flanked by a pair of scrolls, on a punched ground interspersed with flowerheads, on projecting fluted bases, mid-17thC, 42in (106cm).
£1,200-1,600   *S(S)*

A Dutch child's sleigh, the front runner ending in eagle masks, with bobbin turned back handles, the sides with painted panels, c1870, 44in (112cm) long.
£3,500-4,000   *S*

407

ARCHITECTURAL ANTIQUES
Fireplaces

A late Georgian stripped pine fire surround, with leaf carved inner fillet, cut down, 60in (152cm), together with a green marble mantelpiece, 46in (117cm).
£300-400   HSS

An early Victorian white statuary marble fire surround with finely carved brackets, 61in (155cm).
£3,000-3,500   ASH

A cream painted pine and composition fire surround flanked by fluted split Corinthian column stiles, with grey veined white marble fillet with moulded edge, early 19thC, 82in (208cm).
£600-800   HSS

A late Georgian pine and carved walnut mounted chimney piece, carved with central tablet supporting a medallion carved with 'blind Justice', flanked by flaming torchères, 68½in (174cm).
£6,500-7,000   CSK

A pine and gesso fire surround, 19thC, 73in (185cm).
£300-400   CSK

A cast iron fire insert, with brass buttons and double row of egg and dart trim, c1840, 39in (99cm).
£1,200-1,700 ASH

A Louis XV white marble bedroom fire surround, 38in (97cm).
£3,000-4,000   ASH

A George II style pine fire surround, with carved border and plain central tablet, the scrolled jambs carved with flowerheads and bell husks, 60in (152cm).
£500-600   CSK

A pine and gesso chimney piece, the
breakfront shelf above a central
tablet decorated with a figure of
Plenty being driven in a chariot,
19thC, 90½in (230cm).
£800-1,200   CSK

A French statuary marble chimney
piece, Louis XIII style, 55in (140cm).
£6,500-7,500
and fire basket with brass fretwork
apron.
£800-900   ASH

A French/Grecian style white
marble fire surround, the moulded
shelf above a panelled frieze centred
by a medallion of the Goddess Juno,
the projecting end tablets
embellished with rosettes supported
on scroll brackets with guilloche
bands and a large acanthus leaf at
the base, 19thC, 76½in (194cm).
£4,000-5,000   CSK

A George III style steel and brass
basket grate, of serpentine form
with pierced foliate apron and
cluster column front supports
surmounted by urn finials.
£1,500-2,000   Bon

A Regency pine and gesso chimney
piece, with a tablet depicting Cupid
and Psyche, with rosette roundels at
the angles above quiver jambs,
70½in (179cm).
£3,000-4,000   CSK

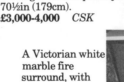

A Victorian white
marble fire
surround, with
half columns,
66in (168cm).
£600-800   ARC

A Victorian white statuary marble
fire surround of architectural
design, 77in (196cm).
£7,000-9,000
and cast iron fire basket with
applied brass rococo decoration.
£1,200-1,500   ASH

A George III style carved pine fire
surround, the shelf above a central
tablet carved with ribbon tied floral
swags flanked by floral scrolls, the
jambs carved with floral trains.
£3,000-3,500   Bon

A Victorian
cast iron
kitchen range,
by James Work,
Liverpool,
restored, c1890.
£1,500-1,800
OLD

A white Sicilian marble fire
surround, c1840, 71in (180cm).
£2,000-2,500
with Carron Co. cast iron insert.
£700-800   *ASH*

A circular iron fire basket, with
dragons heads and sunburst
decoration, c1920.
£350-450   *ASH*

An iron fire basket with cut
fretwork front.
£650-750   *ASH*

An Edwardian fire basket.
£800-1,000   *ASH*

A fire basket, 35in (89cm).
£300-400   *ARC*

An early cast iron fire grate, made
by A. Oakley, Hurst Green,
E. Sussex, c1820, 40in (102cm).
£550-700   *ASH*

A Victorian slate fire surround,
with pink fantasy marble decorated
panels with Victorian cast iron
arched interior, restored, c1870.
£1,500-1,800   *OLD*

An Adams style brass and cast iron
serpentine fronted fire grate, 20thC.
£550-650   *S(S)*

ARCHITECTURAL ANTIQUES

A Victorian brass fender, c1870,
54in (137cm).
£400-500 *ASH*

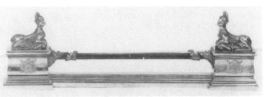

An ormolu and polished steel
fender, with recumbent griffins and
shaped plinths applied with Medusa
masks, with adjustable foliate bar
centre and moulded base, 48in
(122cm) extended.
£1,700-2,000 *C*

A Victorian cast iron fire surround,
with tiled interior and marble
surround, restored.
£2,500-3,000 *OLD*

A gilt metal adjustable fender, of
Empire style with winged griffins
upon plinth ends applied with
flaming winged lightning trophies,
the foliate scrolls joined by a chain,
44in (112cm) closed.
£700-1,000 *C*

A Victorian Patent Eagle
open-and-close firegrate, restored.
£1,500-2,000 *OLD*

A pair of Louis Philippe gilt metal
and bronzed andirons, each with
Jupiter's eagle holding a bolt of
lightning above clouds, with iron
supports, 11in (28cm) high.
£1,700-2,000 *C*

411

A French ormolu and steel fender, of serpentine outline, the scrollwork frieze with pierced and chased meandering foliage, mid-19thC, 60in (152cm).
£800-1,000   *CSK*

A brass fender, c1840, 40in (102cm).
£250-350
ASH

A cast iron fender, 45in (114cm).
£250-350   *ASH*

A set of 3 brass fire irons.
£200-300   *ASH*

A Regency brass fender, 36in (92cm).
£250-350   *ASH*

A set of 3 Victorian brass fire irons.
£250-350   *ASH*

Brass and polished steel shovel and tongs, French, c1820.
£300-400   *ASH*

Fire Irons

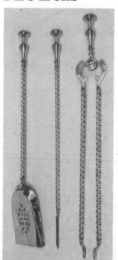

A set of 3 Victorian brass fire irons.
£200-300   *ASH*

A set of 3 early Victorian brass and steel fire irons, each with foliate knop and spirally twisted shaft, comprising a pair of tongs, a pierced shovel and a poker, the tongs 30in (76cm) long.
£600-700   *C*

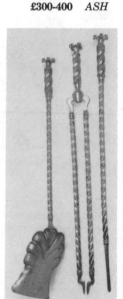

A set of 3 Victorian brass fire irons.
£250-350   *ASH*

A brass coal box, early 20thC, 13 by 15in (33 by 38cm).
£200-300
ASH

An Edwardian oval brass coal box, with decorative fretwork, 16 by 16in (41 by 41cm).
£200-300   *ASH*

A set of brass rests and fire irons, c1870.
£400-500   *ASH*

Furniture

A helmet shaped copper coal scuttle, 19 by 20in (48 by 51cm).
£200-300   *ASH*

A pair of green painted Coalbrookdale type armchairs, of fern leaf design, the pierced backs cast with foliate motif, on wood slatted seats.
£2,000-2,500   *C*

A set of 3 Victorian brass fire irons, c1890.
£200-300   *ASH*

A white painted wrought iron 2 seater garden bench, on straight legs with pad feet, early 19thC, 43in (109cm).
£1,500-2,000   *C*

A Victorian white painted cast iron garden seat, the pierced drop-in seat with stiff leaf back and grape vine feet.
£400-600   *C*

A set of 4 wrought ironwork chairs, the waisted backs above pierced seats, square feet with X shaped cross stretchers, 20thC.
£250-350   *C*

A white painted wrought iron 2 seater seat, on cabriole legs with pad feet, early 19thC, 36in (92cm).
£1,200-1,700   *C*

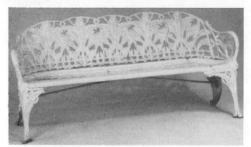

A Coalbrookdale cast iron lily of the valley pattern garden seat, the pierced cast back and arm rests with wood slat seat, 71in (180cm).
£1,500-2,500   *C*

A cast iron garden seat, the scrolled over back with mask surmount and pierced trailing nasturtium decoration, and slatted roll edged wooden seat, 19thC, 53½in (136cm).
£700-1,000   *AH*

This seat was very nearly forgotten in the nettle bed of an estate.

A reeded wrought iron garden seat, with paw feet, early 19thC, 95½in (242cm).
£2,500-3,000   *C*

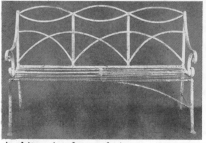

A white painted wrought iron garden seat, early 19thC, 67in (170cm).
£2,000-2,500   *C*

A Regency white painted garden bench, on splayed legs joined by stretchers, 62in (157cm).
£450-650   *CSK*

A cast iron double sided garden bench, the panelled back pierced with foliate motifs, the end pieces similarly decorated with eagle mask hand terminals, on paw feet, with pierced iron slatted seat, 57in (145cm).
£2,500-3,000   *CSK*

A pair of cast iron Coalbrookdale fern leaf pattern armchairs, the pierced cast backs above slatted seats, some slats lacking.
£800-1,200   *C*

A Coalbrookdale cast iron garden seat of unusual small size, of Gothic design, the pierced cast back centred by a crest, with scroll arm rests and iron slatted seat, 37in (94cm).
£1,500-2,000   *C*

A cast iron Coalbrookdale nasturtium pattern seat, the pierced cast back and ends with wood slatted seat, stamped Coalbrookdale, 71in (180cm).
£2,700-3,500   *C*

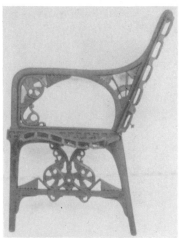

A Coalbrookdale cast iron and polychrome painted nasturtium pattern seat, the pierced cast back above wood slatted seat and scrolled uprights, stamped C.B. Dale and Co., 71in (180cm).
£1,500-2,000 *C*

A set of Coalbrookdale cast iron bench ends, designed by Dr. Christopher Dresser, with elaborate pierced scrolling decorations, each stamped Coalbrookdale and 206162.
£700-900 *C*

A set of 6 white painted cast iron chairs, the waisted backs above pierced seats and cabriole legs.
£850-1,200 *CSK*

A pair of white painted Coalbrookdale cast iron fern leaf pattern seats with pierced backs and uprights above wood slatted seats, 59in (150cm).
£1,200-1,700 *C*

A green painted cast iron bench, the pierced back, sides and seat cast with leafy branches, 50½in (128cm).
£1,200-1,700 *CSK*

A set of 4 cast iron garden chairs, on cabriole legs with paw feet, and a cast iron table, on triple scroll support, 23in (59cm) diam.
£1,000-1,500 *C*

A white painted Coalbrookdale type cast iron bench, the pierced and cast back and sides cast with foliate arabesques, on slatted seat, 73in (185cm).
£2,000-3,000 *C*

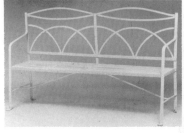

A white painted reeded wrought iron garden seat, with down curved arm rests, the legs with paw feet and curved cross stretcher, early 19thC, 71in (180cm).
£850-1,200 *CSK*

A green painted cast iron garden bench, the pierced scrolled back on S-scrolled end supports pierced with foliate scrolls and wood slatted seat, 28½in (73cm).
£400-700 *CSK*

A white painted cast iron garden seat, with down curved arm rests and wood slatted seat, 47½in (120cm).
£1,200-1,700 *C*

A white painted cast iron
chair, the pierced floral back
above a drop-in pierced seat
and scrolled cabriole legs.
£800-1,000   *CSK*

A pair of white painted cast iron
garden benches, of Gothic design,
the pierced backs with down curved
arm rests and iron slat seats, with
later feet and cross stretchers, 57in
(145cm).
£1,000-1,500   *CSK*

A white painted cast iron garden
bench of Gothic design, with down
curved arm rests and honeycomb
pierced seat, 56½in (143cm).
£1,500-2,000   *CSK*

A pair of green
painted cast iron
rustic garden
armchairs, the
backs and seats
pierced and cast
with foliate
branches.
£1,000-1,500   *C*

A white painted cast iron Gothic
armchair, the pierced back and
down curved arm rests on iron slat
seat.
£450-650   *CSK*

A pair of Verona marble seats, the
curved backs with lion mask
terminals with paw feet, centred by
an anthemion motif, and a table of
rectangular oval form with egg and
dart rim and winged lion supports,
the seat 30in (76cm) high and the
table 57in (145cm) long.
£8,000-10,000   *CSK*

A set of 4 French folding iron
garden chairs, on wicker
work simulated seat and X
frame feet.
£2,000-2,500   *C*

Four white painted galvanised wire
framed garden chairs and a
matching circular table.
£800-1,000   *WW*

A Coalbrookdale cast iron
garden seat of Louis XV
design, the arched pierced
back cast with a central
flower motif, with pierced
trellis work and angled
arm rests, on wood slatted
seat, 75in (191cm).
£2,500-3,000   *C*

416

A white painted cast and wrought iron bench, the swept back and seat on splayed legs, with paw feet, 58in (147cm).
£450-600 *CSK*

Garden Statuary

A rare George V pub table.
£200-250 *ARC*

A pub table, with a cast iron base and wooden top, 24in (61cm) diam.
£100-150 *ARC*

A white marble bust of the Apollo Belvedere, after the antique, the head turned to sinister, with draped shoulders, on socle, 30in (76cm) high.
£3,000-4,000 *CSK*

A stone figure of a dog, ears pricked, on rectangular shaped base with cut corners, 23½in (60cm) high.
£450-650 *C*

A white marble figure of Diana the Huntress, with hound, on square base, 19thC, 52in (132cm) high.
£4,200-5,000 *C*

A white marble figure of Ariadne, the classical figure leaning against a rock signed Calvi, Milano, 19thC, 37in (94cm) high, on cylindrical granite plinth, 20in (51cm) high.
£2,500-3,500 *C*

A large white marble bust depicting The Lord of the Isles, the bearded figure with long flowing hair and draped shoulders, signed on back J. Hutchison Sc, Edinr, 32in (81cm) high.
£1,500-2,000 *CSK*

John Hutchison was born in Lauriston, Edinburgh, in 1833, and died there on 23 May 1910. He was apprenticed to a wood carver but also studied at the Antique and Life School of the Trustees' Academy, Edinburgh, and went to Rome in 1863. He exhibited at the Royal Scottish Academy from 1856, being elected A.R.S.A. in 1862 and R.S.A. 5 years later. He also exhibited at the Royal Academy from 1861 onwards.

A white marble group of Venus and Cupid, on cylindrical marble plinth, fingers and arrow missing, weathered, 19thC, 77in (196cm) high overall.
£2,000-3,000 *C*

A variegated white marble bust, lacking head, the torso dressed as a Roman Emperor, on a later metallic plinth, 15½in (40cm) high.
£1,500-2,000 *CSK*

A pair of white marble figures of seated lions, 19in (48cm) high.
£3,000-4,000 *C*

A white marble figure of Athena, right arm lacking, 19thC, 48in (122cm) high.
£2,000-3,000 *C*

A Coade stone type figure of a recumbent lion, on rectangular shaped base, some chipping, 22in (55cm) wide.
£650-850 *C*

A white marble figure depicting an allegory of Wealth, clasping a wreath of berries with a bird at her feet, a pile of coins below, on circular base, 43in (109cm) high.
£5,000-6,000 *C*

A white marble figure of a classical nymph, seated on an oval base bearing the inscription "Ainsi la volonte de votre père qui est aux cieux n'est pas qu'aucun de ces petits perisse", 27in (69cm) high.
£2,000-3,000 *C*

A white marble figure of Hebe holding a tazza and a ewer, left arm loose, 19thC, 62in (157cm) high.
£3,500-4,500 *C*

A pair of modern white marble figures of lions with heavily carved manes, on rectangular bases, 40in (101cm) wide.
£2,500-3,500 *C*

A pair of lead figures of eagles with wings outstretched, on square bases with cut corners, 24in (61cm) high.
£1,000-1,500 *CSK*

A reconstituted marble fountain mask, depicting a river God with curled coiffure, with water spouts from his eyes and mouth, 30in (76cm) high.
£2,500-3,000   *C*

A composition stone and marble fountain, the centrepiece in composition stone formed as a central vase with 3 standing putti, on circular base, with marble quatrefoil basin with 4 plinths at each corner, 65in (165cm) high.
£6,500-7,500   *C*

A white marble figure of Rebecca at the Well, in pensive mood, with water jar at her feet, signed indistinctly, on naturalistic base, on cylindrical plinth with octagonal base, 19thC, 86in (219cm) high.
£9,000-11,000   *CSK*

An Italian white marble figure of a pensive classical lady, standing on a square base, 19thC, 49in (125cm) high.
£900-1,400   *C*

A lead figure of Cupid, standing on naturalistic base with hand raised above his head, 33in (84cm) high.
£600-800   *C*

A pair of Italian white marble figures of Venus and Venus Victrix after Canova, 19thC, 39in (99cm) high, each on a fluted marble plinth with bronze bell husk mounts and square bases, 50in (127cm) high.
£6,500-7,500   *C*

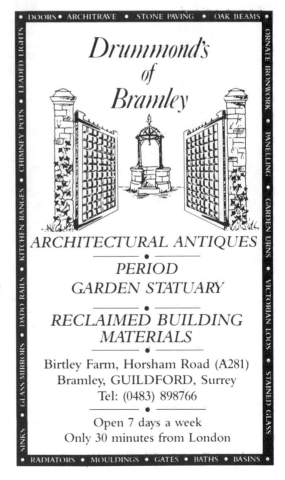

A collection of 10 stone garden
gnomes, some playing bowls, the
others as attendants, 25in (64cm)
high.
£1,800-2,200   *C*

A bronze figure of Venus Disrobing,
standing on a circular base, signed
Ferd. Lepke Fec, also inscribed
Aktien-gessellschaft: Gladenpeck,
Berlin-Friedrichshagen, early
20thC, 72in (183cm) high.
£14,000-20,000   *C*

*Ferdinand Lepke was born in
Coburg on March 23rd, 1866, he
died in Berlin on March 13th, 1909.
He studied at the Berlin Academy
and worked in the studio of the Begas
Brothers.*

A fibreglass statue of Caesar, 90in
(229cm).
£300-400   *ARC*

A white marble figure of Modesty,
the draped female figure holding
flowers, standing on a circular base
and inscribed Modestia, 62in
(157cm) high.
£3,500-4,500   *C*

A Continental carved wood and
polychrome saint, 18thC, 45in
(114cm) high.
£700-900   *ARC*

A pair of lead fountain masks,
depicting 'Winter' and 'Spring', of
Baroque influence, spouts issuing
from their mouths, raised on cloud
motifs, 21in (53cm) high.
£2,500-3,500   *CSK*

A white marble fountain, carved as
a young fisher boy with fish slung
over his back, water spouting from
its mouth, 19thC, 48½in (123cm)
high.
£4,000-5,000   *C*

A Coade stone over life size figure of
a classical maiden, depicting Plenty,
a bunch of grapes in her left hand
and a cornucopia overflowing with
fruits in her right arm, standing on
a rectangular base, stamped Coade,
Lambeth, on a square stepped
plinth, 19thC, 71in (180cm) high.
£43,000-47,000   *C*

Locate the source

*The source of each
illustration in Miller's can
be found by checking the
code letters below each
caption with the list of
contributors*

A pair of stone groups of putti, depicting Day and Night, one group with an owl, the other with a boar, on square bases, restored, 18thC, 29in (74cm) high.
£2,000-2,500   C

A bronze figure fountain, depicting a bearded man in mediaeval costume with peaked cap, holding a goose under each arm, incorporating spouts in their beaks, signed Ch. Lenz, Nuremberg, 19thC, 27in (69cm) high.
£700-1,000   C

An Italian white marble figure of Ariadne dressing her hair, leaning against a tree stump, on oval shaped base, some breaks, 19thC, 69in (175cm) high.
£7,000-8,000   C

A pair of white painted cast iron garden urns, of campana form, the beaded rims with gadrooned lower halves, with looped and mask handles, on circular fluted socles and square bases, 19thC, 31½in (80cm) high.
£1,500-2,000   C

A Neapolitan bronze figure of the Dancing Faun of Pompeii, 19thC, 31in (79cm) high.
£1,000-1,500   C

A pair of white painted cast iron garden urns, raised on stepped square plinths, the sides cast with wreaths, 19thC, 45in (114cm).
£1,500-2,000   C

A pair of lead urns, cast with roseheads with looped crestings, on circular socles and square bases applied with scroll mounts, one damaged, 19thC, 15in (38cm) high.
£2,200-2,600   C

A Coalbrookdale cast iron fountain, formed as 2 putti entwined, supporting a cornucopia, standing on naturalistic rocky base, 35½in (91cm) high.
£750-950   C

A set of 3 white painted cast iron urns, each semi-lobed body moulded with floral scrolls, and with mask hoop handles, on rising circular feet mounted on square tapered pedestals, 19thC.
£900-1,200   Bon

A pair of white painted cast iron
garden urns, on fluted socles, some
damage, 25in (64cm) high.
£250-400   *C*

A decorative pair of floral moulded
lead planters.
£300-350   *Bon*

A Victorian white painted cast iron
garden urn, with looped carrying
handles, the lower half capped with
acanthus leaf scrolls, on fluted socle
and square base, 46½in (118cm)
high.
£2,000-2,500   *C*

A terracotta jardinière, the bowl
with acanthus leaf scroll decoration,
on twist turn support, with 3 figures
of swans, on circular rocky
naturalistic base, 35½in (91cm)
high.
£1,700-2,000   *CSK*

An Italian white marble wall
fountain, the back inset with pink
variegated marble panels, the
mouths incorporating spouts, above
rectangular basin with pedimented
top, 18thC, 43in (109cm).
£7,000-9,000   *C*

A set of 4 white painted cast iron
garden urns, 35in (89cm) high.
£1,000-1,500   *C*

A Doulton terracotta urn, on square
plinth, stamped Doulton Lambeth,
40in (102cm) high.
£500-700   *CSK*

A white marble part urn, the bowl
with fluted mask and loop handles,
carved with anthemion and stiff leaf
decoration, raised on square stepped
base, the rim with stiff leaf
decoration above a frieze centred by
a harp flanked by floral wreaths,
18thC, the base 22in (56cm), the
part urn 11in (28cm) high.
£2,200-2,700   *CSK*

A pair of white painted cast iron
urns, of campana form, with mask
and loop handles, fluted socles and
square bases, 29½in (75cm) high.
£900-1,500   *CSK*

A lead urn, with flambeau finial, the sides applied with lion masks and cartouches with cherubs, on square base with cut corners, mid-19thC, 68½in (174cm) high.
£11,000-15,000   *C*

A cast iron urn, the ovoid fluted body with stiff leaf cast lower halves, with S-scrolled handles, beaded borders and circular base, 30½in (78cm) high.
£700-1,000   *C*

A pair of black painted cast iron urns, each raised on a square plinth, the sides cast with floral panels, on foliate decorated square stepped bases, stamped No. 1, Corneau Alfred, A. Charleville, French, 41½in (105cm) high.
£1,200-1,700   *C*

A pair of stoneware terracotta urns, of campana form, the wide plain rims above gadrooned lower half bodies, with scrolled handles, circular socles with foliate rims, mid-19thC, 18½in (47cm) diam.
£1,500-2,000   *C*

A set of 3 black painted cast iron urns, of Adam design, on circular spreading socles, 2 with gadrooned and foliate capped lids, 37in (94cm) high.
£1,500-2,500   *C*

A pair of lead troughs, in the 18thC style, the sides applied with lion masks within geometrical borders, 18½in (47cm) diam.
£650-900   *C*

A pair of Italian Verona marble tazzas, on central baluster and knopped support with square bases, 29in (74cm) diam.
£6,000-7,000   *CSK*

A set of 3 Regency cast iron urns, of campana form, with ring and mask handles, and another similar, with gadrooned lower half and the frieze depicting a classical scene, 23½in (60cm) high.
£1,700-2,500   *C*

A Doulton stoneware terracotta urn, the circular bowl cast with anthemion motifs, the frieze with trailing grapevine and gadrooned lower half, the foliate capped socle on square base, 22½in (57cm).
£650-850   *C*

A pair of cast iron urns, of campana form, with egg and dart rims, bodies cast with foliate arabesques and gadrooned lower halves, with mask and loop handles, on fluted socles and square bases, 30in (76cm) high.
£1,200-1,700   *C*

A white painted cast iron Medici urn, with classical frieze, mask and loop handles, on fluted circular socle and square base, raised on a square stepped plinth, 27in (69cm) high.
£500-700   *C*

A set of 4 grey painted cast iron garden urns, the beaded borders with waisted bodies, decorated with foliate arabesques, the gadrooned lower halves with loop and mask handles, above fluted socles and square bases, 24in (61cm) high.
£1,500-2,000   *CSK*

A pair of lead jardinières, the sides cast with lion masks, 10½in (27cm) high.
£350-500   *C*

A collection of 12 Georgian wrought iron railing panels, each panel centred by flower motif with friezes above and below, 27 by 35in (69 by 89cm).
£1,000-1,500   *C*

Four cast iron baskets, 18 to 26in (46 to 66cm) long.
£130-170 each   *PH*

An urn shaped two-tier bronze fountain, the bulbous gadrooned dish with foliate capped border with central gadrooned urn, on fluted socle and square base, with central and rim spouts, 26in (66cm) high.
£2,000-3,000   *C*

A pair of white painted cast iron urns, 21in (53cm) high.
£750-1,200   *CSK*

A section of iron railing, comprising a number of panels centred by cartouches and framed by repoussé foliate scrolls, and a number of sections of frieze and alternating half columns with Corinthian capitals, early 20thC, each panel 73 by 47½in (185 by 121cm) approx.
£6,000-7,000   *C*

These panels were made by Mr Starkie Gardner in 1904.

A Coade stone urn, with lion mask ring handles, rosette frieze and stiff leaf decoration, on rectangular base stamped Coade, Lambeth.
£9,000-10,000   *CSK*

A wrought iron conservatory stand, 47 by 37in (119 by 94cm).
£100-150   *ARC*

A white marble trough, the front and sides carved with cherubs riding chariots, raised on winged sphinx supports, cracked, 45½in (115cm) wide.
£9,000-12,000   *C*

A pair of iron gates, each panel centred by scrolling iron work applied with repoussé foliate rosettes, with lower half as dog rail, surmounted by foliate motifs, 68 by 32½in (173 by 83cm).
£400-600   *C*

An Italian rosso antico Grand Tour souvenir modelled as a trough, on solid trestles with fluted sides, on claw feet and rectangular plinth base, base possibly associated, early 19thC, 7½in (19cm).
£4,000-4,500   *C*

A pair of cast and wrought iron gates, the scrolling iron work top with centred breakarched panel decorated with floral scrolling motif, 19thC, each panel 89½ by 42½in (227 by 108cm).
£1,500-2,000   *C*

Did you know

MILLER'S Antiques Price Guide builds up year by year to form the most comprehensive photo-reference system available

Miscellaneous

A pair of carved oak doors, each panel with a moulded surround and carved decorative scrolled crestings centred by a foliate motif within a circle and foliate surround, French, each panel 76 by 27½in (193 by 70cm).
£900-1,200 *C*

An Adam D-shaped fanlight, in pine frame, the sectioned sunburst effect with leaded scrolling work, applied with anthemion motifs, 78 by 40½in (198 by 103cm).
£1,500-2,000 *C*

A pair of stained glass pub with green, red screens, and white frosted glass.
£800-1,000 *ARC*

A door with glass panels painted with birds, 86½ by 28in (220 by 71cm).
£300-400 *ARC*

A door plate, latch and a set of door bells, in original condition, all from one house.
£800-1,200 *ASA*

A pair of double oak doors with bevelled glazed spidersweb oval panels, 90 by 63in (229 by 160cm).
£1,200-1,500 *ARC*

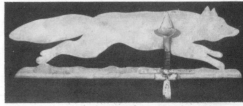

A zinc weather vane, formed as a figure of a running fox, 37 by 28½in (94 by 73cm).
£350-450 *C*

A Coalbrookdale painted cast iron stick stand, with seated whippet between the 2 hoops and loose scallop bases, stamped C.B. Dale Co. No. 20 and Victoria Register Mark.
£3,500-4,000 *WW*

A painted copper weather vane, depicting a running fox, 31in (79cm) long.
£150-200 *CSK*

A pair of stone globes on damaged pedestal bases, late 18thC, 24in (61cm) diam.
£2,000-2,500 *SWO*

A set of 4 gilt bronze capitals, each in 2 sections with scrolled angles, with acanthus leaf scrolled cappings and centred by flowerheads, 25in (64cm) square.
£1,200-1,700   *C*

A Baroque design carved stone plinth, of square squat form, each side carved with inset panels depicting foliate motifs, 25in (64cm) high.
£450-650   *CSK*

A filled terracotta plinth, the shaft decorated with a frieze of classical figures, on circular stepped base, 41in (104cm) high.
£250-300   *CSK*

A set of 3 Regency parcel gilt polychrome arches, each with pointed arch painted in blues with trailing foliage and pierced with a lobed polyfoil above an Indian arch, the jambs with moulded capitals decorated with scrolling foliage, the central arch 125in (318cm) high, the 2 flanking arches 108in (274cm) high.
£800-1,200   *C*

The combination of Gothic and Indian styles would suggest that these arches may have formed part of the re-modellings of the interior of Brighton Pavilion by Robert Jones or Frederick Crace. It is not, however, immediately apparent where, in the Pavilion, the arches were positioned, although they were presumably superseded by further re-modellings.

A terracotta plinth, stamped Doulton Lambeth, the top cracked, mid-19thC, 44in (112cm) high.
£350-500   *C*

A pair of varnished oak fluted columns, with Corinthian capitals, one as three-quarter column, the other virtually a full column, 110½in (280cm) high.
£1,200-1,700   *CSK*

A lead cistern, the front panel cast with geometrical borders with griffin motifs, centred by the initials C.R.A. and dated 1740, 47½ by 36in (121 by 92cm).
£2,000-2,500   *C*

A terracotta plinth, the square top formed as a capital with acanthus leaf scrolls, on square base with cut corners and serpentine sides, indistinctly stamped on base, 41in (104cm) high.
£600-800   *CSK*

A pair of Gothic design terracotta chimney pots, the bases stamped Smith and Co., Old Kent Road, London, 43in (109cm).
£750-850   *C*

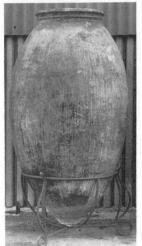

A Spanish terracotta storage jar, of ovoid form, on wrought iron stand, 97in (246cm) high.
£650-750   *C*

A pair of white painted cast iron radiator covers, the front and sides inset with pierced panels cast with foliate flowerheads, birds of paradise and foliate scrolls, each surmounted with a rouge marble top, 58½ by 38in (148 by 97cm).
£1,500-2,000   *C*

A pair of brown glazed terracotta chimney pots, the 'crown' tops above octagonal shafts and square spreading bases, with another unglazed, 37½in (95cm) high.
£100-200   *CSK*

An early Victorian cast iron staircase balustrading, formed as panels pierced and cast with Gothic motifs, alternating with panels interlaced with initials and panels centred by a shield bearing the date of 1834, with newel post with castellated tops.
£800-1,000   *C*

A Victorian black painted cast iron umbrella stand, the backplate modelled with foliate and C-scrolls, the drip tray in the form of a shell, on shaped feet, 30in (76cm) high.
£300-400   *C*

A pair of Suffolk stone gargoyles, the grotesque figures with open oversized mouths, possibly 14thC, 53½in (136cm).
£1,500-2,500   *C*

A pair of stone plaques, of trefoil form, one carved with the fleur de lys and the other with the Tudor rose, 21in (53cm) high.
£400-500 *CSK*

A pair of white painted wirework plant stands, of D-shaped form, with 3 graduated tiers, with scrolled panels below and scrolled feet, 49½in (126cm) high.
£550-700 *C*

A carved stone royal coat-of-arms, flanked by lion and unicorn, supporting shields with George V monogram, the lion 60½in (154cm), the unicorn 58in (147cm), the crest 66½in (169cm) high.
£8,500-10,500 *CSK*

The crest formed part of the Old Royal Hotel in Lowestoft, Suffolk, which was demolished in 1974.

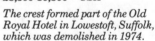

A collection of 6 giltwood carved capitals, of Corinthian design, carved with acanthus leaf scrolls, 2 incomplete, 24 by 21½in (61 by 55cm).
£750-1,000 *C*

A quantity of cast iron balustrading, the cast and pierced balustrades centred by a rosette with foliate scroll motifs with anthemion cresting, early 19thC, 29½in (75cm) high.
£400-500 *C*

A cast iron boot scraper, on scroll uprights centred by lion mask motif, on rectangular base with egg and dart rim, 15½in (39cm), and another 14in (36cm).
£160-220 *C*

A gilt metal bed coronet with swag and rosebud decorations, French, c1880, 19 by 6in (48 by 15cm).
£250-350 *ASH*

An Edwardian cast iron spiral staircase, made by St Pancras Ironworks Company, London, with 14 treads 24in (61cm) wide, with handrail and balustrade, c1907, 114in (290cm) high.
£650-950 *GH*

429

Bracket Clocks

A Victorian brass inlaid rosewood chiming bracket clock, the 7in (18cm) dial signed Benson London, the massive 3-train fusee and chain movement with anchor escapement and chiming on 8 bells and a gong, the front inlaid with brass leaves and stringing, c1885, 29in (74cm). **£2,200-2,700** *S*

A George III mahogany striking bracket clock, with carrying handle, the dial signed Wm Creake Royal Exchange London, with strike/silent ring to the arch, the 5-pillar twin fusee movement with verge escapement, pendulum holdfast to backplate, similarly signed, the case reconstructed, 14in (36cm). **£2,700-3,000** *C*

A walnut bracket clock, the 6in (15cm) silvered dial signed Dent, 61 Strand and 4 Royal Exchange, the twin fusee movement gong striking, with stamped backplate. **£1,500-2,000** *S(S)*

A mahogany bracket clock, the 7in (18cm) brass dial with silvered chapter ring, strike/silent ring and signed at centre Fra. Dorrell, London, date aperture, the fusee movement with replaced verge escapement, pull repeat and leafy scroll engraved backplate, 16½in (42cm). **£1,900-2,500** *S*

A Regency mahogany and brass inlaid bracket clock, on brass ball feet, the white painted dial, chipped, with Roman numerals, inscribed Duncan, London, the twin chain fusee movement striking on a bell, bell missing, 20in (51cm). **£800-1,000** *CSK*

A Regency brass inlaid mahogany bracket clock, with 8in (20cm) convex painted dial signed Brugger London, the 5-pillar bell striking fusee movement with unusual pin wheel escapement, on ball feet, c1820, 18in (45cm). **£1,500-2,000** *S*

An ebonised bracket clock, with a 6in (15cm) brass dial signed Chr. Gould, London, with silvered chapter ring, matted centre and screwed putto spandrels, the movement with 7 latched pillars, verge escapement, foliate engraved backplate and scroll pierced cock, on bun feet, 11½in (30cm). **£7,000-8,000** *S(S)*

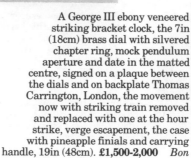

A mahogany striking bracket clock, with 8in (20cm) convex painted dial signed William Grace, Cheapside, London, 2-train fusee movement with anchor escapement, 15in (38cm). **£1,200-1,500** *Bon*

A George III ebony veneered striking bracket clock, the 7in (18cm) brass dial with silvered chapter ring, mock pendulum aperture and date in the matted centre, signed on a plaque between the dials and on backplate Thomas Carrington, London, the movement now with striking train removed and replaced with one at the hour strike, verge escapement, the case with pineapple finials and carrying handle, 19in (48cm). **£1,500-2,000** *Bon*

A rare George III ebonised musical bracket clock, the enamelled and brass dial with chime/not chime and gavot/hornpipe/air/gavot/song/cotillion, the 8-day 3-train fusee movement with a 3in (8cm) cylinder and 13 bells, 2 repeat pulls, by Charles Howse, London, 19in (48cm).
£6,600-7,000 *E*

Charles Howse produced clocks at 5 Great Tower Street, between 1768 and 1794, and was Master of the Clockmakers Company 1787.

A George IV mahogany bracket clock, with an 8in (20cm) painted dial indistinctly signed Frodsham Gracechurch St London, the repeating 5-pillar twin fusee movement with anchor escapement and rack and bell striking, c1830, 17in (43cm). **£800-1,200** *S*

A Victorian chiming bracket clock, in 17thC style, the 7in (18cm) dial signed Thurlow Ryde, with subsidiary dials, the 3-train fusee and chain movement with anchor escapement and chiming on 8 bells and a gong, in a William III style ebonised case with gilt brass basket top, carrying handle and further embellished with gilt brass mounts, side frets and paw feet, c1865, 16½in (42cm). **£2,700-3,200** *S*

An ebonised bracket clock, with a 6in (15cm) brass dial signed at the centre Robt. Henderson, London, date aperture, strike/silent in the arch, the movement with verge escapement, bell striking with pull repeat, the backplate signed, 16in (41cm). **£3,500-4,000** *S*

CLOCKS
Factors influencing prices of clocks

★ **Size.** Small size is a premium factor with most clocks, especially longcase and bracket clocks. Conversely large size is a negative factor except perhaps with special or complicated clocks, where complexity of mechanics may dictate more functional space.

★ **Woods.** The woods used may have a considerable bearing on value with longcase or bracket clocks. Wood is only one of many value factors but if it could be seen in isolation then the order of values based on woods alone would be: ebonised (black stained); oak; pine; mahogany; walnut (with or without marquetry) – all in ascending order. Pine should strictly rate on the lowest level but the scarcity of pine clocks of serious age in good condition tends to lift this level. The woods used will naturally depend to some extent on the period. For example most walnut clocks would date before 1750 and so age is a considerable influencing factor on walnut values.

★ **Auction estimates.** Values given by auctioneers as estimates of anticipated price levels may prove very different from actual bid prices. Prices paid may be much higher than estimates, and often have an added premium of 10% plus VAT on the premium. However high the estimate, some items will fail to sell at all, often for reasons which are not obvious from the illustration alone.

★ **Originality.** Clocks have been subject to more change and alteration than many other antiques, and these changes are seldom apparent from an illustration. A clock not in its original case or with a non-original movement will bring a much lower price than a similar clock in original state. The same applies to a clock with important mechanical functions missing, or even one with such functions replaced later.

★ **Condition.** If a clock is complete it is not particularly important whether its mechanics are in clean condition, as long as the vital components are still present. On the other hand a clock in the lower value ranges may cost more to restore than its total value. Case condition is very important, and a clock in good state with its original patina and colour is much more valuable than a similar one which has had casework restoration, re-polishing, etc. These things can seldom be recognised by a novice.

A George II ebonised striking bracket clock, the dial signed Tho. Martin London, with silvered chapter ring, the matted centre with false pendulum and calendar apertures, pierced blued steel hands, female mask and foliate spandrels, the 5-ringed pillar twin gut fusee movement now with anchor escapement, the pull quarter repeat train removed, 17½in (44cm). **£1,500-2,000** *C*

A walnut bracket clock with an 8in (20cm) brass dial, silvered chapter ring and matted centre, signed on a plate Wm. Smith, London, the movement with replaced verge escapement, pull repeat and with an engraved backplate, the associated case with caddy top, brass handle and on bracket feet, 20in (51cm). **£1,500-2,000** *S(S)*

A mahogany bracket clock, with double fusee movement, silvered chapter ring, glass side panels, date aperture, strikes on bell, by Wm Morgan, London, c1760, 17in (43cm). **£2,000-2,400** *IM*

A George III ebonised bracket clock, the 8in (20cm) silvered dial signed Wm. Ray Sudbury with central calendar and strike/silent dial in the arch, the similarly signed 5-pillar bell striking repeating fusee movement with deadbeat escapement, c1800, 17½in (44cm). **£1,500-2,000** *S*

A mahogany and brass inlaid bracket clock, the 7in (18cm) enamelled dial signed Marriott, London, the associated twin fusee movement quarter striking on 2 bells, 14½in (37cm). **£1,000-1,500** *S(S)*

A mahogany bracket clock, with an 8in (20cm) silvered dial signed Joseph Johnson, Liverpool, pierced gilt hands, the twin fusee movement with pull repeat and engraved backplate, the broken arch case with brass fish scale frets, brass mouldings and ball feet, 17in (43cm). **£1,800-2,200** *S*

A mahogany striking bracket clock, the 8in (20cm) white painted dial with subsidiary date, strike/silent in the arch, anchor escapement, the backplate signed Green, Liverpool, 20½in (52cm). **£1,000-1,500** *Bon*

A Regency mahogany bracket clock, with a 4in (10cm) enamel dial and brass hands, the 5-pillar fusee movement signed Perigal & Duterrau London, with shouldered stepped plates bordered by engraving, the front plate stamped Thwaites and numbered 4835, c1812, 11½in (29cm). **£900-1,200** *S*

A George III ebonised bracket clock, the twin fusee and chain bell striking movement with anchor escapement, 11½in (29cm). **£1,500-2,000** *S*

A George III ebonised chiming bracket clock, with 5in (13cm) painted dial on brass plate, with strike/silent lever above XII and subsidiary dials in the arch for date and regulation, the 5-pillar 3-train fusee movement with anchor escapement and chiming on 8 bells with a further bell for the hour, c1800, 12in (31cm).
£4,000-5,000   *S*

A Regency brass inlaid mahogany bracket clock, with an 8in (20cm) painted dial, the fusee and chain movement with anchor escapement, c1815, 19in (48cm).
£500-800   *S*

A William IV bronze bracket clock, with a 5in (13cm) silvered dial, the bell striking twin fusee movement with anchor escapement, on scroll bracket feet, c1830, 16in (41cm).
£500-700   *S*

A George III striking mahogany bracket clock, with 7in (18cm) white painted convex dial, the 2-train fusee movement with anchor escapement, 13½in (34cm).
£1,200-1,800   *Bon*

A Continental walnut inlaid 8-day bracket clock, with pewter chapter ring, 16½in (42cm).
£5,000-6,000   *SBA*

A French bracket clock veneered with arabesque green boulle supplied by Lee & Son, Belfast, mid-19thC, 12in (31cm).
£500-600 *HSS*

A Victorian carved oak chiming bracket clock, with brass dial, silvered chapter ring and 3 subsidiary dials for chime/silent, regulation and chime select, the triple chain fusee movement chiming on 8 bells, 4 gongs and striking on one gong, 22½in (58cm).
£1,200-1,600 *S(S)*

An Austrian ebonised bracket clock, with 7in (18cm) dial signed Johan Schreibmayr, Wienn and 2 selection dials, dummy pendulum aperture and date, the triple train movement with grande sonnerie striking on 2 bells, the case with caddy top, c1770. **£1,500-2,000** *S(S)*

A South German automaton quarter striking bracket clock, with nun appearing at the quarters and monk appearing at the hours pulling ropes to the bells in the belfry, painted dial with Roman numerals and gilt decoration to the centre, the 3-train skeletonised movement striking the quarters on 2 bells, with pendulum and key, late 19thC, 30in (76cm).
£1,500-2,000 *CSK*

A French boulle bracket clock, the Vincenti movement bell striking and with a 7in (18cm) cartouche dial, in a waisted case with putto mounts and scroll feet and a putto surmount, late 19thC, 24in (61cm), with a bracket en suite.
£1,500-2,000 *S(S)*

A late Victorian mahogany chiming bracket clock, with an 8in (20cm) brass dial, the triple fusee movement chiming on 8 bells and striking on a gong.
£1,500-2,000 *S(S)*

A George III mahogany striking bracket clock, the dial signed Willm. Fleetwood London, on a silvered arc to the arch with subsidiary strike/not strike ring below, silvered chapter ring, the matted centre with false pendulum and calendar apertures, pierced blued hands, foliate scroll spandrels, the 4-pillar twin gut fusee movement with verge escapement, the backplate with profuse inhabited floral engraving, securing brackets to case, 19in (48cm). **£5,000-6,000** *C*

A George III mahogany striking bracket clock, the dial signed John Green London, with false pendulum and calendar apertures, pierced blued hands, foliate scroll spandrels, subsidiary strike/silent ring to the arch, the 5-pillar twin gut fusee movement with anchor escapement, restored and possibly associated, 23in (59cm).
£1,600-2,000 *C*

An ebonised bracket clock, by William Wright, with brass dial, silvered chapter ring and 5-pillar movement, verge escapement and chiming work on 7 bells.
£2,200-2,800 *SWO*

A George III ebonised bracket clock with alarm, the 6in (15cm) silvered dial signed Scandrett Worcester, with an alarm sector in the arch, the 5-pillar fusee movement with later anchor escapement, alarm work missing, c1790, 15½in (39cm).
£650-850 *S*

Carriage Clocks

A George III mahogany bracket clock, with a 7in (18cm) brass dial plate with silvered centre signed Johnson, Grays Inn Passage, the movement with twin fusee and gilt lines, with pull repeat and with replaced anchor escapement, the backplate signed and with an engraved border, 15in (38cm).
£3,500-4,000 *S(S)*

A George V silver mounted tortoiseshell carriage clock by W. Comyns, London 1910, 4½in (11cm).
£2,000-2,500 *Bea*

A repeating carriage clock with alarm, the white enamelled dial with subsidiary alarm dial, the gong striking movement stamped B in a circle, 6in (15cm).
£650-750 *S(S)*

A gilt brass carriage clock, the 2½in (6cm) white enamelled dial signed Barwise, London, 5in (13cm).
£900-1,200 *S(S)*

A gilt brass repeating carriage clock, the dial signed Rowell, Oxford, with engraved gilt mask, subsidiary day, date and alarm dials and gong striking movement, in a gorge case, modern.
£300-400   *S*

A carriage clock with white enamel dial, the repeating movement stamped E.G.L. within an ellipse, lever platform, in Corinthian column case with fluted bands, 6in (15cm).
£600-700   *Bon*

A carriage clock, with white enamel dial, the repeating movement with lever platform, in a moulded gorge case, 6in (15cm).
£750-850   *Bon*

A gilt brass repeating carriage clock, with 3in (8cm) white enamelled dial, gong striking movement and push button repeat, the case with spiral fluted columns and ripple moulded upper and lower friezes, 6½in (16cm).
£700-800   *S(S)*

A brass carriage clock, with repeater movement, 8in (20cm).
£600-700   *AH*

A rare Westminster chiming and repeating carriage clock, the enamel dial with a silent/chime dial below, the 3-train movement with lever escapement and chiming on 4 bells and a gong, with a travelling case, c1880, 7in (17cm).   **£3,000-4,000**   *S*

A rare silver grande sonnerie carriage clock, the dial signed Dent, 1893, 4½in (11cm).
£4,000-4,500   *S*

An English gilt brass and bronze carriage clock, with silvered dial with moon hands, the movement with lever escapement visible through a panel in the top, slow/fast lever in the top, the base with spring clip and recess for the numbered key, both numbered 1069, with velvet lined glazed rosewood travelling case, c1840, 5½in (14cm).
£750-1,200   *Bon*

A miniature gilt brass carriage clock, the gilt dial with silvered scroll engraved mask, with cast scroll handle, in a leather travelling case with a key, 3½in (9cm).
£1,000-1,500   *S(S)*

436

A carriage clock, with white enamel dial, the front sections set with red enamel beads, 6½in (16cm).
£250-300 *Bon*

A 5 minute repeating carriage clock, with an enamel dial, the gong striking GL movement No. 2271 with a ratchet tooth lever escapement and patent twin button 5 minute and hour repeat mechanism, in a numbered corniche case with a later leather travelling case, c1880, 6in (15cm).
£900-1,300 *S*

A French carriage clock, with repeat and alarm by E. Maurice & Co., hour and half hour striking on a gong, in Corinthian column case, late 19thC, 7½in (19cm), with outer carrying case.
£600-700 *Bea*

A carriage clock, the repeating movement numbered 2403, lever platform, with travelling case, 7in (18cm).
£550-750 *Bon*

A gilt brass carriage clock with repeat, the white enamelled dial with moon disc hands, the bell striking movement, stamped Japy Frères, 5in (13cm).
£650-750 *S(S)*

An Austrian grande sonnerie carriage clock with alarm, enamel dial, the repeating 4-train 30-hour gong striking movement with double wheel duplex escapement, in a floral engraved case with Gothic frets and feet, c1840, 7½in (19cm).
£700-900 *S*

437

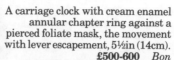

A carriage clock with cream enamel annular chapter ring against a pierced foliate mask, the movement with lever escapement, 5½in (14cm). **£500-600** *Bon*

A gilt brass and enamel carriage clock, with a 2in (5cm) white enamelled dial, with gong striking movement, 6in (15cm). **£1,200-1,500** *S(S)*

A gorge cased carriage clock, Jacot No. 14694, with white enamel dial, the repeating movement bearing the parrot stamp of Henri Jacot, lever platform. **£750-1,200** *Bon*

A brass repeating carriage clock, with painted pale blue dial with leafy scroll pierced mask and side panels, bevelled glasses, 5½in (14cm), in a leather case. **£900-1,200** *S*

A French grande sonnerie calendar carriage clock, the enamel dial with subsidiary chapters for date and alarm, the movement No. 2414 striking on 2 bells and with a later lever escapement, in a gorge case with lever in the base for Gde. Sonnerie/Silence/Pte. Sonnerie, c1865, 6in (15cm). **£1,500-2,000** *S*

A French decorative carriage clock, c1900, 5in (13cm). **£300-400** *SO*

A French brass grande sonnerie and alarm carriage clock, the dials with white chapter on a black and pink enamel ground, the movement, platform lever escapement striking on 2 gongs mounted on the backplate, late 19thC, 7½in (19cm). **£1,000-1,400** *P(M)*

A petite sonnerie alarm carriage clock, with cream enamel dial and subsidiary alarm dial beneath, the movement numbered 7851, quarter striking and repeating on 2 gongs, lever escapement, the sonnerie/silence lever in the base, 6in (15cm), with travelling case. **£750-950** *Bon*

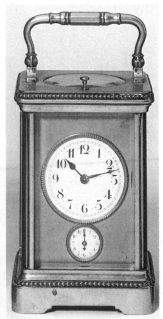

Make the most of Miller's

Unless otherwise stated, any description which refers to 'a set' or 'a pair' includes a valuation for the entire set or the pair, even though the illustration may show only a single item

A French repeating carriage alarm clock, with enamel dials set within a gilt surround, gong striking movement with lever escapement, in a glazed case composed of gilt brass simulated bamboo sticks, c1875, 8½in (21cm).
£700-900   *S*

A petite sonnerie alarm carriage clock, with white enamel dial, subsidiary alarm dial beneath, numbered 7272, with lever platform, the repeating movement quarter striking on 2 gongs, in a moulded case with bands of beading, 5½in (14cm).
£650-750   *Bon*

A brass carriage clock with alarm, with cream chapter ring, 5in (13cm).
£450-550   *S(S)*

Garnitures

An ormolu and porcelain clock garniture, with later bell striking movement, No. 2853-92, contained in a 'bleu-royale' vase case with satyr mask handles, 20½in (52cm), together with a pair of conforming 5-branch candelabra, 23in (59cm). **£600-800** *Bon*

A French white marble and gilt metal clock garniture, the clock striking on single bell, with white enamel dial, 15in (38cm), and a pair of 2-branch matching candelabra. **£1,200-1,700** *C(S)*

A French gilt and porcelain clock garniture, with a 4in (10cm) white enamelled dial and bell striking movement, 12½in (32cm), and a pair of matching 4-light candelabra, with plinths. **£1,200-1,700** *S*

A French gilt mounted green marble garniture, the bell striking movement by Gustav Becker, the case applied with gilt caryatids, swags and trophies, 19in (49cm), and a pair of matching vases, 15in (38cm). **£1,500-1,900** *S*

A black marble Egyptian style garniture clock set, comprising 8-day mantel clock striking with gong, designed as an Egyptian tomb with brass sphinx finial and 2 matching side winged sphinx, the dial marked Victor Emanuel & Co., Gantia De Chile, c1880, 18in (46cm), and a pair of matching stelae, 22in (56cm). **£1,200-1,600** *GH*

A French garniture, late 19thC. **£1,500-2,000** *HSS*

A black marble clock garniture, the 5in (13cm) dial with exposed Brocot escapement and bell striking, 20½in (52cm) and a pair of matching tazzas, 12in (31cm). **£900-1,200** *S*

A French green onyx and champlevé enamel clock garniture, with a 4in (10cm) enamelled dial and gong striking movement, the 4-glass case applied with enamelled mouldings and mercury pendulum, 13in (33cm), and a pair of matching vases, 10½in (26cm). **£700-900** *S*

Lantern Clocks

A brass cased balance wheel lantern clock, with a 6¼in silvered chapter ring and signed on the dial Nicholas Coxeter Neer(sic), Gouldsmiths Hall, Londini, Fecit, the movement with outside countwheel, vertical verge for alarm and balance wheel escapement, hoop and spurs, 15in (39cm). **£2,500-3,000** *S*

A brass cased balance wheel lantern clock, with a 6½in (16cm) narrow silvered chapter ring, with engraved dial, the movement with brass pillars, 16in (40cm). **£2,200-2,700** *S*

A lantern alarm clock, by John Welch of Chesham, with good original anchor escapement, 7in (18cm). **£1,700-1,750** *RFA*

A brass lantern clock, the 6½in (16cm) chapter ring with fleur-de-lys half hour marks, the engraved centre signed Christopher Carter, the 2-train movement in a posted case of typical form, dolphin frets beneath the bell, now with with an oak bracket, anchor escapement, 15in (38cm), **£1,500-2,000** *Bon*

Locate the source

The source of each illustration in Miller's can be found by checking the code letters below each caption with the list of contributors

A brass lantern clock, c1880, 16½in (42cm). **£750-950** *SBA*

Longcase Clocks

An 8-day oak longcase clock, the 12in (31cm) brass dial signed around the arch John Bagnall, Dudley, subsidiary seconds and calendar sector in the scroll engraved centre, 4-pillar movement in a case with canted corners, break arch hood with pagoda pediment and giltwood finials, 94in (238cm).
£2,500-3,500 *Bon*

An 8-day, brass dial longcase clock, with moonwork and tidal dial for high water, by John Baker of Hull, in original oak case crossbanded in mahogany and with shell motif inlays, fully restored, c1770, 92in (234cm).
£3,000-4,000 *BL*

An oak longcase clock, the 12in (31cm) brass dial signed on a disc John Barnet, London, with seconds dial and date aperture, 8-day bell striking movement, 89½in (227cm).
£1,000-1,500 *S*

An oak longcase clock, the 12in (31cm) arched brass dial signed Samuel Bryan, London, with 8-day bell striking movement, the associated case applied with a garland and spiral columns and with plain trunk and plinth, 82½in (209cm).
£1,200-2,000 *S(S)*

An oak longcase clock, with swan neck pediment, painted arched dial with lunar ring, seconds dial and date aperture, inscribed J. Coombes, Melksham, 18thC, 84in (213cm).
£1,200-1,700 *HCH*

An oak longcase clock, with brass dial with pierced spandrels, silvered chapter ring, inscribed Thos. Carswell Hastings, 30-hour birdcage movement, with hour hand only, mid-18thC, 78in (198cm)
£500-600 *DDM*

An Irish mahogany longcase clock, the 13in (33cm) brass dial signed Barny Delahoyde, Dublin, with date aperture and seconds dial, putto spandrels, 8-day bell striking movement, hood with lion mask carved mantling and swan neck pediment, 92½in (235cm).
£1,500-2,000 *S*

An oak and crossbanded longcase clock, the 12in (31cm) brass dial with engraved and signed chapter ring, Wlm. Davison, London, and with date ring and seconds dial, the 8-day bell striking movement with inside countwheel and cut out backplate, the associated oak case with crossbanded trunk door and plinth, 79½in (201cm). **£1,000-1,500** *S(S)*

A James II longcase clock movement, the 10in (25cm) square dial signed James Clowes Londini Fecit at the base, with brass chapter ring, the matted centre with subsidiary seconds and calendar aperture, pierced blued steel hands, latches to the 5-ringed pillar movement with anchor escapement and outside countwheel strike, the purpose built convex moulded walnut case with skirted plinth, lenticle to the trunk door, composite, 71in (180cm).
£3,000-3,500   *C*

An oak crossbanded and inlaid longcase clock, the 14in (36cm) brass dial signed W. Crockford, Coventry, the associated 8-day movement bell striking and signed on the false plate W. Francis, the trunk inlaid and crossbanded, 92½in (234cm).
£1,500-2,000
S(S)

A mahogany and inlaid longcase clock, the 14in (36cm) dial with rolling moon, lunar date sector and subsidiary seconds dial, signed Alker, Wigan, with 8-day bell striking movement, the hood inlaid with fruitwood stringing and shells, 87½in (222cm).
£2,500-3,000   *S*

An oak longcase clock, the brass dial with the maker's name, William Downie Edinburgh, strike/silent, the trunk with quartered reeded columns, the hood with scroll pediment and blind frets, c1770, 83in (210cm).
£4,300-4,500
CLC

A Queen Anne style grandmother marquetry clock, signed Thomas Durman.
£6,500-7,000
GIL

An 8-day brass dial longcase clock by Gardner of Birmingham, in original oak case, fully restored, c1750, 80in (203cm).
£2,300-3,000 *BL*

A mid-Georgian burr walnut longcase clock, in chequer strung and crossbanded case, the dial signed Arl: Dobson London, on a silvered plaque to the matted centre with subsidiary seconds and calendar aperture, silvered chapter ring, urn and scroll spandrels and strike/silent ring in the arch, the 5-pillar movement with rack strike and anchor escapement, 90in (229cm).
£3,500-4,500 *C*

A walnut and marquetry longcase clock, the altered case with marquetry to the skirted plinth and panels, the dial signed Jno. Buffett Colchester on the chapter ring, the matted centre with engraving to the calendar aperture, subsidiary seconds, urn and scroll spandrels, the 5-pillar rack striking movement with anchor escapement, associated, 80in (203cm).
£3,000-4,500 *C*

An 8-day oak longcase clock, with white dial, by Godfrey of Winterton, in original pagoda style case, fully restored, c1790, 86in (218cm).
£2,000-2,500 *BL*

A walnut and marquetry longcase clock, by John Finch of London, 17thC.
£7,500-8,500 *HSS*

An oak longcase clock, the 11in (28cm) brass dial signed W. Dyer, Barnstaple, and applied with foliate spandrels, the dial centre engraved with a coastal scene, the 30-hour bell striking movement with outside countwheel, the associated case with swan neck pediment, crossbanded trunk door and plinth, 80½in (204cm). **£600-900**   *S(S)*

A mahogany longcase clock, with a 12in (31cm) brass dial signed James Gandy, Cockermouth and signed at the centre John Skiner, Rebekah and dated 1741, the movement with outside countwheel, the case with broken arch hood, shaped and crossbanded trunk door and moulded plinth, 90in (228cm). **£1,700-2,000**   *S*

A rare Bentleys Patent Electric earth driven mahogany longcase clock, with 12in (31cm) annular silvered dial and seconds dial, the visible movement with shaped pierced plates, patent No. 19033/10, signed for John Dyson & Sons, Leeds, with a brass pendulum mounted with a coil oscillating over a fixed magnet, in a moulded glazed case with panelled plinth and optional mirror back, c1910, 84in (213cm). **£4,000-5,000**   *S*

Percival Arthur Bentley filed his patent No. 19044 for earth driven clocks on 13 August 1910.

An oak crossbanded longcase clock, the colourful dial with moon phase to the arch, signed Garrat Peterborough, mid-19thC, 81in (205cm).
£3,200-3,500
CLC

A George III black japanned 8-day longcase clock, the 12in (31cm) brass dial signed Daniel Field, Hitchin, with date aperture and subsidiary seconds, the arch with strike/silent, foliate scroll spandrels, 5-pillar movement, the case decorated with gilt chinoiserie designs against a black ground, giltwood finials, 95in (241cm)
£2,500-3,000
Bon

A black and gilt lacquered longcase clock, the 8-day striking movement with anchor escapement, brass dial with cherub mask, dolphin and foliate scroll chased spandrels, silvered chapter ring, subsidiary dial and medallion inscribed William Kipling, London, early 18thC, 89½in (227cm).
£2,800-3,200   *GC*

William Kipling is recorded in London 1705-37, and is regarded as a fine maker.

An 8-day longcase clock, with brass dial, with rocking Father Time, by Robert Henderson of Scarborough, in original dark blue lacquered case, fully restored, c1740, 94in (238cm).
£3,500-4,000   *BL*

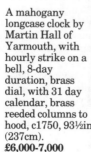

A mahogany longcase clock by Martin Hall of Yarmouth, with hourly strike on a bell, 8-day duration, brass dial, with 31 day calendar, brass reeded columns to hood, c1750, 93½in (237cm).
£6,000-7,000
SBA

A North Country carved oak 8-day longcase clock, with engraved brass dial with silvered chapter ring, date indicator and second hand, cherub head spandrels, moon indicator, trunk with door with key, clock No. 586, maker Kitchen & Lloyd Nantwich, Cheshire, late 18thC, 81in (206cm).
£1,700-2,500   *GH*

The carving on this clock is probably later.

A mahogany longcase clock, the 12in (31cm) dial signed McMaster, Dublin, with 8-day bell striking movement, 81in (206cm).
£1,500-2,000   *S*

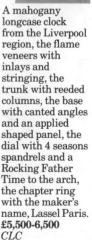

A mahogany longcase clock from the Liverpool region, the flame veneers with inlays and stringing, the trunk with reeded columns, the base with canted angles and an applied shaped panel, the dial with 4 seasons spandrels and a Rocking Father Time to the arch, the chapter ring with the maker's name, Lassel Paris.
£5,500-6,500
CLC

A mahogany longcase clock, by Robert Logie, Edinburgh, the painted dial showing the phases of the moon, subsidiary dial for seconds, 31 day calendar and hourly strike on bell, c1800, 81½in (207cm).
£5,000-5,500
SBA

A painted longcase clock, the 11in (28cm) brass dial with cherub spandrels, raised silvered chapter ring with Roman numerals and Arabic 5 minute divisions with inner minute rings, raised silvered seconds ring, the gilt matted centre with date aperture above the 6 surrounded by engraved decoration, ringed winding holes, signed at the base of the dial Cornelius Herbert, London Bridge, the 4-ringed pillar 8-day movement striking on a bell, with pendulum and 2 weights, in need of restoration, early 18thC, 75in (190cm).
£2,000-3,000   *CSK*

A mahogany pagoda topped longcase clock with 2 ball and spire finials, fluted pillars with brass capitals, the brass dial with raised silvered chapter ring and gilt Indian head spandrels, with raised silvered seconds ring and date aperture, signed on a plaque Joseph Millis, Southwark, silvered ring in the arch inscribed Tempus Fugit, with Father Time to the centre and strike/silent lever below, the ringed pillar 8-day movement striking on a bell, late 18thC, 94in (238cm).
£3,000-3,500
CSK

An oak longcase clock, by Thomas Lumpkin, London, striking by bell, with 11in (28cm) engraved brass and silvered chapter ring dial, second hand, original pierced ornate hands, turned and ringed pillar movement, with key, movement c1700, case slightly later, 72in (183cm).
£2,000-3,000   *GH*

A George III mahogany longcase clock, the enamel dial with moon phase, floral painted spandrels, seconds and date dials and inscribed Parr, Liverpool, the trunk with a flame figured door, 8-day striking movement, 96in (244cm).
£1,200-1,500 *P(S)*

447

An 8-day walnut longcase clock, the door with burr walnut veneer, the brass dial with raised silvered chapter ring, the moulded centre with raised silvered seconds ring and date aperture, gilt Indian head spandrels, signed in the arch on silvered plaque David Pain, London, No. 104, with strike/silent aperture below, mechanism lacking, the 5-ringed pillar movement striking on a bell, some restorations, 91in (231cm).
£3,700-4,500 *CSK*

A mahogany and brass inlaid longcase clock, with 12in (31cm) arched brass dial, silvered chapter ring and signed on a disc Thos. Milner, London, with date aperture and subsidiary seconds dial, 8-day bell striking movement, the hood with broken arch pediment, altered, the plinth inlaid with brass stringing, 92in (234cm).
£1,700-2,500 *S(S)*

A mahogany longcase clock with crossbanding and boxwood stringing, the trunk with reeded columns, the hood with scroll pediment and blind frets, the painted dial with floral decorations, signed D. Norrie, Leith, c1795, 84in (213cm).
£4,000-4,500 *CLC*

An oak longcase clock, the 12in (31cm) brass dial signed Humphrey Mason, Gosport, with date aperture, seconds dial and applied spandrels symbolising the 4 seasons, with 8-day bell striking movement, the pagoda topped hood with brass ball and spire finials, 85in (216cm).
£1,200-1,700 *S(S)*

A George III Lancashire mahogany longcase clock, by William Lawson, Newton-le-Willows, with brass dial with rolling moon, subsidiary seconds and date pointer, 8-day rack striking movement with anchor escapement, c1780.
£3,500-4,500 *P(M)*

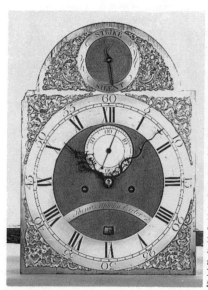

An 8-day oak longcase clock by Thomas Upjohn, Exeter, the movement with 12in (31cm) brass dial, strike/silent in the arch, recessed subsidiary seconds and date aperture, signed on a reserve to the dial centre, 5-pillar rack striking movement with anchor escapement, now contained in an early 19thC inlaid and crossbanded figured mahogany case with swan necked pediment, above free standing spirally fluted columns, 18thC, 81½in (206cm).
£1,500-2,000 *P(M)*

An oak longcase clock, the 12in (31cm) brass dial signed Pattison, Halifax, with 30-hour bell striking movement, outside countwheel, hood with swan neck pediment, fluted columns, shaped trunk door and deep plinth, 86in (219cm).
£650-800 *S*

An oak and crossbanded longcase clock, the 12in (31cm) silvered dial signed Nicklin, Birmingham, with date aperture, subsidiary seconds dial and engraved foliate spandrels, with 8-day bell striking movement, the trunk door with crossbanded borders, 99in (252cm).
£1,000-1,500
S(S)

A mahogany longcase clock, with 12in (31cm) cream painted dial signed Shuttleworth, London, and with subsidiary seconds dial, with 8-day bell striking movement, the hood with scalloped pediment, on bracket feet, 89in (226cm).
£2,000-3,000
S(S)

A walnut longcase clock, the 12in (31cm) dial now with added arch signed on chapter ring Sam. Stevens, London, with subsidiary seconds dial and date aperture, with 8-day bell striking movement, the hood now with broken arch and rebuilt pediment and with plain columns, the trunk door with ebonised mouldings and crossbanded borders, glazed lenticle and resting on a plinth, 101½in (258cm).
£2,200-3,000
S(S)

A George III mahogany longcase clock, the 12in (31cm) dial signed Jno. Price Chichester, with engraved centre, seconds dial, calendar aperture, rococo spandrels and strike/silent dial in the arch, the 5-pillar movement with rack and bell striking and star wheel mounted snail, (229cm).
£2,000-2,500   *S*

A mahogany longcase clock, by William Scott, London, with quarter reeded columns to trunk strung with brass rods, 8-day duration subsidiary dial for seconds and 31 day calendar, c1780, 101½in (258cm).
£8,500-9,500
SBA

A mahogany longcase clock, with 12in (31cm) dial signed Richd. Rooker London on a silvered boss in the arch, with seconds dial, calendar aperture and mask and leaf spandrels, the movement with inside countwheel and later gong striking, the case with a bronzed girl finial, movement c1730, case c1780, 90in (229cm).
£2,700-3,500   *S*

449

An 8-day white dial longcase clock, by Alexander Sim of Aberdeen, in original mahogany case, fully restored, c1800, 87in (221cm). **£2,500-3,000** *BL*

An 8-day oak longcase clock, with 10in (25cm) brass dial with subsidiary seconds and date aperture, the arch signed James Smith, London, 4-pillar movement with anchor escapement, in a case with panelled plinth, the break arch hood with brass ball finials, 85in (216cm). **£1,500-2,000** *Bon*

A walnut longcase clock, the 12in (31cm) brass dial with silvered chapter ring, subsidiary seconds dial, date aperture, urn and scroll spandrels and with matted and engraved centre, signed in the arch Will. Upjohn, Exon. with 8-day bell striking movement, 86½in (220cm). **£4,200-5,000** *S(S)*

An unusual oak longcase clock, by John Seddon (Frodsham), the case profusely carved overall, with brass dial with pointer and penny moon in the arch, silvered chapter, signed, subsidiary seconds and date aperture, with spandrels and incised engraving to the dial centre, the 8-day movement with 4 finned pillars, 3-train movement quarter striking on a carillon of 8 bells, with anchor escapement, 100in (254cm). **£3,500-4,000** *P(M)*

An oak and mahogany longcase clock, the 13in (33cm) arched painted dial signed William Winder, Wreckington, with 8-day bell striking movement, broken arch hood, chamfered trunk and plain plinth, 81½in (206cm). **£1,000-1,500** *S*

A mahogany longcase clock, the 12in (31cm) brass dial with silvered chapter ring and disc now signed Thomas Wagstaffe, with associated 8-day gong striking movement, 106in (269cm). **£3,200-3,700** *S(S)*

A George III oak and mahogany longcase clock, the cream enamelled dial with black Roman numerals and Arabic minutes, enclosing a subsidiary seconds dial, calendar aperture and maker's name Walker, Liverpool, the 8-day movement striking on a single bell, the case crossbanded in mahogany, together with 2 weights, a pendulum and a winding key, 90in (229cm). **£1,400-1,800** *HSS*

An oak cased Nightwatchman's clock, the 5in (13cm) silvered dial signed Vulliamy, London, No. 1835, A.D. 1848, the movement with 4 baluster pillars, the outer dial with lever operated time pegs, 73½in (186cm). **£600-1,200** *S(S)*

Clocks of this type were in service at the Houses of Parliament, c1835-50.

An 8-day brass dial longcase clock, by Henry Watson of Blackburn, in original oak case, fully restored, c1750, 90in (229cm). **£2,500-3,000** *BL*

A mahogany longcase clock, the 13in (33cm) brass dial with rolling moon and signed James Sandiford, Manchester, with date aperture and subsidiary seconds dial, with 8-day bell striking movement, the hood with swan neck pediment and with broken arch trunk with scroll frieze, moulded trunk door and plinth, 84½in (215cm). **£3,000-4,000** *S(S)*

A flame mahogany longcase clock, the trunk with brass inserts to the reeded angles, the hood also with reeded columns, surmounted by a pagoda pediment with pierced sound fret, the dial signed F.B. Roberts, London, c1790, 83in (211cm). **£7,500-8,000** *CLC*

A Lancashire oak crossbanded 8-day longcase clock, with 11in (28cm) brass dial with cherub head spandrels, Roman numerals, striking on the hour, hood supported upon tapering columns, trunk having shaped single door with brass escutcheon, with key, 18thC, by Walker, Preston, 78in (198cm). **£1,200-1,700** *GH*

An unusual mahogany moonphase Masonic longcase clock, with swan neck pediment and central urn finial, the painted dial with Roman numerals and Arabic 5 minute divisions, the centrefield painted with Masonic symbols, subsidiary dials for seconds and date, rolling moon in the arch with lunar calendar, signed Roberts, Burnley, the 8-day movement striking on a bell, 94½in (239cm). **£1,200-1,700** *CSK*

An oak and crossbanded longcase clock, with 14in (36cm) painted dial, date aperture and seconds dial, the false plate stamped Walker, 82in (208cm).
£700-900 *S(S)*

A George III longcase clock with silvered chapter ring and Roman numerals, seconds dial, date aperture and gilt spandrels, a circular plaque to the arch engraved Jn. Walker, Newcastle, with 8-day striking movement, 89in (226cm).
£1,700-2,200 *AG*

A George III 8-day mahogany longcase clock, the 12in (31cm) brass dial signed William Withers, London, subsidiary seconds and date aperture, the arch containing strike/silent, foliate spandrels, the 5-pillar movement in a case with brass inlaid corinthian pilasters to the trunk, 95in (241cm).
£2,500-3,500 *Bon*

A mahogany longcase clock with panelled base, reeded columns to the hood surmounted by a shaped cresting, the brass dial with strike/silent, signed on a cartouche Robert Windsor Newport, c1780.
£5,500-6,000 *CLC*

A late Stuart burr walnut longcase clock, the hood with giltwood capped columns, the dial signed Windmills London on the silvered chapter ring, with subsidiary seconds, ringed winding holes and calendar aperture, mask and foliate spandrels, the 5-ringed pillar rack striking movement with anchor escapement, associated, 84in (214cm).
£6,000-7,000 *C*

An oak and mahogany crossbanded longcase clock, the brass dial with raised silvered chapter ring and Indian head spandrels, Roman numerals and Arabic 5 minute divisions, the engraved centre with pie crust silvered seconds dial, silvered plaque in the arch inscribed Tempus Fugit, the 8-day movement striking on a gong, some restorations, finial missing, 87in (221cm).
£1,600-2,200 *CSK*

A pine longcase clock, c1840, 82in (208cm).
£1,200-1,600 *BH*

An Edwardian inlaid mahogany longcase clock.
£1,200-1,700 *HCH*

A cut down oak cased crossbanded longcase clock, with silvered and brass chapter dial, Roman numerals, date and second hand, foliate spandrels, circular boss, marked William Yeadon, Stourbridge, with key, c1780, 78in (198cm).
£700-800 *GH*

An unusual Continental walnut veneered longcase clock, with inlaid veneered panels, the 9½in (24cm) brass dial with engraved spandrels, raised silvered chapter ring with red Roman numerals and Arabic 5 minute divisions, engraved hatched design to the centre, blued steel moon hands and sweep centre-seconds, date aperture below the 12, the 2-train movement with screwed pillars, maintaining power, anchor escapement with adjustable pallets and rack strike on bell, the pendulum with gimballed suspension from a crutch on the backplate and supported by a strut to the seatboard, 82in (208cm).
£1,600-2,000
CSK

A Victorian mahogany crossbanded 8-day longcase clock, with hand painted white enamel dial, Roman numerals, original hands, moon arched calendar, second hand, all supported upon shaped feet, with key, c1865, 102in (259cm).
£800-1,000 *GH*

A walnut longcase clock, 18thC.
£4,000-4,500
DM

Mantel Clocks

A William IV rosewood mantel clock, with 5in (13cm) painted dial signed Huggins London, the fusee and chain movement with anchor escapement, c1835, 13in (33cm). **£900-1,200** *S*

A mahogany and brass inlaid quarter repeating mantel clock, with an 8in (20cm) cream painted dial, with regulation dial and serpentine hands, the triple train fusee movement chiming on 8 bells and now on a gong, signed on the backplate W.L.M. Partington, Paddington Street, London, now on a rosewood base and brass claw-and-ball feet, 27½in (70cm). **£1,700-2,000** *S*

A French ormolu and porcelain mantel clock, 2-train movement signed Martin & Co., with white enamel dial, 13½in (34cm). **£450-550** *Bon*

An English burr walnut 4-glass clock, glazed to 4 sides and the top, white enamel dial signed F. Dent, 61 Strand, 1466, the single chain fusee movement with anchor escapement and pendulum cock, the pendulum with fine regulation, signed and numbered on the backplate, 10in (25cm). **£3,000-3,500** *CSK*

A gilt brass Gothic mantel clock, with a 3½in (9cm) white enamelled dial signed E. White, 20 Cockspur Street, London, the substantial twin fusee movement gong striking and with a signed backplate, the case with onion dome and leafy scroll pierced frets and baluster finials, 17½in (44cm). **£1,700-2,000** *S(S)*

A late Victorian ebonised quarter chiming mantel clock, with 3 subsidiary dials for chime/silent, slow/fast and Westminster/8 bells, the 3 train fusee movement chiming on 8 bells or 4 gongs, 27in (69cm). **£1,700-2,500** *Bon*

A 4-glass mantel clock with barometer and thermometer, the sunken 3½in (9cm) silvered dial with a gilt bezel set within an engine turned silvered mask, 2 dials mounted below for the thermometer and aneroid barometer, the MS gong striking movement with anchor escapement, c1880, 15in (38cm). **£1,000-1,500** *S*

A William IV burr walnut mantel clock, with silvered brass dial signed Vulliamy, London, single fusee 4-pillar movement with anchor escapement and pendulum with adjustable brass bob, 10½in (26cm). **£4,000-4,800** *P(M)*

A mahogany and chequer strung mantel clock, the 7in (18cm) silvered dial inscribed Willm Ray, Sudbury, the twin train fusee movement with anchor escapement, 20in (51cm).
£650-800   *C*

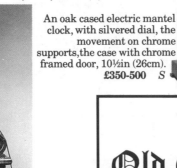

A pale rosewood chiming mantel clock, with an 8in (20cm) silvered dial signed Widenham, London, the triple fusee movement quarter chiming on 8 bells and striking on one, with engraved and signed backplate and pull repeat, on brass bun feet, 18½in (47cm).
£1,000-1,500   *S(S)*

A mahogany and brass inlaid mantel clock, with white painted dial, moon hands, the twin chain fusee movement with pendulum lock striking on a bell, pendulum with fine regulation, early 19thC, 20in (51cm).
£1,300-1,800   *CSK*

An oak cased electric mantel clock, with silvered dial, the movement on chrome supports, the case with chrome framed door, 10½in (26cm).
£350-500   *S*

A walnut mantel clock, with a 7in (18cm) silvered dial signed John Walker and numbered 3001, the substantial movement with twin fusee and pull repeat, 17½in (45cm).
£1,500-2,000   *S*

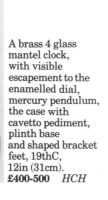

A brass 4 glass mantel clock, with visible escapement to the enamelled dial, mercury pendulum, the case with cavetto pediment, plinth base and shaped bracket feet, 19thC, 12in (31cm).
£400-500   *HCH*

A gilt bronze and marble calendar mantel clock, with enamel dials, the bell striking silk suspension movement with a lever leading from the strike train to the calendar mechanism below indicating the date and the day of the week, the black marble case surmounted by an urn and profusely decorated with gilt and formerly patinated bronze mounts, c1840, 19½in (49cm).
£900-1,200   *S*

A satinwood and inlaid mantel clock, with a 7in (18cm) cartouche dial and bell striking movement, the waisted case with ebonised and mahogany stringing.
£500-600   *S*

A French ormolu and silvered mantel clock, the 2-train movement stamped Cleret, No. 4058, with silk suspension and floral bezel, 20in (51cm).   **£1,000-1,500**   *Bon*

A French porcelain mounted ormolu mantel clock, the 3½in (9cm) porcelain dial signed Bourdin à Paris, the similarly signed bell striking movement with Brocot escapement and outside countwheel, the sides and front inset with porcelain panels, c1850, 12in (31cm).
£2,200-2,700   *S*

A French ormolu mantel clock, the white enamelled dial signed Cachard successor to Ch. Le Roy and signed at the base Dubuisson, the movement with outside countwheel and bell striking, c1800, 22in (56cm).
£4,800-5,500   *S*

An unusual French bronze patinated brass mantel clock, with cast gilt brass dial with blue on white enamel Roman numeral panels, the bell striking 8-day movement inscribed P. Ltre, pendulum missing, 19thC, 23in (59cm).
£400-600   *P(S)*

A French Empire mantel clock, in mahogany case, on gilt bun feet, the white enamel dial signed Devillaine, rue rive. des Pts. Champs No. 35, the large drum shaped movement with outside countwheel strike on a bell, 12in (31cm).
£900-1,200   *CSK*

A French porcelain and ormolu mantel clock, the 2-train movement stamped Deniere à Paris, lacking feet, 14in (36cm).
£1,200-1,600   *Bon*

A Directoire mahogany 4 glass mantel clock, the 5½in (14cm) enamel dial with central calendar ring and signed Pier Le Roy à Paris, the silk suspension movement with anchor escapement, outside countwheel and bell striking, the brass bound glazed case with bun feet, c1795, 16½in (42cm).
£2,000-2,500 *S*

A French ormolu, bronze and marble mantel clock, the white enamel dial inscribed Lacour A Aubigny, the twin train movement with countwheel strike, mid-19thC, 18in (46cm).
£400-500 *CSK*

A French gilt brass and porcelain panel mantel clock, the 4½in (11cm) dial painted with a garland and signed Leroy à Paris, the movement with silk suspension and with stamped backplate, the case mounted with 12 porcelain panels, painted in turquoise borders, c1840, 18½in (47cm).
£1,500-2,000 *S*

A French mahogany portico clock, with gilt dial and engine turned centrefield signed Bernard et fils, Bordeaux, the 8-day movement with outside countwheel strike on a bell, with decorative pendulum, 18½in (47cm), with glass dome, on rectangular ebonised base.
£600-700 *CSK*

A French ormolu mantel clock, with replaced 2in (5cm) silvered dial, the drum movement stamped Robert à Paris, with silk suspension, 11in (28cm). **£300-400** *S(S)*

A French ormolu and marble mantel clock, with a white enamel dial signed S. Devaulx, Palais Royal, the case with bands of green marble, with ormolu appliques, mask feet, 23in (59cm). **£1,500-2,000** *Bon*

A French 4 glass mantel clock, the bell striking movement No. 2483 with enamel dial, visible Brocot escapement and Ellicott pendulum, c1875, 10in (25cm). **£650-750** *S*

A French ormolu and white mantel clock, with white marble dial, raised numerals, 8-day movement with outside countwheel strike on a bell, signed Rollin à Paris, 19thC, 14½in (37cm). **£550-700** *CSK*

A French gilt mounted marble mantel clock, the 4in (10cm) white enamelled dial signed Guydamour à Paris, with bell striking movement, c1800, 16in (40cm). **£1,200-1,700** *S*

An unusual French Empire ormolu and simulated malachite mantel clock, the 2-train movement with silk suspension, 12in (31cm). **£700-800** *Bon*

A French faience mounted gilt brass mantel clock, with gong striking Achille Brocot movement and faience dial decorated against a cream ground, the gilt case flanked by faience columns, c1880, 15½in (39cm). **£750-850** *S*

A French gilt spelter and porcelain mounted mantel clock, on cast gilt feet, with porcelain dial, 8-day movement striking on a bell, bearing the maker's stamp Japy et fils, with pendulum, and giltwood base, 19thC, 14½in (37cm). **£900-1,200** *CSK*

A French 4 glass mantel clock, the 3½in (9cm) enamel dial signed Tiffany & Co., the Japy Frères gong striking movement with Brocot escapement and miniature set pendulum bob, the case with glazed cushion form cresting and a moulded base, c1900, 10½in (27cm). **£1,200-1,700** *S*

A French brass mantel clock, the pendulum bob in the shape of a stewing pot with detachable cresset fender, on rouge marble base with bracket feet, with ivorine dial, the 8-day movement with outside countwheel strike on a gong, 17in (43cm). **£750-850** *CSK*

An ormolu and bronze mantel clock, the countwheel striking movement now with Brocot suspended pendulum, 13in (33cm) wide. **£800-1,000** *C*

A French ormolu and bronze automaton mantel clock, with a bell striking silk suspension movement and silvered engine turned dial with bronze plinth case, the automaton galleon driven by a separate key wound movement, c1840, 17in (43cm). **£1,500-2,000** *S*

A sculptural bronze mantel clock, on Siena marble pedestal, the gilt dial with black on white enamel Roman numeral panels, 19thC, 21in (53cm). **£400-600** *P(S)*

A French brass mounted onyx mantel clock, with bell striking movement, 12½in (32cm). **£550-650** *S(S)*

A Danish coromandel and tortoiseshell veneered mantel clock, with plated and engraved dial, inscribed H.E. Holst, Kløbenhavn, and a Danish bell striking movement, 14in (36cm). **£1,700-2,500** *Bon*

A champlevé enamel mounted 4 glass mantel clock, the 3½in (9cm) enamel dial painted with garlands of flowers and signed for Tiffany & Co., the Japy Frères gong striking movement with a mercury pendulum, c1900, 11in (28cm). **£800-1,200** *S*

A French rouge and black marble perpetual calendar mantel clock, the 6in (15cm) white enamelled dial with exposed Brocot escapement, centre second hand, subsidiary calendar and barometer dials and with glazed pendulum aperture, the case mounted with Fahrenheit and Reamur thermometers, with mercury pendulum, 18in (46cm). **£2,000-2,500** *S(S)*

459

A French vari-coloured marble and gilt mantel clock, surmounted by a marble urn finial, the base with beading, on gilt turned feet, the white enamel dial with quarter hour divisions, with timepiece movement, 8in (20cm).
£350-550
CSK

A bronze and ormolu French Empire mantel clock, 2-train movement with suspension, white enamel dial, in an arched case with ormolu trophies and cherub appliques, urn and butterfly finial, 12in (31cm), on ebonised base with bowfronted glazed dome, cracked.
£900-1,200   *Bon*

A French boulle mantel clock, with a 5½in (14cm) cartouche dial and bell striking movement.
£650-750   *S(S)*

A French gilt mantel clock, with a 3½in (9cm) enamelled chapter ring, the drum movement with silk suspension and outside countwheel, the case in the form of a stylised chariot on a fanciful cloud base, 14½in (38cm).   **£2,200-2,700** *S*

A Dutch mahogany and marquetry mantel clock, with enamel dial, the movement stamped Dales Westbourne, the case inlaid with floral cornucopia with turned columns and plinth base, lacking cresting.   **£900-1,400**   *C*

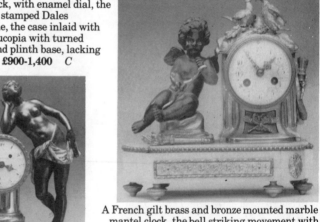

A French gilt brass and bronze mounted marble mantel clock, the bell striking movement with garland painted dial, the case flanked by a reclining putto, on white marble base, 10½in (26cm).   **£600-700**   *S*

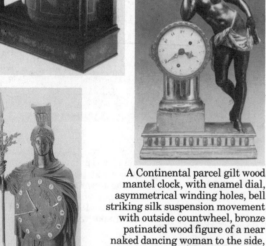

A Continental parcel gilt wood mantel clock, with enamel dial, asymmetrical winding holes, bell striking silk suspension movement with outside countwheel, bronze patinated wood figure of a near naked dancing woman to the side, c1770, 15in (38cm).
£800-1,000   *S*

A French Empire bronzed mantel clock of Centurion form, the 2-train movement signed Alexandre Roussel à Paris No. 515, with silk suspension, on marble base, 28½in (72cm), with associated granite base inscribed Sevastopol 1855.
£4,500-5,500   *Bon*

A French gilt brass and porcelain mantel clock, the 2-train movement with white enamel annular chapter ring, decorated in gilt against a dark blue ground, 16in (41cm).
£1,500-2,000   *Bon*

A striking bracket clock, the brass dial signed J. Lowndes, London, c1685. **£7,000-9,000** *Bon*

A Charles II striking bracket clock, signed Cha. Gretton, London, 12in (30.5cm) **£18,000-22,000** *C*

A Charles II ebonised striking bracket clock, dial signed J. Gerrard, London, strike/silent lever above XII, some restoration, 15in (38cm). **£9,000-12,000** *C*

A William III kingwood quarter repeating bracket clock, the 6 pillar movement signed James Tudman, Londini Fecit, 15in (38cm). **£6,500-8,500** *S*

A George II mahogany striking bracket clock, by Delander, 16in (40.5cm). **£10,000-12,000** *C*

A Charles II ebony veneered bracket clock, signed Joseph Knibb, Londini Fecit, c1670, 14in (35cm). **£40,000-50,000** *S*

An ebony veneered bracket clock, by John Barnett, London, 17thC, 15in (38cm). **£6,500-7,500** *CSK*

A George I ebony grande sonnerie bracket clock, by Dan Delander, altered. **£85,000-95,000** *C*

A Queen Anne striking bracket clock, signed Jos. Windmills. **£14,000-16,000** *C*

461

A French brass carriage clock, with striking movement, 5¹/₂in (12.5cm). **£600-800** *GAK*

A Louis XV boulle bracket clock, dial now signed Glaesner à Lyon, 37in (94cm). **£4,000-6,000** *S*

A William 1V gilt metal carriage timepiece, made by Howell & James, c1835, 4in (10cm). **£6,500-7,500** *S*

A German walnut bracket clock, with quarter strike on 2 gongs, by Lenkirsh, c1880, 10in (25.5cm). **£1,000-1,200** *SO*

A gilt brass striking carriage clock, Japy Frères. **£5,000-6,000** *C*

A miniature 8-day carriage timepiece, restorations, 3in (7cm). **£3,000-4,000** *CSK*

A French repeating and alarm carriage clock, the gong striking movement stamped Pons. Medaille D'or 1827, with lever escapement, c1865, 6in (15cm). **£900-1,200** *S*

A repeating carriage clock, the enamel dial signed for Dent, the bell striking movement No.301 with a lever platform escapement, in gorge case, c1870, 5in (12cm). **£1,800-2,000** *S*

A Louis XV boulle bracket clock, the dial and movement signed Bertrand à Paris, surmounted by a trumpeting angel, c1730, 35in (89cm). **£1,200-1,800** *S*

A French enamel mounted repeating carriage clock, stamped E. M. & Co, later lever escapement, c1900. **£1,500-2,000** *S*

A brass alarm carriage clock, by Henri Jacot. **£900-1,200** *CSK*

A porcelain mounted repeating carriage clock, c1870, 6in (15cm). **£2,000-2,500** *S*

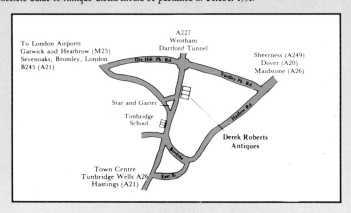

COLOUR REVIEW

A mahogany
longcase clock, by
Blackwood, N.
Shields, c1820.
£3,600-4,200 *PAO*

A country oak
longcase clock by
Friend, Lyme
Regis, 8-day
movement
striking on a
bell, c1830.
£2,000-2,500
PAO

A George III mahogany
longcase clock.
£7,000-8,000 *C*

A mahogany longcase
clock, signed Samuel
Guy, London, c1750.
£4,000-5,000 *S*

A Charles II ebonised
longcase clock, Henry
Jones, c1685.
£28,000-30,000 *S*

A mahogany
longcase clock,
c1830. **£8,000-
9,000** *SO*

A burr elm longcase
clock, the brass dial
signed Jno Clowes,
Russell St., Covent
Garden, the 6-ringed
pillar movement with
bolt and shutter
maintaining power,
late 17thC.
£18,000-20,000 *Bon*

A George II walnut
longcase clock, John
Ellicott, c1740.
£36,000-40,000 *S*

An Edwardian mahogany
chiming longcase clock,
c1905. **£22,000-25,000** *S*

A William & Mary
marquetry longcase
clock. **£5,000-
6,000** *S(NY)*

A burr walnut
longcase clock, signed
Chas. Blanchard,
London, 104in (264cm).
£1,000-1,200 *CSK*

464

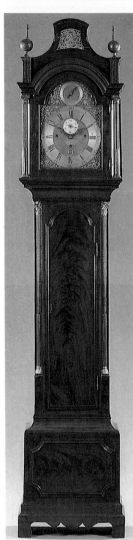

A mahogany longcase clock, by William Scott, London, c1770. **£8,500-9,500** *PAO*

A Charles II burr walnut longcase clock, 78in (198cm). **£30,000-35,000** *C*

A George III longcase clock, Thos. Wilkinson, c1770. **£7,000-8,000** *S*

A William and Mary walnut marquetry longcase clock, J. Wise. **£12,000-14,000** *S*

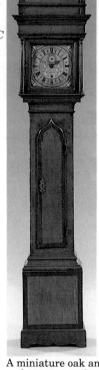

An oak and mahogany longcase clock, c1820. **£2,800-3,200** *PAO*

A William and Mary walnut longcase clock, late 17thC. **£8,500-10,000** *S(NY)*

A miniature oak and mahogany month-going longcase clock, signed J. Windmills, London, early 18thC, 66in (168cm). **£7,000-9,000** *S*

A mahogany longcase clock, James Robertson, c1800. **£4,500-5,500** *PAO*

An ormolu mantel clock, for J. Carter, c1840, **£1,000-1,500** *S*

A French boulle mantel clock, by Japy & Fils. **£350-550** *GAK*

A Louis Philippe ormolu mantel clock, signed Dd Fe Dubois à Paris, 17in (43cm). **£2,000-3,000** *C*

An Empire ormolu mantel clock, by Lesieur, 18½in (47cm) wide. **£4,500-5,500** *C*

An Empire ormolu and mahogany mantel timepiece, the fusee movement signed Barwise, London on the backplate, 23in (59cm). **£7,000-9,000** *C*

A Viennese mantel clock, 19thC. **£6,000-8,000** *C*

An Empire ormolu clock, 15in (38cm). **£3,000-4,000** *C*

A Louis XVIII ormolu and bronze mantel clock, signed, 30in (76cm). **£8,000-10,000** *C*

An Austrian ormolu and bronze troubadour mantel clock of Gothic form, the pinnacle with a bell above a pointed arch, the quarter striking movement with 2 gongs, mid-19thC, 19½in (49cm). **£900-1,200** *C*

A Louis XV1 mantel clock, 19in (48cm) wide. **£12,000-14,000** *C*

A George III ormolu, jasperware and biscuit mounted mantel clock, by Benjamin Vulliamy, c1799, 13½in (34cm). **£10,000-12,000** *S(NY)*

A French 'singing bird' mantel clock, c1880, 16in (41cm). **£5,000-6,000** *S*

An ormolu mantel clock, c1870, 16½in (42cm). **£1,800-2,200** *S*

467

A Charles X ormolu clock, signed Le Roy, 17¹/₂in (44cm). **£2,500-3,500** *C*

A French ormolu mantel clock with calendar, c1850, 17¹/₂in (44cm). **£2,500-3,500** *S*

A 'Sèvres' mounted ormolu clock, signed, 21¹/₂in (54cm). **£5,500-6,500** *S*

A Vienna regulator, c1810. **£30,000-40,000** *GeC*

A Vienna regulator, c1835. **£5,500-6,500** *GeC*

A striking clock, by Vulliamy, London, 19thC, 23¹/₂in (60cm). **£1,250-1,500** *PCh*

A wall clock, by T. Amoore, mid-19thC. **£400-450** *PCh*

A German brass mounted mahogany mantel clock, late 18thC.**£8,500-9,500** *C*

A Vienna regulator,c1825. **£12,000-15,000** *GeC*

A Vienna regulator, c1830. **£25,000-35,000** *GeC*

A Regency mahogany drop dial wall clock with brass inlay. **£450-550** *GAK*

A Louis XVI ormolu mantel clock, signed Peignat A Paris. **£3,000-4,000** *C*

A Louis XV ormolu and tôle mantel clock, signed Thibault A Paris, adapted, 8in (20cm). **£4,000-5,000** *C*

A German brass mounted mahogany obelisk mantel clock, late 18thC, 29in (74cm). **£17,000-20,000** *C*

468

A minute repeating chronograph, by JW Benson, with 18ct gold hunter case, glass missing. **£7,500-8,500** *WW*

An 18ct gold hunter cased keyless lever watch, E. F. Ashley, No.03747, 5cm. **£1,500-2,500** *S*

A Swiss 18ct gold hunter cased minute repeating grande and petite sonnerie watch, signed Invar. **£4,000-5,000** *S*

A gold and enamel musical automaton verge watch, by Isaac Daniel Piguet, quarter repeating on 2 gongs, Numbered 98, 5.8cm. **£23,000-25,000** *C*

A silver and tortoiseshell quarter repeating watch, for Turkish market, 1798. **£11,000-13,000** *S*

A gold and enamel verge watch, by Gregson, c1790. **£3,000-4,000** *S*

A gold and enamel hunter cased minute repeating keyless lever automaton watch, by LeCoultre, c1890. **£6,000-8,000** *S*

A quarter repeating Jacqumart watch, signed Dubois & Comp. No.23114, in silver gilt plain case with push pendant, 5.8cm. **£3,500-4,500** *C*

A gold pocket watch, by Vacheron & Constantin, numbered 319021, 4.5cm. **£1,000-2,000** *CSK*

A gentleman's Patek Philippe keyless lever pocket watch, No.198950, in 18ct gold case, London 1936. **£1,200-1,500** *Bea*

A silver keyless lever Karussell, signed F. A. Chandler. **£3,000-3,500** *S*

A gold repoussé pair case verge pocket watch, by James Cowan, Edinburgh, hallmarked London 1772, 4.7cm, with chain and gold pencil. **£1,800-2,200** *CSK*

A gilt metal striking watch, signed Timy Williamson, c1780. **£7,500-8,500** *S*

A Cartier 18ct gold lady's wristwatch, No.780950832, c1977. **£1,200-1,500** *S*

A stainless steel reverso wristwatch, by Jaeger LeCoultre, with later engraved coat-of-arms, c1940. **£1,200-1,500** *S*

An 18ct gold moonphase calendar chronograph, by Baume & Mercier. **£3,000-3,500** *S*

An 18ct gold five minute repeating keyless lever watch, c1890, stamped J. E. Caldwell & Co. **£2,750-3,500** *S*

An 18ct pink gold single button chronograph, signed Election, subsidiary dials for seconds and minutes, outer telemetric and tachometric scales. **£500-800** *S*

A steel cased Cosmonaut Navitimer chronograph, by Breitling, c1950. **£1,200-2,000** *C*

An 18ct gold and diamond skeleton wristwatch, by Audemars Piguet, with 17 jewels and adjusted to 5 positions, the dial with diamond rope-twist surround, No.B41172, c1975. **£6,000-8,000** *S*

An 18ct gold and steel centre seconds reverso wristwatch, by Jaeger LeCoultre, c1940. **£3,000-3,500** *S*

A 9ct gold reverso wristwatch, signed LeCoultre Co, London import mark for 1936. **£1,500-2,000** *S*

An 18ct gold wristwatch, by Audemars Piguet, c1950. **£1,200-1,500** *S*

A Cartier platinum, gold and diamond lady's wristwatch, signed European Watch & Clock Co Inc., No.429765, c1930. **£4,000-5,000** *S*

A Heuer gentleman's chronograph wristwatch, in 18ct gold case. **£1,000-1,500** *Bea*

An 18ct gold wristwatch, by Audemars Piguet, London import mark for 1959. **£2,200-2,500** *S*

A Cartier nephrite silver, gold, coral and enamel watch set paperknife, blade repaired. **£8,500-9,500** *C*

A steel automatic water resistant calendar chronograph, by Girard Perregaux, 1989 and unworn. **£850-950** *S*

An 18ct gold day/date Rolex Oyster Perpetual wristwatch, 1974. **£4,000-4,500** *S*

A 9ct gold Rolex bubble back Oyster Perpetual wristwatch, c1940. **£1,200-1,500** *S*

A stainless steel wristwatch, by Patek Philippe, c1934. **£1,800-2,000** *S*

A Vacheron & Constantin 18ct pink gold wristwatch, c1945. **£1,200-1,500** *S*

A Rolex 18ct two-colour gold wristwatch, import mark for 1927. **£2,000-2,500** *S*

A Universal 18ct pink gold Tri-Compax chronograph wristwatch, c1940. **£2,500-3,000** *S*

A steel and gold Rolex Datejust Oyster Perpetual wristwatch. **£900-1,200** *S*

A 14ct gold chronograph, Tourneau watch Co, c1945. **£1,800-2000** *S*

A 9ct pink gold Rolex wristwatch, the circular movement with 15 jewels, 1953. **£1,000-1,500** *S*

A Vacheron & Constantin 18ct gold automatic wristwatch, c1960. **£1,000-2,000** *S*

A Rolex 9ct gold wristwatch. **£700-900** *S*

A stainless steel and gold Rolex Oyster Perpetual wristwatch, c1940. **£1,200-1,500** *S*

A lady's Rolex gold and stone set wristwatch, set with rubies and diamonds, numbered 23844 2697. **£800-1,000** *CSK*

An 18ct gold automatic nautilus wristwatch, by Patek Philippe, with intergral bracelet, modern. **£6,000-8,000** *S*

A silver Rolex Prince wristwatch, case worn, 1930. **£1,200-1,500** *S*

A rosewood wheel barometer, with mother-of-pearl inlay, by Bramwell-Alston, c1860.
£850-1,200 *PAO*

A lacquered brass 2¼in reflecting telescope, signed J. Bird, London, the 10in body tube with screw rod focusing , 18thC, 17in (43cm).
£7,000-8,000 *C*

A Smith's 18in (45.5cm) diam celestial globe, by G Phillip & Son Ltd, on turned wood stand, 22in (56cm).
£1,800-2,500 *C*

A rare demonstration orbital globe, by W&S Jones, with painted wood dial, 24in (61cm).
£11,000-12,000 *CSK*

A Spanish gilt brass and silver universal equinoctial dial, signed Juanin Cocart fecit, early 17thC, 5.4cm long. **£40,000-45,000** *CSK*

A 5in reflecting telescope, signed Naire & Blunt, London, replacement mirror, late 18thC, 42in (106.5cm) long.
£5,000-6,000 *CSK*

A 'Solnhofer' stone horizontal dial, signed Isaak Kiening fecit, late 16thC, 10in (26cm) wide.
£8,500-9,000 *CSK*

A celestial globe, the axis through the celestial poles and mounted on a painted wood stand, early 18thC, 16in (39cm) diam.
£9,000-10,000 *CSK*

A brass transit telescope, signed Troughton & Simms, London, with 2 mahogany carrying cases, early 19thC, 20in (50.5cm).
£7,000-9,000 *CSK*

A mahogany wheel barometer, by Borelli, Farnham, c1840, 8in (20cm) diam. **£650-850** *PAO*

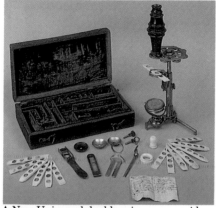

A New Universal double microscope, mid-18thC, 9in (23cm) wide. **£22,000-25,000** *CSK*

An Italian 1½in telescope body tube cum-case, of leather and pasteboard, decorated in gilt with gilt brass and amber cap and fish scale covered outer tube of mother-of-pearl. **£900-1,200** *CSK*

A gilt brass universal ring dial, possibly Flemish, late 17thC, 8in (20cm). **£7,000-8,000** *CSK*

A rosewood wheel barometer, with tulip top, c1860. **£350-450** *PAO*

A Newton's New & Improved Terrestrial pocket globe, dated 1817. **£1,800-2,500** *C*

A pair of 12in (31.5cm) terrestrial and celestial globes, by W & A. K. Johnston Ltd, Edinburgh. **£3,500-4,000** *C*

A 4¼in reflecting telescope, signed on the back plate James Innes 1796, with mahogany carrying case, 26½in (67cm). **£350-450** *C*

A simple orrery, the 2in terrestrial globe with maker's label inscribed S. Fortin Rue de la Harpe, 1773. **£3,500-4,500** *CSK*

A Louis XVI style ormolu barometer and a matching thermometer, 15½in (39cm). **£2,500-3,000** *C*

COLOUR REVIEW

A pair of George II candlesticks, later three-light branches, William Gough, London 1750, branches 19thC, 118oz. £3,500-4,500 *CNY*

A pair of William and Mary cast tablesticks, maker's mark overstruck for Edward Gibson, 6in (15cm), 26oz. £16,500-18,500 *Bon*

A pair of five-light candelabras, c1840. £18,000-20,000 *C*

A pair of French silver gilt candlesticks, by P. Paraud, Paris, 1797, 8½in (21cm), 23oz. £5,500-6,500 *CNY*

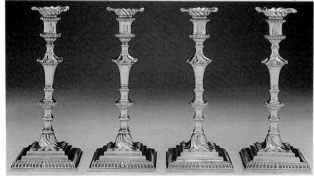

Four George III candlesticks, by William Cafe, London, marked on bases and nozzles, c1766, 10½in (26cm). £9,000-10,000 *CNY*

A George III silver gilt basket, by Thomas Arden, 1805, 13in (33cm), 54oz. £7,000-8,000 *C*

A set of 4 George II table candlesticks, by Edward Wakelin, 1747, 8½in (21.5cm), 79oz. £12,000-15,000 *C*

A centrepiece bowl, the sides decorated with elephants in relief, gilt interior etched with stylised foliage, by Tiffany & Co. New York, marked, c1885, 11in (28cm) diam, 52oz. £10,000-12,000 *CNY*

A George II shaving bowl, by John Edwards II, London 1729, marked on base, 13in (33cm), 28oz. £3,500-4,500 *CNY*

A pair of Charles II candlesticks, maker's mark TD in script monogram, London 1683, 6½in (16cm), 534gr. £13,000-15,000 *S*

A George II punch bowl, Gabriel Sleath, London 1727, 9½in (24cm) diam, 1415gr. £18,000-20,000 *S*

A pair of George III vegetable dishes and covers, by Paul Storr, London 1805, 11in (28cm) diam, 121oz. **£15,000-17,000**   *CNY*

A Victorian centrepiece and cover, by John S Hunt, 1861, 20in (51cm) high, 266oz. **£8,000-10,000**   *C*

A George III centrepiece, on triangular plinth with 3 bracket feet, the base on 3 horned and bearded mask feet, engraved with coat-of-arms, 1815, 18^1/$_2$in (47cm), 233oz. **£28,000-32,000**   *C*

A French parcel gilt centrepiece, signed H. Wadere, 1897, 34^1/$_2$in (87cm), 25,860 gr. gross. **£17,000-18,000**   *C*

A George III epergne, by Emick Romer, fully marked, London 1771, 21in (53cm), 97oz. **£11,000-13,000**   *CNY*

An early Victorian five-light candelabrum centrepiece and mirror plateau, engraved with a coat-of-arms and presentation inscription dated 1843, by Richard Sawyer, Dublin 1843, 25in (64cm), 254oz. **£6,000-8,000**   *C*

A pair of George IV entrée dishes and covers, by Paul Storr, London, marked, 12^1/$_2$in (32cm), 155oz. **£8,000-10,000**   *CNY*

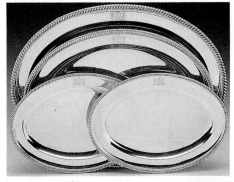

Four George III meat dishes, engraved with a baron's armorials, marked by Robert and Thomas Makepeace, 1794, largest 23in (59cm) wide, 278oz. **£9,000-10,000**   *CNY*

A George III epergne, with removable cut glass dishes, by William Grundy, London 1767, fully marked, 21in (53cm) wide, 86oz. **£12,000-13,000**   *CNY*

A George III epergne, maker's mark IP Pellet between oval punch, London 1799, 15in (38cm). **£9,000-10,000**   *CNY*

A teapot, by William Ball, Baltimore, with script initials 'M.G.' marked twice on base, c1800, 11½in (29cm) high, 28oz gross. **£6,000-8,000** *CNY*

A George I coffee pot, by Humphrey Payne, 1716, 9in (23cm) high, 19oz gross. **£11,000-13,000** *C*

A George II coffee pot, by Paul de Lamerie, 1742, 8½in (21cm) high, 23oz gross. **£45,000-50,000** *C*

A George I chamber pot, Isaac Liger, engraved with contemporary armorials, London 1714, 7in (17.5cm) diam, 861gr. **£20,000-22,000** *S*

A Belgian coffee pot, by Jan Baptist Verberckt I, marked and 19thC control marks, 1781, 14in (35cm), 50oz. **£15,000-18,000** *CNY*

Two George III honey pots, formed as bee skeps, by Paul Storr, c1797, one with clear glass liner, 4½in (11cm) high, 13oz each. **£15,000-20,000 each** *C*

A Belgian chocolate pot, maker's mark and Rome town mark, Mons 1773, 13in (33cm), 1206gr. **£22,000-25,000** *C*

A George III inkstand, with inscription, by John Parker and Edward Wakelin, 1771, 12in (30cm) long, 56oz. **£18,000-20,000** *C*

A George I inkstand, by Lewis Mettayer, London 1716, with later bell, 12½in (32cm) long, 58oz. **£9,000-12,000** *CNY*

A French silver gilt inkstand, by E. D. Tetard, Paris, marked on base, c1870. **£7,500-9,000** *CNY*

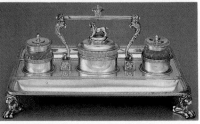

A George III inkstand, by Paul Storr, London 1803, 15in (38cm) wide, 3351 gr. **£45,000-50,000** *S*

A George III tankard, by
Benjamin Smith, 1812, 6½in
(16cm) high, 45oz.
£7,500-8,500 *C*

A tankard, by Philip Syng,
probably Jr, Philadelphia, c1730,
later monograms, 7in (17.5cm),
31oz. **£18,000-20,000** *CNY*

A German parcel gilt coin set
tankard, by David Splitgerber,
Kolberg, c1670, 20in (51cm) high,
233oz. **£115,000-120,000** *CNY*

A pair of Charles I silver
gilt flagons, maker's mark
RS, with mallet above and
below, London 1638, 13in
(33cm) high, 4381 gr.
£60,000-70,000 *S*

A William IV silver gilt
presentation tankard,
inscribed, 13in (33cm) high,
91oz. **£30,000-35,000** *C*

A George II sugar box and matching tea
caddy, by Elizabeth Godfrey, London 1749,
with 6 teaspoons by Jessie McFarlan,
c1754, 40oz. **£17,000-20,000** *CNY*

A French silver gilt part dinner service, by Tetard
Frères, late 19thC, meat dish 17½in (45cm) wide,
286oz. **£10,000-12,000** *CNY*

A pair of George II tea caddies and a matching
sugar box, by Paul de Lamerie, London, 1736,
34oz, with ebony case. **£21,000-23,000** *CNY*

A composite George III/IV tea and coffee service,
by Paul Storr and others, c1820, stand modern,
stand 12in (30.5cm), 136oz. **£9,000-10,000** *CNY*

A set of George III tea caddies, by
Frederick Vonham, 1763, with 12
teaspoons, 18thC, and sugar tongs,
49oz. **£10,000-12,000** *C*

A George III tray, by Robert Garrard, 1809, 30in (76cm) wide, 303oz. **£32,000-35,000** *C*

A George III two-handled soup tureen and cover, by Thomas Robins, 1809, 15in (38cm) wide, 111oz. **£7,000-8,000** *C*

A pair of Brazilian processional lanterns, struck with marks for Oporto, maker's mark A'S, late 18thC, 76in (193cm) high, 300oz weighable silver. **£30,000-35,000** *CNY*

A Mexican hanging lamp, with spurious marks for Miguel Maria Martel, Mexico City, c1800, with 8 later branches, 63in (160cm) high. **£6,500-7,500** *CNY*

A George II cheese stand, by Edward Wakelin, London 1754, 14in (35.5cm) wide, 69.5oz. **£80,000-100,000** *CNY*

An Austrian dressing table set, c1850, 72.75oz silver. **£5,000-6,000** *S*

A pair of George III tea caddies, by Hester Bateman, marked, London 1779, 4¹/₂in (11cm) wide, 24.5oz. **£6,000-8,000** *CNY*

A Victorian model of The Master of a hunt and his mount, by Hunt & Roskell, 1869, 12in (30.5cm) high, 2873gr, on wooden plinth. **£5,000-6,000** *S*

A pair of George III sauce tureens and covers from the Hamilton service, by Paul Storr, London 1806, 10in (25.5cm) wide, 85oz. **£22,000-25,000** *CNY*

A pair of Regency soup tureens and covers, by Kirkby, Waterhouse & Hodgson, Sheffield, 1810, 15in (38cm), 168oz. **£16,000-20,000** *CNY*

A pair of George III wine coolers, by Paul Storr, London 1800, 7¹/₂in (18.5cm) high, 96oz. **£18,000-20,000** *CNY*

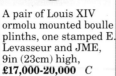

A pair of Louis XIV ormolu mounted boulle plinths, one stamped E. Levasseur and JME, 9in (23cm) high, **£17,000-20,000** *C*

An 18ct gold presentation casket, by Goldsmiths and Silversmiths Company, 1927. **£10,000-12,000** *C*

A pair of George III ormolu candlesticks, possibly Italian, 13in (33cm) high. **£8,500-9,500** *C*

A Roman ormolu vase, by Benedetto Boschetti, on marble pedestal, mid-19thC, 26in (66cm) high. **£30,000-35,000** *C*

A George III ormolu figure of Minerva, on marble plinth and blue john plinth, 13in (33cm). **£3,500-4,500** *C*

An Empire ormolu vase, cast with Cupid and Psyche, with reeded female mask handles, 21^1/$_2$in (54cm) high. **£8,000-10,000** *C*

A Charles X ormolu centrepiece, 20in (51cm) high. **£12,000-14,000** *C*

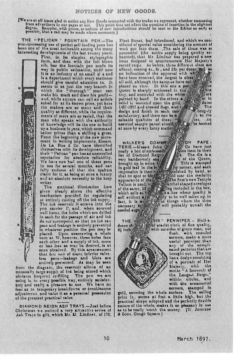

Five ormolu plaques, emblematic of Astronomy and Music, 11in (28cm). **£2,500-3,500** *C*

An ornate 9ct gold Pelican self-feeding pen, with iridium 14ct gold overfed nib, De la Rue, hallmarked 1897. **£5,000-6,000** *Bon*

A pair of Regency bronze, ormolu and marble lions, by Thomas Hope. **£3,000-3,500** *C*

A gilt bronze bust, 'Salammbo', by L. Moreau, 29½in (74.5cm). **£4,500-5,500** *C*

A Franco-Flemish bronze group of Venus and Cupid, late 16thC, 16½in (42cm) high. **£33,000-36,000** *C*

A Venetian bronze centrepiece, some damage, c1674, 6½in (16cm). **£5,500-6,500** *C*

A pair of patinated bronze and ormolu models of deer, possibly Italian, 19thC, 13in (33cm). **£18,000-20,000** *C*

A Florentine bronze group of Diana, mid-17thC, 16in (40cm) high. **£210,000-220,000** *C*

A French silvered bronze figure of Pandora with her open box, silvering rubbed, 19thC. **£4,000-5,000** *C*

An Italian bronze figure of a kneeling satyr, late 16thC, 7in (17cm) high. **£7,000-8,000** *C*

A bronze group, 'Valkyrie', by Stephan Sinding, 22in (56cm). **£3,000-3,500** *C*

A Louis XV gilt bronze and lacquer inkstand, mid-18thC, 13in (33cm) wide. **£6,000-7,000** *S*

A French bronze figure of 'L' Effroi', by Gustave Doré, late 19thC, 23in (59cm). **£5,500-6,500** *C*

An Italian bronze portrait head of Beethoven, by Alfredo Pina, early 20thC. **£7,500-8,500** *C*

A pair of Italian marble busts of a Roman official and his wife, on rouge marble socles and scagliola columns, late 17thC, 25in (64cm) high. **£20,000-22,000** *C*

A marble statue of Cleopatra, early 17thC. **£32,000-35,000** *C*

A pair of Italian marble figures, early 19thC, 53in (135cm). **£27,000-30,000** *C*

An English white marble group of a mother and child, by Edward Gustavus Physick, c1827, 22in (56cm) high. **£14,000-16,000** *C*

A French marble sculpture of Peace, by Albert Carrier-Belleuse, 19thC, 23¹/₂in (60.5cm) high. **£9,000-12,000** *C*

An Italian marble figure of a young street musician, signed J. Bottiglioni. **£12,000-14,000** *C*

A German ivory relief of The Dream of Constantine, attributed to Antonio Leoni, 18thC, 4in (10cm) high. **£10,000-12,000** *C*

An Eastern French Gothic ivory group, early 14thC, 8in (21cm) high. **£13,000-15,000** *C*

An Italian white marble bust of Caesar Augustus, some damage and repair, 30in (76cm) high. **£10,000-12,000** *C*

An Irish marble bust of Pope Clement XIV, by Christopher Heweston, c1772, 25in (63cm) high. **£15,000-17,000** *C*

481

A carved and polychrome painted wood panel, with the Royal arms of King William III, 19thC, 28in (71cm) high. **£4,500-5,500** *C*

A French terracotta bust of Rouget de L'Isle, c1835, on wooden socle, 17½in (45.5cm). **£9,000-10,000** *C*

A pair of Empire carved giltwood columns, early 19thC, **£7,000-8,000** *S*

A Florentine glazed terracotta statue, attributed to Benedetto Buglioni, damage and repairs, c1510. **£45,000-55,000** *C*

An Hispano-Flemish polychrome and giltwood reliquary bust, early 16thC, 22in (56cm) high. **£18,000-20,000** *C*

An Italian variegated white marble urn, distressed, early 19thC, 16in (40.5cm). **£3,000-4,000** *C*

An Italian marble figure of a Greek slave girl, by Scipione Tadolini, some damage, late 19thC, 97in (246cm). **£90,000-100,000** *C*

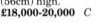

A Tinos marble urn, with gadrooned body and fluted foot, with a beaten copper liner, early 19thC, 11in (28cm) high. **£4,000-5,000** *S(C)*

An Italian white mottled marble mortar, with circular lobed rim, 18thC, 21in (53.5cm) diam. **£1,800-2,200** *C*

A Swabian painted wood group of St.Christopher, some damage, c1500, 31in (79cm). **£13,500-15,000** *S(NY)*

A giltwood figure of a poodle, with brown glass eyes, 19thC, 30½in (77cm), on modern wooden base. **£16,000-18,000** *S*

A gold mounted enamel box, with mythological scenes, emblematic of Love, possibly German, c1770, 3½in (8.5cm) wide. **£2,000-3,000** *C*

A Swiss gold and enamel snuff box, Neuchâtel, c1840, 3½in (9cm) wide. **£2,000-2,500** *CNY*

A George II gold snuff box, with portrait of Mary, Countess of Bute, by Christian Friedrich Zincke, c1750, 7cm wide. **£40,000-42,000** *C*

A Swiss gold and enamel bonbonnière, probably Geneva, c1800, 3in (8cm) wide. **£4,000-5,000** *C*

A gold, enamel and gem set presentation snuff box, mid-19thC, with later French import marks, 3½in (8.5cm) wide. **£4,000-5,000** *C*

A Meissen gold mounted snuff box, with gilt interior, c1755, 9cm wide. **£90,000-100,000** *CG*

A Meissen gold mounted snuff box, c1770, in contemporary leather box with gilt tooling, 8.5cm wide. **£14,000-16,000** *CG*

A Meissen gold mounted snuff box, with gilt interior, enamels rubbed, gilder's numeral 18, c1740, 9cm wide. **£110,000-120,000** *CG*

A Doccia snuff box, painted by J. K. Anreiter, c1750, silver gilt mounts London 1855. **£4,000-5,000** *CG*

A gold snuff box set with a Roman micro-mosaic, by S. Chaligny, Geneva, c1820. **£21,000-23,000** *C*

A Swiss vari-coloured gold, enamel and diamond set presentation snuff box, c1830, 3½in (9cm). **£6,000-7,000** *C*

A German gold mounted hardstone portrait snuff box, set with diamonds, unmarked, c1780, 7.5cm wide. **£6,000-7,000** *CNY*

A Swiss gold presentation snuff box, probably Neuchâtel, maker's mark CCS in a lozenge, c1840. **£5,000-6,000** *C*

A Victorian Diamond Jubilee heavily embossed casket, with leather covered case, **£120-150** *PCh*

A pair of cutlery urns, with enclosed fitted interior, 29in (74cm) high. **£3,500-4,500** *C*

A George III scrolled paper tea caddy, c1790, 8½in (21cm) wide. **£1,200-1,500** *EHA*

An Upper Rhine wooden Minnekästchen, lock replaced, stamped AC, 15thC, 9in (23cm) wide,. **£5,500-6,500** *C*

A Zurich wooden box, 15thC, 11½in (29cm) wide. **£4,500-5,500** *C*

A French oak casket, with bronze mounts, c1850, 8in (20cm) wide. **£500-600** *EHA*

An Upper Rhine Minnekästchen, late 14thC. **£15,000-16,000** *C*

A pair of japanned cutlery urns, 23in (59cm) high. **£10,000-12,000** *C*

A French gilt casket, with silver plated plaques, c1860, 6½in (16cm) wide. **£750-850** *EHA*

An Upper Rhine Minnekästchen, heavily carved, early 15thC, 9½in (24cm) wide. **£4,500-6,000** *C*

A Killarney ware writing slope, c1840, 10in (25.5cm) wide. **£600-650** *EHA*

A papier mâché, mother-of-pearl and gilt decorated box, 19thC, 11in (28cm) wide. **£150-200** *PCh*

An Italian boulle casket, with steel and semi-precious stones inlaid to lid, late 17thC, 14in (35cm) wide. **£2,500-3,000** *EHA*

Regulators

A beechwood and ebonised Vienna regulator, with a 5in (13cm) white enamelled dial and gong striking movement, the case with broken arch pediment and baluster finials, 30½in (77cm). **£500-550** *S(S)*

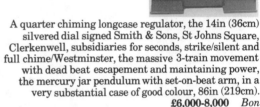

A walnut striking Vienna regulator, 7in (18cm) enamel dial signed M. Schonberger, Vienna, with 2-train weight driven movement, 54in (137cm). **£1,200-1,500** *Bon*

A quarter chiming longcase regulator, the 14in (36cm) silvered dial signed Smith & Sons, St Johns Square, Clerkenwell, subsidiaries for seconds, strike/silent and full chime/Westminster, the massive 3-train movement with dead beat escapement and maintaining power, the mercury jar pendulum with set-on-beat arm, in a very substantial case of good colour, 86in (219cm). **£6,000-8,000** *Bon*

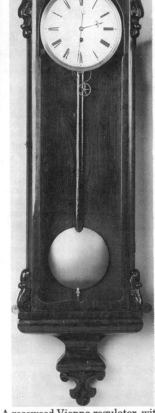

A rosewood Vienna regulator, with a 7in (18cm) white enamelled dial, the movement with dead beat escapement, the case with moulded pediment, ebonised scroll shoulders and baluster knop, 39½in (100cm). **£750-850** *S(S)*

A regulator clock, by Arnold & Dent, The Strand, London, in mahogany case, 19thC, 76in (193cm). **£8,000-9,000** *McC*

Skeleton Clocks

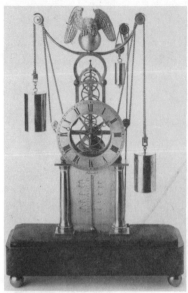

A French Empire weight driven skeleton clock, stamped on the rafter frame Augte. Moirau et Rolland Degrege, No. 33, the bullet shaped weight driving the maintaining power, the suspension chains of square section running over a series of pulleys, the movement supported on 2 brass columns inset with a silvered thermometer, on a walnut veneered base, 23in (59cm).
£3,000-4,000   *Bon*

A brass Cathedral skeleton clock, the pierced silvered chapter ring with black Roman numerals, the double fusee movement striking on a single bell and gong, surmounted on a grey veined white marble plinth under a glass dome, 19thC, 25in (64cm), together with an oak wall bracket.
£1,500-2,000   *HSS*

A Victorian skeleton clock, by Frodsham & Keen, with verge fusee and chain movement beneath a glass dome.
£2,000-2,500   *SWO*

Wall Clocks

A large wall clock in Act of Parliament style, single-train movement with anchor escapement, the moulded shield dial signed Robt. Peake, Dereham, brass spade hands with counter balance, the trunk decorated with florally painted panel against a green ground, 55in (139cm).   **£700-900**   *Bon*

A George III black lacquer wall clock, the convex glazed 11in (28cm) engraved silvered dial signed Jas Higgs Wallingford, with pierced blued hands, the 4-pillar single gut fusee movement with tapered plates, knife-edge verge escapement and bob pendulum, 16in (41cm).
£1,700-2,000   *C*

A Dutch oak alarm staartklok, the movement with turned baluster pillars with countwheel strike on 2 bells, 48in (122cm). **£800-1,000**   *CSK*

An American late Federal mahogany wall clock of banjo type, the dial inscribed Panton on the reverse, the brass movement with 4 front-pinned pillars, anchor escapement, narrow diameter of barrel for the line the weight falling behind a tinplate divider from the pendulum with cranked rod clearing the cannon pinion, in a drum case with spreading shaft and plinth base, mid-19thC.
£1,000-1,500   *C*

A French wall clock, with cream chapter ring, gilt filigree dial centre and replaced electric movement, mounted on a Limoges enamel panel painted on a dark blue ground, in a carved giltwood frame, c1880, 13½in (34cm). **£400-600** *S(S)*

A Louis XV style ormolu cartel clock, with an 8in (20cm) convex enamel dial and a bell striking movement with Brocot escapement, the rococo case cast with scrollwork, c1875, 24in (61cm).
£2,000-2,500 *S*

An Austrian petite sonnerie musical giltwood picture frame wall clock, with annular enamel dial and gilt engine turned centre, the 3-train gong striking movement with silk suspension, a distressed musical movement with 8½in (21cm) pinned cylinder mounted above, in a giltwood picture frame case with egg and dart moulded border, c1840, 20in (51cm) square.
£700-900 *S*

Miscellaneous

A brass cased novelty clock, the case in the form of a ship's bridge telegraph engraved with the lever positions, on pedestal base and wood plinth, now with a replacement movement by Westclox, c1900, 11½in (30cm).
£350-450 *S(S)*

A carved oak cuckoo clock, the twin fusee movement with parchment bellows, stamped Harckell, 28½in (72cm).
£600-800 *S(S)*

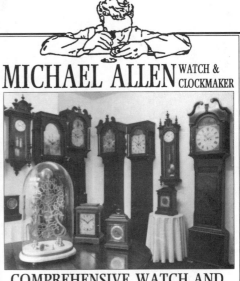

Watches

A gentleman's 18ct gold key-wind open faced pocket watch, the gilt fusee movement with a lever escapement, mask engraved balance cock, the backplate signed Jas. Barclay, London, 2966, with a slow/fast regulator, with blued steel hands, and a key, mid-19thC.
£250-300   *S*

A silver pair case verge pocket watch, in plain outer case, with white enamel chapter ring, outer gilt rim with the motif 'keep me clean, use me well and I to you the truth will tell', the frosted gilt fusee movement signed Richd. Kevitt, London, 6cm.
£450-500   *CSK*

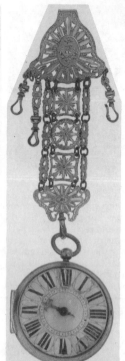

A gilt oignon verge pocket watch, in engraved case, with single steel hand, the frosted gilt fusee movement with silver chased, engraved and pierced bridge cock and pierced Egyptian pillars, signed on the backplate C.D.R. Angers, hinge to the movement broken, with gilt chatelaine, late 17thC, 5.6cm.
£1,500-1,800   *CSK*

An 18ct gold and enamel cylinder watch, with gilded bar movement, the back decorated with dark blue translucent enamel over a guilloche ground, centred with rose diamond set leaves and flowers, 3cm.
£400-450   *Bon*

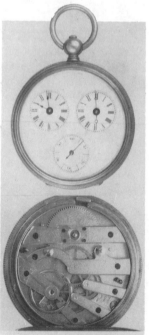

An English verge watch in silver pair cases, with silver regulator disc, plain steel balance, the outer with an engraved monogram and the date 1783, signed John Chapman Sheerness 213, hallmarked London 1781, 5cm.
£450-650   *PT*

A gentleman's 18ct gold keyless wind full hunter cased minute repeating pocket watch, London, 1929, with an unsigned gilt jewelled Swiss lever movement, the cuvette presentation inscribed, with blued steel hands, the side with push-in minute repeat button, the case front monogram engraved, with a box.
£1,500-2,000   *S*

A Swiss cylinder Captain's watch, in a silvered open face case, with keywind gilt bar movement with suspended going barrel, plain 3-arm gold balance with blue steel spiral hairspring and gilt case interior, late 19thC, 5cm.
£350-450   *PT*

A scent bottle containing a verge watch, the movement set in the middle within a sunburst gilt border, with a red paste set silver bezel, on the reverse of the bottle is an enamel plaque within a similar border, which opens to reveal a small compartment through which the watch can be wound, signed Robt Reading London, c1760, 6½in (16cm) high.
£2,500-3,000 *PT*

An 8-day quarter repeating open face keyless pocket watch, with discoloured silvered dial and blued steel hand, minute hand missing, signed Charles Meyer, Montreux, the plated movement under snap-on back, repeating on 2 gongs operated by a pull chord at 6, 10.3cm.
£400-500 *CSK*

A gentleman's keyless wind open faced pocket watch by E. Howard Watch Co., Boston, U.S.A., with a signed jewelled steel lever movement, 935809, adjusted, with a micrometer speed regulator and signed white enamelled dial with blued steel hands.
£450-650 *S*

A gold and enamel keyless cylinder watch, with white enamel dial, the engraved case with back decorated with multi-coloured enamel flowers against pink translucent enamel over a guilloche ground, 2.6cm.
£300-400 *Bon*

A gentleman's 18ct gold keyless wind demi-hunter cased pocket watch, Birmingham 1929, the three-quarter plate jewelled lever movement signed Rotherhams, London, 403398, with a fast/slow regulator, the cuvette presentation inscribed, cased.
£350-450 *S(S)*

A rare 17th Century Verge Watch with Wandering Hours and Calender. Signed: Henou- Emdem.

A gentleman's keyless wind demi-hunter cased pocket watch by Patek Philippe & Cie, Genève, the gilt jewelled lever movement signed and with number 166167, signed and numbered cuvette with signed white enamelled dial, subsidiary seconds and blued steel hands, the case back date inscribed within, the exterior monogram engraved.
£1,500-2,000 *S*

An English verge in decorative silver pair cases, with engraved masked cock, silver regulator disc, fusee and chain with worm and wheel barrel setup between the plates, plain steel balance, later blue steel beetle, silver inner case with silver pendant and bow in a contemporary decorative silver outer case, signed Thos Reynolds London 435, hallmarked London 1742.
£600-700 *PT*

A gold, enamel and diamond mounted fob watch, with gilded keyless lever bar movement jewelled to the centre, gilt dial, the back decorated with blue translucent enamel over a guilloche ground, and old cut diamonds set in a filigree band, with silver ribbon fob, 2.7cm.
£550-750 *Bon*

A silver and enamel Cartier purse watch, the translucent pale blue enamel on guilloche background, chipped, with brushed silvered dial, 4.6 x 3.1cm.
£900-1,200 *CSK*

Wristwatches

A keyless open face Mickey Mouse novelty watch by Ingersoll, in plain white metal case, with unusual outer 13-24-hour ring, subsidiary seconds with 3 Mickeys, the time indicated by Mickey's hands, the signed engine turned back with monometallic balance and lever escapement, 4.9cm.
£450-550 *CSK*

An early stainless steel wristwatch by Rolex, in tonneau case, the discoloured, engine turned silvered dial with subsidiary seconds, the case with hinged back and maker's mark numbered 578 02243, the signed movement jewelled to the third, 3.7 x 2.5cm.
£600-800 *CSK*

A gold steel Cartier automatic calendar wristwatch, the case with protected winder, signed to the reverse by the maker, with integral gold steel flexible bracelet and deployant clasp, 3cm.
£550-750 *CSK*

A stainless steel wristwatch, by International Watch Company, for military use, the black dial with luminous quarter hour marks, sweep centre seconds, the case with screwed back and ordinance number, 3.5cm.
£450-500 *CSK*

A stainless steel Rolex Oyster Perpetual chronometer bubble back wristwatch, the case with screw-down winder and screwed back numbered 2940, the signed movement numbered N18243, 3cm.
£700-900 *CSK*

A gentleman's 9ct gold cased automatic wristwatch by Jaeger le Coultre, London, 1955, with a gilt metal expanding bracelet.
£400-600 *S(S)*

An early silver wristwatch by Rolex, with wire lugs, the case with gilt winder and hinged back with maker's stamp, the signed spotted movement jewelled to the third, 3.3cm.
£200-300   *CSK*

A stainless steel Omega Speedmaster Professional Mark II chronograph wristwatch, the black bezel with tachymetric scale, sweep centre seconds operated by 2 buttons in the band, and the case with screwed back, 4.5cm.
£200-300   *CSK*

An 18ct gold lady's octagonal wristwatch, the 17 jewel movement signed Cartier, the case with fluted stepped bezel containing the winder, 2.4cm.
£650-850   *Bon*

A modern gold steel quartz wristwatch by Baume & Mercier, Genève, in tonneau case, the signed back secured by 4 screws, with integral gold and steel flexible bracelet and B & M deployant clasp, with original packaging and wallet, 2.8 x 2.6cm.
£300-400   *CSK*

A gentleman's circular cased Bulova Accutron electric wristwatch, with visible glazed electric movement, the case with gilt front and steel back, on a sprung gilt bracelet, with the original plastic box.
£280-320   *S*

A Corum gold 20 dollar coin wristwatch, the damascened 18 jewel movement numbered 103038, set in a 1904 20 dollar piece, sapphire set winder, with leather strap, 3.7cm.
£1,100-1,500   *Bon*

An 18ct gold wristwatch by Vacheron & Constantin, with damascened nickel movement, 17 jewels and adjusted to temperatures, No. 473934, 3.3cm.
£1,300-1,700   *Bon*

An 18ct gold calendar wristwatch by Record, the nickel movement jewelled to the centre, the dial with subsidiary seconds, apertures for day, month and moon, concentric date hand, with an associated 9ct gold flexible bracelet, 3.6cm.
£450-550   *Bon*

A duo plan Extra Prima movement wristwatch by Rolex, jewelled to the third and timed to 6 positions, the silvered dial, discoloured, with subsidiary seconds, square, signed Rolex Prince, now in gilt case, 3.2 x 1.7cm.
£1,500-2,000   *CSK*

A gentleman's stainless steel wristwatch by Vacheron & Constantin, Genève, in waterproof case, the discoloured silvered dial with luminous dots to the 5 minute divisions and luminous hands, subsidiary seconds ring, the case with screwed back, 2.8cm.
£900-1,200   *CSK*

A gold backwind wristwatch, the duo-plan nickel lever movement signed European Watch & Clock Co., 16 jewels, damascened dust cover, the white dial signed Cartier, the case mounted with crown at the back, the leather strap with gold Cartier deployant buckle, 3.1 x 2cm.
£4,000-5,000   *Bon*

An 18ct gold cased wristwatch.
£300-400   *HSS*

An 18ct gold wristwatch by Piaget, the 18 jewel movement with bark finish dial, the case with integral 18ct gold bracelet of herringbone design, 2.4cm.
£1,000-1,400   *Bon*

An 18ct gold lady's wristwatch, the nickel movement signed Cartier, the moulded ribbed case with sapphire set winding crown, with leather strap and tooled Cartier box, 3.1 x 2.4cm.
£2,200-2,700   *Bon*

A lady's diamond set wristwatch with diamond scroll and ring link articulated shoulders to a cordette bracelet, the movement signed Syntax, 17 jewels, 4 adjustments.
£550-650   *CSK*

A lady's platinum and diamond wristwatch, with a moiré strap.
£400-500   *CSK*

A lady's platinum, diamond and calibre emerald wristwatch, the dial signed Cito, with milanese bracelet.
£400-450   *CSK*

Chronometers

A 2-day marine chronometer, the silvered dial signed Ja. Edwards, near the West India Docks, No. 282, c1820.
£2,400-2,800   *MAW*

A 2-day marine chronometer, the spotted movement with Earnshaw spring detent escapement, compensation balance, palladium helical spring, free sprung, numbered at the edge 13458, silvered dial signed Kelvin White & Hutton, 11 Billiter St. London, and numbered 6038, in brass box numbered 13458, in later brass bound mahogany carrying case with flush handles and named and numbered roundel, 5in (13cm).
£900-1,200   *S*

An early 2-day marine chronometer, signed on the movement John Arnold London, Invt. et Fecit No. 16, with Arnold's spring detent escapement, early form of 2-armed compensation balance with bi-metallic rims with peripheral adjustment and compensation, gold helical spring with terminal curves and adjustable stud with pointer fitted to the clock, original dial, cracked and chipped, steel hands, in contemporary mahogany box with brass bezel, c1791.
£27,000-30,000   *S*

This chronometer was sold with a framed letter from E. J. Dent to Mr Hawley dated July 11 1832, in which it is stated that this is the chronometer which proved to the House of Commons Committee Mr Arnold's priority of introduction of the spring detent escapement.

Stick Barometers

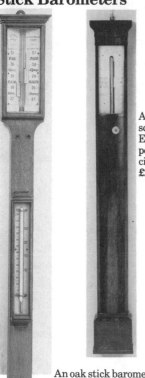

A rosewood barometer, the silvered scales signed Adie & Son, Edinburgh, the case with moulded pediment, bowed front and plain cistern, 41½in (106cm).
£2,000-2,400   *S(S)*

A mahogany 'upside down' stick barometer, by Naime & Blunt, London, with silvered scales signed by the maker with vernier, enclosed mercury tube with ball reservoir at the top and boxed cistern, some restorations, 37½in (95cm).
£750-850   *CSK*

Make the Most of Miller's

CONDITION is absolutely vital when assessing the value of an antique. Damaged pieces on the whole appreciate much less than perfect examples. However a rare, desirable piece may command a high price even when damaged

---

An oak stick barometer with flat top above ivory scales with vernier, knobs lacking, signed J.H. Steward, 457 West Strand, London, cased thermometer with turned cistern cover, 36½in (93cm).
£450-550   *CSK*

A mahogany stick barometer, signed on the silvered register plates Berrenger, London, in a case with crossbanding to the trunk, 38in (96cm).
£900-1,200   *Bon*

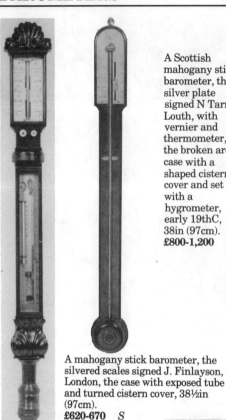

A Scottish mahogany stick barometer, the silver plate signed N Tarra Louth, with vernier and thermometer, the broken arch case with a shaped cistern cover and set with a hygrometer, early 19thC, 38in (97cm).
£800-1,200   *S*

A mahogany stick barometer, the silvered scales signed J. Finlayson, London, the case with exposed tube and turned cistern cover, 38½in (97cm).
£620-670   *S*

A mahogany stick barometer, the plates signed Polti-Exon, the case with hemispherical cistern cover, 39in (99cm).
£500-550   *S*

A rosewood marine barometer by Cameron, Glasgow, with ivory register, the trunk with sympiesometer, thermometer and hygrometer scales, with brass cistern cover and shell pediment, with provision for gimbal mount, 19thC, 40in (102cm).
£2,000-2,500   *P(M)*

A mahogany stick barometer with boxwood and ebony herringbone inlay, the case with visible tube and plain turned cistern cover, the silvered dial with thermometer and vernier, signed F. Pellegrino Fecit, 39in (99cm).
£1,500-2,000   *CSK*

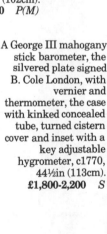

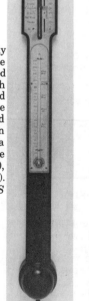

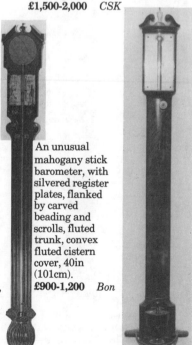

A George III mahogany stick barometer, the silvered plate signed B. Cole London, with vernier and thermometer, the case with kinked concealed tube, turned cistern cover and inset with a key adjustable hygrometer, c1770, 44½in (113cm).
£1,800-2,200   *S*

An unusual mahogany stick barometer, with silvered register plates, flanked by carved beading and scrolls, fluted trunk, convex fluted cistern cover, 40in (101cm).
£900-1,200   *Bon*

A Victorian rosewood marine barometer, the bone plates with vernier and signed B. Biggs Cardiff, the case with a brass cistern cover, later gimbals and set with a thermometer, with a later brass mount and wood shield, c1860, 34in (86cm).
£900-1,200   *S*

An oak stick barometer, the bone scales signed Steward, Strand & Cornhill, London, twin verniers, the case with thermometer on trunk, 39in (99cm).
£500-600   *Bon*

A stick barometer by Carey, London, late 18thC, 37in (94cm).
£3,500-4,000   *McC*

Wheel Barometers

A mahogany cased wheel barometer and thermometer by C. Aiano, Northgate, Canterbury, with 8in (20cm) silvered dial, the case inlaid with shell and leaf ornament, early 19thC, 38in (97cm).
£450-500
GA(W)

A George III inlaid mahogany wheel barometer, with 8in (20cm) silvered dial signed J. Pastorelli, Bowling St., Westminster, the case inset with an alcohol thermometer, c1810, 39in (99cm).
£800-900 *S*

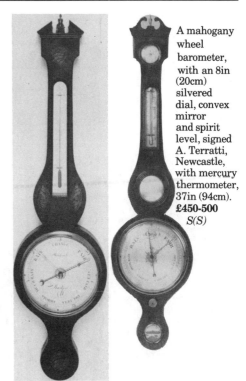

A George IV inlaid mahogany wheel barometer, with an 8in (20cm) silvered dial signed Bullocech Bradford, and thermometer above, the case inlaid and outlined in ebony and box stringing, c1825, 38in (97cm).
£500-600 *S*

A mahogany wheel barometer, with an 8in (20cm) silvered dial, convex mirror and spirit level, signed A. Terratti, Newcastle, with mercury thermometer, 37in (94cm).
£450-500
S(S)

SCIENTIFIC INSTRUMENTS

Dials

A brass compass dial, with folding gnomon and interior printed paper card, the brass circle pierced with Roman numerals, early 20thC, 5½in (14cm) wide.
£200-250   *CSK*

A brass mining dial, signed on the silvered compass rose Cail, Newcastle-upon-Tyne No. 125, the corner engraved with scales for Diff of Hypo & Base, with staff mounting and T. B. Winter trade label, in mahogany case, 19thC, 13in (33cm) wide.
£300-400   *CSK*

A gilt and silvered brass universal equinoctial dial, signed on the under side of the compass box Johan Schrettegger in Augsburg, in leather covered card case, late 18thC, 2½in (6cm) wide.
£1,500-2,000   *CSK*

Globes

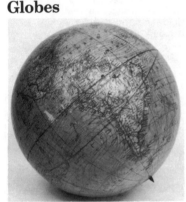

A Smith's 12in (31cm) terrestrial globe, by George Philip & Son Ltd., the paper gores with ocean currents, the continents outlined in colours, with axis pins, 19thC.
£650-750   *CSK*

A 6in (15cm) terrestrial globe, by W & S Jones, London dated 1822, the printed and coloured paper gores with tracks of Admiral Anson, Capt. Cook and other explorers, 10in (26cm) high.
£2,500-3,000   *CSK*

A terrestrial globe, with maker's cartouche inscribed '18 inch Terrestrial Globe by W & A K Johnston Ltd., Geographers, Engravers and Printers, Edinburgh and London, Copyright 1910', the horizon dial 3in (8cm), on a mahogany stand terminating in lion paw feet and ball casters, 48in (122cm) high.
£4,000-5,000   *HSS*

A 1½in (4cm) terrestrial globe, inscribed 'Newton & Berrys New Terrestrial Globe 1831', with varnished and coloured paper gores, Australia as New Holland and with tracks of Capt. Cook and Clarke & Gore, in leather covered drum shaped case, early 19thC, 2in (5cm) high.
£1,700-2,000   *CSK*

A 3in (8cm) thread terrestrial globe, with coloured paper gores, the globe arranged to split and contain a reel of cotton, with interior trade label for Clark & Co., on ebonised stand, late 19thC, 4in (10cm) high.
£350-400   *CSK*

A Betts's patent portable globe, the waxed cotton collapsible sphere with folding umbrella frame, maker's trade label in case, 29in (74cm) long.
£350-500   *CSK*

A 10in (25cm) terrestrial globe by Ludw. Jul. Heymann, Berlin, the axis with part brass base, on turned beechwood stand, the base inset with a compass, 17½in (45cm) high.
£450-550   *CSK*

A 2in (5cm) terrestrial globe, inscribed 'Woodward's Terrestrial Globe 18*6', the coloured and varnished paper gores printed with extensive geographical information, with brass meridian half-circle, on baluster turned support and base, globe cracked, 19thC, 6½in (17cm) high.
£900-1,200   *CSK*

A 1in (3cm) terrestrial globe, unsigned, with varnished and coloured paper gores, in domed mahogany case, 19thC, 2in (5cm).
£1,200-1,500   *CSK*

A 2in (5cm) terrestrial globe, inscribed 'New Terrestrial Globe' and with trade mark, the printed gores delicately coloured, delineated with the tracks of Capt. Cook, and Clarke and Gore, Australia as New Holland, late 18thC.
£600-700   *CSK*

A Betts's portable globe, the calico folding sphere on black japanned umbrella-type frame, in wood box, late 19thC, 29in (74cm) long.
£400-450   *CSK*

An American 6in (15cm) Geographic Educator terrestrial globe, with printed and coloured paper gores, tracks of the transatlantic flights of Lindbergh and Chamberlin, arranged so as to divide into 7 sections containing jig-saw puzzles of the continents, on moulded tripod stand, 11in (28cm) high.
£550-750   *CSK*

A 4in (10cm) Camille Flammarien Mars globe, by E Bertaux 25 Rue Seerpente, Paris, with coloured paper gores, labelled continents and oceans, on ebonised stand, 19thC, 9in (23cm) high.
£900-1,200   *CSK*

A 12in (31cm) terrestrial globe, manufactured by S. S. Edkins Son in Law & Successor to the late T. M. Bardin, Salisbury Square, London', mid-19thC, 18in (46cm) high.
£4,000-5,000   *CSK*

Surveying

A brass surveying level, unsigned, the telescope with a sliding draw-tube focusing, crosswires, bubble level, screw vertical adjustment, the limb with socket staff mounting, in case, 19thC, 13½in (34cm).
£150-200   *CSK*

An oxydised brass surveying compass, signed 'Designed & Made by Andrew Yeates 12 Brighton Place, New Kent Rd, London', with folding wire, prism and slit sights, bubble level, damaged, fixed telescope, finely engraved compass ring and steel bar needle on jewelled pivot, with trade label for Yeates 2 Grafton Street Dublin, in mahogany case, 19thC, 5½in (14cm) wide.
£500-600   *CSK*

A lacquered brass swinging arm protractor, with silvered scale and 2 verniers, signed 'Cail, Newcastle upon Tyne', with rack adjustment, in fitted mahogany case, 19thC, 7in (18cm).
£200-300   *CSK*

A Danish suspended deckhead compass, with dry card signed 'Rasmus Koch I Kiobenhavn 1772', 18thC, 8½in (21cm) diam.
£1,200-1,700   *CSK*

An oxidised and lacquered brass surveying level, signed W. & L.E. Gurley, Troy N.Y., the telescope with rack and pinion focusing, crosswires, eye-piece dust slide, with graduated level on limb with 2 clamps over the silvered horizontal circle with vernier and 4-screw tripod mounting, in carrying case, with maker's trade label, 14in (36cm) wide.
£400-450   *CSK*

An oxidised and lacquered brass theodolite, signed on the silvered compass dial Simms London, on 4-screw tripod mounting, 19thC, 9in (23cm) high.
£800-900   *CSK*

An oxidised brass double frame sextant, signed on the arc, with platina scale, 'Troughton & Simms, London', with rosewood handle, with accessories, in fitted mahogany case, 19thC, 12in (31cm) wide.
£600-800   *CSK*

A geomancers compass, decorated with characters in black and red, the side and underside with other inscriptions, in carrying case, 19thC, 13in (33cm) diam.
£600-700   *CSK*

An oxidised and lacquered brass sextant, signed 'Savill, Maker to the Royal Navy, Liverpool', with adjustable telescope socket, 7 shades, mirrors and index arm, late 19thC, 6½in (17cm), radius with vernier and magnifier, in mahogany case, 10in (25cm) wide.
£500-600   *CSK*

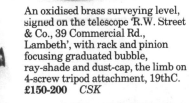

A black enamelled and lacquered brass theodolite, by T. Cooke & Sons Ltd, No. 7105, engraved Fergusson's patent surveying circle No. 6, on 3-screw tripod mounting, 13in (33cm) high.
£400-450   *CSK*

An oxidised brass surveying level, signed on the telescope 'R.W. Street & Co., 39 Commercial Rd., Lambeth', with rack and pinion focusing graduated bubble, ray-shade and dust-cap, the limb on 4-screw tripod attachment, 19thC.
£150-200   *CSK*

Telescopes

An oxidised and lacquered brass sextant, signed on the arc with silvered scale Adams, London, with accessories in mahogany case, late 19thC, 11½in (29cm) wide.
£350-400   *CSK*

A 3in (7.5cm) refracting telescope, by Broadhurst Clarkson & Co., with rack and pinion focusing, lens cap and hood, the black crackle finished body tube with star finder, on trunnion and mahogany tripod, with accessories, in pine carrying case, 49in (125cm) long.
£800-900   *CSK*

A 3in (7.5cm) brass telescope, by Dollond, with rack and pinion focusing, the tube on altitude and azimuth mount with slow motion adjustment, the ring with spirit level and vernier scale, the circular plate with scale, plain turned column support on a cabriole tripod with screw adjustment, 53in (134cm) tube inscribed Dollond, London, mahogany case, early 19thC.
£800-1,000   *P(S)*

A polished brass transit theodolite, by W. Ottway and Son Ltd, with micrometer eyepieces, silvered scales, bubble level and accessories, in mahogany case, 13in (33cm) wide.
£350-400   *CSK*

A 2¾in (7cm) brass reflecting telescope, signed on the backplate 'J. Bird London', the 16½in (42cm) long body tube with pin-hole and bead sights, screw-rod focusing, eyepiece and end cap, with speculum mirrors, on fine geared alt/azimuth mounting, unengraved and on tripod stand, the inswept cabriole legs terminating in scroll feet, late 18thC.
£1,500-2,000   *CSK*

A lacquered brass 2⅛in (5cm) refracting telescope, signed on the backplate 'J.H. Dallmeyer, London', the 27in (69cm) long body tube with rack and pinion focusing, star finder, and mounted by 2 knurled nuts on a quadrant with clamp to an axis on the tapering pillar support, signed 'J.H. Dallmeyer London', on folding tripod stand, with 3 additional eye pieces, in fitted pine case, late 19thC, 38½in (98cm) long.
£750-850   *CSK*

Microscopes

A lacquered brass monocular microscope, unsigned, with rack and pinion coarse and micrometer fine focusing, the rack web with additional in/cm scale by The Lugkin Rule Co. Saginaw U.S.A., with accessories, in mahogany case, late 19thC, 14½in (37cm) wide.
£600-700   *CSK*

A black enamel and satin chrome binocular microscope, by Carl Zeiss Jena No. 207174, with rack and pinion coarse and micrometer fine focusing, quadruple nosepiece, micrometer circuit stage, sub-stage condenser and mirror.
£250-300   *CSK*

An unusual miniature brass microscope, possibly French, unsigned, arranged so as to fold in mahogany case, late 19thC, 5in (13cm) long folded.
£300-400   *CSK*

A lacquered and oxidised brass monocular microscope, signed 'J. Swift & Son, 81 Tottenham Court Rd., London', on horseshoe stand with accessories, in mahogany case, 16in (41cm) high.
£850-1,000   *CSK*

A lacquered brass polarising microscope, signed on the silvered horizontal scale to eyepiece 'W. Ladd & Co., Beak Street, W.' the polariser scale engraved in 2 quadrants with lens train swivel stage and plano concave mirror, in fitted mahogany case, 19thC, 15½in (39cm) wide.
£750-900   *CSK*

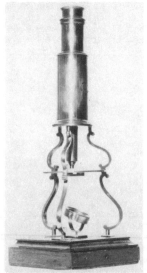

A large brass Culpepper tube microscope, unsigned, the body tube, stage and plinth base with accessory drawer united by scroll supports, in pyramid shaped mahogany case, 20in (51cm) high.
£500-600   *CSK*

A brass folding simple microscope, signed on the stage I. Cuff, Londini, Inv. & Fec. No. 18, with 4 objectives, forceps, talc box, rings and mirror, on oval base in plush lined fishskin case, 18thC, 7in (18cm) wide.
£2,200-2,700   *CSK*

A Nuremburg type tripod monocular microscope, of boxwood and pasteboard construction with 2 sliding body tubes, lens covers, slide clamp and mirror, the underside of the base with brand SIF, 19thC, 13in (33cm) high.
£1,000-1,500 *CSK*

A brass compound monocular microscope, signed 'B. Martin, Invt., London' on the body tube, focusing in the Cuff manner by sliding pillar and sleeve with long fine focus screw, in a red velvet lined fishskin covered case with a range of accessories and slides, late 18thC, 10in (25cm).
£2,000-2,500   *Bon*

Medical Instruments

A lacquered brass enema stomach pump, unsigned, complete with ivory and vulcanite fittings, a set of catheters by Down, London, and a set of Clutton's pattern urethral sounds, all in cases, 19thC, 13in (33cm) wide.
£200-250   *CSK*

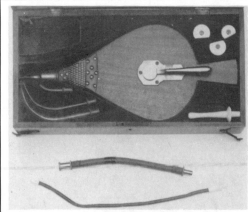

A rare tobacco enema, the fitted mahogany case containing bellows pump, tubing and assorted bone and pewter nozzles, a brass plaque on lid is engraved Bristol Humane Society 1833, 16in (41cm) wide.
£1,500-2,500   *CSK*

This apparatus for resuscitating the apparently drowned, was invented in the late 18thC and distributed by the Royal Humane Society to lock-keepers and docksides, and was used for pumping smoke up the victim's rectum, this practice was discontinued in 1865 after experimenting with pigs and sheep found that it only hastened their deaths!

A mahogany domestic medicine chest, with a steel balance with brass pans and weights, various jars and bottles, and 4-bottle poison compartment to rear, 19thC, 11in (28cm) high.
£600-700   *CSK*

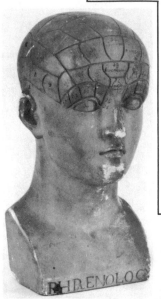

A plaster phrenology bust, inscribed Pub. by J. DeVille, 367 Strand London 11 April 1821, the cranium incised with the numbered areas of the sentiments, 10in (25cm) high.
£250-350   *CSK*

A pair of iron spectacles of 'Martin's' margin pattern, one of the sides with loop ends stamped Froget, the lenses within horn rims, 18thC.
£450-500   *CSK*

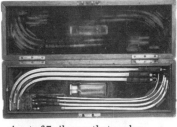

A set of 7 silver catheters, by Ferguson, with chequer grip ebony handles, a solution bottle and other items in plush lined, brass bound, rosewood case, 13½in (34cm) wide.
£200-250   *CSK*

A pair of brown/green tint globe shaped pharmacy carboys, with pontil marks and gilt labels for AQ:ANETH: and TR: RHETI:C, early 19thC, 11in (28cm) high.
£450-500   *CSK*

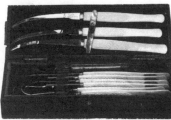

A minor operation set, by Cuzner Bristol, with chequer grip ivory handles with a bistoury knife by Coxeter, University College, in plush lined, gilt tooled leather case, 7½in (19cm) wide, the lid with silver plaque inscribed Bristol Infirmary surgical Prize Essay 1834 Hernia, presented to Mr. G. Cooper, mid-19thC.
£620-670   *CSK*

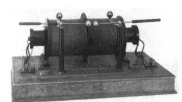

A large induction coil, by Harry W. Cox & Co. Ltd., 159 Great Portland St., London W., with vulcanite insulators, brass fittings, on oak base, late 19thC, 34½in (88cm) wide.
£750-900   *CSK*

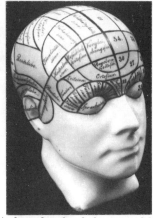

A phrenology head, the areas of the sentiments numbered and named, decorated in colours, late 19thC, 4½in (11cm) high.
£760-820   *CSK*

A part set of surgical instruments, by Arnold & Sons 35 & 36 West Smithfield, in brass bound mahogany case, 19thC, 17in (43cm).
£900-1,200   *CSK*

A fruitwood monaural stethoscope with wide plate, 7in (18cm) long, and a 3-part nickel plated brass and composition stethoscope, repaired, 19thC.
£280-320   *CSK*

A two-piece composition monaural stethoscope, with moulded plate, 19thC, 7in (18cm) long.
£200-250   *CSK*

A collection of surgical instruments, including a trephine, various knives, a tonsil guillotine and a chain lithotrite by S. Garie Gount, with a part mahogany case, 17½in (44cm) wide.
£250-300   *CSK*

A rare fruitwood Lannec monaural stethoscope, arranged in 3 parts, early 19thC, 1½in (4cm) diam, 12in (31cm) long.
£6,500-7,000   *CSK*

A rare Scottish paper cut out of a skeleton, with the inscription 'This representation of the human skeleton cutt with scizars by Thomas Hunter 1791 aged 82 years was presented by him to Doctor John Glendining during his residence at the University of Edinburgh', framed and glazed 10 by 5in (25 by 13cm), 18thC.
£900-1,200   *CSK*

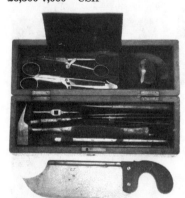

A post mortem set by Brady & Martin, Newcastle-on-Tyne, comprising saw, combination knife and chisels, hammer, skull rest and other items in brass bound mahogany case, late 19thC, 12in (31cm) wide.
£250-350   *CSK*

A burnished and blued steel lithotrite, stamped Charriere and with number 4, 11½in (29cm) long, the ebony handle with chequer grip, a pair of steel perforators, a stone forceps instrument and an ebony handled crochet, 19thC.
£250-300   *CSK*

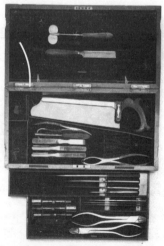

A part set of surgical instruments, by Weiss No. 62 Strand London, one original Liston knife and 3 replacements, in plush lined brass bound mahogany case, 19thC, 17in (43cm) wide.
£600-700   *CSK*

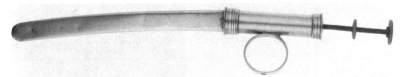

A rare silver concealed tonsillectomy lancet, with sabre shaped steel blade and steel adjustment screws, maker CW, 18thC, 7½in (19cm) long.
£350-450 *CSK*

A burnished steel trepanning drill, unsigned, with tapering trephine perforator and lignum vitae stock, 18thC, 10½in (27cm) long.
£750-850 *CSK*

A rare set of acupuncture needles, the 6 steel needles with brass screw caps contained in a lignum vitae cylindrical case, the cap forming the needle handle, early 19thC, the case 3½in (9cm) long.
£260-320 *CSK*

Dental Instruments

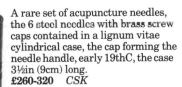

A rare hand operated dental drill, unsigned with spring and ratchet operation, fitted with a single hardened steel 'bit' and ivory handle, 7in (18cm) long, and a collection of 6 burnished iron dental forceps by Pearce, Peyps, Weiss and others, mid-19thC.
£800-900 *CSK*

A dentist's drill, c1925.
£120-170 *RGa*

A set of dental scaling instruments, with ivory handles and mirror, in plush lined leather case, 18thC, 4in (10cm) wide, and a set of scalers in a case, 19thC, 5½in (14cm) wide.
£450-550 *CSK*

A black stained ivory handle tooth key, the moulded shank stamped CAEROM**, an elevator stamped BLANC, and 2 other elevators.
£320-360 *CSK*

A burnished steel tooth key, the cranked shank with claw and chequer grip ivory handle, and 2 shaped elevators with chequer grip bone handles, one stamped Everard, early 19thC.
£300-350 *CSK*

A plaster group of a dentist and patient, The extraction, on plinth, signed J. Pinas, 13in (33cm) high.
£400-600 *CSK*

Cameras

A whole plate brass and mahogany tailboard camera, with a brass bound lens with wheel stops and inset plaque W. Watson & Sons, 313 High Holborn, London. **£300-500** *CSK*

An early dry plate model.

A quarter-plate The Albemarle Postage Stamp camera, with 9 single meniscus lenses, mounted behind a 9 pinhole mask, single metal and wood darkslide, metal photograph holder and instruction card, in maker's original box. **£370-420** *CSK*

A quarter-plate Sibyl De Luxe camera No. D186, by Newman and Guardia, London, with a Carl Zeiss Jena Protarlinse VII 22cm lens No. 167955 and 2 single metal slides, in fitted leather case. **£250-300** *CSK*

A 35mm twin lens Contaflex camera No. Y.84501, with a Carl Zeiss Jena Sucher-Objectiv f/2.8, 8cm viewing lens No. 1513358 and a Carl Zeiss Jena Sonnar f/1.5, 5cm taking lens No. 1753807, in maker's leather ever ready case. **£800-1,000** *CSK*

A mahogany and brass fitted studio camera, with a J. H. Dallmeyer 4b f/3 patent portrait lens with variable soft focus adjustment, repeating back, leather bellows and rack and pinion focusing, mounted on a mahogany studio stand with elevation and adjustable camera geared table. **£370-450** *CSK*

A Retina stereo prism attachment by Kodak A.G., Stuttgart, with sprung framefinder and instruction sheet, in maker's original box. **£130-180** *CSK*

A 35mm Olympus M1 camera No. 122910, with an Olympus M-System G. Zuiko Auto-S f/1.4 50mm lens No. 102161, in maker's leather ever ready case. **£400-450** *CSK*

The Olympus M1 camera was launched at Photokina in 1972 and was rapidly withdrawn and re-launched with the model name OM-1. Leitz had registered the M1 name in 1959. Very few of the M1 marked Olympus cameras found their way on to the open market. The lens engraving was also changed from M to OM-1.

A 35mm Widelux model FV camera No. 340815, by Panon Camera Shoko Co. Ltd., with a Lux f/2.8 26mm lens No. 46243. **£500-600** *CSK*

A 35mm Leica M2 camera No. 1004066 by E. Leitz, Wetzlar, with a Leitz Summilux f/1.4 50mm lens No. 1945430 and lens hood. **£620-670** *CSK*

A 35mm Canon IVSB camera No. 114746, with a Canon Camera Co. 50mm f/1.8 lens No. 95377, in maker's leather ever ready case.
£350-400 *CSK*

An 18 by 24mm film Ducati camera, No. 6909 with rangefinder and a Ducati Vitor f/3.5 35mm lens.
£200-300 *CSK*

A 35mm gilt and black karung leather Leica R3 Electronic camera, No. 1524066 by Leitz, Portugal, and commemorative serial No. 100-333, with a gilt and black Leitz Summilux-R f/1.4 50mm lens No. 2932005, camera top plate engraved O. Barnack, 1879-1979, in maker's fitted mahogany box, instuction booklets and guarantee cards, in maker's box.
£2,500-3,000 *CSK*

This camera was the first prize in the Barnack/Year of the Child Draw and was delivered by E. Leitz (Instruments) Limited Director A. H. Elder on Tuesday 4 March, 1980, to the winner in Wolverhampton. To commemorate the centenary of the birth of Oscar Barnack on 1 November 1879, 1,000 gold and skin covered Leica R3 and M4-2 cameras were produced. The Leitz packaging describes the camera as 24 carat gold plated, lizard skin.

A half plate mahogany wet plate sliding box camera, with removable focusing screen, lacking ground glass, single wet plate holder and a brass bound lens with rack and pinion focusing.
£850-1,000 *CSK*

Viewers

A mahogany body peep box, with 1¼in (3cm) peep hole, hinged legs, front and back mahogany panels, brass fittings and a 7 by 7in (18 by 18cm) linen backed coloured day and night engraving depicting the Thames tunnel. **£900-1,200** *CSK*

A mahogany body Designscope kaleidoscopic viewer, with lacquered brass and ebonised wood viewing column, meniscus viewing lens, 2 internal mirrors and rotating specimen tray.
£600-700 *CSK*

A mahogany body Kinora viewer, with inlaid wood decoration, ornamental embossed metal viewing hood and a picture reel No. 273 showing a white polar bear. **£620-670** *CSK*

A wood body electrically operated wall mounted stereo viewer, with gilt coloured metal decoration, white fascia and text panels proclaiming 40 different pictures, 'You see ten for 3d and 3-D Beauty Parade' featuring stereoscopic pairs of posed nude and semi-nude women.
£1,500-2,000 *CSK*

Use the Index!

Because certain items might fit easily into any of a number of categories, the quickest and surest method of locating any entry is by reference to the index at the back of the book.

SILVER
Baskets

l. A George III silver wirework sweetmeat basket, body with fruiting vine, London 1763, 6½in (16cm), 4½oz.
£400-450

r. A George III sweetmeat basket, embossed and pierced with flowers, London 1767, 6½in (16cm), 5½oz.
£500-550   *P(S)*

A George III boat shaped cake basket, the spreading foot and body pierced and engraved with bright cut scrolls, urns, flowers and foliage, with reeded border and swing handle, engraved with a coat-of-arms within a foliage surround, by Charles Aldridge 1787, 15½in (39cm) wide, 32oz.   **£3,500-4,000**   *C*

The arms are those of Ridell impaling another.

A George III sugar basket, the wirework sides with applied husk and floral swags, medallions and a monogram, engraved oval cartouche with rope twist border, swing handle, by William Pinder or William Peavy, London 1774, 4in (10cm), 5oz, with detachable blue glass liner.
£500-700   *Bon*

A George III sugar basket, with beaded edges, pierced and engraved roundels joined by foliate drapes, erect leafage and scrolls, maker's mark W P, probably William Plummer, London 1775, 5¾oz, with blue glass liner.
£650-750   *P(S)*

A George III fruit basket, engraved with Royal crown and monogram, by John Wakelin and Robert Garrard 1797, 11in (29cm) diam, 41oz.
£6,500-7,500   *C*

The monogram is that of Queen Charlotte, wife of George III.

An Edwardian flower basket, with half pierced body and base, swing handle, London 1909, 17oz.
£500-550   *GAK*

A Victorian swing handled fruit basket, with chased vine pattern edging, on spreading base, by Robert Harper, London 1863, 9½in (24cm) diam, 15.1oz.
£250-300   *Bea*

A late Victorian pierced and fluted shaped cake basket, die stamped with rococo flowers and scrolling foliage and with shell terminals, B.B., Birmingham 1899, 10½in (26cm), 12.5oz.
£360-420   *CSK*

A George III bread basket, with swing handle, engraved with the Godolphin crest and Marquess's coronet, by Peter and William Bateman, 1808, 15in (38cm) long, 34oz.
£2,000-2,500   *C*

A beaded pedestal cake basket, pierced with slats, scrolls and flowerheads and engraved with foliate swags, by Goldsmiths & Silversmiths Co. Ltd., London 1911, 11in (28cm), 19.75oz.
£320-380   *CSK*

A George III sugar basket, with beaded swing handle, London 1783, by Charles Goodwin, 5½in (14cm) high, 6oz, detachable blue glass liner.
£600-800   *Bon*

A George III silver cake basket by R & H Hennell, London 1805, 24oz.
£850-900   *SWO*

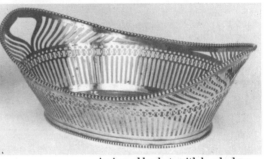

A pierced basket, with bead edges, maker's mark KB, 11in (28cm).
£250-300   *P(S)*

An Austro-Hungarian dessert basket, with platform base centred by a relief moulded pomegranate, Vienna mark, some repair, 13½in (34cm), 9½oz.   **£150-180**   *P(S)*

A foliate pierced moulded cake basket, on trefoil feet, by R. and W. Sorley, London 1913, 25.25oz.   **£700-750**   *CSK*

A George III dessert basket, later embossed and chased with rococo flowers, scrolls, and a cartouche, presentation inscription London 1817, maker Samuel Hennell, 13½in (34cm), 48oz.
£650-850   *P(S)*

A George III bread basket, engraved with a coat-of-arms, by Joseph Felix Podio, 1806, 10½in (26cm) diam, 32oz.
£2,500-3,000   *C*

A pierced basket, with beaded upper edge, by J A Hoeting, Dutch 'Foreign Made' tax mark, 11in (28cm).
£200-250   *P(S)*

Beakers

A Swiss cylindrical beaker, punched with a broad band of matting and with moulded rim, engraved with a Latin presentation inscription and a name, Sion, maker's mark possibly that of Francois-Joseph Ryss, c1700, 3½in (9cm) high, 111gr.
£3,500-4,000   *C*

A French beaker, on a chased foot, the bowl engraved with a monogram and coronet within a rococo cartouche, with a moulded rim, maker's initials possibly B.C., Paris 1744, 4in (10cm).
£900-1,200   *CSK*

A Charles I beaker, the upper part of the body engraved with strapwork and foliage, pricked and engraved with initials, maker's mark I.S. a rosette below, 1640, 3½in (9cm) high, 4oz.
£2,000-2,700   *C*

Bowls

A pair of George III small plain beakers, engraved with a crest and monogram, maker's mark M.S. or S.W., 1773, 3in (8cm) high, 5oz.
£2,500-3,000   *C*

An Irish punch bowl, by John Moore, mid-18thC, 8in (20cm).
£3,000-3,500   *P(S)*

A George III silver gilt bowl, with beaded border, London 1777, 4½in (11cm) diam, 6oz.
£300-350   *HCH*

A silver bowl, with cast figure handles, gilt interior, standing on an oval base, London, 1899, 11oz.
£300-350   *GAK*

An Edward VII punch bowl, the rim with scroll and mask edging, with reeded and beaded lower body, on spreading base, London 1901, 9½in (24cm) diam, and a toddy ladle with twisted whalebone handle, 24.2oz.
£600-700   *Bea*

A George II covered sugar bowl, by John Swift, marked on base and cover, London 1754, 6½in (16cm) high, 13oz.
£1,500-2,000   *CNY*

A Victorian rose bowl, on a spiral fluted rising foot, by Messrs Barnard, London 1888, 11in (28cm), 37.25oz.
£1,500-2,000   *CSK*

An Edwardian two-handled shaped bowl, by Gibson and Co. Ltd., 1905, 28in (71cm) long, 157oz.
£9,000-12,000   *C*

A George III punch bowl, on spreading foot and with reeded borders, by Henry Chawner, 1788, 8in (20cm), 28oz.
£2,500-3,000   *C*

A punch bowl, with everted leaf and scroll border, above foliate, scroll and shell chased sides, on domed chased circular base, crest and motto engraved to side, by The Barnards, London 1898, 12in (31cm) diam, 65oz.
£3,500-4,000   *Bon*

An Elkington & Co. fruit bowl, with elaborate pierced decoration to body and rim, outer gadrooned rim, on 3 tall claw feet, Sheffield 1906, 26oz.
£750-900   *GAK*

A silver gilt bowl, the lower part of the body with a detachable calyx of acanthus leaves, with everted reeded rim, engraved with a later crest and motto, unmarked, late 17thC, 7½in (19cm) diam, 16oz.
£3,500-5,500   *C*

A French silver gilt bowl and cover, with rosette frieze, the cover with cast floral wreath handle, Paris 1st standard mark 1819, 7in (18cm) diam, 36oz.
£4,000-4,500   *RBB*

A French sugar bowl and cover, the body cast and pierced with twin foliate scroll side handles, the fluted domed cover with strawberry finial, c1875, 8in (20cm) including handles, 13oz gross. **£400-600** *S*

A silver mounted wood mazer bowl, the everted rim with stylised foliate border, engraved with an inscription 'Week-end Aerien Arrival Rallye, 2nd Prize, September 1st 1932, Won by Roger the Seligman', foot engraved Omar Ramsden ME FCT, 1931, 6in (15cm) diam.
£1,700-2,200   *C*

A fruit bowl, with beaded wavy rim, pierced top and standing on a stepped circular pedestal base, Sheffield 1913, 15oz.
£400-450   *GAK*

Make the Most of Miller's

In Miller's we do NOT just reprint saleroom estimates. We work from realised prices either from an auction room or a dealer. Our consultants then work out a realistic price range for a similar piece. This is to try to avoid repeating freak results – either low or high

Boxes

BOXES
Please refer to the index to locate boxes elsewhere in this guide

A Queen Anne tobacco box, with moulded borders, the detachable cover engraved with a coat-of-arms, the base engraved 'Ste. Wright, Daventry', by Nathaniel Lock, 1708, 4in (10cm) long, 6oz.
£4,000-5,000 *C*

A George I tobacco box and cover, with moulded borders, the cover engraved with a coat-of-arms within shell and scroll cartouche, by Edward Cornock, 1716, 4in (10cm) long, 3oz.
£1,500-2,000 *C*

A William IV engraved cheroot case, with pull-off cover, by Henry Wilkinson & Co., stamped Wilkinson, Leeds, Sheffield 1832, 5½in (13cm) long, 10oz.
£3,500-4,500 *C*

The view on the case is of Harewood House.

A George IV snuff box, by John Bettridge, Birmingham 1823, 3in (8cm).
£250-300 *WW*

A biscuit box, with shaped sides, marked D M, S'Gravenhage, 1938, 5in (13cm).
£350-400 *P(S)*

A biscuit box, with shaped sides, marked D M, S'Gravenhage, 1938, 6in (15cm).
£320-370 *P(S)*

A Victorian card case, chased in high relief with a view of Windsor Castle amongst strolling foliage, the reverse inscribed with monogram, by Nathaniel Mills, Birmingham 1843, 4in (10cm) long, 73gr.
£500-600 *Bea*

A box, with gadrooned edges, maker's mark G.G., 1860, 6in (15cm).
£350-400 *P(S)*

A Dutch or German decorative box, the hinged cover chased with a battle scene, the body with scroll and flower panels incorporating vacant cartouches, late 19thC, 6½in (17cm) wide, 9oz.
£500-600 *S*

A silver mounted tortoise vesta box, the body with realistically cast head and feet, with hinged tortoiseshell cover, restored, London 1901, 3½in (9cm). **£320-370** *S(S)*

A Spanish spice box, on 4 cast lion's paw feet and with central hinge, gadrooned hinged covers and central detachable grater with baluster finial, Valladolid, with the mark of Juan A. Sanz de Velasco, c1780, 4½in (11cm), 438gr.
£3,700-4,200 *C*

A German silver gilt double spice box, the interior with central divider, the hinged cover engraved with latticework and scrolls on a matted ground, by Johann Pepfenhauser, Augsburg, c1735, 2in (5cm), 80gr.
£2,000-3,000 *C*

A Victorian snuff box, the cover with presentation inscription 'To Donald Davidson Esq., Columbo by a few of his early friends, in Forres', and dated '1845', by Nathaniel Mills, Birmingham 1844, 4in (10cm), 7.5oz.
£1,800-2,500 *Bea*

Starting his career as a junior in a bank in Forres, Scotland, Donald Davidson helped finance and direct many businesses throughout the world, and was held in high esteem. Mount Davidson in Virginia was named after him.

A Victorian novelty cigarette case, in the form of a letter, the name and address and franked postage stamp in enamel to the front, the reverse with a monogram, London 1883, 4in (10cm).
£280-350 *WW*

A Victorian vinaigrette, the hinged cover cast depicting a view of Westminster Abbey, by Wheeler and Cronin, Birmingham 1842, 1½in (4cm).
£470-600 *Bea*

An Edwardian silver embossed jewellery casket, with hinged cover gilded inside, with a silk lining, makers Goldsmiths and Silversmiths Co., London 1901, 17oz.
£760-820 *WW*

A Victorian silver gilt five-light Corinthian column candelabrum, engraved with a crest, motto and Viscount's coronet, by Hawksworth, Eyre Ltd., Sheffield, 1899, 27½in (70cm), weight of branches 103oz.
£3,000-4,000 *C*

A pair of Austro-Hungarian four-light candelabra, with floral moulded knops and floral moulded central finials, the capitals with gadrooned edges, Vienna 1834, 20½in (52cm), 67oz.
£1,400-1,700 *P(S)*

Candelabra

A George IV silver candelabrum centrepiece, the base with engraved coat-of-arms, crests and inscriptions: 'The Bequest of his Mother, 18th January 1833', on 3 foliate scroll feet, inscribed beneath 'Rundel Bridge & Rundell Aurifices Regis Londini', made by John Bridge for Rundell, Bridge & Rundell, fully hallmarked London 1824, 19in (48cm), 157oz.
£5,500-6,000 *HSS*

A pair of George III style three-light candelabra, chased with flutes and with reeded borders, 1933, 17in (43cm), weight of branches 50oz.
£3,500-4,500 *C*

A pair of four-light candelabra, with 3 reeded scroll branches and central light each with similar socket, detachable nozzles and central flame finial, with foliage borders, by Matthew Boulton & Co., c1815, 25in (64cm).
£4,000-4,500 *C*

511

A pair of Continental seven-light candelabra, the stems terminating in foliate sprays and scroll branches, each applied with oak leaves and acorns, L. Janesich, 19thC, 23in (59cm), 3,779gr.
£3,500-5,500   *C*

Refer to index for other candlesticks and candelabra in the lighting section

A pair of George III candelabra, the bases stamped with rams' masks, paterae and husk festoons, engraved with a crest and motto, the two-light branches similarly decorated to the candlesticks, with detachable nozzles, the candlesticks by John Carter, overstriking Sheffield marks, the branches with the mark of John Carter and a lion passant only, 1775, 16in (41cm), weight of branches 70oz.
£6,000-8,000   *C*

Candlesticks

A set of 4 George III Irish candlesticks, with 'cotton reel' nozzles and holders, made by John Walker, Dublin, c1775, 12in (30cm), 111.5oz.
£6,000-7,000   *WW*

A pair of George III candlesticks, with detachable nozzles and gadrooned borders, by William Bennett, 1814, 11in (28cm), 88oz.   **£4,000-4,500**   *C*

A pair of George III silver table candlesticks, by Matthew Boulton, Birmingham 1806, 8½in (21cm).
£1,200-1,700   *P(S)*

A pair of French candlesticks, each with stem, vase-shaped socket and detachable beaded nozzle, applied with husk swags, c1780, 11½in (30cm), 1,297gr.   **£3,000-3,500**   *C*

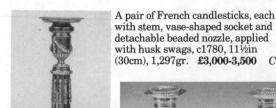

A pair of late Victorian tapersticks in the mid-18thC taste, engraved with a crest and with a waisted socket and detachable nozzle, by Henry Eyre & Co., Sheffield 1897, 4½in (12cm).
£400-500   *CSK*

A pair of Queen Anne table candlesticks, by John Elston, Exeter 1706, 8½in (21cm), 21.8oz.
£9,000-11,000   *Bea*

Three George III Corinthian column candlesticks, by William Cafe, 1764, with a pair of two-light branches, with applied acanthus foliage and central vase finials, with square wax pans and vase shaped sockets, unmarked, 17½in (45cm), 104oz.
£5,000-6,000   *C*

A set of 4 George III cluster column table candlesticks, with detachable shaped circular nozzles, by John Carter, one nozzle unmarked, 1769, 13in (33cm).
£7,500-8,500   *C(S)*

A York chamberstick, the angled handle with rectangular thumbpiece supporting detachable snuffer cone with gadrooned border, the central vase-form socket with detachable nozzle, crests engraved to base, nozzle and cone, by Robert Cattle and James Barber, fully hallmarked York 1812, 4½in (12cm), 15oz.
£700-1,000   *Bon*

A pair of George II style cast silver candlesticks, on shaped square bases with triple knopped stems, London assay, 7in (18cm), 40oz.
£1,200-1,600   *GAK*

A set of 4 Edwardian chamber candlesticks, each with scroll handle, vase-shaped socket, detachable nozzle and conical extinguisher with flame finial, with gadrooned borders, by Martin Hall & Co. Ltd., Sheffield 1901 and 1902, 6in (15cm), 34oz.   **£1,700-2,000**   *C*

Casters

A George III powder caster, with reeded girdle on square plinth base, maker's mark I.M., possibly that of John Merry, London 1789, 6in (15cm), 2.9oz.
£200-250   *Bea*

A George II inverted pear-shaped sugar caster, the pierced domed cover with baluster finial, engraved with a crest and Earl's coronet, by Samuel Wood, 1756, 10in (25cm), 22oz.   **£2,200-2,700**   *C*

The crest and coronet are presumably those of Francis, Earl of Godolphin (d. 1766), whose second daughter and sole heiress, Mary, married Thomas, 4th Duke of Leeds in 1740.

A pair of pierced silver sugar casters, with blue glass liners, by Goldsmiths and Silversmiths Co., London 1924, 5in (13cm), 5oz.
£250-300   *PCh*

A set of 4 George III style baluster casters, engraved with a crest, with pierced corners, on cast collet feet, made by Goldsmiths & Silversmiths Co., Jubilee mark, London 1935, 16oz.   **£650-750**   *WW*

513

Centrepieces

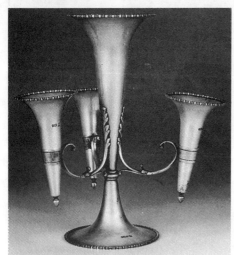

A sugar sifter, the pierced and leaf engraved pull-off cover with baluster finial, monogram engraved to side, by Harrison & Howson, Sheffield 1931, 8in (20cm), 9oz.
£250-350 *Bon*

A George V centrepiece, Sheffield 1913, 906gr.
£560-650 *HSS*

A Victorian centrepiece, the stem formed as 3 heroic female figures in Classical attire, with armorial and presentation inscription engraved to base, by Edward and John Barnard, London 1864, 108oz.
£5,500-7,000 *Bon*

A Continental two-handled centrepiece, import marks for 1897, 16in (41cm), 112oz.
£5,000-6,000 *C*

A Victorian candelabrum centrepiece, with 3 scroll branches each with wax pan and vase-shaped socket, with central foliage support for partly frosted glass bowl, engraved with a presentation inscription to Charles Manby Nainby, dated 16th April 1883, by Robert Hennell IV, 1873, 24in (61cm), 135oz.
£5,000-6,000 *C*

Accompanied by a leather-bound Testimonial.

A Victorian table centrepiece, with 6 finely engraved glass dishes, by Horace Woodward, 1873, 1874 and 1875, 17in (43cm), 93oz.
£4,500-5,000 *C*

Cups

A William IV table centrepiece, engraved with a contemporary coat-of-arms, later crest and presentation inscription, with an associated cut glass liner, by Paul Storr, also stamped Storr & Mortimer, 1833, 18½in (47cm), 110oz.
£4,000-4,500 *C(S)*

The arms are those of Hall of Dunglass, Berwickshire, impaling Walker.

A Victorian silver gilt cup and cover, the bracket handles applied with beading and foliage, the domed cover with hexagonal finial, by James Garrard, 1890, the base stamped R. & S. Garrard, Panton St., London, and with wood plinth applied with 2 silver gilt plaques, one engraved 'The Goodwood Cup, 1892', the other 'Won by Mr. Douglas Baird's 'Martagon' 5 yrs', 18½in (47cm), 163oz, in fitted box.
£10,000-12,000 *C*

514

A Victorian two-handled parcel gilt cup and cover, the foot and body chased with foliage on a matted ground, the body with 2 panels chased with views within applied gilt surround, the handles formed as standing figures of fame, the cover with standing knight in armour finial, by Stephen Smith, 1871, 27½in (69cm), 170oz.
£3,500-5,500   *C*

A Commonwealth wine cup, the bowl chased with flutes, the foot and bowl with matted oval-shaped panels, the base engraved and pricked with initials, maker's mark E.T. crescent below, 1650, 3½in (9cm), 2oz.
£9,000-10,000   *C*

Coffee Pots
Please see the Tea and Coffee Section

A German silver gilt cup and cover, with 8 flattened panels engraved with saints, 17thC, maker's mark only, I.C. a pellet below, for Johannes Clauss of Nuremberg, the standing figure finial and engraved cup rim added at a later date, 20in (51cm), 810gr.
£1,800-2,200   *C*

An Elizabethan spoon, with traces of gilding, the fig-shaped bowl with Exeter town mark, the stem with maker's mark I. Ions for John Jones, c1575, 29gr.   **£1,500-2,000**   *Bea*

Cutlery

A Charles I seal top spoon, the seal with traces of gilding and pricked with the initials P.W., the fig-shaped bowl pricked P.K. 1638, and with Exeter town mark, the stem with maker's mark E.A. for Edward Anthony, Exeter, c1638, 1.6oz.
£900-1,200   *Bea*

A seal spoon is a spoon with a finial shaped like a wax seal – sometimes even engraved like one.

l. & r. A pair of George III Onslow pattern sauce ladles, with swirl fluted shell bowls, maker Thomas Tookey, London 1769, 3.5oz.
£400-450

c. A George III Onslow pattern soup ladle, with a shell fluted bowl, the cast terminal inscribed on the reverse with initials, maker Thomas Evans, London 1772, 4.5oz.
£400-450   *WW*

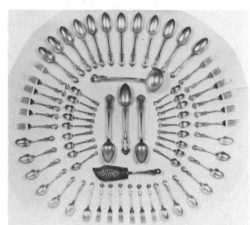

A set of Hanoverian pattern table cutlery, engraved with a crest, comprising 12 of each: 3-pronged table forks, rat tail tablespoons, 3-pronged dessert forks and rat tail dessert spoons, by J. Parkes & Co., 1914-25, 106oz.
£2,500-3,000   *C(S)*

A Victorian Albert pattern silver single-struck table service, comprising 67 pieces, by John James Whiting, 1843, 152oz.
£2,500-3,000   *P(S)*

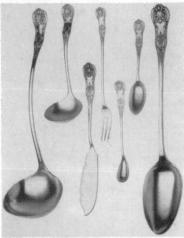

A Victorian Queen's pattern table service, comprising: 36 spoons, 24 forks, a soup ladle, a sauce ladle, a gravy spoon, a butter knife, a pickle fork and a mustard spoon, by Atkin Brothers, Sheffield 1894, 146.6oz.
£3,000-4,000   *Bea*

A composite King's husk pattern table service, each piece engraved with a crest, comprising: 66 forks, 58 spoons, a soup ladle, a cheese scoop, 56 knives, 5 carving implements and 10 fish knives and forks, in fitted wood canteen, the majority by William Eaton, 1828, 1830, etc., and modern, weight of silver 358oz.
£10,000-12,000   *C*

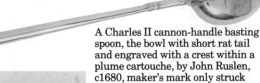

A Charles II cannon-handle basting spoon, the bowl with short rat tail and engraved with a crest within a plume cartouche, by John Ruslen, c1680, maker's mark only struck twice, 16in (41cm), 5oz.
£14,000-15,000   *C*

A graduated set of 5 George III meat skewers, crested with plain ring handles, by Richard Crossley and George Smith, London 1807, graduated in size from 13in (33cm) to 7in (18cm) long, 9.3oz.
£500-700   *Bea*

A composite silver gilt fiddle, thread and shell pattern dessert service, 1802, 1896 and modern, comprising 24 of each: dessert spoons, forks and knives, 88oz excluding knives.
£3,000-4,000   *C*

An early George V composite King's pattern table service.
£2,000-2,500   *HSS*

A set of George IV King's husk pattern table cutlery, each piece engraved with a crest and motto, comprising: 24 forks, 3 by HS Ltd., Sheffield 1920, 24 spoons, 3 by HS Ltd., Sheffield 1920, 10 teaspoons, 2 by HS Ltd., Sheffield 1920, 4 salt spoons, one by HS Ltd., Sheffield 1920, soup ladle, pair of sauce ladles, butter knife and pair of sugar tongs, by William Eley, 1825/6, weight 158oz.
£2,500-3,500   *C(S)*

The crest is that of Dunbar.

A George IV Irish knife tray, with shell and reeded border, engraved twice with a coat-of-arms and with Duke's coronet above, by James Fray, Dublin 1825, 17in (43cm), 67oz.
£3,500-4,000   *C*

The arms are those of Fitz-Gerald presumably for Augustus Frederick, 3rd Duke of Leinster (1791-1874).

Dishes

Six parcel gilt shell-shaped butter dishes, 4 by George Metheun, c1750, 2 by Sebastian and James Crespell, 1763, 4½in (11cm) long, 26oz.
£6,200-7,500   *C*

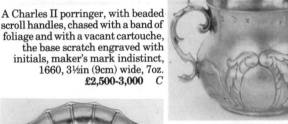

A pair of George II meat dishes, later engraved with a coat-of-arms within a rococo cartouche, by David Willaume II, 1737, 18½in (47cm) long, 114oz.
£4,500-5,500   C

The arms are those of Forde impaling Knox for Matthew Forde of Seaford, M.P. for Downpatrick and Elizabeth Knox, daughter of Thomas Knox of Dungannon, whom he married in 1750.

A Charles II porringer, with beaded scroll handles, chased with a band of foliage and with a vacant cartouche, the base scratch engraved with initials, maker's mark indistinct, 1660, 3½in (9cm) wide, 7oz.
£2,500-3,000   C

A pair of George III Irish meat dishes, each engraved with a coat-of-arms within a rococo cartouche, by John Lloyd, Dublin, c1760, 14in (36cm), 54oz.
£1,700-2,200   C

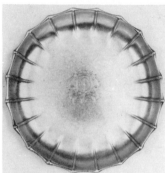

A George I strawberry dish, with lobed border, by John Hugh Le Sage, London 1720, 8½in (21cm), 14.5oz.
£5,500-6,000   P(S)

A French two-handled vegetable dish and cover, the openwork angular handles with pendant rings, the cover with detachable flower finial, engraved with a coat-of-arms, by J. B. C. Odiot, Paris, 1789-1809, 8in (20cm) diam, 1,429gr.
£3,500-4,000   C

A matched pair of George III entrée dishes and covers, engraved with armorials and crest, with gadroon edging, W. Burwash and R. Sibley, London 1807, one dish by another maker, London 1785, 10in (25cm) diam, 79oz.
£1,200-1,500   Bea

Twelve George III dinner plates, each with a gadrooned rim, engraved with the royal arms and crests, by Augustin le Sage, 1766, 9½in (24cm) diam, 196oz.
£16,000-20,000   C

Four George III soufflé dishes, each with foliage handles and gadrooned rim, engraved with a coat-of-arms, by Paul Storr, 1817, 10in (25cm) wide, 96oz.
£4,500-5,500   C

The arms are those of Osborne. The dishes were presumably made for George, 6th Duke of Leeds, but in the absence of a coronet they may possibly have been made for some other member of the family.

A Victorian butter dish, cover and stand, the sides, cover and border to the stand pierced and engraved with scrolling foliage, with vertical handles to the sides and flower finial to the slightly raised cover, by E. J. and W. Barnard, 1837, with frosted glass liner, 20oz.
£2,000-2,500   C

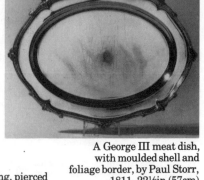

An Edward VII scallop shell shaped
dish, with chased and pierced
decoration on 3 shell feet, by Atkin
Brothers, Sheffield, 1907, 9in
(23cm) long, 10oz. **£250-350** *Bea*

A George III meat dish,
with moulded shell and
foliage border, by Paul Storr,
1811, 22½in (57cm)
long, 85oz.
£2,500-3,000 *C*

A George III Irish dish ring, pierced
with laurel swags, slats, scrolls and
scalework and with oval medallions
enclosing portrait busts, engraved
with a crest, by William Hughes,
Dublin 1773, 8in (20cm) diam, 10oz.
£2,000-3,000 *C*

*The crest is probably that of the
Dukes of Abercorn.*

A set of 4 entrée dishes and
covers, each of the detachable
finials cast as a basket of flowers,
engraved with a coat-of-arms and
crest, by Paul Storr, London,
1801, 12in (31cm)
wide, 228oz, and 4 associated
Sheffield plate, two-handled
hotwater stands on stud feet.
£15,000-18,000 *C(S)*

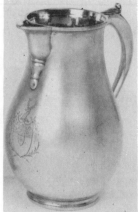

A William IV butter dish, formed as
a pail with a swing handle, the
tapering sides engraved to simulate
staves, engraved with cypher, crest
and Garter motto, by Robert
Garrard, 1834, 5in (13cm) diam,
11oz.
£2,500-3,000 *C*

*The arms are those of Gresley,
presumably for Sir Roger Gresley,
M.P. (1799-1837).*

Inkstands

An inkstandish on 4
scroll and stiff leaf
tab feet, by Mappin
& Webb, London
1925, 10in (25cm),
24oz.
£500-550 *HCH*

A William IV inkstand, fitted with
3 silver mounted clear glass bottles,
the detachable covers chased with
scrolls, foliage and rocaille
ornament, 2 pierced with circular
apertures, by Edward Farrell, 1836,
13in (33cm) long, 59oz.
£3,500-5,500 *C*

A Victorian 2 bottle inkstand, with
2 pen depressions and 2 festoon
chased well holders, with
detachable flame finial covers, on
foliate paw corner panel supports,
fully marked, by Edward Barnard &
Sons, London, 1864, 11in (28cm)
wide, 36oz.
£2,000-3,000 *S*

*The inscription reads, 'Presented to
the Revd. Richard Joseph Farren
Lambert by the Parishioners of
Beckford with Ashton Underhill
annexed, on his leaving that parish,
as a mark of esteem for his Christian
piety & generosity especially to the
poor, during the 4 years he was
Curate, July 1865'.*

Jugs

A George III beer jug,
engraved with a
coat-of-arms,
maker's mark
erased, 1780,
7in (18cm) high, 21oz.
£2,500-3,500 *C*

A George II beer jug, with baluster drop to the curved lip and harp shaped handle, engraved with a coat-of-arms, coronet and motto, by William Darker, 1729, 7½in (19cm) high, 24oz.
£5,500-7,500   *C*

The arms are those of Yorke impaling Cocks for Philip, Baron Hardwicke, later 1st Earl of Hardwicke (b. 1690), and his wife Margaret, daughter of Charles Cocks of Worcester whom he married on 16 May 1719. He became Baron Hardwicke on 23 November 1733 and was elevated to the Earldom on 2 April 1754. He was appointed in 1746 Lord High Steward of England and was one of the Lords Justices for the administration of the Government during the King's absence in 1740, 1748 and 1752.

A pair of Victorian silver mounted claret jugs, each with cylindrical neck, bracket handle, moulded spout and hinged domed cover with lion rampant thumbpiece, the covers each engraved with a coat-of-arms, by C. F. Hancock, 1882, 10½in (27cm) high.
£6,000-7,000   *C*

A pair of Victorian silver gilt mounted glass claret jugs, the neck mounts chased on a matted ground, beaded borders and openwork finials to the domed covers, by W. and G. Sissons, Sheffield, 1869, in fitted wood case, 9½in (24cm) high.
£5,000-5,500   *C*

A George IV silver gilt cream jug, on 3 feet, engraved with a Royal crest and Garter motto, by Paul Storr, 1820, 10oz.
£3,500-4,500   *C*

A Victorian silver mounted claret jug, with bracket handle, shell spout and hinged domed cover with baluster finial, chased with bands of foliage and engraved with a crest, by William Gough, Birmingham, 1869, 11in (28cm) high.
£1,200-1,700   *C*

Mugs & Tankards

A Charles II tankard, the body with applied band and with scroll handle, cherub's mask and scroll thumbpiece and flat topped hinged cover, engraved with a coat-of-arms within plume mantling, by Robert Cooper, 1683, 7in (18cm) high, 27oz.
£7,500-9,000   *C*

A George II tankard, the body with applied rib and with scroll handle, hinged domed cover and scroll thumbpiece, engraved with a coat-of-arms, by John Langlands, Newcastle 1757, the cover unmarked, 7½in (19cm) high, 25oz.
£2,200-2,700   *C*

A James II tankard, with scroll handle, hinged domed cover and corkscrew thumbpiece, engraved with a coat-of-arms within foliate scroll mantling, possibly by Alexander Roode, 1685, 7in (18cm), 27oz.
£4,700-6,000 *C*

A George I tankard, the body with applied rib and scroll handle, hinged domed cover and corkscrew thumbpiece, the handle engraved with initials, by Henry Jay, 1718, 7in (18cm), 27oz.
£4,000-4,500 *C*

A George II tankard, the body with applied moulded band and with scroll handle, hinged domed cover and corkscrew thumbpiece, the handle engraved with initials SP, by John Payne, 1754, 7½in (19cm) high, 27oz.
£2,500-3,000 *C*

A George II tankard and cover, on moulded rim foot, the domed cover with corkscrew thumbpiece, engraved with a coat-of-arms in a Baroque cartouche, by John Fossey, 1733, 7in (18cm), 27oz.
£2,500-3,500 *C*

A George III tankard, the body with applied rib and with scroll handle, hinged domed cover and corkscrew thumbpiece, engraved with initials, by Charles Wright, 1772, 8in (20cm), 24oz.
£2,200-2,700 *C*

A George II pint mug, engraved with a monogram, the underside scratch engraved with initials, maker's initials T.W. or J.W., London 1748, 5in (13cm), 14oz.
£550-650 *CSK*

A pair of George II mugs, with leaf capped double scroll handles, Whipham & Wright, London 1759, 4in (10cm), 16oz.
£1,200-1,700 *CSK*

A George I tapering lidded quart tankard, with scroll handle and later added spout, the body later chased and embossed with a battle scene, maker's mark indistinct, London 1718, Britannia Standard, the spout bearing Victorian hallmarks for London 1878, 7in (18cm), 30oz.
£2,200-2,700 *CSK*

A George III Newcastle tankard, with applied band to belly, scroll handle, the domed hinged cover with volute scroll thumbpiece, later chased with scrolls and flowers and leaves, by John Longlands, 1769, 7in (18cm) high, 20oz.
£1,700-2,000 *Bon*

A George II baluster tankard, with
scroll handle, hinged domed cover
and openwork scroll thumbpiece, by
John Payne, 1754, 8in (20cm) high,
30oz.
£3,000-3,500   *C*

A late George II baluster mug, later
chased with rococo flowers and
scrolling foliage and later engraved
with an armorial and crest, Gurney
and Cooke, London 1756, 5in
(13cm), 11.25oz.
£600-650   *CSK*

A George III tankard, on spreading
foot, the body with applied rib and
with scroll handle, hinged domed
cover and corkscrew thumbpiece, by
John Payne, 1763, 7in (18cm) high,
26oz.
£2,500-3,000   *C*

A George II silver lidded tankard,
the handle with triad initials
M.R.H., the front with engraved
interlaced initials of later date,
London 1759, maker B.C., lid fully
marked, handle with maker's mark,
7in (18cm) high, 23oz.
£1,200-1,700   *HSS*

A Queen Anne tankard, with scroll
handle, hinged domed cover and
bifurcated thumbpiece, by Seth
Lofthouse, 1705, 7in (18cm) high,
27oz.
£3,500-4,500   *C*

A pair of George III tankards, each
with bands of reeding and with
bracket handle, hinged flat cover
and pierced thumbpiece, engraved
with a coat-of-arms, the covers
with crest and monogram, by
Henry Chawner, 1789, 7½in
(19cm) high, 57oz.
£4,000-4,500   *C*

A George III baluster mug, later
chased with scrolls, flowers and
foliage, with leaf capped double
scroll handle, by John Langlands
and John Robertson, Newcastle
1790, 5in (13cm) high, 11oz.
£500-550   *Bea*

An early Victorian campana shaped
half pint mug, with gilt interior, by
John Evans II, London, 1839, 5in
(13cm), 6.5oz.
£500-600   *WW*

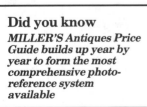

A Victorian lidded trophy jug,
engraved all over, with mare and
foal finial, by Robert Hennell,
London 1861, 13½in (34cm) high,
54oz.
£2,000-3,000   *Bea*

A Queen Anne style tankard, the
flat cover with inscription and twist
thumbpiece, scroll handle and
moulded foot rim, by Carrington &
Co., London 1920, 27.5oz.
£600-700   *WW*

A Victorian gilt lined baluster quart
tankard, with double scroll handle,
chased and embossed with rococo
flowers, and with contemporary
presentation inscription, Houles &
Co., London 1868, 8in (20cm), 22oz.
£1,200-1,500   *CSK*

Salts

A pair of George III salts, each on
4 claw and ball feet, with blue glass
liners, one damaged, by Robert
Hennell, London 1786, 3in (8cm)
long, 3oz.
£160-220   *Bea*

A set of 4 early George III salts, with
gilt interiors, on hoof feet, by David
Hennell, London 1762, 12oz.
£450-500   *WW*

A pair of Victorian salts, in the form
of an hour glass, each applied with a
coat-of-arms and Royal monogram,
the detachable tapering cover with
beaded finial, by James Garrard,
1897, 5in (13cm) high, 12oz.
£3,500-4,000   *C*

*The applied arms are those of the
Salter's Company and the salts were
made to commemorate Queen
Victoria's Golden Jubilee.*

A pair of Victorian salt cellars in the
form of sacks, engraved with
initials, by John Charles Edington,
London 1867, 2in (5cm), 7.3oz.
£850-950   *Bea*

A pair of George III salts, initialled,
with blue glass liners, maker's mark
W.A., London 1781, 3in (8cm) long,
2.6oz.
£200-250   *Bea*

A set of 4 Victorian salts modelled as
figures, each on textured base,
comprising gentleman and female
companion in 18thC dress and a
peasant boy and girl, by E & J
Barnard, London 1863, 8in (20cm)
high, 63oz.
£12,500-15,000   *GA(W)*

A pair of Victorian salts, with blue
glass liners, open chased cast
frames, with rococo scrolls and floral
swags, by Elkington & Co.,
Birmingham 1852, 8oz.
£250-300   *WW*

A set of 4 Victorian salts, with
spoons and blue glass liners, in
fitted case, London 1888, 2½in (6cm)
diam, the spoons 1884/5, 6.6oz.
£300-400   *Bea*

A set of 4 George IV silver salt
cellars, by Richard Cooke, London
1802.
£1,200-1,600   *P(S)*

A pair of Victorian salt cellars, each
on cast simulated coral and seaweed
base and with detachable shell
shaped bowl, by John Mortimer and
John S. Hunt, 1845, 4in (10cm)
wide, 22oz.
£4,000-4,500   *C*

A pair of early Victorian
salt cellars, each cast in
the form of a scallop
shell, on 3 dolphin feet,
maker's mark
overstruck with that of
Joseph and Albert
Savory, 1837, 3in (8cm)
wide, 14oz.
£3,700-4,500   *C*

A matched set of 4 George III salts,
on 4 claw-and-ball feet, with 4 blue
glass liners, maker's mark
indistinct, London 1774 and 1776,
3½in (9cm) long, 7oz.
£450-550   *Bea*

Salvers

A salver, with shaped gadrooned
border, on 3 volute scroll feet, crest
and motto engraved to centre, by
Edward Viner, Sheffield 1961,
12½in (31cm), 29oz.
£350-400   *Bon*

A George III salver, on 4 reeded
scroll feet and with reeded border,
by William Bennett, 1802, 19½in
(49cm), 97oz.
£4,500-5,500   *C*

The arms are those of Gordon.

A Victorian silver Georgian style
salver, with shaped Chippendale
border, the centre with a
coat-of-arms, with gentleman's
helm, Turk's head crest and motto:
'Nemo me impune lacessit', on
4 scroll feet, makers W.C.J.L., made
for Goldsmiths and Silversmiths
Company, 112 Regent Street,
London, 1895, 23in (59cm), 132oz.
£650-750   *HSS*

A set of 4 George III waiters, each on 3 openwork curved feet, engraved with a crest within an oval bright cut cartouche, by John Carter, 1769, 7in (18cm), 32oz.
£4,500-5,500 *C*

A George III salver and a pair of matching waiters, each on 3 leaf capped scroll feet, by Ebenezer Coker, 1765 and 1761, 12 and 7in (31 and 18cm), 51oz.
£2,000-2,500 *C*

The arms are those of Carpenter impaling another, probably Edgecumbe, for Benjamin Carpenter of Mount Tavy and his wife Patience Edgecumbe.

A pair of George III waiters, engraved at the centre with a crest within a gadroon border, on 3 scroll feet, by John Wakelin and Robert Garrard, London 1792, 7½in (19cm), 23.3oz.
£1,500-2,000 *Bea*

A Victorian salver, on 3 scroll supports, by George Richards and Edward Brown, London 1863, 12½in (31cm), 44.6oz.
£550-650 *Bea*

A George III salver, on 4 slightly curved feet and with beaded borders, bright cut engraved with floral swags, the centre engraved with 2 coats-of-arms within drapery mantling, maker's mark of Thomas Lowndes and Edward Lycett overstriking another, 1786, 20in (51cm), 108oz.
£5,000-6,000 *C*

A salver with Chippendale border, on 4 tab feet, Chester 1911, 14in (36cm), 38oz.
£350-400 *HCH*

A Victorian salver, engraved at the centre with a vacant cartouche within a reeded foliate border, on 3 pierced scrolling supports, by Walker and Hall, Sheffield 1894, 14½in (37cm), 32.9oz.
£400-450 *Bea*

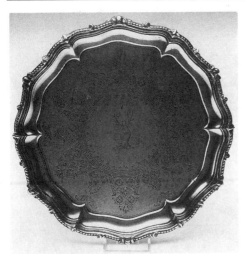

A Victorian salver, on 3 pierced
acanthus supports, by E. J. J. &
W. Barnard, London 1870, 9in
(23cm), 15.2oz.
£350-400   *Bea*

A pair of George III salvers,
engraved with armorials with an
applied cast and pierced border of
tied drapes and foliate oval
medallions, with beaded edging, on
3 feet, by Robert Jones and John
Scofield, London 1775, 9½in (24cm),
33.4oz.
£1,200-1,700   *Bea*

Sauceboats

A pair of George III Irish
sauceboats, each on cast spreading
foot and with leaf capped scroll
handle and gadrooned rim,
engraved with a coat-of-arms, by
Robert Calderwood, Dublin, c1760,
8in (20cm) long, 33oz.
£7,500-8,000   *C*

A pair of George II sauceboats, each
on 3 scroll and hoof feet, with
shaped rims and foliage capped
scroll handles, by Joseph Sanders,
1746, 16oz.
£4,500-5,000   *C*

A pair of George II fluted
sauceboats, engraved with a
coat-of-arms, by John Jacobs, 1739,
7in (18cm) long, 29oz.
£6,200-7,200   *C*

A pair of George III sauceboats,
maker's mark indistinct, 1763, 9in
(23cm) long, 30oz.
£3,500-4,500   *C*

An American
sauceboat, on 4
scroll feet,
complete with
detachable
liner, by
Tiffany & Co.,
c1900, 8½in
(21cm) wide,
25oz.
£1,300-1,700
C(S)

A pair of George III
sauceboats, each on 3
shell feet and with
quilted scroll handle
and gadrooned rim, by
William Cripps, 1763,
8in (20cm), 28oz.
£6,000-7,000   *C*

Services

A George IV partly fluted tea and coffee service, comprising a teapot and coffee pot, with covers with foliage finial, two-handled sugar basin and cream jug, each engraved with a crest, by John Wrangham and William Moulson, 1827 and 1828, 79oz.
£3,000-4,000   *C*

A six-piece tea and coffee service, with ebony handles, bearing London and Birmingham assays 1903, by Mappin and Webb, 137oz. **£1,600-2,000**   *P(M)*

A Victorian four-piece tea and coffee service, by Frederick Elkington, London, 1888, 67.9oz.
£1,700-2,200   *Bea*

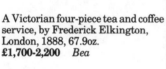

A William IV three-piece tea service, of inverted baluster shape with everted rim, rose and scroll repoussé, on scalloped pedestal foot, London 1831, 48oz.
£650-750   *HCH*

A four-piece tea service, by James Dixon, Sheffield, 1873/1874, 72oz.
£1,200-1,500   *P(M)*

A four-piece tea and coffee set of circular footed form, makers Walker and Hall, Sheffield 1921, 1926 and 1933, 61½oz. **£750-850**   *P(S)*

A George VI four-piece tea and coffee service with a two-handled tray, Sheffield hallmarks for 1939, 160oz.   **£2,000-2,500**   *MAT*

A George V four-piece tea service, with tongue and bead edging, the ribbed bodies decorated with scrolls and acanthus, maker's mark G. Ltd., Sheffield 1931, 65.5oz.   **£650-750**   *Bea*

An Edward VII/George V
three-piece tea service, the teapot
with ivory finial and scroll handle,
London 1908/11, 39.2oz.
£650-750   *Bea*

A George III three-piece tea service, comprising a
teapot, a matching two-handled sugar basin and cream
jug, each with gilt interior, by Alexander Spence, Edinburgh,
1807-10, 37oz.   **£750-850**   *C(S)*

A three-piece tea service in
Georgian style, comprising
teapot, cream jug, sugar
basin, London,
1915, 32oz gross.
£400-450   *GAK*

Trays

A George III tea tray, with reeded
edge and handles, on 4 reeded and
scrolled feet, by John Crouch and
Thomas Hannam, London 1791,
22in (56cm) long, 82oz.   **£2,500-3,000**   *GAK*

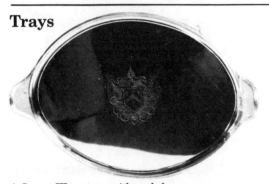

A Victorian tea tray, the border moulded with
shells and scrolls, with presentation inscription
dated 31st December 1906, by Mappin and Webb,
Sheffield 1905, 121oz.   **£1,800-2,500**   *P(S)*

Tureens

A George IV two-handled tray, on
4 shell, foliage and scroll feet, and
with shell, foliage and gadrooned
border, and similar detachable
handles, by Samuel Hennell, 1823,
28½in (73cm) long, 165oz.
£5,000-6,500   *C*

A French two-
handled soup tureen,
cover and stand,
the stand on 4 lion's paw feet,
and with a foliage and beaded
frieze, the cover with rosette
cone finial on a palm leaf and
ground, with narrow
foliage borders and plain
liner, by Jean-Nicolas
Boulanger, Paris, c1800,
14in (36cm), 6,950gr.
£9,000-10,000   *C*

A Victorian tray, on 4 bun feet, with
foliate pierced rim and bracket
handles, bright cut engraved with a
broad band of foliage and
latticework and with a monogram,
by Martin Hall & Co. Ltd., Sheffield
1899, 23½in (60cm) long, 99oz.
£2,000-2,500   *C*

A George III sauce
tureen, crested,
by Paul Schofield,
London 1789,
20oz.
£1,200-1,700   *WW*

A pair of George IV entrée dishes and covers, with flower and foliage borders and similar detachable ring handles, by Marshall & Sons, Edinburgh 1829, 11½in (29cm) long, 112oz.
£4,000-5,000 *C*

A George III style soup tureen and cover of navette form, with looped handles and applied reeded rim, on oval spreading base, London 1902, 54oz.
£1,200-1,700 *P(M)*

A George II quilted two-handled soup tureen and cover, with leaf capped gadrooned scroll handles, the domed cover with similar handle, by Peter Archambo and Peter Meure, 1756, 15½in (40cm) long, 100oz.
£9,000-11,000 *C*

A set of 4 George III sauce tureens and covers, with lion's mask and drop ring handles, each with gadrooned borders and engraved with a coat-of-arms and crest, by John Troby, 1806, 6½in (16cm) long, 93oz.
£5,500-6,000 *C*

The arms are those of Bell impaling another.

Miscellaneous

A pair of George III two-handled sauce tureens and covers, with beaded borders, loop handles and domed covers with urn finials, engraved with a crest, by Thomas Daniell, 1785, 44oz.
£3,500-4,500 *C*

A Victorian nurse's buckle, chased and pierced, London 1898, 6in (15cm) long, 4.2oz.
£200-250 *Bea*

A Continental vase, chased and embossed on a matted ground, London imports for 1899, 10½in (27cm), 23oz.
£700-800 *C(S)*

A George IV silver gilt nutmeg grater, with hinged rasp and container, engraved with Garter motto, crown and monogram GR, by Philip Rundell, 1823, 7in (18cm), 5oz.
£5,000-6,000 *C*

A miniature cow creamer, with hinged oval opening lid to the back of the animal, Chester 1907, 4in (10cm), 2oz.
£400-500 *P(M)*

A Victorian serviette ring, by Atkin Brothers, Sheffield 1899.
£50-60   *TVA*

A serviette ring, with engine turned decoration, Birmingham 1931.
£40-50   *TVA*

An octagonal serviette ring, with engine turned decoration, Birmingham 1921.
£50-60   *TVA*

A pomander formed as a skull, the interior divided into 6 compartments beneath 2 hinged covers, on flat link suspension chain, 17thC, 1½in (4cm).
£900-1,500   *C*

A measure, with moulded borders and tapering cylindrical handle with ring top, engraved with a monogram and coat-of-arms, marks not identified, a script B struck twice and another mark also struck twice, c1800, 4in (10cm) diam, 16oz.
£2,500-3,000   *C*

A George III ear trumpet, with a reeded band to the mid section, by Phipps & Robinson, London 1796, 9½in (24cm).
£2,500-3,000   *C(S)*

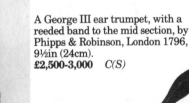

A George II baluster brandy saucepan, with moulded rim and lip and turned wood side handle, engraved with initials, by Robert Bailey, 1729, 6oz gross.
£650-850   *C*

A two-handled replica of the Warwick Vase, the body chased and applied with masks, lions' pelts, foliage and trailing vines, with vine tendril handles and ovolo rim, by Barnard Brothers, on silver-mounted square ebonised wood plinth, the plaques engraved with coats-of-arms, inscription and dates, 1908, 10½in (27cm), 118oz.
£4,500-5,500   *C*

One coat-of-arms is that of the Turners' Company, the other that of William Moore Shirreff, the recipient of the vase.

A pair of George III spurs, of typical form, engraved on the interior E. Agassiz, Exmouth, each applied with a pair of chains, buttons and buckles, by John Faux and George Love, London, c1770, 2½in (7cm), 3oz.
£500-550   *S(C)*

A pair of Victorian grape scissors.
£250-280   *DM*

A pair of William IV cast
naturalistic sugar nips, oak bough
decorated, makers William
Theobalds, London 1834.
£150-200   *WW*

An Edwardian silver-mounted
pencil sharpener, fitted with a
drawer to catch the shavings, A.B.,
London 1908, 4in (10cm).
£700-750   *CSK*

SILVER PLATE

Candlesticks

A pair of George III silver gilt grape
scissors, with reeded and vineous
handles and crowned Newcastle
crest, makers Eley & Fearn, date
letter missing, 3½oz.
£300-400   *GSP*

A pair of old Sheffield plate three-light
candelabra, the central light with
detachable flame finial, c1810, 20in
(51cm).
£1,000-1,500   *C*

A set of 4 table candlesticks, the sockets
with detachable nozzles, monograms
engraved to stems, by S. C. Younge and
Company, Sheffield 1821, 11in (28cm).
£2,500-3,500   *Bon*

A pair of five-light candelabra, each in
Corinthian column form, 21in (53cm).
£850-950   *P(S)*

A pair of early Victorian Sheffield plate
bedroom candlesticks, with leaf scrolls
to the borders, the spool shaped
candleholders with detachable nozzles,
the crested handles with detachable
extinguishers, c1840.
£400-500   *WW*

A Sheffield plate candelabrum
centrepiece, the 4 detachable scroll
branches each with vine border and
vase-shaped sconce, lacking glass liner,
c1830, 18½in (47cm).
£750-850   *C(S)*

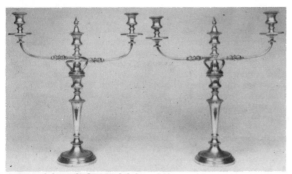

A pair of three-light candelabra, 20in (51cm).
£450-550 *P(S)*

Tureens

An Old Sheffield plate soup tureen and cover, with reeded loop handle, crest to cover and coat-of-arms to side, c1850, 17in (43cm) diam.
£1,000-1,500 *Bon*

Miscellaneous

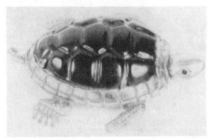

A Dutch silver gilt tobacco box, early 18thC.
£800-900 *P(S)*

A set of 6 Sheffield plate meat dish covers, with gadrooned rims, and detachable shell and foliage ring handles, by Matthew Boulton & Co., c1830.
£1,700-2,000 *C(S)*

A novelty vesta in the form of a turtle, with embossed tortoiseshell back, the head and shoulders hinged, 2in (5cm).
£40-60 *HSS*

An electroplate and cut glass centrepiece.
£2,000-2,500 *Bea*

A soup tureen with 2 stags head handles, ladle with hoof handle and cover with fawn finial, beaded borders, 19thC, 13in (33cm).
£550-650 *E*

A Dixon's patent 24oz. spirit flask, in the form of a leather bound book, with EPNS leaves and quarters, the spine entitled 'A Pleasant Surprise'.
£250-300 *LAY*

A Victorian folding biscuit box, c1880, 10½in (27cm).
£480-580 *TG*

Make the Most of Miller's

Every care has been taken to ensure the accuracy of descriptions and estimated valuations. Price ranges in this book reflect what one should expect to pay for a similar example. When selling one can obviously expect a figure below. This will fluctuate according to a dealer's stock, saleability at a particular time, etc. It is always advisable to approach a reputable specialist dealer or an auction house which has specialist sales

TEA & COFFEE

Ever since tea and coffee were introduced into Britain in the mid-17thC there has been, in addition to the actual tea and coffee pots, an array of equipage which was necessary in their making. Just as roasters and grinders were necessary for coffee, canisters, kettles, strainer spoons and sugar nips for example, were necessary for tea.

The early silversmiths were clearly aware of the commercial opportunities created by the need for tea and coffee accessories as also have all the pottery, porcelain and silver plate manufacturers ever since.

Unfortunately, it is such a big subject that we cannot hope to include all the equipage in this edition.

For coffee we have majored on silver coffee pots whilst for tea, the greater presentation is made on caddies and caddy spoons, tea kettles and urns, teapots and strainers.

It is only natural that as time passes certain items such as sugar nips, ratafia glasses, drip-catchers and even tea cosies can be forgotten, however fashionable they may have been in their day.

A good way for the new collector to understand more about tea and coffee equipment and accessories is to study the 'tea and coffee portrait' paintings which became a popular genre in the paintings of the 18th and 19thC. Such pictures as the poet John Gay and his sisters taking tea (V & A) or the 'Coffee Portrait' by Januarius Zick, Archiv fur Kunst und Geschichte Berlin, proved that tea and coffee had taken its place as an official element of European culture.

Caddy Spoons

These delightful spoons (alas no longer required with a teabag) originated from the strainer spoons which were considered such an essential part of early tea making equipage.

The early Chinese tea canisters with their high rounded turrets used pull off caps which doubled as measures, but since it is easier to measure tea out into a teapot by spoon – rather than shaking – the bowl of the strainer spoon (albeit pierced) would have been used.

This multi-purpose object would not only take tea out of the canister (no other spoon shape would fit into the narrow necks of early caddies) but also acted as a strainer as the tea was poured, and if that was not enough, you could dislodge with the pointed stem any tea leaves stuck in the spout.

The change to the shape associated with the caddy spoon came about around 1760 when the caddy openings became larger and they accepted the broad shell shaped caddy spoon more easily for use within the area of the caddy itself. It is reasonable to suggest that the British, preferring stronger tea to the Chinese, would wish to use more tea and it is significant that as the caddies became more open at the top the strainer spoons disappeared and the caddy spoon emerged triumphant.

A rare collection of English caddy spoons, dating from 1799-1809.
£40-500 each *TBC*

A Victorian leaf bowl caddy spoon, with a hollow vine decorated handle, by George Unite, Birmingham 1869.
£150-200 *WW*

A Victorian caddy spoon, by Hunt and Roskell, London 1867.
£300-350 *WW*

> ### Make the Most of Miller's
>
> *In Miller's we do NOT just reprint saleroom estimates. We work from realised prices either from an auction room or a dealer. Our consultants then work out a realistic price range for a similar piece. This is to try to avoid repeating freak results – either low or high*

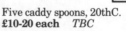

Five caddy spoons, 20thC.
£10-20 each *TBC*

These inexpensive caddy spoons could prove to be an ideal start to a collection.

Coffee Pots

When coffee first came to these shores from the Middle East in the early 17thC it was made by boiling after the Eastern tradition with either the Baghdad boiler, the Ethiopian Jabena, or the Turkish Ibrik.

In the coffee houses however, the coffee made in bulk over the fire grates was decanted into serving pots of ewer shape as depicted on coffee house tokens of the time. To the English silversmith it would have been easier to produce a tapering cylinder or beer tankard shape for coffee with a single seam and this became the mode for our first coffee pots.

Originally, to facilitate serving, the handle was at right angles to the spout, but gradually, as coffee began to be served in the home and people no doubt helped themselves at the table (servants served from a standing position) the handle was made opposite the spout. Ceramic coffee pots followed a similar course.

A George I coffee pot, engraved with armorials, with wood scroll handle, on a base with scratch weight 28:18 and initials I.S., maker's mark worn, Robert Timbrell and Joseph Bell, London 1714, 10½in (26cm) high, 29.1oz gross.
£6,000-8,000   *Bea*

Provenance: By descent in the Hoare family, traditionally known as part of the Kelsey plate. Charles Hoare, born 1767, purchased the estate of Luscombe, near Dawlish. He died in 1851 and bequeathed his property to his nephew, Peter Richard Hoare, of Kelsey Park, near Beckenham, Kent.

A George II coffee pot, with leaf capped fluted curved spout, hinged domed cover and baluster finial, engraved with a coat-of-arms within a rococo cartouche, the base with initials, by John Swift, 1742, 9in (23cm) high, 23oz gross.
£3,000-4,000   *C*

A George IV coffee pot, chased and embossed, engraved with a coat-of-arms, by Benjamin Smith, London 1825, the matched stand on 3 cast foliate feet, complete with burner, 13in (33cm) high, 63oz.
£3,700-4,200   *C(S)*

The arms are those of Bogle. When such pots as this had a support inside for a linen bag to contain the coffee and were held on a spirit heater they were frequently called biggins.

A Staffordshire coffee pot, c1765, 7in (18cm) high.
£3,500-4,000   *JHo*

A Leeds coffee pot, painted with the Miss Pitt decoration, c1780, 9in (23cm).
£2,200-2,600   *JHo*

A Liverpool coffee pot and cover, painted in underglaze blue, iron red and gilding within trellis pattern rims, Philip Christian's factory, c1770, some damage, 9½in (24cm) high.
£350-400   *CSK*

A baluster coffee pot, with an ebonised wood scroll handle, in the French 18thC taste, S.W.S. & Co., London 1920, 7in (18cm), 25.25oz.
£400-450   *CSK*

A George III coffee pot, with Newcastle hallmark, c1755, 8½in (21cm) high, 19.5oz.
£350-450   *HCH*

A George III coffee pot, with a shell polished wood double scroll handle and gadrooned domed hinged cover with spiral twist finial, one side engraved with an armorial within a rococo foliate cartouche, the other side engraved with a crest, maker's initials I.K. with a pellet between, London 1770, 10½in (26cm) high, 29.75oz.
£3,000-4,000   *CSK*

A George III coffee jug on stand with burner, by Paul Storr, London 1803, 13in (34cm), 53.5oz.
£5,500-6,000   *WW*

A George II coffee pot, with curved spout, waisted hinged cover and baluster finial, engraved with a coat-of-arms and flat chased with bands of scrolls, shells, strapwork and latticework, by John White, 1737, 8½in (21cm) high, 24oz.
£3,000-4,000   *C*

An early George III baluster pattern coffee pot with repoussé and chased decoration and blackwood scroll handle, 8in (20cm) high, 18oz.
£1,500-2,000   *P(M)*

A Staffordshire saltglazed coffee pot, c1765, 8½in (21cm) high.
£2,500-3,000   *JHo*

A George II embossed and chased coffee pot, the spout with rocaille decoration, wood scroll handle, by Fuller White, London 1751, 10in (25cm) high, 26.5oz.
£2,000-2,500   *P(S)*

Posters

A further way to study the history of tea and coffee is through its associated ephemera.

A Horniman's Almanac, 1887.
£100-130   *TBC*

An International Stores calendar advertising Ceylindo Tea, 1908.
£100-120   *TBC*

An advertisement for Indian tea depicting Queen Victoria offering tea to President McKinley of the United States, 1897.
£200-250   *TBC*

A Mazawattee Tea Calendar, 1927.
£100-120 *TBC*

A tea chest label, late 19thC.
£100-130 *TBC*

Labels on tea chests were necessary to identify the particular consignment of teas.

The front cover of a song sheet for Lewis's Beautiful Tea, early 20thC.
£100-130 *TBC*

Tea & Coffee Services

Towards the end of the 17thC tea and coffee services on trays became popular, with a servant carrying a tray into the drawing room, stating the social standing of the owners.

A four-piece silver tea set and tray, Mappin and Webb, c1948.
£6,500-7,000 *NH*

A Worcester boxed set of coffee cups and saucers, signed and painted by Harry Stinton, with gilt interiors and 6 silver gilt spoons, marked in puce, date code for 1931.
£2,700-3,500 *P(M)*

A New Hall topographical part tea and coffee service, each piece printed and painted in colours with country views or views of stately homes, some named, gilt line edges, comprising: 8 tea cups, 7 coffee cans, 8 saucers, milk jug, sucrier and cover, slop bowl, teapot stand, saucer dish, some faults, one saucer marked in brown with New Hall within rings, some pieces with puce pattern No. 984, the slop bowl with puce 'fern leaf' and pattern No. 984, 29 pieces.
£800-1,000 *P(S)*

A Victorian tea and coffee service, retailed by Hunt & Roskell, late Storr, Mortimer & Hunt, London 1850, 64.5oz.
£1,700-2,000 *WW*

A Sèvres monogrammed part tea service, printed with the gilt initials LP, the handles and rims enriched with gilding, comprising a teapot and cover, a milk jug, 2 sugar bowls and covers, 5 tea cups and 7 saucers, blue printed marks, some damage, various dates, iron red Château de Tuileries marks, incised marks, c1840.
£500-700 *C*

535

A four-piece silver tea set, by Georg Jensen, designed by Johan Rohde, c1950.
£6,500-7,000 *NH*

An English porcelain part miniature tea service, painted in colours and signed Leighton, comprising a lobed hexagonal teapot and cover, a lobed milk jug, 6 cups and saucers, gilding slightly rubbed.
£320-370 *CSK*

A Staffordshire part tea and coffee service, pattern No. 586, mid-19thC.
£1,000-1,500 *DN*

A Meissen Hausmalerei part tea service, painted in underglaze blue in the Oriental style, enriched in overglaze enamels in the workshop of F. J. Ferner, the borders and underglaze blue decoration enriched with gilding, comprising: a teapot and cover, 4 tea bowls and saucers, with blue crossed sword marks, various painter's initials and numerals, various Dreher's marks and Pressnummern, some damage, the porcelain c1735, the decoration c1750.
£2,000-3,000 *C*

A Japanese export five-piece silver tea set and tray, c1880.
£18,000-20,000 *NH*

A five-piece tea service, with cut card type trefoil terminals, Sheffield 1935, with a matching two-handled tray of oval form with piecrust border, London 1936, 3,599gr total.
£1,600-2,000 *HSS*

A Chinese export silver four-piece tea service with tongs, each engraved with initial, except tongs, in fitted wood box, late 19thC, teapot 5½in (14cm) high, 37.5oz.
£3,000-3,500 *CNY*

A George IV Irish three-piece tea service, by James Fray, each piece richly repoussé and engraved with an armorial crest, Dublin 1826, 1,543gr.
£1,200-1,700 *HSS*

A five-piece tea and coffee set, each piece of square baluster form with broad lobes, wooden handles and finials, the coffee pot Utrecht 1963, maker's mark VKB, the remainder Utrecht 1940/41, maker's mark VKG.
£700-1,000 *P(S)*

An Edwardian Scottish composite eight-piece tea and coffee service, each piece engraved with a crest of a fly above the motto 'Non Sibi', comprising teapot, coffee pot, hot water jug and kettle, all with covers, ebony finials and handles, slop basin, two-handled sugar basin and milk jug and a large two-handled fitted tray, of rounded quatrefoil form, Glasgow 1903/4, by R. and W. Sorley, tea and coffee service, 2,904gr.
£2,200-2,600 *HSS*

A Coalport fluted part tea service, painted between bands in pink and gilding, comprising a teapot, cover and stand, a milk jug, a slop bowl, a sugar bowl and cover, a bread plate, 11 teacups, 4 coffee cans and 10 saucers, some damage.
£550-850 *CSK*

Locate the source

The source of each illustration in Miller's can be found by checking the code letters below each caption with the list of contributors

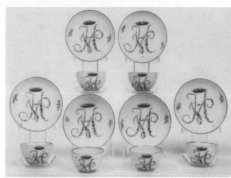

A set of 6 Meissen monogrammed tea cups and saucers, painted with garlands of flowers forming the initials VH beneath a gilt and iron red coronet, flanked by sprays of blue flowers, enriched with gilding, some damage, blue crossed swords and dot marks, blue Bs to cups, various Pressnummern to saucers and 18 to cups, c1770.
£1,500-2,000   *C*

FURTHER INFORMATION
For further information on the subject of Tea and Coffee Equipage, contact:-
The Bramah Tea Collection
3 Oakmount Road
Chandlers Ford
Hampshire SO5 2LG
Tel: (0703) 269443

Tea Caddies

It is not only because caddies take up such little space both to collect and display that we feature them so prominently in this section. They represent all the changes in style for the 18th and 19thC and the popularity and passing of different materials can be studied with total fascination. Tea canisters, tea chests and caddies represent so much of our history.

It was the tea canister from China that came first. Being made of china, silver, tin or pewter they combined the dual function of keeping the tea fresh and a means by which it could be measured out in their pull-off caps.

A fashion developed for placing two or three canisters together in what became known as a tea chest which frequently included sugar nips, a sugar strainer spoon and teaspoons.

The tea 'caddy', being simply a box for tea, came along later in the 18thC and the word is a corruption of 'catty' the Malayan Kati which is about 1⅓lb of tea, which is a convenient measure for packing.

Apart from the essential need to keep tea fresh, the tea chest and caddies coincided with the extremely high cost of tea and so the tea was kept under lock and key. Silver examples date mostly from the 18thC when silversmithing was at its best.

In addition to china and silver caddies, the materials used for either the total constitution or decoration included paper, papier mâché, tortoiseshell, ivory, glass, enamel and a whole host of woods for general marquetry and exotic veneers.

An English blue and white tea caddy, c1750, 4in (10cm) high.
£700-800   *JHo*

A pair of George II silver tea caddies and matching sugar bowl, the caddy covers now pierced and surmounted by cast rocaille finials, by Samuel Taylor, marked on bases, caddies London 1748, 6in (15cm) high, sugar bowl 1749, 5in (13cm) high, 29oz.
£2,000-2,500   *CNY*

A shagreen three-division tea caddy, with spoon compartments, the interior velvet lined, with brass handle and escutcheon plate, on paw feet, 11½in (29cm) wide.
£250-300   *CSK*

A George III silver sugar box and matching tea caddy, with a similar tea caddy, each marked on base and cover, by Pierre Gillois, London 1760 and 1765, each 5½in (14cm) high, 30oz.
£2,000-3,000   *CNY*

A Queen Anne silver tea caddy, by Samuel Thorne, London 1703, marked on side, cover and cap, 5in (13cm) high, 7oz.
£4,700-5,200   *CNY*

A George III silver tea caddy, marked on base and cover, by Pierre Gillois, London 1763, 5in (13cm) high, 8.5oz.
£750-1,200   *CNY*

A George II silver tea caddy, the hinged cover with a cast foliate finial, the sides and cover repoussé and chased with a wave pattern, marked on base and cover, by William Cripps, London 1756, 6in (15cm) high, 12.5oz.
£2,000-3,000   *CNY*

A commemorative tea caddy, depicting George III and Queen Charlotte, c1762, 6in (15cm) high.
£1,000-1,200   *JHo*

A Worcester porcelain tea canister and cover, 18thC.
£300-400   *DM*

A Queen Anne tea caddy and detachable cover with shaped finial, the base engraved with initials, by Ebenezer Roe, 1711, 5in (13cm) high, 6oz.
£2,000-2,500   *C*

A pair of George III enamel tea caddies and a matching sugar box, the caddies inscribed 'Green' and 'Bohea', each enamelled green with 4 polychrome painted landscape scenes surrounded by gilt rocaille, South Staffordshire, c1760, caddies 4in (10cm) high and sugar box 3½in (9cm) high.
£7,000-8,000   *CNY*

Please refer to index for boxes elsewhere in this book

A Worcester tea jar, decorated in colours with the thunder and lightning pattern, c1770.
£150-250   *TBC*

539

A pair of George II tea caddies and a
matching sugar box, the caddies
each with sliding base and cover, the
sugar box on 4 bracket feet, each
engraved with a coat-of-arms within
a rococo cartouche, maker's mark
W.A., contained in a silver mounted
shagreen case on 4 claw and ball
feet, 1756, caddies 5in (13cm) high,
43oz.
£12,500-13,500   C

*The arms are those of Medley
quartering and impaling others.*

A George III fruitwood tea caddy, in
the form of an apple, 4in (10cm)
high.
£800-1,000   CSK

A set of 2 George II tea caddies and a
sugar bowl and cover, the caddies
with sliding bases and cap covers
with shell finials, the sugar bowl on
foliage foot, with domed cover and
bud finial, engraved with a
coat-of-arms and motto and a crest
and motto, by Samuel Taylor, 1748,
with 2 Hanoverian rat tailed
teaspoons, 1887 and a pair of pierced
sugar tongs, c1780, in a silver
mounted fitted wood case, 41oz.
£8,000-9,000   C

*The arms are those of Reid impaling
Clayton for General Sir Thomas
Reid G.C.B. who married in 1835
Elizabeth, daughter of John Clayton
of Enfield Old Park, Middlesex, the
crest and motto are those of Reid.*

A yew veneered and tulipwood
banded tea caddy, the cut corners
with boxwood inlay, the cover and
front with conch shell paterae, late
18thC, 5in (13cm) wide.
£600-700   CSK

Two George II
silver tea caddies,
in a shagreen case,
both with
gadrooned rims,
case with silver
furniture and
later velvet lining,
one by Samuel
Taylor, one
unmarked,
London, c1745,
6in (15cm) high,
25.5oz.
£3,000-4,000   CNY

A pair of George III silver tea
caddies, each marked on base and
cover, maker's mark WT, probably
William Tuite, London 1773, 5in
(13cm) high, 17.5oz.
£1,500-2,000   CNY

A set of 3 bombé tea caddies
and sugar box, by Pierre Gillois,
1755, 33oz.
£5,500-6,000   C

A pair of George II silver tea caddies and a matching sugar box, in shagreen case with hinged cover opening to a velvet lined fitted interior with silver gadrooning, the exterior mounted with silver furniture, marked on bases and covers, by John Sidaway, caddies and sugar box marked WA, London 1759, each 5in (13cm) high, 31oz.
£2,500-3,000 *CNY*

A pair of black japanned and mother-of-pearl inlaid tole peinte tea canisters, with mother-of-pearl mosaic, gilt decoration to neck and lid, some damage, early 19thC, 19in (48cm).
£1,000-1,200 *S(C)*

A George III silver tea caddy and a sugar basket, the caddy surmounted by a figure of a Chinese man, marked in interior, the sugar basket with a red glass liner, marked on the base, in a shagreen case with brass furniture and fitted with a velvet lined interior, c1771, caddy 5in (13cm) high, basket 5in (13cm) diam, 15.5oz.
£3,500-4,500 *CNY*

The maker's mark ED in script may be an unrecorded mark for Edward Darvill, a maker of tea caddies in this period.

A George III silver tea caddy, on 4 foliate scroll feet, marked on base and cover, by William Vincent, London 1768, 5½in (14cm) high, 11oz.
£1,000-1,700 *CNY*

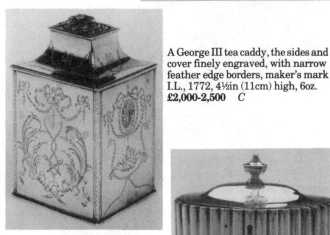

A George III tea caddy, the sides and cover finely engraved, with narrow feather edge borders, maker's mark I.L., 1772, 4½in (11cm) high, 6oz.
£2,000-2,500 *C*

An ivory veneered and tortoiseshell strung tea caddy of decagonal outline, with mother-of-pearl inlaid swag and silver mounts, later re-lined, late 18thC, 4in (10cm) wide.
£1,000-1,200 *CSK*

A George III tea caddy, the cover with urn finial and engraved crest over monogram, marked on base and cover, by William Vincent, London 1785, 5in (13cm) high, 13oz.
£1,500-2,000 *CNY*

A George III silver tea caddy, with an iron lock, marked on base and cover, by Henry Chawner, London 1793, 6in (14cm) high, 12oz.
£3,000-3,500 *CNY*

A wood and paper filigree caddy, early 19thC.
£600-700 *TBC*

A Georgian mahogany and satinwood shell inlaid tea caddy, with fitted interior and 2 glass containers with plated tops.
£700-900 *RID*

A tortoiseshell and mother-of-pearl tea caddy, the hinged top enclosing 2 compartments, on bun feet, in need of restoration, 19thC, 7in (18cm) wide.
£400-450 *S(C)*

A Victorian silver plated tea caddy, on a scrolled base, unmarked, after Paul de Lamerie, 19thC, 5½in (14cm) high.
£450-550 *CNY*

A Regency tortoiseshell tea caddy, the covers with turned ivory handles, the whole outlined and crossed with pewter stringing, upon 4 ball feet, 5in (13cm).
£600-700 *Bon*

A George III silver tea caddy, with inscription 'In remembrance/A mother's gift', and script initials centering a crest, marked on base and cover, by Thomas Holland, London 1806, 5in (12cm) high.
£1,000-1,500 *CNY*

A pair of George III tea caddies, in a fitted silver mounted and ivory case inlaid with flowers and foliage, by Robert Garrard, 1819, the silver mounts also 1819, 35oz.
£10,000-12,000 *C*

The design of these caddies follows that of a set by Thomas Heming of 1752 which is a variation of a model by Paul de Lamerie of 1751. It was later used by a number of goldsmiths including Frederick Vonham in 1763.

A quality veneered tea casket, mid-19thC.
£800-1,000 *TBC*

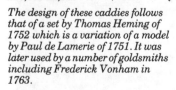

A pair of George II silver tea caddies, by Samuel Herbert & Co., London, marked on base, 1752, 5in (13cm) high, 14.5oz.
£1,700-2,200 *CNY*

The arms are those of Williams-Wynn impaling those of another.

A Georgian mahogany tea caddy, inlaid with stained and coloured woods, with classical columns and medallions containing stylised oak leaves, the hinged cover opening to reveal a zinc lined interior, slight damage, 5in (13cm) high.
£200-250   *HSS*

A Regency burr yew fitted tea caddy, the sides applied with brass lion's mask and ring handles, on 4 brass lion's paw feet, the interior with 2 covered compartments, c1815, 7in (18cm) wide.
£300-400   *CNY*

An early Victorian tortoiseshell tea caddy, the hinged top enclosing 2 compartments, on ivory bun feet, c1840, 7in (18cm) wide.
£600-650   *S(C)*

A George III satinwood and mahogany fitted tea caddy with painted scenes, the compartment covers also painted with reserves labelled 'Bohea' and 'Green', within polychrome bouquets, c1790, 8in (19cm) wide.
£1,500-2,000   *CNY*

A George III silver tea caddy, with an iron lock, marked on base and cover, by Paul Storr, London 1793, 5in (13cm) high, 13.5oz.
£4,500-5,000   *CNY*

A George III fruitwood tea caddy, in the form of a pear, with associate turned ivory knop and steel escutcheon, 7½in (19cm) high.
£1,500-2,000   *Bon*

A George III silver tea caddy, marked on base and cover, by Hester Bateman, London 1789, 5in (13cm) high, 13oz.
£2,000-3,000   *CNY*

A George III tortoiseshell veneered tea caddy, 8in (20cm).
£600-700   *DN*

A George III inlaid yew double tea caddy, the compartment with 2 later covers, the cover and front inlaid with green stained and shaded harewood oval panels, one with fox and grapes and one with heron, the edges with inlaid banding, c1800, 7in (18cm) wide.
£900-1,200   *CNY*

Two George II and George III engraved tea caddies, one by Edward Wakelin, c1755, maker's mark and lion passant only, the other by J. Langford and J. Sebille, 1764, 28oz.
£4,000-5,000   *C*

A Victorian silver tea caddy, engraved with armorials, marked on base, cover and finial, cover with French import control mark, by John Edward Terrey, London 1844, 7in (18cm) high, 35oz.
£1,500-2,000   *CNY*

A late Victorian tortoiseshell veneered tea caddy, the sides with foliate silver handles, the lid with foliate pierced mount, shield shaped escutcheon, raised on bun feet, the mounts with Chester assay office hallmark 1894, 5in (13cm) wide.
£1,500-2,000   *CSK*

A Victorian tortoiseshell veneered and pewter strung 2 division tea caddy, of pagoda shape, the interior with lidded compartments, 9in (23cm) wide.
£900-1,200   *CSK*

A pair of Regency silver tea caddies, marked on side and cover, by Samuel Hennell, London 1819, 5in (13cm) high, 20.5oz.
£2,000-3,000   *CNY*

The arms are those of Lees of Blackrock, Dublin, created baronets in 1804.

A promotional caddy, made by Maling for Ringtons Tea Company, early 20thC.
£100-170   *TBC*

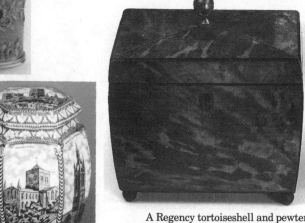

A Regency tortoiseshell and pewter strung tea caddy, interior with 2 lidded compartments, raised on 4 ball feet, 6in (15cm) wide.
£700-800   *CSK*

A William IV 2 division tortoiseshell and pewter strung tea caddy, inlaid with foliate cut mother-of-pearl, pillars to the corners, on shaped base with ivory ball feet, 8in (20cm) wide.
£1,200-1,500   *CSK*

A Regency tortoiseshell veneered 2 division tea caddy, the bow front profusely inlaid with foliate cut brass scrolls, the cover with ball handle, 7in (18cm) wide.
£1,500-2,000   *CSK*

A Regency octagonal tortoiseshell and ivory outlined tea caddy, the lid with silvered loop handle and escutcheon plate, 5in (13cm) wide.
£950-1,200   *CSK*

A Continental silver tea canister, 19thC, 5in (12cm).
£300-350   *HSS*

A Russian silver tea caddy, marked on the base St. Petersburg, 1786, assaymaster Nikifor Moshchalkin, 5in (13cm) high, 9oz.
£1,000-1,500   *CNY*

A George III green stained tortoiseshell and ivory outlined tea caddy, the lid inset with a gold crest, the interior with 2 lidded compartments, 7in (18cm) wide.
£1,800-2,000   *CSK*

A pair of George III tea caddies and matching sugar box, finely cast and chased in the Chinese Chippendale manner, with hinged covers and lizard handles, by Peter Taylor, in original shark skin covered box, scroll handle and pierced escutcheon, London 1747, 4in (10cm) high, 53oz.
£18,000-20,000   *RBB*

An early Victorian tortoiseshell veneered, pewter strung serpentine fronted tea caddy, the cover and front inlaid with mother-of-pearl and haliotis shell designs of song birds amidst foliage, on bun feet, 9in (23cm) wide.
£900-1,200   *CSK*

A Regency boxwood, herringbone banded and paper scroll tea caddy, of navette shape, 8in (20cm) wide.
£600-700 *CSK*

A French glass tea caddy, late 19thC.
£350-450 *TBC*

A Meissen tea caddy and cover, brightly painted in underglaze blue, crossed swords in blue, minute chip, c1735, 4½in (11cm).
£3,000-3,500 *S*

A George IV silver double tea caddy, marked on side and covers, by Joseph Cradock and William K. Reid, London 1825, 7in (18cm) wide, 27oz.
£1,500-2,000 *CNY*

An Austro-Hungarian sugar box or tea caddy, with gilt interior, lock, and maker's mark AK, Vienna 1858, 6in (15cm), 12.25oz.
£350-400 *P(S)*

A Regency Scottish silver tea caddy, fitted with an iron lock, marked on base, by William & Patrick Cunningham, Edinburgh 1818, 6½in (16cm) high, 26oz.
£1,000-1,500 *CNY*

An Austro-Hungarian caddy, the cover with a baluster finial, upper border embossed paterae and husk chains, foliate panel feet, with gilt interior, maker's mark R.O., 5in (13cm) wide, 9.25oz.
£250-350 *P(S)*

A Meissen ormolu mounted tea caddy, painted, beneath a gilt line rim, blue crossed swords mark, the ormolu mount inscribed Escalier de Crystal Paris and the cover cast with foliage, gilding rubbed c1740, 5in (12cm) high.
£2,000-2,500 *C*

A Chinese black lacquer tea caddy inlaid with mother-of-pearl, the top enclosing a well with 2 silk-lined trays, the sides with carrying handles, on a later ebonised stand with square tapering legs, 19thC, 17in (43cm).
£800-1,000 *C*

A late Victorian tortoiseshell veneered tea canister.
£500-600   *HSS*

A Victorian burr elm tea caddy, with rosewood interior, fitted with 2 cut glass caddies and an open sugar bowl, mid-19thC, 14in (36cm) wide.
£350-450   *CNY*

A Russian silver mounted cut glass tea caddy, the silver cap chased with a foliate guilloche border and engraved with a monogram and coronet lifting above a silver rim and inner cover, the mounts marked with the Imperial warrant of Faberge, Moscow, 1899-1908, 6in (15cm) high.
£1,000-1,700   *CNY*

A Chinese silver and enamelled tea canister, made in Peking, c1880.
£1,750-2,200   *HP*

A Meissen Kakiemon tea caddy, painted with sprays of peony and chrysanthemum and scattered insects, the sides each with a flying phoenix and the shoulders with iron red flower heads, Pressnummer 49, c1740, 4in (10cm) high.
£900-1,200   *C*

A Regency silver plated tea caddy, on 4 lion's paw feet, the front engraved with a coat-of-arms, the fitted interior with a pair of caddies and a cut glass sugar bowl, marked on base, c1815, 13½in (34cm) wide.
£1,500-2,000   *CNY*

A Russian silver tea caddy, marked Moscow, maker's mark Cyrillic G L, c1890, 5in (13cm) high, 13oz.
£900-1,500   *CNY*

A tortoiseshell veneered tea caddy, late Georgian, 8in (20cm) wide.
£700-750   *HSS*

Make the Most of Miller's

CONDITION is absolutely vital when assessing the value of an antique. Damaged pieces on the whole appreciate much less than perfect examples. However a rare, desirable piece may command a high price even when damaged

---

An Indian Colonial silver tea caddy, with wood finial, the sides decorated with 4 reeded bands, the front with script monogram, fitted with iron lock, by William Henry Twentyman, marked on base, c1820, 5in (13cm), 18oz.
£2,000-2,500 *CNY*

A Chinese export carved ivory tea caddy, the cover and sides relief-carved, on 4 claw and ball feet, the hinged cover opening to 2 compartments, 19thC, 9½in (24cm) long.
£750-1,000 *CNY*

Tea & Coffee Urns

In spite of their size, urns especially in silver, are outstandingly elegant. The boiling water – or made tea or coffee poured inside – could be kept hot by the red hot iron bar, dropped into a socket inside the urn, or by charcoals kept in the base from which hot air rose through a tub inside the urn, extending up to the lid.

A Scottish coffee urn, on leaf capped shell and paw cabriole supports, with serpent handles and plain spigot with ebony handle, by Hugh Gordon, other marks rubbed, Edinburgh, c1750, 11in (28cm), 53oz.
£1,700-2,000 *C(S)*

A German japanned tea urn, mid-19thC.
£3,000-3,500 *PC*

A German two-handled fluted pear-shaped coffee urn, the customary 3 taps have been removed, the cover has a later plated Walpole crest finial and the body is engraved 'Ye lucke of Walpole', by Johann Georg Kloss, Augsburg, 1747/1749, 12in (31cm).
£2,000-2,700 *C*

A George III silver chinoiserie tea urn, with 2 branch handles and a dolphin-form spigot with wood grip, the cover with a cast finial of a Chinaman, the front engraved with a coat-of-arms within rocaille cartouche, marked on body, base and cover, by Thomas Whipham and Charles Wright, London 1767, 20in (51cm), 97oz.
£10,000-13,000 *CNY*

The arms are those of Daubuz impaling those of Powderdon.

A George III vase shaped tea urn, with foliate scroll handles, shaped tap and detachable cover, engraved with a coat-of-arms within a foliate scroll cartouche, on later detachable wood base, by Daniel Smith and Robert Sharp, 1771, 20in (51cm), 107oz. excluding wood base.
£3,500-4,500 *C*

The arms are those of Stanmore, Middlesex, quartering Port, of Poole, Co. Dorset.

A Staffordshire tea urn, late 19thC.
£150-200 *TBC*

A George III tea urn, the cover with bud finial, with egg and dart and foliage borders and circular detachable lamp, engraved with a coat-of-arms, crest and motto, by Benjamin Smith, 1819, the spirit lamp by Paul Storr, 1812, 15½in (40cm), 181oz.
£4,000-5,000   *C*

The arms, crest and motto are those of Neeld, for Joseph Neeld, the great-nephew and principal beneficiary of Philip Rundell's will, from whom he inherited some £900,000 in 1827. He was M.P. for Chippenham from 1830 until his death in 1856, a governor of his old school, Harrow, from 1828 until 1836, and a member of many learned societies, including the Society of Arts, and the Royal Geographical Society.

A George III coffee urn, on 4 ball feet, with drop ring handles, detachable domed cover and spirally fluted finial, the interior with detachable sleeve, by Peter and Ann Bateman, 1799, 14in (36cm), 43oz.
£2,000-2,500   *C*

Tea Kettles

Since tea was made in the mid-18thC by the lady of the house the constant supply of hot water was catered for by the magnificent tea kettles which filled the delicate teapots. Through the years the tea kettle shape followed the teapot exactly, except for capacity. With the handle above and the tripod table and spirit heater and tray below they stood in total splendour. Towards the end of the 18thC however, the tea kettle was usurped by the tea urn, which with the convenience of a tap was more accurate in its use.

A George III partly fluted tea urn, engraved with a coat-of-arms, the cover with a crest, by John Wakelin and William Taylor, 1785, 18½in (47cm), 110oz.
£5,000-5,700   *C*

The arms are those of Robinson impaling Harris, for the Hon. Frederick Robinson, second son of the 1st Baron Grantham who married Catherine Harris.

A George III silver tea urn, with 2 beaded loop handles and a beaded spigot with stained bone grip, on 4 ball feet, the rim, shoulder and base applied with beaded borders, the front engraved with an oval cartouche enclosing a coat-of-arms in a shield, marked on base, body and cover, by Robert Hennell, London 1781, 13in (33cm), 95oz.
£2,500-3,500   *CNY*

A Japanese silver tea kettle with Shakudo style decoration, c1880.
£3,650-4,000   *NH*

A silver tea kettle, by Richard Gurney, London, 1756.
£3,000-3,500   *DGA*

A Queen Anne tea kettle, stand and lamp, with scrolling swing handle and detachable lamp, engraved with a coat-of-arms in Baroque cartouche, the kettle by John Jackson, 1708, the stand and lamp, c1710, maker's mark only, probably that of William Fawdery, 11in (28cm), 51oz.
£7,000-7,500   *C*

TEA KETTLES

★ made from silver or other metals
★ a vessel intended for boiling water at the table
★ designed to sit over a spirit lamp

A Tetsubin tea kettle, mid-19thC.
£200-250 *TBC*

A Victorian silver tea kettle, stand and burner, fully marked, by George John Richards, London 1851, 16½in (42cm), 75.5oz.
£1,600-1,800 *P(S)*

A German ceramic tea kettle and cover, the body moulded in relief in the Chinese style, the body covered with a red-glazed imitation cinnabar lacquer, chipped, impressed marks, 12½in (32cm).
£100-120 *CSK*

A George II inverted pear-shaped tea kettle, stand and lamp, the kettle with scalework and mask spout, partly wicker covered scroll swing handle and hinged domed cover with wrythen finial, the kettle and lamp engraved with a coat-of-arms, by John Jacobs, 1754, 15in (38cm), 76oz.
£3,500-4,500 *C*

A Tetsubin cast iron tea kettle, mid-19thC.
£300-400 *TBC*

Teapots

Teapots originated in China then went to Japan when a glazed stoneware became the accepted pottery of the Tea Ceremony. Holland was the first European country to see tea porcelains which arrived with the tea which served as the pattern for later productions in both china and silver wares made in Holland, Germany, France and England.

A George III silver teapot, with a hinged cover, an ebonised finial and carved wood handle, by Hester Bateman, marked on base and cover, 5½in (14cm), 12oz.
£1,200-1,700 *CNY*

A silver teapot with chinoiserie decoration, after Chinese export silver model, made by I. E. Terry, 1682 London hallmarks, 1816.
£6,000-6,500 *TBC*

A rare Worcester polychrome teapot and cover, painted with the spinning maiden pattern, with iron red saw-tooth borders, minor damage, c1760, 6in (15cm).
£1,200-1,700 *S*

A Chinese 'famille verte' porcelain teapot, with scroll spout and handle, Kang Hsi, 5in (12cm).
£1,800-2,200   *P(S)*

A Meissen painted teapot and cover, with wishbone scroll handle picked out in gilt, minor chips to knop, crossed swords in underglaze blue, c1760, 3in (7cm).
£600-800   *S*

An American silver tank teapot with similar milk and water tanks, early 1920s.
£12,000-15,000   *NH*

Make the Most of Miller's

CONDITION is absolutely vital when assessing the value of an antique. Damaged pieces on the whole appreciate much less than perfect examples. However a rare, desirable piece may command a high price even when damaged

A Meissen teapot formed as a crowing cockerel, with black, grey and brown plumage, the exotic tail forming the handle and open beak the spout, with iron red wattle and comb beneath a feathered crest, tip of open beak missing, Pressnummer 4, c1740.
£3,000-3,500   *C*

A late George III teapot, with melon fluted ivory finial, raised on 4 ball feet, by T. Robins, London 1811, 498gr.
£350-400   *HSS*

A Japanese earthenware teapot, with cream coloured body, painted in enamels and gilt with wisteria, butterflies and garden flowers, partially rubbed seal mark in gilt, possibly of Meizan, 4in (10cm) high.
£350-500   *HSS*

An early Victorian teapot with floral finial, on scroll cast feet, by Reiley & Storer, London 1843.
£450-500   *P(M)*

A George III silver teapot, with carved wood handle and turned wood finial, by Paul Storr, London, 1793, marked on base and cover, 6in (15cm) high, 15oz.
£1,500-2,000   *CNY*

551

A Regency ogee teapot, chased in
high relief, the cover with cast oak
apple finial, scroll wood handle, on
maiden head/paw feet, by Edward
Cornelius Farrell, London 1817,
24oz.
£900-1,200   *WW*

A George III teapot, with elongated
tapering spout and fruitwood scroll
handle with spur thumbpiece,
matching stand on claw and ball
feet, maker's mark RG, Edinburgh,
with incuse duty mark, 1784, 6in
(15cm), 21oz.
£2,000-2,500   *C(S)*

An English creamware teapot and
cover, painted in puce monochrome,
with leaf handle terminals enriched
in puce and green, restored, c1775,
5in (13cm).
£200-300   *CSK*

A George III teapot with
ebonised wood scroll handle,
wood finial, bright cut with
floral and foliate swags and
later engraved with a
monogram, by John Emes,
London 1804, 5in (13cm),
16.5oz.
£550-650   *CSK*

A George IV silver teapot of
compressed circular form, maker's
mark WH London 1823, 25.75oz.
£400-450   *P(S)*

A George III silver teapot, part
fluted, London 1812.
£300-350   *P(S)*

l. A Victorian silver teapot, London
1856.
£500-550
r. A Victorian silver teapot, by
Charles Thomas Fox and George
Fox, London 1841.
£250-300   *P(S)*

An Austro-Hungarian teapot of
compressed melon shape, with ivory
scroll handle, Vienna 1839, 8in
(20cm) diam, 26oz.
£500-550   *P(S)*

Tea Strainers

Three single cup tea strainers, complete with retaining chains, the forerunner of the teabag, 20thC.
£3-5 plated
£50+ each silver *TBC*

A non-drip plated strainer, the drip catching base is automatically weighted to stay directly below the strainer, early 20thC.
£50-100 *TBC*

A selection of tea strainers, 20thC.
£5-50 each *TBC*

Two spring single cup tea makers, mid-20thC.
£5-10 each *TBC*

An unusual pair of ceramic tea strainers, 19thC.
£100-130 *TBC*

A plated self-balancing tea strainer, ensuring that all drips are caught in the bottom basin, early 20thC.
£50-100 *TBC*

A silver strainer and stand, mid-20thC.
£80-120 *TBC*

Miscellany

A Victorian silk velvet and beadwork tea cosy, of typical form, the purple silk velvet ground applied with thistles and flowers on one side and Tudor roses and flowers on the other, the interior of quilted purple silk, with beaded carrying handle, 19thC, 15in (38cm) wide.
£250-300 *CNY*

Space prohibits us from showing more than one tea cosy in this section!

We wish to pose the question, where is all the miscellaneous tea and coffee equipment?

WINE ANTIQUES

A George III mahogany cellaret, the veneered and rosewood crossbanded top now enclosing a compartment tray, the sides applied with swing handles, on supports of square section with casters, c1790.
£1,200-1,500 *S(C)*

A George III mahogany cellaret-on-stand, the hinged top enclosing compartments on a reduced stand with moulded supports, c1800.
£600-650 *S(C)*

A rosewood liquor cabinet, containing 4 decanters and 12 glasses, the sides inlaid with beechwood lines, c1900, 11½in (29cm) wide.
£600-700 *S(C)*

A late George III mahogany brass bound cellaret on stand, with crossbanded and fruitwood strung hinged lid, with later fitted interior between brass carrying handles, the stand possibly associated, 17½in (44cm) wide.
£1,500-2,000 *CSK*

A late George III mahogany and inlaid cellaret, the hinged lid enclosing a fitted interior, on a fluted banded base, adapted, 25½in (65cm) wide.
£1,500-2,000 *CSK*

A William IV mahogany cellaret, with stepped hinged lid, the interior with compartments, with panelled front on turned reeded legs headed by capitals, with brass caps, 27in (69cm) high.
£1,200-1,500 *C*

A Regency mahogany sarcophagus shaped wine cooler.
£1,800-2,500 *SWO*

A pair of mahogany brass bound wine coolers, zinc lined, 18thC, 14in (36cm) diam. **£3,500-4,000** *McC*

A George III brass bound mahogany wine cooler, the lead lined interior with zinc liner, the ends with brass carrying handles, on square tapering legs with brass caps, 26½in (68cm) wide.
£2,500-3,000 *C*

A George III brass bound mahogany wine cooler, the rim banded in fruitwood, with lead lined interior, the ends with brass carrying handles, 19in (48cm) wide.
£1,800-2,200 *C*

A William IV mahogany wine cooler with later fitted interior, on lotus leaf carved turned feet, stamped W. & C. Wilkinson, 14 Ludgate Hill, 18854, 32in (81cm) wide.
£750-950   *CSK*

W. & C. Wilkinson, a well-known firm of furniture makers of this period who have recorded work at Lowther Castle and Goldsmiths Hall, used this particular stamp from c1830-40.

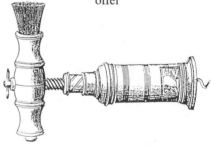

A pair of Sheffield plate two-handled wine coolers, engraved with a coat-of-arms, complete with liners, by Roberts Smith & Co., c1830, 11in (28cm) high.
£1,500-2,000   *C(S)*

A pair of campana shaped wine coolers, the reeded handles issuing from Bacchus masks, complete with liners and associated frosted glass bowls, 10½in (27cm) high.
£4,500-5,000   *C(S)*

A French silvered bronze wine cooler, shaped as a wave with a sea nymph rising to blow her shell trumpet, fitted with 4 light fixtures, marked with the initials N Y, late 19thC, 26½in (68cm) high.
£3,000-3,500   *C*

A pair of Georgian lacquered wine coasters, the sides painted in gilt with a running vine leaf border, 5in (13cm).
£250-300   *Bon*

WINE COOLERS OR WINE CISTERNS

★ a wine cooler is a container designed to hold wine bottles and water or ice
★ it has a lead lining
★ wine coolers have been in use from Tudor times, in silver, marble, granite or solid mahogany
★ they had to be massive until c1760 to hold wide wine bottles, and then became increasingly deep

A pair of George III wine coasters, pierced with slats and with gadrooned borders and wood bases, each engraved with a crest, by Thomas Jackson, 1772.
£3,000-4,000   *C*

A pair of Sheffield plate wine coasters, with everted fluted sides with applied vine borders and turned wooden bases, c1860, 7in (18cm).
£300-350   *Bon*

Five London delft bin labels named for Sherry and
Champaign in manganese, and Cyder, Perry and Lisbon
in underglaze blue, pierced for hanging, some restorations,
c1780, 5½in (14cm) long.
£1,000-1,400 *C*

Four George III wine coasters, with
trelliswork sides and gadrooned
borders, the silver bases engraved
with a coat-of-arms in plume
mantling, by W. Burwash and
R. Sibley, 1810.
£8,000-9,000 *C*

*The arms are those of Henchman or
Hinchman, Co. Northampton.*

A Battersea enamel and gilt metal
mounted wine funnel, the white
ground painted in puce with sprays
of flowers, 18thC, 3½in (9cm).
£350-400 *CSK*

A pair of Sheffield plate wine
coasters, each with scalloped
foliate pierced edges, scroll and
bead embossed edge, and
turned wood base, 6in (15cm).
£120-170 *HCH*

A George III Irish silver wine
funnel and stand, by
James le Bas, Dublin,
1822, 4.5oz.
£150-200 *RID*

A pair of silver wine coasters, with
turned fruitwood bases, Sheffield,
1925, 5in (13cm).
£550-600 *HCH*

A wine funnel with embossed decoration,
by Charles Fox, London 1818.
£350-400 *HSS*

A brass barrelled King's
Screw corkscrew with bone
handle and steel side
winding handle, applied
with a Royal coat-of-arms
plaque, the brush lacking.
£300-350 *CSK*

A nickel plated A1
double lever
corkscrew, by
James Heeley &
Sons Ltd.
£150-200 *CSK*

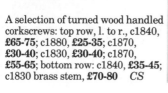

A selection of turned wood handled
corkscrews: top row, l. to r., c1840,
£65-75; c1880, **£25-35**; c1870,
£30-40; c1830, **£30-40**; c1870,
£55-65; bottom row: c1840, **£35-45**;
c1830 brass stem, **£70-80** *CS*

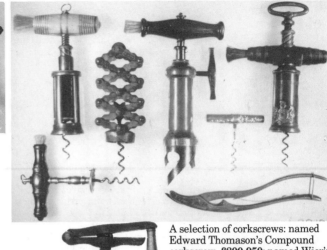

A selection of corkscrews: Thomason type double action corkscrews with applied oblong tablet, **£200-275**; brass Farrow and Jackson corkscrew, marked FJ on wing nut handle, open frame, **£100-200**; Thomason double action type, the brass barrel embossed with autumnal fruits, **£350-450**; brass Continental open frame corkscrew, **£100-200**; early open brass frame corkscrew, **£200-300** *CS*

An incomplete Henry Schrapnel Patent steel corkscrew. **£800-1,000** *CSK*

A selection of corkscrews: named Edward Thomason's Compound corkscrew, **£800-950**; named Wier's Patent Double Lever, **£400-450**; Thomas Lund's bottle grips 'Queen's Patent', **£300-575**; American embossed silver pocket corkscrew, **£200-250**; Edward Thomason's Varient corkscrew, **£350-480**; Henshall Button type corkscrew, named Wilmot & Roberts, **£80-100**; 'The Incisor', Lund patentee, champagne wire cutters, **£80-95** *CS*

A Victorian claret jug, with hobnail cut glass body with chased collar and pierced thumbpiece, by Sissons Brothers, Sheffield, 1871, 10in (25cm). **£750-850** *Bon*

A Victorian claret jug, London, 1851, 11in (28cm). **£2,200-2,700** *McC*

A George II brandy warming saucepan, initialled and monogrammed, with turned wood side handle, by John Swift, London, 1729, together with a detachable cover, apparently unmarked, 6.1oz. **£400-500** *Bea*

A Victorian claret jug, with loop handle, plain silver collar and domed hinged cover, with monogram engraved to centre, London, 1890, 8in (20cm). **£350-550** *Bon*

METALWARE
Gold

A gold mounted double ended hardstone desk seal, formed as an agate column with bloodstone matrices, one engraved with the crest, coronet and garter motto of the Prince of Wales, the base engraved 'to err is human, to forgive divine', the upper mount chased and engraved with foliate scrolls and a reeded band, the lower engraved with chevrons, c1820. **£1,500-2,000** *C*

A Louis XVI gold mounted bonbonnière, the cover set with a miniature under glass, bordered by entwined gold wirework and seed pearls, 2 panels cracked, with the décharge of Henry Clavel, Paris, 1783-89, 2in (5cm) diam. **£2,000-2,500** *C*

Pewter

A Scottish lidded pewter flagon, the interior bearing touch mark for J. Gardiner, Edinburgh, 19thC, and a similar unmarked flagon, each 10in (25cm) high. **£600-700** *C(S)*

Brass

A brass tavern tobacco box with central carrying handle, flanked by 2 lidded compartments, the right hand one having coin slot, retaining original mechanism, raised on bun feet, mid-19thC. **£200-300** *P(M)*

A cylindrical brass hand lantern with hinged door, the candle guard with pierced foliage, late 18thC, 4in (10cm) high. **£120-170** *CSK*

A quart wine measure, West of England, c1850, 6½in (16.5cm). **£170-200** *KEY*

An English or Dutch brass brazier, with pierced stand, on tripod scroll feet, with turned wood handle, 18thC, 12in (31cm) long, and 2 copper castellated jelly moulds. **£300-400** *CSK*

A French copper and brass grape hod of tapering form, embossed with 2 figures carrying a vine branch, coat-of-arms and a cartouche inscribed within 'Armand Lesange, Longnoy, Anno 1749', with iron ring carrying handles, early 19thC, 36in (92cm) high. **£550-650** *P(S)*

A group of 4 English brass spice and pepper shakers, 18thC, 4-5in (10-12cm) high. **£50-100 each** *KEY*

A brass shoe snuff box, c1795, 4½in (11cm). **£300-400** *KEY*

A Victorian cast brass door stop, 24in (61cm) high. **£200-250** *HSS*

A brass warming pan, the cover pierced and engraved with a deer shot by an arrow, within a foliate border and the inscription 'In God is all my trust', with iron handle, late 17thC.
£400-500 *CSK*

An English brass snuffer and stand, c1740, 6½in (17cm). **£350-400** *KEY*

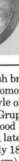

A brass warming pan, the cover incised with a leaping dog, surrounded by foliate motifs and pierced borders, with engraved steel handle, late 17thC.
£400-600 *CSK*

Bronze

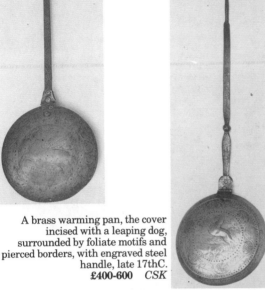

A Flemish bronze bust of Pomona, in the style of Gabriel Grupello, on gilt wood pedestal, late 17th/early 18thC, 5½in (14cm).
£1,500-2,000 *C*

An Italian bronze bust of a young faun, on painted plaster socle, 19thC, 18in (46cm) high.
£3,000-4,000 *C*

A bronze bust of King George IV, wearing the Order of the Golden Fleece, after Pistrucci, 8in (20cm) high, on a white marble socle, 19thC.
£400-500 *CSK*

A pair of French bronze busts of Bacchantes, after Clodion, on marble socles and bronze bases, 19thC, 10½in (27cm).
£1,200-1,600 *C*

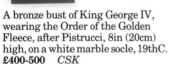

An English bronze bust of Wellington, early 19thC, 12in (31cm) high.
£750-1,000 *C*

The casting and quality of this bronze are similar to the work of Samuel Parker (fl. 1820-31), who made a series of small bronze busts, some of which are in the Scottish National Portrait Gallery and the Ashmolean Museum, Oxford.

An Italian bronze figure of Bacchus, after Jacopo Sansovino, from the workshop of Massimiliano Soldani-Benzi, some damage, 18thC, 12in (31cm) high.
£1,500-2,500 *C*

A bronze figure of a harvester by Charles Levy, signed Faneur Par Ch. Levy, Salon des Beaux-Arts and with foundry stamp, brown patination, c1880, 16½in (42cm).
£1,500-2,000   *S(S)*

A French bronze model of a walking bear, cast from a model by Isidore Bonheur, signed I. Bonheur, 19thC, 5in (13cm).
£2,500-3,000   *C*

An Austrian cold painted bronze figure group of a quail and 3 chicks, 3in (8cm) high.
£650-750   *HSS*

A bronze group of 2 bloodhounds, signed A. Dubucard, traces of gilt patination now worn, c1870, 12in (31cm) long.
£1,500-2,000   *S(S)*

A Viennese cold painted bronze of a rock dove, the underside of the tail stamped, 5in (13cm) high.
£800-900   *CSK*

A French bronze model of a bull, cast from a model by Isidore Bonheur, on naturalistic base, signed I Bonheur, numbered underneath in ink, golden brown patina, 19thC, 15in (38cm) high.   **£4,500-5,000**   *C*

A French bronze figure of a Fribourg milking cow, cast from a model by Isidore Bonheur, the base signed I. Bonheur, the velvet base with title plaque inscribed 'Vache Laitiere Fribourgeoise, 1er Prix, Exposition Universelle 1889', late 19thC, 11in (28cm) high.
£1,200-1,700   *C*

A bronze group of 'Chasse à la Perdrix', cast after a model by Pierre-Jules Mêne (1810-79), signed P.J. Mêne, 9in (23cm) high.
£1,700-2,200   *Bon*

This is possibly one of Mêne's best known groups. It was first exhibited in wax at the Salon in 1848.

A French bronze group of 2 stallions, 'L'Accolade', cast from a model by Pierre-Jules Mêne, on naturalistic base signed P J Mêne, reddish gold patina, indistinct ink inscription under base, 19thC, 8in (20cm) high.
£2,500-3,500   *C*

A French bronze equestrian group of Louis XIV, cast from a model by Baron Francois-Joseph Bosio, signed Baron Bosio, mid-19thC, 18in (46cm) high.
£1,800-2,500   *C*

This sculpture is a reduction of the original commissioned in bronze by the King in 1819. It was cast in 1822 and erected in the Place des Victoires, Paris.

A French bronze group of 2 stalking hounds, cast from a model by Jules Moigniez, signed J. Moigniez, c1865, 8in (20cm) high.
£2,000-2,500   *C*

A pair of French bronze groups of Clorinda and Tancred, Clorinda in the process of clubbing her foe, Tancred drawing his sword, respectively inscribed Clorinde and Tancrede, mid-19thC, Clorinda 19in (48cm) and Tancred 18½in (47cm) high.
£1,200-2,000   *C*

The subject of Clorinda and Tancred derives from Torquato Tasso's epic of the first Crusade 'Jerusalem Delivered'. The Christian knight, Tancred, was in love with a maiden from his Saracen opposition, Clorinda. Unfortunately, he did not recognise her in her armour during the ensuing battle, and mortally wounded her.

A French bronze group of a mare and dog, cast from a model by Pierre-Jules Mêne, signed P.J.Mêne, c1865, 10in (25cm) high.
£1,500-2,000   *C*

A French bronze model of a heron, with wings displayed and a fish in its beak, on naturalistic base cast with leaves and reeds, 19thC, 9in (23cm).
£450-550   *C*

Both Alfred Jacquemart and Jules Moigniez worked on similar models of herons.

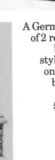

A German bronze group of 2 rearing horses, on bronze base with stylised foliate trim, on marble pedestal base, 19thC, 13in (33cm) high.
£2,500-3,000   *C*

A pair of French bronzes of Henri IV and Charles I, above brass, tortoiseshell and ebonised 'boulle' plinths, dark brown patination, 19thC, 17½in (45cm).
£1,700-2,200   *S(S)*

A French bronze group of 2 stallions, cast from a model by Jules Moigniez, the base signed J. Moigniez, with pale golden brown patina, on veined marble base, c1860, bronze 13in (33cm) high.
£3,500-4,000   *C*

A pair of Italian bronze figures of a horse and a bull, after Giambologna, probably cabinet figures, on marble bases, 17th or 18thC, 4½ and 4in (11 and 10cm) high.
£2,500-3,000   *C*

A French bronze model of a walking lion, cast from a model by Antoine-Louis Barye, on naturalistic ground and stepped integrally cast base, signed Barye and with FB stamp for Barbedienne, 19thC, 9in (22cm) high.
£2,000-2,700   *C*

A pair of bronze lions, on moulded hexagonal bases edged with a band of ropetwist, mid-19thC, 14½in (37cm) high.
£1,700-2,200   *C*

A bronze model of a standing rhinoceros, 4½in (11cm) high.
£900-1,200   *CSK*

A French bronze model of a stag, cast from a model by Pierre-Jules Mêne, signed P.J. Mêne, late 19thC, 23½in (60cm) high.
£2,700-3,200   *C*

A bronze model of a racehorse, saddled and bridled, on a shaped naturalistic base, signed Willis Good, 9in (23cm) high.
£1,200-1,700   *CSK*

A Russian bronze group of 3 cavalrymen on horseback, signed in Cyrillic E.A. Lanceray, and with the date 1880, Chopin foundry mark, 16in (41cm) high.
£10,000-12,000   *CSK*

A bronze figure of Albert Edward, Prince of Wales, after the painting by Franz Xaver Winterhalter, dressed in a sailor suit, English, mid-19thC, 21in (53cm) high.
£2,000-2,500   *C*

The celebrated painting of the Prince of Wales by Winterhalter is now in the Royal collection at Osborne House. Prince Albert commissioned the portrait in 1846, and included it amongst his 1846 Christmas presents to Queen Victoria.

A bronze figure of a nymph representing the river Thames, with the arms of the City of London on the ewer, English, mid-19thC, 11 by 17in (28 by 43cm).
£2,000-2,500   *C*

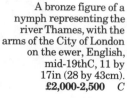

A bronze figure allegorical of Autumn, mid to dark brown patination, 15½in (39cm) high.
£400-600   *Bon*

A French bronze group of The Rape of A Sabine, after Giambologna, bearing the signature Jean de Bologne, on rococo ormolu base numbered 51765 and with bronze label Houdebine Bronzier Paris, on a lacquered wood pedestal with pierced arches, 19thC, 38in (96cm) high.   **£3,500-5,500**   *C*

A seated figure of a young girl by Ruth Milles, signed Ruth Milles on base, brown/green patination, c1910, 6½in (16cm) high.   **£800-1,200**   *S(S)*

A pair of French bronze figures of Tragedy and Comedy, cast from models by Albert Carrier-Belleuse, both signed on the base A. Carrier, 19thC, 20½in (52cm) high.
£2,500-3,500   *C*

A bronze study of a crouching boy, cast from a model by Alfred Drury R.A., signed A. Drury, 1918, upon a marble plinth, dark green/black patination, 10in (25cm) high.
£2,000-2,500   *Bon*

A. Drury (1856-1944) first studied at the Oxford School of Art before going to South Kensington, where he studied under Jules Aimé Dalou, whom he accompanied to Paris in 1879. Although Drury became most famous for his portrait busts and large public commissions, such as his work for the Victoria Memorial 1901-24, he continued to produce small works in bronze, many of which, in the immediacy of their interpretation, reveal the lasting influence of Dalou.

A French bronze figure of a naked nymph, cast from a model by Henri Marius Ding, the base of the harp inscribed H. Ding, the circular base with founder's seal, on marble base with gilt bronze border, 19thC, 18in (46cm) high.
£1,500-2,000   *C*

A bronze figure of Henry Irving, shown as Mathias in 'The Bells', signed and dated E. Onslow Ford 1893 and inscribed Henry Irving as Mathias, presented by his comrades of the Lyceum Theatre on the 21st Anniversary of his first appearance Bells 25th Nov 1871 25th November 1892, c1892, 21½in (54cm) high.
£9,000-12,000   C
Sir Henry Irving (1838-1905), was renowned during his lifetime as the greatest actor in England. It was through his outstanding efforts that the Lyceum Theatre became nationally acclaimed for its dramatic acting and plays. The present bronze is not only a rare work of the contemporary 'New Sculpture' and of a contemporary subject, but also an interesting example of the rediscovered 'lost-wax' technique.

A French gilt bronze group of putti playing with a sedan chair, cast from a model by Louis Gossin, the 5 putti tumbling as the rococo chair is tilted, on naturalistic white marble base, signed L. Gossin, late 19th/early 20thC, 9½in (24cm) high.
£2,200-2,700   C

A bronze figure of Joan of Arc by Henri Chapu, the base signed H. Chapu and inscribed F. Barbedienne, fondeur, Paris and with A. Collas reduction stamp, pale brown patination, c1870, 18in (46cm) high.
£800-1,200   S(S)

A pair of French bronze cupids, one holding a scroll entitled Contrat de Mariage, the other holding a heart pierced by an arrow, the bases signed Drouot upon moulded spreading Siena marble plinths, 14in (36cm) high.
£1,500-2,000   C

A pair of French bronze groups of Bacchantes, after Clodion, on shaped veined marble socles, late 19thC, 20in (51cm) high.
£2,700-3,200   C

A bronze group of a girl and her lover, on marble base, signed O. Hertel, late 19thC, 11in (28cm) high.   £600-900   S(S)

A bronze group of 2 nymphs and a putto, after Claude Michel Clodion, clad in flowing dresses with vine leaves in their hair, on circular base signed Clodion, dark brown patination, mid-19thC, 21in (54cm).
£1,700-2,000   S

A French bronze figure of Cupid, after Charles Gabriel Lemire, the naked winged figure seated on a draped outcrop stringing a bow, pale brown patination, mid-19thC, 16in (41cm) high.
£1,000-1,200   S

A bronze of a nude bather, 'Venus', inscribed J. Mardi, 19thC, 28½in (72cm) high.
£1,800-2,200   WW

A bronze figure of a huntsman entitled 'Hallali' by Eugene Marioton and signed Eug. Marioton, brown patination, 40in (101cm).
£2,000-2,500   *S*

A French bronze figure of Father Time, standing scantily-clad, green/black patination, base missing, early 19thC, 11½in (30cm) high.
£400-450   *S*

An Italian bronze group of Venus and Cupid, in the style of Pietro Tenerani, underside lined with resin, early 19thC, 25in (64cm) long.
£2,500-3,500   *C*

A French bronze figure of a young naked woman, reclining on a bear skin rug, signed L. Pradier, 19thC, 9in (23cm) long.
£300-350   *CSK*

A bronze group of 2 children by Francois Hippolyte Moreau, signed Hte. Moreau and titled Un Secret par Hte. Moreau, Medaille au Salon, on veined marble base, patination rubbed, c1880, 17in (43cm) high.
£1,500-2,000   *S(S)*

An Italian bronze figure of Apollo Sauroctonus, after the Antique, perhaps from the Zoffoli workshops, on Siena marble base, late 18thC, 11in (28cm) high.
£1,500-2,000   *C*

The Hellenistic Apollo Sauroctonus, formerly in the Borghese Collection, is now in the Musée du Louvre, Paris. During the 18thC, particularly thanks to Winckelmann's enthusiasm for the figure, the Apollo became popular. Bronze reductions were made at this time for the Grand Tourists. The present bronze example is probably one of these, and varies from the marble in some details, particularly in the position of Apollo.

A pair of French bronze figures of Hungarian warriors, by Emile Picault, clad in chainmail, armour and helmet, one holding a sword, the other an oil lamp, the base signed E. Picault, mid-brown patination, late 19thC, 18in (46cm).
£800-1,200   *S*

A pair of French bronze figures of semi-naked infants in the attitude of the dance, in the manner of Clodion, on marble stands, 19thC.
£650-750   *CSK*

A French gilt bronze and plated encrier, signed J. Moigniez, 19thC, 12in (31cm) wide.
£370-420   *CSK*

An Italian bronze figure of Marshal Ney, cast from a model by Giuseppe Grandi, inscribed Ney, late 19thC, 13in (33cm) high.
£5,500-6,500   *C*

A bronze on plaster figure of a classical male, numbered 122241, late 19thC, 50½in (129cm) high.
£1,500-2,000   *HSS*

A bronze figure of a fisherboy, signed Lavergne, pale brown patination, c1880, 12in (31cm).
£650-850   *S(S)*

A bronze figure of an Italian shepherd boy, indistinctly signed, dark brown patination, c1870, 16½in (42cm).
£750-1,000   *S(S)*

An Italian bronze figure of the seated Mars, after the Antique, green/brown patination, late 19thC, 19½in (49cm) high.
£650-750   *S*

An Italian bronze inkwell of a monkey playing with terrapins, cast from a model by Guido Righetti, one of the terrapins lifts to reveal an inkwell, on black marble base, signed G. Righetti, early 20thC, 7½in (19cm) long including base.
£1,500-2,000   *C*

Guido Righetti (1875-1958) was born in Milan. He was a pupil of Paul Troubetzkoy, but for most of his life worked in isolation at his estate in the Brianza region.

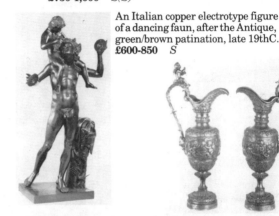

An Italian copper electrotype figure of a dancing faun, after the Antique, green/brown patination, late 19thC.
£600-850   *S*

A pair of French gilt bronze ornamental ewers, the handles modelled with putti, with satyr terminals, the bodies with raised bands of fruiting vines and amorini emblematic of the Arts, on stepped circular bases, 19thC, 22½in (57cm).
£350-450   *C*

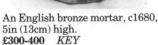

An English bronze mortar, c1680, 5in (13cm) high.
£300-400   *KEY*

An Italian bronze hand bell, the sides cast in relief, the centre inscribed with the initials G di B F and dated 1560, the handle in the form of a female figure ringing a bell with an urn at her side, bell body cracked, c1560, 7in (18cm) high.
£1,500-2,000   *C*

A Northern Italian bronze vessel, the vessel cast in the shape of a mortar with the addition of 4 hollow lateral cylinders, the central vessel and cylinders with waisted decorative band, with feet in the form of seated lions, late 16th/early 17thC, 4in (10cm) high.
£800-1,200   *C*

An Italian bronze bell, surmounted with the Papal Tiara, the body with raised figure subjects, 19thC, 5½in (14cm) high.
£100-150   *C*

Locate the source

The source of each illustration in Miller's can be found by checking the code letters below each caption with the list of contributors

Copper

A graduated set of 6 Victorian bulbous copper measures, from quarter gill to quart capacity.
£650-1,000 *CSK*

A Limoges enamel and copper reliquary casket, in 12thC Mosan style, the lid and sides enamelled with biblical scenes and florets in blues, green, yellow and red, the reverse with a hinged opening, some damage, 6½ by 6in (16 by 15cm).
£4,500-5,500 *C*

This casket is inspired by 4 Mosan 12thC plaques in the Louvre, Paris, which entered their collection in 1820. They were until recently assumed to form part of a casket, but have now been associated with other similar plaques in various museums, and, in fact, form part of a large crucifix.

A North European copper lidded urn with brass banding, 28in (71cm) high.
£300-400 *S(S)*

The District Fire Office, copper, c1860, 7½in (19cm).
£50-60 *KEY*

Firemarks

The Salop Fire Office, copper, c1830, 8in (20cm).
£50-80 *KEY*

The Alliance British and Foreign Fire and Life Insurance Co., copper, c1830, 9in (23cm).
£50-80 *KEY*

The Sun Fire Office, copper, c1850, 6in (15cm) diam.
£50-70 *KEY*

A tôleware bottle carrier, the 2 co-joined cylindrical canisters with a central carrying handle, the painted blue ground heightened in gilt with fruiting vine and painted with reserves of Italianate landscapes, 19thC, 13in (33cm).
£600-700 *CSK*

Tole peinte is a French 18thC method of varnishing sheet iron vessels so that the surfaces can be painted; and by derivation, painted metal panels applied to furniture.

Iron

An iron strong box of Armada type, the hinged lid opening to reveal a complex polished iron lock, the front with false cartouche key plate and a carrying handle to each side, late 17thC, 43in (109cm) wide.
£2,200-2,500 *CSK*

A cast iron fire back, c1685, 22in (56cm).
£400-500 *KEY*

A cast iron water font back, with a lion couchant in high relief, on moulded shelf with D-shaped back, 19thC, 33in (84cm) wide.
£500-600 *RBB*

A cast iron fireback, c1720, 18in (46cm).
£120-150 *KEY*

A blacksmith made wrought iron trivet, c1760, 14in (36cm) high.
£180-220 *KEY*

An iron weathervane, 19thC, 39in (99cm) long.
£400-500 *KEY*

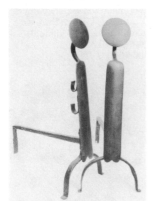

A pair of wrought iron spit dogs, 18thC, 22in (56cm) high.
£200-250 *KEY*

A wrought iron kettle tilt, English, c1770, 20in (51cm).
£100-130 *KEY*

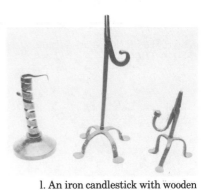

l. An iron candlestick with wooden base, c1850, 7½in (19cm) high.
£90-110
c. An iron rushnip, c1780, 12in (31cm) high.
and r. Another iron rushnip, 7in (18cm) high.
£120-140 each *KEY*

Ormolu

A pair of ormolu and white marble urn stands, on toupie feet, late 19thC, 8½in (21cm) wide.
£1,500-2,000 *C*

A pair of ormolu and mother-of-pearl comports on plinth bases, 19thC.
£400-500 *HCH*

A pair of ormolu and bronze cassolettes, fitted for electricity, restorations, one arm detached, 19thC, 13in (33cm) high, excluding fittings.
£800-1,200 *C*

ARTS & CRAFTS

A Bretby bowl, c1895, 8½in (21cm) diam.
£85-110   *BLO*

An unusual tea set, showing the influence of William Burgess, maker's mark A.L. unidentified, Chester, 1912.
£700-900   *DID*

A Bretby earthenware 'bamboo' stick stand, with a seated monkey at the base, his arms wrapped around the stand, the monkey painted in naturalistic colours, the stand shading from yellow to amber and green, rim crack, impressed mark, 23in (59cm) high.
£350-450   *Bon*

A William de Morgan red lustre vase and cover, the white ground decorated in red, cover restored, the base impressed W. De Morgan, Sand Pottery, with Morris & Co. paper label, 13in (33cm) high.
£2,500-3,000   *C*

A pair of Bretby vases, c1885, 14in (36cm) high.
£500-600   *BLO*

A Minton's majolica teapot and cover in the form of a monkey, impressed marks and year code for 18?, 7in (17cm) high.
£1,200-1,700   *Bon*

A William De Morgan jar, decorated in the Persian style, in turquoise, blue, dark purple and grey with stylised floral arabesques, 16in (41cm) high.
£3,500-4,000   *P*

A pair of candle sconces, attributed to Edward Spencer and the Artificers Guild, in steel, 12in (31cm) high.
£2,000-2,500   *P*

A Minton pottery plaque, painted by W. S. Coleman, in pastel colours, printed Minton Art Pottery Studio, Kensington Gore, c1870, 18in (46cm) wide.
£3,200-3,700   *Bon*

A pair of Moser engraved glass vases, each deeply engraved with flowering daffodils, engraved mark 3, 13in (33cm) and 13½in (34cm) high.
£350-550   *C*

A Cotswold School dresser, in plain oak, 53½in (136cm) wide.
£800-1,200   *P*

A Rookwood pottery vase, by Albert R. Valentien, decorated with yellow floral blooms with long curving tendrils against a dark brown ground, exhibiting in part a glimmering lustre, impressed 'Rookwood 1886', incised A.R.V. artist's monogram, 28½in (73cm) high.
£1,200-1,700   *P*

An oak bedroom suite decorated with coloured glass panels, comprising a breakfront wardrobe, 83in (210cm) wide, a dressing table with swing-frame mirror, 48in (122cm) wide, a marble topped washstand with spindle turned superstructure, 50in (127cm) wide, and a pedestal bedside cupboard, 17in (43cm) wide.
£1,600-2,000   *CSK*

An oak cabinet designed by Ambrose Heal, the cupboard doors with elaborate locking mechanism, 44in (112cm) wide.
£800-1,200   *C*

An oak chair, probably by William Birch, with drop-in rush seat with stretchers below, on pad feet.
£500-600   *P*

An Edward Barnsley oak pedestal desk, with beaten metal handles, 53½in (136cm) wide.
£2,000-2,500   *P*

The records of the Barnsley Education Trust show that this desk was commissioned in 1923 – the year that Edward Barnsley established his workshop at Froxfield.

An inlaid oak desk, the top covered in red leather, with brass handles, one door enclosing 3 short drawers, the other a single shelf, the front, sides and back of the desk decorated with stylised foliate panels of marquetry, 59in (149cm) wide.
£1,700-2,200   *C*

A brooch, embellished with wirework, garnet cabochons and a moonstone and opal cabochon, and dragonflies amid foliage, with garnet drops, 2in (5cm) wide.
£400-500 *P*

An important necklace by Edward Spencer of the Artificers' Guild, set with aquamarines, moonstones, rubies, emerald and opal, c1890, showing influences by Henry Wilson.
£2,300-2,800 *DID*

A large rock crystal, crysophase and moonstone heart-shaped pendant, English, c1930, probably by Sybil Dunlop.
£800-1,200 *DID*

Martin Bros.

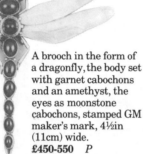

A brooch in the form of a dragonfly, the body set with garnet cabochons and an amethyst, the eyes as moonstone cabochons, stamped GM maker's mark, 4½in (11cm) wide.
£450-550 *P*

A Martin Brothers stoneware bottle vase incised and painted with an insect, game birds and reeds, the neck with a geometric pattern in shades of blue and brown, 10in (25cm).
£300-400 *Bea*

Two Martin Brothers stoneware cache pots, l. the sides moulded with lizard-like creatures on a waved ground, coloured overall in shades of olive and brown, incised Martin Bros. London & Southall, 10-1900; r. the rim decorated with ovals, the sides moulded with various species of jellyfish on a hatched ground, coloured overall in shades of olive and brown, incised Martin Bros. London & Southall, 10-1900, 4½in (11cm) high.
£1,200-1,700 each *Bon*

MARTIN BROTHERS

★ Robert, Charles, Walter and Edwin founded the pottery in 1873, moved to Southall in 1877 and continued in production until 1914
★ Martinware is the Art Pottery made by the Martin brothers between 1873 and 1914, characterised by Grotesque human and animal figures in stoneware

---

A Martin Brothers stoneware spill vase, incised and painted with birds on the branches of a fruit tree, in shades of blue on a light brown ground, inscribed R.W. Martin, Southall, 7½in (19cm).
£200-300 *Bea*

A Martin Brothers stoneware jug of compressed globular form, with narrow neck modelled and incised with peonies and foliage on a scaly ground, in shades of beige, brown and black, incised Martin Bros. London & Southall, 5in (12cm).
£450-550 *Bon*

ART NOUVEAU
Ceramics

A Brannam egg separator, c1910.
£60-70 *BLO*

A German tile, tube lined with a maiden in purple dress, contained within a wooden wall bracket embellished with gilt metal floral detail, 19in (49cm).
£600-800 *P*

An Ault vase, the design attributed to Christopher Dresser, 5½in (14cm) high.
£130-160 *BLO*

CHRISTOPHER DRESSER 1835-1905

★ an influential English pottery and glass designer who was inspired by Japanese art and worked for Tiffany as well as the pottery firms of Ault, Linthorpe and Pilkington

---

A Poole blue and white geometric vase, 10in (25cm) high.
£500-550 *CHa*

Make the Most of Miller's

Every care has been taken to ensure the accuracy of descriptions and estimated valuations. Price ranges in this book reflect what one should expect to pay for a similar example. When selling one can obviously expect a figure below. This will fluctuate according to a dealer's stock, saleability at a particular time, etc. It is always advisable to approach a reputable specialist dealer or an auction house which has specialist sales

---

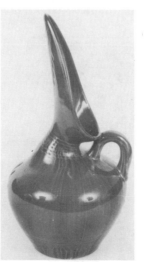

A Linthorpe jug, by Christopher Dresser, shape No. 346, 10in (25cm).
£600-700 *BLO*

A Goldscheider ceramic wall head, c1930.
£400-600 *ASA*

A Pilkingtons Royal Lancastrian highly decorated lustre bowl, by Mycock, c1900, 5in (13cm) diam.
£200-300 *ASA*

A Linthorpe vase, designed by Dr. Christopher Dresser, decorated with 4 grotesque heads, each forming a handle, covered in a streaky green glaze, running and pooling, impressed facsimile signature Chr Dresser 254, 9in (23cm) high.
£1,000-1,500 *C*

A Royal Dux porcelain centrepiece, in tones of pink, green and mauve heightened with gilt, raised pink triangle to base, numbered 710, 16½in (42cm).
£700-1,000   *P*

A Gallé faience model of a cat, with green glass eyes, glazed yellow and decorated with blue hearts and circles, unsigned, 13½in (35cm).
£600-800   *P*

A Minton Pottery Secessionist jardinière and stand, slip trailed and painted with a stylised design of candles and leaves, glazed in blood red and green enamels on a cream ground, printed mark, design No. 55, 41½in (105cm).
£750-1,000   *Bea*

A Rookwood ceramic vase, on 4 splayed feet, the white ground shaded into blue, with painted decoration of narcissi, with stamped monogram RP and numbered 597z, initialled R.F., 13½in (35cm).
£450-650   *C*

A Gallé tin glazed earthenware flowerholder, covered in a white glaze, decorated with polychrome flowersprays and a pink ribbon, on an oval naturalistic base with a tree trunk vase, inset with red glass eyes, signed Gallé Nancy, 8in (20cm) high.
£2,300-2,700   *C*

Clocks

A Tiffany and Co. clock, the face square with canted corners, set in a thin section of lapis lazuli, mounted in a gold coloured and enamelled bezel, the face signed Tiffany & Co. and etched to the base VAN 19539, 4½in (12cm).
£400-500   *P*

A pewter clock, probably Liberty in the manner of C. F. A. Voysey, with a brass dial above a row of stylised poplars in relief, 11½in (29cm).
£1,500-2,000   *P*

A Gouda glazed earthenware clock case painted with colourful swirling flowers and plant forms, 16½in (42cm).
£300-400   *PCh*

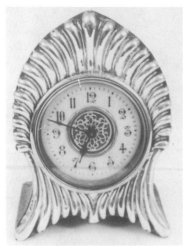

A clock, inscribed on the bezel St. Moritz 1900, with an interesting hallmark, c1891, 5in (12cm) high.
£400-450   *RFA*

A corner table with inlaid chrysanthemum design, 18½in (47cm) high.
£150-160   *BEV*

A Liberty & Co. pewter and enamelled clock, embossed with a stylised leafy tree, the blue/green enamelled clock face with Roman numerals, the door on the reverse with a pierced tree, stamped marks, made in England, Tudric, c1900, 13in (33cm).
£2,500-3,000   *S(C)*

Furniture

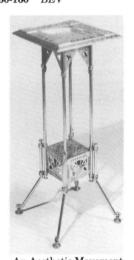

A Liberty & Co. mahogany side table, the octagonal top with a lighter inlaid band, on square section legs, tapering to pad feet, with slotted stretchers between, with maker's label, 36in (92cm) diam.
£800-900   *P*

A pair of Morris & Co ebonised side chairs, each with toprails and cross splat, the rush seats on turned legs straight and curved bar stretchers.
£1,200-1,700   *C*

An Aesthetic Movement brass pedestal, the top with shallow well, on 4 angled tubular legs, with pierced and repoussé linear and foliate decoration, moulded marks PAT APL^D FOR, 32in (82cm) high.
£700-800   *C*

An Aesthetic Movement ebonised chest stool, decorated front and back with carved gilt emblematic roundels, supported on turned legs above a gallery, the seat upholstered in black horse hair 35½in (90cm) wide.
£2,500-3,000   *C*

A Liberty's style mahogany three-piece suite, comprising a two-seater settee and a pair of armchairs, with rosewood veneered backs with inlay, upholstered in Liberty's Peacock Feather linen, settee 54in (137cm) wide, armchairs 30in (76cm) wide.
£3,000-4,000   *Bon*

A chair designed by J. M. Olbrich, the back inlaid with stylised flowers in mother-of-pearl and fruitwoods, with upholstered seat and back, supported on tapering square section legs with pad feet.
£700-800   *P*

An inlaid display cabinet.
£800-1,200   *ASA*

An oak dining table, designed by M. H. Baillie-Scott, on 2 trestle supports, each composed of twin turned baluster columns and shaped transverse base, c1897, 72in (183cm) long.
£4,000-5,000   *C*

Figures

A German plated pewter lady holding a jewellery box, 13½in (35cm).
£400-600   *ASA*

An English Aesthetic Movement bedroom suite, comprising a wardrobe, dressing table and a bedside cabinet, each decorated with panels of fruitwood marquetry with hammered and pierced hinges and handles, the wardrobe 70in (177cm) high.
£2,200-2,700   *C*

A gilt bronze figure lamp by Agathon Léonard, the lamp concealed in the drape held above the female head, signed in the bronze, c1900.
£10,000-15,000   *ASA*

A bronze figure by Eloe, signed.
£800-1,200   *ASA*

Locate the source

The source of each illustration in Miller's can be found by checking the code letters below each caption with the list of contributors

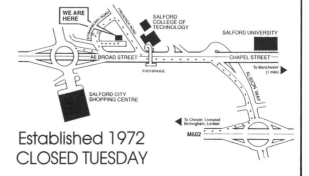

Six enamelled glasses, each
decorated in either blue, red or
yellow with a painted
flowerhead, each with
gilt linear decoration,
6½in (16cm) high and smaller.
£1,700-2,200   *C*

A gilt bronze and
ivory figure by Preiss,
signed, c1930, 11in
(28cm) high.
£1,500-2,500   *ASA*

An Austrian bronze figure
on marble base.
£400-600   *ASA*

A Gallé cameo glass bottle vase, the
compressed onion body and slender
attenuated trumpet neck carved in
relief with hollyhocks rising from
dark to pale tint, signed, c1900, 15in
(38cm) high.
£1,500-2,000   *PCh*

*Emile Gallé (1846-1904) was the
founder of a talented circle of
designers based around Nancy.
Simultaneously, in the 1880s, he
designed delicate furniture
embellished with marquetry and
began experimenting with new glass
techniques. In 1889 he developed
cameo glass; in 1897 marquetry
glass. After his death factories
continued to produce his wares,
signed Gallé but marked with a star,
until the 1930s.*

Glass

An orange and green satin glass
vase, the undulating rim folded to
form 3 handles, acid etched and
carved to reveal green fronds, with
gilt decorated border,
monogrammed L.G. and
indistinctly inscribed, chipped, 6in
(15cm) high.
£300-350   *HSS*

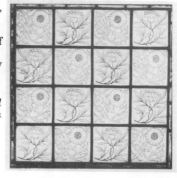

Twelve Austrian enamelled glass goblets, the bowls decorated with a
variety of stylised petals in shades of orange, blue, yellow, pink and
green, with gilt highlights, most enamelled with letters or numerals,
the largest 9in (23cm) high.
£1,700-2,200   *CNY*

A Morris & Co. stained glass panel,
the pale yellow stained glass
painted with red, yellow and white
decoration in alternating designs of
open and budding flowers, within
charcoal border, 17½ by 18in (46 by
44cm).
£320-500   *C*

*The decorative features of this panel
can be seen in a pair of windows with
minstrel figures which are in the
Victoria and Albert Museum.*

A Gallé cameo glass vase.
£3,500-4,000   *HSS*

Fourteen wine glasses and 2 liqueur glasses, attributed to Heckart Petersdorfer Glashütte, on long green stems, with various gilt and polychrome enamelled stylised floral designs, 8½in (21cm) and 5½in (14cm) high.
£2,000-2,500 C

A Daum cameo class landscape lamp, in mottled orange/yellow glass, overlaid in green with trees on the bank of a lake, repeated on the wavy rimmed shade, cameo mark, Daum Nancy, Cross of Lorraine, c1900, 16½in (42cm).
£10,000-12,000
S(C)

Jewellery

A Liberty & Co. silver belt buckle, in the style of Archibald Knox, with stylised spade-shaped flowers, supported on entwined entrelacs, the surface beaten, stamped marks, L & Co. Cymric, Birmingham 1901, 2in (5cm).
£150-200 *S(C)*

A large 9ct gold pendant, by Murlle Bennett & Co., set with an opal flanked by 2 pale aquamarines and 2 citrines, c1900.
£700-900 *DID*

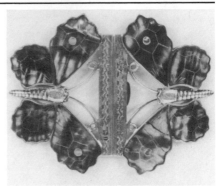

A silver buckle, each piece in the form of a butterfly with shaded mother-of-pearl wings, marked R.P. Birmingham 1910, 3½in (9cm) wide.
£100-150 *P*

A French 18ct gold brooch, the sculpture effect hand finished, c1900.
£600-800 *DID*

A rose diamond and plique à jour enamel butterfly brooch, with baroque pearl, untested, rose diamond and gem body.
£2,500-3,000 *CSK*

A diamond and rose diamond cluster brooch, the pierced and chased floral scrollwork shoulders each set with 2 rose diamonds.
£350-400 *CSK*

An unusual plique à jour and diamanté pendant, the ivory and mother-of-pearl bust mounted in a gilt white metal setting, the wings and fan tail with shades of green and turquoise plique à jour enamel, set with white and pink gems, in fitted leather case, 13in (33cm).
£3,200-3,700 *C*

A Liberty & Co. silver and enamel belt buckle, attributed to Archibald Knox, enamelled in mottled blue and green, some enamel replaced, stamp marks L & Co. Cymric, Birmingham 1901, 3in (8cm).
£200-250 *S(C)*

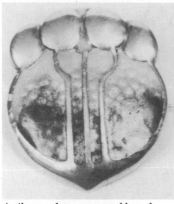

A silver and green enamel brooch, signed and dated, c1900.
£50-100   ASA

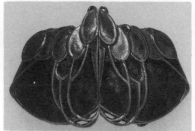

A Liberty & Co. Cymric enamelled silver belt buckle, decorated with pendant honesty against a blue/green enamel background, with stamped mark L & Co. Cymric and Birmingham hallmarks for 1903.
£400-450   C

A green paste and tourmaline brooch, by Arthur Gaskin, c1900.
£450-550   DID

Lamps

An Austrian bronze lamp, the shade set with coloured stones, c1900, 20in (51cm).
£500-800   ASA

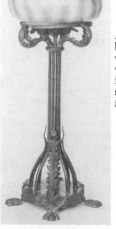

An orange ground and blue fleck inverted glass ceiling light fitting, with 3 flower shape glass light fittings, signed Müller Frère.
£200-300   PCh

A decorative gilt metal table lamp, modelled as a maiden, on marble base, 29in (74cm).
£500-700   P

A Quezal iridescent glass and bronze table lamp, the shade with white interior, decorated externally with green and silver-blue iridescent feathering, the shade signed Quezal, 25in (64cm).
£1,700-2,200   P

A flower girl gilt bronze table lamp, cast from a model by Louis Chalon, signed in the bronze L. Chalon, 16in (41cm).
£6,000-7,000   C

A German bronze desk light, the cowl shade with tin glazed liner, printed signature Julius Pintsch, Berlin, mounted on horse shoe shaped pedestal stand on shaped foot cast with reeded and foliage decoration, fitted for electricity, 11in (28cm).
£800-1,000   C

An iridescent glass and metal table lamp, with domed Palme Konig shade of pink tone with pale web-like stringing, 15in (38cm).
£1,500-2,000   *P*

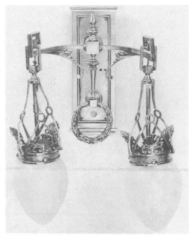

A set of 4 brass twin light wall lights, the frosted glass shades suspended by arms from rectangular backplates with laurel wreath terminals, 11½in (29cm) high.
£800-1,200   *CSK*

A copper and brass table lamp, by W. A. S. Benson.
£550-650   *BLO*

Metal

A Tudric pewter biscuit box with enamelled lid, the design attributed to Archibald Knox, 4in (10cm) high.
£600-700   *BLO*

A pair of pewter W.M.F. candelabra, with nymphs, entwined around tendrils which form the sconces, on spreading bases, 10in (25cm).
£1,000-1,200   *P(M)*

A W.M.F. silver plated punchbowl and ladle, on stepped base, each side with figure of Minerva in high relief, dedicated to Rev. Joseph Larzan, bowl and ladle impressed with firm's marks, 20in (51cm) high.
£2,000-2,500   *CNY*

A W.M.F. pewter jug, c1900, 15in (38cm).
£400-500   *ASA*

A Guild of Handicraft silver chalice, lightly hammered, stamped marks G of H Ltd, with London hallmarks for 1902, 8½in (22cm), 275gr.
£450-650   *C*

A pewter mirror, probably Osiris, c1900.
£600-800   *DID*

A Tudric vase, the design attributed
to Archibald Knox, 7½in (19cm).
£150-250 *BLO*

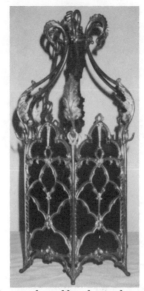

An ormolu and hand cut coloured
glass lantern, 16in (41cm) high.
£375-425 *HAE*

A Guild of Handicraft toast rack,
designed by C. R. Ashbee, the end
panels with repoussé decoration of
stylised trees, stamped G of H Ltd.,
with London hallmarks for 1906,
5in (13cm), 220gr.
£1,500-2,000 *C*

A laminated copper frame, c1900.
£25-50 *BLO*

A W.M.F. dish with female figure,
10½in (27cm) diam.
£300-500 *ASA*

A silver hand mirror, with
embossed cherubs,
London 1896.
£75-125 *PCh*

A peal gong, as illustrated in
Liberty's 1898 Yuletide catalogue.
£250-350 *Ced*

A Tudric pewter muffin dish and cover,
stamped Tudric C293, 9½in (24cm) diam.
£250-300 *P*

A silver repoussé picture frame,
decorated in relief with kingfishers
and water plants, stamped maker's
marks W.N and Chester hallmarks
for 1904 Patent 9616, on wood back
panel, 12½in (32cm).
£1,500-2,000 *C*

A W.M.F. pewter dish, 14in (36cm).
£200-300 *ASA*

A pair of Tudric pewter candlesticks,
the design attributed to Archibald
Knox, 9in (23cm).
£650-750 *BLO*

A Cymric Liberty & Co. bowl, designed by Oliver Baker, set with Connemara marble discs, Birmingham 1901, 8½in (21cm) diam.
£3,000-3,500 *DID*

A Mappin and Webb vase, the handles with heart shaped terminals, the base with inverted hearts in relief, with inscription, maker's mark, London 1903, 5in (13cm).
£180-250 *P*

A plated pewter pen and inkstand, 8½in (22cm) high.
£100-120 *P*

A Liberty & Co. silver pen tray, each end decorated with a cabochon turquoise, with owner's initials A.M.W., stamped marks L & Co. and Birmingham hallmarks for 1912, 7in (17cm) long, 60gr.
£250-300 *C*

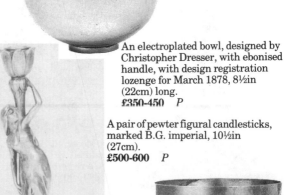

An electroplated bowl, designed by Christopher Dresser, with ebonised handle, with design registration lozenge for March 1878, 8½in (22cm) long.
£350-450 *P*

A pair of pewter figural candlesticks, marked B.G. imperial, 10½in (27cm).
£500-600 *P*

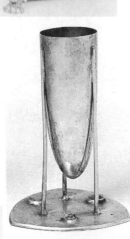

A C. R. Ashbee hammered silver goblet, the foot with a radiating repoussé pattern of stylised buds, stamped C R A with London hallmarks for 1899, 5in (12cm).
£600-650 *C*

A Liberty & Co. Cymric silver vase, designed by Archibald Knox, the base with 3 turquoise cabochons and 3 wire supports, maker's marks, Birmingham 1903, stamped Cymric 2126, 4½in (11cm).
£500-600 *P*

A W.M.F. silvered metal tea set, comprising a teapot, coffee pot, covered sugar and creamer, with two-handled lobed tray, all cast with curvilinear foliage, tray 24½in (62cm) diam.
£1,500-2,000 *CNY*

W.M.F.
Short for the Austrian Württembergishe Metallwarenfabrik, one of the principal producers of Art Nouveau silver and silver plated objects, early 20thC.

Moorcroft

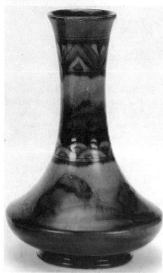

A rare Moorcroft flambé Eventide vase, tube-lined with trees in a hilly landscape and richly coloured in mauve, orange and red, minor chip restored on foot, impressed Moorcroft, Made in England and signed in blue W. Moorcroft, 8in (20cm).
£2,000-2,500 *S*

A Moorcroft Eventide vase, decorated with green and brown trees and hills against a flame coloured sky, impressed mark, signature in green, 5½in (14cm).
£750-850 *AH*

A Moorcroft Apple Blossom bowl, tube-lined with branches of flowers and berries in tones of green, hair crack, impressed Moorcroft Burslem 1914, signed in green W. Moorcroft and dated 1914, 10in (25cm).
£800-1,200 *S*

A Moorcroft Pottery vase, the body painted with the Anemone pattern on a red ground, 6½in (17cm).
£260-300 *Bea*

A Moorcroft pottery vase, painted with the Hibiscus design on a deep red ground, impressed marks and painted signature, 8½in (21cm).
£300-350 *Bea*

A Moorcroft Florian ware bottle vase with fluted rim, decorated in blue and green with the Poppy design on a white ground, pattern No. 401753, printed Florian ware mark and signed, 6in (15cm).
£400-450 *Bea*

A Moorcroft MacIntyre pottery baluster vase with 2 loop handles, polychrome floral decoration on a white ground with gilt banding, 7½in (19cm).
£600-700 *AH*

A Moorcroft pottery vase, painted with the Pomegranate and Grape design on a deep blue ground, impressed marks and painted signature, 6½in (17cm).
£170-220 *Bea*

A Moorcroft Florian ware vase, tube-lined with yellow and blue flowerheads and green foliage on a light and dark blue ground, printed Florian ware mark and signed in green W. Moorcroft, c1902, 11½in (30cm).
£1,500-2,000 *S*

l. A Moorcroft MacIntyre Florian ware two-handled vase, decorated in the Peacock Feathers pattern, the rim glazed in tones of blue, yellow, grey and green, printed mark and painted initials in green W.M. des, c1902, 5in (13cm).
£650-750

r. A Moorcroft MacIntyre vase decorated in the Daisy pattern, in tones of blue, green and white, painted mark in green W. Moorcroft, des, 1899-1900.
£1,500-2,000   *Bon*

A Moorcroft Moonlit Blue vase, with flaring rim, tube-lined with a tree-lined landscape in tones of blue and green against a blue sky, impressed W. Moorcroft signature and Royal Warrant, blue painted signature W. Moorcroft, c1925, 9½in (24cm).
£900-1,200   *S*

A Moorcroft Pomegranate pattern vase, with white piped decoration, covered in a puce, green, red and blue glaze, with green facsimile signature W. Moorcroft, 12½in (32cm).
£2,000-2,500   *C*

A pair of William Moorcroft Florian ware candlesticks.
£400-450   *DM*

A Moorcroft Florian ware jardinière.
£700-750   *DM*

A Moorcroft bottle vase painted with the Pomegranate and Grape pattern, impressed marks and painted signature, 10½in (26cm).
£350-450   *Bea*

A Moorcroft Burslem candlestick, decorated in the Cornflower pattern, c1914, 9in (23cm).
£600-700   *Bon*

A Moorcroft Liberty pewter mounted Eventide landscape vase, the cylindrical body tube-lined with tall trees in a hilly landscape, set against a red to orange-red ground, mounted in a flared beaten pewter base, restored, c1928, 7½in (19cm).
£250-350   *S(C)*

DOULTON

A Doulton figure of a mandarin, wearing a yellow tunic with circular motifs over a plain blue full length skirt, his jacket with larger motifs on a black ground, small chip to hat, dated 7.24, HN 611, 10in (25cm).
£650-1,000   *S(C)*

A pair of Doulton Lambeth salt glazed stoneware bookends, one with a single monkey, the other with a monkey and child, on a foliate base under a green glaze, stamped factory mark, Doulton, Lambeth, England, c1890, 6in (15cm).
£300-400   *S(C)*

A 1930s style Doulton dinner service entitled 'Dubarry', comprising: 4 tureens and covers, 2 ladles, 5 graduated meat plates, 2 sauceboats, 22 plates and 2 petal edged plates, on a cream ground, with a geometric pattern of intersecting lines and semi-circles edged in green with a central motif of a stylised flower in orange, some plates worn.   **£300-400**   *P(M)*

A Doulton Lambeth stoneware vase, decorated by Edith Lupton, carved and glazed with flowers and grasses over a beige background with painted florets, dated 1887, 16in (41cm).
£450-550   *PCh*

A Doulton figure, 'Contentment', decorated mainly in yellow, light green and pink, slight pitting to glaze, HN 395, 7½in (19cm).
£450-650   *S(C)*

A Doulton salt glazed stoneware vase, by Hannah B. Barlow, impressed factory marks and date, incised monogram, BHB and LAB for Lucy A. Barlow, c1884, 12in (31cm).
£650-750   *S(C)*

ROYAL DOULTON

A figure 'Coquette', HN 37, No. 258, cracked, 9½in (24cm) high.   **£700-800**   *S(C)*

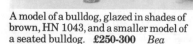

A model of a bulldog, glazed in shades of brown, HN 1043, and a smaller model of a seated bulldog.   **£250-300**   *Bea*

'A Yeoman of the Guard', HN 2122, 6in (15cm) high.
£350-450   *DN*

584

ART NOUVEAU ROYAL DOULTON

Town Crier, 2119, 1953-76, 8in (20cm).
£180-220 *TP*

The Winner, 1407, 1930-38, 6in (15cm).
£1,000-1,250 *TP*

A bay mare with foal, 2522, 1938-60, 6in (15cm).
£350-450 *TP*

A Treasure Island loving cup, limited edition of 600, c1934.
£300-400 *TP*

The Organ Grinder, 2173, 1956-75, 8in (20cm).
£300-350 *TP*

A seated collie, model 47, c1920. **£250-350** *TP*

A pair of Royal Doulton vases,
c1900, 11in (28cm).
£150-180   *HAE*

A pair of flambé models of penguins,
set on an alabaster ashtray with
silver mounts, with assay mark for
London 1919, 6½in (17cm).
£250-300   *Bea*

A pair of salt glazed stoneware
vases, by Hannah B. Barlow, in
green and brown with tube lined Art
Nouveau swirling motifs in a band
above and below, large chip to rim of
one, impressed factory marks,
incised monogram, BHB and others
of Assistants, c1885, 11in (28cm).
£900-1,200   *S(C)*

A coffee service,
'Reynard the Fox',
with printed
marks and pattern
number H4927.
£300-400   *DN*

A group, 'The Love Letter',
HN 2149, withdrawn 1976.
£150-200   *Bea*

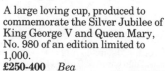

A brown and white model of a
standing bulldog, HN 1045.
£350-400   *Bea*

A large loving cup, produced to
commemorate the Silver Jubilee of
King George V and Queen Mary,
No. 980 of an edition limited to
1,000.
£250-400   *Bea*

'Simon the Cellarer', a white
character jug, 3in (8cm).
£150-200   *DN*

A salt glazed metal mounted
stoneware biscuit barrel, by
Hannah B. Barlow, highlighted
in blue, with impressed factory
mark and date, and incised
monogram Hannah B Barlow,
1880, 7½in (19cm).
£450-550   *S(C)*

A pottery vase, the body
decorated with an
extensive fox hunting scene
between bands of flowers,
2 cracks, 22½in (57cm).
£200-300   *Bea*

A porcelain vase, dated
5.11, by Arthur Leslie,
decorated with a
maiden holding a white
dove in a landscape, 9in
(23cm). **£400-450**   *S(C)*

'Collinette',
HN 1999, withdrawn
£250-300   *Bea*

ART DECO
Lalique Glass

An opalescent bowl with beads graduating inside and forming a swirling pattern, with R. Lalique in upper case, 8in (20cm).
£300-400   *P(M)*

A Lalique blue tinted opalescent glass bowl, moulded with fishes.
£700-800   *GIL*

A frosted desk clock, 'Roitelets', the glass face surrounded by a band of wrens in flight, with Omega timepiece, stencilled R. Lalique France, 8in (20cm).
£3,000-3,500   *Bon*

An opalescent table clock, 'Inseperables No. 765', minor damage, 4½in (11cm).
£850-1,000   *Bea*

An opalescent bowl, 'Vase Coquilles', 9½in (24cm).
£350-400   *Bea*

An opalescent bowl, 'Perruches', moulded with a frieze of budgerigars perched on flowering branches, heightened with blue staining and etched R. Lalique France, 9½in (24cm).
£3,000-3,500   *Bon*

An opalescent glass bowl, entitled 'Lys', moulded with a frieze of 4 lilies, the stems tapering to form legs, stencil mark R. Lalique, France, c1925, 9½in (23cm).
£850-1,200   *P(M)*

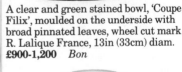

A clear and green stained bowl, 'Coupe Filix', moulded on the underside with broad pinnated leaves, wheel cut mark R. Lalique France, 13in (33cm) diam.
£900-1,200   *Bon*

A clear and frosted glass clock, 'Naïdes', intaglio moulded with a band of mermaids with fanned and beaded hair, their limbs entwined, heightened with pale brown staining, etched R. Lalique France, 4in (11cm) diam.
£1,000-1,500   *P*

An opalescent and sienna stained dish, 'Anges', moulded in intaglio with facing pairs of kneeling angels, wheel cut R. Lalique France, 14½in (37cm) diam.
£3,500-4,000   *Bon*

An opalescent dish, decorated with birds, 8in (20cm).   **£400-500**   *ASA*

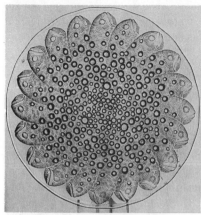

A clear blue stained dish, 'Roscoff', the underside moulded with radiating fish, the centre with a myriad of bubbles, engraved R. Lalique France, 14in (36cm).
£1,000-1,500   *Bon*

A glass pendant, in white metal frame, the foil backed and black stained glass with relief decoration of a nymph in a wooded landscape, the reverse with mirror, with engraved signature R. Lalique France, 3in (8cm) long.   **£1,500-2,000**   *C*

A dark blue frosted dish, 'Phalènes', moulded to the underside with a stylised flower, the flat rim moulded in intaglio with moths, slight reduction to rim, wheel cut R. Lalique France, 15in (38cm).
£3,500-4,500   *Bon*

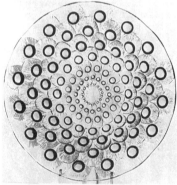

An opalescent dish, moulded on the underside with a peacock feather motif, engraved R. Lalique France, 12in (30cm).
£700-800   *Bon*

A glass pendant in white metal frame, the gold foil backed and black stained glass with relief decoration of a maiden's face framed with flowers, the reverse with mirror, the frame stamped Lalique, 3in (8cm) long.
£1,500-2,000   *C*

A green glass brooch, 'Sauterelles', signed LALIQUE, 3in (8cm) long.
£3,000-4,000   *CNY*

A frosted glass plaffonier of hemispherical form, 'Charmes', moulded in relief with overlapping beach leaves, with suspension chain and ceiling rose, moulded R. LALIQUE, 13½in (35cm) diam.
£650-850   *CSK*

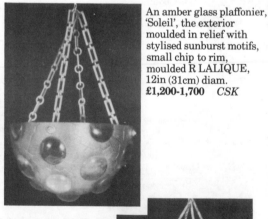

An amber glass plaffonier, 'Soleil', the exterior moulded in relief with stylised sunburst motifs, small chip to rim, moulded R LALIQUE, 12in (31cm) diam.
£1,200-1,700   *CSK*

A frosted glass plaffonier, 'Stalactites', moulded as pendant icicles, minor chips, wheel cut R. LALIQUE, 10½in (26cm).
£1,500-2,000   *CSK*

A black opaque pendant, moulded with 2 panels of wasps, heads facing inwards and with down-curved bodies, pierced at the top and base for suspension cord and tassel, engraved R. Lalique, 2in (5cm).
£1,500-2,000   *Bon*

A clear and frosted glass chandelier, 'Charmes', moulded twice R LALIQUE, 14in (36cm) diam.
£1,500-2,500   *CNY*

A hanging light, 'Boule de Gui', composed of 2 hemispherical and 8 rectangular glass panels, linked by metal rings to form a globe, moulded with mistletoe, with metal hanging ring and wired for electricity, 17½in (45cm) high.
£12,000-15,000   *C*

A frosted plafonnier, 'Deux Sirénes', moulded with 2 swimming water nymphs, their hair forming streams of bubbles, with matching ceiling rose, moulded R. Lalique, 15½in (39cm) diam.
£8,000-9,000   *Bon*

An opalescent glass and chromium plated metal table lamp, 'Coquilles', moulded with 4 clam shells, suspended from a C-shaped mount on stepped circular base, wheel cut R. Lalique France, 12in (31cm).
£2,000-2,500   *Bon*

A frosted glass vase, 'Druids', moulded with entwined sprigs of mistletoe with polished clusters of berries in relief, moulded to base R. Lalique, 7in (18cm) high.
£500-700   *P*

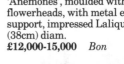

A rare, early frosted mirror, 'Anemones', moulded with flowerheads, with metal easel support, impressed Lalique, 15in (38cm) diam.
£12,000-15,000   *Bon*

A vase, 'Laurier', with raised leaves and berries in blue, etched near the base R. Lalique, 7in (17cm) high.
£300-400   *P(M)*

A clear glass vase, 'Paquerettes', moulded in relief with stylised daisy-like blooms against a heavily textured ground heightened with black staining, etched R. Lalique France, 7½in (19cm) high.
£700-900   *P*

A turquoise stained vase, 'Oursin', the clear and satin finished glass moulded with protruding bubbles, with acid stamped signature R. Lalique France, 7½in (19cm) high.   **£1,500-2,000**   *C*

A clear and frosted vase, 'Annecy', moulded with alternating waved and serrated horizontal bands, stencilled R. Lalique France, 6in (15cm).   **£600-700**   *Bon*

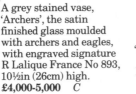

A grey stained vase, 'Archers', the satin finished glass moulded with archers and eagles, with engraved signature R Lalique France No 893, 10½in (26cm) high.
£4,000-5,000   *C*

An opalescent, clear and blue stained ashtray, 'Cendrier Statuette', in the centre a miniature 'Source de la Fontaine' figure, holding a lotus, etched R. Lalique, 4½in (12cm) high.
£700-900   *Bon*

Ceramics

A hand painted yellow and black vase, by Myott & Son, 8½in (22cm).
£55-85   *LB*

A Beswick wall mask, with brown hair, wearing a green and yellow necklace, with blue and yellow petalled flowers behind, impressed Beswick, Made in England, 436, late 1930s, 12in (31cm).
£200-300   *S(C)*

A Pilkington's Royal Lancastrian lapis-ware wall plate, decorated by W. S. Mycock, in grey on an orange ground, with impressed Pilkington mark and underglaze artist's monogram, 12½in (32cm) diam.
£100-150   *C*

A Charlotte Rhead Burslem ware jug, c1920, 9in (23cm).
£65-70   *SCO*

A Pilkington's Royal Lancastrian vase, by Mycock, 8½in (21cm).
£400-500   *ASA*

A Shelley Regent shape coffee service, transfer printed with a Lakeland scene, comprising coffee pot and cover, milk jug, sugar basin, 6 cups and 6 saucers, c1935, printed factory mark, Shelley, England, registration number 781613, painted number 12336.
£250-350   *S(C)*

A Pilkington's Royal Lancastrian vase, by Mycock, 8½in (21cm).
£350-450   *ASA*

A Pilkington's Royal Lancastrian vase, by Cundall, 9in (23cm).
£400-500   *ASA*

A Shelley porcelain tea service, each piece decorated with irises and stylised flowers on a pink and white ground, comprising: a teapot and cover, hot water jug, sugar basin, milk jug, 2 bread and butter plates, 12 tea plates and 12 teacups and saucers, slight damage to sugar basin.
£500-700   *Bea*

A Shelley tea service, with abstract black pattern, some slight damage, 20 pieces, No. 756533.
£350-450   *IM*

A Limoges porcelain tea set, glazed a lustrous faux malachite with silver trim, with firm's printed mark, tray 15½in (40cm) long.
£600-700   *CNY*

A cased Crown Devon coffee service, decorated in yellow, purple and gilt, with silver plastic beaded spoons, chip to saucer, black printed factory mark, Crown Devon, Fieldings, England, painted number 2258, c1930.
£300-500   *S(C)*

A Pilkington's Royal Lancastrian lapis-ware wall plate, decorated by W. S. Mycock, in grey on an orange ground, with impressed Pilkington mark, underglaze artist's monogram and date code for 1935, 12in (31cm).
£100-150   *C*

A Shelley fluted tea service with cottage scene, in black, white and yellow, 37 pieces, No. 11604131.
£350-450   *IM*

Clarice Cliff

A Clarice Cliff Bizarre plate, from the Circus Series designed by Dame Laura Knight, all printed in pink overpainted in green, black, yellow and iron red heightened with gilt, printed marks, impressed year mark for 1934, 9in (23cm).
£600-750   *Bon*

A Clarice Cliff Fantasque Hiawatha bowl, the interior decorated in the Broth pattern in red, green, blue and black, with multi-banded exterior, minor wear to exterior, rubber stamp mark, 9½in (24cm).
£300-500   *CSK*

A Clarice Cliff Fantasque Isis vase, hand painted with repeating panels in the Sunrise pattern of a sunburst in green, orange, blue, yellow and brown, factory marks and facsimile signature to base, 10in (25cm).
£450-600   *P*

A Clarice Cliff Blue Firs flower bowl, painted with tall black stemmed trees, with various blue foliage on treetops with a half hidden cottage between the hills, some surface scratching, black printed factory mark, Hand Painted, Bizarre, by Clarice Cliff, Newport Pottery, England, c1930, 9in (23cm).
£250-300   *S(C)*

A Clarice Cliff Bizarre sandwich set, decorated in the Idyll pattern, painted in colours with black and yellow banded borders, lithograph marks, the large plates 9in (23cm), tea plates 6in (15cm).
£1,700-2,000   *CSK*

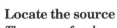

Locate the source

The source of each illustration in Miller's can be found by checking the code letters below each caption with the list of contributors

---

591

A Clarice Cliff Inspiration plate, painted with pink lilies, with black stems and black lily pads, on a green ground, black printed factory mark, Hand Painted, Bizarre, by Clarice Cliff, Wilkinson Ltd., England, 1931, 10in (25cm).
£300-400   *S(C)*

A Clarice Cliff Persian Inspiration pottery vase, in vibrant azure blue with spiral and ogee motif in turquoise, lavender and amber, signed Persian and with printed Bizarre marks, 10in (25cm).
£800-1,000   *CNY*

A Clarice Cliff Melons plate, decorated with a band of fruits in yellow and orange with blue sections and green dots, minor damage to edge, printed mark, hand painted, Fantasque, by Clarice Cliff, Wilkinson Ltd., England, 10in (25cm).
£200-300   *S(C)*

A pair of Clarice Cliff cottage bookends, decorated in red on a green ground with a blue sky, one cracked, the other chipped, black printed mark, Clarice Cliff, Wilkinson Pottery, retailer's mark, Lawleys, Regent Street, late 1930s, 5½in (14cm).
£450-650   *S(C)*

A Clarice Cliff Bizarre Sliced Circle pattern single handled lotus jug, painted in bright colours, printed factory marks and facsimile signature, 10in (25cm).
£1,800-2,200   *P*

A Clarice Cliff pierced floral wall plaque, moulded in low relief with various flowers, printed factory mark, hand painted, Bizarre, Newport Pottery, England, painted The property of Threlfalls Brewery, signed on front Clarice Cliff, c1930, 13in (33cm).
£200-250   *S(C)*

A Clarice Cliff Apples Isis vase, painted with apples and grapes, in pink, orange, black, yellow and green, fitted as lamp base, with electric fittings and shade, black printed factory mark, Fantasque, Hand Painted, Bizarre, by Clarice Cliff, Newport Pottery, England, c1932, 10in (25cm).
£900-1,200   *S(C)*

A Clarice Cliff Isis vase, boldly painted with trees in Latona glazes, 10in (25cm).
£470-520   *Bea*

A Clarice Cliff Fantasque Summerhouse pattern vase, hand painted in colours around the 3 sides with a red roofed summerhouse and trees with pendant blooms, with orange banding top and bottom, facsimile signature and factory mark for Newport Pottery, 8in (20cm).

Did you know
MILLER'S Antiques Price Guide builds up year by year to form the most comprehensive photo-reference system available

592

A Clarice Cliff Bizarre plate, painted with the Delicia Pansies pattern, 9in (23cm).
£200-250 *Bea*

A pair of Clarice Cliff vases, shape 451, in the Oranges and Lemons pattern, of large red, orange and yellow fruit with black leaves against a white ground, base, 8in (20cm).
£1,000-1,500 *P*

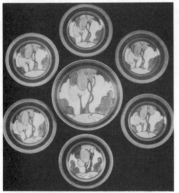

A Clarice Cliff Fantasque Bizarre part tea set, decorated in the Pastel Autumn pattern, painted in colours, comprising: milk jug, 5 cups and 6 saucers, 6 tea plates and a sandwich plate, chips to foot of milk jug, lithograph marks.
£1,200-1,500 *CSK*

A Clarice Cliff Berries part coffee service, the coffee pot painted with orange and red berries with blue and purple foliage, comprising: coffee pot and cover, 6 coffee mugs, 5 saucers, milk jug and sugar bowl, minor surface scratching, printed mark Fantasque, hand painted, Bizarre, by Clarice Cliff, Newport Pottery, England, c1930, the pot 6½in (17cm).
£600-800 *S(C)*

A Clarice Cliff Bizarre Lightning pattern single handled lotus jug, painted in black, blue and purple, red, orange and yellow, printed factory marks and facsimile signature to base, 10in (25cm).
£2,500-3,000 *P*

A Latona Bizarre wall plaque, decorated in the Dahlia pattern, painted in colours, printed and painted marks, 13in (33cm) diam.
£1,500-2,000 *CSK*

A Clarice Cliff Fantasque sandwich set decorated in the Geometric Flowers pattern, painted in colours, some damage, gilt rubber stamp marks, the oblong plate 11½in (29cm), tea plates 5½in (14cm) wide.
£750-1,000 *CSK*

Ceramic Figures

A Goldscheider figure of a nude female, signed Lorenzl, No. 3802, 11in (28cm).
£500-550   *IM*

A Cathaussen ceramic figure, 13in (33cm) long.
£300-550   *ASA*

Metal Figures

An Art Deco chrome lamp, 12in (31cm) high.
£95-110   *HAE*

A green patinated bronze figure of a dancing girl, on green onyx base, pitted and rubbed, marked Lorenzl and Argentor Wien, c1930, 14in (36cm).
£800-1,000   *S(C)*

A cold painted silvered bronze figure of a nude girl, holding a bronze and ivory opened fan, on arched mottled marble base, Etling, Paris, 15½in (40cm).
£750-850   *P(M)*

'O Mighty Woman', a bronze group cast from a model by J. J. Nielsons, on a naturalistic base, her distraught lover at her feet, signed in the bronze J.J. Nielsons, 14½in (37cm) high.
£600-800   *C*

'Sword Dance' a bronze figure, cast from a model by F. Ouillon Carrere, on bronze base, on black marble plinth, signed in the bronze F. Ouillon Carrere 1919, 21in (54cm) high.
£1,200-1,500   *C*

A green patinated bronze figure of a dancing maiden, on an alabaster and marble circular base, 16in (41cm) high.
£400-600   *C*

A bronze figure, by Phillipe, on square marble base, signed P. Phillipe, R.U.M., 16in (41cm) high.
£1,200-1,500   *ASA*

Bronze & Ivory Figures

A pair of bronze and ivory figures, 6in (15cm) high.
£1,500-1,800   *ASA*

A bronze and ivory figure of a dancer by Lorenzl, 15in (38cm) high.
£1,800-2,600   *ASA*

A figure of a bronze and ivory dancer, on a large onyx dish, 8in (20cm) high.
£700-900   *ASA*

A Preiss carved ivory figure of a young girl with a skipping rope, on an onyx base, signed F. Preiss, 6in (15cm) high.
£600-800   *P*

A gilded bronze and ivory figure of a dancing girl, on a green onyx pedestal, signed in the bronze H. Fugiere, the base plate stamped Fabrication Francaise Paris – G.M., little finger of right hand missing, 19in (48cm) high.
£1,500-2,000   *MAT*

A bronze and ivory statue in the style of Preiss, the girl balancing an iridescent glass ball, minor damage to hands and feet, 12in (31cm).
£1,500-2,000   *LAY*

A bronze and ivory figure, by Claire J. Colinet, 12in (31cm).
£4,000-5,000   *ASA*

Furniture

A silvered bronze and ivory figure, by Lorenzl, modelled as a 1920s girl in short graduated party dress, on square marble base, signed Lorenzl, 7½in (19cm) high.
£300-400   *P*

The Respectful Splits, a cold painted bronze and ivory figure, cast from a model by Paul Phillipe, on a green onyx base, signed P. Phillipe, 7in (18cm) high.
£2,500-3,000   *Bon*

A games/music cabinet, in brown lacquer, the drop front opening to reveal shelves and partitions, above a pair of chequer doors with carved ivory chess pieces, 63in (161cm) high.
£1,200-1,700   *P*

A burr walnut and satinwood bedroom suite comprising a 'Lit Double', a pair of bedside cabinets with grey and white striated marble panels, a dressing mirror and a wardrobe.
£2,000-3,000   *C*

A French calamander and maple veneered occasional table, the rectangular twin-flap top above 2 frieze drawers, on solid rectangular supports, 23½in (60cm) wide.
£400-500   *CSK*

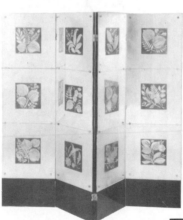

A tub chair, upholstered in beige suede, 30½in (78cm) high.
£1,000-1,500   *CNY*

An inlaid wood cabinet, attributed to Leleu, with mirrored back, above two-door cabinet, inlaid with mother-of-pearl blossoms against parquetry ground, 47½in (120cm).
£1,200-1,700   *CNY*

A French three-fold screen, with mirrored glass decoration by Pierre Lardin, the white painted sections of perforated form, mounted with large rectangular acid-etched, gold-leafed and painted glass panels depicting a mermaid and 2 sea sprites, 66in (168cm) high, each section 24in (61cm) wide.
£1,500-2,000   *C*

A French four-fold lacquer screen, with mirrored glass decoration by Max Ingrand, each section mounted with 3 square mirrored panels decorated with acid-etched amber and gold autumn leaves, 74in (188cm) high, each section 21in (53cm) wide.
£2,000-2,500   *C*

Glass

A Robert 'Mouseman' Thompson oak double bed, on casters, one leg with carved mouse signature, 80½in (204cm) long.
£1,200-1,800   *C*

A Robert 'Mouseman' Thompson oak buffet, carved with mouse signature, 72in (182cm) wide.
£2,000-2,700   *C*

A frosted green glass bowl, set in a chromed metal stand on a bakelite base, inscribed under the base 'Designed and Manufactured in our own works, Joseph Lucas Ltd'.
£120-180   *Bea*

A pair of French frosted glass decanters, decorated with female forms.
£600-900
ASA

A black and clear glass decanter, 9in (23cm), and 6 glasses.
£300-400 *ASA*

Jewellery

A cameo vase by Le Verre Francais, 8½in (21cm) high.
£700-900 *ASA*

A black and clear glass decanter, c1930.
£100-200 *ASA*

A Georg Jensen brooch, with Danish maker's marks and numbered 70, 2in (6cm) diam.
£200-250 *P*

A black and white enamelled dress set comprising: a pair of cufflinks, 4 buttons and 3 studs, all depicting a gentleman in tuxedo, in original fitted case.
£450-550 *CSK*

A Georg Jensen silver ring, designed by Henning Koppel, of openwork almost heart-shape amoebic form, Danish marks, numbered 89 and bearing London import marks for 1967.
£80-100 *P*

A pearl bracelet, each section interspersed by 3 diamonds and with all diamond set white gold clasp, 2ct approx.
£1,200-1,600 *GA(W)*

A silver and enamel pendant watch, the reverse with green, black, yellow, blue and red enamel stripe design, the champagne dial with Arabic numerals, signed Fresard, Lucerne, the signed oval movement jewelled to the third with 3 adjustments, the hinged case with the maker's mark.
£250-350 *CSK*

A lady's Continental two-colour bracelet watch, the black dial signed Titus with square cut synthetic ruby twin line borders and diamond and synthetic ruby panel, scroll shoulders to the twin row Brazilian link bracelet.
£700-900 *CSK*

Make the most of Miller's

Unless otherwise stated, any description which refers to 'a set' or 'a pair' includes a valuation for the entire set or the pair, even though the illustration may show only a single item

A lady's Continental sprung bangle watch, with scrollwork terminals, the movement signed Periam Watch Co., with black dial.
£1,200-1,700 *CSK*

597

Metal

A Continental silver gilt and enamel cigarette box with cedar interior, in pale blue, pink and black design on a white ground, stamped import marks for London 1927, 4½in (11cm) wide.
£900-1,200 *CSK*

A sterling silver oblong cigarette case with sunburst cast decoration and gold coloured clasp set with a blue stone, 4½in (11cm) wide.
£300-350 *P(M)*

A silver chalice by Charles Boyton, 1936, 7in (18cm).
£400-500 *ASA*

A pair of brass candlesticks, 11in (28cm) high.
£40-50 *SCO*

A James Dixon silver candelabra, c1920, 8in (20cm) high.
£400-600 *ASA*

A pair of Liberty pewter candlesticks, with separate sconces, maker's marks.
£300-400 *ASA*

A silver dish, London, c1930, 11in (28cm) diam.
£350-450 *ASA*

A Georg Jensen hammer beaten beaker, marked Denmark Sterling, Georg Jensen, 296A, c1925, 4in (10cm).
£500-600 *S(C)*

Georg Jensen (1886-1935) was a Danish designer of silverware and jewellery, whose workshop was established in 1904 in Copenhagen.

A Georg Jensen silver butter dish and butter knife in the Blossom pattern, maker's marks and import marks for 1928 and 1930.
£400-500 *P*

A German electroplate cocktail shaker modelled as a Zeppelin, the interior containing flask, lemon squeezer, strainer, graduated cups, corkscrew box and cover, and spoon.
£1,200-1,500 *CSK*

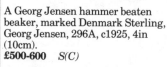

A pair of bonbon dishes with applied ivory handles, by William Hutton & Sons, Sheffield 1935, 9in (23cm) wide **£900-1,200** *P(M)*

A tea and coffee service, designed by Georg Jensen, comprising: teapot with ebonised wooden handle, terminating at the top in twin fruit cluster finial, London import marks for 1931, coffee pot, London import marks for 1929, 9½in (24cm) high, sugar bowl and milk jug, London import marks for 1931, and tea tray, marks for 1928, each with oval mark and crown, oval .925 mark, and Sterling Denmark, with GS import mark for George Stockwell, marked Dessin GI.
£4,000-5,000 *P*

A three-piece coffee set, by R. E.
Stone, London, 1947.
£700-800 *DID*

A Georg Jensen four-piece lightly
hammered coffee service, with
ebonised handles and finials,
stamped with usual Georg Jensen
marks and dated 1918, coffee pot 6in
(15cm) high, 788gr.
£1,500-2,000 *C*

A pewter coffee set with tray,
marked Liberty & Co.
£300-400 *ASA*

A W.M.F. electroplated pewter
mirror, stamped factory marks, B,
1/O, OX, piece missing from top,
c1900, 19in (48cm).
£550-650 *S(C)*

A four-piece tea service comprising:
teapot, hot water jug, sugar and
cream jug, of octagonal form,
decorated with bands of chased
scrollwork, Birmingham 1933, 58oz.
£600-700 *P(M)*

A three-piece silver tea service of
panelled rectangular design,
comprising: teapot, sugar basin and
cream jug, Birmingham 1932/3,
39oz gross.
£350-450 *GAK*

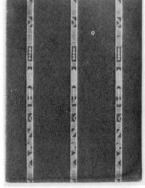

Miscellaneous

A Wiener Werkstätte embossed
leather wallet, 'Gesiba', with popper
fastener, with embossed gilt
decoration of 3 bands each with a
geometric pattern, stamped on the
inside Gesiba Wiener Werkstätte,
6in (15cm) long.
£250-350 *C*

A Donegal tufted woollen carpet,
the sage green field with central
blue rose flowerhead within rose
leaf and stem motifs in green and
brown, 68½ by 37½in
(173 by 96cm).
£600-700 *C*

A bronze and ivory figure and
clock, by Ferdinand Preiss,
9in (23cm).
£2,000-2,500 *ASA*

A clock made in the Isle of Man, and
featured on the front cover of
Collectable Clocks, the rocking ship
and changing background light are
very effective, particularly at night,
c1943, 13in (33cm) high.
£400-500 *RFA*

An enamelled and chromed metal
table lamp, on circular base, the
curved part reeded column
supporting swivel mounted reeded
shade, 16½in (42cm) high.
£250-350 *CSK*

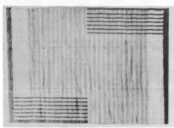

A Donegal tufted woollen carpet, the mushroom ground with patterns in shades of green, the reverse with printed number 1936, 159½ by 107½in (404 by 273cm).
£450-650 *C*

Post-War Design

Jean Cocteau, a terracotta bust by Arno Breker, signed, numbered 5/50, on a rectangular dark grey stone base, 13½in (35cm) high.
£2,000-2,500 *C*

A terracotta plate, designed by Jean Lurçat, with polychrome enamels, signed under the plate J. Lurçat Sant-Vicens, N.Z.C. III Dessin, 10in (25cm) diam.
£1,200-1,800

Pipistrello, a table lamp designed by Gae Aulenti, for Martinelli Luce, marked Modello 620, Pipistrello, Martinello Luce design Gae Aulenti, Made in Italy, 35½in (91cm).
£1,000-1,500 *C*

A Vistosi metal and glass stylised bird, the free-blown smoky grey glass internally decorated with a triple row of irregular blue and green rectangles, with applied millefiori eyes and mounted on folded metal legs with claw feet, 10½in (27cm).
£1,000-1,500 *C*

A Scandinavian blue tinted fruit bowl, signed and dated 1960, 15in (38cm) wide.
£60-80 *PCh*

A set of 8 Fornasetti plates, each with painted polychrome decoration of the sun in various shapes, with black printed signature 12 Mesi, 12 Soli, Fornasetti Milano, Made in Italy, 10½in (26cm) diam.
£3,200-4,000 *C*

Berthe Hill, 'Chippie', 1920s jazz singer, in fibreglass, by John Clinch, 34in (86cm).
£800-900 *ABS*

A Vistosi metal and glass stylised bird, the free-blown blue tinted glass internally decorated with a red spiral, with applied millefiori eyes and mounted on folded metal legs with claw feet, 7½in (19cm) high.
£1,000-1,500 *C*

A James Powell & Sons (Whitefriars) Ltd. vase, decorated with a spiral ribbon, in amethyst glass, 11in (28cm) high.
£150-200 *P*

IVORY

A Siculo-Arabic ivory casket, the lid and body with gilt copper mounts and lock plate, the lid with one side panel lacking, minor damage, 12th/13thC, 4½in (12cm) wide.
£3,200-5,000   *C*

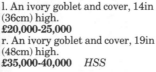

A set of 6 Austrian carved ivory figures of musicians, on turned boxwood and ebonised barrel bases, 6in (15cm).
£2,500-3,500   *CSK*

A pair of South German ivory and wood figures of beggars, on naturalistically carved wooden bases, minor damage to one hat, early 18thC, 11in (28cm).
£4,500-5,000   *C*

These figures are stylistically very close to the style of Veit Grauppensberg (1698-1774).

l. An ivory goblet and cover, 14in (36cm) high.
£20,000-25,000
r. An ivory goblet and cover, 19in (48cm) high.
£35,000-40,000   *HSS*

An unusual Anglo Indian carved ivory miniature chiffonier, the upper section with mirror back and scroll supports, the base with 2 doors, enclosing a selection of bottles, goblets and jugs, slight damage, 19thC, 7in (18cm).
£500-550   *Bea*

A German or Austrian ivory and boxwood figure of a tonsured monk leaning on a wine barrel, dated 1895, 6in (15cm) overall.
£450-650   *CSK*

An ivory opera glass, three-draw with turned eyepiece and barrel, signed on the draw G. & C. Dixey, 3 New Bond Street, London.
£350-500   *S*

A German ivory figure of Venus with Cupid, on naturalistic base, on turned wooden socle, 19thC, 9in (23cm).
£2,000-3,000   *C*

A French ivory statuette of Parsifal, in period costume, on cylindrical turned socle, hand repaired, 19thC, 8in (20cm).
£1,000-1,500   *CSK*

A carved ivory portrait bust of a gentleman, raised on a black marble socle, 19thC, 3in (8cm). **£450-550**   *CSK*

A Dutch ivory handled knife and fork set, the handles carved in the round with a king and queen holding their sceptres, the steel knife blade with cutler's mark, the steel fork with 2 tines, in cuir bouilli case, some splits, late 17thC, the knife 8in (20cm) overall. **£1,000-1,500**   *C*

MARBLE

An English white marble bust of a young girl, by Donald Campbell Haggart, inscribed and dated on the back D.G. Haggart. SCR.1902, on an ebonised wood pedestal base, early 20thC, 59½in (150cm) high. **£1,500-2,000**   *C*

Donald Campbell Haggart worked primarily in Glasgow during the late 19th and early 20thC. He exhibited at the Royal Academy in 1882.

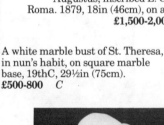

An Italian sculpted white marble bust of the young Emperor Augustus, inscribed L. Clerici. Roma. 1879, 18in (46cm), on a socle. **£1,500-2,000**   *C*

A white marble bust of St. Theresa, in nun's habit, on square marble base, 19thC, 29½in (75cm). **£500-800**   *C*

An Italian white marble bust of a faun, the smiling figure with tightly curling hair, set on a waisted socle, c1880, 22in (56cm). **£650-850**   *S(S)*

A white marble bust of a young woman, in Renaissance style, late 19thC, 21½in (54cm). **£3,500-4,000**   *C*

A reconstituted marble bust of a young clown, smiling and wearing a ruff, on a waisted socle, 20in (51cm). **£170-220**   *CSK*

Make the Most of Miller's

CONDITION is absolutely vital when assessing the value of an antique. Damaged pieces on the whole appreciate much less than perfect examples. However a rare, desirable piece may command a high price even when damaged

A Victorian white marble figure of a Classical style maiden, by John Randolph Rogers, signed Randolph Rogers, Rome, base detached, some chipping, 42in (107cm).
£2,000-3,000   *Bon*

John Randolph Rogers (1825-92). Born in New York, he studied both in Florence and Rome under Bartolini. Major commissions include many monuments to the American Civil War as well as a pair of doors for the Capitol. Smaller pieces include Biblical and Classical subjects such as Ruth and Nydia.

An Italian white marble bust of a pensive girl in a lace mantilla, by C. Lapini, signed and dated on the reverse C. Lapini Firenze 1888, associated green marble fluted column with rotating capital, the bust 20½in (52cm).
£2,500-3,500   *C*

A pair of Italian white marble busts, Venus and Adonis, after the Antique, on socles, with grey marble pedestals, 69in (175cm) high overall.
£3,000-3,500   *P(S)*

A white marble armorial keystone, the face carved with a coat-of-arms flanked by foliate scrolls, 18thC, 5½in (14cm).
£300-400   *S*

An Italian white marble figure of a young boy, late 19thC, 22in (56cm).
£1,200-1,700   *S*

An Italian white marble portrait relief of a lady, in Florentine Renaissance style, within an oval giltwood frame with flowerheads at corners, 14½ by 11in (37 by 28cm).
£3,500-4,000   *C*

A white marble armorial plaque, the face with a coat-of-arms supported by a lion and a slave, inscribed Furth fortune and fill the fetters, 18thC, 9in (23cm).
£500-600   *S*

The arms are those of Murray, Alexander Sutherland.

An Italian marble mortar, the sides richly carved in relief, and with the initials IN-B-G-M, 2 of the spouts carved for pouring, the other 2 plain, 17thC, 16in (41cm) wide.
£1,500-2,000   *C*

A Victorian white marble female figure, wearing a long skirt, monogrammed L.S., 25in (64cm).
£350-450   *CDC*

A pair of marble and gilt bronze urns, the mottled white and green marble forming the baluster body, stepped domed lids with pine cone finials, with gilt bronze feet decorated with stylised foliage, the body with gilt bronze satyr masks and swags of leaves and berries, the gilt bronze neck with guilloche design, 19thC, 6in (15cm).
£1,500-2,000 *C*

An Italian white marble figure of Jesus of Nazareth, with a young boy at his side, some chips and weathering, late 19thC, 55in (140cm).
£1,000-1,500 *HSS*

An Italian serpentine marble inkwell, the lid and sides decorated with plaster cameos after the Antique, enclosing a fitted interior with slightly ribbed body, mid-19thC, 5½in (14cm) diam.
£1,000-1,500 *C*

An English white marble relief of Diana, probably from a chimneypiece, shown seated against a tree trunk, her quiver at her side and a boar's head and dead stag in the background, holding aloft a bird, at which her 2 hounds look, 18thC, 21 by 8in (53 by 20cm). **£1,800-2,200** *C*

TERRACOTTA

Vertue records Rysbrack making the statuettes of Van Dyck, Rubens and Fiammingo (sic) in 1743, during the period that his popularity was briefly eclipsed by Scheemaker's successful Monument to Shakespeare of 1740 in Westminster Abbey. The 3 statuettes were, nevertheless, much admired at the time, and by 1744 the Daily Advertiser was carrying an advertisement for the casting in plaster of the 3 figures 'now in the Collection of Mr. Joseph van Hacken' for the price of seven and a half guineas the set, subscriptions to be taken by Mess. Claessens and Ven Hagen, at Mr. Rysbrack's in Vere Street. The production of these casts was continued after van Hacken's death in 1749 by John Cheere and Charles Harris. Although examples of the Rubens and van Dyck figures are relatively common, the figure of Duquesnoy, referred to in contemporary literature as Fiammingo, is very rare.

An English white terracotta figure of François Duquesnoy, cast from a model by Michael Rysbrack, leaning against the Belvedere Torso, which is partially draped with an embroidered coverlet, right and left foot missing, minor arm chips, late 18thC, 21½in (54cm). **£4,500-5,500** *C*

A French painted terracotta bust of Marie Antoinette, with manufacturer's mark to the reverse, on an integral socle, 19thC, 30in (76cm).
£500-800
CSK

WOODCARVINGS

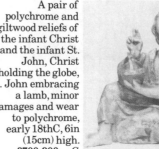

A pair of polychrome and giltwood reliefs of the infant Christ and the infant St. John, Christ holding the globe, St. John embracing a lamb, minor damages and wear to polychrome, early 18thC, 6in (15cm) high.
£700-900 *C*

A rare English carved oak figure
of St. John, 16thC.
£3,500-4,000   *B*

A set of 5 Tyrolean wood figures
of peasants, the wood stained to
resemble marquetry, one figure
lacking right arm, another
lacking left hand, other minor
losses, 18th/19thC,
approximately 12½in
(32cm) high.
£2,000-3,000   *C*

A German polychrome wood group
of 3 winged putti, some repainting,
later shaped wooden base, early
18thC, 21½in (55cm) high.
£5,000-6,000   *C*

A pair of Anglo-Flemish wood
figures of courtiers, one figure
lacking right forearm, some
damages, early 17thC, 24in (61cm).
£2,000-3,000   *C*

A South German boxwood figure of
St. John, formerly from a
Crucifixion group, on wooden socle,
tip of nose and base chipped, c1700,
7½in (19cm).
£1,500-2,000   *C*

*The present boxwood figure with its
delicate modelling is similar in style
to a boxwood figure of approximately
the same height in the Staatliche
Museen zu Berlin.*

A Neopolitan
polychrome carved
wood figure of the
Christ Child, with
inset glass eyes,
on the associated
wooden plinth,
18thC, 20½in
(52cm).
£400-500   *CSK*

A Hispano-Flemish polychrome and
giltwood group of St. Martin, sword
lacking, some worming and minor
damages, later wooden base, early
16thC, 31½in (80cm).   **£6,200-7,000**   *C*

A Franconian limewood relief of a
bishop saint, traces of polychrome,
staff and fingers lacking from right
hand, early 16thC, 38in (97cm).
£2,500-3,500   *C*

A pair of Italian carved
giltwood and gesso figures
of amorini, on stepped
square bases, late 18thC,
23in (59cm) high overall.
£1,000-1,200   *CSK*

A carved oak cartouche, the cresting with 2 putti interspersed with 'rays of light' above a panel of the Virgin Mary framed by leafy scrolls, c1750, 54 by 36in (137 by 92cm).
£700-1,000   *S(S)*

A South German or Austrian wood appliqué, carved in high relief with a demi-figure of a bishop, later pierced wooden background with strapwork, 18thC, 11in (28cm) high.
£2,000-2,500   *C*

Two wood carvings in the style of Grinling Gibbons, one depicting pine cones, fruit and peas in the pod, 23in (59cm) high, the other flowers and ears of wheat, 26in (66cm), 18thC.
£220-270   *PCh*

A Neapolitan polychrome wood figure of an ox, probably from a crib group, with glass eyes, on later wooden base, late 18th/early 19thC, 11½in (29cm) high.
£1,700-2,200   *C*

A pair of Italian giltwood and painted wall plaques, centred with scallop shells, within fruit and foliate surrounds, 28in (71cm).
£800-1,000   *CSK*

A German 16thC style oak panel, carved in high relief with Adam and Eve, after Albrecht Durer, head of serpent lacking, 26in (66cm) wide.
£1,500-2,000   *C*

A pair of German pearwood reliefs, within ebonised wood mounts and giltwood frames, the oak reverse with old label, late 17th/early 18thC, 6in (15cm) high.
£4,000-5,000   *C*

The labels on the reverse of these reliefs read 'William of Orange landed at Torbay 1688. This carving was one of the panels round top of one of the ornamental vats which were brought over for his dining room so that he could always get at his favourite drink. When these vats in possession of the L. Victuallers Co. were broken up, a parishioner on Epping Green secured the Panels for Rev. H. L. Neave'.

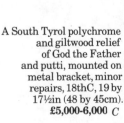

A South Tyrol polychrome and giltwood relief of God the Father and putti, mounted on metal bracket, minor repairs, 18thC, 19 by 17½in (48 by 45cm).
£5,000-6,000   *C*

ANTIQUITIES
Marble

A Roman marble head of Caracalla, 2nd Century A.D., 11½in (29cm). **£18,000-22,000** *S*

A Roman marble funerary relief, with inscription between the acroteria at either corner, reading 'Ioulianos, son of Menios, aged 35, farewell. Chrysea, wife of Ioulianos, (?age), farewell', the recessed niche below carved with 2 busts, Eastern Mediterranean, 3rd Century A.D., 23½in (60cm) high. **£6,500-7,000** *S*

A Roman marble cinerary urn, 3rd Century A.D., 27in (69cm) wide. **£8,000-10,000** *S*

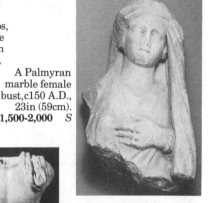

A Palmyran marble female bust, c150 A.D., 23in (59cm). **£1,500-2,000** *S*

A Roman marble male figure, wearing a bulla decorated with a mask, his himation worn diagonally so as to leave his chest bare, the garment with notched edges, 1st Century A.D., 39½in (100cm). **£6,000-8,000** *S*

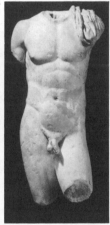

A Roman marble male torso, nude except for a fragment of drapery over the left shoulder, restored, 1st-2nd Century A.D., 31in (79cm). **£25,000-30,000** *S*

A Roman marble head, from a togatus or palliatus figure, his himation drawn up over the back of his head, the face with furrowed brow and ageing features, 1st Century B.C. /1st Century A.D., 9½in (24cm). **£10,000-12,000** *S*

Metalware

An Egyptian bronze figure of a cat, Late period, c600 B.C., 4½in (11cm). **£4,500-5,500** *S*

A fragmentary Greek marble grave loutrophoros, carved in shallow relief, inscribed above the heads of the 2 principal figures, 'Polykrates and Polystratos', foot, handles and neck of loutrophoros broken away, 4th Century B.C., 44in (111cm). **£22,000-25,000** *S*

Polykrates and Polystratos appear as son and father on a gravestone from Peiraeus (IG II 1771); on this loutrophoros the order of relationship seems reversed. It could perhaps be the same family, but neither are rare names in Athens.

An Egyptian bronze figure of a lion, reclining, with its left paw resting on its right paw, Late period, 712-30 B.C., 4½in (11cm). **£4,500-5,000** *S*

An Egyptian bronze figure of Osiris, the God, of mummified form, standing holding the crook and flail, with plumed headdress and central uraeus, 26th Dynasty, c664-525 B.C., 8½in (21cm).
£3,200-4,000 S

A Roman bronze candelabrum, standing on 3 dolphin shaped feet with palmettes, 3 shell shaped dishes between, one foot restored, 1st-2nd Century A.D., 32½in (82cm).
£8,000-10,000 S

A Roman bronze lamp, with the inward curving handle terminating in a theatrical mask, a palmette under its chin, 3rd Century A.D., 6in (15cm).
£2,000-2,500 S

An Italic bronze helmet, of the Pilos type, 2 appliques resembling wings to either side of the crown, mid-4th Century B.C., 10in (25cm).
£5,000-5,500 S

Pottery

An Iranian grey pottery vessel in the form of a bird, 1st millennium B.C., 10in (25cm), a Middle Eastern bronze chariot, and a Middle Eastern bronze male figure.
£8,000-10,000 S

The item has a thermoluminescence test certificate verifying its authenticity.

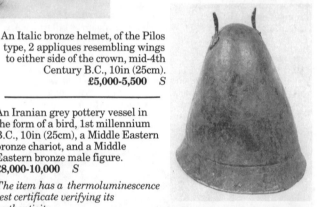

A Corinthian pottery round bodied aryballos, decorated with the figure of a siren, standing with open wings between a panther and a goose, with added purple details, c600 B.C., 5in (13cm).
£1,500-2,000 S

Miscellaneous

A Palmyran limestone female bust, carved in relief, with an Aramaic inscription in the top left hand corner, nose restored, c150-200 A.D., 21in (53cm).
£5,000-6,000 S

A Roman limestone relief, with a male figure holding a scroll in his left hand, the head surmounted by a ?bird, 3rd Century A.D., 31in (79cm). £3,500-4,500 S

A Greek terracotta female figure, 6th Century B.C., 8in (20cm). £600-800 S

A Roman green glass single handled flask, a strap handle attached to the shoulder and neck, the base moulded with 3 concentric circles, with some weathering, 2nd-3rd Century A.D., 10in £800-1,000 S

A Greek terracotta female figure, probably East Greek, early 5th Century B.C., 7in (18cm). **£600-800** *S*

A boulle sewing box with original fittings, c1850, 9in (23cm) wide. **£1,700-2,000** *EHA*

An Attic terracotta doll, in the form of a nude female figure, depicted only to the upper part of the legs, the arms not moulded, 5th Century B.C., 6in (15cm). **£1,700-2,000** *S*

A Roman limestone draped female torso, 1st-2nd Century A.D., 49in (124cm). **£6,500-7,000** *S*

SEWING

A collection of 51 lace bobbins, comprising 33 bearing names or messages, 6 pewter banded, 12 plain, 5 bobbins chipped, 19thC. **£600-650** *S*

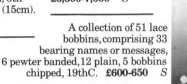

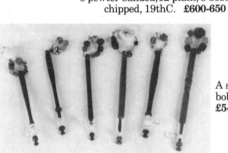

A selection of wooden lace bobbins, 4-6in (10-15cm). **£5-10 each** *VB*

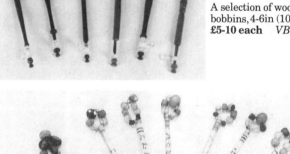

Nine variously named bone bobbins. **£140-170** *Bea*

A silver mounted tortoiseshell novelty sewing case, in the form of an egg, mounted with the cast head of an emerging chick, its feet protruding from the base, containing a gilt thimble, silver gilt scissors, silver needle case and silver bodkin, London, 1901, 4in (10cm). **£600-700** *S(S)*

An ivory and brass inlaid sewing case, the cover and escutcheons inlaid with brass scrolls and stained mother-of-pearl, containing carved mother-of-pearl spools, 2 silver thimbles and various sewing items, including an ivory tape measure case. **£450-500** *S*

A selection of bone lace bobbins, 3½-4½in (9-12cm). **£17-40 each** *VB*

609

A brass container for packets of needles, made by W. Avery, c1880.
£20-25 *PC*

A Chelsea porcelain thimble, brightly painted within gold line bands, inscribed Souvenez vous de moy, hair crack, 1in (2cm).
£2,500-3,000 *Bea*

A Meissen style porcelain needlecase, with hinged cover, in the form of a baby, swathed in yellow and florally decorated clothes, 4½in (12cm). **£450-550** *Bea*

A Meissen gilt metal mounted etui, of cigar shape, painted with 4 scenes of gallants and ladies, in iron red, minute rim chips, c1770, 6½in (17cm).
£900-1,200 *S*

An enamel bodkin case, painted with urns and trophies in gilt cartouches on a turquoise ground, inscribed Amor and A Pledge of Love, and a group of 4 bodkins.
£250-300 *S*

A Meissen porcelain thimble, reserved on a powder-blue ground, the top with a flowerhead, with gilt interior, c1740.
£1,700-2,000 *Bea*

A Meissen porcelain thimble, the top painted with a gold flowerhead, c1740.
£2,500-3,000 *Bea*

A set of 6 buttons, each engraved with a dog, George Cray, London, c1780, 1in (2cm) diam, in fitted case. **£300-350** *CSK*

A Ward's arm and platform machine, No. 15851, with gilt and coloured decoration. **£470-550** *CSK*

A decoupage sewing box, French, c1850.
£900-1,200 *EHA*

A selection of wooden netting tools – 2 needles and 3 gauges or meshes.
£3-10 *PC*

A Grover & Baker No. 24 treadle sewing machine, No. 233295, with japanned arm, gilt decoration, patent dates to 1863, open treadle with drawer, instruction book, sales literature and original invoice; Bainbridge & Co., Newcastle, date June 11, 1870, for £8.8.0.
£1,500-2,000 *CSK*

TEXTILES
Costume

A trained dress of white cotton, the sleeves, bodice and hem with deep muslin insertions embroidered in white silk with laurel wreaths and key pattern borders, the bodice also worked with monogram C.M., c1800. **£2,000-4,000** *CSK*

A trained dress of white muslin, the sleeves and borders embroidered with garlands of white flowers outlined in black, c1800. **£5,000-5,500** *CSK*

A set of viscount's and viscountess's ceremonial robes, by Ede and Ravenscroft, comprising a pair of coronets trimmed with ermine and silver balls, a scarlet velvet gown and matching cape trimmed with ermine, tasselled sash, an ermine trimmed waistcoat with matching cape, with deep ermine collar and trim, all in a wooden case, early 20thC. **£1,000-1,500** *S*

A dress of yellow cotton printed with vignettes of palm trees and shells, in red, with gigot sleeves, and a miniature version of the same dress for a little girl, both c1828. **£2,000-2,500** *CSK*

A printed cotton gown, in black, gold and rust, c1810. **£700-900** *S*

A dress of grey silk, embroidered in emerald green, yellow and white silk, trimmed with green velvet and black lace, with sleeved and sleeveless bodice, one bodice altered, French, c1865. **£900-1,200** *CSK*

A Schiaparelli evening gown and cape, the gauze striped with bands of orange and gold, the skirt with asymmetrical fishtail, complete with silk underslip, labelled Schiaparelli, Paris, numbered 41677, c1935. **£2,500-3,000** *S*

A trained wedding dress of ivory silk and cream silk, with a spray of artificial orange blossom at the neck, the Vandyked hem trimmed with a blue bow and a spray of heather, c1878. **£300-350** *CSK*

A sleeveless evening dress of crushed raspberry pink velvet, the off the shoulder bodice trimmed with a large velvet flourish, labelled Chanel, 1930s. **£2,000-4,000** *CSK*

Napoleon Bonaparte's black silk socks, contained in purpose made leather presentation book shaped case, together with letter of provenance from Mr. Dixon dated 1916, early 19thC. **£4,000-4,500** *C*

Provenance: these socks were allegedly presented by Madame Bertrand to W. Dixon Esq., Surgeon on H.M. Camel at St. Helena. In a letter dated 1916 a descendant of his, H. Dixon, donates the socks to raise money for the war effort.

A wedding dress of ivory silk, with high waist and slight train, with matching bolero and cloak, some alterations, unlabelled, probably by Balenciaga, c1968.
£700-900 *CSK*

A pair of brocaded satin ankle boots, the soles stamped Hird, the gold and white striped satin woven with yellow, pink and pale blue flowers, and fastened with 9 gold buttons, 2in (5cm) heels, c1885. **£650-700** *S*

A straw hat, c1920. **£25-35** *CLH*

A brocaded silk shoe and clog, woven in pale blue and ivory, the clog of pale blue satin, c1760.
£600-700 *S*

Five Bes Ben hats, American, some damage, c1950. **£300-500** *S*

A woven Kashmir shawl, with central quatrefoil ground densely bordered by green, pink, scarlet and blue intertwined botehs, c1840. **£400-600** *S*

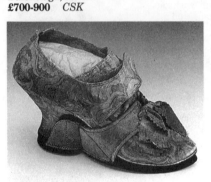

A pair of lady's court shoes of navy blue satin figured with gilt thread arabesques and printed with bold floral designs, with long pointed tongue, stamped Made Expressly for Mme Neal Ltd, Bradford, c1910.
£200-300 *CSK*

A Bes Ben crystal water lily toque, American, of black felt applied with huge blooms and enamelled leaves, with veil, c1950.
£150-200 *S*

A topi. **£30-60** *MSh*

A Paisley shawl, woven with a border of blue hooked vines against an ivory ground, with red veined cones and corner ornaments, 1840, 58 by 112in (147 by 285cm).
£550-600 *CSK*

A Paisley shawl, woven with fresh colours, towards the black silk central medallion, c1860, 72in (183cm) square. **£500-550** *CSK*

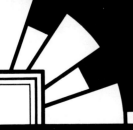

A Clarice Cliff 'Age of Jazz' figural group, modelled as a two-dimensional pianist and banjo player in evening dress, 5in (12cm). **£4,000-4,500** *P*

A Linthorpe vase, by C. Dresser. **£720-780** *C*

A Clarice Cliff Bizarre pottery chocolate pot, in the form of a chicken, with lid, on circular orange foot, some damage, 6in (15cm) high. **£120-150** *HCH*

A Lorenzl Goldscheider earthenware figure of an odalisque, marked Lorenzl c1925, 18in (46.5cm). **£1,500-2,000** *S*

Two Clarice Cliff Fantasque pottery comports: l. Hollyhock pattern. **£230-260** r. Melon pattern. **£80-120** *HCH*

A Goldscheider glazed earthenware figure of a female dancer, marked, c1930, 15½in (39.5cm).**£850-950** *S*

A Gallé faience bulldog, enamelled mark E Gallé à Nancy, c1880, 12½in (31.5cm). **£5,500-6,000** *S*

A Coronaware vase, by Hancock & Sons, designed by Molly Hancock, 10in (25.5cm) high. **£130-150** *CHa*

A Clarice Cliff Bizarre pottery vase, 8in (20cm). **£300-350** *HCH*

A Lenci figure on a turtle, c1930. **£2,000-2,600** *ASA*

A New Hall plate, by Lucien Bollumier, signed, c1925, 11½in (29cm). **£180-220** *CHa*

A bronze and
ivory figure,
marked Bruno
Zach, 15in
(38.5cm).
£2,500-3,500 *S*

A bronze figure,
c1930. **£1,800-
2,500** *CNY*

A gold and enamel
buckle, now fitted with
a watch, stamped
Vever Paris, c1900, 3in
(7.5cm).**£9,000-10,000**S

A parcel gilt cold
painted bronze figure,
23¹/₂in (60cm).
£6,500-7,500 *CNY*

A gilt and
enamelled bronze
figure of a snake
dancer, by Otto
Poertzel, c1930,
20¹/₂in (52cm).
£5,500-7,500 *ASA*

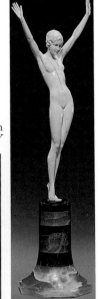

A bronze and ivory group, by Otto
Poertzel, 16¹/₂in (41.5cm).
£9,500-11,000 *C*

A bronze and ivory
figure, by Philippe,
14in (35cm).
£5,000-7,000 *ASA*

A parcel silvered bronze
and ivory figure of an
archer, by Pierre le
Faguays, early 20thC, 17in
(43cm). **£3,000-3,500** *CNY*

An ivory figure of a
nude, Ecstasy, by
Ferdinand Preiss,
early 20thC,
17in (43cm).
£5,000-6,000 *CNY*

A cold painted bronze and ivory female
figure, by Ferdinand Preiss, early 20thC,
9in (23cm). **£5,500-6,000** *CNY*

A Chiparus bronze and ivory figure of a
dancer, 'Alméria', c1925, 25in (64cm).
£45,000-50,000 *S*

A bronze and
enamel clock,
with enamelled
dial, on marble
base, marked
Maple & Cie
Paris, c1920,
10¹/₂in (27cm).
£8,000-9,000 *S*

An Art Deco bronze and ivory figure, by
Demètre Chiparus, 21in (54cm).
£50,000-60,000 *P*

615

Four Daum vases.
£2,500-4,500 each *C*

A Daum internally
decorated glass lamp,
17in (43cm).
£4,000-5,000 *CNY*

A Daum cameo
glass and wheel
carved vase,
signed in
intaglio, c1900,
7¹/₂in (18cm).
£1,600-1,900
PSG

A Daum enamelled
vase, enamelled
mark Daum Nancy,
c1900, 13in (33cm).
£24,000-26,000 *S*

A Daum overlaid and
etched glass lamp, 18in
(45.5cm).
£13,000-15,000 *CNY*

Three Daum carved, and
enamelled painted vases,
painted signatures and cross of
Lorraine. **£5,000-8,000 each** *C*

A Daum carved cameo
and marqueterie sur
verre glass vase,
engraved mark Daum
Nancy, c1900, 8in
(20.5cm).
£10,000-12,000 *S*

A Daum enamelled
glass lamp, with mark
Daum Nancy, c1900,
24¹/₂in (62cm).
£35,000-40,000 *S*

A Daum etched and
enamelled cameo glass
vase, signed, c1900,
7¹/₂in (18cm).
£3,500-4,000 *PSG*

An etched, enamelled
and applied glass vase,
Daum Nancy, 8in (20cm).
£35,000-40,000 *CNY*

Two Daum carved and acid
etched lamps, carved
signatures Daum Nancy.
£7,000-10,000 each *C*

A Daum
carved,
acid
etched
vase,
with
signature
Daum
Nancy,
with
Cross of
Lorraine,
12¹/₂in
(31cm)
high.
**£8,500-
9,500** *C*

A Daum carved and
acid etched overlay
vase, 9in (23cm).
£15,000-18,000 *C*

An Edgar Brandt
wrought iron lamp,
c1925. **£6,500-7,500** *S*

A Daum etched and enamelled glass vase, signature, 19½in (49cm). **£24,000-26,000** *CNY*

A Gallé double overlaid and etched glass chandelier, the domed shade with frosted ground overlaid and etched to depict blossoms, cameo signature, 17½in (44cm). **£5,500-6,500** *CNY*

A Daum vase, signed Daum Nancy, 9½in (24cm). **£2,700-3,200** *P*

A Daum glass vase, with Cross of Lorraine, 7½in (19cm). **£1,500-2,000** *P*

A Gallé carved and acid etched double overlay plafonnier, carved signature, 19in (49cm) diam. **£13,000-15,000** *C*

A Daum overlaid and carved glass vase, cameo signature, 16in (40cm). **£6,000-8,000** *CNY*

A Gallé overlaid and etched glass chandelier, cameo signatures, 18in (46cm) diam. **£20,000-22,000** *CNY*

A Gallé overlaid, glass lamp, 22in (56cm) high. **£13,000-15,000** *CNY*

A Gallé carved and acid etched double overlay table lamp, signed. **£35,000-45,000** *C*

A Gallé double overlaid etched glass lamp, 25in (64cm). **£12,000-15,000** *CNY*

A Gallé carved and acid etched triple overlay lamp. **£24,000-26,000** *C*

A Gallé carved, acid etched and fire polished double overlay table lamp, signed. **£22,000-25,000** *C*

A Gallé carved and acid etched lamp, 15½in (39cm) high. **£28,000-30,000** *C*

617

A Gallé intrecalaire, intaglio carved 'verrerie parlante' vase, signed, 4½in (11cm) high. **£30,000-35,000** *C*

A Gallé glass vase, the frosted ground overlaid and etched to depict wisteria, cameo signature, 24½in (61cm). **£80,000-85,000** *CNY*

A Gallé vase, signed in cameo, 12in (30.5cm) high. **£3,500-4,500** *ABS*

A Gallé carved and acid etched double overlay landscape vase, carved Gallé signature, 33in (83cm). **£90,000-100,000** *C*

A Gallé cameo glass vase, signed, c1900, 8½in (21cm). **£4,500-5,000** *PSG*

A Gallé decorated martelé enamel vase, 12in (30.5cm) **£7,500-8,500** *C*

A Gallé vase, carved signature, 6½in (16.5cm). **£7,000-8,000** *C*

A Gallé triple overlaid and etched glass table lamp base, cameo signature, 15in (38cm), with metal mount, **£20,000-25,000** *CNY*

A Gallé glass vase, c1900, 14in (35.5cm). **£10,000-12,000** *S*

A Gallé cameo glass 'Iris' vase, cameo mark, c1900, 20½in (51.5cm). **£30,000-32,000** *S*

A Gallé internally decorated carved cameo vase, c1900. **£35,000-40,000** *S*

A Gallé double overlaid and etched vase, signature, 17in (43cm). **£16,000-18,000** *CNY*

A Gallé carved and acid etched double overlay vase, cameo signature 17½in (43.5cm) high. **£40,000-45,000** *C*

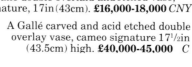

A frosted glass and bronze luminaire, the arched glass moulded with 3 peacocks and set in an electricfied bronze base, etched R Lalique France, 36in (91.5cm) wide. **£90,000-100,000** *CNY*

A Lalique glass vase, 'Languedoc', moulded in high relief with overlapping stylised leaves, engraved mark R Lalique France, 1929, 9in (22.5cm). **£7,000-8,000** *S*

A Lalique opalescent glass vase, 'Bacchantes', 9¹/₂in (24cm). **£14,000-16,000** *Bon*

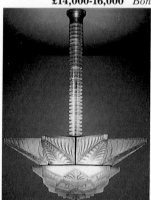

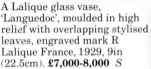

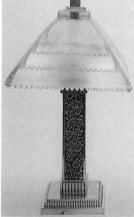

A Lalique opalescent figure, 'Suzanne', engraved R. Lalique France, 9in (23cm). **£10,000-12,000** *C*

A frosted glass chandelier, 'Stockholm', moulded R. Lalique. **£5,000-6,000** *CNY*

A pair of Lalique glass and nickel plated metal lamps, one shade with stencilled mark R Lalique, the other with wheel cut R Lalique France, c1928, 20in (50cm). **£9,000-10,000** *S*

A Lalique table lamp, the base acid stamped, 10in (26cm). **£12,000-15,000** *C*

A Lalique wall light, 18¹/₂in (47cm) diam. **£10,000-12,000** *C*

'Le Jour et la Nuit' clock, stencilled mark R Lalique, 15in (38cm). **£80,000-90,000** *Bon*

A Lalique glass clock, 'Sirènes', marked, c1928, 11in (28cm). **£5,500-6,500** *S*

An Argy-Rousseau pâte-de-verre glass vase, marked, c1920, 4in (9,5cm). **£20,000-22,000** *S*

A clear and frosted Alexandrite vase, 'Tortues', intaglio moulded R Lalique, 10½in (26cm). **£22,000-25,000** *Bon*

A Muller Frères cameo glass vase, cameo mark, 12in (30.5cm). **£7,000-8,000** *S*

A Lalique opalescent vase, 'Bacchantes', with engraved signature R Lalique, France, 9½in (24cm). **£19,000-21,000** *C*

A leaded glass and earthernware table lamp, the shade by Tiffany, the base by Ruth Erikson. **£10,000-12,000** *CNY*

A double overlaid and etched glass table lamp, cameo signature Muller Frères, Luneville, 21½in (54cm). **£8,000-10,000** *CNY*

A blue and clear glass scent flaçon, 'Bouchon Mûres', chip to underside, moulded R Lalique, 4½in (11cm). **£35,000-40,000** *Bon*

A Gabriel Argy-Rousseau pâte-de-verre table lamp, marked on both shade and base, 15½in (39.5cm). **£58,000-62,000** *C*

A diamond, glass and yellow gold brooch, stamped Lalique, 3½in (9cm). **£45,000-50,000** *CNY*

A French blue vase, 'Penthièvre', stencilled R Lalique, 10in (25.5cm). **£26,000-28,000** *Bon*

A glass table, 'Cactus', by Lalique et Cie, engraved No 37 le 3/12/82, 60in (152cm) diam. **£13,500-15,000** *CNY*

A Georges Dumoulin vase, with applied vertical grips, internally decorated with air bubbles, engraved G. Dumoulin, c1930. **£1,800-2,500** *C*

An Argy-Rousseau enamelled glass vase, gilded mark, 1920s, 6in (15cm). **£3,000-4,000** *S*

A Venini bottle vase, designed by Fulvio Bianconi, acid stamped mark, 9in (23cm). **£7,000-8,000** *C*

A set of 6 Liberty & Co silver and turquoise enamel buttons, with an entrelac design of Celtic inspiration, stamped L&Co, cymric with Birmingham hallmark for 1907, original fitted case. **£500-600** *C*

An Art Deco brooch, set with calibre cut black onyx and round diamonds, mounted in platinum, by Cartier. **£25,000-30,000** *CNY*

A plique à jour pendant, German, Pforzheim, c1910, 2½in (6cm). **£800-1,200** *DID*

An Art Deco jade, rock crystal, diamond and enamel desk clock, signed Cartier, c1930, in fitted case. **£28,000-32,000** *CNY*

Three Liberty & Co silver pendants. **£100-250 each** *DID*

Two Liberty pendants and one by Murlle Bennett & Co. **£100-200 each** *DID*

A Georg Jensen silver coloured metal necklace, monogrammed 'GJ', c1910, 9in (23cm) long. **£1,500-2,000** *S*

An Art Deco carved emerald, diamond and enamel bracelet, by Cartier. **£45,000-50,000** *CNY*

622

A Gabriel Argy-Rousseau pâte-de-verre vase, 'Loupes', moulded signature, 9¹/₂in (24cm) high. **£40,000-45,000** *C*

A glass sculpture, by Clifford Rainey, 'Blue Figure', cast signature, 1989, 28in (71cm). **£3,500-4,500** *C*

A copper and mica table lamp, the ginger jar vessel with 4 arms supporting a sweeping shade, stamped with windmill mark and Dirk Van Erp, c1911, 27in (69cm) high, with broken box. **£34,000-38,000** *CNY*

A wrought iron and hammered copper five-light chandelier, by Gustav Stickley, c1905. **£4,500-5,500** *CNY*

A leaded glass and copper table lamp, by the Roycrofters, stamped with the firm's orb mark, 18¹/₂in (47cm). **£5,000-6,000** *CNY*

A glass sculpture, 'Cosmic Tides', by Ray Flavell, cut, polished and sand blasted, deeply engraved, engraved signature, 1990, 16¹/₂in (41cm). **£4,000-5,000** *C*

A copper and mica table lamp, by Dirk Van Erp, stamped and windmill mark, c1919. **£5,000-6,000** *CNY*

A copper and glass hanging ceiling light, by the Roycrofters. **£4,500-5,500** *CNY*

A copper and mica table lamp, by Dirk Van Erp, stamp and windmill mark, c1912, 15¹/₂in (39cm). **£25,000-30,000** *CNY*

An engraved glass globe, 'Walking the Earth', by Ronald Pennell, the hand blown glass body on cylindrical stem, wheel engraved with various animals, 1990, 10in (25cm). **£2,000-3,000** *C*

A pair of Art Deco burr walnut bedside cabinets, by Mercier Frères, 23in (58cm) wide. **£3,500-4,000** *C*

An oak sewing cabinet, by Gustav Stickley, firm's red decal, c1905, 20in (51cm) wide. **£2,800-3,200** *CNY*

A walnut, maple and chrome display cabinet, by Gordon Russell workshops, c1930. **£3,500-4,500** *S*

An oak smoker's cabinet, by Gustav Stickley, c1903, 17in (43cm) wide. **£3,000-4,000** *CNY*

A carved mahogany, and marquetry cabinet, by Louis Majorelle, 25in (64cm). **£30,000-35,000** *CNY*

An inlaid oak music cabinet, designed by Harvey Ellis for Gustav Stickley, c1903. **£4,000-4,500** *CNY*

A carved mahogany and marquetry cabinet, by Louis Majorelle, 68in (173cm) high. **£20,000-25,000** *CNY*

A mahogany and marquetry side cabinet, c1900, 55in (139cm) wide. **£3,000-4,000** *S*

An oak hanging trophy case, by Gustav Stickley, c1904, 60½in (154cm) wide. **£4,500-5,500** *CNY*

An Art Deco three-piece bedroom suite, comprising grand lit and 2 bedside tables, branded Leleu. **£6,000-7,000** *C*

A carved mahogany and marquetry cabinet, by Louis Majorelle, boldly carved and inlaid, 75in (190.5cm) high. **£28,000-32,000** *CNY*

An Art Deco ebony, macassar and vellum daybed, 86in (220cm) long. **£5,500-6,500** *C*

A set of 8 Everaut pressed metal stacking chairs, c1930. **£4,000-5,000** *S*

A pair of Apelli and Varesio side chairs, by Carlo Mollino, c1945. **£5,500-6,500** *C*

A suite of leather furniture, comprising three-seater settee and 2 armchairs, c1930. **£2,000-3,000** *S*

An aluminium chair, designed by Frank Lloyd Wright for the H. C. Price Company tower, c1954. **£9,000-10,000** *CNY*

A 'Kota' chair, by Sue Golden, of fibreboard and steel construction, 1987. **£800-1,200** *C*

An Italian three-piece suite, comprising a chaise longue and 2 armchairs, c1950. **£1,200-2,000** *C*

A Cassina chaise longue. **£1,200-1,500** *S*

An inlaid oak side chair, designed by Harvey Ellis, produced by Gustav Stickley, red decal, model No.338, c1904. **£2,200-3,000** *CNY*

An English Art Deco leather upholstered three-piece suite. **£4,000-5,000** *C*

An Irish pearwood Art Nouveau three-piece suite, by James Hayes, upholstered in brown leather, labelled Millar and Beatty Ltd, c1902. **£6,000-7,000** *C*

A Carlo Bugatti painted vellum ebonised and inlaid side chair, seat restored, painted signature. **£4,000-5,000** *C*

A pair of Liberty and Co., oak armchairs, with leather upholstery, manufacturers label. **£2,500-3,000** *C*

A set of 6 dining chairs, designed by Harvey Ellis, produced by Gustav Stickley, model Nos 353 and 353A, c1910. **£2,500-3,500** *CNY*

COLOUR REVIEW

An oak wardrobe, by
Peter Waals.
£2,500-3,500 *C*

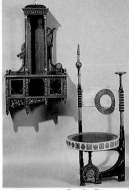

A Carlo Bugatti
inlaid chair and
hanging shelf.
**£4,000-5,000
each** *CNY*

'Metropole', a Memphis
clock, designed by
George J. Sowden,
made in Italy, 1982.
£1,500-2,000 *C*

An oak dressing table mirror,
1906, 23in (58cm) wide.
£5,000-6,000 *S*

An oak blanket chest, by Gordon
Russell, dated 20.6.27, 65in
(166cm) wide. **£4,500-6,000** *C*

An oak sideboard, by Gustav Stickley,
firm's branded mark, model No.804, 54in
(137cm) wide. **£8,000-10,000** *CNY*

A Liberty and Co. oak
revolving bookcase,
c1900. **£6,000-7,000** *S*

A Carlo Bugatti
ebonised and inlaid
pedestal, 51in (130cm).
£3,000-4,000 *C*

A black lacquered dining table, top
with curved corners, on U-shaped
base, c1930, 66in (168cm) long.
£2,000-3,000 *S*

'Three Thirds of a Table', by Ron Arad,
of mirror polished stainless steel, c1989,
98in (250cm) wide. **£12,000-15,000** *C*

An oak serving table,
by Gustav Stickley,
firm's branded mark,
c1912. **£2,500-3,500** *CNY*

A carved mahogany
and marquetry
cupboard, by Louis
Majorelle, 46in
(117cm).
£6,000-7,000 *CNY*

A carved mahogany and marquetry
sideboard, by Louis Majorelle,
signed. **£8,000-10,000** *CNY*

A spruce coffee table, designed by
Frank Lloyd Wright, c1950, 74in
(188cm). **£8,500-9,500** *CNY*

A Shapland and Petter oak
sideboard, the central reserve
decorated with a copper relief
panel of stylised flowers, 90in
(228cm) wide. **£5,000-6,000** *C*

A Fontana Arte glass topped bronze
coffee table, attributed to Gio Ponti,
stamped, 1950s. **£4,000-5,000** *C*

An E. Bingham & Co electroplated table service, designed by Charles Rennie Mackintosh, comprising 42 pieces. **£8,000-10,000** *C*

A silver and rosewood powder box, bowl and circular box, made by Puiforcat, marked, 1927, 21¹/₂ oz gross. **£5,000-6,000** *CNY*

A silver two-handled tea tray, by Georg Jensen, 830 standard, inscribed and dated 1925, marked, 34in (86cm) wide. **£10,000-12,000** *CNY*

A set of 12 silver plates, designed by Johan Rohde, 1930, made by Georg Jensen, post 1945, marked, 11in (28cm) diam. **£6,000-8,000** *CNY*

A nickel plated metal smoker's companion, 1930s, 10¹/₂in (26cm) long. **£3,000-4,000** *S*

A WMF electroplated metal photograph frame, marks, c1900, 14¹/₂in (36cm). **£1,500-2,000** *S*

A Liberty and Co. silver and enamel ceremonial spoon, by Archibald Knox, Birmingham 1900. **£3,500-5,000** *C*

A parcel gilt silver pitcher, by Georges Lecomte, Paris, marked, c1945, 18in (46cm), 133¹/₂oz. **£9,000-10,000** *CNY*

A canteen of Georg Jensen cutlery, comprising 77 pieces, various Jensen marks. **£5,000-6,000** *S*

A George Jensen muffin dish, cover and stand, various marks, c1920 and c1940. **£3,000-4,000** *S*

A four-piece silver and glass tea and coffee service and tray, by Puiforcat, post 1973. **£12,000-14,000** *CNY*

A silver and fluorite covered tureen, by Puiforcat, marked post 1973, 54oz gross. **£8,000-10,000** *CNY*

A silver eight-piece tea and coffee service and tray, Georg Jensen, post 1945. **£30,000-35,000** *CNY*

A Hukin & Heath electroplated tantalus, designed by Dr Christopher Dresser, stamped H&H, c1879, 11in (28cm) high. **£6,000-8,000** *C*

A James Dixon & Son three-piece electroplated tea set, designed by Christopher Dresser, stamped, c1880. **£8,500-10,000** *C*

A Hukin & Heath electroplated metal three-piece tea set, designed by Christopher Dresser, stamped H&H, c1878. **£5,000-7,000** *C*

A silver ivory mounted vase, by Tétard Frères, Paris, marked, c1935, 15in (38cm), 170oz gross. **£8,000-10,000** *CNY*

A silver vase, by Risler, Paris, marked, c1935, 22in (56cm) high, 164oz. **£8,000-10,000** *CNY*

A silver covered soup tureen, by Tétard Frères, Paris, marked, c1935, 9¹/₂in (24cm) high, 101oz gross. **£7,000-8,000** *CNY*

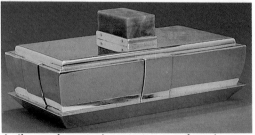

A silver and aventurine quartz covered serving dish, by Puiforcat, marked, c1935, 9in (23cm) long, 41oz gross. **£13,500-15,000** *CNY*

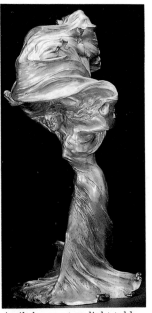

A Flamand gilt bronze figural lamp, marked G. Flamand, c1900, 33in (84cm). **£3,500-4,500** *S*

A gilt bronze two-light table lamp, 'Loie Fuller', by Raoul Larche, early 20thC. **£6,000-8,000** *CNY*

A Gurschner bronze and nautilus shell lamp, marked, c1900, 21in (53cm). **£10,000-12,000** *S*

A Cartier silver and lapis lazuli humidor, 1928, 9½in (24cm) long. **£7,000-8,000** *S*

A WMF style electroplated metal tazza, c1900, 18in (45cm). **£2,000-3,000** *S*

An Albert Cheuret alabaster and metal lamp, c1925. **£8,000-10,000** *S*

A pair of Bouval gilt bronze Art Nouveau lamps, marked M Bouval and with foundry mark 'Thiébaut Frères', c1900, 20in (50.5cm). **£10,000-12,000** *S*

A wrought iron lamp, with Muller Frères etched glass shade, c1925, 41in (104cm). **£1,500-2,000** *S*

A pair of Georg Jensen silver tureens and covers, 1928. **£7,000-8,000** *S*

A pair of silver five-light candelabra, by Georg Jensen, marked, c1930, 10½in (26cm). 185½oz. **£24,000-28,000** *CNY*

A napkin ring, by Henri Husson, c1905, 2½in (5cm). **£1,500-2,000** *S*

629

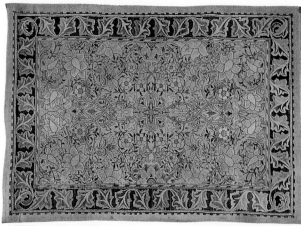

A William Morris 'Redcar' hand knotted carpet, probably woven at Merton Abbey, c1890, 135 by 98in (345 by 249cm). **£38,000-45,000** *S*

A woollen tapestry, 'Moonlight', designed by Howard Hodgkin, woven at the West Dean Tapestry Studio by Dilys Stinson, dated 1983. **£4,500-5,000** *C*

A pair of Liberty jardinières on pedestals, 31½in (80cm) high. **£2,000-3,000** *C*

An Edgar Brandt wrought iron firescreen, marked, c1925, 36½in (93cm) high. **£10,000-12,000** *S*

A spun silk wall hanging, by Sally Greaves-Lord, 1990, 75 by 35in (190 by 90cm). **£600-800** *C*

A leaded glass window c1913, 72in (183cm) high. **£4,000-5,000** *CNY*

A Nigel Coates woollen carpet, 'L'Europea', signed, 1990, 110 by 63in (280 by 160cm). **£2,500-3,500** *C*

A pair of Morris & Co woven compound twill Peacock and Dragon curtains, c1878. **£2,500-3,000** *S*

A gilt bronze and glass sconce, designed by Frank Lloyd Wright, c1902, 13½in (34cm). **£4,500-5,500** *CNY*

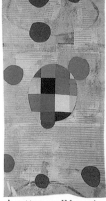

A cotton wall hanging, 'Core', by Ruston Aust, 1989. **£800-1,000** *C*

A set of steel Dupré Lafon fireguards, with flat rectangular section and tubular crossbar, c1930, 40in (102cm) wide. **£2,500-3,500** *S*

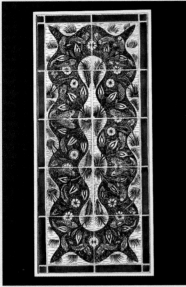

A stoneware sack form, by Hans Coper, with bronze disc top, seal, c1970, 7¹/₂in (19cm). **£7,500-8,500** *Bon*

An hour glass vase, by Hans Coper, c1963. **£9,500-10,500** *Bon*

A cup form stoneware pot, by Hans Coper, impressed HC seal, c1970, 6in (15cm). **£6,000-8,000** *Bon*

A Hans Coper vase, impressed HC seal, c1965, 7¹/₂in (19cm). **£10,000-12,000** *S*

An early thistle form pot, by Hans Coper, impressed HC seal, c1958, 12in (31cm). **£6,500-7,500** *Bon*

A Hans Coper spade vase, chip restored, impressed HC seal, c1970, 7in (17.5cm). **£5,500-6,500** *S*

A hand painted and glazed vase, by Raoul Dufy, signed, marked, numbered 17, 12¹/₂in (32cm). **£45,000-50,000** *S*

An early stoneware bottle form, by Hans Coper, 11in (28cm). **£4,000-5,000** *Bon*

A stoneware form, Hans Coper, impressed seal, c1970, 7in (18cm). **£7,000-9,000** *Bon*

An early bottle form by Hans Coper, impressed seal, c1956, 13in (34cm). **£14,000-16,000** *Bon*

A spade form, by Hans Coper, impressed HC seal, c1965, 8in (20cm). **£7,000-8,000** *Bon*

A Hans Coper vase, impressed HC seal, c1965, 7in (18.5cm). **£9,000-10,000** *S*

An enamelled terracotta plaque, 'Le Prophète', by Jean Arp, comprising 6 painted and partially glazed ceramic tiles, signed, inscribed XI on the reverse, 22in (56.5cm) high. **£8,000-9,000** *S*

A cup and disc stoneware form, by Hans Coper, c1965. **£3,000-4,000** *Bon*

An Elizabeth Fritsch bowl, with bright blue interior, green exterior with wide rim border, 18in (45.5cm). **£4,500-5,500** *S*

A stoneware swollen sack form, by Elizabeth Fritsch, with brown glaze to rim and interior, 1983, 16in (41cm). **£6,000-8,000** *C*

A stoneware flask, by Elizabeth Fritsch, c1984, 16in (41cm). **£3,500-4,500** *Bon*

An Elizabeth Fritsch vase, decorated and incised with a geometric design, rim chip, 1975, 7^{1}/$_{2}$in (19cm). **£2,000-3,000** *S*

A stoneware vase, by Elizabeth Fritsch, white with tinges of green, the rim with an ochre band, the interior in pale blue, 10in (26cm). **£3,000-3,500** *Bon*

A stoneware charger, by Bernard Leach, impressed BL and St Ives Pottery seals, 13^{1}/$_{2}$in (34cm). **£3,500-4,500** *C*

A stoneware container of 3 stacking compartments, by Kanjiro Kawai, c1950, 6^{1}/$_{2}$in (16.5cm). **£3,000-4,000** *Bon*

An elliptical cup and saucer, by Elizabeth Fritsch, saucer 9in (23cm). **£5,000-6,000** *Bon*

A stoneware vase, by Bernard Leach, glazed in tehmoku, impressed BL and St Ives seals, c1963. **£4,000-5,000** *Bon*

A stoneware lidded bowl, by Bernard Leach, the rust brown body with sgraffito decoration, impressed BL and St Ives seals, c1967, 9in (23cm) diam. **£3,500-5,000** *Bon*

An earthenware bowl, by George Ohr, stamped G.E. OHR Biloxi, Miss, 8in (20cm) diam. **£1,200-1,500** *CNY*

A hand painted and glazed plate, by
Pablo Picasso, signed and dated 7 juin
54, 18½in (22cm) wide.
£35,000-40,000 *S*

A plate, by Pablo Picasso,
inscribed 188/200, 1953,
9in (23cm).
£1,200-1,500 *Bon*

A painted and partially glazed
pitcher, by Pablo Picasso,
inscribed, No 27/50, 14in (35.5cm).
£40,000-50,000 *S*

A painted white earthenware vase, by
Pablo Picasso, No. 12/25, 1951, 22in
(55cm) high. **£40,000-45,000** *S*

A hand painted and glazed plate, 'Oseau
sur fond bleu', stamped, by Pablo Picasso,
1949, 14½in (37.5cm) long.
£50,000-60,000 *S*

A hand painted and glazed vase,
by Pablo Picasso, No. 2/62, 22½in
(57cm) high. **£40,000-45,000** *S*

A hand painted and glazed plate, 'Oiseau
Mangeant un ver', by Pablo Picasso, 1949.
£55,000-60,000 *S*

A painted white earthenware
pitcher, 'Taureau', stamped
Edition Picasso, Madoura plein
feu, No. 17/100, 1955, 12in
(30.5cm). **£45,000-50,000** *S*

A painted and partially glazed
plate by Pablo Picasso, 1956,
16½in (42cm).
£10,000-12,000 *S*

A painted and partially glazed
terracotta vase, by Pablo Picasso,
dated 19.12.53, stamped and
inscribed. **£10,500-12,000** *S*

A hand painted and glazed plate,
by Pablo Picasso, dated 25.3.48,
stamped on reverse, 25½in (65cm)
wide. **£60,000-70,000** *S*

A painted and glazed pitcher,
'Visage aux yeux rieurs',
by Pablo Picasso, stamped and
inscribed.
£15,000-18,000 *S*

A Lucie Rie stoneware compressed bowl, impressed LR seal, c1968, 11in (28cm) wide. **£4,000-5,000** *C*

A Lucie Rie bowl, impressed LR seal, c1968, 9¹/₂in (24cm) diam. **£6,000-7,000** *Bon*

A Lucie Rie porcelain bowl, with impressed LR seal, c1960, 6in (15cm) high. **£4,000-5,000** *C*

A Lucie Rie stoneware bowl, impressed LR seal, c1972, 10¹/₂in (27cm) diam. **£4,000-5,000** *Bon*

A Lucie Rie porcelain bowl, with feathered rim, impressed LR seal, c1968, 9in (23cm) **£3,800-4,200** *Bon*

A Lucie Rie bowl, with yellow uranium glaze and running bronze rim, impressed LR seal, c1960, 5in (13cm) diam. **£2,500-3,000** *S*

A Lucie Rie porcelain bowl, with bronze fluxed rim, impressed LR seal, c1965, 9in (23cm) diam. **£2,000-3,000** *Bon*

A Lucie Rie porcelain bowl, with one inlaid circular line, LR seal, c1960, 7in (18cm) diam. **£3,500-4,500** *Bon*

A Lucie Rie white porcelain bowl, with bronze running rim, impressed LR seal, c1975, 10in (26cm) diam. **£3,000-4,000** *Bon*

A Lucie Rie stoneware inlaid sgraffito bowl, with brown vertical sgraffito, impressed LR seal, c1950, 14¹/₂in (37cm) diam. **£4,500-5,500** *C*

A Lucie Rie stoneware 'knitted' bowl, with inlaid criss-cross lines, impressed LR seal, c1975, 7¹/₂in (19cm) diam. **£2,500-3,500** *Bon*

A Lucie Rie porcelain bowl, impressed LR seal, c1968, 5in (12.5cm) diam. **£4,000-5,000** *Bon*

A Lucie Rie porcelain bowl, impressed LR seal, c1978, 5in (12.5cm) diam. **£1,800-2,500** *Bon*

A Lucie Rie bowl, with sgraffito decoration, c1965, 8in (21cm). **£5,000-5,500** *S*

A Lucie Rie stoneware bowl, with feathered rim, LR seal, c1985, 9in (23cm) diam.**£3,000-4,000** *Bon*

A Lucie Rie stoneware bowl, LR seal, c1982, 9in (23cm). **£3,000-4,000** *Bon*

A Lucie Rie porcelain vase, with wide flaring rim, impressed LR seal, c1978, 9$\frac{1}{2}$in (24cm). **£11,000-12,000** *Bon*

A Lucie Rie bronze porcelain vase, LR seal, c1972, 9$\frac{1}{2}$in (24cm). **£3,000-4,000** *Bon*

A stoneware vase by Lucie Rie, impressed LR seal, c1965, 12in (31cm) high. **£2,500-3,500** *Bon*

A Lucie Rie stoneware vase, LR seal, c1960, 11$\frac{1}{2}$in (29cm) high. **£6,500-7,500** *Bon*

A Lucie Rie stoneware pot, in a pitted 'volcanic' glaze, unglazed base, impressed LR seal, c1958, 6in (15.5cm) high. **£7,000-8,000** *Bon*

A Lucie Rie porcelain bowl, the terracotta foot and well with a ring of turquoise, impressed LR seal, c1986, 9in (23cm) diam. **£4,500-5,500** *Bon*

A Lucie Rie stoneware bottle, impressed LR seal, c1960, 13$\frac{1}{2}$in (34.5cm) high. **£5,000-6,000** *C*

A Lucie Rie bowl, impressed LR seal, c1975, 7in (43cm) diam. **£6,000-7,000** *Bon*

A Lucie Rie stoneware vase, with a heavily pitted glaze, impressed LR seal, c1960, 7in (19cm) high. **£2,000-3,000** *Bon*

A Lucie Rie stoneware bowl, with a pitted white and beige glaze, impressed LR seal, c1980, 9$\frac{1}{2}$in (24cm) wide. **£4,000-5,000** *Bon*

A Lucie Rie tall vase, the shoulder and rim with sgraffito, impressed LR seal, c1965, 10in (25cm) high. **£6,000-7,000** *Bon*

A Lucie Rie porcelain vase, LR seal, 11in (28in) high. **£1,500-2,000** *Bon*

A Lucie Rie stoneware bowl, impressed LR seal, c1984, 8in (21cm) diam. **£3,200-3,800** *Bon*

636

A gentleman's sleeved waistcoat of linen, the borders worked with exotic leaves in corded and knotted work, with small ball-shaped self-embroidered buttons to the hem, the buttonholes finish at pocket height, c1690. **£2,500-3,000** *CSK*

A gentleman's pale grey-green grosgrain coat embroidered in colours with floral garlands and bows, and with embroidered buttons, c1775.
£550-650 *WHB*

A red facecloth suit, comprising wide trousers, with gilt thread embroidered front, fastening with gilt covered buttons, and outer jacket with open embroidered sleeves, 19thC.
£200-300 *CSK*

A jacket of red cotton woven with a quilted effect and printed with sprays of berries, with pouched hem and wrap over, three-quarter length sleeves, with large ceramic buttons, labelled Schiaparelli, 12 Place Vendome, Paris, inscribed on the reverse 82542, 1940s.
£900-1,200 *CSK*

Dunn & Co. travelling salesman's samples, trousers 10in (25cm), jackets 9in (23cm).
£40-70 *CLH*

A suit of pink and apple green checked bouclé wool, the jacket weighted with a chain at the hem, with matching pale pink sleeveless blouse, the jacket labelled Chanel, 1960s. **£250-450** *CSK*

A lady's waistcoat of linen embroidered in brightly coloured red, blue and green silks, against a yellow herringbone motif, bound with yellow silk braid, enlarged down the sides, English, early 18thC. **£5,000-8,000** *CSK*

An apron of ivory silk embroidered in gold thread in various stitches, the scalloped border edged with gold lace, English, c1735.
£1,500-2,000 *CSK*

A rare pair of gentlemen's trousers, of olive green silk woven with satin stripes, with fall front buttoned with self covered buttons, with silk braid ties at the ankles, c1790. **£1,500-2,000** *CSK*

An Italian miniature linen robe for an effigy, embroidered in pink silk, the central medallion with the IHS symbol and the 2 side ones with hearts and the initials S.A.N. and M.R.A., 17thC. **£500-700** *CSK*

A Queen Victoria souvenir beadwork purse, the gilt clasp marked 'Victoria June 28th 1938', together with another Victorian beadwork purse, a beadwork bracelet, a muff purse and a beadwork cuff.
£80-120 WW

Such combined lots are quite common at auction, and can prove very good value.

A Swiss linen handkerchief, embroidered in red silk, the centre with clasped hands, the symbol of fidelity, and the initials H.S. and K.P., the border with a zigzag pattern of leaves and acorns, trimmed with lace, probably commemorating an engagement, 17thC, 18in (46cm) square.
£1,700-2,200 CSK

A miniature corset, possibly for a doll but probably an apprentice's masterpiece of linen, the front woven in silk damask with a pattern of berries and trimmed with lacing, boned and laced at the back, c1770, 6in (15cm) high.
£1,500-2,000 CSK

A reticule of ivory silk, embroidered in coloured silks, the edges trimmed with green braid and blue and pink flowers, lined with ivory silk, c1820, 7in (18cm) long.
£500-600 CSK

Embroidery

An English needlework picture, embroidered in coloured silks, on an ivory satin ground, c1660, 9 by 11in (23 by 28cm), framed and glazed.
£2,500-3,000 CSK

A linen border, woven with a repeating pattern in green silk, depicting pairs of dragons between castles and fountains, trimmed with braid, joined, probably Italian, 16thC, 3 by 96in (8 by 243cm).
£900-1,200 CSK

A Swiss linen cushion cover, embroidered in scarlet coloured silk, trimmed with lace, c1650, 15 by 13in (38 by 33cm).
£2,000-2,500 CSK

A pair of needlework panels, embroidered in coloured silks, mounted on a stretcher, late 16thC, 23in (59cm) square.
£1,700-2,000 CSK

A needlework pelmet, worked in coloured silks, with large bizarre type flowerheads among smaller blossoms and petals, against a dark brown ground, with scalloped edge, c1680, 14 by 168in (36 by 426cm).
£1,500-2,000   *CSK*

A silkwork picture on silk ground, depicting a woman watching a boy feeding 2 pigs, church and cottages to background, in gilt gesso frame, early 19thC, 16½ by 20in (42 by 51cm).
£500-800   *S*

A needlework picture, worked in coloured silks, against an ivory satin ground, unfinished, with drawing visible, framed and glazed, English, mid-17thC, 9 by 8in (23 by 20cm).
£4,500-5,000   *CSK*

A needlework mirror, embroidered in coloured silks and gilt threads, with the initials MD at the top, dated 1652, 24 by 20in (61 by 51cm), in a black and gold painted chinoiserie 19thC frame.
£2,500-3,000   *CSK*

Lace

A pair of needlework pictures, worked in coloured silks, one depicting a shepherdess, the other with a shepherd, early 18thC, 8 by 11in (20 by 28cm), framed and glazed.
£2,000-2,500   *CSK*

A linen point de Saxe cover, worked within an elaborate strapwork frame, the details worked with white silk embroidery and drawn thread work, Dresden, c1730, 68 by 64in (172 by 162cm).
£5,000-6,000   *CSK*

A pair of Brussels bobbin lace lappets with oval cartouches containing asymmetric floral sprays, c1745.
£350-400   *CSK*

A border of Italian needlelace, composed of framed vignettes of birds and mythical beasts and devices from the arms of the Colona family, 16th/17thC, 3 by 30in (8 by 76cm).   **£500-600**   *CSK*

A panel of Spanish needlelace, worked with 2 rows of framed vignettes, including ships, birds and horse riders, 16th/17thC, 6 by 33in (15 by 84cm).
£2,000-2,500   *CSK*

A panel of fine Italian filet, worked with leafy scrolls with 2 mermaids bearing a cup, 17thC, 7 by 28in (18 by 71cm).
£700-800   *CSK*

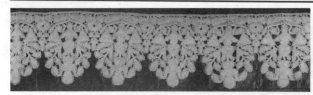

A length of Flemish bobbin lace, Vandyked border, worked with flowers and bows, 17thC, 3 by 82in (8 by 208cm).
£900-1,000 *CSK*

Two borders of bobbin lace worked with stylised figures and trees, possibly Italian, 17thC, 18 and 44 by 2in (46 and 111 by 5cm).
£100-150 *CSK*

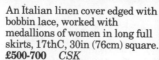

A length of Italian bobbin lace with a Vandyked edge with pendant florets and perching birds, 16th/17thC, 3 by 17in (8 by 43cm).
£350-400 *CSK*

A flounce of point de France large scale lace, worked with bold designs, c1710, 25 by 108in (64 by 274cm).
£3,000-5,000 *CSK*

A border of needlelace, worked with a top edge of scrolling carnations, with a Vandyked edge of pendant carnations, with crown like motifs above, Italian, 17thC, 30 by 5in (76 by 13cm).
£700-800 *CSK*

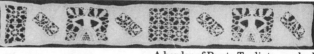

A border of Punto Tagliato, worked with alternating blocks of figures, geometric cutwork and reticella patterns, 17thC, 2½ by 18½in (6 by 47cm).
£250-300 *CSK*

A panel of drawn thread work depicting crowned lions and birds among flowers, with a border of animals, Norwegian Harlanger, 19thC, 10 by 25in (25 by 64cm).
£200-300 *CSK*

An Italian linen cover edged with bobbin lace, worked with medallions of women in long full skirts, 17thC, 30in (76cm) square.
£500-700 *CSK*

An Italian linen cover, with a lace border worked with scrolling foliage and an angel with knotted hair at each corner, 17thC, 5in (13cm) square.
£500-700 *CSK*

A cap back of Mechlin lace, worked with a pair of rearing stags below a castle, 18thC.
£1,200-1,500 *CSK*

A filet altar frontal, worked with the story of Adam and Eve, showing Adam beseeching God to give him a companion, the birth of Eve, the eating of the apple and the expulsion from the Garden, worked with an inscription HOC OPUS F F PRIORES S MI ROSARII 1596, 33 by 50in (84 by 127cm).
£12,000-15,000 *CSK*

An Italian long panel of Punto Tirato, worked with an undulating ribbon with palmette flowers, 18thC.
£80-120 *CSK*

A pair of Brussels bobbin lace lappets, with attached cap back, worked with flowers and devices against a scrolling ground, c1735, lappets 24 by 4in (61 by 10cm).
£450-500 *CSK*

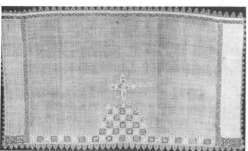

An Italian altar cloth, worked with a border of bobbin lace scallops of geometric patterns and with an inset band of similar lace, late 17thC, cloth later, 59 by 38in (149 by 96cm).
£350-400 *CSK*

An altar cloth of fine linen, worked with a border of Punto in Aria, the cloth worked with cutwork insertions of animals and birds alternating with whitework birds, animals and angels, early 17thC, 24 by 40in (61 by 101cm).
£3,500-4,500 *CSK*

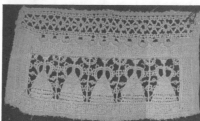

A linen cuff, worked with an elaborate smocked border surrounding a cutwork panel of needlelace ladies, Abruzzi, 17thC, 10 by 5in (25 by 13cm).
£550-650 *CSK*

A panel of Vierländer lacis, worked with a pair of doves in a tree, German, 18thC, 14 by 28in (36 by 71cm).
£500-600 *CSK*

A filet panel, worked with motto and a coat-of-arms surrounded by oak leaves and surmounted by a firebreathing dragon, inscribed 1450.
£500-800 *CSK*

Use the Index!

Because certain items might fit easily into any of a number of categories, the quickest and surest method of locating any entry is by reference to the index at the back of the book.
This has been fully cross-referenced for absolute simplicity

Samplers

An English sampler, worked in shades of blue, green and cream silk, with bands of patterns, including rows of flowers and vines, and an alphabet, mid-17thC, 39in (99cm) long.
£1,500-2,000 *CSK*

An early Victorian needlework sampler, 1845.
£350-450 *HCH*

A darning sampler, worked in coloured silks, framed and glazed, late 18th/early 19thC, 17 by 13in (43 by 33cm).
£850-950 *CSK*

An English sampler by Isbel Hall, embroidered in coloured silks, 1653, 26 by 7in (66 by 18cm).
£1,700-2,000 *CSK*

A William IV needlework sampler by Elizabeth Lammiman, aged 10, depicting Holwood House, Kent, the seat of the Rt. Hon. William Pitt, November 25th 1832, 17 by 13in (43 by 33cm).
£550-650 *P(M)*

A needlework sampler by Hannah Carter, worked in cross stitch with verse above Adam and Eve and the Tree of Life, dated 1832, 17½ by 16in (45 by 41cm).
£450-500 *HSS*

Tapestries

A silkwork sampler, Louisa Benford Aged 9 years, 1818, in plain gilt frame, 16 by 12½in (41 by 32cm).
£1,000-1,200 *S*

A long sampler, by Mary Smith, worked in coloured silks, framed and glazed, 1692, 34 by 10in (86 by 25cm).
£1,200-1,700 *CSK*

An Aubusson tapestry portière, woven in many colours, trimmed with fringing, French, late 19thC, 63 by 80in (160 by 203cm).
£1,200-1,700 *CSK*

A tapestry lunette, worked in many colours, depicting the Annunciation to the Virgin after Filippo Lippi, from the workshop of Morris and Company, in gesso frame, damaged, c1912, 80 by 34in (203 by 86cm).
£17,000-22,000   *CSK*

This tapestry was woven by the weavers John Martin and Gordon Berry for St Mary's Convent, Chiswick.

A woolwork picture of H.M.S. Victoria, 19thC.
£1,500-2,000   *SWO*

A needlework book binding, embroidered in coloured silks, the front and back depicting Adam and Eve and the Tree of Knowledge, unfinished, with the pattern drawn on the ground, English, mid-17thC, framed and glazed, 12 by 19in (31 by 48cm).
£3,000-5,000   *CSK*

A gros point wool picture, Summer, by Edna Oddy, 1810, in moulded frame, 34 by 24in (86 by 61cm).
£2,500-3,000   *AH*

FANS

A Dutch fan, the guards pierced with chinoiseries, the sticks with Chinese figures carrying umbrellas, c1760.
£400-500   *S(S)*

Miscellaneous

A Charles II beadworked picture, the satin ground densely covered with glass beads and pearls, in softwood frame, c1660, 9 by 11½in (23 by 29cm).
£1,200-2,000   *S*

The autograph fan of Miss Katherine Grant, 'White Lady' of Sir Hubert Herkomer R.A., with wooden stick, one guardstick inlaid with mother-of-pearl chrysanthemum, in green kid box tooled in gold with sprays of flowers by Johanna Birkenroth, London, lined with grey and pink figured silk, with a tall booklet listing many of the autographs bound in the same silk, c1880, 13in (33cm).
£2,000-2,500   *CSK*

A patchwork cover top, with original templates intact, one dated 1853, 82in (208cm) square.
£200-250   *CSK*

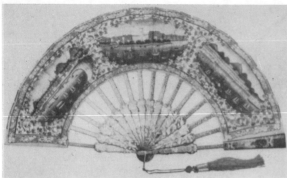

An Italian fan, the leaf centred by a painted panel of 2 bound slaves being assessed by a lady and attendants flanked by medallions and vignettes, plain ivory sticks and guards.
£400-500   *S(S)*

A telescopic fan, the leaf painted with 3 topographical views of The Hongs at Canton, with shipping in the foreground, the verso with figures on a terrace, their faces of ivory, their clothes of silk, with lacquer sticks, verso rubbed, 10in (25cm) extended, in lacquer box for a non-telescopic fan.
£700-1,000   *CSK*

A fan, the leaf painted with a country dance, the figures dressed in pink, blue and mauve, the ivory sticks carved and pierced with figures, c1720, 10in (25cm), in 19thC fan box.
£1,500-2,000   *CSK*

A fan, the leaf printed with an oval hand coloured stipple engraving of Apollo, by Thomas Kirk, the ivory sticks carved and pierced with flowers, in contemporary red morocco fan box, c1800, 9in (23cm).
£300-400   *CSK*

Five Neapolitan School fan designs, gouache on kid skin, 19thC, overall 21in (53cm) wide.
£1,700-2,000   *P(S)*

A Royal Marriage fan, commemorating the marriage of King George III and Queen Charlotte, with silver paper decoupe leaf, the ivory sticks carved and pierced and painted with chinoiserie and crowns, with a gold tassel, probably 1761, 11in (28cm).
£1,700-2,200   *CSK*

An English fan, the ivory sticks carved and pierced and painted with chinoiserie and cloute with mother-of-pearl and decorated with glitter, c1740, 12in (31cm).
£400-800   *CSK*

The fan appears to have been designed for larger sticks and to have been cut down slightly at the sides.

A fan, the leaf painted with Chinese ladies in a garden, the wooden sticks painted with figures in European dress, the guardstick painted with a musician, Chinese, for the European market, late 17th/early 18thC, in glazed fan case inscribed: One of the Court fans for the Wedding of William the 3rd and Mary of England Nov. 4.1677, leaf damaged.
£250-450   *CSK*

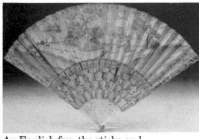

An English fan, the sticks and guards pierced and painted with chinoiserie panels, and 2 painted ivory fans, c1760.
£2,000-2,500   *S(S)*

A Cantonese mandarin fan, the leaf painted with a multitude of ivory faced figures, the gilt filigree guards and sticks pierced with figures of tortoiseshell, stained ivory and mother-of-pearl, in a lacquer case, c1880.
£350-550   *S(S)*

A French fan, the leaf painted with 3 vignettes in 18thC style, against a pink ground painted with putti en grisaille, the verso with monogram J.E.L., c1840, in fan box, 11in (28cm).
£600-700   *CSK*

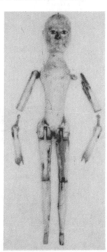

Souvenir de l'Exposition Universelle de 1867, Paris, a printed fan, designed by Guilletat, 48 rue de Belleville and engraved by Tuillot, with wooden sticks, 10in (25cm).
£400-500   *CSK*

Les Riches du Jour, a printed fan, the leaf a stipple engraving printed in blue with 3 scenes, c1790, 9in (23cm).
£400-600   *CSK*

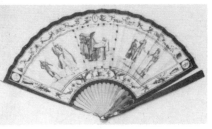

DOLLS

Wooden Dolls

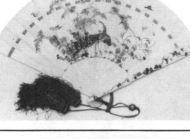

A Japanese ivory brisé fan, lacquered in gold with peacocks, the eyes on their tails cloute with mother-of-pearl, the guardsticks decorated with shibayama work fruit and insects, late 19thC, 3 stones missing from guardsticks, 11in (28cm), in bamboo box.
£3,000-4,000   *CSK*

A carved and painted wooden doll, with dark inset stitched eyes, rouged cheeks, carved ears, the cream painted body and limbs jointed at shoulders, elbows, hips and knees, damaged, English, 18thC, 16in (41cm) high.
£700-900   *CSK*

It is likely that there was one maker who constructed dolls in this manner, with fine joints, all-over painted flesh tones and well shaped body and limbs.

A late Georgian painted wooden doll, with painted rouged cheeks, red mouth and nostrils, inserted black pupil-less eyes, blonde mohair wig, the body with high pigeon chest, wooden peg-jointed hips and knees with hoof feet, wound linen upper arms nailed to the shoulders, the kid lower arms each having 3 stitched fingers, unmarked, 15in (38cm) high.
£800-1,000   *Bon*

A wooden pedlar doll, with painted hair and features, wearing red cape and printed dress, carrying basket of wares including lace and buttons, 11½in (29cm) high, under glass dome, on ebonised wood plinth base.
£300-350   *HCH*

A pair of wooden head and shoulder character dolls, each with a carved and painted wig, features, wooden lower limbs and stuffed fabric body, wearing national costume, 20thC, 14in (35cm) high.
£250-350   *HSS*

A wax over papier mâché headed doll, with pink kid arms and separated fingers in original pink silk spencer with matching quilted bonnet, white piqué dress, pantaloons, lace edged cap, petticoat and pink figured cotton laced boots and extra clothes, English, c1812, 18in (46cm) high.
£1,200-1,700   *CSK*

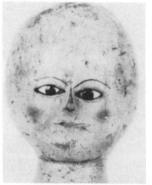

A painted wooden doll's torso, with inset enamel eyes, rouged cheeks and remains of kid arm, wearing printed cotton frock and petticoat, English, early 19thC, 9in (23cm) high.
£650-850   *CSK*

An English poured shoulder-wax doll, with fixed blue glass eyes, inserted blonde hair and cloth body with poured wax lower limbs, in original lace panelled and pintucked white dress, one leg bandaged, head and shoulder colour faded, late 19thC, 25in (64cm).
£500-700   *S*

A wax over composition pumpkin headed doll, with dark inset eyes, and moulded blonde hair, the stuffed body with squeaker, papier mâché lower section and wooden limbs, dressed in contemporary blue and white cotton print frock, c1860, 12in (31cm) high.
£250-350   *CSK*

Wax

A wax over composition headed doll, with fixed blue eyes, wearing original underclothes and faded pink silk frock trimmed with lace and ribbons, c1865, 16in (41cm) high.
£500-600   *CSK*

A waxed shoulder composition bride doll, with fixed spiralled blue glass eyes, painted mouth, applied ringletted blonde real hair, kid leather body, with separately stitched fingers, earrings, wax and fabric floral headdress, wearing underclothes, ivory brocaded satin lace trimmed wedding gown with train and heeled light brown shoes, some lace frail, German, c1890, 14½in (37cm).
£600-800   *S*

A pair of wax over composition dolls, one with blue eyes the other with black weighted eyes, painted mouths, fabric bodies with leather lower arms, dressed in matching maroon silk lace trimmed gowns, bead necklaces, and pearlised brown shoes with silk trim, minor cracking to faces, one shoe to each doll with hole in sole, German, c1890, 15in (38cm).
£1,000-1,500   *S*

A poured wax baby doll, with fixed blue eyes, inset short blonde wig and stuffed body, with wax limbs attached through metal eyelets, wearing a petticoat, with Lucy Peck square stamp on the body reading "FROM Mrs Peck THE DOLL'S HOME 131 REGENT STREET W", 20in (51cm) high.
£400-500 *CSK*

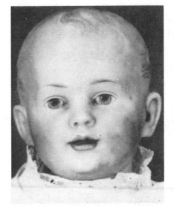

A bisque headed character baby doll, with brown painted eyes with red line above, open/closed mouth, dressed in white, impressed 131 2, 11½in (29cm) high.
£450-600 *CSK*

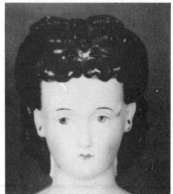

A bisque doll's shoulder head, with painted features, pierced ears, moulded and painted hair, marked 18, 5in (13cm) high.
£150-200 *CSK*

Bisque & Papier Mâché

A bisque headed character baby doll, with blue sleeping eyes, feathered brows, brown mohair wig and bent limbed composition body, marked Jutta 1914 12½. by Cuno & Otto Dressel, one finger damaged, 23in (59cm) high.
£350-400 *CSK*

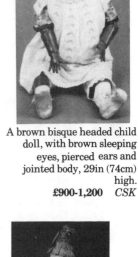

A brown bisque headed child doll, with brown sleeping eyes, pierced ears and jointed body, 29in (74cm) high.
£900-1,200 *CSK*

A bisque headed child doll, with fixed blue eyes, pierced ears and jointed body dressed in cream silk gauze over satin, underclothes, shoes and socks, impressed DEP 12, and on the body 12, 28in (71cm) high.
£800-1,200 *CSK*

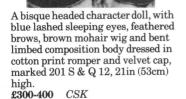

A bisque headed character doll, with blue lashed sleeping eyes, feathered brows, brown mohair wig and bent limbed composition body dressed in cotton print romper and velvet cap, marked 201 S & Q 12, 21in (53cm) high.
£300-400 *CSK*

A bisque flange necked fashionable doll, with unusual construction allowing the head to turn only 90° on a bisque protrusion, remains of skin wig and gussetted kid body wearing black kid slippers, Swiss straw hat, tortoiseshell comb, and later dress, c1870, 14½in (37cm) high.
£700-900 *CSK*

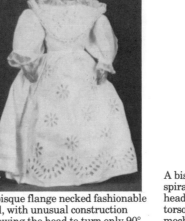

A bisque headed doll, with fixed spiralled blue glass eyes, Belton head, closed painted mouth, metal torso and skirt with clockwork mechanism within, in red satin skirt, black velvet bodice peasant costume and matching hat, impressed N/9, costume frail, German, c1885, 11in (28cm).
£350-500 *S*

A bisque swivel head fashion doll, with fixed blue glass eyes, fair mohair wig over cork pate and gussetted kid body with separately stitched fingers, unclothed except for leather boots with silk rosettes, impressed 1, French, c1875, 15in (38cm).
£900-1,200   *S*

A Kohl Wengenroth bisque character doll, with weighted brown glass eyes, open mouth, 5 piece curved limb composition body, replaced brown human hair, redressed in underclothes, white gauze dress, knitted pants and vest, brown shoes, impressed KW in an oval /12, German, c1910, 21in (53cm).
£600-700   *S*

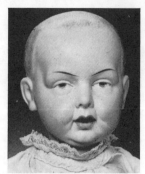

An 'Einco' Kaiser-baby type bisque character doll, with intaglio blue eyes, open/closed mouth, brushstroked hair, curved limb 5 piece composition body, in white shift, hands rubbed, impressed Einco Germany 3, c1910, 15in (38cm).
£400-500   *S*

A bisque headed bébé, with blue yeux fibres, feathered brows, pierced ears, dark brown wig, the jointed wood and composition body dressed in navy and green striped woollen frock, underwear and brown leather shoes, small chip to neck, marked 10 1, 24in (61cm).
£2,000-2,500   *CSK*

A brown bisque headed character doll, with brown sleeping eyes and rigid limb body, impressed 34 – 26, by Gebruder Kuhnlenz, 16½in (42cm).
£850-950   *CSK*

A bisque swivel headed Parisienne, with blue eyes, feathered brows and blonde mohair wig, the gussetted kid body with replaced composition arms dressed in white cotton gown, body marked with faint Simonne stamp, Passage Delorme, Paris circa 1860, 17½in (45cm).
£1,200-1,500   *CSK*

A pair of Laurel and Hardy bisque head and shoulder dolls, the stuffed bodies with bisque lower limbs dressed in felt costumes, 18 and 21in (46 and 53cm).
£60-100   *Bon*

Bru

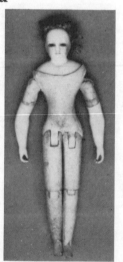

A rare early bisque shoulder headed Parisienne, with short blonde mohair curls, cork pate, fixed bright blue eyes, unpierced ears and kid over wood jointed body, the bisque arms with pink tinting at elbow and back of hand, possibly by Bru, c1870, 10½in (27cm) high.
£1,500-2,000   *CSK*

Gebruder Heubach

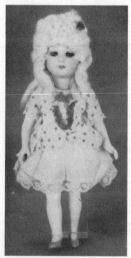

A bisque headed character doll, with blue sleeping eyes, and rigid limb child body with moulded shoes and socks, in original 18thC style fancy dress and powdered wig, impressed Gebruder Heubach 5½ O G. 5/0½ H, 11½in (29cm).
£250-350   *C*

A rare bisque headed character doll, moulded hair and composition baby's body, impressed Gebruder Heubach square mark and 8191 27 5, 11½in (29cm).
£800-1,000 *C*

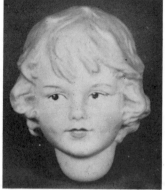

A bisque character doll's head, with open/closed mouth, light blue intaglio eyes and moulded blonde hair, impressed Heubach square mark 79, late production, 3½in (9cm).
£700-900 *C*

A bisque headed bébé, with pale blue eyes, fixed wrist papier mâché body dressed in blue, impressed DEPOSE E 8 J, and with painter's mark, the body stamped Jumeau Medaille d'Or Paris, the shoes marked EJ Depose, 19in (48cm).
£5,500-6,500 *CSK*

A bisque character doll, with weighted brown glass eyes, brown mohair wig and ball jointed wood and composition body in orange and white dress, impressed 8192 5, c1912, 20in (51cm).
£700-900 *S*

Jumeau

A bisque doll, with jointed wood and composition body, dressed in white cotton dress edged with lace, stringing loose, paint worn on body, stamped in red DÉPOSÉ TÊTE JUMEAU Bte. S.G.D.G. 7 and with red check mark, c1880, 17in (43cm).
£2,500-3,500 *S*

An English poured shoulder wax doll, with fixed blue glass eyes, one inside head, blonde mohair and cloth body with poured wax lower limbs, in original dress and cream cape, quilted cream satin bonnet, 22in (56cm), together with extra clothes including a pair of Jumeau ice blue satin shoes stamped on sole in gold BÉBÉ JUMEAU MED'OR PARIS DÉPOSÉ.
£900-1,200 *S*

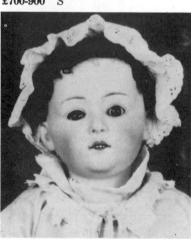

A bisque headed child doll, with blue sleeping eyes and jointed composition body, impressed with the Gebruder Heubach square mark and 10532 13, 31in (79cm).
£700-900 *C*

A Mulatto bisque doll, with black real hair wig and jointed wood and composition body, in pink ribbed dress with lacy top, slight damage and repair, embossed with a J, c1885, 17in (43cm).
£500-700 *S*

An early pressed bisque headed bébé, with closed mouth, blue almond shaped eyes, light brows, pierced ears, skin wig and fixed wrist jointed body, dressed in red with original cream satin and lace hat, impressed 3 over 0 and stamped on the body JUMEAU MEDAILLE d'OR, c1880, 13½in (34cm).
£5,500-6,500 *CSK*

A swivel head bisque fashion doll, wearing yellow metal thread brocaded top, pink figured silk bloomers and pink and yellow striped silk shawl and headscarf, marked with red check marks and incised 4, with stamp on back JUMEAU MEDAILLE d'OR PARIS, c1880, 14in (36cm).
£1,000-1,500 *S*

An 'Oriental Jumeau' bisque doll, with fixed brown glass eyes, lined in black, with stiffened shaped black wig on wooden pate, pierced ears, wood and composition straight limbed body with fixed wrists, in attractive original Chinese style robe and leggings, and matching raised slippers, hands rubbed, impressed 6, late 19thC, 19in (48cm), complete with silk covered wooden stand.
£1,200-1,700 *S*

A bisque doll, with 8 ball jointed wood and composition body, very slight wig pull on left side of face and raised firing line at left of mouth, blue stamp on bottom JUMEAU MEDAILLE D'OR PARIS, in later blue and white dress, brown kid shoes with cut silk rosettes incised 8 E. JUMEAU MÉD d'OR 1878 PARIS, c1875, 23in (58cm).
£3,000-4,000 *S*

A bisque walking/talking doll, with brown glass eyes, blonde real hair wig and jointed wood and composition body with straight walking legs causing the head to turn and the voice box to scream, firing line from left ear to centre of cheek, one wrist joint loose, hand paint scuffed, impressed 1907 10, 22½in (57cm), c1907, together with an extra white bonnet.
£1,000-1,500 *S*

An unusual 'crying' bisque doll, with open/closed mouth, fixed brown glass eyes, pierced applied ears, black wig over cork pate and wood and composition jointed body containing pull string 'Mama' voice box, in brown and white spotted silk dress, some chips and cracks, impressed 8 on head, c1880, 17in (43cm).
£1,500-2,500 *S*

A bisque doll, with fixed blue eyes, auburn real hair wig and jointed wood and composition body, crack from wig socket to right eyebrow, one finger missing and body paint scuffed, impressed 8 and 0 and indistinctly stamped TÊTE, c1905, 19in (49cm), together with a bodice and a blue and white striped extra bonnet.
£800-1,000 *S*

A bisque headed bébé, dressed in pale blue with shoes and socks, impressed 7, and stamped in red TETE JUMEAU, and on the body BÉBÉ JUMEAU Diplome d'Honneur, 18in (46cm).
£2,000-2,500 *CSK*

Did you know
MILLER'S Antiques Price Guide builds up year by year to form the most comprehensive photo-reference system available

A bisque doll, French head on German body, with auburn wig, jointed wood and composition body, in cream lacy dress with maroon tartan overdress, hairline crack from wig socket to edge of right eye, impressed 6, c1880, 17in (43cm).
£400-600 *S*

A bisque headed character baby doll, with painted hair, brown sleeping eyes and composition body dressed in silk robe, bib and bonnet, impressed J D K 20, 24in (61cm).
£600-700 *C*

A bisque doll with blue glass eyes, blonde mohair wig over plaster pate, jointed wood and composition body in original pink dress and bonnet, impressed 1924, c1910, 14in (35cm), and her trunk covered in cream linen and metal studs, containing clothing and trinkets.
£1,500-2,000 *S*

J. D. Kestner

Lenci

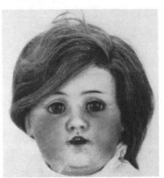

A large Kaiser baby type bisque character doll, with weighted brown glass eyes, open/closed mouth, brown mohair wig, 5 piece curved limb composition body, in long infant gown, napkin, knitted socks and bib, probably Kestner, impressed 50 at neck, c1910, 18½in (47cm).
£800-1,200 *S*

A bisque headed child doll, with blue lashed sleeping eyes, feathered brows, fair wig and jointed wood and composition body, dressed in white, 5 fingers broken, marked 13 J.D.K. 249, 24in (61cm).
£450-550 *CSK*

A cloth soldier doll, with felt face, painted lips and brown eyes, auburn hair and stitched ears, the body jointed at shoulders and hips and with joined middle fingers, in original sludge green serge uniform and hat, brown leather boots with metal studs and backpack, Italian, c1930, 17in (43cm).
£850-1,200 *S*

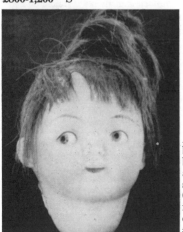

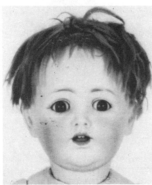

A bisque headed character baby doll, with quivering tongue, brown sleeping flirting eyes, short fair wig and baby's body, impressed J.D.K. 257 51, 19in (48cm).
£350-550 *CSK*

An all bisque googlie eyed doll, with blue eyes, water melon mouth, brown wig and painted blue socks and black shoes, probably a wigged swivel necked version of the Campbell Kid, chip to back of neck, impressed on legs 179 0, by Kestner, c1930, 6½in (16cm).
£450-550 *C*

A pair of cloth dolls of Laurel and Hardy, featuring felt, hand finished faces, wearing 18thC costumes including tri-cornered hats, 10in (25cm) each.
£1,500-2,000 *CNY*

A cupid cloth doll, with felt face, painted blue eyes, knotted red felt hair, swivel neck, butterfly wings in red, orange and yellow discs, blue felt top and brown shorts embroidered with red hearts, yellow felt socks in brown sandals with red straps, red felt gloves holding a blue tipped bow in one hand, an arrow in the other, a blue and yellow painted wooden sheath holding 4 red shafted arrows round his neck, c1930, 7½in (19cm).
£1,700-2,000 *S*

Armand Marseille

A bisque socket head girl doll, 390 ASM, 22½in (57cm).
£300-400 *HSS*

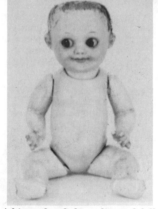

A bisque headed googlie eyed doll, with brown sleeping eyes, smiling closed mouth and composition baby's body, impressed 323 A 5/0 M, 8½in (22cm).
£500-600 *CSK*

A bisque shoulder headed doll, with brown eyes, blonde wig and stuffed body, with chamois leather breeches, leather gaiters and boots, impressed 370 AM 2½ DEP, 23in (59cm).
£400-500 *CSK*

A bisque socket head doll, with mohair wig, painted features, blue eyes, composition body and bent limbs, wearing a lemon petticoat under a cream lace dress with rosebuds and matching bonnet tied with pink ribbon, head and neck impressed Armand Marseille, Germany 990,A5/0M, 11in (28cm).
£200-300 *HSS*

A bisque headed googlie eyed doll, with blue eyes and rigid limb composition body, dressed in combinations, impressed 323 A 3/0 M, 11½in (30cm).
£900-1,200 *C*

S.F.B.J.

A French bisque character boy doll, with open/closed mouth, fixed blue glass eyes, domed brush stroked head and jointed wood and composition body, in blue sailor outfit, impressed 226, c1910, 16in (41cm).
£700-1,000 *S*

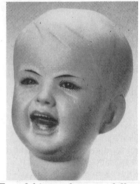

A French bisque character doll, with open/closed mouth showing tongue and teeth, fixed blue glass eyes, moulded hair and curved limb composition body, unclothed and unstrung, body paint flaked on legs and hands, impressed 233 4, c1910, 13in (33cm).
£1,200-1,700 *S*

Make the Most of Miller's

CONDITION is absolutely vital when assessing the value of an antique. Damaged pieces on the whole appreciate much less than perfect examples. However a rare, desirable piece may command a high price even when damaged

A French bisque doll, with brown glass eyes, pierced ears, red-blonde real hair wig and wood and composition jointed body, in cream fine lawn dress, cream calf fur shoes with pom-poms, lacy bonnet with lace flowers and green silk and satin ribbons, 3 fingers cracked, impressed 13, c1900, 28in (71cm).
£1,200-1,500   *S*

Simon & Halbig/ Kammer & Reinhardt

A Simon and Halbig bisque headed doll, with blue sleeping eyes, pierced ears and composition ball jointed body, in cream embroidered net dress, impressed Simon and Halbig DEP 1079 Germany 12, 25½in (65cm).
£500-550   *HCH*

A Kammer & Reinhardt/Simon & Halbig bisque headed doll, with sleeping blue eyes, auburn wig, composition ball jointed body, in blue velvet dress with straw bonnet, impressed K star R Simon and Halbig 117n, 32in (81cm).
£900-1,200   *HCH*

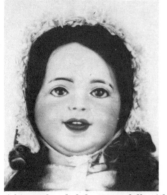

A bisque headed character doll, with open/closed mouth, blue sleeping eyes, brown wig, and baby's body wearing embroidered dress with lace insertions, impressed S.F.B.J. 236 Paris 11, 25in (64cm).
£800-1,200   *CSK*

A Kammer & Reinhardt bisque character doll, with blue eyes, blonde mohair plaited wig and jointed wood and composition body in blue-grey striped dress and white pinafore, impressed 114 23, c1909, 9in (23cm).
£1,000-1,500   *S*

A Simon & Halbig swivel head bisque doll, with fixed blue eyes, real hair over cork pate and canvas covered French wooden body with joints at shoulders, elbows, hips, knees and ankles, with bisque forearms, in rose pink cotton dress embroidered with blue flowers, black and blue bonnet with linen flowers, one little finger chipped, unmarked, c1880, 17in (43cm), together with broken glass dome.
£1,200-1,700   *S*

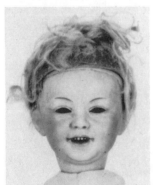

A rare bisque headed character boy doll, with fixed blue laughing eyes, blonde wig and jointed body, impressed S.F.B.J. 229 Paris 6, 16in (41cm).
£1,800-3,000   *CSK*

A bisque swivel headed doll, with kid neck lining, closed mouth, blue fixed eyes and blonde mohair wig, on a stuffed body with composition limbs, impressed S 14 H 949, 26½in (68cm).
£1,500-2,000   *CSK*

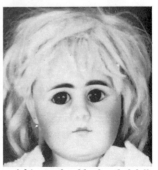

A bisque shoulder headed doll, with pierced ears and brown eyes, the cloth and kid body with bisque arms, dressed in white, impressed S 1 1 H 950, 20in (51cm).
£1,000-1,400   *CSK*

A Martin swimming doll, the French body with German head, with open mouth and upper teeth, fixed blue glass eyes, pierced ears, auburn wig and the pink jointed wooden body with metal hands, with keywind swimming mechanism, in original eau-de-nil swimming suit, impressed 1079 S & H 2½, c1895, 16in (41cm).
£1,000-1,500 *S*

A Simon & Halbig Oriental bisque doll, with brown eyes, black mohair wig, jointed wood and composition body, in mustard silk short robe, pale blue and white striped trousers, stringing loose, small firing fault under left eye, c1910, 13in (33cm).
£800-1,000 *S*

A Kammer & Reinhardt/Simon & Halbig flirty eyed bisque character doll, with five-piece curved limb composition body, in knitted pink dress and cotton underslip, stringing loose, hands and feet rubbed, replaced wig, impressed K star R Simon & Halbig 126/46, c1920, 18½in (47cm).
£400-600 *S*

A bisque headed character doll, with grey painted eyes and jointed composition body, wig pulls at back, body washed, impressed K star R 114 43, 15½in (40cm).
£1,700-2,200 *CSK*

A Simon & Halbig bisque doll, with weighted blue glass eyes, original brown mohair wig, pierced ears, wood and composition body, in original cream costume, lacking shoes and socks, impressed 1078/14½, c1895, 30in (76cm).
£1,000-1,500 *S*

Jules Steiner

A Simon & Halbig Gibson Girl bisque character doll, with fixed blue eyes, pierced ears, original wig, jointed wood and composition body, in original costume, lacking one earring, impressed 1159 Simon & Halbig DEP 6, c1894, 18½in (47cm).
£700-1,000 *S*

A French bisque doll, with moving blue eyes, pierced ears, dark real hair wig and jointed papier mâché body, in blue and white checked dress, straw bonnet and with small white teddy bear, some damage, impressed J. Steiner Bte. S.G.D.G. Paris FIre. A.11, c1895, 17in (43cm).
£1,000-1,200 *S*

A French bisque doll, with blue eyes, pierced ears, dark mohair wig and jointed papier mâché body, in white dress with blue sash, some damage, impressed J. Steiner Bte. S.G.D.G. Paris Fre., A 17, c1880, 24in (61cm).
£600-800 *S*

Dolls Houses

A dolls house designed as a double fronted Georgian residence with front gable pilaster and gallery, with hinged front gable and interior with furniture, 19thC, 29in (74cm) high.
£250-350   *GH*

A painted and furnished wooden dolls house, with slate roof, opening at the front to reveal 3 rooms with staircase, the base with shaped apron, 41in (104cm) high.
£600-700   *CSK*

A dolls house chair made of yellow beads, 7in (18cm) high.
£18-25   *LB*

A George III three-storey painted wooden baby house, opening at the front to reveal 6 rooms, hall, staircase, landings, interior doors and chimney breasts, 50in (127cm) high.
£2,500-4,000   *CSK*

A set of dolls bedroom furniture, comprising: bed, wardrobe, night cupboard and dressing table, with ebonised tops and brass handles, the dressing table 15½in (40cm) high.
£200-250   *CSK*

A German miniature kitchen, early 20thC, 20in (51cm) high.
£1,000-1,500   *S*

Six pieces of silver dolls house furniture, hallmarked variously 1896-1907, some restorations, the tallest 2in (5cm) high.
£350-550   *S*

A selection of German, English and French dolls house dolls and furniture, the 4 dolls missing original arms and legs, some damage, 1820-1900.
£600-800   *S*

A collection of dolls house miniatures and furniture, of approximately 150 pieces, the majority in good condition, c1920.
£800-1,000   *S*

Two Hepplewhite shield style chairs, one of mahogany decorated with Prince of Wales feathers, and both with front tapering square legs with splayed feet, made and signed by A.C. Lowe Esq., 1935-1985, 7in (18cm) and 7½in (19cm) high.
£400-500   *CSK*

A group of 'cherry wood' dolls house furniture, with embossed Art Nouveau decoration, one armchair upholstered in plum velvet, and an elaborate bronze painted soft metal fireplace, with shop label from The Bon Marché Liverpool.
£250-400   *CSK*

The Bon Marché was founded by David Lewis in 1879, and is mentioned in the Liverpool Directory in 1880 as 'millinery, haberdashery and fancy repository 10-18, Basnett Street'. The shop is now a part of the John Lewis Partnership.

A quantity of dolls house furnishings and chattels, including 4 Waltershausen pieces, a helmet coal scuttle and shovel, a gilt metal vase with lamp shade and a china headed dolls house doll, with cloth body with china limbs, the doll c1865.
£650-750   *C*

A quantity of dolls house furniture and chattels, including a Waltershausen bureau and 4 chairs, a fender and fire irons.
£450-550   *CSK*

A selection of dolls house furniture, c1900.
£1,000-1,200   *S*

A pair of German fabric dolls, by Käthe Kruse, Cristabel with painted hazel eyes, applied blonde hair, in blue and white striped dress, with red handbag; Friedebald with painted brown eyes, applied blonde hair, in khaki shorts; each doll in original green cardboard box complete with head support and descriptive leaflet, c1950, each 19in (48cm).
£1,400-1,800   *S*

Miscellaneous

A talking doll with movable limbs, dressed in modern fabric, c1945, 19in (48cm).
£50-60   *LB*

A German shoulder parian doll, with painted blue eyes, bald head with black yarn wig, fabric body with kid leather arms, in original peasant costume, c1860, 19in (48cm).
£600-800   *S*

A Russian doll in peasant costume, 9in (23cm).
£60-80   *PCh*

Two early English paper dolls, one in ivory silk dress with hand painted rose border to hem, dress frail, 10in (25cm); the other in gauze dress with applied paper leaf and flower decoration, inscribed to the back of head 'E G Ludlow, The Gift of the Bishop of Northumberland, 1809', 13in (33cm); together with a cut-out figure of a man in a frock coat, 10½in (27cm), and a watercolour portrait of a woman with 6 overlay transformation images, each labelled with inscription to reverse, and cut-out images of Prince Albert and Sir Walter Scott, c1810.
£350-450   *S*

A composition headed clockwork walking doll, mounted on a green painted three-wheeled platform, with movable front wheel and head movement, wearing original straw padded bonnet and later blue wool frock and cotton pinafore, some damage and repainting, probably by Theroude, c1860, 11in (28cm).
£1,000-1,500   *CSK*

A set of Punch and Judy hand puppets, the painted wooden heads on original felt and cotton outfits and wooden legs, some damaged, mid-19thC, Punch head 5½in (14cm).
£1,000-1,500   *S*

Two miniature French prams, the larger of cream painted metal wire with cream cotton interior and folding canopy, on 4 spoked flat metal wheels, with curved handle, some paint loss, 7in (18cm) long; the other similar and smaller, with pink cotton lining and canopy, paint loss, 5in (12cm), both early 20thC.
£250-350   *S*

657

TOYS
Automata

A Roullet et Decamps musical rabbit in cabbage automaton, the moving mouth chewing a cabbage leaf, pricking up his ears and turning his head, with keywind stop/start musical movement, slighty soiled, nose rubbed, French, c1890, 10½in (27cm).
£900-1,200   *S*

A maracca playing Roullet et Decamps fur covered rabbit automaton, with amber and black glass eyes, tall pricked up ears, clockwork mechanism, with integral keywind causing him to dance and play his celluloid maraccas, French, early 20thC, 15in (38cm).
£750-850   *S*

A Hoyt smiling negro automaton picture, the clockwork mechanism causing the negro's face to change from a sleeping to a smiling expression, German, back cover missing, late 19thC, 27 by 22in (69 by 56cm) framed.
£3,000-3,500   *S*

A Roullet automaton of a drumming bear, the brown fur covered and muzzled beast with black and white glass eyes, with wooden hands holding metal drumsticks playing a metal drum, with keywind clockwork mechanism inoperative, French, c1900, 12in (31cm).
£400-500   *S*

A Decamps walking pig automaton, the kid covered animal with glass eyes, raised on 4 wheels, mechanism causing him to walk haltingly and emit grunting noise, with key, leather faded, some soiling, c1900, 12in (31cm) long.
£650-750   *S*

A rare Hoyt smiling lady automaton picture, the clockwork mechanism causing her eyes, mouth and head to move from sleeping to smiling expression, back cover and key missing, spring broken, German, late 19thC, 27 by 22in (69 by 56cm) framed.
£2,500-3,000   *S*

Teddy Bears

A Decamps walking cat automaton, the white rabbit fur covered animal with green and black glass eyes, pink painted nose, opening mouth, long tail, on 4 black painted wooden wheels, mechanism overwound, whiskers missing, c1900, 10in (25cm).
£400-600   *S*

A French singing bird automaton, the cage with feathered bird on perch, gessoed gilded base containing musical movement, carrying ring to top, some wear, early 20thC, 17in (43cm).
£1,000-1,500   *S*

A Steiff cinnamon plush teddy bear, with button in ear and white label 5328, swivel joints and excelsior stuffed, inoperative growler, some small holes, c1905, 16in (41cm).
£900-1,200   *S*

A Steiff cinnamon plush teddy bear, with blank button in ear, black boot button eyes, hump back, swivel joints, inoperative voice box, some plush sparse, German, c1904, 13½in (34cm).
£1,500-2,000　*S*

A Steiff gold plush teddy bear, with button in ear, swivel joints, excelsior stuffed, with growler, c1910, 18in (46cm).
£1,700-2,000　*S*

A honey coloured plush teddy bear, with stitched nose and one boot button eye, with blank Steiff button in ear, lacks most of his stuffing through small hole from the missing eye, inoperative squeaker, some re-stitching, c1904, 13in (33cm).
£1,200-1,500　*CSK*

A brown plush covered bear on all fours, with swivel head, cut muzzle, glass eyes, with white tips, 9in (23cm) long.
£150-200　*CSK*

A Steiff gold plush teddy bear, with button in ear, brown and black glass eyes, excelsior stuffed and with swivel joints and back hump, c1925, 21in (53cm).
£1,500-2,000　*S*

A German blond plush teddy bear, with brown stitched snout, brown glass eyes, hump back, swivel joints, excelsior stuffed, with brown leather shoes, c1910, 19in (48cm).
£400-600　*S*

A Bing gold plush mechanical bear, in red felt military tunic with braid trim and brass buttons, red and white felt cap, black painted metal feet, torso with clockwork mechanism causing him to walk, several holes in tunic, c1910, 10in (25cm).
£3,000-3,500　*S*

A long blond plush teddy bear, with brown stitched nose and mouth, cotton pads, brown stitched claws, swivel limbs, straw and fibre filled, snout worn, amber and black glass eyes replaced, possibly American, c1920, 26in (66cm).
£450-650 *S*

A Steiff dark golden plush covered roly poly bear, with boot button eyes, pronounced snout and wide apart ears, missing half an arm, small patches of wear, c1909, 5½in (14cm).
£450-600 *CSK*

A Steiff blond plush teddy bear, excelsior filled, with black boot button eyes, black stitched snout, humped back, long arms and pale felt paws, button to ear, growl box inoperative, early 20thC, 18in (46cm).
£3,000-3,500 *HSS*

A Steiff blond plush covered teddy bear, with boot button eyes, elongated limbs, slight hump, pronounced cut muzzle and felt feet pads, dressed as a sailor in blue trousers, white jersey and blue beret, worn, 8½in (21cm).
£300-400 *CSK*

A Steiff gold plush teddy bear, with button in ear, wide apart pricked ears, hump back, swivel joints, excelsior stuffed, some plush sparse, stuffing shifted, snout stitching sparse, c1908, 24in (61cm).
£1,500-2,000 *S*

A golden plush covered teddy bear, with elongated limbs, cut muzzle, glass eyes, wide apart ears, cloth pads, stitched nose with 2 outer edges extended, hump and growler, 21in (53cm).
£750-1,000 *CSK*

A Steiff blond teddy bear, with button in ear, brown and black glass eyes, brown stitched snout, hump back, swivel joints, excelsior stuffed, small holes to pads, c1930, 13½in (35cm).
£800-1,200 *S*

A Steiff blond plush teddy bear, with button in ear, swivel joints, some stitching worn, stuffing shifted at joints, one foot detached, c1908, 25in (64cm).
£600-800 *S*

A Steiff gold plush teddy bear, with button in ear, amber and black glass eyes, black stitched nose and mouth, straw filled, swivel limbs, ball growler, stuffing slipped, left ear torn and partially detached, early 20thC, 19in (48cm).
£650-750 *S*

A Steiff gold plush teddy bear, with button in ear, black stitched snout, black glass eyes, hump back, swivel joints, excelsior stuffed, inoperative growler, c1930, 18in (46cm).
£650-750 *S*

A Steiff gold plush polar bear, with button in ear, swivel head with brown glass eyes, black stitched nose on white snout, tail key moving head from side to side, large hole on one paw, minor holes to 2 others, ears torn, c1930, 9in (23cm).
£1,700-2,000 *S*

A straw gold plush covered teddy bear, with pronounced snout, glass eyes, felt pads, hump, growler, stitched nose and Steiff button in ear, probably c1909, 24in (61cm).
£2,000-2,500 *CSK*

A set of 12 miniature painted lead foxhunting figures and hounds.
£100-150 *HSS*

An early Steiff Burlap bear on wheels, with black stitched snout, black boot button eyes and swivel neck, hole in one paw, c1896, 20in (51cm) long.
£500-700 *S*

Lead Soldiers & Figures

A collection of 19 Britains painted lead anthropomorphic animals.
£150-200 *HSS*

A set of 5 Britains painted lead bandsmen.
£100-150 *HSS*

A collection of 20 rare Lucotte Napoleonic figures, exceptionally well hand painted, French, paint chipped and lifting on some figures.
£1,400-2,000 *S*

A Tipp & Co. 'Führerwagen' Mercedes tinplate clockwork staff car, with one composition figure in SS uniform, and key, in original box, together with 4 Lineol and 16 Elastolin figures, including Hitler with moving arm, in Jungfolk (Hitler Youth) uniform, Hess Goebbels, Jungfolk standard and flag bearers, Labour Corps flagbearer and worker, SS Motorcycle Corps with flagbearer, SS guard with flagbearer and others, some figures with fatigue, c1936.
£3,000-3,500 *S*

A set of 5 Britains painted lead Salvation Army figures.
£150-200 *HSS*

Money Banks

A cast iron savings bank featuring Andy and Bim Gump standing at each side, with a cast iron money bag at the slot area, 6in (15cm), together with a tinplate lithographed Andy Gump thrift bank, 4in (10cm).
£450-500 *CNY*

A John Harper & Co. Kiltie cast iron money bank, a coin placed in the figure's hand is placed into his shirt pocket, some damage and paint loss, English, c1935, 7in (18cm).
£600-700 *S*

Tinplate

A Shepherd Hardware Co. Uncle Sam cast iron money bank, coin trap with patent date June 8 1886, with key, paint loss and chipping, operating lever missing, American, c1890, 11½in (30cm).
£500-700 *S*

A Fischer clockwork lithographed tinplate six-light limousine, with chauffeur, finished in buff, red and ochre with ochre lining, in original box, 1920s, 13in (33cm) long.
£1,700-2,000 *CSK*

A Shepherd Hardware Co. Humpty Dumpty cast iron mechanical bank, hand depositing coin in clown's mouth, causing him to roll his eyes, with orange hat, blue and orange costume, American, paint loss and lacking coin trap, c1885, 7½in (19cm).
£300-400 *S*

A German lithographed tinplate money box, with lever action eyes and extending tongue, c1925, 7½in (19cm).
£350-450 *C*

A Bing tinplate sedan, lithographed in pale blue with dark blue lining, some repairs and repainting, wheels and edges rubbed, c1920, 12in (31cm).
£500-600 *S*

A Japanese Trademark tinplate open topped vintage car, with spring driven motor, patent No. 27579, 5½in (14cm) long.
£100-150 *HSS*

A large scale Lesney Massey Harris farm tractor, 8in (20cm) long.
£100-150 *HSS*

A Spanish tinplate wind-up Charlie Chaplin on a tricycle, a highly lithographed, smiling Charlie pedals the three-wheeled cycle while looking over his shoulder, c1920, 3½in (9cm).
£1,000-1,200 *CNY*

A German tinplate clockwork 4 seat open tourer, finished in off-white with orange lining, yellow spoked wheels, and scarlet seats, damage to paint, tyres distressed or missing, maker unknown, c1912, 10½in (27cm) long.
£2,000-2,500 *S*

A Günthermann Mutt and Cicero tinplate toy, lithographed in yellow and green, when wound father and son play, 5½in (14cm).
£1,700-2,000 *CNY*

Six Dinky boxed No. 23c die cast Mercedes racing cars, painted in red, royal blue, light blue, silver, yellow and light green, in original trade box with insert, English, c1938, 7½in (19cm) wide.
£700-800 *S*

A Martin La Petite Marchande d'Oranges tinplate clockwork toy, the figure clothed in cotton, with walking action, pushing cart of oranges, the cart containing the simple clockwork mechanism, shoulders of blouse restitched, some paint damage, French, catalogue No. 184, c1901.
£600-700 *S*

A Tipp & Co. tinplate clockwork Royal Mail van, lithographed in red, black, yellow and cream, the sides lettered G.R., with trade mark on dashboard, needs restoring, German, No. T.C.903, c1930.
£400-600 *S*

A Louis Marx tinplate Popeye Express, a wind-up toy featuring Popeye carrying a trunk in a wheelbarrow, on which sits a squawking stationary parrot, in original box, 8in (20cm).
£600-700 *CNY*

A Linemar tinplate Bubble Blowing Popeye figure, battery operated, a highly lithographed Popeye, using his pipe, blows soap bubbles when operated, boxed, 8½in (21cm).
£1,200-1,700 *CNY*

A collection of 10 Dinky boxed die cast vehicles, some with slight chips and play wear, boxes in fair to good condition, English, c1960.
£500-700 *S*

A Linemar tinplate Smoking Popeye, battery operated, featuring Popeye with pipe in hand, seated on a can of spinach and waving, with original box, 8½in (21cm).
£2,500-3,000 *CNY*

Make the most of Miller's

Unless otherwise stated, any description which refers to 'a set' or 'a pair' includes a valuation for the entire set or the pair, even though the illustration may show only a single item

A Günthermann 'Major Seagrave's Golden Arrow' record car, the clockwork vehicle finished in gold paint with lithographed driver and Union Jack, in original cardboard box, distressed, German, c1930, 21in (53cm).
£450-650 *S*

Major H. Seagrave recorded a speed of 231.44 mph at Daytona Beach, Florida, on 11th March 1929 in his 'Golden Arrow'.

A Günthermann 'Kaye Don's Silver Bullet' tinplate clockwork record car, lithographed in silver and blue, with key, in original cardboard box, lid worn and distressed, c1930, 22in (56cm) long.
£900-1,200 *S*

A Chad Valley lithographed tinplate caravan and menagerie set, comprising: Invicta type steam roller, menagerie and Romany caravan, in original box, some rusting to one wheel, c1945, 22in (56cm).
£600-700 *C*

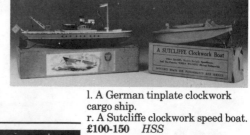

l. A German tinplate clockwork cargo ship.
r. A Sutcliffe clockwork speed boat.
£100-150 *HSS*

A Bing tinplate torpedo boat, the hull painted in light and dark grey with lithographed portholes, twin funnels, 2 lifeboats on davits (detached), 2 ventilators, searchlight, 4 guns, 2 masts, forward deck detached, one flag missing, some surface pitting, guardrail loose around stern, c1912, 15½in (40cm).
£600-700 *S*

Miscellaneous

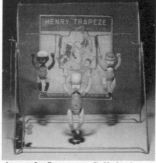

An early Japanese Celluloid and metal Henry Trapeze wind-up toy, with original box, box 10½ by 11½in (27 by 30cm).
£1,500-2,000 *CNY*

A Rosenthal ceramic Mickey Mouse saxophone player, Mickey with pie-cut eyes, finished in black and white, standing on self base, 3½in (9cm).
£1,000-1,500 *CNY*

A Stollwerck toy gramophone by Junghans, with stained wood case, floating Puck type reproducer and wood grained tinplate horn with brass bell, 11½in (29cm) long.
£1,500-2,000 *CSK*

Designed to play 3in records made either of chocolate (with a foil covering) or laminated and coated card. Two models are known, the other pattern being of tinplate with a circular case and a hollow turntable to store the records.

A Spanish Oswald and Mickey tinplate pushchair, the seat lithographed with Mickey running in a diamond and square pattern, and the back depicting Oswald pushing a pushchair, 5in (13cm).
£750-900 *CNY*

A Meccano Number 10 set, in original cabinet on casters, 2 drawer pulls missing, together with 2 boxed Meccano motors, and an instruction manual for Outfit 10 in folder, c1960.
£750-900 *S*

A painted wooden Noah's ark, with sliding side and approximately 140 painted animals and 7 turned wooden figures, by Sonneburg, mid-19thC, 15in (38cm) long.
£800-900   *CSK*

A Flowerpot Man glove puppet by Palitoy, together with a quantity of other toys including The Tricky Tractor, Penguin Clyde Cruiser, Roll Over Cat, etc., some boxed.
£160-200   *Bon*

A Steiff cloth Humpty Dumpty figure.
£1,200-1,700   *CNY*

A painted wooden toy carter's dray with carved and painted dapple grey horses, the cart painted yellow, with original contents, the horses with manes, tails and leather harness, possibly English, c1900, 36in (92cm) long.
£350-450   *CSK*

A pair of chalkware figures of Mutt and Jeff, in appropriate clothes and individual top hats, some repairs to Mutt, Mutt 21in (53cm).
£250-300   *CNY*

A Celluloid Mickey Mouse riding a wooden hobby horse, featuring Mickey in full colour, with large red shoes, riding on hand painted hobby horse, c1935, 4½in (11cm).
£1,500-2,000   *CNY*

A French flock covered carton Boston terrier, with chain pull growl, moving lower jaw and glass eyes, 21in (53cm) long.
£350-550   *CSK*

MODELS

A Bing for Bassett-Lowke electric gauge 1 express locomotive, 4-6-0, Sir Sam Fay, No. 423, German, finished in Great Central Railways livery with matching six-wheeled tender, slight wear and rubbing to paint and transfers, headlamps missing, with quantity of three-rail track, original Bassett-Lowke pro-forma invoice, 1926, and sales catalogues, c1922.
£1,500-2,000   *S*

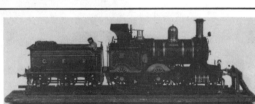

A 6in gauge engineered model of an 0-4-0 coal fired Jubilee locomotive, of largely brass construction, with matching six-wheeled tender, bearing brass plaque reading T Hall, 1897, in GWR livery, lined in red and white, some paint loss and rubbing, 1897, 40in (101cm) long.
£3,500-4,000   *S*

This model was made for Lord Derby, on the occasion of Queen Victoria's Jubilee, and ran upon an elevated track in his garden.

A Märklin bo-bo 'Gothard'-type 110 volt AC locomotive, Catalogue Ref. 1302, c1923.
£3,000-3,500   *C*

A Bing gauge 3 live steam spirit fired 4–4–0 locomotive, Clyde, No. 1932, with brass boiler dome, finished in black with red and white lining, lacking chimney stack, spirit burner, rusted and dusty condition, lacking tender, with Bing gauge 3 L & N W R fitted First Class carriage and fitted guards/goods van, both with hinged lids lifting to reveal interiors, both chipped, crazed and rusted in places, 1904.
£2,000-2,500 *S*

A Hornby 0 gauge tinplate snow plough, with original working drive belt, pre-war.
£200-250 *HSS*

A 2½in gauge model locomotive, probably American, mounted on a green painted chassis, boiler and firebox door detached, with a caged tender, lettered De Witt Clinton, carrying 2 barrels and spare wood, one wheel missing, and a yellow and gold painted stage coach, mounted on a 2½in gauge railway chassis, all pieces dusty and with minor damage, c1890.
£1,400-2,000 *S*

A rare Märklin gauge 1 4–6–2 Swiss electric locomotive, catalogue No. HS 65/13021, finished in green with white roof livery with brown lining, red wheels and buffer plates, slight chips and crazing to paint, with quantity of Märklin gauge 1 track, c1932.
£3,500-4,000 *S*

A model of the brig Marie Sophie, by L. D. Taylor, painted in blue and white, with 2 lifeboats, 2 life belts, 2 anchors and cabins, on a wooden stand, 32in (81cm) high.
£900-1,200 *HSS*

A model boat, c1900, 48in (122cm) long.
£900-1,200 *SAn*

Chess Sets

A Cantonese carved ivory chess set, one side stained red, natural side as European royalty, rooks as knights as horsemen, complete, some damage, mid-19thC, white king 4in (10cm) high.
£500-600 *S*

A large Cantonese ivory chess set, red and natural, each carved piece with concentric pedestal bases, some old repairs and damage, kings 6½in (17cm) high, with lacquered chess/backgammon board with mother-of-pearl white squares, late 19thC, with velum transit case.
£550-750 *S*

A Spanish pulpit form bone chess set, each piece within an acanthus gallery, one side stained brown/black, one side natural, rooks as castellated towers, knights with horses heads, 7 pieces detached from bases, 5 pieces with losses, white queen lacking crown finial, late 18thC, the kings 5½in (14cm) high.
£8,000-9,000   *S*

A natural and red stained carved ivory chess set, kings 4in (10cm) high.
£300-500   *CSK*

Miscellaneous

A boxed games compendium, the burr thuya veneered box with ivory and ebony decorative edging with fitted interior, some replacements and damage, c1880, box 18½in (47cm) wide.
£4,500-5,500   *S*

A carved wood and cast iron cribbage board, 19thC, 11in (28cm) long.
£100-150   *HSS*

A Victorian burr walnut games compendium, the interior with ivory retailer's label, W. Thornhill & Co., 144 New Bond Street, with a compartmented tray containing counters, shells, dominoes, chessman and other pieces, fitted below with 2 drawers containing a miniature croquet set, cards and other counters, 16in (41cm) wide.
£1,200-1,500   *CSK*

An oak cased penny operated Worlborl game, c1920, 26½in (67cm) high.
£200-250   *HSS*

Locate the source
The source of each illustration in Miller's can be found by checking the code letters below each caption with the list of contributors

An Embriachi horn and ivory games board, the sides decorated with intarsia pattern 'alla certosina', minor losses, restored, 15thC, 12in (30cm).
£3,000-3,500   *C*

An oak cased playball machine, all win with 9 winning chutes, c1920.
£150-200   *HSS*

An oak cased old penny operated skill machine, c1920, 18in (46cm) high.
£150-200   *HSS*

A coin operated Throw a Dice game, early 20thC, 14½in (37cm) wide.
£100-150   *HSS*

MUSICAL
Musical Instruments

A single action pedal harp by J. Erat, of Wardour Street, Soho, London, the body and scroll arm veneered with maple, painted in black and gilt, the base carved with recumbent lions and on paw feet, with 43 strings, 8 pedals and 5 louvre boards, the brass machine head inscribed with maker's name and numbered 488, slight damage, some strings missing, early 20thC, 69in (175cm) high. **£800-1,000** *HSS*

An Astor & Company chamber barrel organ, the 27cm cylinder playing 10 tunes on 6 rack and wood and metal pipes, contained in mahogany Gothic revival case with winding handle, set of simulated organ pipes and 6 organ stops at the front, tune changing knife at the side, English, early 19thC, 80in (203cm) high. **£1,800-2,200** *S*

A grand pianoforte by John Broadwood & Sons, in a mahogany case with simple inlaid lines and a rosewood interior, the legs and pedal board enriched with ebony, with music desk, c1817, 97in (246cm) long. **£6,500-8,000** *C*

An English violoncello by Arthur Richardson, labelled Made By/Arthur Richardson/Crediton Devon 1921, the varnish of a golden orange colour, length of back 30in (76cm), in case. **£5,000-6,000** *C*

A violin, the two-piece back with medium to narrow near horizontal curl, the ribs and head of a similar wood, the table with narrow grain, the varnish of a mid-brown colour, with short neck, ebonised finger board and rosewood turners, together with a violin bow, the silver plated button and ebony frog inlaid with mother-of-pearl, late 19thC, length of back 14½in (37cm). **£400-450** *HSS*

An English violin by John Byrom, labelled John Byrom :..... Liverpool 1902, with red-brown colour varnish over a golden ground, in case with silver mounted bow branded G.A. Chanot, length of back 14in (36cm). **£2,500-3,000** *C*

A six-keyed glass flute by Claude Laurent, engraved C. Laurent à Paris 1819/Brevete, with silvered keys and end cap, set with coloured glass, silver mounts, sounding length 21in (53cm), in fitted case. **£6,200-7,500** *C*

An I. Willis & Co. chamber barrel organ, the 18 key movement playing on 4 racks of wooden and metal pipes, with 6 pinned wooden barrels each playing 10 popular airs and hymns, contained in mahogany case with winding handle on the front, together with panel of simulated organ pipes and 4 stops, the base housing spare cylinders, mid-19thC, 70in (178cm) high. **£3,000-4,000** *S*

A German rosewood cased boudoir grand pianoforte by Blüthner, on bold turned and fluted tapering legs ending in brass cappings and casters, c1887, 78in (198cm) long. **£1,500-2,000** *S*

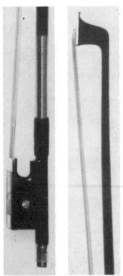

A gold and tortoiseshell mounted violin bow, attributed to Persois, unbranded, the octagonal stick mounted with a gold and tortoiseshell frog with Paris eye and gold and mother-of-pearl faceted adjuster, 62.5gr.
£5,000-7,000   C

A figured walnut musical box, playing 6 airs, No. 20119, 19thC, 21in (53cm) wide.
£1,000-1,200   HSS

Musical Boxes

A Swiss rosewood cased musical box, by Nicole Frères, playing 6 airs, No. 38459, 19thC, 24in (61cm) wide.
£1,500-2,000   HSS

A George Bendon & Co. bells-in-sight musical box, Swiss, the 23.5cm cylinder playing 8 airs as listed on tune sheet, in walnut veneer case with cast brass carrying handles at side, tune sheet badly torn, comb with 4 missing teeth, some veneer missing from lid, c1870, 19in (48cm) wide.
£1,000-1,500   S

A Lochmann Original bells disc musical box, 24½in, the periphery driven movement playing on 4 combs with 12 tubular bells, in glass cabinet with coin chute and winding handle at the side, c1905, together with 14 metal discs, 46in (117cm) high.   **£5,200-5,700   S**

A rare musical Valentine, probably French, the case covered in purple satin and decorated with gold thread and seed pearls, the hinged lid activating a small cylinder musical movement when opened and revealing a small simulated pond with flowers and a humming bird, c1880, 12½in (32cm) long, in original wooden case.
£1,500-2,000   S

Gramophones

An 11⅞in Symphonion rococo disc musical box, German, Style 25C, the 'sublime harmonie' arrangement of 2 combs together with 12 metal discs, 18½in (47cm) wide.
£3,000-3,500 *S*

An early His Master's Voice gramophone.
£400-500 *WW*

An E. M. Ginn Expert Senior hand made gramophone with Expert 4 spring sound box, electric motor, counter-balanced goose neck tone arm and papier mâché horn, 28in (71cm) diam.
£2,000-2,500 *CSK*

A rare HMV Model 251 console cabinet gramophone, with No. 4 sound box and folded internal horn enclosed by louvres and doors flanked by record compartments, finished in Chinese lacquer on black ground, c1925.
£900-1,200 *CSK*

The last of the Gramophones Company's derivatives of the 'Humpbacked Victrola', and the only one to appear with the new acoustic system of October 1925. The lacquer finish does not figure in HMV catalogues, and was probably applied for Harrods, whose label is in the machine.

A rare hand-cranked Berliner gramophone, German, with cast iron base, mounted with 5in turntable, flywheel and handcrank, original sound box and papier mâché horn, distressed, c1899, 10in (25cm) long, together with one damaged disc. **£3,500-4,000** *S*

BOXES

An early Victorian ebony, red tortoiseshell and boulle artist's box, inlaid in brass and pewter, the lid enclosing trays on 2 levels with paint holders, mixing tray and brush holders and green leather portfolio folder, lock stamped Turners Patent Hampton, 16½in (41cm) wide.
£750-1,000 *C*

A pair of Regency amboyna boxes, each hinged top inset with a boulle, red tortoiseshell, mother-of-pearl, copper and brass panel, one with a satyr and snakes, the other with putti, birds and snakes, enclosing a red velvet interior with pen tray, 10in (25.5cm) square.
£1,200-1,500 *C*

A Victorian biscuit box on stand, with hinged action opening to reveal pierced liners with cast handles and ornate cast legs terminating in hoof feet, 7½in (19cm) wide.
£350-400 *P(M)*

A mahogany, chequer strung and painted knife box, the interior converted for stationery, 19thC, 18½in (47cm) high.
£1,700-2,200 *C*

A Britannia metal biscuit box,
c1890, 8½in (21cm) high.
£250-275   TG

A Japanese export black and gilt
lacquer bow fronted decanter box,
the top enclosing a fitted green
velvet lined interior, with a set of
6 cut glass decanters with stoppers
and 2 smaller glass bottles, the sides
with carrying handles, on later bun
feet, late 18thC, 11in (28cm) wide.
£1,700-2,200   C

A calamander dressing box, the
hinged top with an initialled brass
plaque, enclosing a fitted interior
with cut glass fittings with silver
mounts, above a sprung drawer,
19thC, 7½in (19cm) high.
£870-950   S(C)

A French ivory counter box, the
cover with games marker, painted
and engraved with figures and
foliage, with a collection of counters,
18thC, 3in (7.5cm) wide.
£300-400   CSK

A George III mahogany and chequer
banded serpentine fronted knife
box, with later fitted interior, 13½in
(34cm) high.
£450-500   CSK

A snakewood and ebony decanter
box, with quarter veneered top
enclosing a cut glass decanter
with stopper, 6in (15cm) wide.
£1,000-1,200   C

A George III burr elm and
marquetry knife box, crossbanded
overall with fruitwood and inlaid
with boxwood and ebonised
stringing, enclosing a green baize
lined interior, the front with an oval
inlaid with an urn, possibly Dutch,
15½in (39cm) high.   **£700-900   C**

A George IV rosewood and brass
bound dressing case,
countersunk handles and an
engraved plaque, the velvet lined
interior with a concealed mirror
above trays and compartments
including engraved silver
mounted cut glass containers,
hallmarked London 1822, 14½in
(37cm).   **£1,200-1,500   S(S)**

A Regency penwork
games box, decorated
with acorns and other
foliage, the interior
with compartments
and gaming counters,
11in (28cm) wide.
£650-700   CSK

A Regency rosewood jewellery box.
£400-500   LT

A Sheraton period mahogany knife
box, crossbanded in satinwood, with
original interior and silver plated
mounts.
£450-500 DEN

A Victorian rosewood and boulle
jewellery casket, inlaid overall à
premiere partie with brass and
pewter, the hinged lid enclosing an
interior with tray containing a glass
fronted silver gilt red leather
display box, the reverse embossed in
gilt, Honble. Elizabeth Ingram,
Mrs. Hugo Meynell, enclosing an
ormolu saucer, on a moulded base,
13in (33cm) wide.
£400-550 C

A George II red stained shagreen
veneered knife box, the cover with
brass handle and escutcheon plate,
the interior fitted and lined with silk
and velvet and braid, 8in (20cm)
high. **£200-250 CSK**

A pair of George III mahogany
stationery boxes, inlaid overall with
chevron banding, the top banded
with rosewood and inlaid with later
compass medallions with waved
front, enclosing a later fitted
interior, 13in (33cm) high.
£1,500-2,000 C

A George III mahogany cutlery urn,
inlaid with chevron stringing, the
domed top with later turned finial,
the chamfered stem on a later
hexagonal base, 25in (64cm) high.
£700-900 S(S)

A French gold mounted portrait
box, with reeded mounts, the box of
green lacquer with plain mounts
and tortoiseshell lining, c1790.
£450-550 S

A pair of George III urn-shaped
mahogany knife boxes, the lids and
bodies with boxwood and ebony
stringing, the pedestal bases with
tulipwood banding, on ogee bracket
feet, interiors missing, 27in (68cm)
high. **£2,000-3,000 WHB**

A French enamel powder box,
painted with young lovers strolling
through countryside, 8cm.
£450-500 S

A Victorian pierced gilt brass scent
casket, with carrying handle, the
interior velvet lined and with 3 clear
and blue flashed glass scent bottles,
decorated in gilt, 5in (12.5cm) wide.
£450-550 CSK

A Regency Anglo-Indian ivory
sewing box, in the form of a house,
6in (15cm) wide.
£1,500-2,500 C

A gilt lined snuff box with reeded sides, the lid engraved with a two-masted sailing ship in a floret border and, on the inside, 'The passenger on The Falcon, Capt. John Adams to accept this small token in admiration of his Seamanship on the passage to Port Sydney, 21st Day of May 1829', the base stamped Dick, 4 pseudo-hallmarks, and N.S.W.
£20,000-25,000 *WW*

A gold snuff box, the cover engraved with a scene of a Roman ruin, the borders chased and carved with leafy scrolls, engine turned base and sides, 19thC, 8cm.
£1,500-2,000 *S*

An English gold mounted ivory snuff box, the cover engraved, the base piqué and engraved, with plain reeded mount, c1720, 3½in (8cm) wide.
£1,500-2,000 *C*

An English gold mounted tortoiseshell snuff box, with reeded mounts and hinge, the cover set with a gold plaque engraved with a coat-of-arms, c1725, 3in (8cm) wide.
£2,000-2,500 *C*

The similarity of the engraving of the cartouche to a number of coats-of-arms on silver by Paul de Lamerie may suggest that it is the work of Ellis Gamble.

A South Staffordshire enamel snuff box, the cover painted on a raised white scroll cartouche, the sides and base with similar cartouches enclosing flowersprays, against a green ground with raised white trelliswork, restored, c1765, 3in (7.5cm) wide.
£650-750 *C*

A Viennese enamel and silver mounted snuff box, painted all over with figures in landscapes and buildings in riverscapes, 19thC, 3in (7.5cm) wide.
£450-500 *CSK*

A French enamel snuff box, the red ground with raised white scrolls, painted with panels of flowers, 3in (7.5cm) wide.
£150-200 *CSK*

A French enamel snuff box, the blue ground with raised scrolls, painted with reserves of flowers, 19thC, 3in (7.5cm) wide.
£150-200 *CSK*

A gold and enamel mounted toothpick case, applied with a turquoise enamel panel and bordered with ivory beads, mirrored interior, c1800, 3½in (9cm).
£350-500 *S*

A pair of Dutch mahogany and fruitwood hanging tobacco jars, banded with ebonised mouldings with pierced roundel above a hinged lid, one with pottery jar, 19thC, 11½in (29cm) high.
£1,500-2,000 *C*

A domino vesta box. **£25-30** *SCO*

A Victorian walnut and marquetry nautical theme work box, 13in (33cm) wide. **£550-600** *HSS*

A Victorian walnut and marquetry nautical theme work box, 13in (33cm) wide. **£550-600** *HSS*

A mid-Victorian rosewood and mother-of-pearl inlaid travelling box, 10½in (26cm) wide. **£350-400** *P(M)*

An early Victorian rosewood work box, with inlaid brass work, opening to reveal a Tunbridge Ware style inlay to the interior, 10in (25cm). **£250-300** *DEN*

A Victorian figured walnut dome-top writing box, with key, 8in (20cm). **£100-150** *PCh*

A Fabergé nephrite box, with gold lappet hinges set with sapphires and rose diamonds, rose diamond collet set thumbpiece, marked with workmaster's mark HW for Henrik Wigstrom, full Fabergé mark and scratched inventory number 7185, 56 Kokoshnik Standard marks for St. Petersburg, early 20thC, 2 by 1in (5 by 2.5cm). **£15,000-20,000** *DN*

A Sèvres style casket, the gros bleu ground with a central reserve on the cover, enriched with gilt scrolling in the rococo manner around the outside, 8½in (21cm) wide. **£750-1,200** *P(M)*

A George III satinwood box, painted overall with polychrome floral bouquets with hinged lid enclosing a paper lined interior, the sides with carrying handles, 10½in (26cm) wide. **£600-700** *C*

A brass bound tin box, 35½in (90cm) wide. **£200-250** *AL*

A silver mounted ebonised casket, with blue velvet lined interior, the front, back and sides with grotesque masks and scrolling foliage, late 17thC, 11in (28cm) wide.
£300-500   *C*

A William IV rosewood and mother-of-pearl inlaid lady's necessaire cabinet, opening to reveal a compartmented tray, with 2 drawers and a writing slope below, enclosed by a pair of panel doors, on fluted bun feet, 12in (30.5cm) wide. **£350-450**   *CSK*

A Regency horn veneered work box of sarcophagus outline, 11in (28cm) wide.
£270-350   *CSK*

A late Victorian burr walnut, satinwood and Tunbridge Ware table cabinet, the top with a view of Windsor Castle, on a sloping base with squat bun feet, 14½in (37cm) high.
£1,000-1,500   *CSK*

The underside of each drawer is stamped by the maker Boyce, Brown & Kemp, Camden Road, Tunbridge Wells, Tunbridge Ware Manufacturers.

A William and Mary oak boarded box, the moulded front with iron escutcheon and hasp, c1690, 19in (48cm) wide.
£320-400   *S(S)*

A Regency blonde tortoiseshell and pewter strung work box, outlined with horn, the interior with decorated paper, the lid inset with a silk screen print of a woman and a cornucopia, on 4 silvered ball feet, 9in (23cm) wide.
£650-800   *CSK*

A William and Mary oak boarded desk box, the front carved with initials T.H. dated 1688 and branded T.K., 30in (76cm) wide.
£600-700   *S(S)*

A blued and etched steel casket, the corners mounted in ormolu with figures of robed dignitaries banded with strapwork and foliate borders, Bohemian, late 18thC.
£450-550   *CSK*

A gold mounted shagreen necessaire, with leaf engraved mount, containing a mirror, 2 scent bottles, ivory slip and 5 implements, c1780, 8cm.
£500-650   *S*

A Charles II carved oak boarded box, with hinged cover, the sides with lunette motifs, the front with triple roundels and iron escutcheon, c1680, 22in (55cm) wide.
£400-500   *S(S)*

ELECTRICAL

A Gecophone 'Victor 3' three-valve receiver, in crinkle finish metal case with hinged lid, and an Orphean horn speaker.
£200-250 *CSK*

A Pilot Model U-650 six-valve receiver, in upright walnut veneered case with circular tuning dial with 'Magic Eye', 19½in (49cm) high.
£300-350 *CSK*

A Pye Model 350 four-valve receiver, in horizontal walnut case with sloping control panel above fret, 17in (43cm) wide, and a Celestion Model 79 speaker in case
£250-300 *CSK*

An Ekco Model 313 AC mains receiver, in horizontal brown Bakelite case, c1930, 17in (43cm) wide, and a Celestion speaker in mahogany case.
£200-250 *CSK*

An Ekco R.S.2 three-valve mains receiver, in Art Deco style brown Bakelite case, with triple speaker grille, 16in (41cm) high.
£150-200 *CSK*

A Magneto telephone, by Ericsson Telephones Ltd., in an oak case.
£250-300 *HSS*

Miscellaneous

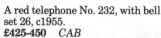

A red telephone No. 232, with bell set 26, c1955.
£425-450 *CAB*

A Sterling intercommunication telephone, c1910.
£50-100 *SM*

A 328 G.P.O. telephone, with bell on/off facility, c1955.
£75-80 *CAB*

A Siemens
neophone, c1938.
£100-120 *CAB*

A red Federal telephone, used on the
Government system, c1948.
£250-300 *CAB*

An ivory telephone
No. 232, with
bell set 26, c1955.
£350-380 *CAB*

A Post Office neophone, black
Bakelite with cast iron base, c1929.
£300-600 *SM*

A Salter Improved No. 5 typewriter,
No. 2694, with gilt lining and
decoration, mahogany baseboard
and japanned and gilt lined steel
cover, by Geo. Salter & Co., West
Bromwich.
£3,000-3,500 *CSK*

A 52in (132cm)
Ordinary bicycle,
the backbone with
mounting step,
stamped Humber
& Co., Makers,
c1885.
£2,200-2,700 *S*

TRANSPORT

Vehicles

A Dursley Pederson bicycle, size 3,
with chain guard and tool box,
c1910.
£950-1,200 *S*

A 50in (127cm) Ordinary
bicycle, with sprung leather
saddle, mounting step,
and turned wood handles
mounted on shaped bar,
c1885.
£2,000-2,500 *S*

A Dursley Pederson bicycle, with
string saddle, tubular cross frame,
gears and bell, painted green,
size 5,
c1910.
£1,000-1,200 *S*

Car Mascots

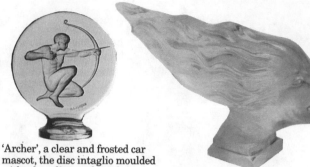

'Epsom', a frosted modelled head of a racehorse, relief moulded mark R. Lalique, 7in (18cm) high, on chromed radiator mount, base with shallow rim chip.
£8,500-9,500 *Bon*

'Archer', a clear and frosted car mascot, the disc intaglio moulded with a kneeling male archer, moulded R. Lalique, wheel cut France, 5in (13cm).
£1,500-1,700 *Bon*

A red Ashay car mascot, c1930, 9in (23cm) long.
£1,000-1,300 *ASA*

'Tête de Bélier', a clear glass car mascot with amethyst tinge, in the form of a ram's head, the face exhibiting a waxy translucence, 4in (9cm) high, complete with Breves Galleries metal mount on illuminated square wooden stand, signed R. Lalique France and Breves Galleries Knightsbridge SW3, stand 8½in (21cm) high.
£5,000-5,500 *P*

'Barbillon', a frosted and clear car mascot, moulded as a fish with upright fin, on rectangular block base, stencilled R. Lalique, 3in (8cm).
£350-400 *Bon*

Leather & Luggage

A bound domed top canvas covered trunk, late 19thC, 32in (81cm) wide.
£50-70 *PCh*

Top. A photographic equipment trunk, covered in zinc and brass bound, with leather carrying handles, the interior fitted with polished wood and labelled Louis Vuitton Paris, London P1073, lock No. 0376752, 24in (61cm) wide.
£2,700-3,000
Bottom. A cabin trunk, vermin proof for use in the tropics, covered in zinc and brass bound, with carrying handles, on casters, interior finished in white cotton and labelled Louis Vuitton London, Paris No. N32043, lock No. 0215, lacking tray, 33½in (85cm) wide.
£2,500-2,800 *ONS*

A shoe secrétaire, covered in LV material, on casters bound in leather and brass, fitted with 29 shoe boxes with lids, one drawer and tray, all lined in white felt, labelled inside twice Louis Vuitton, Paris, Nice, Cannes, Vichy, London, number indistinct, lock No. 078463, 44½in (112cm) high.
£4,500-5,000 *ONS*

A gentleman's tan pigskin dressing case, with ivory fittings, monogrammed C.E.F., 15in (38cm) wide.
£250-300 *ONS*

A Fortnum and Mason travelling drinks set, comprising 3 shaped flasks and centre container with cups and lemon squeezer, in brown leather case, 8in (20cm) high.
£100-150 *PCh*

A Regency leather covered and gilt metal mounted lady's dressing table compendium, the chamfered, reeded top with gilt metal plaque inscribed Eliza B. Swayne, March 5th 1817, revealing a secret sprung jewellery compartment, the tan leather interior with 2 short and 3 long drawers, fitted with a paint box, a sewing box with thimbles, thread, ivory measuring tape and other items, the lower drawer with a pull-out writing slope containing 2 compartments and twin bottles, raised on claw feet, 12in (31cm) wide.
£920-970 *CSK*

On opening the writing slope a watermark can be detected which reads Ansell 1807.

A German trunk with leather, brass and wood trim, fitted interior, with drawers, some lined with silk, by Madler Koffer, 46in (116cm).
£155-165 *AL*

A gentleman's tan leather fitted dressing case, the interior finished in polished hide lined leather, fitted with real ebony hair, hat and clothes brushes, silver topped glass bottles initialled G.P.R., and other accessories, nickel plated locks, Harrods, 26in (66cm) wide.
£300-350 *ONS*

A leather trunk banded in wood with brass fittings, with interior tray.
£200-220 *AL*

A William and Mary leather and iron mounted travelling trunk, the hinged cover with Royal coronet and initials M.R., with iron carrying handles and key, standing on later twin rectangular oak stands with turned feet, the interior now unlined, c1690, 45½in (115cm) wide.
£4,500-5,000 *S(S)*

This trunk reputedly was the property of Queen Mary, wife of William, Prince of Orange.

A crocodile skin travelling dressing case, the interior lined in maroon watered silk and fitted with silver mounted bottles, brushes, manicure set and curling tongs, further fitted with writing folder with ivory paper knife, pen and pencil, various maroon leather wallets, instrument case, French clock etc., makers Samuel Summers Drew and Earnest Drew, and CD, London, c1905, 18½in (47cm) wide.
£550-750 *P(S)*

A car trunk with 3 matching trunks inside, all with white cotton interiors and straps, all labelled Louis Vuitton, Paris, Nice, Lille, London, Nos. 190383 to 190386, with monogram locks.
£4,000-4,500 *ONS*

SPORTS
Cricket

J. Wisden's Cricketers' Almanack
for 1879, original soft covers, spine
distressed.
£260-290 *Bon*

J. Wisden's Cricketers' Almanack
for 1881, original soft covers, spine
distressed.
£170-200 *Bon*

A metal admission ticket, obverse
die-stamped with a central 'W' and
name 'Darnall Cricket Ground',
reverse with scene of a cricket field
with inscription 'Grand Match
Admission Ticket' on surround, 1in
(3cm) diam.
£350-400 *CSK*

Locate the source
*The source of each
illustration in Miller's can
be found by checking the
code letters below each
caption with the list of
contributors*

J. Wisden's Cricketers' Almanack
for 1880, original soft covers, spine
distressed, covers loose.
£240-270 *Bon*

J. Wisden's Cricketers' Almanack
for 1882, original soft covers.
£170-200 *Bon*

A Parian bust of W. G. Grace, by
Robinson and Leadbetter, 6½in
(17cm).
£400-600 *CSK*

England Australia Official Cricket
Souvenir, Season 1911-12, souvenir
programme issued by Authority of
the Board of Control, with half tone
portraits of the England Eleven and
individual team members, original
pictorial wrappers.
£200-300 *CSK*

*A rare tour programme not listed by
Padwick.*

Fishing

A 3in Ogden Smith of London
Improved Zefer reel, 1930s.
£30-40 *JMG*

A 3in Allcock of Redditch 'the Ousel'
reel, made by Walter Dingley,
c1930.
£20-25 *JMG*

680

A 1¼in unnamed brass reel, with
crankwind handle, early 1800s.
£30-40 *JMG*

A 4in Uniqua, the ivorine handle
replaced by a brown one, c1915.
£25-30 *JMG*

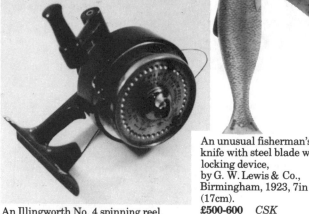

An Illingworth No. 4 spinning reel,
brought out for salmon, in very good
condition, rare, c1930.
£35-45 *JMG*

An unusual fisherman's
knife with steel blade with
locking device,
by G. W. Lewis & Co.,
Birmingham, 1923, 7in
(17cm).
£500-600 *CSK*

A Hardy Altex No. 1, Mk. 1, with
unusual right hand wind, first
model from 1932.
£25-30 *JMG*

A 3¾in Uniqua, with ivorine
handle, c1915.
£30-40 *JMG*

A rare Scottish vintage fishing
tackle dealer, c. 1924, with a deep
knowledge of old reels, grey beard,
ruddy-ish patina, and a most
generous nature towards owners of
fine tackle; buys up to £1000 *JMG*

A 4in Ogden Smith of London brass
reel, not found in Ogden Smith
catalogues, unusual design and
handles, c1914.
£30-40 *JMG*

A 3³⁄₁₆in LRH Lightweight, with
3 screw latch, and duplicated Mk. II
check, post-war model but the first
type made.
£50-60   *JMG*

A 2½in Farlow brass reel, crank
wind handle made specially for the
top to be bent down for protection
while travelling, pre-1880.
£50-65 *JMG*

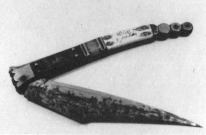

A 4in Allcock of
Redditch the
Marvel salmon
reel, probably
wartime.
£30-40   *JMG*

A Spanish knife,
with tortoiseshell and
ivory handle, and
brass picture of a
mounted spearing
soldier, probably
pre-war, 13½in
(35cm).
£15-20   *JMG*

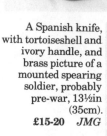

A small spinning reel by Allan of
Glasgow, the Spinet, c1912.
£40-50   *JMG*

A carved painted wood half model of
a salmon, 48in (122cm).
£1,800-2,200   *WW*

A 2⁵⁄₈in Moscrop brass reel, many
unusual mechanisms, only designed
by Moscrop, who died 1903.
£40-50   *JMG*

A 4in spinning reel, made by
Young's of Redditch, named the
Windex, post-war but collectable.
£20-30   *JMG*

A 2½in brass reel with embossed
fisherman on back and front, rare,
but poor condition.
£30-40   *JMG*

A mahogany fishing rod cabinet and
contents, 19thC, 25in (64cm) wide.
£3,500-4,000   *HSS*

A 2⅝in Uniqua, a wartime model when there was a shortage of the blacklead finish, so lacquered over the aluminium, now known as the Spitfire model, c1945.
£60-70 *JMG*

A 4½in Westley Richards of Birmingham, by Walter Dingley, with elaborate ball bearings.
£40-50 *JMG*

Football

A Hardy Test Montague black japanned fly box, with special compartment outside lid, very good condition, pre-1940.
£20-25 *JMG*

A Staffordshire pottery mug, transfer printed in blue, depicting a football match on a pale brown ground, the interior rim with a garland of flowers, mid-19thC, 4in (10cm) high.
£430-480 *CSK*

Welsh Football Union Winners 1901-02 Triple Crown, 17 oval head and shoulders portrait photographs of the team, all mounted in one frame with central caption.
£200-250 *CSK*

A bronze statue of a footballer about to throw a ball into play, on wooden base, early 20thC, 13in (33cm).
£170-220 *P*

An Art Deco style clock, surmounted by a spelter statue of a footballer in action, 11in (28cm).
£250-300 *P*

Miscellaneous

Four early badminton rackets, contained in a wood box with other relics of a lawn tennis and badminton set.
£300-400 *CSK*

Golfing

A William Park Transitional and scared and head brassie, with lead insert and horn sole, restored.
£220-260 *Bon*

A Standard Golf Co. Mills Patent aluminium head putter, SS model Medium Lie, 10oz.
£40-60 *Bon*

Did you know

MILLER'S Antiques Price Guide builds up year by year to form the most comprehensive photo-reference system available

A half size mahogany billiard table,
by Thurston & Co., with 6 turned
and fluted tulip legs, c1880.
£2,000-3,000   *AC*

A billiard/pool wall scoring board in
mahogany, with centre slate
marker, roller numbering, lower
ball storage and coin sections, c1875.
£1,200-1,800   *AC*

A yellow silk World Champion
Cycling sash, embroidered with
white metal thread with inscription
'Union Cycliste Internationale
Champion Du Monde Fond
Amateur 1908'.
£200-300   *CSK*

A Victorian style billiard table,
with turned legs, c1900.
£2,500-3,500   *AC*

An Olympic torch in steel with
outline of the route taken by the
runners from Olympia to Berlin,
inscribed at the top 'Organisations-
Komitee für die XI. Olympiade
Berlin 1936, Als Dank Dem Trager',
and on the underside 'Stiftung der
Fried. Krupp A.G., Essen, Krupp
Nirosta V2A Stahl', 11in (28cm).
£6,000-6,500   *CSK*

A full size mahogany billiard table,
by Orme & Sons, c1900.
£8,000-12,000   *AC*

A full size mahogany billiard table
by Burroughes & Watts, c1870.
£8,000-10,000   *AC*

A full size light oak billiard table, by
Burroughes & Watts, with
matching lights and other
accessories and adjustable legs for
levelling, c1890.
£18,000-22,000   *AC*

A circular mahogany carousel cue
stand, to hold 12 cues, c1900.
£400-500   *AC*

A half size mahogany billiard/dining
table, by Burroughes & Watts,
shown with dining leaves removed
and raised ready for play, c1890.
£3,500-4,500   *AC*

Use the Index!

*Because certain items
might fit easily into any of
a number of categories,
the quickest and surest
method of locating any
entry is by reference to the
index at the back of the
book.
This has been fully cross-
referenced for absolute
simplicity*

LIGHTING

A miniature chamber candlestick, the feather moulded base painted with flowers within a gold rim, by J. Rose & Co., Coalport, 4in (9cm).
£350-400 *Bea*

A Worcester, Flight, Barr & Barr pink ground and gilt chamber candlestick, impressed and script marks, c1820, 4in (10cm) wide.
£1,200-1,500 *C*

A pair of brass candlesticks, the tall shafts with ejectors, on domed bases, early 19thC, 20in (51cm) high. **£450-650** *C*

A pair of Dutch brass candlesticks, each with knopped stem on a slightly dished base, c1700.
£850-950 *C*

A pair of stained beech candlesticks, the turned knopped columns with wide drip pans, on spreading conforming bases, late 19thC, 53in (134cm).
£750-800 *CSK*

A pair of bronze and gilt bronze candlesticks after the antique, of tripod form with paw feet, concave sided platforms, circular bases, applied gilt bronze florettes and gilt bronze sconces, 19thC, 11in (28cm).
£700-800 *P(S)*

A pair of bronze and gilt bronze candlesticks, on bronze bronze stepped bases, engine turned and moulded key patterns, 19thC, 6in (15cm).
£250-350 *P(S)*

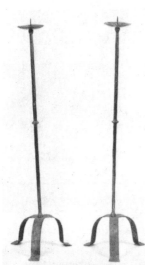

A pair of Northern bronze pricket candlesticks, raised on 3 stylised lion's feet, the knopped faceted stems with spirally twisted prickets, one pricket broken, bases with splits, 14th/15thC, 10in (25cm) high.
£3,200-3,600 *C*

A pair of late 18thC style wrought iron floor standing pricket candlesticks, with knopped columns on trefoil bases, 49½in (126cm) high.
£420-600 *CSK*

A bronzed metal three-light candelabrum, in the form of a street lamp, modelled with a figure of a swaggering young man, the base formed to simulate cobblestones and with a cartouche shaped plaque inscribed SIFFLEUR, early 20thC, 36in (92cm) high.
£400-600 *CSK*

A large pair of six-light bronze patinated brass candelabra, in the form of male and female partially clad figures each supporting the 6 scrolling foliate branches, on open rococo bases, 19thC, 27in (69cm) high.
£650-850   *P(S)*

A pair of George III cut glass two-branch candelabra, 23in (59cm) high.   **£750-850**   *DN*

A pair of ormolu ornate three-branch candelabra, 19thC, 20in (51cm) high.
£400-500   *GH*

A pair of gilt metal five-branch, six-light candelabra with cut glass drops, 26in (66cm) high.
£500-600   *AG*

A pair of bronze and ormolu five-light candelabra, on a stepped alabaster plinth and toupie feet, fitted for electricity, one plinth restored, 18in (46cm) high.
£3,000-3,500   *C*

A pair of French ormolu table candelabra, raised on 3 acanthus leaf sheathed knurl feet, 30½in (77cm) high.
£800-1,000   *HSS*

A George II gilt metal hall lantern, with 4 double arched panels, one forming the door with arched ribs, door panel missing, c1750, 17½in (44cm) diam.
£1,500-2,000   *S(S)*

A pair of French ormolu and black painted seven-light candelabra, the concave bases with variegated marble plinths and acanthus decoration, late 19thC, 31in (79cm) high.
£1,200-1,800   *CSK*

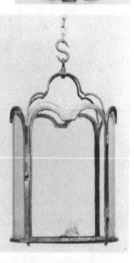

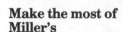

Make the most of Miller's

Unless otherwise stated, any description which refers to 'a set' or 'a pair' includes a valuation for the entire set or the pair, even though the illustration may show only a single item

A Georgian glass and bronze hall lantern, the tapering cylindrical glass body with guilloche decorated metal rim with 3 hooks for chains, the base with a screw-on candle nozzle with urn pendant finial, c1810, 16½in (42cm).
£1,500-2,000   *S(S)*

A French style pentagonal hall lantern, with an open scroll corona, late 18thC, 41in (104cm) high.
£3,000-3,500 *CSK*

A pair of George III style gilt bronze framed four-light hall lanterns, of pentagonal outline, with curved glass panels and scroll corona, 32in (81cm) high.
£3,500-4,500 *CSK*

A French brass framed eight-light hall lantern of square section with canted corners, the frame with applied stylised caryatid figures, with open scrollwork corona, 48in (122cm) high.
£2,000-2,500 *CSK*

A George III style hexagonal brass hall lantern, the glazing bars surmounted by anthemion leaves, below an open scrollwork corona, 30in (76cm) high.
£500-600 *CSK*

A green painted wrought iron hexagonal hall lantern, with stylised foliate and open scrollwork corona and terminal, 36in (92cm) high.
£350-400 *CSK*

A Royal Worcester female Bringaree Indian lamp base, her clothes coloured rust-brown and green, a cream coloured staff held in her right hand, after a model by James Hadley, puce printed crowned circle, shape number 2028 and Rd. No., impressed mark, c1898, 26in (66cm).
£2,500-3,000 *S*

A tôleware adjustable twin-light table lamp, the pierced shades heightened in gilt, 19thC, 19½in (49cm) high.
£350-400 *CSK*

A black painted wrought iron hexagonal hall lantern in the form of a castle, with a central spire flanked by 2 smaller turrets, the base with stylised foliate mounts, 30in (76cm) high.
£450-550 *CSK*

An ormolu three-light electrolier, the scrolling foliate chased branches emanating from a circular lobed corona, late 19th/early 20thC, 21in (53cm) high.
£650-700 *CSK*

An Edwardian brass two-branch table lamp, with adjustable shade.
£70-100   *PCh*

A spelter and gilt metal figural lamp stand, after Auguste Moreau, on a waisted onyx plinth, fitted for electricity, 49in (124cm) high.
£1,500-2,000   *Bon*

A Regency bronze student's lamp, with adjustable candle sconce and shade attached to a rod surmounted by a handle cast with leafage and raised on a moulded base, c1815, 18½in (47cm) high.
£950-1,200   *S(C)*

An early Victorian brass two-light oil lamp, 33in (84cm) high.
£1,200-1,700   *CSK*

An Austrian twin-light oil lamp, the globular green glass reservoirs with applied acorns and oak leaves, emanating from 6 point antlers, centred by a carved wood and polychrome figure head of Diana the Huntress with bow and sheaf of arrows, 19thC, 38in (96cm) wide.
£750-850   *CSK*

A pair of 17thC style Dutch type brass six-light chandeliers, the scrolling mounted branches emanating from bulbous knopped columns, 17½in (44cm) high.
£600-800   *CSK*

A pair of Victorian brass table oil lamps, the hobnail cut glass reservoirs on fluted tricolumnar supports, terminating in hoofed feet, on concave bases, 24in (61cm) high.
£250-400   *CSK*

A gilt bronze and glass centre light fitting, the dish with diamond and fan cutting, the gilt bronze rim moulded with acorns and oak foliage and Egyptianesque lion mask motifs, 9 lamp holders, the central stem with an urn knop supporting the chains, 19thC, 39in (99cm) high.
£5,500-6,500   *P(S)*

A set of 4 French ormolu six-light wall appliqués, the arms supported on a central column with acanthus leaf chased capital and terminal, supported by a cartouche shaped backplate, 42in (106cm) high.
£2,000-3,000   *CSK*

A French gilt bronze adjustable table lamp, the column with finial, on a wreath applied circular base, with a glass shade, 19thC, 22in (56cm) high. **£300-400**   *C*

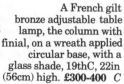

A George IV gilt brass and glass four-light Colza hanging oil lamp, hung with chains from a foliate corona, the burners with later frosted glass shades, 20in (51cm) diam. **£6,000-7,000** *CSK*

A pair of Empire style ormolu eight-light chandeliers, with pineapple terminal and suspension chains below a stellar corona, 58in (147cm) high.
£3,000-5,000 *CSK*

A set of 5 French twin-light wall appliqués, late 19thC, 17½in (45cm) high. **£1,200-1,700** *CSK*

A pair of Victorian silver plated on copper Adam style oil lamps/candlesticks, with removable cranberry glass reservoirs. **£250-350** *GD*

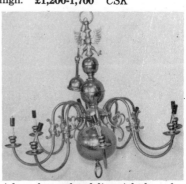

A large brass chandelier, eight-branch electric candle fitments with eagle mount to top. **£550-650** *MGM*

A set of 4 gilt bronze twin-light wall appliqués, of Empire design, the fluted branches emanating from narrow backplates, centred by a laurel wreath and hung with ribbon tie surmount, 17½in (44cm) high. **£1,500-2,000** *CSK*

A set of 6 French gilt bronze wall lanterns, the glazing bars with foliate mounts, crown surmount and pineapple terminal, late 19thC, 18½in (47cm) high. **£2,000-2,500** *CSK*

A pair of French ormolu five-branch wall lights of Louis XVI design, 12in (31cm). **£650-1,000** *S*

A collection of 4 gilt metal Louis XVI style wall lights, the foliate candle arms with cast acanthus leaves and berries attached to quiver backplates, the central arms above putti blowing twin trumpets, with frosted glass torch shades, one wall bracket slightly damaged, 24½in (62cm) high. **£600-700** *Bon*

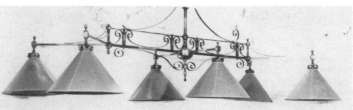

A six-light snooker table electric light fitting with highly decorative wrought oxidised metal frame. **£850-1,000** *WIL*

A Tami Island bowl, carved in relief with a stylised mask to one end with zigzags about the eyes, the carved teeth heightened with lime, a frigate bird to each side below the rim, a serrated band in high relief to each side joining the tail, dark glossy patina, tail broken, 23in (58cm) long.
£400-600 *CSK*

A Hawaiian bowl, of flaring form tapering in from the shoulder, a hooked projection emerging from one side, shiny smooth yellow brown turning to dark brown patina, 7in (18cm) diam.
£4,000-5,000 *S(NY)*

A Yoruba horseman, wearing a turban and holding a flywhisk, his jacket with incised chevrons the horse wearing striped collar, painted in red, blue, black and white, crack to base, left arm and reins repaired, from Ota, 19thC, 10in (25cm) high.
£700-900 *CSK*

This fine small carving shows all the characteristics of the work of the carving house in Ota which produced the carvers Labitan and Olaniyan at the beginning of this century.

Two Borneo figures, male and female, the male with conical hat and concave face, the female with hands curving about the swollen abdomen, wood bases, 28 and 24½in (71 and 63cm) high.
£900-1,000 *CSK*

A Nias large female figure, the hands holding an object against the chest, wood stand, 26in (66cm) high.
£650-750 *CSK*

A Senufo female figure, the median crest terminating in two knobs at nape of neck, thick crusty patina, 15in (38cm) high.
£3,500-4,000 *CSK*

A Yoruba helmet mask, in the form of a compressed oval head with typical features, remains of white, black, blue and red pigment, 17½in (44cm) high.
£2,000-3,000 *S(NY)*

A Yoruba female figure, the blued coiffure with 2 tufts at the top, the eyes with metal stud pupils, carved wearing several bracelets and band about the waist, wearing 3 necklaces of coloured beads, from Ilobu, 16in (41cm) high.
£600-800 *CSK*

Two West African animal face masks, painted in red, white and black, one with incised details in white, 31 and 18in (79 and 46cm) high.
£1,500-3,000 *S(NY)*

A Maprik river ancestral figure, Abelam people, of openwork form, with a stylised lizard supporting a large standing male figure, decorated with dotted and geometric details in yellow, white, black and dark red, 74½in (189cm) high.
£1,200-1,700   *S(NY)*

A Yaka initiation mask, surmounted by a double tiered canvas headdress supporting an embracing couple, painted in bright blue, red, yellow and white, 24in (61cm) high.
£1,500-3,000   *S(NY)*

A Middle Sepik river ancestral board, with details painted in dotted outline white against a faded red, yellow and black field, together with a Southern New Britain war shield, decorated with opposed stylised figures, flanking a broad rectangular projection emerging to bracket handles, bound at the centre and either end with red dyed raffia, 47 and 52in (119 and 132cm) high.
£1,500-2,000   *S(NY)*

A Hawaiian Islands ivory pendant, of hooked form, strung on bundled thinly plaited human hair strands, bound at the top and attached to an olana fibre cord, 14in (36cm) long.
£4,000-5,000   *S(NY)*

A Mossi helmet mask, in the shape of a bird's head, the hemispherical lower part with a long narrow pointed beak surmounted by a backward turning jagged crest, the whole covered by a rich brown patina with traces of white, black and red painted designs on the sides of the helmet and the crest, 11in (28cm) high.
£1,700-2,500   *S(NY)*

The Wagadugu style masks are small, wooden zoomorphic masks. They are coloured with patterns in dark earth red, black and white, and represent animals commonly found in Mossi country. The type of animal represented can usually be recognised by certain stylised features of the animal. Thus, the hawk and other birds of prey are recognised by their short powerful beak and tri-lobed head crest feathers.

A Marquesan Islands stilt step, dark brown patina, 12in (31cm) high.
£2,500-3,000   *S(NY)*

A Lower Sepik river mask, 21½in (54cm) high.
£500-700   *S(NY)*

A Makonde ceremonial staff with zig-zag and diamond scarification on the face, smooth black patina, 19in (48cm) high.
£2,000-3,000   *S(NY)*

A Maori adze, with hooked cylindrical handle surmounted on the curved top by a seated figure covered with typical scrolling motifs, the pommel bound with twisted fibre, a rectangular jade blade emerging from the mouth of a stylised animal's head, pierced through the base for attachment of a wrist cord, reddish brown patina on the shaft, turning to darker brown, mottled green jade, 14in (36cm) long.
£2,500-3,000   *S(NY)*

A Western Australian Aborigine shield, decorated with angular and grooved parallel lines on the front, striated lines on the back and arched handle, remains of red, white and black pigment, 31in (79cm)
£2,000-2,500   *S(NY)*

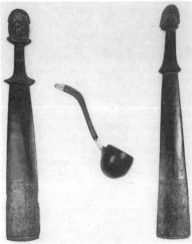

An Australian Aborigine bull roarer, of oval form, incised on each side with 5 spirals and crescents, dark glossy patina, 13in (33cm) long.
£2,000-2,500 *CSK*

A Kongo staff, the finial carved as a kneeling female, the cloth revealing three rows of ornaments at the back, incised swag headgear with topknot, a band of cowrie shell ornament at base, dark glossy patina, inagaki wood stand, 12½in (32cm) high.
£1,200-2,000 *CSK*

l.&r. Two Massim sword clubs incised on both sides with scroll designs, 26½in (67cm).
£170-200 each
c. An Oceanic ladle with stained coconut bowl, ivory and wood shaped handle, 13½in (34cm).
£80-120 *P(S)*

A Solomon Islands model boat, in the form of a narrow dug-out canoe, inset with serrated mother-of-pearl geometric elements into the pitched surface, a long row of seashells attached to a ladder shaped device bound in red cloth on one end, broken off and reattached with native repair, an arched tapering element bound in similar cloth on the other end, 73½in (187cm) long.
£550-700 *S(NY)*

A Kongo flywhisk, the grip decorated with typical geometric design and surmounted by a human torso, eyes inset with metal discs, and coiffure in the form of a long braid hanging on the nape, animal's hair inset into the whisk with a wooden peg, brown patina with metal inlays, some missing, 16½in (42cm) high.
£300-350 *S(NY)*

A pair of Benin brass armlets, each with repoussé bands of heads of Portuguese, alternating with quatrefoils, a border of interlaced geometric ornament, each applied with 12 Maltese crosses in darker metal, minor damage, 19thC, 5½in (14cm) high.
£250-350 *CSK*

ORIENTAL

Cloisonné & Enamel

A pair of Japanese cloisonné vases, worked in silver wire with birds among flowering trees on green grounds, signed Ota Kichishaburo, 6in (15cm) high.
£550-900 *CSK*

Two Marquesan Island objects, a stone pounder with curved base, tapering sides and cylindrical shaft, surmounted by a Janus head with broad upturned mouth and scrolling ears, and a wood bowl with cylindrical base and rounded sides, decorated with traditional scrolling geometric elements and stylised human faces, pounder 9½in (24cm) high, bowl 12in (31cm) diam.
£2,000-2,500 *S(NY)*

A Japanese cloisonné vase, worked in silver wire with a writhing dragon on a dark blue ground, minor scratches, 9½in (24cm) high.
£650-800 *CSK*

A Chinese cloisonné baluster vase of diamond cross section with mask ring handles, decorated on a turquoise ground, 19in (48cm) high.
£400-600 *CSK*

A Japanese cloisonné vase, decorated with chyrsanthemum sprays, on a dark blue ground, signed Tamura, 7½in (19cm) high.
£200-300 *CSK*

A Chinese cloisonné bottle decorated on a turquoise ground, Qianlong, 5½in (14cm) high.
£350-450 *CSK*

Costume

A Chinese image robe of green silk, embroidered in coloured silks and couched gilt threads, the lining with inscription, early 18thC.
£2,500-4,000 *CSK*

The inscription translates: This robe was offered on the 2nd day of the 2nd month, the sixth year of Qianlong (ie 1741 AD), followed by a list of the officers then the signature of the person who prepared the offering note.

A Chinese robe of bronze coloured silk, embroidered in coloured silks and gilt threads against a gilt thread lattice ground, with a sea-wave border at the base, with inscription in lining, fastened by ribbons, 19thC.
£650-1,000 *CSK*

The inscription translates: In the peach month (the third lunar month) of the sixth year of the Guangxu period (ie 1880) written under auspicious circumstances.

A Japanese 'furisode' of midnight blue silk, embroidered in gilt threads and coloured silks, lined with red silk crepe, with padded hem, mid/late 19thC.
£600-800 *CSK*

A Chinese dragon robe, of brown kossu silk, woven in many coloured silks and gilt threads, with horseshoe cuffs, trimmed with fur, late 19thC.
£1,500-2,000 *CSK*

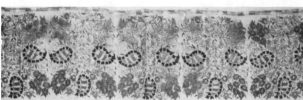

A ceremonial cover of three natural linen panels, each end embroidered with a band of pink florets, boteh outlined with blue hearts, and metal thread flowersprays, late 18thC, 108 by 54in (274 by 137cm).
£600-1,000 *CSK*

It is thought that these covers were placed on the marriage bed.

A Chinese dragon robe of blue silk, embroidered with coloured silks and gilt threads, lined with blue silk, early/mid 19thC.
£900-1,200   *CSK*

A Chinese formal robe, of blue kossu silk, woven in coloured silks and gilt threads, mid/late 19thC.
£1,200-1,700   *CSK*

A 'kosode' of pale blue cotton, printed with a bold overall design in yellow, white, brown and black, also with large hats and tassels, lined with red, padded, early 19thC.
£400-500   *CSK*

A Chinese lady's informal jacket of midnight blue silk, embroidered in coloured silks, the sleeve bands of sea green embroidered silk, lined with red silk damask, with jade buttons, 19thC.
£450-650   *CSK*

Furniture

A Chinese lady's informal jacket of red silk, embroidered in coloured silks and gilt threads, the sleeve bands and trimmings of yellow silk embroidered with blossom and butterflies, lined with red silk, padded, mid/late 19thC.
£300-500   *CSK*

A Chinese lady's informal robe, of red silk, embroidered in coloured silks, trimmed with black embroidered braid, the sleeve bands of ivory embroidered silk, lined with blue silk, mid-19thC.
£1,000-1,500   *CSK*

A Chinese wood six-leaf screen, the leaves set with a total of 92 'famille rose' porcelain plaques variously depicting Immortals in landscapes or scrolling foliage, each leaf 40½ by 12½in (103 by 32cm).
£1,700-2,000   *CSK*

A Japanese gold and black lacquered wood two-leaf screen with cloisonné panels, the exterior with panels of gold lacquer on wood, some damage, 67in (170cm) high.
£2,500-2,700   *CSK*

A Chinese export black and gilt lacquered tripod table, with tilt-top, mid-19thC, 36in (92cm) wide.
£2,500-3,000   *C*

A pair of Oriental hardwood jardinière stands, the marble tops above prunus carved friezes, on cabriole supports headed by masks and ending in claw-and-ball feet, 18in (46cm) diam.
£700-1,000   *CS*

A Chinese lacquered sewing table, the hinged top enclosing a fitted interior, on lyre shaped end supports with floral carved scrolled feet tied by a turned stretcher, 19thC.
£250-350   *Bon*

A Chinese hardwood corner table, the serpentine top inset with marble, above a profusely carved and pierced frieze, on three massive carved cabriole supports and claw-and-ball feet, tied by a roundel and curved stretcher, 19thC, 41½in (105cm) wide.
£600-900   *Bon*

Glass

A Chinese black and gold japanned tray-on-stand, with hoof feet, early/mid-18thC, 32in (81cm) wide.
£1,700-2,000   *CSK*

A Chinese huanghualiwood stool, with rimmed top above beaded edge with pierced frieze and bowed supports joined by a shaped stretcher, 16½in (42cm) wide.
£400-700   *CSK*

A Peking yellow glass bottle shaped vase, with tapering neck decorated in relief with birds among prunus branches, 7in (18cm) high.
£1,000-1,200   *CSK*

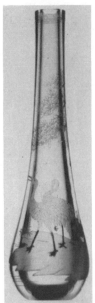

A Chinese hardwood side cabinet, with raised sides to the cleated top, 3 frieze drawers, 2 doors to the panelled front, flanked by pierced and carved side sections and on square supports, 85in (216cm) wide.
£500-700   *Bea*

A Japanese padouk wood netsuke cabinet, 38in (96cm) wide.
£2,500-3,000   *HSS*

A Chinese hardwood window seat, carved with bamboo throughout, the solid seat enclosing a compartment and flanked by raised side sections, pierced underframe below, on cabriole legs, some restoration, 40in (101cm) wide.
£300-400   *Bea*

A Peking aquamarine green glass pear-shaped vase, 20in (51cm) high.
£1,000-1,200   *CSK*

Ivory

A Japanese ivory figure group, depicting three warriors in a circle wielding swords and weapons, some damage, signed sword blades and some digits, 5in (13cm) high.
£700-750   *RBB*

An ivory okimono of Kanyu and Chohi, 3in (8cm) high.
£500-600   *HSS*

A Japanese sectional ivory carving of a farmer with a wood frame of bundles of sticks on his back, a bird in a bird's nest in his left hand, a hare at his feet and an eagle perched on the frame watching the bird, the details in black, signed Gyokushi, 16½in (42cm) high.
£3,000-4,000   *CSK*

A Japanese ivory group of a farmer supporting a wood frame of bundles of wheat and a small child, a further child at his left with a basket of fruit and a rake, minor damage, signed on a red lacquer tablet, 9in (23cm) high.
£1,500-2,000   *CSK*

An ivory okimono of a lady peering into the ear of a grimacing man, his elbow resting on his cabinet, a pipe in his left hand, a case in his right, pipe bowl broken off, signed Munehiro, 2in (5cm) long.
£700-800   *CSK*

A Japanese ivory carving of a man, standing wearing a loosley fitting jacket with a large straw hat slung over his back, holding a tobacco pipe in his left hand and a pouch in his right, the details in black, signed on a red lacquer tablet, Hideyuki wood stand, 13in (33cm) high.
£2,500-3,000   *CSK*

A Japanese ivory carving of a girl dressed in a girl guides' uniform, holding a bunch of peony, 8in (20cm) high.
£350-400   *CSK*

An ivory okimono of Kakkio and his family, 3in (8cm) high.
£500-600   *HSS*

A Cantonese ivory box, 19thC, 10½in (27cm) wide.
£900-1,200   *P(W)*

A Japenese marine ivory carving of Shoki, 2 onis and 3 skeletons, the reverse with a lady pouring sake for a further skeleton, 4½in (12cm) high.
£300-400   C

Jade

A Japanese ivory carving of a figure, holding a bird of prey on his right arm, a basket slung at his waist, damaged, signed on a red lacquer tablet, 6in (15cm) high.
£100-200   CSK

An ivory netsuke style okimono of Daikoku holding his sack on which he plays with a drum and two mice, signed, 1½in (4cm) high.
£320-500   CSK

A Japanese ivory group of two farmers, the details in black, signed on a red lacquer tablet, Sekizan wood stand, 11½in (30cm) high.
£2,500-3,000   CSK

A jade and white metal mounted mirror, attached by an incised white metal frame to a pale celadon jade belt hook handle carved with an openwork chilong, Qing Dynasty, 10½in (26cm) long, with box.
£1,500-2,000   C

A pair of Chinese mottled green and brown jadeite carvings of ladies seated on deer, each holding a ruyi spray, the animals heads turned left and right, one broken at the ankles, 10in (25cm) high, on pierced wood stands.
£1,000-1,200   CSK

A Chinese apple green jadeite saddle ring, with slight russet inclusions, 1in (3cm) wide.
£500-800   CSK

A Chinese decorative jade carving on stand, early 19thC, 5in (13cm) long.
£300-400   Wai

A Chinese pale celadon jade figure group, 12½in (32cm) high.
£1,200-1,500   HSS

A Chinese dark green nephrite jade bowl of shallow form, the everted rim rising from a short foot, 8in (20cm) diam., with box.
£800-900   CSK

Metal

A pair of Japanese silvered bronze Manchurian cranes, on wood stand, some damage, signed Hidehisa, 9½ and 14½in (24 by 37cm) high.
£700-900 *CSK*

A pair of bronze mythical beasts, the bushy upright tails resembling flames, traces of gilt and red lacquer remaining, some wear, 17thC, 21in (54cm) high.
£7,200-7,700 *C*

A Chinese bronze figure of Buddha, with tightly curled hair and pendulous earlobes, the cloak falling over both shoulders, some degrading, late Ming Dynasty, 12½in (32cm) high.
£1,500-2,000 *CSK*

A Japanese bronze jardinière, cast in relief with several monkeys playing, some holding persimmon, signed Genryusai (Seiya Zo), 14in (36cm) diam.
£4,200-5,000 *CSK*

An archaic Ordos bronze dagger, the tapered blade of thin lozenge section, deeply patinated with some malachite encrustation, small losses to blade edges, 4th Century B.C., 13in (35cm) long.
£2,500-3,500 *C*

A Chinese bronze gilt and white metal inlaid twin headed duck, each head in opposite direction, late Ming Dynasty, 3½in (9cm) long.
£620-700 *CSK*

An Oriental silver coloured incense burner, with dragon handles supported by 3 elephant heads, on carved hardwood stand, 16in (41cm) high.
£350-450 *PCh*

A set of 12 Japanese bronze lanterns, with pagoda type tops and pierced doors and panels with foliage and cherry blossom, on shaped bases, 13in (33cm) high.
£2,500-3,000 *E*

A silver inlaid bronze figure of Guanyin, inlaid in silver with scrolling lotus, one finger missing, 17thC, 11in (28cm) high, on wood stand.
£1,500-2,000 *C*

A pair of Chinese bronze
ornamental elephants supporting
vases, on hardwood stands, late
19thC, 10in (25cm).
£120-150 *PCh*

A Chinese bronze tripod globular
vessel and hinged cover, with a
bird's head style hinged spout, the
extended square handle incised
with an inscription, Ming Dynasty,
7in (18cm) wide.
£420-620 *CSK*

A Chinese gilt bronze figure of
Bodhisattva, wearing jewels in her
hair and a jewelled necklace, 18thC,
6in (15cm) high.
£1,000-1,500 *P(S)*

An archaic bronze bell, cast to each
side with three bands of raised
knops above scrollwork to one side,
earth and malachite encrustation,
Western Zhou Dynasty, 15in (39cm)
high, wood stand.
£1,200-1,700 *C*

A Japanese bronze sleeve vase,
details picked out in gilt, late 19thC,
12in (30cm) high.
£550-650 *HSS*

A Japanese
bronze model
of a snarling
tiger, the
stripes well
delineated,
signed, 11½in
(29cm) long.
£320-400 *CSK*

A pair of Japanese bronze pigeons,
the eyes gilt, possibly replacement
feet, 4in (10cm) long.
£600-700 *CSK*

A pair of early Chinese cast iron
heads of Guanyin, each face with
long pendulous ear lobes, traces of
gilt around mouth and eyes, later
wood stands, 7½in (19cm).
£700-1,000 *P(S)*

An Oriental bronze animalier group
depicting 3 tigers attacking an
elephant, on carved hardwood
stand, seal mark, 19thC, 22in
(56cm) wide.
£1,500-2,000 *AH*

Netsuke

An ivory netsuke of a man standing clasping a bear, the animal's head turned, the details stained black, minor chips, signed, 2in (5cm) high.
£100-150 *CSK*

An ivory netsuke of a recumbent karashishi scratching its back with a hind leg, the eyes inlaid, signed, 2in (5cm) long.
£300-350 *CSK*

A boxwood mask netsuke of Bugatu, signed Hozan and inscribed Shichi ju issai, aged 71.
£320-370 *CSK*

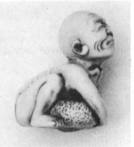

An ivory netsuke of an ox carrying wheat, with a girl by its side holding a pipe, signed, 2in (5cm) wide.
£320-400 *CSK*

A large ivory manju netsuke, carved in deep relief with 2 tennin wearing flowing robes and celestial scarves, one holding a lotus and necklace the other beating a drum with 2 sticks, the reverse with a pine tree, signed Insai, 3in (8cm) diam.
£850-950 *CSK*

An ivory netsuke of a blind man straining to lift a large stone, the details in red, signed on a rectangular reserve Ryoun.
£500-600 *CSK*

Use the Index!

Because certain items might fit easily into any of a number of categories, the quickest and surest method of locating any entry is by reference to the index at the back of the book.
This has been fully cross-referenced for absolute simplicity

Snuff Bottles

An agate snuff bottle, the darker skin in relief with a horseman holding a banner, 3in (7cm) high.
£400-600 *CSK*

An amber snuff bottle carved as a gourd, with leaves and tendrils in relief, 2in (5cm) high.
£450-500 *CSK*

An amber snuff bottle and stopper modelled as a lingzhi fungus, 2½in (7cm) high.
£250-300 *CSK*

Miscellaneous

Two Oriental brass inlaid hardwood jewel boxes, with trays, 9 by 8in (23 by 20cm).
£70-100 *PCh*

A C.I.J. tinplate clockwork P2 Alfa Romeo, some damage, 21½in (54cm) long, with original box and key. **£2,500-3,000** *S*

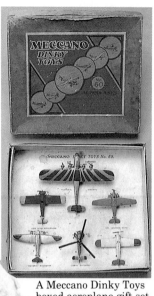

A Meccano Dinky Toys boxed aeroplane gift set, No. 60, play worn, c1940. **£800-900** *S*

A Bing spirit fired fire engine, re-painted, mechanism restored, hose missing, c1902, 10in (26cm) long. **£2,000-2,500** *S*

A Merrythought Mickey Mouse doll, 14in (35.5cm). **£40-60** *Pch*

A German Baroque painted sledge, early 18thC, 109in (277cm) long. **£9,000-12,000** *S*

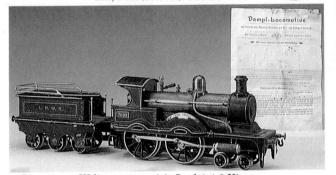

A Bing gauge III live steam spirit fired 4-4-0 King Edward Locomotive, damaged, c1902. **£6,000-7,000** *S*

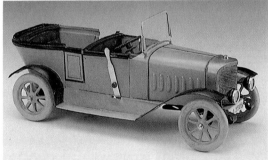

A Marklin tinplate clockwork open tourer, steering mechanism detached from front axle, c1927, 11in (28cm). **£4,000-5,000** *S*

A Musical automaton, French, c1870, 26in (66cm) high. **£6,000-7,000** *S*

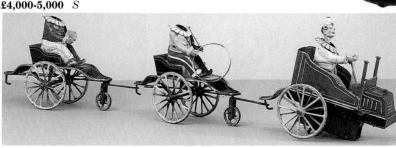

A Marklun tinplate 'Fidelitas' clown car train, hand painted, No. 8965, car lacking. **£14,500-16,000** *S*

A carved flag horse, with American flag blanket, 54in (137cm) long.
£4,500-6,000 *CNY*

A set of 2 carved wood rounding boards.
£1,400-1,600 *CNY*

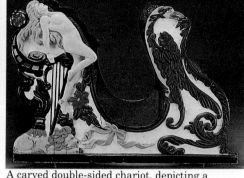

A carved double-sided chariot, depicting a woman riding a swan, 54in (137cm) long.
£1,600-1,800 *CNY*

A carved wood 'Uncle Sam' chariot, with carved images.
£4,000-5,000 *CNY*

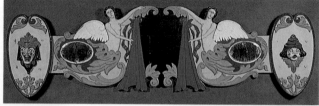

A set of carved wood rounding boards, with carved nude angels.
£600-800 *CNY*

A carved wood horse.
£1,200-1,500 *CNY*

A carved prancing horse, with jewelled trappings, 53in (135cm) long.
£12,000-15,000 *CNY*

A set of carved wood rounding boards.
£600-800 *CNY*

A carved wood stork, carrying a baby, 67in (168cm) high.
£14,000-15,000 *CNY*

A carved wood Zebra, 42in (107cm) **£5,000-6,000** *CNY*

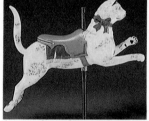

A carved wood cat, in leaping pose, 49in (125cm) long.
£11,000-12,000 *CNY*

A carved wood carousel dog, with deeply carved fur and carved collar, chains and saddle, 53in (134.5cm) long.
£8,000-10,000 *CNY*

A carved wood cat, with expressive face, 51in (130cm) long. **£7,000-8,000** *CNY*

A carved wood leaping frog, 41in (104cm) high. **£9,000-10,000** *CNY*

A carved wood dog, with deep markings, carved buckle, collar and saddle, 43in (109cm) long.
£4,000-5,000 *CNY*

A carved wood carousel horse 47in (119cm) long.
£2,200-2,800 *CNY*

A Lenci cloth doll of a Russian lady, c1930s, 41in (104cm). **£5,000-6,000** *S*

A F. E. Winkler bisque doll, with Bahr and Proschild head, body by Adolf Wislizenus. **£3,000-5,000** *S*

A Kammer & Reinhardt bisque googlie eyed doll, c1914, 14¹/₂in (34cm). **£2,000-3,000** *S*

A French bisque doll, with ball jointed wood and composition body, impressed J1. **£3,000-4,000** *S*

A Jumeau bisque doll. **£12,000-15,000** *S*

A Steiff plush teddy bear, c1908, 29in (74cm). **£3,000-3,500** *S*

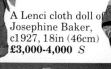

A Lenci cloth doll of Josephine Baker, c1927, 18in (46cm) **£3,000-4,000** *S*

A J D Kestner bisque doll, c1914, 13¹/₂in (34cm). **£4,000-5,000** *S*

A Jumeau bisque doll, some damage, impressed EJ ALO, c1875, 26in (66cm) high. **£20,000-25,000** *S*

A Steiff plush teddy bear, with growler, button in ear, c1908, 27¹/₂in (70cm). **£4,400-5,500** *S*

A Steiff golly, with button in ear, c1913, 17in (43cm). **£5,000-6,000** *S*

A Steiff plush teddy bear, with button in ear, some wear, c1920, 30in (76cm). **£5,000-6,000** *S*

An Etruscan bronze helmet,
Vetulonia type, 480-460 BC, 8in
(21cm). **£11,000-13,000** *S*

A Hellenistic terracotta figure of a
woman, 2nd-1st Century BC, 21¹/₂in
(54cm). **£7,000-8,000** *S*

An Egyptian limestone head of
a goddess, 19th-21st Dynasty.
£4,500-5,500 *S*

An Apulian pottery pyxis
and cover, associated with
the Baltimore painter,
4thC BC. **£2,500-3,000** *S*

An Attic cup, 540 BC.
£7,000-8,000 *S*

A Roman marble head, 1st
Century AD, 9¹/₂in (24cm).
£9,000-11,000 *S*

A Greek terracotta head of a
Kouros, early 5th Century BC.
£9,000-12,000 *S*

A Roman glass flask,
restored, 1st Century BC,
31¹/₂in (9cm). **£25,000-
28,000** *S*

A Roman bronze figure
of youth, 2nd Century
AD, 5¹/₂in (14cm).
£9,000-10,000 *S*

An Apulian pottery krater,
late 4th Century BC.
£30,000-35,000 *S*

An Egyptian limestone
stele, c1075-30 BC,
11in (28cm) high.
£3,500-4,500 *S*

An Attic krater, 540-530 BC,
11in (28cm) high.
£6,000-8,000 *S*

An Egyptian bronze head of a
cat, with a beryl scarab inset
in the crown of its head,
712-730 BC, 3in (7.5cm).
£5,000-6,000 *S*

704

A celadon jade 'champion' vase and cover, Qianlong.
£17,000-20,000 *C*

A Jadeite figure of a maiden, in flowing robe, 8¹/₂in (22cm) high, wood stand.
£2,500-3,500 *C*

A bronze figure of Guanyin, losses, Song Dynasty, 9in (22cm).
£4,000-5,000 *C*

A pottery cocoon jar, the oviform body with waisted neck, Han Dynasty, 18¹/₂in (47cm) wide.
£3,000-3,500 *C*

Two painted pottery Zodiac figures, one ear missing, six Dynasties, 9¹/₂in (24cm). **£4,000-5,000** *C*

An archaic bronze wine vessel and cover, Western Zhou Dynasty. **£30,000-40,000** *C*

A Bronze group of Zhenwu, Ming Dynasty, 43in (110cm) high, with wood stand. **£9,000-11,000** *C*

A celadon and russet jade boulder, carved with 2 deer on a river bank, 18thC, 7¹/₂in (19cm) long wood stand. **£4,000-5,000** *C*

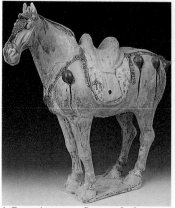

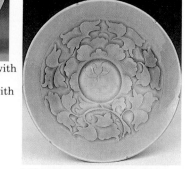

A Sancai pottery figure of a horse, 20in (50cm) high. **£11,000-13,000** *C*

A Dingyao floral dish incised with a single lotus stem, rim chips, Song Dynasty, 5¹/₂in (14cm), with box. **£7,000-8,000** *C*

A recumbent jade bull, the mottled grey stone with scattered deep russet inclusions, small chip to nostril, Ming Dynasty, 51¹/₂in (13.5cm) long, wood box and stand.
£6,500-8,000 *C*

A Yaozhou celadon bowl, the exterior incised with petal ribs, under a translucent celadon glaze suffused with bubbles, Song Dynasty, 8in (20cm) diam.
£10,000-12,000 *C*

A silver and shibuichi box and cover, decorated in gold wire and translucent enamels, signed, late 19thC, 5in (12.5cm) long. **£1,800-2,200** *C*

A gilt bronze figure of Wei To, 17thC, 9in (23cm) high, wood stand. **£3,500-4,500** *C*

A Ming style gilt copper seated figure of Buddha, with inscriptions, incised Qianlong Seven-character mark. 12¹/₂in (31cm). **£3,500-4,500** *C*

A silver Kogo, decorated in takabori and gilt takazogan, signed Setsuho sei, late 19thC, 3in (7cm) diam. **£7,000-9,000** *C*

A pair of archaic Ordos bronze openwork plaques, extensive malachite encrustation, Warring States, 5in (12cm) long. **£4,500-5,500** *C*

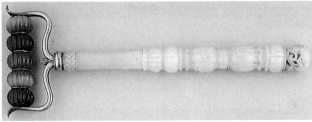

A celadon jade back massager, with revolving beads of lapis lazuli, coral and jade, mid-Qing Dynasty, 10¹/₂in (26cm) long. **£4,500-6,000** *C*

A pair of inscribed beaten gold lotus cups, Tang Dynasty, 4in (9cm) diam. **£22,000-25,000** *C*

A Shibuichi migaki-ji kogo and cover, signed Isshuhoru, late 19thC, 2¹/₂in (6cm) square. **£2,000-3,000** *C*

An iron box, decorated in uchidashi, takabori and silver takazogan, late 19thC, 5in (12cm). **£900-1,200** *C*

A jade carving of a finger citron, 18thC, 4in (10.5cm). **£1,200-1,500** *C*

A celadon jade sceptre, 18thC, 14in (35cm). **£3,500-4,500** *C*

An ivory netsuke, signed Shugetsu, 18thC, 6in (15cm) high. **£50,000-55,000** *C*

An ivory netsuke of the God of Longevity, unsigned, 18thC, 3¹/₂in (8.5cm) high. **£18,000-20,000** *C*

A rogin box and cover formed as Hotei's treasure bag, late 19thC, 4in (10cm) wide. **£8,000-9,000** *C*

A bronze vase, signed in seal form Yuasa zo, late 19thC, 7in (18cm) high. **£3,500-4,500** *C*

A silver box and cover, signed Yukiteru, late 19thC, 6¹/₂in (17cm) wide. **£4,500-5,500** *C*

A bronze moon flask, base signed Shoami Katsuyoshizo, c1880, 7in (18cm) high. **£8,000-9,000** *C*

A silver lined shibuichi box and cover, base signed Kogyokusai, late 19thC, 5¹/₂in (13.5cm) wide. **£10,000-12,000** *C*

A Korean gilt bronze seal, inscription probably removed, Yi Dynasty, 15th/16thC. **£4,500-6,000** *C*

An inlaid silver ox and ceremonial cart, with lapis lazuli, turquoise, mother-of-pearl and amber, late Qing Dynasty, 18¹/₂in (7cm) long. **£4,500-5,500** *C*

A Shibuichi-ji natsume, unsigned, 19thC, 4in (10.5cm) high. **£1,700-2,000** *C*

A Komai iron box and cover, shaped as a folding fan overlapping a gourd, signed Kyoto ju Komei sei, late 19thC, 7in (17.5cm) wide. **£2,000-3,000** *C*

An archaic gold and silver inlaid bronze axe head, some encrustations, Warring States, 5in (13cm) wide. **£8,000-9,000** *C*

A suzuribako, decorated in fundame, silver heidatsu, aogai okibirame, the interior similarly decorated, damaged, unsigned, late 17thC, 8¹/₂in (21cm) high. **£1,500-2,000** *C*

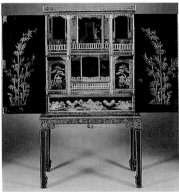

A Chinese Export gilt decorated black lacquer cabinet-on-stand, restoration to decoration, early 19thC, 35½in (90cm) wide. **£8,000-10,000** *S(NY)*

A lacquer Momoyama period domed chest, latch replaced, c1600. **£3,500-4,000** *C*

A Chinese six-leaf screen, 80in (203cm) high. **£80,000-90,000** *C*

A Chinese painted four-leaf screen, the reverse painted with waterfront scenes and domestic utensils, 19thC, 74in (188cm) high. **£4,000-5,000** *C*

An ebonised cabinet-on-stand, inset with pietra paesina panels, restorations, cabinet early 18thC, 35in (89cm) wide. **£5,000-6,000** *C*

A Chinese six-leaf screen, 19thC, 81½in (206cm). **£15,000-18,000** *C*

A Chinese Export black and gold lacquer coffer, mid-18thC. **£17,000-20,000** *C*

A lacquer storage coffer, 18th/19thC, 69in (175cm) long. **£120,000-130,000** *CNY*

An eight-leaf black lacquer hardwood screen, painted with a continuous scene, the reverse with landscape, 19thC, 72in (182cm) high. **£5,000-6,000** *C*

A black lacquer tsuitate, 19thC, 51in (130cm) high. **£14,000-16,000** *C*

COLOUR REVIEW

A cloisonne enamel censer and cover, 19thC. **£3,000-4,000** *C*

A Sino-Tibetan cloisonne enamel qilin, old enamel losses, Qianlong, 24in (62cm) high. **£7,500-8,500** *C*

A carved marbled lacquer stand, chip to foot, 17th/18thC, 9in (23cm) wide. **£4,000-5,000** *C*

A lacquer tray, some damage, late 19thC, 28¹/₂in (73cm) wide. **£25,000-28,000** *C*

A cloisonne enamel bronze mounted vase, early 19thC, 33¹/₂in (85.5cm) high. **£4,000-5,000** *C*

An enamelled silver koro and cover, minor damage, signed on a gilt tablet Hiratsuka, late 19thC, 5¹/₂in (13cm). **£4,500-6,000** *C*

A lady's leather card case, with ivory spine and covers, leather torn, unsigned, Meiji period. **£2,500-3,500** *C*

A carved marbled lacquer bowl, 15th/16thC, 7¹/₂in (19cm). **£5,500-6,500** *C*

A lacquer dish, age cracks, mid-Ming Dynasty. **£8,000-9,000** *C*

A leather laced armour, c1860. **£15,000-18,000** *C*

A pair of wood sculptures, old wear and damage, Kamakura period, 19¹/₂in (50cm) high. **£55,000-60,000** *C*

A Chinese mirror painting mid-18thC, in George III style giltwood carved frame. **£8,000-9,000** *C*

A pair of Regency gilt bronze candelabra, c1820, 26in (66cm) high. **£7,000-8,000** *S(NY)*

A pair of George III ormolu and giltwood candelabra, drilled for electricity, one base cracked, 27in (168cm) high. **£35,000-40,000** *C*

A pair of Regency candlesticks, 13¹/₂in (34cm). **£1,500-2,000** *C*

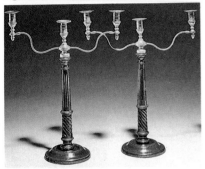

A pair of George III mahogany and brass candelabra, 20¹/₂in (52cm) high. **£5,500-6,500** *C*

A pair of bronze and ormolu candelabra, early 19thC, 28in (71cm) high. **£40,000-45,000** *C*

A pair of Irish George III giltwood and composition candelabra, restored, 44in (113cm). **£8,000-10,000** *C*

A pair of Empire bronze and ormolu candelabra, supported on spreading triangular shafts, 7 later drip pans, 39¹/₂in (100cm) high. **£25,000-30,000** *C*

A pair of Napoleon III bronze candelabra. **£5,000-6,000** *CKS*

A set of 4 gilt bronze candlesticks, French or English, c1775, 16¹/₂in (42cm) high. **£70,000-80,000** *S*

A pair of Louis XVI ormolu and Meissen porcelain candelabra, some damage. **£5,000-6,000** *C*

A pair of Regency ormolu candelabra, one drip pan lacking, one associated. **£7,000-8,500** *C*

A pair of ormolu and bronze two-light candelabra, on marble plinths, 17¹/₂in (44cm) high. **£4,000-5,000** *C*

A pair of Charles X bronze and ormolu candlesticks, 13in (33cm). **£2,500-3,500** *C*

A pair of French bronze and ormolu twin-light candelabra, mid-19thC, 19in (48cm). **£18,000-20,000** *C*

A pair of Restauration bronze candelabra, c1820, 32in (81cm). **£12,000-13,000** *S*

A pair of George III paktong candlesticks, 11in (28cm). **£3,000-4,000** *C*

A pair of Charles X ormolu candelabra, the central branches with flaming nozzles, 16¹/₂in (42cm) high. **£3,000-4,000** *C*

A pair of Empire ormolu and polished steel candlesticks, each foliate nozzle on turned tapering applied with stars, with triple paw socle and stepped base with anthemia, 10in (25cm) high. **£1,400-1,600** *C*

A pair of ormolu candlesticks in Louis XV style, after Meissonnier, 13in (33cm) high. **£25,000-30,000** *C*

A pair of ormolu seven-light candelabra, 29in (74cm) high. **£2,000-3,000** *C*

An ormolu and marble four-light candelabra, with beaded drip pans, drilled for electricity, 21in (53cm) high. **£2,000-3,000** *C*

A brass six-light chandelier, surmounted by an eagle, late 17th/early 18thC, fitted for electricity, 26¹/₂in (67cm) high. **£2,200-2,800** *C*

A pair of gilt bronze candlesticks, supported by seated male and female figures with cornucopia, 19thC, 13in (33cm) high. **£1,800-2,500** *S*

A pair of Regency black painted plaster, gilt gesso and cut glass candelabra, 34in (86cm) high. **£4,500-5,500** *C*

712

An ormolu and cut glass eight-light chandelier, mid-19thC. **£2,500-3,500** *C*

A brass chandelier, the scroll arms with flat drip pans and ovoid nozzles, early 18thC, 39in (99cm) diam. **£8,500-10,000** *S*

A cut glass chandelier, fitted for electricity, slight chips, 46in (117cm) high. **£4,000- 5,000** *C*

A Restauration gilt bronze and glass chandelier, c1820, 44in (112cm) high. **£9,000-10,000** *S*

A German giltwood seven-light chandelier, 18thC, 41in (104m) high. **£8,000-9,000** *C*

A brass twelve-light chandelier in 2 graduated tiers, 18thC, 25¹/₂in (65cm) diam. **£4,000-5,000** *C*

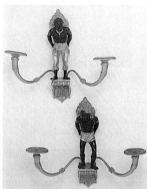

A pair of ormolu and bronzed twin-branch wall lights, later nozzles, fitted for electricity, 11in (28cm) high. **£3,500-5,000** *C*

A pair of ormolu wall lights, bored for electricity, basically early 19thC, 9¹/₂in (24cm) wide. **£2,000-2,500** *C*

A pair of ormolu four-branch wall lights, fitted for electricity, 12in (30cm) high. **£3,000-4,000** *C*

A gilt metal, tôle and soft paste porcelain chandelier, fitted for electricity, 29in (74cm) high. **£2,500-3,500** *C*

A William IV brass colza oil hanging light, lacking burners, 45in (114cm) high. **£3,500-4,500** *C*

A pair of early Victorian painted and parcel gilt torchère lamps, 65in (165cm) high. **£2,500- 3,000** *C*

713

A Louis XV style ormolu eight-branch chandelier, lacking one branch, 53in (134.5cm) high. **£7,000-8,000**   *C*

A pair of French ormolu torchères, the bases with inset jasper limoges plaques, c1900, 72in (182cm). **£2,500-3,500** *CSK*

A pair of Venetian parcel gilt polychrome and ebonised blackamoor torchères, lacking trays, mid-19thC, 66in (168cm) high. **£15,000-18,000**   *C*

A Second Empire torchère, 84¹/₂in (214cm) high. **£5,000-6,000**   *C*

A Regency gilt brass and glass colza light, c1815, with modern shades, 36in (91cm) high. **£13,500-15,000**   *S*

A pair of giltwood torchères, one as a merman and one as a mermaid, on simulated porphyry bases, one with damage to shell, redecorated, 18thC, 57¹/₂in (146cm) high. **£6,000-8,000**   *C*

A Regency ormolu colza oil hanging lamp, in Gothic style, later fitments and frosted glass shades, restorations, 51in (130cm) high. **£20,000-22,000**   *C*

A William IV glass chandelier, c1830, 64in (162cm) high. **£13,500-15,000**   *S*

An ormolu, cut and moulded glass chandelier, fitted for electricity, late 19thC. **£8,000-9,000**   *C*

A pair of Louis XVI style ormolu and cut glass electroliers, 48in (122cm) high. **£4,000-5,000**   *CSK*

An alabaster dish light, with crenellated top, painted with signs of the Zodiac, c1830, 11in (28cm) diam. **£4,500-5,500** *C*

A pair of Louis XVI gilt bronze wall lights, c1785. **£12,000-14,000** *S*

A pair of Regence style silvered wall lights, 29½in (75cm) high. **£5,500-6,500** *C*

A pair of Viennese ormolu, tôle and enamel wall lights, mid-18thC. **£20,000-22,000** *C*

A pair of Louis XV gilt bronze wall lights, mid-18thC, 22in (56cm) high. **£15,000-16,000** *S*

A pair of Charles X ormolu lamps. **£11,000-12,000** *C*

A gilt bronze and cut glass lamp. **£7,000-8,000** *C*

A pair of Louis XV gilt bronze wall lights, mid-18thC. **£3,500-4,500** *S*

A pair of Empire gilded and patinated bronze wall lights, each with a blackamoor mask. **£4,000-5,000** *S*

A set of 6 ormolu and twin-branch wall lights, fitted for electricity, 24in (61cm). **£5,000-6,000** *C*

A pair of early Louis XVI gilt bronze wall lights, attributed to Pitoin, c1775. **£11,000-13,000** *S*

A pair of Louis XVI ormolu lamps, fitted for electricity. **£10,000-12,000** *C*

A pair of Empire ormolu and bronze wall lights, 9½in (24cm) wide. **£7,500-8,500** *C*

A brass and engraved glass hanging light, fitted for electricity, 19thC, 25in (64cm). **£5,500-6,000** *C*

A pair of Louis XV ormolu, tôle and Vincennes lights, 13in (33cm) high. **£15,000-16,000** *C*

A pair of Louis XV gilt bronze wall lights, mid-18thC. **£3,000-4,000** *S*

The Most Noble
Order of the
Garter, Lesser
George sash badge,
in fitted case.
£22,000-25,000 *C*

The Most Noble Order of
the George, Lesser George
sash badge, mid-18thC.
£42,000-45,000 *C*

The Most Noble Order
of the Garter.
£11,000- 12,000 *C*

Order of the Golden
Fleece, Spain,
Kingdom, late 18thC
£6,000-8,000 *C*

The Most Noble Order of
the Garter, Lesser George
badge. **£10,000-12,000** *C*

The Most Noble Order of
the Garter, Lesser George.
£19,000-22,000 *C*

The Most Noble Order of
the Garter, Lesser George,
c1650. **£28,000-30,000** *C*

The Most Noble Order
of the Garter, Lesser
George, early 18thC.
£20,000-22,000 *C*

The Most Noble Order of the
Garter, breast star, gold, silver
and enamel, mid-19thC.
£3,000-4,000 *C*

The Most Noble Order of the
Garter, breast star, gold, silver
and enamel. **£3,500-4,500** *C*

The Most Noble Order of
the Garter, Lesser George,
mid-17thC.
£46,000-50,000 *C*

Order of the
Osmanieh,
Grand Cordon
set of insignia,
badge, Turkey.
£600-800 *C*

716

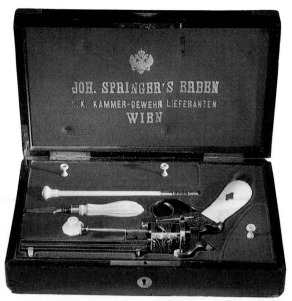

A Continental cased 12mm six-shot pifire double-action revolver, No. 125656 and 641, c1875. **£7,500-8,500** *S(NY)*

A 12-gauge Winchester model 101 Silver Anniversary Edition custom selective, single trigger over/under gun. **£1,800-2,500** *CNY*

A French model of an armourer's shop, signed Au Pere Masselin, Armurier du Roi, early 16thC. **£5,500-6,500** *S(NY)*

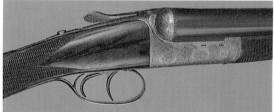

A pair of 12-bore round-action ejector guns, by J Dickson, No. 7067/8, 28in (71cm) barrels. **£16,500-18,500** *CSK*

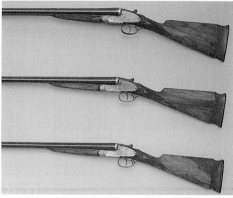

A composed set of 3 12-bore Churchill 'Premiere XXV' assisted-opening sidelock ejector gun, 25in (63cm). **£24,000-26,000** *CSK*

A factory engraved Winchester model 1886 Takedown rifle, by Angelo J Stokes, No. 145592, 24in (61cm) barrel. **£22,000-24,000** *CNY*

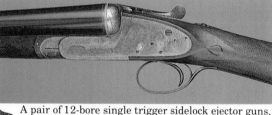

A pair of 12-bore single trigger sidelock ejector guns, No. 7083/4, standard easy-opening action, 29in (73.5cm) barrels. **£20,000-22,000** *CSK*

A pair of 12-bore self-opening sidelock ejector guns, by J. Purdey, No. 27437/8, 28in (71cm) barrels. **£31,000-33,000** *CSK*

A factory engraved and cased Winchester model 1892 lever-action carbine, No. 60909, 44-40 calibre, 20 in (50.5cm) barrel, with brass and hickory cleaning rod. **£20,000-25,000** *CNY*

A pair of 12-bore sidelock ejector guns, by F. Beesley, No. 2221/2, 28in (71cm) barrels, with oak and leather case . **£19,000-20,000** *CSK*

717

A Heriz silk rug, with floral cartouche and vine border, 76 by 53in (193 by 134cm). **£17,000-20,000** *C*

An Aubusson carpet, areas of repair, stained, backed. **£1,200-1,500** *C*

An Agra carpet, the brickred field with herati patern, with flowering vine border, 144 by 120in (365 by 304cm). **£6,000-7,000** *C*

An Aubusson runner, the border with leafy cartouches, areas of wear and damage, backed, 168 by 46in (416 by 117cm). **£3,000-3,500** *C*

An Aubusson carpet, slight-staining, backed, 203 by 159in (515 by 403cm). **£16,500-18,000** *C*

An Aubusson carpet, with central moulded medallion and bouquet, slight damage, 256 by 124in (650 by 314cm). **£17,000-19,000** *C*

An Aubusson carpet, areas of repair, 122in (309cm) long. **£3,000-4,000** *C*

An Aubusson carpet, with tracery flowering vine around a central medallion, areas of staining and repair, backed, 138 by 133in (350 by 337cm). **£4,500-5,500** *C*

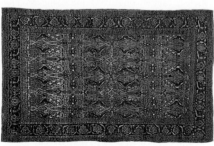

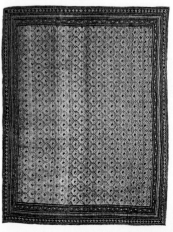

A bidjar carpet, 221 by 136in (560 by 345cm). **£7,000-8,000** *C*

An Agra carpet, striped border, 131 by 100in (332 by 254cm). **£5,500-6,500** *C*

A Melas prayer rug, a short kilim strip at each end, minor repairs, 71in (180cm) long. **£2,500-3,500** *C*

A Kirman part silk pictorial rug, with minor damage, 93 by 63in (236 by 160cm). **£5,500-6,500** *C*

A Senneh Hamadan rug, short kilim at each end, some damage, 81in (205cm) long. **£7,000-8,000** *C*

A Kashan Mochtasham rug with Royal Hawkers, in floral boarder with calligraphic cartouches, between calligraphic cartouche stripes, 91 by 55in (231 by 140cm). **£5,000-6,000** *C*

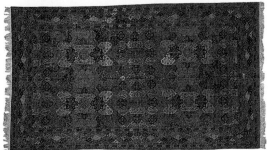

A Kashan carpet, areas of extensive re-piling, 283 by 161in (718 by 408cm). **£11,000-12,000** *C*

A Pontremoli carpet, the ivory field with a variety of loose open sprays, in a serrated minor border, signed JMP, 146 by 97in (370 by 246cm). **£19,000-22,000** *C*

A Kashan Mochtasham rug, with pictorial scene of Bahram Gur, 82in long. **£4,000-5,000** *C*

A Savonnerie carpet, with a central floral roundel with a moulded leaf frame, some damage and wear, 200in (762cm) long. **£25,000-30,000** *C*

A Kashan carpet, with an angular lattice of palmettes, flowerheads and floral lozenges surrounding a central medallion, 200 by 121in (508 by 307cm). **£11,000-12,000** *C*

A Bakshaish carpet, with flowerheads and floral motifs around a serrated and indented panel, areas of slight wear, one end rewoven, 130 by 116in (330 by 294cm). **£10,000-12,000** *C*

A Regency Axminster carpet, with large floral bouquets, ribbons and bunches of leaves around an octagonal panel, with leafy border, reduced, 130 by 120in (330 by 304cm). **£5,000-6,000** *C*

A Kashan carpet, with palmettes and floral sprays around a palmette medallion, 147 by 106in (373 by 296 cm). **£12,000-13,000** *C*

A Heriz carpet, with radiating floral medallion, and flowering vine and serrated leaf border, areas of wear, some tinting, 228 by 179in (579 by 454cm). **£13,000-15,000** *C*

A Kashan mochtacham carpet, with flowering vine and perching bird striped border, 130 by 93in (330 by 236cm). **£16,000-18,000** *C*

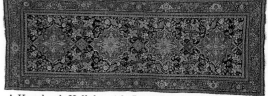

A Karabagh Kelleh, with flowering vine border, 222 by 66in (563 by 167cm). **£3,500-4,500** *C*

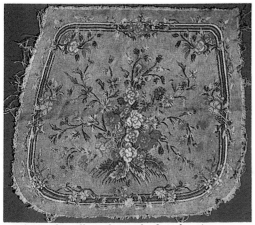

A set of needlework panels, for a bergère chair, worked in silks and wools, French, c1760. **£600-800** *CSK*

A pieced and appliqued cotton quilted coverlet, North Carolina, c1850, 88½in (224cm). **£900-1,200** *CNY*

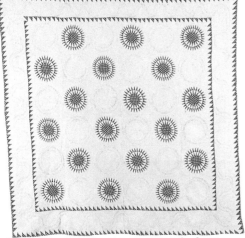

A pieced appliqued and trapunto quilted cotton coverlet American, 19thC, 90in (230cm) long. **£2,000-30,000** *CNY*

A Charles I stumpwork picture, probably depicting Charles I and Henrietta, mounted in black and gilt frame, c1645, 12in (30cm) wide. **£4,000-5,000** *S(NY)*

A Charles I embroidered picture, c1685, 17in (43cm) wide. **£7,500-8,500** *S(NY)*

A velvet coat, stencilled in gold with thistles and roses, labelled Mariano Fortuny Venise, c1920. **£2,000-4,000** *CSK*

A Charles II silver thread, needlework and stumpwork picture, c1660, in 18thC box, 13in (33cm) wide. **£7,500-9,500** *S(NY)*

A pair of lady's shoes, in spotted kid, with low heels, labelled Edwd. Hogg, St James's, London, c1795. **£700-1,000** *CSK*

A pair of lady's mules, embroidered in white thread wrapped in silver, with sunbursts with sequins, square toes, c1665. **£12,000-14,000** *CSK*

'Autumn', a tapestry depicting peasants at grape harvest, losses and restoration, 232½in (590cm). **£20,000-25,000** *CNY*

An Aubusson tapestry, late 18thC, 93in (236cm) wide. **£11,000-15,000** *S(NY)*

'Summer', a tapestry depicting harvest, losses and restorations, 248½in (631cm). **£20,000-25,000** *CNY*

A Brussels mythological tapestry, early 18thC, 99in (252cm) wide. **£16,000-18,000** *S(NY)*

A Flemish biblical tapestry, probably depicting the continence of Scipio, within a floral and foliate border, 17thC, 166in (421cm). **£12,000-15,000** *S(NY)*

A Bruges woven silk and wool tapestry, late 17thC, 99in (252cm) wide. **£35,000-40,000** *C*

A Bruges woven tapestry, after an engraving by Lucas Vorsterman after the painting by Rubens, in silk and wool, mid-17thC, 81in (205cm) wide. **£35,000-40,000** *C*

A suite of Spanish vestments 18thC. **£4,000-5,000** *P(M)*

The detail of the embroidered borders of a velvet suit, altered, c1760. **£4,000-5,000** *CSK*

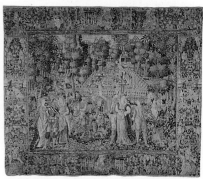

A Flemish tapestry, c1600, 148in (375cm) wide. **£11,000-15,000** *S(NY)*

A Besson echo cornet.
£550-750 *AK*

A Bechstein vertical strung
iron framed piano, c1880.
£400-700 *SPX*

A Victorian English vertical strung
piano, repolished burr walnut case.
£450-750 *SPX*

An overstrung iron framed
boudoir grand piano, by Ernest
Kaps, Dresden, No. 21849.
£950-1,500 *GAK*

A violin, by Antonio
Stradivari, the two-
piece back of broad curl
descending from the
centre joint, c1720,
length of back 14in
(35.5cm).
£900,000-1,000,000 *C*

An English overstrung under
damped piano, repolished
mahogany case, c1920.
£550-850 *SPX*

A Composite
Cremonese Violoncello,
with two-piece back,
c1670.
£16,000-18,000 *C*

An Italian violin, by
Bernardo Calcagni,
with one-piece back,
c1751, 14in (35.5cm).
£30,000-40,000 *C*

A French Violoncello,
school of Bernadel,
with two-piece back,
29½in (75cm).
£18,000-22,000 *C*

A violin, by David
Tecchler, with two-
piece back, 18thC, 14in
(35.5cm). **£16,000-
20,000** *C*

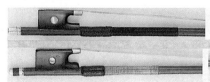

A silver mounted violin
bow, by Grand Adam.
£8,000-10,000 *C*

A silver mounted violin
bow, by Francois Tourte.
£20,000-30,000 *C*

Sangorski & Sutcliffe, binders, The Complete Angler, John Major, 1824. **£2,500-3,000** *CNY*

Zaehnsdorf, binders, Burns Poetical works, Macmillan & Co., 1879. **£2,000-3,000** *CNY*

Zaehnsdorf, binders, The Parson's Horn-Book, by the Comet Literary and Patriotic Club, London, Effingham Wilson, 1832. **£240-280** *CNY*

Trautz-Bauzonnet Bindery, Epithalamion, Edmund Spenser, George D. Sproul, 1902. **£300-500** *CNY*

Zaehnsdorf, binders, Posthumous Poems, J & H. L. Hunt, 1824. **£1,400-1,600** *CNY*

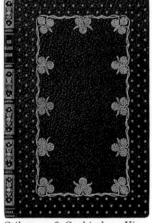

Stikeman & Co, binders, King of England, Vale Pres, London 1903. **£400-800** *CNY*

Webb of Liverpool, The Sketch Book of Geoffrey Crayon, John Murray, 1822. **£450-550** *CNY*

Sangorski & Sutcliffe, Poems by Alfred Tennyson, Edward Moxon, 1842. **£600-800** *CNY*

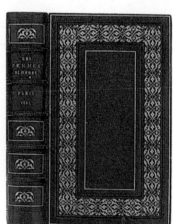

Masson-Debonelle, binders, Les Femmes Blondes, Paris, Aubry 1845. **£900-1,200** *CNY*

Sangorksi & Sutcliffe, binders, a Complete View of the Dress and Habits of the People of London, H. G. Bohn, 1843. **£450-550** *CNY*

Zaehnsdorf, binders, Chastelard A Tragedy, by A. C. Swinburne, Camden Hotten, 1866. **£300-400** *CNY*

ISLAMIC ART

A Tibetan gilt bronze figure of a monk, seated in dhyanasana on a waisted throne, a vajra in relief in front of him, his hands in bhumisparsa and dhyana mudra, wearing a patchwork sanghati, with closely cropped black hair, the face with painted features, re-sealed, 17th/18thC, 9in (23cm).
£2,000-2,500 *S*

A Qajar pottery dish, decorated in dull blue and purple, with a Persian poem at the rim in 8 cartouches separated by rosettes, at the centre a hunter with his bow has just shot a lion, a tree between, the hunter wears pantaloons and boots with curled tips, a pointed helmet with chain mail and a shield on his back, beside his head are the Arabic numbers 82, 9in (23cm) diam.
£500-600 *S*

An Islamic inlaid table, the top inlaid with mother-of-pearl and various woods decorated with a geometric pattern and a central inscription against arabesques within a cube band border, the sides with inscribed panels above pairs of lobed arches supporting 8 legs, early 20thC, 24in (61cm) high.
£1,200-1,500 *S*

A large Qajar pottery tile, with a moulded design, decorated in cobalt blue, yellow, turquoise, purple and light brown with dark brown outlines, and a raised border with a grapevine, 19thC, 20 by 16in (51 by 41cm).
£2,000-2,500 *S*

A pair of Channakale pottery horses, of reddish ware with mottled greenish glaze and opaque red splashes, and with a filler hole on their hindquarters, decorated with a moulded rosette on their chests and a bridle lying curled on their saddles, the tubular legs with a ridge at the centre, 19thC, 9in (23cm) high. **£2,500-3,500** *S*

A panel of 10 Syrian pottery tiles, decorated in underglaze greyish blue, apple green, olive green, turquoise and purple with black outlines, with an elaborate design based on a tall flower filled vase decorated with cintimani holding a bouquet of flowers, other flowers and floral borders on either side, the stems of the central bouquet clasped together, mid/late 16thC, tiles 9in (23cm) square. **£1,300-1,500** *S*

An Ottoman inlaid wooden table, the octagonal recessed top inlaid with mother-of-pearl and coloured woods in a geometric design with the tughra of Abdülhamid II at the centre, the sides with pointed arches and inlaid geometric panels above, late 19th/early 20thC, 21in (54cm) high.
£400-600 *S*

A Safavid tinned copper bowl, with squat bulbous sides and waisted neck, the decoration consisting of 3 continuous inscribed bands round the neck, shoulder and body, a cable band on the shoulder and a festoon frieze below the inscriptions, 8in (20cm) diam.
£600-800 *S*

A Qajar pottery tile, decorated in cobalt blue, turquoise, pale yellow, brown and purple with black outline, 19thC, 10in (25cm) square.
£1,000-1,500   *S*

An Armenian silver gilt plaque of the Virgin and Child, decorated in repoussé with engraved details, the Virgin holding the Child in the crook of her left arm, both gesturing with their right hands towards a cross hanging from the Virgin's neck, the Virgin with a triple pointed crown and a cross at the centre, with a pleated and scalloped robe, the lower half of the plaque with a rectangular chevron frame, 16thC, 5½in (14cm) high.
£1,400-1,600   *S*

An Ottoman silver bowl, with a raised boss at the centre, and decorated in repoussé in high relief, 19thC, 7in (17cm) diam.
£1,800-2,200   *S*

A pair of Channakale pottery jugs, of green glazed earthenware with traces of unfired gold decoration, 19thC, 20in (51cm) high.
£2,000-2,500   *S*

An Indo-Persian steel axe, the watered blade with gold damescening on edges and hammer, the lacquered shaft with a floral trellis on the upper and lower halves and spiral floral sprays in the middle section, 18thC, 26in (66cm) long.
£500-700   *S*

A Turkish bronze stirrup, the sides and top with chiselled floral motifs within a double lined frame, with openwork scrolls on top corners, 18thC, 5in (13cm) wide.
£500-700   *S*

A carved black basalt Islamic tombstone, each face with a panel containing a lengthy inscription on a stippled ground including the name of the deceased, an arched panel above with pendant mosque lamp, slight damage and staining, Arabia 12th-14thC, 18in (46cm) high.
£1,500-2,000   *C*

A Persian silver bowl with flat base, rounded sides and thick rim, the rim extruded at one side into a cusped lobed panel, areas of slight corrosion, c14thC, 5in (13cm) diam.
£1,500-2,000   *C*

An Indo-Persian tinned copper bowl, with inscribed band interrupted by a roundel and framed by 2 scrolling foliate friezes, below a band of interlacing floral scrollwork and a row of trilobed escutcheons, the inscription calling God's blessing on the Fourteen Innocents, 18th/19thC, 11in (28cm) diam.
£600-900   *S*

An Ottoman mail shirt, composed of interlocking riveted rings, a rectangular inscribed button on the front left side near the edge, 16thC, 38in (96cm) long.
£1,400-1,800   *S*

A Safavid tinned copper bowl, with squat bulbous sides, waisted neck and everted rim, incised on the rim with a large band containing 2 lines of inscription framed by 2 friezes of quadrilobes, the body with an overall intricate design of overlapping palmette and arabesque patterns within a scrolling foliate frieze and a strapwork border, late 17thC, 8in (20cm) diam. **£1,000-1,200** *S*

A Sino-Tibetan brass figure of Vajrabhairava, standing in pratyalidhasana on birds, animals and Hindu deities, on a lotus throne, clasping his sakti in yab-yum, with 34 arms and numerous heads, the central one that of a ferocious bull, wearing typical garments and jewellery, traces of colour, c1800, 7in (18cm).
£1,200-1,300 *S*

A south Indian bronze figure of Buddha, standing on a waisted throne on a square base, his hands in abhaya and varada mudra, wearing a long diaphanous sanghati, the hair with flamiform finial, the separately cast aureole with columnar supports and scroll edged arch flanked by openwork floral medallions, the base inscribed, c17thC, 17in (43cm).
£2,500-3,000 *S*

Three Qajar pottery tiles, each of moulded design with floral borders at the top, painted in underglaze polychrome colours with an equestrian figure holding a hawk in a floral landscape, 2 of them with buildings in the background, 19thC, largest 8 by 5in (20 by 13cm).
£1,100-1,300 *S*

A Qajar pottery tile, of moulded design, decorated in underglaze polychrome colours with a crowned figure in profile holding a sword in her left hand and seated on a throne between floral sprays against a blue ground, framed by a frieze of flowers, 19thC, 13 by 11in (33 by 28cm). **£700-900** *S*

A Qajar pottery tile, with moulded frame and central design, decorated in underglaze blue, green, yellow, purple, grey and brown with black outlines, 19thC, 11in (28cm) square.
£1,000-1,500 *S*

An Egyptian carved and inlaid wooden corner cupboard, the central shelf with 2 lobed arches surmounted by a mashrabiyyah panel, the 2 other shelves with a central arch surrounded by 4 smaller, decorated with carved arabesques and inlaid mother-of-pearl rosettes, with trefoil cresting, late 19thC, 69½in (176cm) high. **£1,500-2,000** *S*

An Indo-Persian tinned copper pedestal bowl, the inscription of calling God's blessing on the Twelve Innocents, owner's mark in a pointed medallion, 18th/19thC, **£600-900** *S*

A Qajar pottery tile, decorated in shades of grey, blue, purple and turquoise with black outlines, framed, 19thC, 11½ by 10in (29 by 25cm). **£1,000-1,800** *S*

EPHEMERA

Pop Ephemera

An album, Beatles For Sale, Parlophone Records, 1964, signed on the cover by each member of the group.
£1,500-2,000   *CSK*

A set of 4 glasses, each transfer printed with a portrait of a Beatle and his name, c1964, 4in (10cm) high.
£200-300   *CSK*

A souvenir table lamp, with yellow metal base and paper shade printed with the Beatles portraits and their facsimile signatures, 12in (31cm) high.
£250-450   *CSK*

A presentation Gold disc 'Reel Music', by the Beatles, the album mounted above a 'Gold' cassette, a reduction of the album cover and a plaque bearing the R.I.A.A. Certified Sales Award and inscribed Presented to Gary Benson to commemorate the sale of more than 500,000 copies of the Capitol Records Inc. album and cassette 'Reel Music', framed, 21 by 17in (53 by 43cm).
£1,000-1,500   *CSK*

A single sided acetate, I am The Walrus, by the Beatles, on white Emidisc label, inscribed with artists and song details and dated 2-10-67, with unpublished variations from the final release.
£1,200-1,500   *CSK*

A piece of paper signed by the 4 Beatles and inscribed Love to Barbara from Paul McCartney, framed, 7 by 5in (18 by 13cm).
£500-600   *CSK*

A set of 4 plastic dolls with movable heads, each labelled with a printed facsimile signature, and a set of 4 rubber character dolls, each 4in (10cm) high, another plastic Beatle doll dressed in a grey suit, 7in (18cm) high, and a John Lennon puzzle poster in box, 16 by 11½in (41 by 29cm).
£170-250   *CSK*

A presentation Gold disc, Dancing Machine, inscribed Presented to The Jackson Five to commemorate the sale of more than 500,000 copies of the Motown Records album, cassette and C.D. 'Dancing Machine', 21 by 17in (53 by 43cm).
£500-800   *CSK*

A Kalamazoo Oriole acoustic guitar, Serial No. 971 F27, in maple with solid spruce top, rosewood fingerboard, simulated tortoiseshell scratchplate and trim, the body signed Jon Bon Jovi in black felt pen, in case, 41in (104cm) long.
£500-1,000   *CSK*

Peter Sander's TV cartoon series, The Performing Beatles, gouache on celluloid, window mounted and framed, 1964, 8½ by 13½in (22 by 35cm).
£600-700   *CSK*

This image was used on the cover of a Beatles Tour programme, 1965.

A tooled leather guitar strap decorated with artist's name Bill Haley, and a floral pattern, 49in (124cm) long, used by Haley in the late 1970s, accompanied by a printed itinerary for Bill Haley and The Comets British Tour, March-April 1979, featuring a machine print photograph of Haley playing guitar and wearing this strap, signed and inscribed To Jerry – a pleasure working with you pal, Bill Haley.
£1,500-2,500   *CSK*

An illustrated souvenir concert programme, New Victoria Theatre, London, 24th August, 1976, signed on the cover Luck, Fats Domino, accompanied by a piece of paper, signed and inscribed Luck and Love to Jerry from your Boy, Fats Domino.
£300-400   *CSK*

Four Beatles Christmas flexi-discs in original sleeves, 1966, two 1967 and 1968, 2 demonstration singles, Lady Madonna and All You Need is Love, Parlophone Records, green labels with white 'A' motif, 45 r.p.m., 1967 and 1968 respectively, and 4 other Parlophone Records factory sample singles.
£560-650   *CSK*

An original photomontage artwork for Fashion, 12in and 7in single covers, 1980, signed and inscribed by artist Edward Bell on mount, framed, 10½ by 10½in (26 by 26cm).
£800-1,200   *CSK*

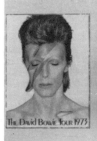

A typescript letter, signed by David Bowie, to a fan thanking him for his card, on headed paper, in common mount with 2 machine print photographs, framed, 19 by 32in (48 by 81cm).
£500-600   *CSK*

An ivory crepe shirt and a rust coloured cotton cap, the peak decorated with silver painted letters G.C., both garments worn by David Bowie in the 1969 film Love You Till Tuesday, accompanied by a letter of authenticity.
£600-1,200   *CSK*

The initials G.C. stand for Ground Control.

An original photomontage artwork for Scary Monsters album cover, signed by artist Edward Bell, dated 1980 and inscribed in artist's hand giving various instructions including one for Bowie's hair colour Dye red, window mounted and framed, 10½ by 13in (27 by 33cm).
£2,200-2,700   *CSK*

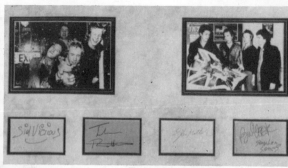

Four pages from an autograph book bearing the signatures of The Sex Pistols, in common mount with 2 publicity photographs of the band, overall measurement 16 by 29in (41 by 74cm).
£1,200-1,800 *CSK*

A mask of black net trimmed with black and gold lace, worn by Prince in the 1984 Warner Bros film Purple Rain accompanied by a copy of a letter from co-star Apollonia Kotero.
£600-800

A pair of ornate 17thC style gauntlets of black and silver lace also worn by Prince in the film Purple Rain.
£800-1,000

A pair of high heeled ankle boots brocaded in a purple and gold Paisley pattern, hand made by Franco Puccetti and worn by Prince in the film Purple Rain.
£3,500-4,500 *CSK*

All the above items accompanied by a letter of authenticity from co-star Apollonia.

A large collection The Sex Pistols and others punk clothing, including approximately 40 punk T-shirts, all decorated with various slogans, logos and band names.
£300-400 *CSK*

A rare handwritten playlist for a Beatles concert 1964, with 10 abbreviated song titles, signed and inscribed on the reverse To Wendy love from John Lenon xx, 4 by 2½in (10 by 6cm).
£2,000-2,500 *CSK*

The song titles included in the playlist suggest that it was written some time between January and April 1964.

A polished bronze of John Lennon by John Somerville entitled Imagine, number 4 from a limited edition of 20, with certificate signed by sculptor, 1983, 25in (64cm) high including marble base.
£1,800-2,200 *CSK*

The Great Rock N Roll Swindle, 1979, Sid Vicious, 5 gouache on celluloid, window mounted, 9 by 12in (23 by 31cm).
£1,700-2,000 *CSK*

A wide brimmed black felt hat allegedly owned by John Lennon and worn by him in the photograph on the cover of A Spaniard In The Works, 1965, accompanied by an affidavit confirming the provenance and John Lennon, A Spaniard In The Works, Jonathan Cape, 1965, illustrations, original boards.
£900-1,200 *CSK*

A bronze of Mick Jagger, numbered 2 from an edition limited to 20 by John Somerville, with a certificate of authenticity, signed by the sculptor, 25in (64cm) high, including marble base.
£1,200-2,200 *CSK*

A sheriff's badge inscribed Captain-Deputy Sheriff Shelby County, State of Tennessee, 2½ by 2½in (6 by 6cm), and corresponding identification card No. 499 with a head and shoulders photograph of Vernon Presley on the obverse, accompanied by a certificate of authenticity from The Elvis Presley Museum.
£1,700-2,200   *CSK*

The bicycle allegedly used in the 'Heaven' sequence of The Rocky Horror stage show, 1960s, the frame applied with gilded press-metal leaves, foliate scrolls and flowerheads.
£1,200-1,800   *CSK*

Film & Theatre

A black trilby of pure wool, stamped Cacharel in gilt lettering on inside leather band and silk lining, and letter of authenticity from Apollonia, Prince's co-star in the film Purple Rain, stating that she…received this black felt hat from Prince while we were working on the film…
£300-500   *CSK*

Twelve polychrome film posters, the majority featuring Humphrey Bogart and Errol Flynn, various titles include The Left Hand Of God, The Harder They Fall, Too Much Too Soon, African Queen, Sabrina Fair and In A Lonely Place, 2 framed, majority 40 by 30in (101 by 76cm).
£150-200   *CSK*

A signed and inscribed photograph of Ingrid Bergman, obtained in person at 14 Hill Street, London, where she was staying whilst she starred in 'The Constant Wife', 1970, 10 by 8in (25 by 20cm).
£80-100   *VS*

A concert bill for Jerry Lee Lewis's cancelled tour, advertising a concert at the Gaumont Theatre, Doncaster, 1958, with a Rank Organisation printed announcement slip fixed to the front withdrawing Lewis's name … The Rank Organisation feel they are carrying out the wishes of the majority in withdrawing this name from the bill…, 15 by 10in (38 by 25cm).
£400-600   *CSK*

Jerry Lee Lewis's fortunes plummeted in 1958 when news of his marriage to his 13-year-old second cousin Myra broke whilst he was on a concert tour of England. The condemnation was so great that concerts were cancelled.

A shirt of cream silk woven with purple stripes and trimmed with purple and cream braid, worn by Rudolph Valentino as Ahmed, The Sheik in the early scenes of his last film The Son of the Sheik, United Artists, 1926, and 2 stills of subject wearing the shirt in the film, in common frame, overall measurement 36 by 27in (92 by 69cm).
£4,500-6,500   *CSK*

A portrait still of Marlene Dietrich in the 1941 film Manpower, signed in blue ink, 9½ by 7½in (24 by 19cm).
£250-300   *CSK*

Make the most of Miller's

Unless otherwise stated, any description which refers to 'a set' or 'a pair' includes a valuation for the entire set or the pair, even though the illustration may show only a single item

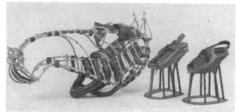

A silver foil, cane and leather theatrical mask shaped as a life size horse's head, 30in (76cm) long, and a corresponding pair of leather and painted metal shoes resembling hooves, the soles shaped as horseshoes, 10in (25cm) high, worn in Peter Schaeffer's Equus, produced by the National Theatre at the Old Vic, July 26th 1973. **£500-800**   *CSK*

A collection of assorted tricks, props and novelties, and a letter of authenticity from Mrs Gwen Cooper confirming that these tricks and props were taken by Tommy Cooper for his final performance at Her Majesty's Theatre, April 1984. **£1,200-1,800**   *CSK*

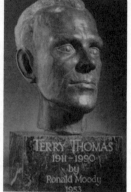

A Ronald Moody bronze portrait head of Terry Thomas, inscribed with gilt lettering, on marble base, 13in (33cm) high.   **£200-300**   *CSK*

A collection of correspondence from Stan Laurel to Mr and Mrs Wray, fans from Tyneside, and one corresponding envelope. **£450-650**   *CSK*

A theatre programme with Gracie Fields on the bill, c1930.   **£8-10**   *COB*

A theatre programme signed on front cover by Vivien Leigh, Duel of Angels, at the Apollo Theatre, London, 24th April 1958, obtained in person.   **£80-100**   *VS*

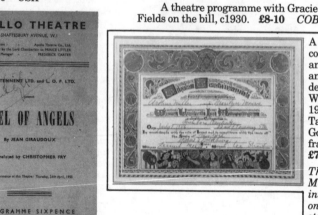

A Ketubbah/Jewish marriage contract, inscribed with the bride and groom's names Arthur Miller and Marilyn Monroe and further details including the city Lewisboro, Weschester, the secular date July 1, 1956 and Hebrew date 22nd of Tammuz 5716, Rabbi Robert E. Goldburg, window mounted and framed, 20½ by 13½in (52 by 34cm). **£7,000-9,000**   *CSK*

The marriage between Arthur Miller, one of America's greatest intellectuals, and Marilyn Monroe, one of America's most famous film stars, caused an orgy of publicity. Marilyn was instructed in the Jewish faith by Rabbi Robert Goldburg, and a double-ring ceremony took place in Katonah at the home of Kay Brown, Arthur Miller's literary agent. Lee Strasberg gave Marilyn away and also signed the contract as one of the 2 witnesses, the other being Miller's brother Kermit. The Millers flew to England for their honeymoon to work on The Prince and the Showgirl, the couple and their 27 pieces of luggage were met at the airport by Laurence Olivier and Vivien Leigh, and a thirty-car caravan took them to a large rented estate at Egham in the grounds of Windsor Park.

A publicity photograph of Vivien Leigh as Scarlet O'Hara in the Twelve Oaks barbeque sequence signed by subject, 4 by 5in (10 by 13cm) window mounted and framed, and an illustrated Atlanta premiere programme for Gone With The Wind, 1939, in common frame, overall measurements 16½ by 24in (42 by 61cm). **£450-650**   *CSK*

A worn black leather wallet, stamped inside with gilt lettering James Dean, made by Rolfs, 7 by 4in (18 by 10cm), accompanied by an affidavit confirming the provenance and a photograph of the vendor with Dean and an actress, Kathleen Case, at Santa Barbara race track 2 months before Dean's fatal accident, 10 by 8in (25 by 20cm). **£5,500-6,500** *CSK*

John Lennon In His Own Write Jonathan Cape, London, 1964, signed and inscribed by Lennon on fly leaf To John god help you from John Lennon and illustrated with a cartoon caricature saying We're growing a hen! **£1,200-1,700** *CSK*

Posters

A Lambert & Butler Navy Cut Royal Salute poster, framed, with screw holes to frame, 23 by 17½in (59 by 44cm). **£300-350** *VS*

A Hignett's Sunflower poster, framed and glazed, with 2 screw holes to frame, 14 by 18in (36 by 46cm). **£700-750** *VS*

A Hignett's Wild West poster, framed and glazed, with 2 screw holes to frame, slight scuffing and surface creasing, 14 by 19in (36 by 48cm). **£1,200-1,500** *VS*

A Hignett's True Bird's Eye poster, framed and glazed with 2 screw holes to frame, some scuffing, 19 by 14in (48 by 36cm). **£500-550** *VS*

A Marcella Cigars poster, comedy of
old man at bookstall, framed,
2 screw holes to frame, some foxing,
14 by 10in (36 by 25cm).
£90-120 *VS*

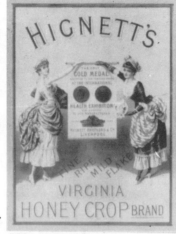

A Hignett's Virginia Honey Crop
poster, framed and glazed with
2 screw holes to frame, some
creasing and tears to edges, 19½ by
14½in (49 by 37cm). **£80-90** *VS*

An Ogden's Special Mixture poster,
framed and glazed, with 2 screw
holes to frame, some cracking and
surface damage, 19 by 14in (48 by
35.5cm).
£60-90 *VS*

A Pacific Line brochure, 1930s.
£10-15 *COB*

A felt newspaper
advertisement,
1930s.
£18-25 *COB*

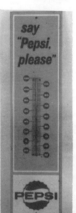

A Pepsi thermometer, American,
c1950, 28in (71cm) high.
£50-70 *AAM*

PHENOMENAL SUCCESS
1d. 2   1d. 2
STAR
LARGEST CIRCULATION
OF ANY EVENING PAPER

A Hignett's True Bird's Eye poster,
showing a yokel smoking a pipe,
framed and glazed, with 2 screw
holes to frame, 14½ by 11½in (37 by
29cm).
£100-120 *VS*

A Hignett's Cavalier Brand poster,
showing Cavalier with horse, on
canvas, framed and glazed
with 2 screw holes to
frame, cracking and scuffing
to canvas, 23 by
16in (59 by 41cm).
£50-80 *VS*

A Hignett's Honey-Crop Brand
poster, showing plantation workers
tending tobacco plants, framed and
glazed, with 4 screw holes to frame,
creases, 11½ by 16½in (29 by 42cm).
£170-200 *VS*

CRAFTS

An earthenware cider flagon, by Henry Hammond, in dark brown with trailed ochre slip decoration, impressed HH seal, 14½in (37cm).
£250-350 *Bon*

A Bernard Leach vase, covered with a grey and orange peel glaze, incised with a band of stylised flying birds, impressed BL and St. Ives, c1965, 7in (18cm).
£1,900-2,200 *S*

A stoneware bottle vase, by William Marshall, covered in an iron brown glaze beneath mottled dark caramel, with incised floral decoration, impressed WM and St. Ives seals, 11½in (29cm).
£300-400 *C*

A stoneware bottle vase, by Ewen Henderson, covered in textured mottled green glazes, 12½in (31.5cm).
£500-650 *C*

A Bernard Leach slab bottle, grey oatmeal and dark brown quartered and decorated with red tree motifs, impressed BL and St. Ives seals, c1955, 8in (20cm).
£4,000-4,500 *S*

A Bernard Leach incense box and cover, decorated with a rich brown and 'tenmoku' glaze, the domed cover incised with a quartered design, impressed BL and St. Ives seals, c1950, 4in (10cm).
£850-1,000 *S*

A stoneware bowl, by Hans Coper, the interior covered in a matt manganese glaze, the underside with a bluish matt glaze burnished to reveal matt manganese beneath, rim restored, impressed seal HC, 11in (28cm) diam.
£3,000-5,000 *C*

A stoneware flared bowl, by Lucie Rie, the slate grey body covered in a pitted thick white glaze, the exterior running and pooling, slight restoration by artist, seal, c1980, 12in (30cm).
£600-800 *C*

A deep porcelain bowl, by Mary Rich, covered in a mottled lavender blue and pink glaze with gilt bands of zig-zag and cross-hatched cell motif and purple band with gilt rim, impressed M seal, 10½in (26.5cm) diam.
£400-450 *C*

Locate the source

The source of each illustration in Miller's can be found by checking the code letters below each caption with the list of contributors

PAPIER MÂCHÉ

A papier mâché bread basket, decorated in colours and gilt against a black ground, the base impressed Clay, King St., Covt. Garden, c1820, 13½in (34cm) wide.
£400-500 *S(C)*

Henry Clay, working 1772-1822, achieved wealth and fame after patenting in 1772 his 'new improved paper ware'. In 1792 he claimed the title 'Japanner to His Majesty', he died in 1812, the business continuing until 1822 at the King St. address.

A lacquered papier mâché blotter, heightened with tinted inlaid mother-of-pearl leaves and petals, within a gilt penwork and mother-of-pearl border, c1835, 12 by 9in (30.5 by 23cm).
£100-150 *Bon*

A Victorian papier mâché and parcel gilt lady's chair, the back inlaid with mother-of-pearl and painted with a flowerspray, above a caned seat, on cabriole legs.
£200-300 *Bon*

A pair of early Victorian black lacquered papier mâché pole screens, with adjustable panels, mother-of-pearl inlaid and gilt patterned with differing designs of exotic birds, flowers and scrolls, on triple splay supports.
£1,200-1,700 *GC*

A Victorian papier mâché tray, inlaid with mother-of-pearl, the border decorated in gilt and with a hatched border, 31in (79cm) wide.
£350-450 *CSK*

JEWELLERY

A Victorian gold and banded onyx locket back brooch, the solitaire centre with banded onyx and half pearl floral border.
£300-350 *CSK*

A Victorian Golden Jubilee ring, 1887.
£100-150 *PVH*

A Victorian silver Aesthetic locket pendant, with applied two-colour owl, bird and linear decoration against an engraved background, suspended from a silver shield link collar.
£400-450 *CSK*

A Victorian gold and cabochon
garnet three-stone twin strand
flexible bracelet.
£1,000-1,200 *CSK*

A Victorian gold set turquoise and
freshwater pearl bracelet.
£150-200 *WW*

A Victorian foliate engraved
panelled bracelet, set with a
turquoise spray on 2 scallops.
£600-700 *WW*

A Victorian gold locket, enamelled
with the monogram G.L. above date
1864, enclosing a portrait of a
gentleman with a lock of hair.
£320-400 *CSK*

*George Lock, 1803-64, partner in the
family firm of Lock & Co., Hatters of
St. James's.*

A Victorian gold bracelet and
padlock.
£400-500 *C(S)*

A Victorian gold tile link collar
necklace, the clasp with stamped
registration mark.
£1,700-2,000 *CSK*

A Victorian Tara brooch, set with
malachite, the reverse with applied
registration plaque and raised
maker's name, West & Son, College
Green, Dublin, Reg.
£200-300 *CSK*

A Victorian graduated diamond
crescent brooch.
£1,000-1,500 *CSK*

PINE FURNITURE
Beds

A pine cot/cradle, c1850, 34in (86cm) long. **£300-350** *AL*

A pine cot, with porcelain handles, 41in (104cm) long.
£145-175 *CHA*

A pine single bed head and foot from an Austrian sleigh bed, 75in (190cm).
£300-400 *CHA*

A pine sleigh bed, c1880.
£120-160 *TPF*

Bookcases

An open bookcase, early 19thC, 46in (116cm) high. **£650-800** *DN*

A glazed bookcase, with broken pediment, 50in (127cm).
£900-1,200 *RK*

A Victorian grey painted pine bookcase, in the Gothic taste, the upper section with a moulded cornice, the base with Gothic panelled cupboard doors, on a plinth, slightly reduced in length, late 19thC.
£30,000-35,000 *Bon*

Chairs

A primitive small chair, c1840.
£100-120 *AL*

A Scottish primitive chair, new rush seat, c1840.
£100-120 *AL*

An armchair, with new rush seat, c1870.
£200-280 *AL*

Chests

A six-drawer chest of drawers, c1860.
£550-650 *SSD*

A six-drawer chest, with original handles, c1860.
£550-600 *SSD*

A South German chest of drawers, c1880. **£200-265** *TPF*

A five-drawer chest of drawers, c1860, 45in (114cm). **£420-480** *SSD*

A flight of 6 drawers, c1860, 16in (41cm) high. **£100-150** *AL*

A Scandinavian bowfront chest of drawers, 38in (96cm). **£300-350** *BEL*

A five-drawer chest of drawers, c1870, 45in (114cm). **£420-480** *SSD*

A three-drawer chest, c1890, 39in (99cm). **£250-300** *SSD*

A Scottish mule chest, 42in (106cm). **£250-300** *RK*

A Victorian chest of drawers, 36in (91.5cm).
£250-300 *FP*

A blue painted kitchen chest of drawers, with brass knobs, late 19thC, 61in (155cm).
£350-400 *PCh*

A miniature chest, 12in (30.5cm) high.
£145-150 *SCO*

A pine coffer, c1800, 66in (167.5cm).
£240-300 *SSD*

A German original painted pine box, c1854, 45in (114cm).
£750-800 *CHA*

A domed top box, with wrought iron straps, candle box and secret drawer, c1773, 46in (116.5cm).
£350-450 *CHA*

An Austrian pine chest, dated 1861.
£140-160 *TPF*

A pine mule chest, with drawer, c1840, 42½in (107cm).
£325-350 *AL*

A tool chest, with 2 trays, c1860, 36in (92cm).
£140-180 *AL*

A sea chest with fitted tray, 27in (69cm).
£125-150 *AL*

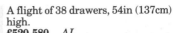

A flight of 38 drawers, 54in (137cm) high.
£520-580   *AL*

A spice rack, possibly a child's dresser, with black porcelain handles, 28in (71cm) high.
£200-250   *AL*

A pine flight of drawers, c1850, 56½in (143cm).
£600-650   *AL*

A German painted pine chest, 19½in (49cm).
£275-325   *CHA*

A box shaped chest of drawers, with locking fall front, c1860, 31in (78.5cm).
£420-500   *AL*

A mid-European chest of drawers, 37in (94cm).
£300-360   *RK*

A painted pine box, with original lock and key, dated 1868, 44in. **£425-475**   *CHA*

A domed top box, with original lock and key, 39in (99cm). **£225-275**   *CHA*

A pine box, with candle box, c1840, 41in (104cm).
£170-200 *AL*

A Swedish painted pine marriage chest, 18thC, 43in (109cm).
£400-450 *DN*

Clocks

A Danish pine eight-day grandfather clock, with original paint, by J. M. Kofoed, 73in (185cm) high.
£950-1,200 *BEL*

A Danish pine eight-day grandfather clock, with later paint, c1860, 73in (186cm) high.
£950-1,200 *BEL*

A Danish eight-day grandfather clock, with painted dial, c1862, 76in (192cm) high.
£950-1,200 *BEL*

Commodes

A mid-Victorian commode, 17in (43cm) square.
£70-100 *FP*

A commode, with initials TD on lid and date 1890.
£100-150 *CHA*

A painted pine bowfronted corner cupboard, with panelled doors, original paint, 19thC, 46in (118cm).
£850-950 *BEL*

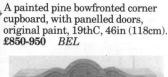

A glazed cupboard with arched top, 36in (91.5cm). **£250-300** *CHA*

Cupboards

An English corner cupboard, 80in (203cm) high.
£450-500 *RK*

A Scandinavian pine bowfront corner cupboard, with panelled doors enclosing 2 shelves, c1845, 48in (122cm).
£750-850 *BEL*

A Swedish pot cupboard, c1910, 24½in (62cm). **£140-180** *BEL*

A hanging corner cupboard, 19thC, 28in (71cm).
£350-400 *CHA*

An Austrian hanging corner cupboard, with 3 coloured glass panels in the single door, 31½in (80cm) high.
£165-185 *CHA*

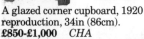

A glazed corner cupboard, 1920 reproduction, 34in (86cm).
£850-£1,000 *CHA*

A warming cupboard, c1830, 43in (109cm). **£325-375** *AL*

A hanging cupboard,
19thC, 33in (84cm) high.
£75-100   *CHA*

A pot cupboard, with marble
top, no back, c1910, 25in
(63cm).   **£120-150**   *BEL*

A food cupboard,
19thC, 50in (127cm).
£800-850   *RK*

A Victorian upright chest,
with false front, 31in (79cm).
£140-180   *FP*

A French display cupboard,
c1890.   **£250-300**   *TPF*

A glazed painted pine hanging
cupboard, c1840, 42in (106.5cm).
£250-300   *KEY*

An English
cupboard, 32in
£150-200   *RK*

A French
food
cupboard,
c1860.
£240-300
TPF

A Welsh corner cupboard, 71in
(180cm) high.
£700-900   *RK*

A Scandinavian cupboard, with
secrétaire front, 38in (96.5cm).
£400-450   *RK*

An Irish food cupboard, 58in (147cm).
£1,400-1,800   *RK*

An Irish cupboard, with drawers, 72in (182cm).
£1,700-2,000   *RK*

A French bedside cupboard, c1870.   **£75-85**   *TPF*

A Scandinavian painted pine secrétairo, with fitted interior, c1845, 36in (93cm).
£950-1,200   *BEL*

A pair of South German bedside cupboards, c1900.
£70-90 each   *TPF*

A Danish glazed food cupboard, with ventilators in the back, drawers under, 65in (165cm) high.
£400-450   *CHA*

A mid-European pot cupboard, 17in (43cm).
£90-120   *RK*

A Danish cupboard, with fall front, 40in (101cm).
£650-700   *RK*

A Regency pine tapered leg pot cupboard, 32in (81cm) high.
£130-150   *AL*

A painted sycamore cupboard, East German or Polish border, c1818, 24in (61cm).
£350-400   *CHA*

A German painted pine cobblers cupboard, 27in (68.5cm).
£150-200   *CHA*

Desks

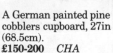

An English writing desk, 74in (188cm).
£550-600   *RK*

An English kneehole desk, 47in (119cm).
£700-750   *RK*

Dressers

A dresser base, c1840, 39in (99cm).
£550-600   *SSD*

A Yorkshire serpentine front dresser, 54in (137cm).
£1,500-2,000   *SSD*

A painted arched top dresser, 19thC, 98in (249cm).
£2,000-2,500   *RK*

A George III dresser, with moulded cornice above plate rack, the lower section with 3 frieze drawers above a pair of fielded arched panel cupboard doors, on square section feet, 54in (137cm).
£1,800-3,500   *Bon*

A miniature dresser, 26in (66cm).
£250-300   *RK*

A Shetland Islands dresser, with iron handles, c1880, 51in (130cm).
£550-650   *AL*

A pine dresser, replacement to drawer bases, c1870, 45in (114cm).
£550-600   *AL*

A French dresser, c1860
£475-575   *TPF*

An Irish country dresser, 54in (137cm).
£675-750   *RK*

A Bavarian pine kitchen dresser, replacement handles, 49in (124.5cm).   **£600-700**   *CHA*

A Scottish dresser, 51in (129.5cm).
£650-700   *RK*

An Austrian dresser, 40in (101.5cm).
£700-750   *RK*

Dressing Tables

A dressing table, c1870, 39in (99cm). **£500-550** *SSD*

A pitch pine dressing chest, c1870, 42in (106.5cm). **£470-520** *SSD*

A hazel pine dressing chest, c1890, 36in (92cm). **£475-525** *SSD*

A hazel pine dressing chest, c1890, 42in (106.5cm). **£500-600** *SSD*

Stools

A pine stool, 7in (17.5cm) high. **£30-40** *AL*

A pine stool, 10in (25cm) diam. **£12-15** *AL*

Hazel pine is a more correct name for the timber that has previously been described as satinwood or satin walnut. Hazel pine is an accepted alternative, and more commercially attractive name for American red gum – Liquidambar Styraciflua.

A stool or small table, c1860, 15in (38cm) diam. **£35-45** *AL*

Tables

A gateleg table, with drawer under, 48in (122cm). **£425-500** *AL*

A pair of pine potboard bases, c1880, 46in (117cm). **£650-750** *AL*

A sycamore and pine cricket table, mid-18thC, 30in (76cm) diam.
£350-400   *CHA*

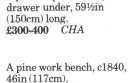

A pine drop leaf table, with a drawer under, 59½in (150cm) long.
£300-400   *CHA*

A pine work bench, c1840, 46in (117cm).
£150-200   *AL*

A cricket table, c1840, 26in (66cm) diam.   **£200-250**   *AL*

A picnic table and 4 folding chairs, c1930.
£300-350   *MCA*

A French side table, c1890.
£95-120   *TPF*

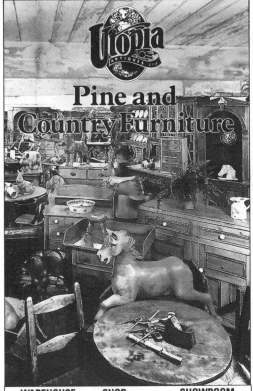

747

A farmhouse table, c1870, 66in (167.5cm) long. **£450-500** *SSD*

A lift top table, c1840, 34in (86cm). **£250-300** *AL*

A pair of French cream painted pine console tables, with cloven hoof feet tied by a curved stretcher surmounted by a figure of a putto playing a harp, originally gilt, 18thC, 36in (92cm). **£2,500-3,000** *HSS*

A drop leaf table, with drawer under, c1840, 60in (152cm). **£200-250** *AL*

Wardrobes

A cricket table, c1840, 28in (71cm). **£200-250** *AL*

A Regency bowfronted side table, 36in (92cm). **£175-225** *AL*

A pine double wardrobe, c1870, 66in (167cm) wide. **£650-700** *SSD*

A pine wardrobe/
armoire, 19thC,
78in (198cm) high.
£600-700   *CHA*

A Hungarian wardrobe,
c1885. **£450-550**   *TPF*

A hazel pine wardrobe,
c1890, 54in (137cm).
£450-550   *SSD*

A hazel pine combination
wardrobe, with feature panels
in East Indian satinwood,
dated 1891, 72in (182.5cm).
£1,500-2,000   *SSD*

An Austrian painted armoire,
c1807, 73in (185cm) high.
£6,000-7,000   *CHA*

A Dutch carved linen
press, 93in
(236cm) high.
£2,300-2,700   *RK*

A Danish wardrobe, 76in
(193cm) high.   **£750-800**   *RK*

A Danish single door
wardrobe,
72in (182cm) high.
£350-400   *RK*

Washstands

A single pine washstand, c1860, 24in (61cm) wide.
£225-275 *SSD*

A hazel pine, marble top, washstand, c1890, 42in (106cm) wide.
£275-325 *SSD*

A pine cupboard washstand, with marble top, c1910, 42½in (107cm) high.
£135-200 *BEL*

Miscellaneous

A pine luggage rack, c1880, 25in (64cm) wide. **£80-90** *AL*

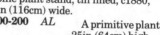

A pine plant stand, tin lined, c1880, 46in (116cm) wide.
£100-200 *AL*

A primitive plant stand, c1840, 25in (64cm) high. **£60-65** *AL*

An Austrian grape barrel, 28in (71cm) high.
£100-120 *RK*

Liberty pine shelves, 31in (79cm) high. **£60-70** *AL*

A counter with panelled back, English, 76in (193cm) wide. **£700-750** *RK*

A pine over mantel, c1860, 44in wide. **£80-100** *AL*

KITCHENALIA

A selection of horn beakers, 2½ to 4in (6 to 11cm) high.
£10-20 each   *SCO*

A wooden lemon squeezer, 6in (15cm) long.
£15-20   *SCO*

An apple corer, 6in (15cm) long.
£14-15   *SCO*

A bone apple corer, 4in (10cm) long.
£25-28   *SCO*

A wooden bowl scoop, 8in (20cm) diam.
£15-18   *SCO*

A Scottish oatmeal bowl, 19thC, 7in (18cm) diam.
£30-35   *SCO*

A German painted pine bread board, c1833, 23in (59cm) diam.
£40-50   *CHA*

A 19thC shaving soap bowl, 4in (10cm) diam.
£10-15   *SCO*

A German painted pine bread board, dated 1890, 24in (61cm) diam.   **£70-80**   *CHA*

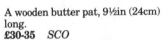

A wooden butter pat, 9½in (24cm) long.
£30-35   *SCO*

A selection of butter stamps, 19thC.
£25-50 each   *SCO*

Wooden butter moulds, 5½ by 3½in (14 by 9cm).
£35-40   *SCO*

A 19thC butter whisk, 7½in (19cm) long.
£15-20   *SCO*

A coffee grinder, 7½in (19cm) high.
£28-30   *SCO*

A 19thC butter churn, 17in (43cm) high.
£80-85   *SCO*

A thatcher's mallet, 12½in (32cm) long.
£8-10   *SCO*

A butter stamp and bowl with acorn pattern, bowl 4½in (11cm) diam.
£75-80 *SCO*

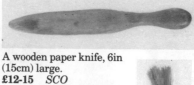

A wooden paper knife, 6in (15cm) large.
£12-15 *SCO*

An oak, metal banded measure, 7in (18cm) high.
£55-60 *SCO*

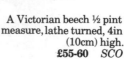

A Victorian pastry brush, 8in (20cm) long.
£15-16 *SCO*

A 19thC wooden grain measure, 7½in (19cm) diam.
£35-40 *SCO*

A Victorian beech ½ pint measure, lathe turned, 4in (10cm) high.
£55-60 *SCO*

A lemon squeezer, 9½in (24cm) long.
£35-40 *SCO*

A selection of brass pastry tools, 4½ to 6½in (11 to 16cm) long.
£24-30 each *SCO*

A pastry press, 5in (13cm) long.
£30-32 *SCO*

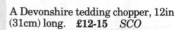

A set of Mintons Art Deco storage jars, early 20thC.
£70-100 *S(S)*

A Devonshire tedding chopper, 12in (31cm) long. **£12-15** *SCO*

A French wooden spoon, 8in (20cm) long. **£15-18** *SCO*

A pine spoon rack, 13in (33cm) high, with spoons. **£50-55** *SCO*

A wooden spoon rest, 5½in (14cm) long.
£5-10 *BEE*

A carved wooden spoon, 10in (25cm) long. **£18-20** *SCO*

A cheese press with lid and liner, 19thC, 8in (20cm) diam.
£48-50 *SCO*

A chrome sieve, 6in (15cm) high.
£18-20 *SCO*

A wool comb, 6in (15cm) wide.
£28-30 *SCO*

A cheese thermometer and holder, 10in (25cm) long. **£25-30** *SCO*

Crocodile nut crackers, 8in (20cm) long. **£20-25** *SCO*

Treen

A spice tin, 7in (18cm) diam, with brass handle. **£45-50** *SCO*

A French wire egg basket, 19thC. **£30-35** *SCO*

Three darners, 5 to 6½in (13 to 17cm). **£5-6 each** *SCO*

A pair of travelling olivewood candlesticks, each with a shallow cylindrical socket, on a detachable dished circular base, the 2 bases screwing together to form a cushioned circular box, together with a conical extinguisher, 4in (10cm) diam. **£150-200** *HSS*

A wooden lemon squeezer, the semi-ovoid shaped body with finial shaped nozzle to the base and screw-off cover fitted with threaded plunger and T shaped handle, 19thC, 7in (18cm) high. **£200-250** *HSS*

A brass and copper Aladdin's lamp, 18in (46cm) high. **£30-35** *SCO*

A washboard with glass panel, early 20thC, 28in (71cm) high. **£20-25** *SCO*

Tools

Smoking & Snufftaking

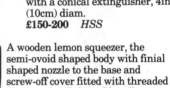

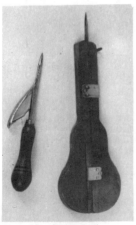

A leather marker, 6½in (17cm). **£9-10** *SCO*

A meerschaum pipe, the bowl modelled as an open flowerhead, and carved with a running deer, amber stemmed, the bowl 3in (8cm) high, in a case. **£150-200** *CSK*

A Victorian Scandinavian pipe, 12in (31cm) long. **£30-50** *HOW*

Two rug making tools, 6½in (16cm). **£5-6** 11½in (29cm). **£14-18** *SCO*

A pig scraper, 9in (23cm). **£40-42** *SCO*

A massive meerschaum pipe bowl, carved with figures and hounds hunting bears, 7½in (19cm) long. **£220-270** *CSK*

WALKING STICKS & CANES

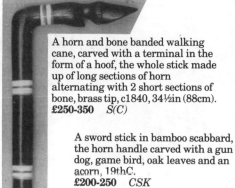

A horn and bone banded walking cane, carved with a terminal in the form of a hoof, the whole stick made up of long sections of horn alternating with 2 short sections of bone, brass tip, c1840, 34½in (88cm).
£250-350 *S(C)*

A sword stick in bamboo scabbard, the horn handle carved with a gun dog, game bird, oak leaves and an acorn, 19thC.
£200-250 *CSK*

A pair of walking canes, the carved nut grips modelled with grimacing and smiling infants, 19thC.
£200-250 *CSK*

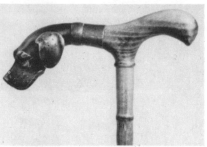

A gentleman's malacca cane, the ivory grip with piqué inlay, with initials and date, I.I. 90.
£1,000-1,400 *CSK*

A bamboo walking stick, the handle carved with the head of a gun dog, with overlaid silvered metal and inset glass eyes.
£400-500 *CSK*

A bamboo walking cane, the carved nut grip modelled in the form of a bulldog's head, the white metal collar stamped BRIGG, 19thC.
£250-350 *CSK*

A malacca cane, with gilt metal collar, the ivory knop carved with the head of a child emerging from the beak of a chick, and a bamboo walking cane, the carved ivory grip modelled with an Arab's head.
£200-250 *CSK*

A German malacca cane, the silver and gilt hinged pommel inset with an automaton of an insect with cut and coloured glass wings and body, 19thC.
£1,400-1,800 *CSK*

A simulated bamboo walking cane, the ivory grip carved in the form of a cat's head, with inset glass eyes and yellow metal collar, and another with the wooden handle carved in the form of a cat's head.
£900-1,000 *CSK*

A Continental rose quartz, seed pearl, enamel and silver coloured metal parasol handle, decorated with engine turned bands and encircled by a husk garland, rose quartz terminal, part of original wooden shaft, in original Dreyfou tooled leather case, terminal 3in (7cm).
£200-250 *S(C)*

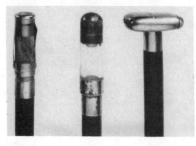

A simulated rosewood cane, the plated silver top formed as a vesta, incorporating a sovereign case and with 2 pencils, a malacca cane, the silver top with glass scent phial, and an ebonised cane with silver metal match case handle.
£300-400 *CSK*

TUNBRIDGE WARE

A Regency Tunbridge ware rosewood sewing box, the cover with cube parquetry inlay, the sides with a Vandyke border, the compartmented interior with a tray and various Tunbridge ware tools and implements, 12½in (32cm) wide.
£1,000-1,500   *CSK*

A Tunbridge ware work box, veneered in amboyna and sycamore, the lined interior with a sectional tray and various accessories including mother-of-pearl reels, bearing trade label of W. Childs Farney Repository, 51 Kings Road, Corner of Middle Street, Brighton, c1850, 8½in (22cm) wide.
£600-700   *S(S)*

A Tunbridge ware banjo, by Ward of Islington, c1880, 34in (86cm) long.
£465-500   *STR*

A Tunbridge ware card box, the cube pattern top with specimen veneers within Vandyke borders, the sides veneered in kingwood, on brass ball feet, 8½in (22cm) wide, with associated playing cards and mother-of-pearl counters, c1820.
£600-700   *S(S)*

A Tunbridge ware box, with label on the base, Edward Nye, Mount Ephraim Parade, Tunbridge Wells, 8in (20cm) wide.
£450-500   *STR*

A Tunbridge ware six-sided Barton/Nye sewing box/pin cushion, with floral lid and Barton label, late Nye, 6in (15cm) wide.
£295-325   *STR*

A Tunbridge ware stamp box, 2½in (7cm) wide.
£110-120   *STR*

A Tunbridge ware box by R. Russell, with label on base, 7in (18cm) wide.
£500-550   *STR*

A Tunbridge ware postal card box, 5½in (14cm) wide.
£175-190   *STR*

A Tunbridge ware pin cushion, in the form of a stickware kettle, 2in (5cm) diam.
£150-180   *STR*

A Tunbridge ware pins and needles box, 3 by 2in (8 by 5cm).
£70-80   *STR*

A Tunbridge ware money box, 4in (10cm).
£125-150   *STR*

A triangular Tunbridge ware cribbage board, with a central motif of rose, shamrock and thistle, 7½in (19cm).
£225-250   *STR*

A Tunbridge ware sewing clamp, 2in (5cm) wide.
£175-200   *STR*

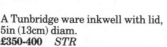

A Tunbridge ware tray with cube pattern, 4 by 3in (10 by 8cm).
£95-100   *STR*

A Tunbridge ware inkwell with lid, 5in (13cm) diam.
£350-400   *STR*

A Tunbridge ware dressing box with floral band to sides of pin cushion, jewellery tray under scent bottles on either side, on 4 stickware feet, 9in (23cm) wide.
£400-420   *STR*

A Tunbridge ware desk box, with fitted interior and geometric pattern on lid, 7in (18cm) wide.
£275-300   *STR*

A Tunbridge ware watch stand, with decorated base, 6½in (17cm) high.
£225-250   *STR*

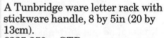

A Tunbridge ware glove darner, 5½in (14cm) long.
£85-100   *STR*

A Tunbridge ware letter rack with stickware handle, 8 by 5in (20 by 13cm).
£325-350   *STR*

Stickware is when wood is fashioned long ways, not cut in cube design.

A Tunbridge ware standish desk set, with Vandyke pattern, c1840, 13in (33cm) wide.
£600-700   *STR*

A Tunbridge ware sewing box, original interior fitted with various compartments and 2 inlaid lids, top with view of Penshurst Place, 8in (20cm) wide.
£650-700 *STR*

A Tunbridge ware needle booklet, 2½ by 2in (6 by 5cm).
£75-80 *STR*

A Tunbridge ware puzzle, 2in (5cm) square.
£95-120 *STR*

A Tunbridge ware paper knife, 9½in (24cm) long.
£40-50 *STR*

A Tunbridge ware lady's toilet box, decorated with an intricate floral motif mainly in bird's-eye maple, with key and 3 perfume/toilet water bottles, 6in (15cm) wide.
£675-700 *STR*

Bilbouquet, a very expensive toy, 8in (20cm) long.
£500-550 *STR*

A Tunbridge ware napkin ring, 2in (5cm) diam.
£30-40 *STR*

Three Tunbridge ware items, a scent bottle, taperstick and box with glass lining, 1 to 1½in (3 to 4cm) high.
£95-150 each *STR*

Tunbridge ware book ends showing Herstmonceux and Hever castles, base in rosewood, 13in (33cm) long.
£450-485 *STR*

A Tunbridge ware folding lectern, with original pegs, 16½in (42cm) high.
£565-600 *STR*

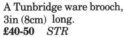

A Tunbridge ware brooch, 3in (8cm) long.
£40-50 *STR*

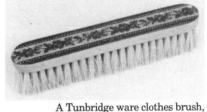

A Tunbridge ware clothes brush, 6in (15cm) long.
£25-30 *STR*

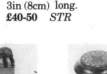

A Tunbridge ware sewing item with pin wheel to base, tape measure and pin cushion.
£100-120 *STR*

A Tunbridge ware seam weight, 2in (5cm).
£145-165 *STR*

A Tunbridge ware thermometer by Henry Hollamby and bearing his name, 5½in (14cm) high.
£265-300 *STR*

> ### Did you know
> *MILLER'S Antiques Price Guide builds up year by year to form the most comprehensive photo-reference system available*

ARMS & ARMOUR
Armour

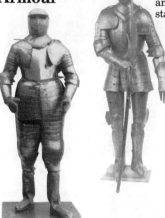

A complete suit of armour, in 16thC style, all etched with floral sprays and trophies of arms, mounted on stand. **£1,200-1,700** *Bon*

A reproduction suit of 16thC armour. **£1,500-2,000** *ASB*

A Continental breast and back plate, etched overall with religious scenes, c1680. **£1,000-1,500** *ASB*

A suit of armour, the visor with rising peak above fretted eye pieces and fretted front, the breast plate with period indented test mark, articulated thigh and knee cover, on a stand covered in blue velvet and with later leather boots, on a dwarf panelled oak pedestal, early 17thC, 70in (177cm) high. **£6,000-6,500** *B*

Helmets

l. A north Italian 'Spanish' morion, with skull rising to a stalk, slightly cracked, late 16thC, 11½in (29cm) high.
£5,500-6,500
r. A pikeman's pot, of russet iron, pierced and shaped iron plume-pipe, and retaining some original gilding throughout, c1630, probably Flemish, 12in (31cm) high.
£6,000-7,000 *C*

A Saxon electoral guard comb morion, with roped comb and brim, the base of the skull encircled by 16 gilt brass lion masks capping the lining rivets, laminated ear pieces, one replaced, the brim struck with the Nuremberg mark, c1580, 12in (31cm) high. **£13,000-15,000** *C*

A Milanese Spanish morion, the base of the skull and brim with strapwork and guilloche borders, and remains of original red silk lining, late 16thC, 9in (23cm) high. **£8,000-10,000** *C*

A composite German, 'Maximilian' close helmet, shaped at the bottom to form a neck plate, the lower edges recessed, painted black throughout, minor repairs, the skull early 16thC, 12in (31cm) high. **£4,000-5,000** *C*

Daggers

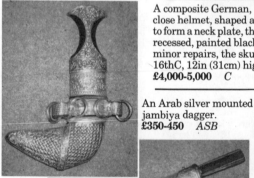

An Arab silver mounted jambiya dagger. **£350-450** *ASB*

An Indian pesh-kabz dagger, with stone hilt, 19thC. **£500-650** *ASB*

A British midshipman's dirk, c1800. **£150-200** *ASB*

A Scottish dirk, complete with small knife and fork, c1870. **£300-450** *ASB*

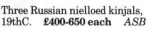

Three Russian nielloed kinjals, 19thC. **£400-650 each** *ASB*

A medieval English dagger. **£600-800** *ASB*

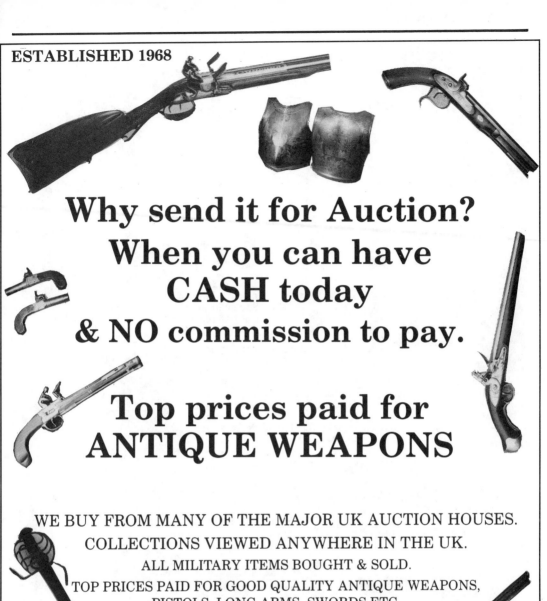

Knives

An American bowie knife, with engraved blade and American eagle in centre panel of hilt.
£2,000-3,000 *ASB*

An American hunting knife, c1800.
£350-450 *ASB*

Swords

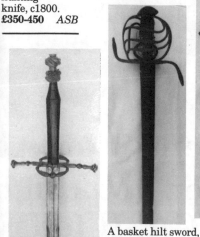

A Spanish Bilbao rapier, c1720.
£300-350 *ASB*

A basket hilt sword, Scandinavian or North German, c1650.
£650-850 *ASB*

A French officer's sword, by Le Page, c1810.
£4,000-5,000 *ASB*

A two-handled processional sword in 16thC style, etched and gilt throughout with bands and panels of scrollwork against a gilt ground, and bottle shaped leather covered wooden grip, with coloured fringe at the top, some worming to wooden grip, 46in (116cm) blade.
£3,000-4,000 *C*

Swords – Eastern

A bronze sword from Luristan.
£350-450 *ASB*

A sword from Tibet, with gilt brass sheath, 19thC.
£200-300 *ASB*

Blunderbuss

A brass barrelled flintlock blunderbuss, by Coner, Dublin, 18thC.
£1,200-1,700 *ASB*

Pistols

A pair of flintlock duelling pistols, by H. Nock, cased, c1780.
£4,000-5,000 *ASB*

A pair of English percussion pocket pistols, c1840.
£250-350 *ASB*

A pair of silver mounted flintlock pistols, c1770.
£2,500-3,500 *ASB*

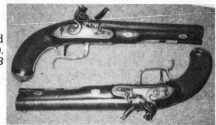

A French military percussion pistol.
£150-250 *ASB*

An English all brass tap flintlock action pistol, c1790. **£300-400** *ASB*

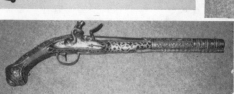

A silver mounted Turkish flintlock pistol, c1800. **£350-450** *ASB*

A flintlock box-lock pocket pistol, 19thC, 5in (13cm).
£650-750 *C*

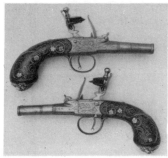

A pair of double barrelled flintlock box-lock pistols, with brass turn-off cannon barrels numbered from 1 to 4, brass actions engraved with rococo ornament, signed within a ribbon on the right side and with sliding cut-off on the left, engraved steel trigger-guard safety catches, rounded walnut butts finely inlaid with silver wire scrolls and flowers, some restoration, vacant silver escutcheons, and silver grotesque mask caps, by Joseph Bunney, London, Birmingham silver hallmarks, maker's mark of Charles Freeth, c1780, 8in (20cm).
£2,000-2,500 *C*

Sporting

A .450 express martini-action sporting rifle by G. E. Lewis, No. 8632/42380, with some original blued finish, well-figured stock with iron butt-plate, horn-capped fore-end, sling-eyes, the barrel with matt top-flat and open-sights, 29in (74cm) barrel, black powder proof.
£650-800 *C*

Miscellaneous

A German sporting crossbow, with robust steel bow struck with a mark and retained by its original cords, original string of twisted cord, together with a cranequin, probably original, curved crank handle with swelling wooden grip, and later belt hook, some wear, early 17thC, 26 and 13in (66 and 33cm).
£6,000-8,000 *C*

A pair of bronze cannon, each with tapering barrel with prominent muzzle ring, a blank shield with ermine lined mantling, date 1668, on 19thC wheeled pierced bronze carriages, probably French, 24½in
£6,200-7,000 *C*

Uniforms & Bits

A 'Greener' Light Model martini action harpoon gun, by W. W. Greener, No. 79, nickel-plated finish, worn in places, manual lever-safe, cocking-indicator, stock with butt-plate, the forestock with brass mounting for a line-release frame, 20in (51cm) barrel, nitro proof, for 10oz harpoon, in its wooden case with instruction label, 5 stainless-steel barbed-harpoons, approx. 11oz, 2 line-release frames, a spare line and miscellaneous cleaning accessories.
£800-1,000 *C*

The harpoon fits over the barrel and the gun must not be used with any other projectile.

A cow's horn powder flask, all over decorated with scrimshaw work with hinged brass cover, 19thC, 9in (22cm) long.
£200-300 *HSS*

A Danish military shako.
£120-160 *ASB*

A selection of 19thC tipstaffs.
£100-350 each *ASB*

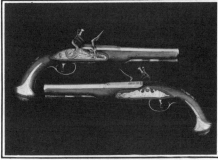

AUCTIONEERS

TENTERDEN Antique Auction Rooms

Monthly auction sales throughout the year

Sales and Valuation Advice always available

102 High Street
Tenterden, Kent
(05806) 2083

Probate Valuations

Insurance Valuations

FINE ART
HALIFAX PROPERTY SERVICES
(Formerly John Hogbin & Son)
COUNTRY AUCTIONEERS

Regular sales of antique furniture, paintings, porcelain, silver, glass and objets d'art

SALEROOMS IN KENT

53 HIGH STREET
TENTERDEN
(05806) 3200

15 CATTLE MARKET
SANDWICH
(0304) 614369

D.M. NESBIT & Company

CHARTERED SURVEYORS AUCTIONEERS & VALUERS

Monthly sales to include furniture, porcelain, pottery, glassware, silver, jewellery, paintings and collectors' items. Valuations for insurance probate and family division.

Fine Art and Auction Department, Southsea Salerooms, 7 Clarendon Rd., Southsea, Hants. PO5 2ED
Tel: (0705) 864321   Fax: (0705) 295522

Burstow & Hewett

Robert Ellin F.S.V.A.
Abbey Auction Galleries
Battle, East Sussex. Tel: (04246) 2302

*Monthly Sales of Antique and Fine Furniture, Silver, Jewellery, Paintings etc.
Valuations for all Purposes.
House Clearance Undertaken.*

DESMOND JUDD, Associates
(Wealden Auction Galleries, Cranbrook, Kent)

800 Lot Monthly Evening Auction Sales:
Jewellery, Silver, Country Pursuits, Weapons, Fine Paintings, Ceramics, Furniture.

**Telephone: Cranbrook (0580) 714522
(9.00 am — 8.00 pm)**

Chancellors AUCTIONS

SALES EVERY THURSDAY
Antique Furniture, Works of Art, Silver, Jewellery, Pictures and Ceramics
ONCE A MONTH
General Furniture and Household Effects
THREE TIMES A MONTH

74 London Road, Kingston-upon-Thames, Surrey KT2 6PX

081-541 4139

PETER S. WILLIAMS & CO.
Auctioneers

**"Orchard End", Sutton Valence
Maidstone, Kent ME17 3LS
Telephone Maidstone (0622) 842350**

Regular Auctions held in Maidstone, and other venues as appropriate, of antique and quality modern furniture and effects.
Auctions held in private residences.
Single items or complete house clearances dealt with.
Valuations for Insurance, Probate or Family Division.

MAY & SON

(Established 1925)

*Auctioneers & Estate Agents
The long established Family Firm. Well experienced in Auctioneering and property matters.
Regular Monthly Auctions*

18 Bridge Street, Andover (0264) 323417

AUCTIONEERS

Auctioneers
in the South of England

AUCTIONEERS

AUCTIONEERS

McCARTNEYS

THE ANTIQUES AND FINE ART AUCTIONEERS
OF THE WELSH MARCHES

In a prominent centre of the antiques and tourist trade

Our specialities include antique pottery, porcelain,
silver, jewellery, clocks,
books and furniture

Wide London and International clientele

for details of regular sales
Telephone Ludlow (0584) 872636

PORTCULLIS SALEROOMS, LUDLOW, SHROPSHIRE

FINE ART
AUCTIONEERS AND VALUERS
Located in
THE HEART OF THE WEST MIDLANDS

GILES HAYWOOD

CHARTERED SURVEYORS • VALUERS • FINE ART AUCTIONEERS

•

The Auction House • St Johns Road • Stourbridge • West Midlands DY8 1EW

•

Stourbridge (0384) 370891

Arthur Johnson & sons

The Nottingham Auction Centre

**The Largest Furniture
Auction Complex in the
Midlands**

SPECIALIST SALEROOMS
Around 1,800 lots every Saturday

Salerooms, Meadow Lane
Nottingham (0602) 869128

Gilding's
AUCTIONEERS & VALUERS

- Regular Fine Art, Antique and Specialist Sales.
- Fortnightly Victoriana and Collectable Sales.
- Valuations for Insurance, Probate, and Family Division.
- Confidential Valuation service in your own home.
- Specialists available at all times, for free verbal Valuations and Consultations.
- From a single item to a full house clearance.

A COMPREHENSIVE SERVICE TO SUIT YOUR NEEDS.

Roman Way, Market Harborough, Leics. LE16 7PQ.
Tel: (0858) 410414 Fax: (0858) 432956

AYLSHAM
◁◦▷
SALEROOMS

SALES OF
★ ANTIQUES (3-WEEKLY)
★ PICTURES (BI-MONTHLY)
★ BOOKS AND COLLECTORS SALES (BI-MONTHLY)

WEEKLY HOUSEHOLD FURNITURE ETC

**AYLSHAM (0263)
733195**
8 MARKET PLACE, AYLSHAM,
NORFOLK NR11 6EH

Fine Toy Shop Display Case
Sold At Aylsham Saleroom
For £2,800

G. A. KEY

VALUATIONS FOR SAL
INSURANCE & PROBAT
PURPOSE

THOS. WM. GAZE & SON
ESTABLISHED 1857

FRIDAY SALES
at the
DISS AUCTION ROOMS
Over 1500 Lots every week
including
500 LOT CATALOGUE SALE
of ANTIQUE and COTTAGE FURNITURE

10 Market Hill, Diss, Norfolk IP22 3JZ
Tel: DISS (0379) 650306. Fax: (0379) 651936

Established 1846
Monthly Specialist Sales
FURNITURE
WORKS of ART
PORCELAIN & POTTERY
SILVER
PEWTER
CLOCKS
MUSICAL BOXES
BRONZES
BOOKS and PICTURES
BYGONES
ORIENTAL CARPETS

RUSSELL, BALDWIN & BRIG

VALUATIONS for all purposes carried out by our qualified staff.
SALES by AUCTION of the contents of Town and Country Houses conducted throughout th
West Midlands and Wales
Enquiries to: The Fine Art Saleroom, Ryelands Rd. Leominster, Herefordshire. HR6 8NZ (0568)61

768

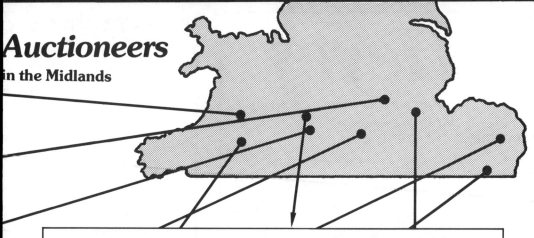

Walker Barnett & Hill
Est. 1780
Auctioneers

**Fortnightly Sales of Victorian
and General Household Furniture.
Monthly Antique Sales, Country House
and Specialist Sales.**

*Valuations and Inventories Compiled for Insurance,
Probate, and Family Division Purposes.*

**Waterloo Road Salerooms, Clarence Street,
Wolverhampton WV1 4DL.**

Tel No. (0902) 773531 ● Fax No. (0902) 712940

William H. Brown
FINE ART
— Fine Art Auctioneers and Valuers —

SALES

- *Regular auction sales of antique and fine art at our main salerooms*
- *Regular auction sales of general furniture and effects at all salerooms*
- *Contents sales on vendors' premises*
- *Total House clearance for executors*

VALUATIONS

Valuations and Inventories for Insurance, Probate, Capital Transfer, Capital Gains Tax and Family Division

ADVICE

Free Advisory Service at the salerooms

SALEROOMS

William H. Brown
10 Regent Street
Barnsley
South Yorkshire S70 2EJ
(0226) 299221

William H. Brown
Paskells Rooms
14 East Hill
Colchester
Essex CO1 2QX
0206 868070

William H. Brown
Stanilands Auction Rooms
28 Netherhall Road
Doncaster
South Yorkshire DN1 2PW
(0302) 367766

William H. Brown
Westgate Hall
Westgate
Grantham
Lincolnshire NG31 6LT
(0476) 68861

William H. Brown
Morphets
4-6 Albert Street
Harrogate
North Yorkshire HG1 1JL
(0423) 530030

William H. Brown
The Warner Auction Rooms
16-18 Halford Street
Leicester LE1 1JB
(0533) 519777

William H. Brown
Oliver's Rooms
Burkitts Lane
Sudbury
Suffolk CC10 6HB
(0787) 880305

Brown and Merry
Brook Street
Tring
Hertfordshire
(044282) 6446

REGIONAL OFFICES

1 Market Place
Beverley
North Humberside HU17 8BB
(0482) 864588

1 West Street
Buckingham MK18 1HL

3 Market Place
Dereham
Norfolk NR19 2AW
(0362) 691017

24 Queen Street
Maidenhead
Berkshire SL6 1HZ
(0628) 21608

19 Market Square
Northampton NN1 2DX
(0604) 231866

37-39 Church Street
Sheffield S1 2GL
(0742) 762064

48 Goodramgate
York YO1 2LF
(0904) 640094

770

Auctioneers

n Scotland and the North of England

Lithgow Sons & Partners
(Established 1868)
North East Auctioneers

Antique House
Station Road, Stokesley
Middlesbrough
Cleveland TS9 7AB
Tel: 0642 710158
Fax: 0642 712641

Wright-Manley

Beeston Sales Centre, Near Tarporley,
Cheshire CW6 9NJ

Regular Furniture and Fine Art Sales

Fortnightly Collective Sales of
Antique and Modern Furniture

Information: Gerald Tilston
Tel: (0829) 260318

CUMBRIA AUCTION ROOMS
Fine Art, Antiques and Furniture
Auctioneers and Valuers
Regular Catalogue Sales of Antiques
and Works of Art
Weekly Sales of General Furniture
and Effects

12 LOWTHER STREET, CARLISLE, CUMBRIA CA3 8DA
Telephone: Carlisle (0228) 25259

J R Parkinson Son and Hamer Auctions
Auctioneers
Fine Art, Antique & Modern Furnishings
**THE AUCTION ROOMS, ROCHDALE ROAD
(KERSHAW STREET), BURY, LANCS.**
Tel: (061) 761 1612 & 761 7372
Fax: (061) 762 9310

Anderson & Garland

The Fine Art Sale Rooms
Marlborough House, Marlborough Crescent
Newcastle upon Tyne NE1 4EE
Telephone: (091 232) 6278

Tennants

AUCTIONEERS

A complete, nationwide service with free advice
on values and reserves for either a single item, a
complete home clearance or a country house sale.

Tennants, 27 Market Place, Leyburn,
North Yorkshire, DL8 5AS. Tel: 0969 23780

Write for copies of our free full colour News Bulletin.

DIRECTORY OF SPECIALISTS

This directory is in no way complete. If you wish to be included in next year's directory or if you have a change of address or telephone number, please could you inform us by April 1st 1992. Entries will be repeated in subsequent editions unless we are requested otherwise. Finally we would advise readers to make contact by telephone before a visit, therefore avoiding a wasted journey, which nowadays is both time consuming and expensive.

Any entry followed by (R) denotes a specialist who undertakes restoration work.

ANTIQUITIES DEALERS

London
Astarte Gallery,
Britannia Hotel, Grosvenor Square, W1
Tel: 071-409 1875

Charles Ede,
37 Brook Street, W1
Tel: 071-493 4944

Faustus Fine Art,
Upper Gallery, 90 Jermyn Street, SW1
Tel: 071-930 1864

Hadji Baba,
36 Davies Street, W1
Tel: 071-499 9363/9384

Thomas Howard Sneyd,
35 Furscroft, George Street, W1
Tel: 071-723 1976

Khalili Gallery,
15c Clifford Street, Bond Street, W1
Tel: 071-734 0202

Jonathan Mankowitz,
Grays in the Mews, Davies Street, W1

C J Martin,
85 The Vale, Southgate, N14
Tel: 081-882 1509

Nigel Mills,
51 Crescent Road, South Woodford, E18
Tel: 081-504 2569

Pars Antique,
H 16/17 Grays in the Mews, Davies Street, W1
Tel: 081-399 8801

Simmons & Simmons,
K 37/38 Grays in the Mews, Davies Street, W1
Tel: 071-629 9321

Surena,
Grays Mews Antique Market, Davies Mews, W1
Tel: 071-493 6762

Annie Trotter and Ian Parsons,
A 30 Davies Mews, W1
Tel: 071-629 2813

Nicholas Wright,
42A Christchurch Avenue, NW6
Tel: 081-459 7123

Dorset
Ancient Forum
PO Box 356, Christchurch
Tel: (0202) 478592

Hants
Phil Goodwin,
3 Apollo Drive, Crookhorn, Portsmouth
Tel: (0705) 266866

Michael Harrison,
Truelocke Antiques,
109 High Street, Odiham
Tel: (0256) 702387

Herts
David Miller,
51 Carlisle Avenue, St Albans
Tel: (0727) 52412

Kent
C J Denton,
PO Box 25, Orpington
Tel: (0689) 873690

Lancs
H & M J Burke,
Old Packet House Building, South Worsley

Middx
M & H Kashden,
19 The Lawns, Pinner
Tel: 081-421 3568

Somerset
Fox & Co,
30 Princes Street, Yeovil
Tel: (0935) 72323

Sussex
Agora,
18 Regent Arcade, East Street, Brighton
Tel: (0273) 26663

Yorks
Wilton House Gallery,
95 Market Street, Pocklington
Tel: (0759) 4858

ARCHITECTURAL ANTIQUES

London
Antique Fireplace Warehouse,
194-196 Battersea Park Road, SW11
Tel: 071-627 1410

Nigel Bartlett,
67 St Thomas Street, SE1
Tel: 071-378 7895

H Crowther Ltd,
Garden Leadwork (R),
5 Chiswick High Road, W4
Tel: 081-994 2326

Davis & Davis,
Architectural Antiques, Arch 266, Urlwin Street, Camberwell SE5 0NF
Tel: 071-703 6525

Fortress,
23 Canonbury Lane, Islington, N1
Tel: 071-359 5875

Lassco,
Mark Street, EC2
Tel: 071-739 0448

Lamont Antiques,
151 Tower Bridge Road, SE1

Miles D'Agar Antiques,
533 Kings Road, SW10
Tel: 071-352 6143

H W Poulter & Son,
279 Fulham Road, SW10
Tel: 071-352 7268

Westland Pilkington Antiques,
The Clergy House, Mark Street, EC2
Tel: 071-739 8094

Avon
Robert Mills,
Unit 3, Satelite Business Park, Blackswarth Road, Redfield, Bristol
Tel: (0272) 556542

Walcot Reclamation,
108 Walcot Street, Bath
Tel: (0225) 444404

Berks
The Fire Place (Hungerford) Ltd,
Old Fire Station, Charnham Street, Hungerford
Tel: (0488) 683420

Cheshire
Antique Fireplaces,
The Manor House, Tarvin Village, Cheshire
Tel: (0829) 40936

Nostalgia,
61 Shaw Heath, Stockport
Tel: 061-477 7706

Cumbria
The Holme Firth Company,
Holme Mill, Holme, Nr. Carnforth
Tel: (0524) 781423

Derbyshire
Havenplan's Architectural Emporium,
The Old Station, Station Road, Killamarsh, Nr. Sheffield
Tel: (0742) 489972

Devon
Architectural Antiques,
Westley, Alswear Old Road, South Molton
Tel: (076 95) 3342

Ashburton Marbles,
Englands Antique Fireplaces, Grate Hall, North Street, Ashburton
Tel: (0364) 53189

Bellevue House Interiors,
Fort House, 36 East Street, South Molton
Tel: (07695) 3761

Cantabrian Antiques,
16 Park Street, Lynton
Tel: (0598) 53282

Dorset
Talisman Antiques,
The Old Brewery, Wyke, Gillingham
Tel: (0747) 824423

Glos
Architectural Heritage,
Taddington Manor, Taddington, Nr. Cutsdean, Cheltenham
Tel: (0386) 73414

Hayes & Newby,
The Pit, 70 Hare Lane, Gloucester
Tel: (0452) 301145

Gt Manchester
Antique Fireplaces,
1090 Stockport Road, Levenshulme
Tel: 061-431 8075

Hereford & Worcester
Bailey's Architectural Antiques,
The Engine Shed, Ashburton Industrial Estate, Ross-on-Wye
Tel: (0989) 63015

Lancs
W J Cowell & Sons,
Church Hill House, D'urton Lane, Broughton, Preston
Tel: (0772) 862034

Leics
Britains Heritage,
Shaftesbury Hall, 3 Holy Bones, Leicester
Tel: (0533) 519592

Middx
Crowther of Syon Lodge,
London Road, Isleworth
Tel: 081-560 7978/7985

Oxon
Oxford Architectural Antiques
The Old Depot, Nelson Street, Jericho, Oxford
Tel: (0865) 53310

Shropshire
Architectural Antiques,
140 Corve Street, Ludlow
Tel: (0584) 876207

Somerset
Wells Reclamation Company,
The Old Cider Farm, Wells Road, Coxley, Nr. Wells, Somerset
Tel: (0749) 677087 or evenings and weekends (0749) 677484

Staffordshire
Old Flames,
133-139 Church Street, Stoke-on-Trent
Tel: (0782) 744985

Surrey
Drummond's of Bramley,
Birtley Farm, Horsham Road, Bramley, Guildford
Tel: (0483) 898766

Glover and Stacey Ltd,
Grange Farm, Grange Road, Tongham, Nr. Farnham
Tel: (02518) 2993

Sussex
Brighton Architectural Salvage,
33 Gloucester Road, Brighton
Tel: (0273) 681656

Tyne & Wear
Shiners,
123 Jesmond Road, Jesmond, Newcastle-upon-Tyne
Tel: (091) 281 6474

Yorks
Andy Thornton Architectural Antiques Ltd,
Ainleys Industrial Estate, Elland
Tel: (0422) 3775595

Cupid Architectural,
West Royd Cottage, West Royd Avenue, King Cross, Halifax
Tel: (0422) 3763585

The Main Pine Co,
Grangewood, Green Hamerton, York
Tel: (0423) 330451

Manor House Fireplaces,
Bankgate Mills, Bankgate,
Slaithwaite, Huddersfield
Tel: (0484) 846055

Robert Aagaard Ltd,
Frogmire House, Stockwell Road,
Knaresborough
Tel: (0423) 864805

Wilts

David J Bridgwater,
112 High Street, Marshfield, Nr.
Chippenham
Tel: (0225) 891623

Relic Antiques,
Brillscote Farm, Lea, Nr
Malmesbury
Tel: (0666) 822332

Wales

An Englishman's Home,
Old Stores, Sudbrook, Newport
Tel: (0291) 423414

M & A Main Architectural
Antiques (R),
The Old Smithy, Cerrig-y-
Drudion, Corwen
Tel: (049 082) 491

The Pumping Station,
Penarth Road, Cardiff
Tel: (0222) 221085

Victorian Fireplaces (Simon
Priestley),
Saturdays only: Ground Floor,
Cardiff Antique Centre, 69-71 St
Mary Street, Cardiff
Tel: (0222) 30970
Any other time: Tel: (0222) 26049

ARMS & MILITARIA

London

Armada Antiques,
Gray's Antique Market, 58 Davies
Street, W1
Tel: 071-499 1087

The Armoury of St James's,
17 Piccadilly Arcade, SW1
Tel: 071-493 5082

Colin C Bowdell,
Gray's Antique Market, 58 Davies
Street, W1
Tel: 071-408 0176

Michael C German,
38b Kensington Church Street, W8
Tel: 071-937 2771

Tradition,
5a Shepherd Street, W1
Tel: 071-493 7452

Avon

Chris Grimes Militaria,
13 Lower Park Row, Bristol
Tel: (0272) 298205

Co. Durham

Matched Pairs Ltd,
20 High Street, Spennymoor
Tel: (0388) 819500 or (0740) 20667
evenings

Glos

HQ 84,
82-84 Southgate Street, Gloucester
Tel: (0452) 27716

Hants

Romsey Medal Centre,
5 Bell Street, Romsey
Tel: (0794) 512069

Lancs

Rod Akeroyd & Son Antiques,
101-103 New Hall Lane, Preston
Tel: (0772) 794947

Norfolk

Anglian Arms,
Market House, Harleston
Tel: (0379) 852184 or (0986)
875115

Northumberland

David A Oliver,
Pennystane, Church Lane,
Thropton, Nr. Morpeth
Tel: (0669) 20618

Surrey

Casque & Gauntlet Antiques,
55/59 Badshot Lea Road, Badshot
Lea, Farnham
Tel: (0252) 20745

Alan S Cook,
132 Rydens Road, Walton-on-
Thames
Tel: (0932) 228328 home

West Street Antiques,
63 West Street, Dorking
Tel: (0306) 883487

Sussex

Military Antiques (by
appointment only),
42 Janes Lane, Burgess Hill
Tel: (0444) 233516 & 43088

Michael Miller,
The Lamb, 8 Cuckfield Road,
Hurstpierpoint
Tel: (0273) 834567

Wallis & Wallis,
West Street Galleries, Lewes
Tel: (0273) 480208

Worthing Gunshop,
80 Broadwater Street West,
Worthing
Tel: (0903) 37378

Warwickshire

Arbour Antiques Ltd,
Poet's Arbour, Sheep Street,
Stratford-upon-Avon
Tel: (0789) 293453

Yorks

The Antique & Bargain Store,
6 Sunny Bar, Doncaster
Tel: (0302) 344857

Doncaster Sales & Exchange,
20 Copley Road, Doncaster
Tel: (0302) 344857

The Antique Shop,
226 Harrogate Road, Leeds
Tel: (0532) 681785

Andrew Spencer Bottomley (by
appointment only),
The Coach House, Thongsbridge,
Holmfirth
Tel: (0484) 685234

Wales

Hermitage Antiques,
10 West Street, Fishguard
Tel: (0348) 873037

ART DECO & ART NOUVEAU

London

Bizarre,
24 Church Street, NW8
Tel: 071-724 1305

Henry Boxer Galleries,
58-60 Kensington Church Street,
W8
Tel: 071-376 0425/081-948 1633

Butler & Wilson,
189 Fulham Road, SW3
Tel: 071-352 3045

Chilton,
Stand A11/12, Chenil Galleries,
181-183 King's Road, SW3
Tel: 071-352 2163

Church Street Antiques,
8 Church Street, NW8
Tel: 071-723 7415

T Coakley,
Stand D13, Chenil Galleries,
181-183 King's Road, SW3
Tel: 071-351 2914

Cobra & Bellamy,
149 Sloane Street, SW1
Tel: 071-730 2823

Editions Graphiques Gallery,
3 Clifford Street, W1
Tel: 071-734 3944

The Facade,
196 Westbourne Grove, W11
Tel: 071-727 2159

Galerie 1900,
267 Camden High Street, NW1
Tel: 071-485 1001

Gallery '25,
4 Halkin Arcade, Motcomb Street,
SW1
Tel: 071-235 5178

Patrick & Susan Gould,
L17, Grays Mews, Davies Mews,
W1
Tel: 071-408 0129

Jazzy Art Deco,
67 Camden Road, Camden Town,
NW1
Tel: 071-267 3342/081-960 8988

John Jesse,
160 Kensington Church Street, W8
Tel: 071-229 0312

Helen Lane,
212 Camden High Street, NW1
Tel: 071-267 6588

Lewis M Kaplan Associates Ltd,
50 Fulham Road, SW3
Tel: 071-589 3108

The Lamp Gallery,
355 New Kings Road, SW6
Tel: 071-736 6188

John & Diana Lyons Gallery,
47-49 Mill Lane, West Hampstead,
NW6
Tel: 071-794 3537

Pruskin Gallery,
73 Kensington Church Street, W8
Tel: 071-937 1994

Ziggy,
Portwine Galleries, 175 Portobllo
Road W11

Cornwall

Judith Gunn,
25 Fore Street, Fowey, Cornwall
Tel: (072683) 2595

Cheshire

Nantwich Art Deco & Decorative
Arts,
87 Welsh Row, Nantwich
Tel: (0270) 624876

Gt Manchester

AS Antiques,
26 Broad Street, Salford
Tel: 061-737 5938

Herts

Ziggy,
2 Morley Cottages, Chells Manor,
Stevenage
Tel: (0438) 727084

Humberside

Carlton Gallery,
Main Street, Swanland, Hull
Tel: (0482) 443954

Kent

Rowena Blackford, Penny
Lampard's Antique Centre,
31 High Street, Headcorn
Tel: (0622) 890682/861360

Lancs

Decoroy,
105 New Hall Lane, Preston
Tel: (0772) 705371

Leics

Birches Antique Shop,
18 Francis Street, Stoneygate,
Leicester
Tel: (0533) 703235

Merseyside

Osiris Antiques (Paul & Carol
Wood),
104 Shakespear Street, Southport
Tel: (0704) 60418 (Eve)
(0704) 500991 (Day)
(Closed Tues)

Shropshire

Antiques on the Square,
2 Sandford Court, Church Stretton
Tel: (0694) 724111

Expressions,
17 Princess Street, Shrewsbury
Tel: (0743) 51731

Somerset

Decoration, Rosamund Morgan,
Taunton Antique Centre, Silver
Street, Taunton, every Monday
Tel: (0460) 40958 evenings

Suffolk

Victoria & Alan Waine,
Country Collectables, The Old
Surgery, Hall Street, Long Melford
Tel: (0787) 310140

Surrey

Peter & Debbie Gooday,
20 Richmond Hill, Richmond
Tel: 081-940 8652

Sussex

Armstrong-Davis Gallery,
The Square, Arundel
Tel: (0903) 882752

Warwickshire

Art Deco Ceramics
The Ocsbury, 10 Mill Street,
Warwick
Tel: (0926) 498068

West Midlands

Smithsonia,
15/16 Piccadilly Arcade, New
Street, Birmingham
Tel: 021-643 8405

Yorks

Dragon Antiques,
10 Dragon Road, Harrogate
Tel: (0423) 562037

Mr Muir Hewitt,
Halifax Antiques Centre, Queens
Road, Gibbet Street, Halifax
Tel: (0422) 366657

Scotland

The Rendezvous Gallery,
100 Forest Avenue, Aberdeen
Tel: (0224) 323247

Wales

Paul Gibbs Antiques,
25 Castle Street, Conway
Tel: (0492) 593429

ARTS & CRAFTS

LONDON

Paul Reeves,
32B Kensington Church Street,
W8
Tel: 071-937 1594

Simon Tracy Gallery
18 Church Street, NW8
Tel: 071-724 5890

BOXES, TREEN & WOODEN OBJECTS

London
Simon Castle,
38B Kensington Church Street,
W8
Tel: 071-937 2268

Halcyon Days,
14 Brook Street, W1
Tel: 071-629 8811

Alistair Sampson Antiques,
156 Brompton Road, SW3
Tel: 071-589 5272

Avon
Gloria Gibson,
2 Beaufort West, London Road,
Bath
Tel: (0225) 446646

Berks
Mostly Boxes,
92-52b High Street, Eton
Tel: (0753) 858470

Charles Toller,
Hall House, 20 High Street,
Datchet
Tel: (0753) 42903

Bucks
A & E Foster (by appointment
only),
Little Heysham, Forge Road,
Naphill
Tel: (024 024) 2024

Hants
Gerald Austin Antiques,
2A Andover Road, Winchester
Tel: (0962) 869824 Ext 2

Millers of Chelsea,
Netherbrook House, 86
Christchurch Road, Ringwood
Tel: (0425) 472062

Oxon
Key Antiques,
11 Horse Fair, Chipping Norton
Tel: (0608) 643777

Shropshire
Parmenter Antiques,
5 Central Court, High Street,
Brignorth
Tel: (0746) 765599

Sussex
Michael Wakelin & Helen Linfield,
10 New Street, Petworth
Tel: (0798) 42417

CAMERAS

London
Cliff Latford Photography,
Stand G006 Alfie's Antiques
Market, 18/25 Church Street, NW8
Tel: 071-724 5650

Jessop Classic Photographica,
67 Great Russell Street, WC1
Tel: 071-831 3640

Vintage Cameras Ltd,
254/256 Kirkdale, Sydenham
Tel: 081-778 5416 & 5841

Essex
Cliff Latford,
91A East Hill, Colchester
Tel: (0206) 564474

Herts
P Coombs,
87 Gills Hill Lane, Radlett
Tel: (0923) 856949

774

CARPETS

London
David Black Oriental Carpets,
96 Portland Road, Holland Park,
W11
Tel: 071-727 2566

Mayfair Carpet Gallery,
9 Old Bond Street, W1
Tel: 071-493 0126/7

Vigo Carpet Gallery,
6a Vigo Street, W1
Tel: 071-439 6971

Vigo Sternberg Galleries,
37 South Audley Street, W1
Tel: 071-629 8307

Dorset
J L Arditti (Old Oriental Rugs),
88 Bargates, Christchurch
Tel: (0202) 485414

Essex
Robert Bailey (by appointment
only),
PO Box 1110, Ongar
Tel: (0277) 362662

Glos
Alan Du Monceau,
Millswood, Chalford
Tel: (0453) 886970

Herts
Oriental Rug Gallery,
42 Verulam Road, St Albans
Tel: (0727) 41046

Kent
Persian Rugs, R & G King,
Vines Farm, Mathews Lane,
W Peckham, Maidstone
Tel: (0732) 850228

Somerset
Sheelagh Lewis (by appointment
only),
The Garden House, Selworthy
Tel: (0643) 862344

M & A Lewis,
Oriental Carpets & Rugs, 8 North
Street, Wellington
Tel: (082 347) 667430

Sussex
Lindfield Galleries,
59 High Street, Lindfield
Tel: (04447) 3817

Yorks
Danby Antiques,
61 Heworth Road, York
Tel: (0904) 415280

Gordon Reece Gallery,
Finkle Street, Knaresborough
Tel: (0423) 866219/866502

London House Oriental Rugs &
Carpets,
London House, High Street,
Boston Spa By Wetherby
Tel: (0937) 845123

Omar (Harrogate) Ltd,
8 Crescent Road, Harrogate
Tel: (0423) 503675

Scotland
Whytock & Reid,
Sunbury House, Belford Mews,
Edinburgh
Tel: 031-226 4911

CLOCKS WATCHES & BAROMETERS

London
Asprey PLC,
165-169 New Bond Street, W1
Tel: 071-493 6767

Bobinet Ltd,
102 Mount Street, W1
Tel: 071-408 0333/4

Aubrey Brocklehurst,
124 Cromwell Road, SW7
Tel: 071-373 0319

Camerer Cuss & Co,
17 Ryder Street, St James's, SW1
Tel: 071-930 1941

Capital Clocks,
190 Wandsworth Road, SW8
Tel: 071-720 6372

Partic Capon,
350 Upper Street, N1
Tel: 071-354 0487

Chelsea Clocks,
479 Fulham Road, SW6
Tel: 071-731 5704
Also at:
69 Portobello Road
Tel: 071-727 5417

City Clocks (R),
31 Amwell Street, EC1
Tel: 071-278 1154

The Clock Clinic Ltd,
85 Lower Richmond Road, SW15
Tel: 081-788 1407

Philip & Bernard Dombey,
174 Kensington Church Street, W8
Tel: 071-229 7100

Gerald Mathias (R),
R5/6 Antiquarius, 136 King's
Road, SW3
Tel: 071-351 0484

North London Clock Shop Ltd (R),
72 Highbury Park, N5
Tel: 071-226 1609

Pieces of Time,
1-7 Davies Mews, W1
Tel: 071-629 2422

Roderick Antiques Clocks,
23 Vicarage Gate, W8
Tel: 071-937 8517

R E Rose, FBHI,
731 Sidcup Road, Eltham, SE9
Tel: 081-859 4754

Strike One (Islington) Ltd,
51 Camden Passage
Tel: 071-226 9709

Temple Brooks,
12 Mill Lane, NW6
Tel: 081-452 9696

Philip Whyte,
32 Bury Street, SW1
Tel: 071-321 0353

Avon
David Gibson,
2 Beaufort West, London Road,
Bath
Tel: (0225) 446646

John & Carol,
Hawley CMBH1, The Orchard,
Clevedon Lane, Clapton Wick,
Clevedon
Tel: (0275) 852052

Berks
Richard Barder Antiques,
Crossways House, Near Newbury
Tel: (0635) 200295

The Clock Workshop,
17 Prospect Street, Caversham,
Reading
Tel: (0734) 470741

Medalcrest Ltd,
Charnham House, Charnham
Street, Hungerford
Tel: (0488) 84157

Times Past Antiques Ltd,
59 High Street, Eton
Tel: (0753) 857018

Bucks
The Guild Room,
The Lee, Great Missenden
Tel: (024 020) 463

Cheshire
Peter Bosson Antiques,
10B Swan Street, Wilmslow
Tel: (0625) 525250 & 527857

Coppelia Antiques
Holford Lodge, Plumley Moor
Road, Plumley
Tel: (056 572) 2197

Cranford Clocks,
12 Princess Street, Knutsford
Tel: (0565) 633331

Derek Rayment Antiques (R),
Orchard House, Barton Road,
Barton, Nr Farndon
Tel: (0829) 270429

Cumbria
Don Burns,
CMBH1, The Square, Ireby,
Carlisle
Tel: (096 57) 477

Derbyshire
Derbyshire Clocks,
104 High Street West, Glossop
Tel: (0457) 862677

Devon
Musgrave Bickford Antiques,
15 East Street, Crediton
Tel: (03632) 5042

Dorset
Good Hope Antiques,
2 Hogshill Street, Beaminster
Tel: (0308) 862119

Tom Tribe & Son,
Bridge Street, Sturminster
Newton
Tel: (0258) 72311

Essex
It's About Time (R),
863 London Road, Westcliff-on-Sea
Tel: (0702) 72574 & 205204

Littlebury Antiques,
58/60 Fairycroft Road, Saffron
Walden
Tel: (0799) 27961

Mark Marchant,
3 Market Square, Coggeshall
Tel: (0376) 561188

Trinity Clocks,
29 East Hill, Colchester
Tel: (0206) 868623

Glos
J & M Bristow Antiques,
28 Long Street, Tetbury
Tel: (0666) 502222

Gerard Campbell,
Maple House, Market Place,
Lechlade
Tel: (0367) 52267

Montpellier Clocks Ltd,
13 Rotunda Terrace, Montpellier
Street, Cheltenham
Tel: (0242) 224414

Colin Elliott,
4 Great Norwood Street,
Cheltenham
Tel: (0242) 528590

Saxton House Gallery,
High Street, Chipping Camden
Tel: (0386) 840278

Southbar Antiques,
Digbeth Street, Stow-on-the-Wold
Tel: (0451) 30236

Hants
Charles Antiques,
101 The Hundred, Romsey
Tel: (0794) 512885

Evans & Evans,
40 West Street, Alresford
Tel: (096 273) 732170

Gerald E Marsh,
32A The Square, Winchester
Tel: (0962) 844443

A W Porter & Sons,
High Street, Hartley Wintney
Tel: (025126) 2676

Hereford & Worcester
Barometer Shop,
New Street, Leominster
Tel: (0568) 3652
also at:
3 Lower Park Row, Bristol
Tel: (0272) 272565

G & V Taylor Antiques,
Winforton Court, Winforton
Tel: (054 46) 226

Herts
Country Clocks (R),
3 Pendley Bridge Cottages, Tring
Station, Tring
Tel: (044 282) 5090

Isle of Wight
R. Taylor,
Alum Bay
Tel: (0983) 754193

Kent
Atropos Antiques,
21 St Johns Hill, Sevenoaks
Tel: (0732) 454179

John Chawner Antiques,
44 Chatham Hill, Chatham
Tel: (0634) 811147 & (0843) 43309

Hadlow Antiques,
No. 1 The Pantiles, Tunbridge
Wells
Tel: (0892) 29858

Apollo Gallery,
19 Market Square, Westerham
Tel: (0959) 62200

The Old Clock Shop,
63 High Street, West Malling
Tel: (0732) 843246

Derek Roberts Antiques,
24/25 Shipbourne Road, Tonbridge
Tel: (0732) 358986

Rochester Fine Arts,
88 High Street, Rochester
Tel: (0634) 814129

Malcolm G Styles (R),
Tunbridge Wells
Tel: (0892) 30699

Anthony Woodburn,
Orchard House, Leigh,
Nr Tonbridge
Tel: (0732) 832258

Lancs
Kenneth Weigh, Signwriting &
Numbering,
9 Links Road, Blackpool
Tel: (0253) 52097

Leics
Bonington Clocks,
12 Market Place, Kegworth
Tel: (05097) 672900

Clock Replacements (R),
239 Welford Road, Leicester
Tel: (0533) 706190

G K Hadfield (R),
Blackbrook Hill House, Tickow
Lane, Shepshed
Tel: (0509) 503014

C Lowe & Sons Ltd (R),
37-40 Churchgate, Loughborough
Tel: (0509) 217876

Lincs
George Clocks,
3 Pinfold Lane, Ruskington
Tel: (0526) 832200

Merseyside
T Brown Horological Restorers (R),
12 London Road, Liverpool 3
Tel: 051-709 4048

Norfolk
Delawood Antiques & Clock
Restoration (R),
10 Westgate, Hunstanton
Tel: (04853) 2903

Norfolk Polyphon & Clock Centre,
Wood Farm, Bawdeswell, Nr. East
Dereham
Tel: (036 288) 230

Oxon
Laurie Leigh Antiques,
36 High Street, Oxford
Tel: (0865) 244197

Rosemary & Time,
42 Park Street, Thame
Tel: (084421) 6923

Telling Time,
57 North Street, Thame
Tel: (084 421) 3007

Witney Antiques,
96-98 Corn Street, Witney
Tel: (0993) 703902

Somerset
Michael & Judith Avis (R),
The Barton, Simonsbath,
Minehead
Tel: (064383) 428

Shelagh Berryman,
15 The Market Place, Wells
Tel: (0749) 76203

Bernard G House,
Mitre Antiques, 13 Market Place,
Wells
Tel: (0749) 72607

Edward A Nowell,
12 Market Place, Wells
Tel: (0749) 72415

Matthew Willis,
88 Bove Town, Glastonbury
Tel: (0458) 32103

Staffordshire
James A Jordan,
7 The Corn Exchange, Lichfield
Tel: (0543) 416221

Suffolk
AN Antiques,
Home Farm, South Green, Eye
Tel: (0379) 870367

R L Fryatt, Grad BHI (R),
10 Amberley Court, Oulton Broad,
Lowestoft
Tel: (0502) 560869

Antique Clocks By Simon Charles,
The Limes, 72 Melford Road,
Sudbury
Tel: (0787) 75931

Surrey
BS Antiques,
39 Bridge Road, East Molesey
Tel: 081-941 1812

Bryan Clisby,
86B Tilford Road, Farnham
Tel: (0252) 716436

The Clock Shop,
64 Church Street, Weybridge
Tel: (0932) 840407 & 855503

Roger A Davis, Antiquarian
Horologist,
19 Dorking Road, Great Bookham
Tel: (0372) 57655 & 53167

Douglas Dawes (by appointment
only),
Antique Clocks, Linfield
Tel: (0342) 834965

Hampton Court Antiques,
75 Bridge Road, East Molesey
Tel: 081-941 6398

E Hollander Ltd,
The Dutch House, Horsham Road,
South Holmwood, Dorking
Tel: (0306) 888921

Horological Workshops,
204 Worplesdon Road, Guildford
Tel: (0483) 576496

R Saunders Antiques,
71 Queens Road, Weybridge
Tel: (0932) 842601

Geoffrey Stevens,
26-28 Church Road, Guildford
Tel: (0483) 504075

Surrey Clock Centre,
3 Lower Street, Haslemere
Tel: (0428) 4547

Sussex
Adrian Alan Ltd,
4 Frederick Place, Brighton
Tel: (0273) 25277

W F Bruce Antiques,
Gardner Street, Herstmonceux
Tel: (0323) 833718

Sam Orr Antique Clocks,
36 High Street, Hurstpierpoint
Tel: (0273) 832081

David & Sarah Pullen,
Bexhill-on-Sea
Tel: (0424) 222035

R W Wren, MBHI (R),
4 The Ridge, Hastings
Tel: (0424) 445248

Tyne & Wear
T P Rooney, Grad BHI (R),
191 Sunderland Road, Harton
Village, South Shields
Tel: 091-456 2950

Warwickshire
The Grandfather Clock Shop,
2 Bondgate House, Granville
Court, West Street, Shipston on
Stour
Tel: (0608) 62144

Mason Antique Clocks,
Glympton House, 3 New Road,
Water Orton
Tel: (021 747) 5751

West Midlands
M Allen (R),
76A Walsall Road, Four Oaks,
Sutton Coldfield
Tel: 021-308 6117

Ashleigh House Antiques,
5 Westbourne Road, Birmingham
Tel: 021-454 6283

Osborne's (R),
91 Chester Road, New Oscott,
Sutton Coldfield
Tel: 021-355 6667

Wiltshire
Allan Smith Clocks,
Amity Cottage, 162 Beechcroft
Road, Upper Stratton, Swindon
Tel: (0793) 822977

Avon Antiques,
26-27 Market Street, Bradford-on-
Avon
Tel: (022 16) 2052

P A Oxley,
The Old Rectory, Cherhill, Nr
Calne
Tel: (0249) 816227

The Salisbury Clock Shop,
107 Exeter Street, Salisbury
Tel: (0722) 337076

Yorks
Arcadia Antiques,
The Ginnel Antique Centre,
Harrogate
Tel: (0704) 64441

Brian Loomes,
Calf Haugh Farm, Pateley Bridge
Tel: (0423) 711163

Clocks & Gramophones,
11 Walmgate, York
Tel: (0904) 611924

The Clock Shop,
Hilltop House, Bellerby, Nr
Leyburn
Tel: (0969) 22596

Haworth Antiques (R),
Harrogate Road, Huby, Nr Leeds
Tel: (0423) 734293
Also at:
26 Cold Bath Road, Harrogate
Tel: (0423) 521401

Keith Stones Grandfather Clocks,
5 Ellers Drive, Bessacarr,
Doncaster
Tel: (0302) 535258

Scotland
Browns Clocks Ltd,
203 Bath Street, Glasgow
Tel: 041-248 6760

DOLLS, TOYS &
GAMES
London
Antique Dolls,
Stand L14, Grays Mews, W1
Tel: 071-499 6600

Dr Colin Baddiel,
Stand C12, Grays Mews,
1-7 Davies Mews, W1
Tel: 071-629 2813

Jilliana Ranicar-Breese,
Martin Breese International,
8 Portwine Arcade, 175 Portobello
Road (Sats only). Tel: 071-727 9378

Steve Clark, (Chelsea Lion),
Chenil Gallery, 181-183 Kings
Road, Chelsea, SW3
Tel: 071-352 8653

Stuart Cropper,
Gray's Mews, 1-7 Davies Mews,
W1
Tel: 071-499 6600

Dolly Land,
864 Green Lanes, Winchmore Hill,
N21
Tel: 081-360 1053

Donay Antiques,
35 Camden Passage, N1
Tel: 071-359 1880

Engine 'n' Tender,
19 Spring Lane, Woodside, SE25
Tel: 081-654 0386

Pete McAskie,
Stand D10-12 Basement, Grays
Mews Antiques, 1-7 Davies Mews,
W1
Tel: 071-629 2813

The Dolls House Toys Ltd,
29 The Market, Covent Garden,
WC2
Tel: 071-379 7243

The Singing Tree,
69 New King's Road, SW6
Tel: 071-736 4527

Yonna,
C17 Grays Mews, W1
Tel: 071-629 3644

Avon
Bristol Doll's Hospital,
50-52 Alpha Road, Southville,
Bristol
Tel: (0272) 664368

The China Doll,
31 Walcot Street, Bath
Tel: (0225) 465849

Chester
Dollectable,
53 Lower Bridge Street, Chester
Tel: (0244) 344888

Cornwall

Mrs Margaret Chesterton,
33 Pentewan Road, St Austell
Tel: (0726) 72926

The Millcraft Rocking Horse
Company,
Lower Trannack Mill, Coverack
Bridges, Helston
Tel: (0326) 573316

Dorset

Hobby Horse Antiques,
29 West Allington, Bridport
Tel: (0308) 22801

Essex

Blackwells of Hawkwell,
Dept C, 733 London Road,
Westcliffe-on-Sea
Tel: (0702) 72248

The Doll Cupboard,
63 High Street, Epping
Tel: (0378) 76848

Glos

Lilian Middleton's Antique Dolls'
Shop & Dolls' Hospital,
Days Stable, Sheep Street,
Stow-on-the-Wold
Tel: (0451) 30381

Park House Antiques,
Park Street, Stow-on-the-Wold
Tel: (0451) 30159

Hampshire

Past & Present Crafts,
19 Ditton Close, Stubbington
Tel: (0329) 661377

Hereford & Worcester

Antiques Centre,
Blackwell Street, Kidderminster
Tel: (0562) 829000

Kent

Hadlow Antiques,
1 The Pantiles, Tunbridge Wells
Tel: (0892) 29858

The Magpie's Nest,
14 Palace Street, Canterbury
Tel: (0227) 764883

Pantiles Spa Antiques,
4, 5, 6 Union House, The Pantiles,
Tunbridge Wells
Tel: (0892) 541377

Staffs

B H Bates (Amusement Machine
Specialist),
Fairview, Maerway Lane, Maer,
Newcastle
Tel: (0782) 680667

Surrey

Heather & Clifford Bond,
Victoriana Dolls
Tel: (073 72) 49525

Dorking Dolls House,
Gallery, 23 West Street, Dorking
Tel: (0306) 885785

Elizabeth Gant,
52 High Street, Thames Ditton
Tel: 081-398 0962

Sussex

Dolls Hospital, Hastings
17 George Street, Hastings
Tel: (0424) 444117

Doll & Teddy Bear Restorer (R),
Wendy Foster, Minto, Codmore
Hill, Pulborough
Tel: (0798) 872707

Rathbone Law,
7-9 The Arcade, Worthing
Tel: (0903) 200274

West Midlands

Robert Taylor,
Windyridge, Worcester Lane, Four
Oaks, Sutton Coldfield
Tel: 021-308 4209

Woodsetton Antiques,
65 Sedgley Road, Woodsetton,
Dudley
Tel: (0384) 277918

Yorks

The Antique & Bargain Store,
6 Sunny Bar, Doncaster
Tel: (0302) 344857

Doncaster Sales & Exchange,
20 Copley Road, Doncaster
Tel: (0302) 344857

John & Simon Haley,
89 Northgate, Halifax
Tel: (0422) 822148

Second Childhood,
20 Ryram Arcade, Westgate,
Huddersfield
Tel: (0484) 530117/603854

Wales

Museum of Childhood Toys & Gift
Shop,
1 Castle Street, Beaumaris,
Anglesey, Gwynedd
Tel: (0248) 712498

EPHEMERA

London

Jilliana Ranicar-Breese, Martin
Breese Ltd,
Martin Breese International,
8 Portwine Arcade, 175 Portobello
Road (Sats only)
Tel: 071-727 9378

Dodo (Posters),
286 Westbourne Grove, W11 (Sat
7-4 or by appointment)
Tel: 071-229 3132
also at:
8 Portwine Arcade, 175 Portobello
Road (Sats only)
also at:
Alfie's Antiques Market, NW8
Tel: 071-706 1545

Donay,
35 Camden Passage, N1
Tel: 071-359 1880

M & R Glendale,
Antiquarian Booksellers, 9A New
Cavendish Street, W1
Tel: 071-487 5348

The Old Ephemera & Newspaper
Shop,
37 Kinnerton Street, SW1
Tel: 071-235 7788

Jubilee,
1 Pierrepont Row, Camden
Passage, N1
Tel: 071-607 5462

Pleasures of Past Times,
11 Cecil Court, Charing Cross
Road, WC2
Tel: 071-836 1142

Danny Posner,
The Vintage Magazine Company,
39/41 Brewer Street, W1
Tel: 071-439 8525

Avon

Michael & Jo Saffell,
3 Walcot Buildings, London Road,
Bath
Tel: (0225) 315857

Bucks

Omniphil Ltd,
Germains Lodge, Fullers Hill,
Chesham
Tel: (0494) 771851
Also at:
Stand 114, Gray's Antique
Market, 58 Davies Street, W1
Tel: 081-629 3223

Essex

G K R Bonds Ltd,
PO Box 1, Kelvedon
Tel: (0376) 571138

Hants

Cobwebs,
78 Northam Road, Southampton
Tel: (0703) 227458

Kent

Mike Sturge,
39 Union Street, Maidstone
Tel: (0622) 754702

Notts

Neales of Nottingham,
192 Mansfield Road, Nottingham
Tel: (0602) 624141

T Vennett-Smith,
11 Nottingham Road, Gotham
Tel: (0602) 830541

Surrey

Richmond Antiquary,
28 Hill Rise, Richmond
Tel: 081-948 0583

FISHING TACKLE

Dorset

Yesterday Tackle & Books,
42 Clingan Road, Southbourne
Tel: (0202) 476586

Kent

Alan Clout,
36 Nunnery Fields, Canterbury
Tel: (0227) 455162

Sussex

N Marchant-Lane
The Old Bakery, Golden Square,
Petworth
Tel: (0798) 42872

Scotland

Jamie Maxtone Graham,
Lyne Haugh, Lyne Station,
Peebles
Tel: (07214) 304

Jess Miller,
PO Box 1, Birnam, Dunkeld,
Perthshire
Tel: (03502) 522

FURNITURE

London

Antiquum (R),
147 Highgate Road, NW5
Tel: 071-485 9501

Asprey PLC,
165-169 New Bond Street, W1
Tel: 071-493 6767

John Bly,
27 Bury Street, St James's, SW1
Tel: 071-930 1292

F E A Briggs Ltd,
73 Ledbury Road, W1
Tel: 071-727 0909 & 071-221 4950

Butchoff Antiques,
233 Westbourne Grove, W11
Tel: 071-221 8174

Rupert Cavendish Antiques
(Biedermeir),
610 King Road, London, SW6
Tel: 071-731 7041/071-736 6024

Eldridge,
99-101 Farringdon Road, EC1
Tel: 071-837 0379 & 0370

Hampstead Antique Emporium,
12 Heath Street, Hampstead, NW3
Tel: 071-794 3297

John Keil Ltd,
154 Brompton Road, SW3
Tel: 071-589 6454

C H Major (Antiques) Ltd,
154 Kensington Church Street, W8
Tel: 071-229 1162

Mallett & Son (Antiques) Ltd,
40 New Bond Street, W1
Tel: 071-499 7411

M & D Seligmann,
37 Kensington Church Street, W8
Tel: 071-937 0400

Michael Marriott Ltd,
588 Fulham Road, SW6
Tel: 071-736 3110

Murray Thomson Ltd,
152 Kensington Church Street, W8
Tel: 071-727 1727

The Old Cinema,
160 Chiswick High Road, W4
Tel: 081-995 4166

Oola Boola Antiques,
166 Tower Bridge Road, SE1
Tel: 071-403 0794

Phelps Ltd,
133-135 St Margaret's Road,
E Twickenham
Tel: 081-892 1778 & 7129

Reindeer Antiques,
81 Kensington Church Street, W8
Tel: 071-937 3754

Alistair Sampson Antiques,
156 Brompton Road, SW3
Tel: 071-589 5272

Arthur Seager Ltd,
25a Holland Street, Kensington,
W8
Tel: 071-937 3262

Stair & Co,
120 Mount Street, W1
Tel: 071-499 1784/5

William Tillman,
30 St James's Street, SW1
Tel: 071-839 2500

O F Wilson Ltd,
Queen's Elm Parade, Old Church
Street, SW3
Tel: 071-352 9554

Robert Young Antiques,
68 Battersea Bridge Road, SW11
Tel: 071-228 7847

Zal Davar Antiques,
Unit 4, Hurlingham Business
Park, Sulivan Road, SW6
Tel: 071-736 2559/1405

Avon

Cottage Antiques,
The Old Post Office, Langford
Place, Langford, Nr Bristol
Tel: (0934) 862597

Berks

Mary Bellis Antiques,
Charnham Close, Hungerford
Tel: (0488) 682620

Biggs of Maidenhead,
Hare Hatch Grange, Twyford
Tel: (0734) 403281

The Old Malthouse,
Hungerford
Tel: (0488) 682209

Medalcrest Ltd,
Charnham House, Charnham
Street, Hungerford
Tel: (0488) 684157

Charles Toller,
Hall House, 20 High Street,
Datchet
Tel: (0753) 42903

Bucks

Jeanne Temple Antiques,
Stockwell House, 1 Stockwell
Lane, Wavendon, Milton Keynes
Tel: (0908) 583597

A & E Foster (by appointment
only),
Little Heysham, Forge Road,
Naphill
Tel: (024 024) 2024

Lloyd Loom,
Western Turville
Tel: (0296 61) 5121 (R)

Cambs

Clover Antiques,
5-6 Soham Road, Fordham
Tel: (0638) 720250

Cheshire

Coppelia Antiques,
Holford Lodge, Plumley Moor
Road, Plumley
Tel: (056 581) 2197

Townwell House Antiques,
52 Welsh Row, Nantwich
Tel: (0270) 625953

Cornwall

Pydar Antiques & Gallery,
People's Palace, Off Pydar Street,
Truro
Tel: (Michelle) (0872 51) 510485
(Newquay) (0637) 872034

Cumbria

Anthemion,
Broughton Hall, Cartmel,
Grange-over-Sands
Tel: (044 854) 234

Haughey Antiques,
Market Street, Kirkby Stephen
Tel: (0930) 71302

Fenwick Pattison,
Bowmanstead, Coniston
Tel: (0534) 41235

Shire Antiques,
The Post House, High Newton,
Newton in Cartmel, Nr
Grange-over-Sands
Tel: (0448) 31431

Townhead Antiques,
Newby Bridge
Tel: (0448) 31321

Derbyshire

Maurice Goldstone & Son,
Avenel Court, Bakewell
Tel: (0629) 812487

Spurrier-Smith Antiques,
28, 39 & 41 Church Street,
Ashbourne
Tel: (0335) 43669 and (home)
(0629) 822502

Yesterday Antiques,
6 Commercial Road, Tideswell, Nr
Buxton
Tel: (0298) 871932

Devon

Robert Byles,
7 Castle Street, Bampton
Tel: (0398) 31515

McBain of Exeter,
Exeter Airport, Clyst Honiton,
Exeter
Tel: (0392) 66261

Dorset

Dodge & Son,
28-33 Cheap Street, Sherborne
Tel: (0935) 815151

Johnsons of Sherborne Ltd,
South Street, Sherborne
Tel: (0935) 812585

Talisman Antiques,
The Old Brewery, Wyke,
Gillingham
Tel: (0747) 824423

Durham

Bygone Antiques, Victorian &
Edwardian Furniture,
3/5 McMullen Road, Darlington
Tel: (0325) 461399/380884

Essex

F G Bruschweiler,
41-67 Lower Lambricks, Rayleigh
Tel: (0268) 773761

Stone Hall Antiques,
Trade Warehouse, Down Hall
Road, Matching Green, Nr Harlow
Tel: (0279) 731440

Glos

Baggott Church Street Ltd,
Church Street, Stow-on-the-Wold
Tel: (0451) 30370

Paul Cater,
High Street, Moreton-in-Marsh
Tel: (0608) 51888

Country Life Antiques,
Grey House, The Square,
Stow-on-the-Wold
Tel: (0451) 31564

Gloucester House Antiques,
Market Place, Fairford
Tel: (0285) 712790

Huntington Antiques Ltd,
The Old Forge, Church Street,
Stow-on-the-Wold
Tel: (0451) 30842

Painswick Antiques & Interiors,
Beacon House, Painswick
Tel: (0452) 812578

Antony Preston Antiques Ltd,
The Square, Stow-on-the-Wold
Tel: (0451) 31586

Stone House Antiques,
St Mary's Street, Painswick
Tel: (0452) 813540

Studio Antiques Ltd,
Bourton-on-the-Water
Tel: (0451) 20352

Denzil Verey Antiques,
(Specialists in Country & Pine
Furniture)
Barnsley House, Barnsley, Nr
Cirencester
Tel: (0285) 740402

Hants

C W Buckingham,
Twin Firs, Southampton Road,
Cadnam
Tel: (0703) 812122

Cedar Antiques,
High Street, Hartley Wintney
Tel: (025 126) 3252

Mark Collier Antiques,
24 The High Street, Fordingbridge
Tel: (0425) 52555

R C Dodson,
85 Fawcett Road, Southsea
Tel: (0705) 829481

Lita Kaye of Lyndhurst,
13 High Street, Lyndhurst
Tel: (042 128) 2337

Millers of Chelsea Antiques Ltd,
Netherbrook House, 86
Christchurch Road, Ringwood
Tel: (0425) 472062

Truelocke Antiques,
109 High Street, Odiham
Tel: (0256) 702387

Hereford & Worcester

Gavina Ewart,
60-62 High Street, Broadway
Tel: (0386) 853371

Great Brampton House Antiques
Ltd,
Madley
Tel: (0981) 250244

Jean Hodge Antiques,
Peachley Manor, Lower
Broadheath, Worcester
Tel: (0905) 640255

Jennings of Leominster,
30 Bridge Street, Leominster
Tel: (0568) 2946

Lower House Fine Antiques (R),
Far Moor Lane, Winyates Green,
Redditch
Tel: (0527) 25117

Herts

C Bellinger Antiques
91 Wood Street, Barnet
Tel: 081-449 3467

John Bly,
50 High Street, Tring
Tel: (044 282) 3030

Collins Antiques,
Corner House, Wheathampstead
Tel: (058283) 3111

Phillips of Hitchin (Antiques) Ltd,
The Manor House, Hitchin
Tel: (0462) 432067

Humberside

Geoffrey Mole,
400 Wincolmlee, Hull
Tel: (0482) 27858

Isle of Wight

Chris Watts,
60 High Street, Cowes
Tel: (0983) 298963 &
(0860) 342558

Kent

Atropos Antiques,
21 St Johns Hill, Sevenoaks
Tel: (0732) 454179

Castle Antiques,
No 1 London Road, Westerham
Tel: (0959) 62492

Chislehurst Antiques,
7 Royal Parade, Chislehurst
Tel: 081-467 1530

Conquest House Antiques,
Conquest House, 17 Palace Street,
Canterbury
Tel: (0227) 464587

Furnace Mill,
Lamberhurst
Tel: (0892) 890285

Garden House Antiques,
118 High Street, Tenterden
Tel: (058 06) 3664

John McMaster,
5 Sayers Square, Sayers Lane,
Tenterden
Tel: (058 06) 2941

The Old Bakery Antiques (Mr &
Mrs D Bryan),
St Davids Bridge, Cranbrook
Tel: (0580) 713103

Pantiles Spa Antiques,
4, 5, 6 Union House, The Pantiles,
Tunbridge Wells
Tel: (0892) 541377

Steppes Hill Farm Antiques,
Stockbury, Sittingbourne
Tel: (0795) 842205

Swan Antiques,
Stone Street, Cranbrook
Tel: (0580) 712720

Sutton Valence Antiques,
Sutton Valence, Maidstone
Tel: (0622) 843333 & 843499

Lancs

Preston Antique Centre,
The Mill, New Hall Lane, Preston
Tel: (0772) 794498

West Lancs Exports,
Victoria Mill, Victoria Street,
Burscough
Tel: (0704) 894634

Leics

Leicester Antiques Complex,
9 St Nicholas Place, Leicester
Tel: (0533) 533343

Lowe of Loughborough,
37-40 Church Gate, Loughborough
Tel: (0509) 217876

Lincs

Kirkby Antiques Ltd,
Kirkby-on-Bain, Woodhall Spa
Tel: (0526) 52119 & 53461

Harwood Tate,
Church Mill, Caistor Road,
Market Rasen
Tel: (0673) 843579

Laurence Shaw Antiques,
Spilsby Road, Horncastle
Tel: (06582) 7638

Middlesex

Binstead Antiques,
21 Middle Lane, Teddington
Tel: 081-943 0626

J W Crisp Antiques,
166 High Street, Teddington
Tel: 081-977 4309

Phelps Ltd,
133-135 St Margaret's Road,
E Twickenham
Tel: 081-892 1778

Norfolk

Joan Adams Antiques,
Rossendale, The Street,
Rickinghall, Diss
Tel: (0379) 898485

Arthur Brett & Sons Ltd,
40-44 St Giles Street, Norwich
Tel: (0603) 628171

Peter Howkins Antiques,
39, 40 & 135 King Street, Great
Yarmouth
Tel: (0493) 851180

Pearse Lukies,
Bayfield House, White Hart
Street, Aylsham
Tel: (0263) 734137

Rossendale Antiques (Ian Shaw),
Rossendale, The Street,
Rickinghall, Diss
Tel: (0379) 898485

Northants

Paul Hopwell Antiques,
30 High Street, West Haddon
Tel: (078 887) 636

Oxon

David John Ceramics,
11 Acre End Street, Eynsham
Tel: (0865) 880786

Elizabethan House Antiques,
28 & 55 High Street, Dorchester-
on-Thames
Tel: (0865) 340079

Key Antiques,
11 Horse Fair, Chipping Norton
Tel: (0608) 643777

Peter Norden Antiques,
High Street, Burford
Tel: (099 382) 2121

Manfred Schotten Antiques,
The Crypt, High Street, Burford
Tel: (099 382) 2302

Telling Time,
57 North Street, Thame
Tel: (084 421) 3007

Zene Walker,
The Bull House, High Street,
Burford
Tel: (099 382) 3284

Witney Antiques,
96-98 Corn Street, Witney
Tel: (0993) 703902

Shropshire

Castle Gate Antiques,
15 Castle Gate, Shrewsbury
Tel: (0743) 61011 (evenings)

R G Cave & Sons Ltd,
17 Broad Street, Ludlow
Tel: (0584) 3568

Dodington Antiques,
15 Dodington, Whitchurch
Tel: (0948) 3399

Doveridge House of Neachley,
Long Lane, Nr Shifnal
Tel: (090 722) 3131/2

F C Manser & Son Ltd,
53/54 Wyle Cop, Shrewsbury
Tel: (0743) 51120

Parmenter Antiques,
5 Central Court, High Street,
Bridgnorth
Tel: (0746) 765599

Paul Smith,
The Old Chapel, Old Street,
Ludlow
Tel: (0584) 2666

M & R Taylor (Antiques),
53 Broad Street, Ludlow
Tel: (0584) 4169

Somerset

Peter Murray Antique Exports,
Station Road, Bruton
Tel. (0749) 813728

Edward A Nowell,
12 Market Place, Wells
Tel: (0749) 72415

Staffs

Richard Midwinter Antiques,
13 Brunswick Street, Newcastle
under Lyme
Tel: (0782) 712483

Suffolk

David Gibbins Antiques,
21 Market Hill, Woodbridge
Tel: (039 43) 3531

Hubbard Antiques,
16 St Margaret's Green, Ipswich
Tel: (0473) 226033

Michael Moore Antiques,
The Barns, Clare Hall, Cavendish
Road, Clare
Tel: (0787) 277510

Peppers Period Pieces (R),
23 Churchgate Street, Bury St
Edmunds
Tel: (0284) 768786

Randolph,
97 & 99 High Street, Hadleigh
Tel: (0473) 823789

Oswald Simpson,
Hall Street, Long Melford
Tel: (0787) 77523

Surrey

Albany Antiques,
8-10 London Road, Hindhead
Tel: (0428) 605528

Churchill Antiques Gallery Ltd,
65 Quarry Street, Guildford
Tel: (0483) 506662

Richard Deryn Antiques,
7 Paved Court, The Green,
Richmond-upon-Thames
Tel: 081-948 5005

Dorking Desk Shop,
41 West Street, Dorking
Tel: (0306) 883327 & 880535

Hampshires of Dorking,
51 West Street, Dorking
Tel: (0306) 887076

J Hartley Antiques,
186 High Street, Ripley
Tel: (0483) 224318

Heath-Bullock,
8 Meadrow, Godalming
Tel: (048 68) 22562

Ripley Antiques,
67 High Street, Ripley
Tel: (0483) 224981

Swan Antiques,
62a West Street, Dorking
Tel: (0306) 881217

Anthony Welling Antiques,
Broadway Barn, High Street,
Ripley
Tel: (0483) 225384

Wych House Antiques,
Wych Hill, Woking
Tel: (0483) 764634

Sussex

A27 Antiques Warehouses,
Chaucer Industrial Estate, Dittons
Road, Polegate
Tel: (032 12) 7167 & 5301

Bursig of Arundel,
The Old Candle Factory, Tarrant
Street, Arundel
Tel: (0903) 883456

Dycheling Antiques,
34 High Street, Ditchling,
Hassocks
Tel: (0273) 842929

Humphry Antiques,
North Street, Petworth
Tel: (0798) 43053

Richard Davidson,
Lombard Street, Petworth
Tel: (0798) 42508

The Grange Antiques,
High Street, Robertsbridge
Tel: (0580) 880577

Lakeside Antiques,
The Old Cement Works, South
Heighton, Newhaven
Tel: (0273) 513326

John G Morris Ltd,
Market Square, Petworth
Tel: (0798) 42305

The Old Mint House,
High Street, Pevensey, Eastbourne
Tel: (0323) 762337

David and Sarah Pullen,
29/31 Sea Road, Bexhill-on-Sea
Tel: (0424) 222035

Village Antiques,
2 & 4 Cooden Sea Road, Little
Common, Bexhill-on-Sea
Tel: (042 43) 5214

Tyne & Wear

Harold J Carr Antiques,
Field House, Rickleton,
Washington
Tel: (091) 388 6442

West Midlands

John Hubbard Antiques,
224-226 Court Oak Road,
Harborne, Birmingham
Tel: 021-426 1694

Rock House Antiques & Collectors
Centre,
Rock House, The Rock, Tettenhall,
Wolverhampton
Tel: (0902) 754995

Warwickshire

Apollo Antiques,
The Saltisford, Birmingham Road,
Warwick
Tel: (0926) 494746

Coleshill Antiques,
High Street, Coleshill
Tel: (0675) 462931

Ferneyhough Antiques,
11 Chapel Street, Stratford-upon-
Avon
Tel: (0789) 293928

Don Spencer Antiques,
Unit 2, 20 Cherry Street, Warwick
Tel: (0926) 499857

Wilts

Avon Antiques,
26-27 Market Street, Bradford-
upon-Avon
Tel: (022 16) 2052

Robert Bradley,
71 Brown Street, Salisbury
Tel: (0722) 333677

Combe Cottage Antiques,
Castle Combe, Nr Chippenham
Tel: (0249) 782250

Ian G Hastie, BADA,
46 St Ann Street, Salisbury
Tel: (0722) 22957

Robert Kime Antiques,
Dene House, Lockeridge
Tel: (067 286) 250

Melksham Antiques,
8A King Street, Melksham
Tel: (0225) 707291

Monkton Galleries,
Hindon
Tel: (074 789) 235

K & A Welch,
1a Church Street, Warminster
Tel: (0985) 214687 & 213433
(evenings)

Worcs

Gavina Ewart,
60-62 High Street, Broadway
Tel: (0386) 853371

Yorks

Robert Aagaard Ltd,
Frogmire House, Stockwell Road,
Knaresborough
Tel: (0423) 864805
(Specialises in fireplaces)

Barmouth Court Antiques,
Abbeydale House, Barmouth
Road, Sheffield
Tel: (0742) 582160 & 582672

Derbyshire Antiques Ltd,
27 Montpellier Parade, Harrogate
Tel: (0423) 503115/564242

Bernard Dickinson,
Estate Yard, West Street
Tel: (0756) 748257/749285

W F Greenwood & Sons Ltd,
2 & 3 Crown Place, Harrogate
Tel: (0423) 504467

Old Rectory Antiques,
The Old Rectory, West Heslerton,
Malton
Tel: (094 45) 364

Robert Morrison & Son,
Trentholme House, 131 The
Mount, York
Tel: (0904) 655394

R M S Precious,
King William House, High Street,
Settle
Tel: (072 92) 3946

Scotland

John Bell of Aberdeen Ltd,
Balbrogie, By Blackburn,
Kinellar, Aberdeenshire
Tel: (0224) 790209

Paul Couts Ltd,
Linkfield Road, 8-10 High Street,
Musselburgh
Tel: 031-665 7759

Letham Antiques,
20 Dundas Street, Edinburgh
Tel: 031-556 6565

Roy Sim Antiques,
21 Allan Street, Blairgowrie,
Perthshire
Tel: (0250) 3860 & 3700

Unicorn Antiques,
65 Dundas Street, Edinburgh
Tel: 031-556 7176

FURNITURE – PINE
London

Abbotts Antiques,
109 Kirkdale, SE26
Tel: 081-699 1363/5729

Adams Antiques,
47 Chalk Farm Road, NW1
Tel: 071-267 9241

At the Sign of the Chest of
Drawers,
281 Upper Street, Islington, N1
(open 7 days a week)
Tel: 071-359 5909

The Barewood Company,
58 Mill Lane, West Hampstead,
NW6
Tel: 071-435 7244

Islington Artefacts,
12-14 Essex Road, Islington, N1
Tel: 071-226 6867

Olwen Carthew,
109 Kirkdale, SW26
Tel: 081-699 1363/5729

Scallywag,
187-191 Clapham Road,
Stockwell, London, SW9
Tel: 071-274 0300

This & That (Furniture),
50 & 51 Chalk Farm Road, NW1
Tel: 071-267 5433

Avon

Abbas Combe Pine,
4 Upper Maudlin Street, Bristol
Tel: (0272) 299023

Pennard House Antiques,
3/4 Piccadilly, London Road, Bath
Tel: (0225) 313791

Bucks

For Pine,
340 Berkhampstead Road,
Chesham
Tel: (0494) 776119

The Pine Merchants,
52 High Street, Gt Missenden
Tel: (024 06) 2002

Devon

The Ark Antiques,
76 Fore Street, Topsham
Tel: (0392) 876251

Chancery Antiques,
8-10 Barrington Street, Tiverton
Tel: (0884) 252416/253190

Country Cottage Furniture,
The Old Smithy, Back Street,
Modbury
Tel: (0548) 830888

Fine Pine,
Woodland Road, Harbertonford
Tel: (080 423) 465

Glos

Bed of Roses Antiques,
12 Prestbury Road, Cheltenham
Tel: (0242) 231918

Country Homes,
61 Long Street, Tetbury
Tel: (0666) 502342

Denzil Verey Antiques,
(Specialists in Country & Pine
Furniture),
Barnsley House, Barnsley, Nr
Cirencester
Tel: (0285) 740402

Gloucester House Antiques,
Market Place, Fairford
Tel: (0285) 712790

Hants

C W Buckingham,
Twin Firs, Southampton Road,
Cadnam
Tel: (0703) 812122

Craftsman Furniture Ltd,
Castle Trading Estate,
Portchester, Portsmouth
Tel: (0705) 219911

Millers of Chelsea Antiques Ltd,
Netherbrook House,
86 Christchurch Road, Ringwood
Tel: (0425) 472062

The Pine Cellars,
39 Jewry Street, Winchester
Tel: (0962) 867014

The Pine Co,
104 Christchurch Road, Ringwood
Tel: (0425) 473932

Hereford & Worcester

Jennings of Leominster,
30 Bridge Street, Leominster
Tel: (0568) 2946

La Barre Ltd,
The Place, 116 South Street,
Leominster
Tel: (0568) 4315

Marshall Bennett Restorations,
Eagle Lane, High Street, Cleobury
Mortimer,
Nr Kidderminster, Worcester
Tel: (0299) 270553

SW Antiques,
Abbey Showroom 1, Newlands,
Pershore
Tel: (0386) 555580

Herts

Out of Town,
21 Ware Road, Hertford
Tel: (0992) 582848

Humberside

Bell Antiques,
68 Harold Street, Grimsby
Tel: (0472) 695110

The Hull Pine Co,
Bean Street, 2/6 Anlaby Road, Hull
Tel: (0482) 227169

Paul Wilson Pine Furniture,
Perth Street West, Hull
Tel: (0482) 447923 & 448607

Kent

Empire Antiques,
The Old Council Yard, Gazen
Salts, Strand Street, Sandwich
Tel: (0304) 614474

Penny Lampard,
31 High Street, Headcorn
Tel: (0622) 890682

Old English Pine
100 Sandgate High Street,
Folkestone
Tel: (0303) 48560

The Old Bakery Antiques (Mr &
Mrs D Bryan),
St Davids Bridge, Cranbrook
Tel: (0580) 713103

The Plough Pine Shop,
High Street, Eastry, Dover
Tel: (0304) 617418

Sissinghurst Antiques,
Hazelhurst Cottage, The Street,
Sissinghurst, Nr Cranbrook
Tel: (0580) 713893

Traditional Furniture,
248 Seabrook Road, Seabrook,
Hythe
Tel: (0303) 39931

Up Country,
The Corn Stores, 68 St John's
Road, Tunbridge Wells
Tel: (0892) 23341

Lancs

Cottage Furniture,
Queen Street, Farnworth, Bolton
Tel: (0204) 700853

Enloc Antiques,
Birchenlee Mill, Lenches Road,
Colne
Tel: (0282) 861417

Utopia Pine,
Holme Mills, Carnforth
Tel: (0524) 781739

Leics

Richard Kimbell Antiques,
Riverside, Market Harborough
Tel: (0858) 33444

Riverside Trading,
Riverside Industrial Estate,
Market Harborough
Tel: (0858) 464110/464825

Lincs

Allens Antiques,
Moor Farm, Stapleford
Tel: (052 285) 392

StowAway (UK) Ltd,
2 Langton Hill, Horncastle
Tel: (065 82) 7445

Norfolk

Rossendale Antiques (Ian Shaw),
Rossendale, The Street,
Rickinghall, Diss
Tel: (0379) 898485

Northants

Acorn Antiques,
The Old Mill, Moat Lane,
Towcester
Tel: (0327) 52788

The Country Pine Shop,
Northampton Road, West Haddon
Tel: (0788) 510430

Oxon

Julie Strachey,
Southfield Farm, Weston-on-the-
Green
Tel: (0869) 50833/2

Somerset

Chalon,
Hambridge Mill, Hambridge, Nr
Langport
Tel: (0458) 252374

Crewkerne Antiques Centre,
42 East Street, Crewkerne
Tel: (0460) 76755

Peter Murray Antique Exports,
Station Road, Bruton
Tel: (0749) 813728

Pennard House Antiques,
East Pennard, Shepton Mallet
Tel: (074 986) 266

Staffs

Anvil Antiques Ltd,
Cross Mills, Cross Street, Leek
Tel: (0538) 371657

Aspleys Antiques,
Compton Mill, Compton, Leek
Tel: (0538) 373396

Directmoor Ltd,
The Coppice Farm, Nr Moorcourt,
Oakamoor
Tel: (0588) 702419

Gemini Trading,
Limes Mill, Abbotts Road, Leek
Tel: (0538) 387834

Johnsons,
Park Works, Park Road, Leek
Tel: (0538) 386745

Stone-Wares,
The Stripped Pine Shop,
24 Radford Street, Stone
Tel: (0785) 815000

Suffolk

Michael Moore Antiques,
The Barns, Clare Hall, Cavendish
Road, Clare
Tel: (0787) 277510

Surrey

Richard Deryn Antiques,
7 Paved Court, The Greens,
Richmond-on-Thames
Tel: 081-948 5005

Manor Antiques,
2 The New Shops, Old Woking
Tel: (0483) 724666

Odiham Antiques,
High Street, Compton, Guildford
Tel: (0483) 810215

F & L Warren,
The Sawmills, Firgrove Hill,
Farnham
Tel: (0252) 726713

Wych House Antiques,
Wych Hill, Woking
Tel: (0483) 764636

Sussex

Drummer Pine,
Hailsham Road, Herstmonceux
Tel: (0323) 833542/833661

Hillside Antiques,
Units 12-13, Lindfield Enterprise
Park, Lewes Road, Lindfield
Tel: (044 47) 3042

Bob Hoare Antiques,
Unit Q, Phoenix Place, North
Street, Lewes
Tel: (0273) 480557

Ann Lingard,
Ropewalk Antiques, Ropewalk,
Rye
Tel: (0797) 223486

Polegate Antique Centre,
Station Road, Polegate
Tel: (0323) 485277

Graham Price Antiques Ltd,
A27 Antiques Complex, Unit 4,
Chaucer Industrial Estate, Dittons
Road, Polegate
Tel: (0323) 487167 or 487681

Touchwood (Mervyn & Sue),
The Square, Herstmonceux
Tel: (0323) 832020

Michael Wakelin & Helen
Lindfield,
10 New Street, Petworth
Tel: (0798) 42417

Wilts

Ray Coggins Antiques,
The Old Brewery, Newtown,
Bradford-on-Avon
Tel: (02216) 3431

Yorks

Early Days,
7 Kings Court, Pateley Bridge,
Harrogate
Tel: (0423) 711661

Michael Green,
Library House, Regent Parade,
Harrogate
Tel: (0423) 560452

Manor Barn Pine,
Burnside Mill, Main Street,
Addingham, Ilkley
Tel: (0943) 830176

Pine Finds,
The Old Corn Mill, Bishop
Monkton, Harrogate
Tel: (0765) 677159

Smith & Smith Designs,
58A Middle Street North, Driffield
Tel: (0377) 46321

Ireland

Old Court Pine,
The Square, Collon, Co Louth
Tel: (010 353 41) 26270

Albert Forsythe,
Mill House, 66 Carsontown Road,
Saintfield, Co Down, Northern
Ireland
Tel: (0238) 510398

Delvin Farm Galleries,
Gormonston, Co Meath
Tel: (0001) 412285

Luckpenny Antiques,
Kilmurray House, Shinrone, Birr,
Co Offaly, Southern Ireland
Tel: (010 353 505) 47134

Scotland

A & P Steadman,
Unit 1, Hatston Industrial Estate,
Kirkwall, Orkney
Tel: (0856) 5040

Wales

Heritage Restorations,
Maes y Glydfa, Llanfair,
Caereinion, Welshpool, Powys
Tel: (0938) 810384

Maclean,
Dudley & Marie Thorpe, Tiradda,
Llansadwrn, Dyfed
Tel: (0550) 777-509

Pine Furniture,
Station Stores, Station Yard,
Goodwick, Fishguard
Tel: (0348) 872634

GLASS

London

Asprey PLC,
165-169 New Bond Street, W1
Tel: 071-493 6767

Phyllis Bedford Antiques,
3 The Galleries, Camden Passage,
N1
Tel: 071-354 1332;
home 081-882 3189

Christine Bridge,
78 Castelnau, SW13
Tel: 081-741 5501

W G T Burne (Antique Glass) Ltd,
11 Elystan Street, SW3
Tel: 071-589 6074

Delomosne & Son Ltd,
4 Campden Hill Road, W8
Tel: 071-937 1804

East Gates Antiques,
Stand G006, Alfies Antique
Market, 13-25 Church Street, NW8
Tel: 071-724 5650

Eila Grahame,
97C Kensington Church Street,
W8
Tel: 071-727 4132

Lloyds of Westminster,
5A Motcomb Street, SW1
Tel: 071-235 1010

S W Parry (Old Glass),
Stand A4-A5 Westbourne Antique
Arcade, 113 Portobello Road, W11
(Sat only)
Tel: 081-740 0248 (Sun to Fri)

Pryce & Brise Antiques,
79 Moore Park Road, Fulham, SW6
Tel: 071-736 1864

Gerald Sattin Ltd,
25 Burlington Arcade, Piccadilly,
W1
Tel: 071-493 6557

Mark J West,
Cobb Antiques Ltd,
39B High Street, Wimbledon
Village, SW19
Tel: 081-946 2811

R Wilkinson & Son (R),
5 Catford Hill, SE6 4NU
Tel: 081-314 1080

Avon

Somervale Antiques,
6 Radstock Road, Midsomer
Norton, Bath
Tel: (0761) 412686

Dorset

A & D Antiques,
21 East Street, Blandford Forum
Tel: (0258) 455643

Quarter Jack Antiques,
The Quarter Jack, Bridge Street,
Sturminster Newton
Tel: (0258) 72558

Hants

Stockbridge Antiques,
High Street, Stockbridge
Tel: (0264) 810829

Todd & Austin Antiques & Fine
Art
2 Andover Road, Winchester
Tel: (0962) 869824

Kent

Castle Antiques,
1 London Road, Westerham
Tel: (0959) 62492

779

Somerset
Abbey Antiques,
52-54 High Street, Glastonbury
Tel: (0458) 31694

Surrey
Shirley Warren (by appointment only),
42 Kingswood Avenue, Sanderstead
Tel: 081-657 1751

Shirley Warren (shop),
333B Limpsfield Road, Sanderstead
Tel: 081-651 5180

Sussex
Rusthall Antiques,
Chateaubriand Antique Centre, High Street, Burwash
Tel: (0435) 882535 & (0892) 20668 (evenings)

Warwickshire
Sharon Ball (Antique glass & collectables),
Unit 1, Stratford-on-Avon Antique Centre, Ely Street, Stratford-on-Avon
Tel: (0789) 204180

Stratford-on-Avon
Antique Centre,
Ely Street, Stratford-on-Avon
Tel: (0789) 204180

Scotland
William MacAdam (appointment only),
86 Pilrig Street, Edinburgh
Tel: 031-553 1364

GRAMOPHONES, PHONOGRAPHS & RADIOS
Avon
The Vintage Wireless Co,
Tudor House, Cossham Street, Mangotsfield, Bristol
Tel: (0272) 565472

Devon
Brian Taylor Antiques,
24 Molesworth Road, Stoke, Plymouth
Tel: (0752) 569061

Yorks
Clocks & Gramophones,
11 Walmgate, York
Tel: (0904) 611924

ICONS
London
Maria Andipa,
Icon Gallery, 162 Walton Street, SW3
Tel: 071-589 2371

Mark Gallery,
9 Porchester Place, Marble Arch, W2
Tel: 071-262 4906

JEWELLERY
London
Hirsh Fine Jewels,
Diamond House, Hatton Garden, EC1
Tel: 071-405 6080/071-404 4392

Glos
South Bar Antiques (Cameos),
Digbeth Street, Stow-on-the-Wold
Tel: (0451) 30236

Hereford & Worcester
B B M Jewellery,
8 & 9 Lion Street, Kidderminster
Tel: (0562) 744118

Old Curiosity Antiques,
11 Tower Buildings, Blackwell Street, Kidderminster
Tel: (0562) 742859

Herts
Forget Me Not Antiques,
23 George Street, St Albans
Tel: (0923) 26472

Kent
Castle Antiques,
1 London Road, Westerham
Tel: (0959) 62492

Norfolk
Peter & Valerie Howkins,
39, 40 & 135 King Street, Great Yarmouth
Tel: (0493) 844639

Somerset
Edward A Nowell,
12 Market Place, Wells
Tel: (0749) 72415

Sussex
Rusthall Antiques,
Chateaubriand Antique Centre, High Street, Burwash
Tel: (0435) 882535 (0892) 20668 (evenings)

KITCHENALIA
Lancashire
Kitchenalia,
36 Inglewhite Road, Longridge, Nr Preston
Tel: (077 478) 5411

Shropshire
Tiffany Antiques,
Unit 3, Shrewsbury Antique Centre, 15 Princess House, The Square, Shrewsbury
Tel: (Home) (0270) 257425
also at:
Unit 15, Shrewsbury Antique Market, Frankwell Quay Warehouse, Shrewsbury
Tel: (0270) 257425

LIGHTING
London
Judy Jones,
194 Westbourne Grove, W11
Tel: 071-229 6866

The Lamp Gallery,
355 New Kings Road, SW6
Tel: 071-736 6188

Hereford & Worcester
Fritz Fryer,
12 Brookend Street, Ross-on-Wye, Hereford
Tel: (0989) 67416

Hertfordshire
J Marsden,
Magic Lanterns and Vestalia Antique Lighting Ltd, 23 George Street, St Albans
Tel: (0727) 65680 & 53032

LOCKS & KEYS
Notts
The Keyhole, Dragonwyck (R),
Far Back Lane, Farnsfield
Tel: (0623) 882590

MARINE ANTIQUES
Devon
Temeraire,
63 Brownston Street, Modbury
Tel: (0548) 830317

Essex
Littlebury Antiques,
58/60 Fairycroft Road, Saffron Walden
Tel: (0799) 27961

METALWARE
London
Christopher Bangs (by appointment only),
Tel: 071-223 5676

Jack Casimir Ltd,
The Brass Shop, 23 Pembridge Road, W11
Tel: 071-727 8643

Arthur Davidson Ltd,
78-79 Jermyn Street, SW1
Tel: 071-930 6687

Alistair Sampson Antiques,
156 Brompton Road, SW3
Tel: 071-589 5272

Avon
Cottage Antiques,
The Old Post Office, Langford Place, Langford, Nr Bristol
Tel: (0934) 862597

Beds
Christopher Sykes Antiques,
The Old Parsonage, Woburn, Milton Keynes
Tel: (052 525) 259/467

Bucks
Albert Bartram,
177 Hivings Hill, Chesham
Tel: (0494) 783271

Cumbria
Stable Antiques,
Wheelwright Cottage, 15-16 Back Lane, Sedbergh
Tel: (05396) 20251

Glos
Country Life Antiques,
Grey House, The Square, Stow-on-the-Wold
Tel: (0451) 31564

Oxon
Robin Bellamy Ltd,
97 Corn Street, Witney
Tel: (0993) 704793

Elizabethan House Antiques,
28 & 55 High Street, Dorchester-on-Thames
Tel: (0865) 340079

Key Antiques,
11 Horse Fair, Chipping Norton
Tel: (0608) 643777

Suffolk
Brookes Forge Flempton (R),
Flempton, Bury St Edmunds, Suffolk
Tel: (02848) 728473 business (0449) 781376 home

Sussex
Michael Wakelin & Helen Linfield,
10 New Street, Petworth
Tel: (0798) 42417

Wilts
Avon Antiques,
26-27 Market Street, Bradford-on-Avon
Tel: (022 16) 2052

Combe Cottage Antiques,
Castle Combe, Chippenham
Tel: (0249) 782250

Rupert Gentle Antiques,
The Manor House, Milton Lilbourne, Nr Pewsey
Tel: (0672) 63344

Yorks
Windsor House Antiques (Leeds) Ltd,
18-20 Benson Street, Leeds
Tel: (0532) 444666

MUSICAL INSTRUMENTS
London
Mayflower Antiques,
117 Portobello Road, W11
Tel: 071-727 0381
(Sats only 7am-3pm)

Essex
Mayflower Antiques,
2 Una Road, Parkeston, Harwich
Tel: (0255) 504079

Glos
Vanbrugh House Antiques,
Park Street, Stow-on-the-Wold
Tel: (0451) 30797

Oxon
Laurie Leigh Antiques,
36 High Street, Oxford
Tel: (0865) 244197

Somerset
Shelagh Berryman,
Musical Boxes,
15 The Market Place, Wells
Tel: (0749) 76203

Sussex
Sound Instruments,
Worth Farm, Little Horsted, Nr Uckfield
Tel: (082 575) 567

ORIENTAL
London
Kotobuki,
F100 Alfies Antique Market, 13-25 Church Street, NW8
Tel: 071-402 0723

Sussex
Linda Loveland Restorations,
18-20 Prospect Place, Hastings
Tel: (0424) 441608

PORCELAIN
London
Armin B Allen,
3 Bury Street, St James's, SW1
Tel: 071-930 4732/0729

Albert Amor Ltd,
37 Bury Street, St James's, SW1
Tel: 071-930 2444

Antique Porcelain Co Ltd,
149 New Bond Street, W1
Tel: 071-629 1254

Susan Becker,
18 Lower Richmond Road, SW15
Tel: 081-788 9082

David Brower Antiques,
113 Kensington Church Street, W8
Tel: 071-221 4155

Cale Antiques,
24 Cale Street, Chelsea Green, SW3
Tel: 071-589 6146

Belinda Coote Antiques,
29 Holland Street, W8
Tel: 071-937 3924

Craven Antiques,
17 Garson House, Gloucester Terrace, W2
Tel: 071-262 4176

Marilyn Delion,
288 Westbourne Grove, Stand 7, Portobello Market, W11
(Sat only by appointment)
Tel: 071-937 3377

Delomosne & Son Ltd,
4 Campden Hill Road, W8
Tel: 071-937 1804

H & W Deutsch Antiques,
111 Kensington Church Street, W8
Tel: 071-727 5984

Graham & Oxley (Antiques) Ltd,
101 Kensington Church Street, W8
Tel: 071-229 1850

Grosvenor Antiques Ltd,
27 Holland Street, Kensington, W8
Tel: 071-937 8649

Harcourt Antiques,
5 Harcourt Street, W1
Tel: 071-723 5919

Hoff Antiques Ltd,
66A Kensington Church Street,
W8
Tel: 071-229 5516

Klaber & Klaber,
2A Bedford Gardens, Kensington
Church Street, W8
Tel: 071-727 4573

Mayfair Gallery,
46 South Audley Street, W1
Tel: 071-499 5315

Mercury Antiques,
1 Ladbroke Road, W11
Tel: 071-727 5106

St Jude's Antiques,
107 Kensington Church Street, W8
Tel: 071-727 8737

Gerald Sattin Ltd,
14 King Street, St James's, SW1
Tel: 071-493 6557

Jean Sewell (Antiques) Ltd,
3 Campden Street, Kensington
Church Street, W8
Tel: 071-727 3122

Simon Spero,
109 Kensington Church Street, W8
Tel: 071-727 7413

Constance Stobo,
31 Holland Street, W8
Tel: 071-937 6282

Nicholas Vandekar Ltd,
138 Brompton Road, SW3
Tel: 071-589 8481/3398

Venner's Antiques,
7 New Cavendish Street, W1
Tel: 071-935 0184

Avon
Andrew Dando,
4 Wood Street, Queen Square, Bath
Tel: (0225) 422702

Brian & Angela Downes,
9 Broad Street, Bath
Tel: (0225) 465352

Berks
The Old School Antiques,
Dorney, Windsor
Tel: (0628) 603247

Cornwall
Mrs Margaret Chesterton,
33 Pentewan Road, St Austell
Tel: (0726) 72926

Devon
Paul & Dorothy Stockman,
Newton Abbot Antiques, 55 East
Street, Newton Abbot
Tel: (0803) 215188

David J Thorn,
2 High Street, Budleigh Salterton
Tel: (039 54) 2448

Glos
Gloucester House Antiques,
Market Place, Fairford
Tel: (0285) 712790

L Greenwold,
Digbeth, Digbeth Street,
Stow-on-the-Wold
Tel: (0451) 30398

Pamela Rowan,
High Street, Blockley, Nr
Moreton-in-Marsh
Tel: (0386) 700280

Studio Antiques Ltd,
Bourton-on-the-Water
Tel: (0451) 20352

Hants
Gerald Austin Antiques,
2A Andover Road, Winchester
Tel: (0962) 869824 Ext 2

Goss & Crested China Ltd,
62 Murray Road, Horndean
Tel: (0705) 597440

Rogers of Alresford,
16 West Street, Alresford
Tel: (0962) 732862

Hereford & Worcs
Gavina Ewart,
60-62 High Street, Broadway
Tel: (0386) 853371

Antiques Centre,
11 Tower Buildings, Blackwell
Street, Kidderminster
Tel: (0562) 829000

M Lees & Sons,
Tower House, Severn Street,
Worcester
Tel: (0905) 26620

Kent
Beaubush Antiques,
95 Sandgate High Street,
Folkestone
Tel: (0303) 49099

Castle Antiques,
No 1 London Road, Westerham
Tel: (0959) 62492

The History in Porcelain Collector,
High Street, Shoreham Village,
Nr Sevenoaks
Tel: (095 92) 3416

Kent Cottages Antiques,
39 High Street, Rolvenden
Tel: (0580) 241719

Steppes Hill Farm Antiques,
Stockbury, Sittingbourne
Tel: (0795) 842205

Wakefield Ceramic Fairs (Fred
Hynds),
1 Fountain Road, Strood,
Rochester
Tel: (0634) 723461

W W Warner (Antiques) Ltd,
The Green, Brasted
Tel: (0959) 63698

Lancs
Burnley Antiques & Fine Arts Ltd,
336A Colne Road, Burnley
Tel: (0282) 20143/65172

Leics
Charnwood Antiques,
Coalville, Leicester LE6 3RN
Tel: (0530) 38530

Norfolk
T C S Brooke,
The Grange, Wroxham
Tel: (0603) 782644

Margaret Corson,
Irstead Manor, Neatishead
Tel: (0692) 630274

Notts
C B Sheppard Antiques,
122/124 Chesterfield Road North,
Mansfield
Tel: (0773) 872419

Oxon
Castle Antiques,
Lamb Arcade, Wallingford, Oxon
Tel: (0491) 35166

David John Ceramics,
11 Acre End Street, Eynsham,
Oxford
Tel: (0865) 880786

Shropshire
Castle Gate Antiques,
15 Castle Gate, Shrewsbury
Tel: (0743) 61011 evenings

F C Manser & Son Ltd,
53-54 Wyle Cop, Shrewsbury
Tel: (0743) 51120

Teme Valley Antiques,
1 The Bull Ring, Ludlow
Tel: (0584) 874686

Tudor House Antiques,
33 High Street, Ironbridge
Tel: (0952) 433237

Peter Wain,
7 Nantwich Road, Woore
Tel: (0630) 817118

Suffolk
Crafers Antiques,
The Hill, Wickham Market,
Woodbridge
Tel: (0728) 747347

Surrey
Elias Clark Antiques Ltd,
1 The Cobbles, Bletchingley
Tel: (0883) 843714

Whittington Galleries,
22 Woodend, Sutton
Tel: 081-644 9327

Sussex
Barclay Antiques,
7 Village Mews, Little Common,
Bexhill-on-Sea
Tel: (0797) 222734 home

Geoffrey Godden,
Chinaman, 17-19 Crescent Road,
Worthing
Tel: (0903) 35958

William Hockley Antiques,
East Street, Petworth
Tel: (0798) 43172

Leonard Russell,
21 King's Avenue, Newhaven
Tel: (0273) 515153

Warwickshire
Coleshill Antiques,
High Street, Coleshill
Tel: (0675) 462931

Wilts
The China Hen,
9 Woolley Street, Bradford-on-
Avon
Tel: (022 16) 3369

Mark Collier Antiques,
High Street, Downton
Tel: (0725) 21068

Melksham Antiques,
8A King Street, Melksham
Tel: (0225) 707291

Yorks
Angela Charlesworth,
99 Dodworth Road, Barnsley
Tel: (0226) 282097/203688

David Love,
10 Royal Parade, Harrogate
Tel: (0423) 565797

Nanbooks,
Roundabout, Duke Street, Settle
Tel: (072 92) 3324

Wales
Station Stores,
Station Yard, Goodwick,
Fishguard
Tel: (0348) 872634

POTTERY
London
Britannia,
Stand 101, Gray's Market,
58 Davies Street, W1
Tel: 071-629 6772

Nicolaus Boston,
Chenil Galleries, 181-183 Kings
Road, SW3
Tel: 071-352 8790

Cale Antiques,
24 Cale Street, Chelsea Green,
SW3
Tel: 071-589 6146

Gerald Clark Antiques,
1 High Street, Mill Hill Village,
NW7
Tel: 081-906 0342/958 4295

Belinda Coote Antiques,
29 Holland Street, W8
Tel: 071-937 3924

Marilyn Delion,
228 Westbourne Grove, Stand 7,
Portobello Market, W11
(Sat by appointment only)
Tel: 071-937 3377

Richard Dennis,
144 Kensington Church Street, W8
Tel: 071-727 2061

Graham & Oxley (Antiques) Ltd,
101 Kensington Church Street, W8
Tel: 071-229 1850

Jonathan Horne,
66C Kensington Church Street,
W8
Tel: 071-221 5658

Valerie Howard,
131e Kensington Church Street,
W8 7PT
Tel: 071-792 9702

J & J May,
40 Kensington Church Street, W8
Tel: 071-937 3575

Mercury Antiques,
1 Ladbroke Road, W11
Tel: 071-727 5106

Sue Norman,
L4 Antiquarius, 135 Kings Road,
SW3
Tel: 071-352 7217

Oliver Sutton Antiques,
34C Kensington Church Street,
W8
Tel: 071-937 0633

Jacqueline Oosthuizen,
Shop 12, Georgian Village
(Wed & Sat) Tel: 071-226 5393
23 Cale Street, Chelsea
Tel: 071-352 6071/352 5581

Rogers de Rin,
76 Royal Hospital Road, SW3
Tel: 071-352 9007

Alistair Sampson Antiques,
156 Brompton Road, SW3
Tel: 071-589 5272

Constance Stobo,
31 Holland Street, W8
Tel: 071-937 6282

Nicholas Vandekar Ltd,
138 Brompton Road, SW3
Tel: 071-589 8481 & 3398

Avon
Andrew Dando,
4 Wood Street, Queen Square, Bath
Tel: (0225) 5422702

Robert Pugh,
2 Beaufort Mews, St Saviours
Road, Larkhall, Bath
Tel: (0225) 314713

Cornwall
Mrs Margaret Chesterton,
33 Pentewan Road, St Austell
Tel: (0826) 72926

Cumbria
Kendal Studio Pottery,
2-3 Wildman Street, Kendal
Tel: (0539) 723291

Devon
Paul & Dorothy Stockman,
Newton Abbot Antiques, 55 East
Street, Newton Abbot
Tel: (0803) 215188

David J Thorn,
2 High Street, Budleigh Salterton
Tel: (039 54) 2448

Hants
Goss & Crested China Ltd,
62 Murray Road, Horndean
Tel: (0705) 597440

Millers of Chelsea,
Netherbrook House, Christchurch
Road, Ringwood
Tel: (0425) 472062

Rogers of Alresford,
16 West Street, Alresford
Tel: (0962) 732862

Humberside
The Crested China Company,
The Station House, Driffield
Tel: (0377) 4702

Kent
Beaubush House Antiques,
95 High Street, Sandgate,
Folkestone
Tel: (0303) 49099

W W Warner (Antiques) Ltd,
The Green, Brasted
Tel: (0959) 63698

Lancs
Burnley Antiques & Fine Arts Ltd
(appointment only),
336A Colne Road, Burnley
Tel: (0282) 65172

Roy W Bunn Antiques,
34/36 Church Street,
Barnoldswick, Colne
Tel: (0282) 813703

Norfolk
Margaret Corson,
Irstead Manor, Neatishead
Tel: (0692) 630274

Northants
Heyford Antiques,
9 Church Street, Nether, Heyford,
Northampton
Tel: (0327) 40749

Shropshire
Peter Wain,
7 Nantwich Road, Woore
Tel: (0630) 817118

Suffolk
Crafers Antiques,
The Hill, Wickham Market,
Woodbridge
Tel: (0728) 747347

Surrey
Elias Clark Antiques Ltd,
1 The Cobbles, Bletchingley
Tel: (0883) 843714

Whittington Galleries,
22 Woodend, Sutton
Tel: 081-644 9327

Sussex
Ron Beech,
1 Brambledean Road, Portslade
Tel: (0273) 423355

Ray & Diane Ginns,
PO Box 129, East Grinstead
Tel: (0342) 326041

Leonard Russell,
21 King's Avenue, Newhaven
Tel: (0273) 515153

Warwickshire
Beehive Antiques,
125 Warwick Road, Kenilworth
Tel: (0926) 55253

Wilts
Bratton Antiques,
Market Place, Westbury
Tel: (0373) 823021

Yorks
The Antique & Bargain Store,
6 Sunny Bar, Doncaster
Tel: (0302) 344857

Doncaster Sales & Exchange,
20 Copley Road, Doncaster
Tel: (0302) 344857

Nanbooks,
Roundabout, Duke Street, Settle
Tel: (072 92) 3324

Wales
Howards Antiques,
10 Alexandra Road, Aberystwyth,
Dyfed
Tel: (0970) 624973

Islwyn Watkins,
1 High Street, Knighton, Powys
Tel: (0547) 520145/528940

Isle of Man
Rushton Ceramics,
Tynwald Mills, St Johns
Tel: (0624) 801618

RESTORATION
London
Plowden & Smith,
190 St Ann's Hill, SW18
Tel: 081-874 4005

Devon
Alastair Paul & Company Ltd,
Challenge House, 12 Walkham
Business Park, Burrington Way,
Plymouth
Tel: (0752) 770049

Kent
Antique Restoration & Polishing,
etc.,
K J Garrett (Clocks), 48 Henley
Fields, St Michaels, Tenterden
Tel: (0797) 270250

Sussex
Richard Davidson,
Lombard Street, Petworth
Tel: (0798) 42508/43354

Robin S Johnson
Unit 2, Church Street, Dorking
Tel: (0306) 884244

Wiltshire
Cooks of Marlborough,
High Trees House, Savernake
Forest, Marlborough
Tel: (0672) 513017/515745

Scotland
Traditional Antique Restoration,
The Stable, Altyre Estate, Forres,
Moray
Tel: (0309) 72572

SCENT BOTTLES
Kent
Kent Cottage Antiques,
39 High Street, Rolvenden
Tel: (0580) 241719

SCIENTIFIC INSTRUMENTS
London
Jilliana Ranicar-Breese, Martin
Breese International,
8 Portwine Arcade, 175 Portobello
Road (Sat only)
Tel: 071-727 9378
(Optical Toys/Illusion)

Arthur Davidson Ltd,
78-79 Jermyn Street, SW1
Tel: 071-930 6687

Mariner Antiques Ltd,
55 Curzon Street, W1
Tel: 071-499 0171

Mayflower Antiques,
117 Portobello Road, W11
Tel: 071-727 0381
(Sats only 7am-3pm)

Arthur Middleton Ltd,
12 New Row, Covent Garden, WC2
Tel: 071-836 7042/7062

Trevor Philip & Sons Ltd,
75A Jermyn Street, St James's,
SW1
Tel: 071-930 2954/5

David Weston Ltd,
44 Duke Street, St James, SW1
Tel: 071-839 1051-2-3

Harriet Wynter Ltd (by
appointment only),
50 Redcliffe Road, SW10
Tel: 071-352 6494

Beds
Christopher Sykes Antiques,
The Old Parsonage, Woburn,
Milton Keynes
Tel: (0525) 290259/290467

Essex
Mayflower Antiques,
2 Una Road, Parkeston, Harwich
Tel: (0255) 504079

Glos
Country Life Antiques,
Grey House, The Square,
Stow-on-the-Wold
Tel: (0451) 31564

Hereford & Worcester
Arcadia Antiques,
The Ginnel Antique Centre,
Harrogate
Tel: (0704) 64441

Kent
Hadlow Antiques,
No. 1 The Pantiles, Tunbridge
Wells
Tel: (0892) 29858

Norfolk
Margaret Corson,
Irstead Manor, Neatishead
Tel: (0692) 630274

Humbleyard Fine Art,
3 Fish Hill, Holt
Tel: (0263) 713362
or (0362) 637793

Turret House (Dr D H Morgan),
27 Middleton Street, Wymondham
Tel: (0953) 603462

Surrey
Whittington Galleries,
22 Woodend, Sutton
Tel: 081-644 9327

SILVER
London
Asprey PLC,
165-169 New Bond Street, W1
Tel: 071-493 6767

N Bloom & Son (Antiques) Ltd,
40-41 Conduit Street, W1
Tel: 071-629 5060

Bond Street Galleries,
111-112 New Bond Street, W1
Tel: 071-493 6180

J H Bourdon-Smith,
24 Mason's Yard, Duke Street, St
James's, SW1
Tel: 071-839 4714

H & W Deutsch Antiques,
111 Kensington Church Street, W8
Tel: 071-727 5984

Howard Jones,
43 Kensington Church Street, W8
Tel: 071-937 4359

London International Silver Co,
82 Portobello Road, W11
Tel: 081-979 6523

S J Phillips Ltd,
139 New Bond Street, W1
Tel: 071-629 6261/2

Gerald Sattin Ltd,
25 Burlington Arcade, Piccadilly,
W1
Tel: 071-493 6557

S J Shrubsole Ltd,
43 Museum Street, WC1
Tel: 071-405 2712

Cheshire
Watergate Antiques,
56 Watergate Street, Chester
Tel: (0244) 44516

Hereford & Worcester
Lower House Fine Antiques (R),
Far Moor Lane, Winyates Green,
Redditch
Tel: (0527) 25117

Castle Antiques,

Kent
Castle Antiques,
1 London Road, Westerham
Tel: (0959) 62492

Ralph Antiques,
40A Sandwich Industrial Estate,
Sandwich
Tel: (0304) 611949/612882

Steppes Hill Farm Antiques,
Stockbury, Sittingbourne
Tel: (0795) 842205

Middlesex
London International Silver Co
Ltd,
Hampton
Tel: 081-979 6523

Oxon
Thames Gallery,
Thameside, Henley-on-Thames
Tel: (0491) 572449

Shropshire
F C Manser & Son Ltd,
53-54 Wyle Cop, Shrewsbury
Tel: (0743) 51120

Somerset
Edward A Nowell,
12 Market Place, Wells
Tel: (0749) 72415

Warwickshire
Coleshill Antiques,
High Street, Coleshill
Tel: (0675) 462931

Yorks
Georgian House,
88 Main Street, Bingley
Tel: (0274) 568883

SPORTS & GAMES

London

Sarah Baddler,
The Golf Gallery, B12 Grays In
The Mews, Davies Mews, W1
Tel: 071-408 1239/081-452 7243

Oxon

The Crypt Antiques,
109 High Street, Burford
Tel: (099382) 2302

Surrey

Academy Antiques (Billiard
Tables),
No 5 Camphill Industrial Estate,
West Byfleet
Tel: (0932) 352067

TEXTILES

London

Act One Hire Ltd,
2a Scampston Mews, Cambridge
Gardens, W10 6HX
Tel: 081-960 1456/1494

Matthew Adams,
A1 Rogers Antique Galleries,
65 Portobello Road, W11
Tel: 081-579 5560

Gallery of Antique Costume &
Textiles,
2 Church Street, Marylebone,
NW8
Tel: 071-723 9981

Linda Wrigglesworth,
Grays Inn, The Mews, 1-7 Davies
Mews, W1
Tel: 071-408 0177

Kent

The Lace Basket,
1A East Cross, Tenterden
Tel: (05806) 3923

Norfolk

Mrs Woolston,
Design House, 29 St Georges
Street, Norwich
Tel: (0603) 623181
Also at:
Long Melford Antique Centre

Sussex

Celia Charlotte's Antiques,
7 Malling Street, Lewes
Tel: (0273) 473303

WINE ANTIQUES

London

Brian Beat,
38 Burlington Gardens, W1
Tel: 071-437 4975

Richard Kihl,
164 Regent's Park Road, NW1
Tel: 071-586 3838

Avon

Robin Butler,
20 Clifton Road, Bristol
Tel: (0272) 733017

Beds

Christopher Sykes Antiques,
The Old Parsonage, Woburn,
Milton Keynes
Tel: (0525) 290259 & 290467

Cumbria

Bacchus Antiques,
Longlands at Cartmel
Tel: (05395) 36475

WRITING MATERIALS

London

Jasmin Cameron (R),
Stand J6 Antiquarius,
131-141 Kings Road, SW3 5ST
Tel: 071-351 4154

FAIR ORGANISERS

London

KM Fairs,
PO Box 1568, London, N6
Tel: 071-794 3551

Philbeach Events Ltd,
Earl's Court Exhibition Centre,
Warwick Road, SW5
Tel: 071-385 1200

Berks

Bridget Fraser,
Granny's Attic Antique Fairs,
Dean House, Cookham Dean
Tel: (062 84) 483658

Silhouette Fairs (inc Newbury
Antique & Collectors' Fairs),
44 Donnington Square, Newbury
Tel: (0635) 44338

Cheshire

Antique & Collectors Fair,
The Guildhall, Watergate Street,
Chester
(no telephone number)

Susan Brownson,
Antique Fairs North West,
Brownslow House, Gt Budworth,
Northwich
Tel: (0606) 891267

Pamela Robertson,
8 St George's Crescent, Queen's
Park, Chester
Tel: (0244) 678106

Cornwall

Richard Castle Fairs,
Bake Barton, Trerulefoot, Saltash
Tel: (05034) 694

Devon

West Country Antiques &
Collectors Fairs (Gerry Mosdell),
The Dartmoor Antiques Centre,
Ashburton
Tel: (0364) 521821

Essex

Robert Bailey Antiques Fairs,
PO Box 1110, Ongar
Tel: (0277) 362662

Hereford & Worcester

Northern Antiques Fair,
9 Emson Close, Saffron Walden
Tel: (0799) 26699

Unicorn Fairs,
PO Box 30, Hereford
Tel: (061 773) 7001

Herts

Bartholomew Fairs,
Kings Mews, 49-51 London Road,
Sawbridgworth
Tel: (0279) 600005 & 725809

Humberside

Seaclef Fairs,
78 Humberston Avenue,
Humberston, Grimsby
Tel: (0472) 813858

Kent

Wakefield Ceramic Fairs (Fred
Hynds),
1 Fountain Road, Strood,
Rochester
Tel: (0634) 723461

Norfolk

Broadland Fayres,
Dakenham Hall, Salhouse,
Norwich
Tel: (0603) 721360

Notts

Top Hat Exhibitions Ltd,
66-72 Derby Road, Nottingham
Tel: (0602) 419143

Oxon

Portcullis Fairs,
20 High Street, Wallingford
Tel: (0491) 39332

Staffs

Waverley Fairs,
at Kinver
Tel: (021 550) 0309 & (0905)
620697

Suffolk

Camfair (Ros Coltman),
Longlands, Kedington, Haverhill
Tel: (0440) 704632

Emporium Fairs,
Longlands, Kedington, Haverhill
Tel: (0440) 704632

Surrey

Antiques & Collectors' Club,
No. 1 Warehouse, Horley Row,
Horley
Tel: (0293) 772206

Cultural Exhibitions Ltd,
8 Meadrow, Godalming
Tel: (048 68) 22562

Historic and Heritage Fayres
Tel: 081-398 5324

Sussex

Ron Beech,
1 Brambledean Road, Portslade
Tel: (0273) 423355

Penman Antique Fairs,
PO Box 114, Haywards Heath
Tel: (0444) 482514

Penman Antique Fairs,
Cockhaise Mill, Lindfield,
Haywards Heath
Tel: (044 47) 2514

Yorks

Bowman Antique Fairs,
PO Box 37, Otley
Tel: (0532) 843333
Also in:
Cheshire, Cleveland, Lincs, Staffs
and Yorks

SHIPPERS

London

Featherston Shipping Ltd,
24 Hampton House, 15-17 Ingate
Place, SW8
Tel: 071-720 0422

Lockson Services Ltd,
29 Broomfield Street, E14
Tel: 071-515 8600

Stephen Morris Shipping Ltd,
318 Green Lanes, N4
Tel: 071-354 1212

Pitt & Scott Ltd,
20/24 Eden Grove, N7
Tel: 071-607 7321

Avon

A J Williams,
607 Sixth Avenue, Central
Business Park, Petherton Road,
Hengrove, Bristol
Tel: (0272) 892166

Dorset

Alan Franklin Transport,
Unit 8, 27 Black Moor Road,
Ebblake Industrial Estate,
Verwood
Tel: (0202) 826539 & 826394 &
827092
Fax: (0202) 827337

Hants

Colin Macleod's Antiques
Warehouse,
105 Albert Road, Southsea,
Portsmouth
Tel: (0705) 864211

Humberside

Geoffrey Mole,
400 Wincolmlee, Hull
Tel: (0482) 27858

Lancs

GG Antique Wholesalers,
25 Middleton Road, Middleton,
Morecambe
Tel: (0524) 51565

West Lancs Antique Exports,
Black Horse Farm, 123 Liverpool
Road, South Burscough, Nr
Ormskirk
Tel: (0704) 894634/35720

Lincs

Laurence Shaw Antiques,
Spilsby Road, Horncastle
Tel: (0507) 527638

Middx

Burlington Specialised
Forwarding Ltd,
Unit 8, Ascot Road, Clockhouse
Lane, Feltham
Tel: (0784) 244152

Phelps Ltd,
133-135 St Margaret's Road,
E Twickenham
Tel: 081-892 1778/7129

Staffs

Aspleys Antiques,
Compton Mill, Compton, Leek
Tel: (0538) 373396

Sussex

British Antiques Exporters Ltd,
Queen Elizabeth Avenue, Burgess
Hill
Tel: (0444) 6245577

Graham Price Antiques Ltd,
A27 Antiques Complex, Unit 4,
Chaucer Industrial Estate, Dittons
Road, Polegate
Tel: (032 12) 7167 & 7681

Peter Semus Antiques,
The Warehouse, Gladstone Road,
Portslade
Tel: (0273) 420154

Wiltshire

C&C Transport Services,
The White House, Winterbourne
Monkton, Swindon
Tel: (06723) 375

TRADE SUPPLIERS

London

Air Improvement Centre Ltd,
23 Denbigh Street, London, SW1
Tel: 071-834 2834
Fax: 071-821 8485

Green & Stone of Chelsea – Art
Supplies, Framing Service,
Restorers,
259 King's Road, London, SW3
Tel: 071-352 6521/0837

Devon

Optimum Brasses,
7 Castle Street, Bampton, Tiverton
Tel: (0398) 331515

Kent
C & A J Barmby,
Fine Art Accessories, 68 Judd
Road, Tonbridge, Kent
Tel: (0732) 356479

Lancs
GG Antique Wholesalers,
25 Middleton Road, Middleton,
Morecambe
Tel: (0524) 51565

Sussex
Loveland Antiques,
18-20 Prospect Place, Hastings
Tel: (0424) 441608

West Midlands
Retro Products,
174 Norton Road, Stourbridge
Tel: (0384) 373332

Yorks
Stanley Tools,
Woodside, Sheffield, S Yorkshire
Tel: (0742) 768888

ANTIQUE CENTRES & MARKETS
London
Atlantic Antique Centres,
15 Flood Street, SW3
Tel: 071-351 5353

Alfies Antique Market,
13-25 Church Street, NW8
Tel: 071-723 6066

Antiquarius Antique Market,
135/141 King's Road, Chelsea,
SW3
Tel: 071-351 5353

Bermondsey Antique Market &
Warehouse,
173 Bermondsey Street, SE1
Tel: 071-407 2040

Bond Street Antique Centre,
124 New Bond Street, W1
Tel: 071-351 5353

Camden Passage Antique
Centre,
357 Upper Street, Islington, N1
Tel: 071-359 0190

Chenil Galleries,
181-183 King's Road, SW3
Tel: 071-351 5353

Georgian Village,
Camden Passage, Islington, N1
Tel: 071-226 1571

Grays,
1-7 Davies Mews, 58 Davies
Street, W1
Tel: 071-629 7034

Hampstead Antique
Emporium,
12 Heath Street, NW3
Tel: 071-794 3297

Kensington Church Street
Antique Centre,
58-60 Kensington Church
Street, W8

London Silver Vaults,
Chancery House, 53-
65 Chancery Lane, WC2
Tel: 071-242 3844

The Mall Antiques Arcade,
359 Upper Street, Islington, N1
Tel: 071-351 5353

The Old Cinema,
160 Chiswick High Road, W4
Tel: 081-995 4166

Avon
Bath Antique Market,
Guinea Lane, Paragon, Bath
Tel: (0225) 422510

Clifton Antiques Market,
26/28 The Mall, Clifton
Tel: (0272) 741627

Great Western Antique Centre,
Bartlett Street, Bath
Tel: (0225) 424243

Beds
Woburn Abbey Antiques
Centre,
Woburn Abbey
Tel: (052 525) 290350

Berks
Loddon Lily Antiques Centre,
1 High Street, Twyford
Tel: (0734) 342161

Bucks
Great Missenden Antique
Arcade,
76 High Street, Gt Missenden
Tel: (024 06) 2819 & 2330

Cambs
Collectors' Market,
Dales Brewery, Gwydir Street
(off Mill Road), Cambridge

Cheshire
Davenham Antique Centre,
461 London Road, Davenham,
Northwich
Tel: (0606) 44350

Cumbria
Cockermouth Antiques
Market,
Main Street, Cockermouth
Tel: (0900) 824346

J W Thornton Antiques,
Supermarket, North Terrace,
Bowness-on-Windermere
Tel: (0229) 869745 (0966) 22930
& 25183

Devon
Barbican Antiques Market,
82-84 Vauxhall Street, Barbican,
Plymouth
Tel: (0752) 266927

New Street Antique Centre,
27 New Street, The Barbican,
Plymouth
Tel: (0752) 661165

Sidmouth Antiques Market,
132 High Street (next to Fords),
Sidmouth
Tel: (03955) 77981

Dorset
Antique Market,
Town Hall/Corn Exchange,
Dorchester
Tel: (0963) 62478

Antique Market,
Digby Hall, Sherborne
Tel: (0258) 840224

Antiques Trade Warehouse,
28 Lorne Park Road, Bournemouth
Tel: (0202) 292944

Barnes House Antiques Centre,
West Row, Wimborne Minster
Tel: (0202) 886275

Essex
Antique Centre,
Doubleday Corner, Coggeshall
Tel: (0376) 562646

Baddow Antiques & Craft Centre,
The Bringy, Church Street, Great
Baddow
Tel: (0245) 76159

Maldon Antiques & Collectors'
Market,
United Reformed Church Hall,
Market Hill, Maldon
Tel: (078 72) 22826

Trinity Antiques Centre,
7 Trinity Street, Colchester
Tel: (0206) 577775

Glos
Antique Centre,
London House, High Street,
Moreton-in-Marsh
Tel: (0608) 51084

Cheltenham Antique Market,
54 Suffolk Road, Cheltenham
Tel: (0242) 529812

Cirencester Antique Market,
Market Place (Antique Forum
Ltd), Cirencester
Tel: 071-240 0428

Gloucester Antique Centre,
1 Severn Road, Gloucester
Tel: (0452) 29716

Tewkesbury Antique Centre,
78 Church Street, Tewkesbury
Tel: (0684) 294091

Hants
Winchester Antique & Craft
Market,
King's Walk, Winchester
Tel: (0962) 862277

Hereford & Worcester
Antiques Centre (Old Curiosity),
11 Towers Buildings, Blackwell
Street, Kidderminster
Tel: (0562) 829000

Leominster Antiques Market,
14 Broad Street, Leominster
Tel: (0568) 2189

Herts
The Herts & Essex Antiques
Centre,
The Maltings, Station Road,
Sawbridgeworth
Tel: (0279) 722044

St Albans Antique Market,
Town Hall, Chequer Street,
St Albans
Tel: (0727) 50427

Kent
The Antiques Centre,
120 London Road, Sevenoaks
Tel: (0732) 452104

Canterbury Weekly Antique
Market,
Sidney Cooper Centre, Canterbury
(No telephone number)

Hythe Antique Centre,
The Old Post Office, 5 High Street,
Hythe
Tel: (0303) 269643

Noah's Ark Antique Centre,
King Street, Sandwich
Tel: (0304) 611144

Rochester Antiques & Flea
Market, Rochester Market,
Corporation Street, Rochester
Tel: 071-262 5003

Sandgate Antiques Centre,
61-63 Sandgate High Street,
Sandgate (Nr Folkestone)
Tel: (0303) 48987

Lancs
The A & D Centre
56 Garstang Road, Preston
Tel: (0772) 882078

Castle Antiques,
Moore Lane, Clitheroe
Tel: (0254) 35820

Levenshulme Antique Village,
Levenshulme, Old Town Hall, 965
Stockport Road, Levenshulme
Tel: 061-224 2410

North Western Antique Centre,
New Preston Mill (Horrockses
Yard), New Hall Lane, Preston
Tel: (0772) 794498

Preston Antique Centre,
The Mill, New Hall Lane, Preston
Tel: (0772) 794498

Leics
Oxford Street Antique Centre Ltd,
16-26 Oxford Street, Leicester
Tel: (0533) 553006

Lincs
Lincolnshire Antiques Centre,
Bridge Street, Horncastle
Tel: (06582) 7794

Norfolk
Antique & Collectors Centre,
St Michael at Plea, Bank Plain,
Norwich
Tel: (0603) 619129
Open 9.30-5pm

Coltishall Antiques Centre,
High Street, Coltishall
Tel: (0603) 738306

Fakenham Antique Centre,
Old Congregational Chapel,
14 Norwich Road, Fakenham
Tel: (0328) 862941 or home (0263)
860543

Norwich Antique & Collectors'
Centre,
Quayside, Fye Bridge, Norwich
Tel: (0603) 612582

The Old Granary Antique &
Collectors' Centre,
King Staithe Lane, off Queen's
Street, King's Lynn
Tel: (0553) 5509

Northants
Finedon Antiques Centre,
3 Church Street, Finedon
Tel: (0933) 681260

The Village Antique Market,
62 High Street, Weedon
Tel: (0327) 42015

Northumberland
Colmans of Hexham (Saleroom &
Antique Fair),
15 St Mary's Chare, Hexham
Tel: (0434) 603812/605522

Notts
Nottingham Antique Centre,
British Rail Goods Yard, London
Road, Nottingham
Tel: (0602) 54504/55548

Top Hat Antiques Centre,
66-72 Derby Road, Nottingham
Tel: (0602) 419143

Oxon
The Antique Centre,
Laurel House, Bull Ring, Market
Place, Deddington
Tel: (0869) 38968

Shropshire
Ironbridge Antique Centre,
Dale End, Ironbridge
Tel: (095 245) 3784

Shrewsbury Antique Market,
Frankwell Quay Warehouse
(Vintagevale Ltd), Shrewsbury
Tel: (0743) 50916

Stretton Antiques Market,
Sandford Avenue, Church Stretton
Tel: (06945) 402
also: (0694) 723718

Somerset
Crewkerne Antiques Centre,
42 East Street, Crewkerne
Tel: (0460) 76755

Taunton Antiques Centre,
27/29 Silver Street, Taunton
Tel: (0823) 289327

Staffs

The Antique Centre,
7A The Digbeth Arcade, Walsall
Tel: (0922) 725163/5

Barclay House,
Howard Place, Shelton,
Stoke-on-Trent
Tel: (0782) 657674/274747

Rugeley Antique Centre,
161/3 Main Road, Rugeley
Tel: (088 95) 77166

Suffolk

Old Town Hall Antique Centre,
High Street, Needham Market
Tel: (0449) 720773

Waveney Antique Centre,
The Old School, Peddars Lane,
Beccles
Tel: (0502) 716147

Surrey

Antique Centre,
22 Haydon Place, Corner of Martyr
Road, Guildford
Tel: (0483) 67817

Dukes Yard Antique Market,
1A Duke Street, Richmond-upon-
Thames
Tel: 081-332 1051

Farnham Antique Centre,
27 South Street, Farnham
Tel: (0252) 724475

Maltings Market,
Bridge Square, Farnham
Tel: (0252) 726234

The Old Smithy Antique Centre,
7 High Street, Merstham
Tel: (0737) 642306

Victoria & Edward Antiques,
61 West Street, Dorking
Tel: (0306) 889645

Sussex – East

Antique Market,
Leaf Hall, Seaside, Eastbourne
Tel: (0323) 27530

Bexhill Antiques Centre,
Old Town, Bexhill
Tel: (0424) 210182

Chateaubriand Antique Centre,
High Street, Burwash
Tel: (0435) 882535

The Collectors Market,
The Enterprise Centre (next to
Railway Station), Station Parade,
Eastbourne
Tel: (0323) 32690
(Open: Tues-Sat 9.30-5pm)

Heathfield Antiques Centre,
Heathfield Market, Heathfield
Tel: (042 482) 387

Lewes Antiques Centre,
20 Cliffe High Street, Lewes
Tel: (0273) 476148

Newhaven Flea Market,
28 South Way, Newhaven
Tel: (0273) 517207

St Leonards Antique Dealers,
Norman Road, St Leonards-on-Sea
Tel: (0424) 444592

Seaford's 'Barn Collectors'
Market',
The Barn, Church Lane, Seaford
Tel: (0323) 890010

Sussex – West

Mamie's Antiques Market,
5 River Road, Arundel
Tel: (0903) 882012

Midhurst Antiques Market,
Knockhundred Row, Midhurst
Tel: (073 081) 4231

Mostyns Antiques Centre,
64 Brighton Road, Lancing
Tel: (0903) 752961

Petworth Antiques Market,
East Street, Petworth
Tel: (0798) 42073

Robert Warner & Son Ltd,
South Farm Road, Worthing
Tel: (0903) 32710

Treasure House Antiques Market,
Rear of High Street, in Crown
Yard, Arundel
Tel: (0903) 883101

Warwickshire

Bidford-on-Avon Antiques Centre,
High Street, Bidford-on-Avon
Tel: (0789) 773680

Rugby Antiques Centre,
22 Railway Terrace, Rugby
Tel: (0788) 62837

Vintage Antique Market,
36 Market Place, Warwick
Tel: (0926) 491527

Warwick Antique Centre,
16-18 High Street, Warwick
Tel: (0962) 492482

West Midlands

The City of Birmingham Antique
Market,
St Martins Market, Edgbaston
Street, Birmingham
Tel: 071-624 3214

Wiltshire

Salisbury Antique & Collectors
Market,
37 Catherine Street, Salisbury
(open 9-6pm)
Tel: (0722) 26033

Yorks – North

Grove Collectors' Centre,
Grove Road, Harrogate
Tel: (0423) 561680

Harrogate Antique Centre,
The Ginnel, Corn Exchange
Building, Harrogate
Tel: (0423) 508857

West Park Antiques Pavilion,
20 West Park, Harrogate
Tel: (0423) 561758

York Antique Centre,
2 Lendal, York
Tel: (0904) 641445

Yorks – South

Treasure House Antiques and
Antique Centre,
4-10 Swan Street, Bawtry
Tel: (0302) 710621

Yorks – West

Halifax Antique Centre,
Queen's Road/Gibbet Street,
Halifax
Tel: (0422) 366657

N. Ireland

London Street Antique Market,
4 London Street, Londonderry
Tel: (0504) 371551

Scotland

Bath Street Antique Centre,
203 Bath Street, Glasgow
Tel: 041-248 4229

The Victorian Village,
53 & 57 West Regent Street,
Glasgow
Tel: 041-332 0808

Wales

Cardiff Antique Centre,
69-71 St Mary Street, Cardiff
Tel: (0222) 230970 or 700834
(Open Thurs & Sat)

DIRECTORY OF AUCTIONEERS

This directory is by no means complete. Any auctioneer who holds frequent sales should contact us for inclusion in the next Edition. Entries must be received by April 1992. There is, of course, no charge for this listing. Entries will be repeated in subsequent editions unless we are requested otherwise.

London

Academy Auctioneers & Valuers,
Northcote House,
Northcote Avenue, Ealing, W5
Tel: 081-579 7466

Bonhams, Montpelier Galleries,
Montpelier Street, Knightsbridge,
SW7
Tel: 071-584 9161

Bonhams, Lots Road, Chelsea,
SW10
Tel: 071-351 7111

Christie Manson & Woods Ltd,
8 King Street, St James's, SW1
Tel: 071-839 9060

Christie's Robson Lowe,
47 Duke Street, London, SW1
Tel: 071-839 4034/5

Christie's South Kensington Ltd,
85 Old Brompton Road, SW7
Tel: 071-581 7611

City Forum Auctioneers,
108 Belsize Avenue, NW3
Tel: 071-433 1305

Forrest & Co,
79-85 Cobbold Road, Leytonstone,
E11
Tel: 081-534 2931

Stanley Gibbons Auctions Ltd,
399 Strand, WC2
Tel: 071-836 8444

Glendining's,
101 New Bond Street, W1
Tel: 071-493 2445

Hamptons Fine Art Auctioneers
and Valuers,
6 Arlington Street, London, SW1
Tel: 071-493 8222

Harmers of London Stamp
Auctioneers Ltd,
91 New Bond Street, W1
Tel: 071-629 0218

Hornsey Auctions Ltd,
54/56 High Street, Hornsey, N8
Tel: 081-340 5334

Jackson-Stops & Staff,
14 Curzon Street, W1
Tel: 071-499 6291

Lewisham Auction Rooms,
165 Lee High Road, SE13
Tel: 081-852 3145

Lots Road Chelsea Auction
Galleries,
71 Lots Road, Worlds End,
Chelsea, SW10
Tel: 071-351 7771

MacGregor Nash & Co,
Lodge House, 9-17 Lodge Lane,
North Finchley, N12 8JH
Tel: 081-445 9000

Thomas Moore,
217-219 Greenwich High Road,
SE10
Tel: 081-858 7848

Onslow's,
Metrostore, Townmead Road, SW6
Tel: 071-793 0240

Palmers,
New Octagon House, 17-31
Gibbons Road, London, E15
Tel: 081-555 0517

Phillips,
Blenstock House, 7 Blenheim
Street, New Bond Street, W1
Tel: 071-629 6602

Phillips,
10 Salem Road, London W2 4BU
Tel: 071-229 9090

Rippon Boswell & Co,
The Arcade, Sth Kensington
Station, SW7
Tel: 071-589 4242

Rosebery's Fine Art Ltd,
Old Railway Booking Hall,
Crystal Palace, Station Road,
SE19 2AT
Tel: 081-778 4024

Michael Shortall,
22a Jay Mews, Knightsbridge,
London, SW7
Tel: (0831) 308666

Sotheby's,
34-35 New Bond Street, W1
Tel: 071-493 8080

Southgate Antique Auction
Rooms,
Munro House, Munro Drive, Cline
Road, New Southgate, N11
Tel: 081-886 7888

Greater London

Chancellors,
Kingston upon Thames
Tel: 081-541 4139

Croydon Auctions Rooms
(Rosan & Co)
144-150 London Road, Croydon
Tel: 081-688 1123/4/5

Parkins,
18 Malden Road, Cheam, Surrey
Tel: 081-644 6633 & 6127

Avon

Alder King, Black Horse Agencies,
The Old Malthouse, Comfortable
Place, Upper Bristol Road, Bath
Tel: (0225) 447933

Aldridges, Bath,
The Auction Galleries, 130-132
Walcot Street, Bath
Tel: (0225) 462830 & 462839

Allen & Harris,
Bristol Auction Rooms, St. Johns
Place, Apsley Road, Clifton, Bristol
Tel: (0272) 737201

Clevedon Salerooms,
Herbert Road, Clevedon
Tel: (0272) 876699

Phillips Auction Rooms of Bath,
1 Old King Street, Bath
Tel: (0225) 310609 & 319709

Phillips Fine Art Auctioneers,
71 Oakfield Road, Clifton, Bristol
Tel: (0272) 734052

Taviner's Ltd,
Prewett Street, Redcliffe, Bristol
Tel: (0272) 265996

Woodspring Auction Rooms,
Churchill Road, Weston-super-
Mare
Tel: (0934) 628419

Bedfordshire
Wilson Peacock,
The Auction Centre, 26 Newnham
Street, Bedford
Tel: (0234) 266366

Berkshire
Dreweatt Neate,
Donnington Priory, Donnington,
Newbury
Tel: (0635) 31234

R. Elliott,
Chancellors, 32 High Street, Ascot
Tel: (0344) 872588

Holloway's,
12 High Street, Streatley, Reading
Tel: (0491) 872318

Martin & Pole,
12 Milton Street, Wokingham
Tel: (0734) 790460

Thimbleby & Shorland,
31 Great Knollys Street, Reading
Tel: (0734) 508611

Duncan Vincent Fine Art &
Chattel Auctioneers,
105 London Street, Reading
Tel: (0734) 594748

Buckinghamshire
Hamptons,
10 Burkes Parade, Beaconsfield
Tel: (0494) 672969

Nationwide Anglia,
Amersham Auction Rooms,
125 Station Road, Amersham
Tel: (0494) 729292

Geo Wigley & Sons,
Winslow Sale Room, Market
Square, Winslow
Tel: (029 671) 2717

Cambridgeshire
Cheffins Grain & Comins,
2 Clifton Road, Cambridge
Tel: (0223) 358721/213343

Phillips Auctioneers,
Station Road, St Ives
Tel: (0480) 68144

Grounds & Co
2 Nene Quay, Wisbech
Tel: (0945) 585041

Hammond & Co,
Cambridge Place, off Hills Road,
Cambridge
Tel: (0223) 356067

Maxey & Son,
1-3 South Brink, Wisbech
Tel: (0945) 584609

Cheshire
Andrew, Hilditch & Son,
Hanover House, 1A The Square,
Sandbach
Tel: (0270) 762048/767246

Robert I Heyes,
Hatton Buildings, Lightfoot
Street, Hoole, Chester
Tel: (0244) 328941

Highams Auctions,
Waterloo House, Waterloo Road,
Stalybridge
Tel: 061-303 2924/061-303 1091
also at:
Southgate House, Southgate
Street, Rhodes Bank, Oldham
Tel: 061-626 1021

Frank R Marshall & Co,
Marshall House, Church Hill,
Knutsford
Tel: (0565) 653284

Phillips North West,
New House, 150 Christleton Road,
Chester
Tel: (0244) 313936

Phillips Fine Art Auctioneers,
Trinity House, 114 Northenden
Road, Sale, Manchester
Tel: 061-962 9237

Sotheby's
Booth Mansion, 28-30 Watergate
Street, Chester
Tel: (0244) 315531

Henry Spencer Inc. Peter Wilson,
Victoria Gallery, Market Street,
Nantwich
Tel: (0270) 623878

Wright Manley,
Beeston Sales Centre, 63 High
Street, Tarporley
Tel: (0829) 260318

Cleveland
Lithgow Sons & Partners,
The Auction Houses, Station Road,
Stokesley, Middlesbrough
Tel: (0642) 710158 & 710326

Cornwall
Lambrays, incorporating
R J Hamm ASVA,
Polmorla Walk, The Platt,
Wadebridge
Tel: (020 881) 3593

W H Lane & Son,
St Mary's Auction Rooms,
65 Morrab Road, Penzance
Tel: (0736) 61447

David Lay,
Penzance Auction House,
Alverton, Penzance
Tel: (0736) 61414

Phillips Cornwall,
Cornubia Hall, Par
Tel: (072 681) 4047

Pooley and Rogers,
Regent Auction Rooms, Abbey
Street, Penzance
Tel: (0736) 68814

Jeffery's
5 Fore Street, Lostwithiel
Tel: (0208) 872245

Cumbria
Cumbria Auction Rooms,
12 Lowther Street, Carlisle
Tel: (0228) 25259

Mitchells,
Fairfield House, Cockermouth
Tel: (0900) 822016

Alfred Mossops & Co,
Loughrigg Villa, Kelsick Road,
Ambleside
Tel: (05394) 33015

James Thompson,
64 Main Street, Kirkby Lonsdale
Tel: (05242) 71555

Thomson, Roddick & Laurie,
24 Lowther Street, Carlisle
Tel: (0228) 28939 & 39636

Derbyshire
Noel Wheatcroft & Son,
The Matlock Auction Gallery,
39 Dale Road, Matlock
Tel: (0629) 584591

Devon
Bearnes,
Avenue Road, Torquay
Tel: (0803) 296277

Bonhams West Country,
Devon Fine Art Auction House,
Dowell Street, Honiton
Tel: (0404) 41872/3137

Michael J Bowman,
6 Haccombe House, Nr Netherton,
Newton Abbot
Tel: (0626) 872890

Eric Distin Chartered Surveyors,
2 Bretonside, Plymouth
Tel: (0752) 663046

Peter J Eley,
Western House, 98-100 High
Street, Sidmouth
Tel: (0395) 513006

Robin A Fenner & Co
Fine Art & Antique Auctioneers,
The Stannary Gallery, Drake
Road, Tavistock
Tel: (0822) 617799/617800

Kingsbridge Auction Sales,
85 Fore Street, Kingsbridge
Tel: (0548) 856829

Michael Newman,
Kinterbury House, St Andrew's
Cross, Plymouth
Tel: (0752) 669298

Phillips,
Alphin Brook Road, Alphington,
Exeter
Tel: (0392) 439025
and
Armada Street, North Hill,
Plymouth
Tel: (0752) 673504

Potbury's,
High Street, Sidmouth
Tel: (0395) 515555

Rendells,
Stone Park, Ashburton
Tel: (0364) 53017

G S Shobrook & Co,
20 Western Approach, Plymouth
Tel: (0752) 663341

John Smale & Co,
11 High Street, Barnstaple
Tel: (0271) 42000/42916

Spencer Thomas & Woolland,
Church Street Auction Rooms,
Exmouth
Tel: (0395) 267403

Taylors,
Honiton Galleries, 205 High
Street, Honiton
Tel: (0404) 42404

Ward & Chowen,
1 Church Lane, Tavistock
Tel: (0822) 612458

Whitton & Laing,
32 Okehampton Street, Exeter
Tel: (0392) 52621

Dorset
Cottees, Bullock & Lees,
The Market, East Street,
Wareham
Tel: (0929) 554915/552826

Hy Duke & Son,
Fine Art Salerooms, Weymouth
Ave, Dorchester
Tel: (0305) 265080
also at:
The Weymouth Saleroom,
St Nicholas Street, Weymouth
Tel: (0305) 783488

Garnet Langton Auctions,
Burlington Arcade, Bournemouth
Tel: (0202) 552352

House & Son,
Lansdowne House, Christchurch
Road, Bournemouth
Tel: (0202) 556232

Southern Counties Auctioneers,
Shaftesbury Livestock Market,
Christy's Lane, Shaftesbury
Tel: (0747) 51735

William Morey & Sons,
The Saleroom, St Michaels Lane,
Bridport
Tel: (0308) 22078

Riddetts of Bournemouth,
26 Richmond Hill, Bournemouth
Square, Bournemouth
Tel: (0202) 555686

County Durham
Denis Edkins,
Auckland Auction Room,
58 Kingsway, Bishop Auckland
Tel: (0388) 603095

Thomas Watson & Son,
Northumberland Street,
Darlington
Tel: (0325) 462559/463485

Wingate Auction Co,
Station Lane, Station Town,
Wingate
Tel: (0429) 837245

Essex
Abridge Auction Rooms,
Market Place, Abridge
Tel: (099281) 2107/3113

Black Horse Agencies,
Ambrose, 149 High Road,
Loughton
Tel: 081-502 3951

William H Brown,
The Auction Rooms, 11-14 East
Hill, Colchester
Tel: (0206) 868070

Cooper Hirst,
The Granary Saleroom, Victoria
Road, Chelmsford
Tel: (0245) 258141/260535

Saffron Walden Saleroom,
1 Market Street, Saffron Walden
Tel: (0799) 513281

Grays Auction Rooms,
Ye Old Bake House, Alfred Street,
Grays
Tel: (0375) 381181

Hamptons Fine Art/J. M. Welch &
Son,
The Old Town Hall, Great
Dunmow
Tel: (0371) 873014

John Stacey & Sons,
Leigh Auction Rooms, 86-90 Pall
Mall, Leigh-on-Sea
Tel: (0702) 77051

Gloucestershire
Bruton, Knowles & Co,
111 Eastgate Street, Gloucester
Tel: (0452) 521267

Fraser Glennie & Partners,
The Old Rectory, Siddington,
Nr Cirencester
Tel: (0285) 659677

Hobbs & Chambers,
Market Place, Cirencester
Tel: (0285) 654736
also at:
15 Royal Crescent, Cheltenham
Tel: (0242) 513722

Ken Lawson t/as Specialised
Postcard Auctions,
25 Gloucester Street, Cirencester
Tel: (0285) 659057

Mallams,
26 Grosvenor Street, Cheltenham
Tel: (0242) 235712

Moore, Allen & Innocent,
33 Castle Street, Cirencester
Tel: (0285) 651831

Nationwide, Wotton-under-Edge,
Wotton Auction Rooms,
Tabernacle Road, Wotton-under-
Edge
Tel: (0453) 844733

Hampshire
Andover Saleroom,
41A London Street, Andover
Tel: (0264) 364820

Fox & Sons,
5 & 7 Salisbury Street,
Fordingbridge
Tel: (0425) 652121

GA Fine Art & Chattels,
The Romsey Auction Rooms,
86 The Hundred, Romsey
Tel: (0794) 513331

Hants & Berks Auctions,
82, 84 Sarum Hill, Basingstoke
Tel: (0256) 840707
also at:
Heckfield Village Hall, Heckfield,
Berks

Jacobs & Hunt,
Lavant Street, Petersfield
Tel: (0730) 62744/5

May & Son,
18 Bridge Street, Andover
Tel: (0264) 323417

D M Nesbit & Co,
7 Clarendon Road, Southsea
Tel: (0705) 864321

Nationwide Lymington,
New Forest Auction Rooms,
Emsworth Road, Lymington
Tel: (0590) 677225

Phillips Fine Art Auctioneers,
54 Southampton Road, Ringwood
Tel: (04254) 473333
also at:
The Red House, Hyde Street,
Winchester
Tel: (0962) 862515

Hereford & Worcester
Carless & Co,
58 Lowesmoor, Worcester
Tel: (0905) 612449

Andrew Grant,
St Mark's House, St Mark's Close,
Worcester
Tel: (0905) 357547

Griffiths & Co,
57 Foregate Street, Worcester
Tel: (0905) 26464

Hamptons,
69 Church Street, Malvern
Tel: (0684) 892314

Philip Laney & Jolly,
12a Worcester Road, Gt Malvern
Tel: (0684) 892322

Phipps & Pritchard,
Bank Buildings, Kidderminster
Tel: (0562) 822244/6 & 822187

Russell, Baldwin & Bright,
Fine Art Saleroom, Ryelands
Road, Leominster
Tel: (0568) 611166

Nationwide Broadway,
41-43 High Street, Broadway
Tel: (0386) 852456

Village Auctions,
Sycthampton Community Centre,
Ombersley
Tel: (0905) 421007

Nigel Ward & Morris,
Stuart House, 18 Gloucester Road,
Ross-on-Wye, Herefordshire
Tel: (0989) 768320

Richard Williams,
2 High Street, Pershore
Tel: (0386) 554031

Hertfordshire
Bayles,
Childs Farm, Cottered,
Buntingford, Herts
Tel: (076 381) 256

Brown & Merry,
41 High Street, Tring
Tel: (044 282) 6446

Norris & Duvall,
106 The Fore Street, Hertford
Tel: (0992) 582249

Pamela & Barry Auctions,
The Village Hall, High Street,
Sandridge, St Albans
Tel: (0727) 861180

Sworders,
Northgate End Salerooms,
Bishops Stortford
Tel: (0279) 651388

Humberside North
Gilbert Baitson, FSVA,
The Edwardian Auction Galleries,
194 Anlaby Road, Hull
Tel: (0482) 223355/645241/865831

H Evans & Sons,
1 Parliament Street, Hull
Tel: (0482) 23033

Humberside South
Dickinson, Davy & Markham,
10 Wrawby Street, Brigg
Tel: (0652) 53666

Isle of Man
Chrystals Auctions,
Majestic Hotel, Onchan
Tel: (0624) 673986

Isle of Wight
Watson Bull & Porter,
Nationwide,
Isle of Wight Auction Rooms,
79 Regent Street, Shanklin
Tel: (0983) 863 441

Phillips Fine Art Auctioneers,
Cross Street Salerooms, Newport
Tel: (0983) 822031

Ways Auction House,
Garfield Road, Ryde
Tel: (0983) 62255

Kent
Albert Andrews Auctions & Sales,
Maiden Lane, Crayford, Dartford
Tel: (0322) 528868

Black Horse Agencies,
Geering & Colyer, Highgate,
Hawkhurst
Tel: (0580) 753463

Bracketts,
27-29 High Street, Tunbridge
Wells
Tel: (0892) 33733

Castle Antiques Centre,
1 London Road (next to Post
Office), Westerham
Tel: (0959) 62492

Lambert & Foster,
102 High Street, Tenterden
Tel: (05806) 2083/3233

Canterbury Auction Galleries,
40 Station Road West, Canterbury
Tel: (0227) 763337

Stewart Gore,
100-102 Northdown Road,
Margate
Tel: (0843) 221528/9

Edwin Hall,
Valley Antiques,
Lyminge, Folkestone, Kent
Tel: (0303) 862134

Hobbs Parker,
Romney House, Ashford Market,
Elwick Road, Ashford
Tel: (0233) 622222

Ibbett Mosely,
125 High Street, Sevenoaks
Tel: (0732) 452246

Kent Sales,
'Giffords', Holmesdale Road, South
Darenth
Tel: (0322) 864919

Lawrence Butler & Co, (inc. F W
Butler & Co),
Fine Art Salerooms, Butler House,
86 High Street, Hythe
Tel: (0303) 266022/3

B J Norris,
'The Quest', West Street,
Harrietsham, Nr Maidstone
Tel: (0622) 859515

Phillips,
11 Bayle Parade, Folkestone
Tel: (0303) 45555

Phillips Fine Art Auctioneers,
49 London Road, Sevenoaks
Tel: (0732) 740310

Halifax Property Services,
Fine Art Department, 53 High
Street, Tenterden
Tel: (05806) 3200
also at:
15 Cattle Market, Sandwich
Tel: (0304) 614369

Michael Shortall,
Tunbridge Wells Auction Centre,
Southborough Hall, Western
Road, Southborough
Tel: (0892) 514100

Walter & Randall,
7-13 New Road, Chatham
Tel: (0634) 841233

Peter S Williams, FSVA,
Orchard End, Sutton Valence,
Maidstone
Tel: (0622) 842350

Lancashire
Artingstall & Hind,
29 Cobden Street, Pendleton,
Salford
Tel: 061-736 5682

Capes Dunn & Co,
The Auction Galleries, 38 Charles
Street, Manchester
Tel: 061-273 6060/1911

Entwistle Green,
The Galleries, Kingsway, Ansdell,
Lytham St Annes
Tel: (0253) 735442

Robt. Fairhurst & Son,
39 Mawdsley Street, Bolton
Tel: (0204) 28452/28453

Highams Auctions,
Southgate House, Southgate
Street, Rhodes Bank, Oldham
Tel: 061-626 1021/061-665 1881/
061-624 8580
also at:
Onward Buildings,
207 Deansgate, Manchester
Tel: 061-834 0068

McKennas, formerly Hothersall,
Forrest, McKenna & Sons,
Bank Salerooms, Harris Court,
Clitheroe
Tel: (0200) 25446/22695

Mills & Radcliffe,
101 Union Street, Oldham
Tel: 061-624 1072

David Palamountain,
1-3 Osborne Grove, Morecambe
Tel: (0524) 423941

J R Parkinson Son & Hamer
Auctions, The Auction Rooms,
Rochdale Road, Bury
Tel: (061 761) 1612/7372

Phillips,
Trinity House, 114 Northenden
Road, Sale, Manchester
Tel: 061-962 9237

Smythe, Son & Walker,
174 Victoria Road West, Cleveleys
Tel: (0253) 852184 & 854084

Warren & Wignall Ltd,
The Mill, Earnshaw Bridge,
Leyland Lane, Leyland
Tel: (0772) 453252/451430

Leicestershire
Churchgate Auctions,
The Churchgate Saleroom,
66 Churchgate, Leicester
Tel: (0533) 621416

Gildings,
64 Roman Way, Market
Harborough
Tel: (0858) 410 414

Noton Salerooms,
76 South Street, Oakham
Tel: (0572) 722681

David Stanley Auctions,
Stordon Grange, Osgathorpe,
Loughborough
Tel: (0530) 222320

William H Brown,
The Warner Auction Rooms,
16/18 Halford Street, Leicester
Tel: (0533) 519777

Lincolnshire
William H Brown,
Fine Art Dept, Westgate Hall,
Westgate, Grantham
Tel: (0476) 68861

Dowse,
89 Mary Street, Scunthorpe
Tel: (0724) 842569/842039

Henry Spencer & Sons,
42 Silver Street, Lincoln
Tel: (0522) 536666

Thomas Mawer & Son,
63 Monks Road, Lincoln
Tel: (0522) 524984

Nationwide, Bourne,
Bourne Auction Rooms, Spalding
Road, Bourne
Tel (0778) 422686

John H Walter,
1 Mint Lane, Lincoln
Tel: (0522) 525454

Merseyside
Hartley & Co,
12 & 14 Moss Street, Liverpool
Tel: 051-263 6472/1865

Kingsley & Co,
3-4 The Quadrant, Hoylake,
Wirral
Tel: 051-632 5821

Outhwaite & Litherland,
Kingsway Galleries, Fontenoy
Street, Liverpool
Tel: 051-236 6561/3

Eldon E Worrall & Co
13-15 Seel Street, Liverpool
Tel: 051-709 2950

Norfolk
Ewings,
Market Place, Reepham, Norwich
Tel: (0603) 870473

Thos Wm Gaze & Son,
10 Market Hill, Diss
Tel: (0379) 651931

Glennie's,
Marchants Court, St Georges
Street, Norwich
Tel: (0603) 633558

Nigel F Hedge,
28B Market Place, North
Walsham
Tel: (0692) 402881

Hilhams,
Baker Street, Gorleston, Great
Yarmouth
Tel: (0493) 662152 & 600700

James Norwich Auctions Ltd,
33 Timberhill, Norwich
Tel: (0603) 624817/625369

G A Key,
8 Market Place, Aylsham
Tel: (0263) 733195

Northamptonshire
Corby & Co,
30-32 Brook Street, Raunds
Tel: (0933) 623722

Heathcote Ball & Co,
Albion Auction Rooms, Old Albion
Brewery, Commercial Street,
Northampton
Tel: (0604) 37263

Lowery's,
24 Bridge Street, Northampton
Tel: (0604) 21561

Nationwide, Moreton Pinkney,
28 High Street, Daventry,
Northants
Tel: (0327) 703917

Southam & Sons,
Corn Exchange, Thrapston,
Kettering
Tel: (08012) 4486

H Wilford Ltd,
Midland Road, Wellingborough
Tel: (0933) 222760 & 222762

Northumberland

Louis Johnson Auctioneers,
Morpeth
Tel: (0670) 513025/55210

Nottinghamshire

Arthur Johnson & Sons Ltd,
The Nottingham Auction Rooms,
The Cattle Market, Meadow Lane,
Nottingham
Tel: (0602) 869128

Neales of Nottingham,
192 Mansfield Road, Nottingham
Tel: (0602) 624141

John Pye & Sons,
Corn Exchange, Cattle Market,
London Road, Nottingham
Tel: (0602) 866261

C B Sheppard & Son,
The Auction Galleries, Chatsworth
Street, Sutton-in-Ashfield
Tel: (0773) 872419

Henry Spencer & Sons Ltd,
20 The Square, Retford
Tel: (0777) 708633

T Vennett-Smith,
11 Nottingham Road, Gotham,
Nottinghamshire
Tel: (0602) 830541

Oxfordshire

Green & Co,
33 Market Place, Wantage
Tel: (02357) 3561/2

Holloways,
49 Parsons Street, Banbury
Tel: (0295) 253197/8

Mallams,
24 St Michael's Street, Oxford
Tel: (0865) 241358

Messengers,
27 Sheep Street, Bicester
Tel: (08692) 52901

Phillips Inc Brooks,
39 Park End Street, Oxford
Tel: (0865) 723524

Simmons & Sons,
32 Bell Street, Henley-on-Thames
Tel: (0491) 571111

Shropshire

Cooper & Green,
3 Barker Street, Shrewsbury
Tel: (0743) 232244

Ludlow Antique Auctions Ltd,
29 Corve Street, Ludlow
Tel: (0584) 875157

McCartneys,
25 Corve Street, Ludlow
Tel: (0584) 872636

Perry & Phillips,
Newmarket Salerooms,
Newmarket Buildings, Listley
Street, Bridgnorth
Tel: (07462) 762248

Somerset

Dores, The Auction Mart,
Vicarage Street, Frome
Tel: (0373) 62257

John Fleming,
4 & 8 Fore Street, Dulverton
Tel: (0398) 23597

Greenslades,
13 Hamet Street, Taunton
Tel: (0823) 277121
also at:
Priory Saleroom, Winchester
Street, Taunton

Gribble Booth & Taylor,
13 The Parade, Minehead
Tel: (0643) 702281

Black Horse Agencies,
Alder King,
25 Market Place, Wells
Tel: (0749) 73002

The London Cigarette Card Co Ltd,
Sutton Road, Somerton
Tel: (0458) 73452

Nationwide Frome,
Frome Auction Rooms, Frome
Market, Standerwick, Nr Frome
Tel: (0373) 831010

Nuttall Richards & Co,
The Square, Axbridge
Tel: (0934) 732969

Wellington Salerooms, Mantle
Street, Wellington
Tel: (0823) 664815

Staffordshire

Hall & Lloyd,
South Street Auction Rooms,
Stafford
Tel: (0785) 58176

Louis Taylor,
Britannia House, 10 Town Road,
Hanley, Stoke-on-Trent
Tel: (0782) 260222

Wintertons,
Lichfield Auction Centre,
Woodend Lane, Fradley, Lichfield
Tel: (0543) 263256

Suffolk

Abbotts (East Anglia) Ltd,
The Hill, Wickham Market,
Woodbridge
Tel: (0728) 746321

Boardman Fine Art,
Station Road Corner, Haverhill
Tel: (0440) 730414

Diamond, Mills & Co,
117 Hamilton Road, Felixstowe
Tel: (0394) 282281

William H Brown,
Ashford House, Saxmundham
Tel: (0728) 603232

Lacy Scott,
Fine Art Department, The Auction
Centre, 10 Risbygate Street, Bury
St Edmunds
Tel: (0284) 763531

Neal Sons & Fletcher,
26 Church Street, Woodbridge
Tel: (0394) 382263

Olivers, William H Brown,
Olivers Rooms, Burkitts Lane,
Sudbury
Tel: (0787) 880305

Phillips,
Dover House, Wilsey Street,
Ipswich
Tel: (0473) 255137

Surrey

Ewbank Fine Art,
Welbeck House, High Street,
Guildford
Tel: (0483) 232134

Clark Gammon,
The Guildford Auction Rooms,
Bedford Road, Guildford
Tel: (0483) 66458

Crows Auction Gallery,
Rear of Dorking Halls, Reigate
Road, Dorking, Surrey
Tel: (0306) 740382

Hamptons, Fine Art Auctioneers
& Valuers,
93 High Street, Godalming
Tel: (04834) 23567

Lawrences,
Norfolk House, 80 High Street,
Bletchingley
Tel: (0883) 743323

Phillips Fine Art Auctioneers,
Millmead, Guildford
Tel: (0483) 504030

Wentworth Auction Galleries,
21 Station Approach, Virginia
Water
Tel: (0344) 843711

P F Windibank,
Dorking Halls, 18-20 Reigate
Road, Dorking
Tel: (0306) 884556

Sussex – East

Ascent Auction Galleries,
11-12 East Ascent, St Leonards-on-
Sea, E Sussex
Tel: (0424) 420275

Burstow & Hewett,
Abbey Auction Galleries and
Granary Salerooms, Battle
Tel: (04246) 2374/2302

Clifford Dann Auction Galleries,
20-21 High Street, Lewes
Tel: (0273) 480111

Fryers Auction Galleries,
Terminus Road, Bexhill-on-Sea
Tel: (0424) 212994

Gorringes Auction Galleries,
15 North Street, Lewes
Tel: (0273) 472503

Graves, Son & Pilcher, Fine Arts,
71 Church Road, Hove
Tel: (0273) 735266

Hove Auction Galleries,
115 Church Road, Hove
Tel: (0273) 736207

Raymond P Inman,
Auction Galleries, 35 & 40 Temple
Street, Brighton
Tel: (0273) 774777

Lewes Auction Rooms (Julian
Dawson),
56 High Street, Lewes
Tel: (0273) 478221

Rye Auction Galleries,
Rock Channel, Rye
Tel: (0797) 222124

Michael Shortall,
120 Marina, St Leonards-on-Sea
Tel: (0424) 434854

Wallis & Wallis,
West Street Auction Galleries,
Lewes
Tel: (0273) 480208

Watsons,
Heathfield Furniture Salerooms,
The Market, Burwash Road,
Heathfield
Tel: (0435) 862132

Sussex – West

Bannister & Wellers,
59 Perrymount Road, Haywards
Heath
Tel: (0444) 412402

Peter Cheney,
Western Road Auction Rooms,
Western Road, Littlehampton
Tel: (0903) 722264 & 713418

Denham's,
Horsham Auction Galleries,
Warnham, Horsham
Tel: (0403) 53837/55699

R H Ellis & Sons,
44-46 High Street, Worthing
Tel: (0903) 38999

Nationwide Midhurst,
Midhurst Auction Rooms, Bepton
Road, Midhurst
Tel: (073081) 2456

Phillips Fine Art Auctioneers,
Baffins Hall, Baffins Lane,
Chichester
Tel: (0243) 787548

Sotheby's in Sussex,
Summers Place, Billingshurst
Tel: (0403) 783933

Stride & Son,
Southdown House, St John's
Street, Chichester
Tel: (0243) 780207

Sussex Auction Galleries,
59 Perrymount Road, Haywards
Heath
Tel: (0444) 414935

Tyne & Wear

Anderson & Garland,
The Fine Art Sale Rooms,
Marlborough House, Marlborough
Crescent, Newcastle-upon-Tyne
Tel: 091-232 6278

Boldon Auction Galleries,
24a Front Street, East Boldon
Tel: 091-537 2630

Thomas N Miller,
18-22 Gallowgate, Newcastle-
upon-Tyne
Tel: 091-232 5617

Sneddons,
Sunderland Auction Rooms,
30 Villiers Street, Sunderland
Tel: 091-514 5931

Warwickshire

Bigwood Auctioneers Ltd,
The Old School, Tiddington,
Stratford-upon-Avon
Tel: (0789) 269415

John Briggs & Calder,
133 Long Street, Atherstone
Tel: (0827) 718911

Locke & England,
18 Guy Street, Leamington Spa
Tel: (0926) 427988

West Midlands

Biddle & Webb,
Icknield Square, Ladywood
Middleway, Birmingham
Tel: 021-455 8042

Cariss Residential,
20-22 High Street, Kings Heath,
Birmingham 14
Tel: 021-444 0088

Ronald E Clare,
Clare's Auction Rooms, 70 Park
Street, Birmingham
Tel: 021-643 0226

Frank H Fellows & Sons,
Augusta House, 19 Augusta
Street, Hockley, Birmingham
Tel: 021-212 2131

Giles Haywood,
The Auction House, St Johns
Road, Stourbridge
Tel: (0384) 370891

James & Lister Lea,
42 Bull Street, Birmingham
Tel: 021-200 1100

Phillips,
The Old House, Station Road,
Knowle, Solihull
Tel: (0564) 776151

K Stuart Swash, FSVA,
Stamford House, 2 Waterloo Road,
Wolverhampton
Tel: (0902) 710626

Walker Barnett & Hill,
3 Waterloo Road, Wolverhampton
Tel: (0902) 773531

Walton & Hipkiss,
111 Worcester Road, Hagley
Tel: (0562) 885555

Weller & Dufty Ltd,
141 Bromsgrove Street,
Birmingham
Tel: 021-692 1414

Wiltshire

Allen & Harris,
Saleroom & Auctioneers Dept,
The Planks (off The Square), Old
Town, Swindon
Tel: (0793) 615915

Hamptons,
20 High Street, Marlborough
Tel: (0672) 513471

Woolley & Wallis,
The Castle Auction Mart, Castle
Street, Salisbury
Tel: (0722) 411422

Yorkshire – East

Dee & Atkinson,
The Exchange, Driffield
Tel: (0377) 43151

Yorkshire – North

Boulton & Cooper (Fine Arts),
Forsyth House, Market Place,
Malton
Tel: (0653) 692151

H C Chapman & Son,
The Auction Mart, North Street,
Scarborough
Tel: (0723) 372424

M W Darwin & Sons,
The Dales Furniture Hall, Bedale
Tel: (0677) 422846

GA Fine Art & Chattels,
Royal Auction Rooms, Queen
Street, Scarborough
Tel: (0723) 353581

Hutchinson Scott,
The Grange, Marton-Le-Moor,
Ripon
Tel: (0423) 324264

Morphets of Harrogate,
4-6 Albert Street, Harrogate
Tel: (0423) 530030

Nationwide/Wells Cundall,
15 Market Place, Malton
Tel: (0653) 695581

Stephenson & Son,
Livestock Centre, Murton, York
Tel: (0904) 489731

Nationwide Fine Arts,
27 Flowergate, Whitby
Tel: (0947) 603433

Geoffrey Summersgill, ASVA,
8 Front Street, Acomb, York
Tel: (0904) 791131

Tennants,
Harmby Road, Leyburn
Tel: (0969) 23780

D Wombell & Son,
Bell Hall, Escrick, York
Tel: (090 487) 531

Yorkshire – South

Eadon Lockwood & Riddle,
Western Saleroom, Crookes,
Sheffield
Tel: (0742) 686294

William H Brown,
10 Regent Street, Barnsley
Tel: (0226) 733456

William H Brown,
Stanilands Auction Room,
28 Nether Hall Road, Doncaster
Tel: (0302) 367766

Roland Orchard,
Fine Art & Chattels Valuers &
Auctioneers, 55 Copley Road,
Doncaster (Call Monday)
Tel: (0302) 340499

Henry Spencer & Sons Ltd,
1 St James Row, Sheffield
Tel: (0742) 728728

Wilkinson & Beighton,
Woodhouse Green, Thurcroft,
Nr Rotherham
Tel: (0709) 700005

Yorkshire – West

Audsley's Auctions (C R Kemp
BSc)
11 Morris Lane, Kirkstall, Leeds 5
Tel: (0532) 758787

de Rome,
12 New John Street, Westgate,
Bradford
Tel: (0274) 734116

Eddisons,
Auction Rooms, 4-6 High Street,
Huddersfield
Tel: (0484) 533151

Andrew Hartley,
Victoria Hall Salerooms, Little
Lane, Ilkley
Tel: (0943) 816363

Malcolms No. 1 Auctioneers &
Valuers,
(7) Finkle Hill, Sherburn-in-
Elmet, Nr Leeds
Tel: (0977) 684971/685334
(24 hours)

Nationwide (Whitby),
Whitby Auction Rooms, West End
Saleroom, The Paddock, Whitby
Tel: (0947) 603433

New Bond Street Auctions,
76 Harry Street, Batley Car,
Dewsbury
Tel: (0924) 469381

Phillips,
17a East Parade, Leeds
Tel: (0532) 448011

John H Raby & Son,
The Sale Rooms, 21 St Mary's
Road, Manningham, Bradford
Tel: (0274) 491121

Windle & Co,
The Four Ashes, 535 Great Horton
Road, Bradford
Tel: (0274) 572998

Channel Islands

Langlois Auctioneers & Valuers,
Westway Chambers, 39 Don
Street, St Helier, Jersey
Tel: (0534) 22441

Le Gallais Auctions Ltd,
36 Hillgrove Street, St Helier,
Jersey
Tel: (0534) 66689

Martel, Maides & Le Pelley,
50 High Street, St Peter Port,
Guernsey
Tel: (0481) 21203

Ireland

James Adam & Sons,
26 St Stephens Green, Dublin 2
Tel: 010 3531 760261

Northern Ireland

Dunmurry Auctions Ltd,
Barbour Gardens, Dunmurry,
Belfast
Tel: (0232) 602815/6

Morgans Auctions Ltd,
Duncrue Crescent, Duncrue Road,
Belfast
Tel: (0232) 771552

Temple Auctions Limited,
133 Carryduff Road, Temple,
Lisburn, Co Antrim
Tel: (0846) 638777

Scotland

John Anderson,
33 Cross Street, Fraserburgh,
Aberdeenshire
Tel: (0346) 28878

Christie's Scotland,
164-166 Bath Street, Glasgow
Tel: (041 332) 8134

B L Fenton & Sons,
Forebank Auction Halls,
84 Victoria Road, Dundee
Tel: (0382) 26227

Frasers (Auctioneers),
28-30 Church Street, Inverness
Tel: (0463) 232395

J & J Howe,
24 Commercial Street, Alyth,
Perthshire
Tel: (08283) 2594

Loves Auction Rooms,
The Auction Galleries, 52-
54 Canal Street, Perth
Tel: (0738) 33337

Robert McTear & Co (Auctioneers)
Ltd,
Royal Exchange Salerooms,
6 North Court, St. Vincent Place,
Glasgow
Tel: 041-221 4456

John Milne,
9 North Silver Street, Aberdeen
Tel: (0224) 639336

Robert Paterson & Son,
8 Orchard Street, Paisley,
Renfrewshire
Tel: (041 889) 2435

Phillips in Scotland,
207 Bath Street, Glasgow
Tel: 041-221 8377
also at;
65 George Street, Edinburgh
Tel: 031-225 2266

L S Smellie & Sons Ltd,
Within the Furniture Market,
Lower Auchingramont Road,
Hamilton
Tel: (0698) 282007

West Perthshire Auctions,
Dundas Street, Cowie, Perthshire

Wales

Dodds Property World,
Victoria Auction Galleries,
9 Chester Street, Mold, Clwyd
Tel: (0352) 752552

Graham H Evans, FRICS,
FRVA,
Auction Sales Centre, The
Market Place, Kilgetty, Dyfed
Tel: (0834) 812793 & 811151

Spencer's John Francis,
Curiosity Salerooms, 19 King
Street, Carmarthen
Tel: (0267) 233456

King Thomas,
Lloyd Jones & Company,
36 High Street, Lampeter,
Dyfed
Tel: (0570) 422550

Morgan Evans & Co Ltd,
30 Church Street, Llangefni,
Anglesey, Gwynedd
Tel: (0248) 723303/77582

Morris Marshall & Poole,
10 Broad Street, Newtown,
Powys
Tel: (0686) 625900

Phillips in Wales Fine Art
Auctioneers,
9-10 Westgate Street, Cardiff
Tel: (0222) 396453

Rennies,
1 Agincourt Street, Monmouth
Tel: (0600) 712916

Wingett's,
22 Holt Street, Wrexham,
Clywd
Tel: (0978) 353553

INDEX

A

Adam, Robert 359, 410, 426
Adams 499
Adie & Son 493
Aesthetic Movement 573–4
Agassiz, E. 529
Agra 718
Aiano, C. 495
albarelli 73
Aldridge, Charles 506
ale flutes 210
ale glasses 90, 208–9, 212, 223
Alker 443
amethyst 89, 91
Amoore, T. 468
Angers, C.D.R. 488
Anglo-Indian 263
Annamese 173
Anreiter, J.K. 483
Anthony, Edward 515
antique upholstery pointer
  280
antiquities 607–9
  marble 607
  metalware 607–8
  pottery 608
Apeli and Varesio 625
architects' tables 313
architectural antiques 408–
  29
  fenders 332, 411–12
  fire grates 332
  fire irons 332, 412–13
  fireplaces 408–12
  furniture 413–17
  garden statuary 417–25
  miscellaneous 421–9
Arden, Thomas 474
Argy-Rousseau 621–3
Arita,
  bowls 171, 174
  dishes 171, 181–2, 186
  figures 178–9
  jars 87
  plates 183, 187
  tureens 87
  vases 193, 196, 198
armchairs 234–5, 274–81,
  294–7, 414, 625
  library 280–1, 294–6
  open 234–5, 295–7
  panel back 234
  Windsor 234
  wing back 235, 280–1, 294
armoires 241–2, 326, 348
armour 710, 758
arms and armour 717, 758–61
  armour 710, 758
  blunderbusses 760
  cannon 761
  daggers 758
  guns 717
  helmets 608, 704, 758
  knives 760
  pistols 760–1
  revolvers 717
  sporting 761
  swords 760
  uniforms 761
Arnold & Dent 485
Arnold & Sons 502
Arnold, John 493
Arp, Jean 632
Art Deco 587–600
  ceramics 590–1, 594
  Clarice Cliff 591–3, 614
  figures 594–5, 615
  furniture 595–6, 624–7
  glass 229, 591–7
  jewellery 597, 622
  Lalique glass 587–9, 678
  metal 594–5, 598–9
  miscellaneous 599
Art Nouveau 571–86
  ceramics 571–2
  clocks 572–3
  Doulton 584
  figures 574, 576
  furniture 573–4
  glass 571–7

jewellery 577–8
lamps 578–9
Martin Bros. 570
metal 579–81
Moorcroft 583–4
Royal Doulton 584–6
artist's necessaires 407
Arts & Crafts 568–70
Ashbee, C.R. 580–1
Ashley, E.F. 469
Astor & Co. 668
Atkin Brothers 516, 518, 529
Aubusson 718, 722
Aulenti, Gae 600
Ault 571
automata 658, 701

B

Baccarat 91, 224, 228, 230
Bacchus 224–5
bachelor's chests 299, 337
badges 716
Bagnall, John 442
Bailey, Robert 529
Baillie-Scott, M.H. 574
Baker, John 442
Bakshaish 720
Baldwyn, C.H.C. 156
Balenciaga 612
Ball, William 476
baluster mugs 223
Barber, James 513
Barclay, Jas. 488
Barlow, Hannah 584, 586
Barnack, O. 505
Barnard Brothers 529
Barnard, E. & J. 522
Barnard, E.J.J. & W. 525
Barnard, Edward 514
Barnard, Edward, & Sons
  518
Barnard, John 514
Barnard, W. 517
Barnards 509
Barnett, John 442, 461
Barnsley, Edward 569
barometers 472–3, 493–5
  stick 493–4
  wheel 472, 495
Barr, Flight & Barr 112, 114,
  153, 155
Barwise 435, 467
Barye, Antoine-Louis 561
baskets 78, 101–3, 474, 501–7
Bateman, Ann 549
Bateman, Hester 478, 543,
  550
Bateman, Peter 507, 549
Bateman, William 507
Battersea 556
Baume & Mercier 470, 491
Becker, Gustav 440
bed steps 327
beds 231, 252–3, 288, 624, 738
bedside tables 313
bedsteads 252
beer jugs 89
Beesley, F. 717
Bell, Joseph 533
benches 286, 312, 413–17
Bennett, William 512, 523
Benson, J.W. 469
Bentley, Percival Arthur
  445
bergères 279–81, 294–6, 370
Berlin,
  boxes 105
  cups 113
  figures 118, 126
  plaques 80, 145–6
  plates 135
  services 152
  tureens 83
  vases 157
Bernard et fils 457
Bernier 158
Berrenger 493
Bertion, L. 159

Bertrand 462
Bes Ben 612
Beswick 590
Bettridge, John 510
Betts 497
Bevington 106
bicycles 677
Bidjar 718
Biedermeier 327, 370, 384,
  388, 390
Biggs, B. 494
bijouterie tables 389
billiards tables 684
bin labels 556
binders 724
Bing 659, 662, 664–6, 701
Bird, J. 472, 499
Blackwood 464
blanc de chine 201
Blanchard, Chas. 464
blunderbusses 760
bobbins 609
bodkins 610
Bohemian 215, 225–6
Bologne, Jean de 562
bonbonnières 99, 483
Bonheur, Isidore 560
bonheurs du jour 253–4, 292
bonnet glasses 227
book cabinets 257
bookcases 289–91, 330
  on chests 258
  pine 330, 738
boot stands 373
Boschetti, Benedetto 479
Bosio, François-Joseph 560
Böttger 76, 113, 136
Bottiglioni, J. 481
bottle holders 327
bottles,
  glass 89, 202–3
  oriental 170
  porcelain 75, 103
  pottery 29, 69
Boulanger, Jean-Nicholas
  527
Boulton, Matthew, and Co.
  511–12, 531
Bourdin 456
Bow,
  baskets 78
  bottles 75
  bowls 103
  cups 110
  cutlery 160
  dishes 132
  figures 77–8, 118–19
  sauceboats 147
  vases 153
bowl stands 310
bowls 171, 174
  glass 203
  oriental 170–7
  porcelain 75, 84, 103–5,
  635–6
  pottery 29–30, 98, 100
  silver 474, 508–9
boxes 239, 251, 483–4, 670–5
  enamel 483
  ivory 671
  porcelain 76, 105–6
  pottery 30
  silver 510–11, 708
  wooden 484, 670–5
bracket clocks 431–5, 461
Brady & Martin 502
Bramwell-Alston 472
Brandt, Edgar 616, 630
Brannam 571
brass 685, 687–8
breakfast tables 318, 377–9
breakfront bookcases 254–5,
  289
breakfront cabinets 269
breakfront library bookcases
  254–5
breakfront secretaire
  bookcases 255
breakfront sideboards 307,
  370–1

Breitling 470
Breker, Arno 600
Bretby 568
Bridge, John 511
Bristol 29, 44–6, 50, 64–5, 81,
  160, 205
Britains 661–2
Britannia metal 671
Broadhurst Clarkson & Co.
  499
Brocot, Achille 440, 458–9,
  487
bronze 685–8, 704, 707–8
  busts 480, 559
  candelabra 685–6
  candlesticks 685
  figures 480, 560–5, 574–5,
  595, 615, 701–7
brooches 621, 731–7
Brown, Edward 524
Bru 648
Brugger 430
brush pots 88
Brussels 639, 641
Bryan, Samuel 442
buckets 259–60
Buddha 707
buffets 240, 287
Buffett, Jno. 444
Bugatti, Carlo 625–6
Buglioni, Benedetto 482
Bullocech 495
Bulova Accutron 491
bureau bookcases 231, 251–7,
  286, 290
bureau cabinets 265–6, 290
bureau mazarin 292
bureaux 260–4, 286, 291–2,
  302
  oak & country 231–2
bureaux plats 324–5, 404–5
Burgess, William 568
Burslem 590
Burwash, W. 517
busts,
  bronze 480, 559
  ivory 602
  marble 481, 602–3, 704
  porcelain 76
  pottery 31
  terracotta 482, 600, 604,
  704
butler's trays 327
butter dishes 29
butter tubs 65, 152
buttons 610

C

C.I.J. 701
cabinet bookcases 258
cabinets 265–72, 292–3, 624
  oak & country 232
cabinets en armoire 326
cabinets on stands 232, 269,
  292–3, 709
Cachard 456
caddy spoons 532
Cafe, William 474, 513
Cail 496, 498
Calderwood, Robert 525
Caldwell, J.E., & Co. 470
cameras 504–5
Cameron 494
campaign beds 253
campaign chairs 297
canapes 308–9, 367–9
candelabra,
  bronze 685–6
  glass 686
  silver 474–5, 511–12, 629,
  711
candle snuffers 161
candlestands 250, 374
candlesticks,
  bronze 685
  pottery 69
  silver 474, 512–13, 711
  silver plate 530–1, 689
canes 754

cannon 761
canterburies 272–4
canterburies pointer 274
Capodimonte 77
car mascots 678
carafes 89
card tables 313–14, 379–82
Carey 494
carousel animals 702
carpets 630, 718–20
carriage clocks 435–9, 462
Carrier-Belleuse, Albert 481
562
Carrington & Co. 521
Carrington, Thomas 430
Carswell, Thos 442
Carter, Christopher 441
Carter, John 512–13, 524
Cartier 470, 490–2, 629
carton-pierre mirrors 304
caskets 106, 407, 479, 484,
674–5
cassolettes 567
Castel Durante 73
Castelli 72
casters 513
Cathaussen 594
Cattle, Robert 513
Caughley 101, 104, 109, 132–
3, 141
celadons 170–1, 174, 200
cellarets 321–7, 554
censers 710
centre lights 688
centre tables 246, 315–16,
325, 383–5
centrepieces 101–7, 474–5,
480, 514, 531
ceramics 571–2, 590–1, 594
Chad Valley 664
chairs 232–8, 281–4, 286, 295–
8, 333–6, 413–16, 625
arm 294–7, 414, 625
child's 237
corner 237, 281
dining 232, 298
hall 298
high 237
ladder back 236
lambing 235
nursing 236, 336
oak & country 232–8
occasional 336
Orkney 237
pine 738
side 234
spindle back 232, 236
turner's 237
wainscot 236
Windsor 234–6, 286
chaises longues 308, 367–9
Chaligny, S. 483
chamber pots 476
Chamberlain's Worcester
113, 115, 133–4, 144, 153
champagne flutes 210
Chanakale 725–6
chandeliers 617, 688–9
Chandler, F.A. 469
Chanel 611
Chantilly 76
Chapman, John 488
Chapu, Henri 563
chargers 45
Charriere 502
Chawner, Henry 509, 521,
542
cheese stands 478
Chelsea,
beakers 80
bowls 39, 103
cups 109–10
dishes 132–3, 135
figures 71–7, 119–20
jugs 79
salts 161
teapots 81
thimbles 610
tureens 81
vases 83, 153
Chelsea/Derby 109, 118
chenets 332
chess sets 661–7
Chesterfield 369
chests 238–40, 286, 299–300,
709

oak & country 238–40
pine 330, 738–42
chests of drawers 238, 299,
302, 330, 337–41
chests on chests 341–2
chests on stands 343–4
cheval mirrors 360, 363
chimneypieces 332
Chinese 84
*Chinese dynasties and marks
pointer* 173
Chinese porcelain pointers
171, 173
Chippendale 282, 357, 360,
366, 388
chocolate pots 476
Christian, Philip 533
chronographs 469–71
chronometers 493
Cito 492
claret jugs 557
Clark & Co. 496
Clauss, Johannes 515
Clavel, Henry 558
Cleret 456
Clerici, L. 602
Clichy 224–5
Cliff, Clarice 591–3, 614
Clinch, John 600
clocks 430–71, 485–92
Art Nouveau 572–3
bracket 431–5, 461
carriage 435–9, 462
garnitures 440
lantern 441
longcase 442–53, 464, 466
mantel 454–60, 467–8
miscellaneous 487
porcelain 107–8
regulators 468, 485
skeleton 486
wall 468, 481–7
watches 469–71, 488–92
wristwatches 490–2
clocks pointer 431
Clodion, Claude Michel 563
cloisonné 692–3, 710
clothes presses 349–50
Clowes, James 443
Clowes, Jno 464
coal boxes 412–13
coal scuttles 413
Coalbrookdale 413–16, 426
Coalport,
dishes 132
miscellaneous 161
plates 134
services 148–9, 151, 537
trays 139
vases 154
Coalport/Chamberlain's
Worcester 134
coffee pots 74, 81, 476, 533–4
coffee services 477, 535–8,
628
coffee tables 626
coffee urns 548–9
coffers 238–40, 251, 286, 709
coin set tankards 227, 477
Coker, Ebenezer 524
Cole, B. 494
collectors cabinets 266, 293
collectors desks 355
commemorative 30–1, 539
commode chests 345–7
commodes 300–1, 344–5, 742
comports 567, 614
Comyns, W. 435
console brackets 317
console tables 311–18, 385–6
conversation settees 308
Cooke, T., & Sons 499
Coombes, J. 442
Cooper, Robert 519
Copeland 31, 51, 119, 134, 148
Copeland & Garrett 63, 133
Coper, Hans 532
copper 623
cordial glasses 210–12, 217
corkscrews 551–7
corner cabinets 270, 272, 296
corner chairs 237, 281
corner cupboards 241, 348–9
corner tables 317
cornets 721
Cornock, Edward 510

cornucopias 99
corsets 638
Corum 491
costume 611–12, 637–8, 693–4
cottages 32, 108
counter tables 246
cow creamers 32
Cowan, James 469
Cox, Harry W., & Co. 501
Coxeter, Nicholas 441
Creake, Wm 430
cream jugs 80, 89
creamware,
baskets 94
boxes 30
coffee pots 74
cow creamers 32
dovecotes 74
figures 34–7, 69–71
flatware 48
jugs 51, 55–6, 73–4
mugs 60
plaques 61
teapots 552
credence cupboards 242
credenzas 270–2
Crespell, James 516
Crespell, Sebastian 516
crested china 162–9
cricket 680
cricket tables 250
Cripps, William 525, 539
Crockford, W. 443
Crossley, Richard 516
Crouch, John 527
Crown Devon 591
cruet sets 202–3
Cuff, I. 500
Cunningham, Patrick 546
Cunningham, William 546
cup stands 201
cupboard dressers 287
cupboards 240–2, 328, 330,
348–51, 626
corner 241
oak & country 240–2
pine 328, 330, 742–4
cups,
oriental 177
porcelain 76, 109–14
pottery 33
silver 514–15
cutlery, silver 515–16, 627
cutlery urns 484, 672
Cuzner 502
cylinder bureaux 263–4, 292
Cymric 581

D

daggers 758
Dales 460
Dallmeyer, J.H. 499
Daniell, Thomas 528
Darker, William 519
Daum 577, 611–17
Davenport 73, 95, 149
davenports 302, 351–2
davenports pointer 352
Davis, Harry 151–7
Davison, Wm 442
day beds 252–3, 288, 624
day beds pointer 252
De la Rue 479
decanters, glass 89, 204–8,
597
Degrege, Rolland 486
Dehua 179, 192
Delahoyde, Barny 442
Delander, Dan 461
delft,
Bristol 44–6, 50, 65
Dutch 47–51, 67, 73
English 29, 69, 71
Lambeth 46, 50
Liverpool 33, 52
London 29, 33, 45–6, 49–51,
64, 69, 75
Southwark 71
delft racks 328
Dent, F. 436, 454, 462
dental instruments 503
Derby,
baskets 101
cups 114
dishes 134

figures 116, 119–22
jugs 141
mugs 143–4
plates 135–6
sauceboats 84, 147–8
services 149
tureens 153
vases 83, 153–5
desk boxes 251
desk chairs 295–6
desks 302, 326, 353–8
kneehole 302, 353–8
partners' 302, 354–8
pedestal 302, 326, 353–7
pine 744
dessert plates 72
Devaulx, S. 458
Devillaine 456
dials 472–3, 496
Dickson, J. 717
Dillwyn & Co. 47
Ding, Henri Marius 562
dining chairs 232, 237, 282–4,
298, 333–5, 625
dining tables 246, 250, 318,
381–8
Dinky 663, 701
dish lights 715
dishes 171, 181–2, 186
porcelain 81–7, 132
pottery 100
silver 475, 511–18
display cabinets 261–9, 289,
291, 330
display tables 389
Dixey, G. & C. 601
Dixon, James 526
Doccia 110
Dollond 499
dolls 645–57, 703
Armand Marseille 652
bisque 647–54
Bru 648
clockwork 657
dolls' houses 655–6
Gebrüder Heubach 648–9
Jules Steiner 654
Jumeau 649–51, 703
Kammer & Reinhart 653–
4, 703
Kestner, J.D. 651, 703
Lenci 651, 703
miscellaneous 657
papier mâché 647–8
S.F.B.J. 652–3
Simon & Halbig 653–4
wax 641–7
wooden 645–6
dolls' houses 655–6
Donegal 599–600
door stops 558
Dore, Gustave 480
Dorrell, Francis 430
Doulton 422–3, 584
dovecotes 74
Down 501
Downie, William 443
dram glasses 222–3
drawleaf tables 246
Dresden 67, 128, 157
dresser bases 243, 328
Dresser, C. 614, 628
dresser and racks 244
dressers 242–5, 287, 328
oak & country 242–5
pine 745
dressing chests 300, 302, 330
dressing commodes 300
dressing table sets 478
dressing tables 389–90
pine 746
drinking glasses 208–23
dropleaf tables 390
Drouot 563
drum tables 318–19
Drury, Alfred 562
Dubois & Comp. 467, 469
Dubou 456
Dubuisson 456
Ducati 505
Duesbury Derby 119
duet stands 373–4
Dufy, Raoul 632
dumb waiters 310, 358
Duncan 430
Dunlap II, John 321

Durman, Thomas 443
dwarf bookcases 257
dwarf cabinets 270–2
Dyer, W. 445
Dyson, John, & Sons 445

E
easels 373
Eaton, William 516
Edington, John Charles 522
Edkins, S.S. 497
Edwards, James 493
Edwards II, John 474
egg cups 99
Election 470
electrical 671–7
electroliers 714
Eley & Fearn 530
Eley, William 516
Elkington & Co. 509, 522
Elkington, Frederick 526
Ellicot, John 458, 464
Elston, John 512
Emanuel, Victor, & Co. 440
embroidery 638–9
Emes, John 552
Empire chairs 298
enamel 483, 539, 692–3
encriers 84
entrée dishes 475
épergnes 475
ephemera 729–33
   film 731–3
   pop 728–31
   posters 733
   theatre 731–3
equinoctial dials 472
escritoires 290
European Watch & Clock Co.
   492
Evans, John 521
Evans, Thomas 515
Everaut 625
ewers 33, 84, 86, 115, 178
exportware 86
Eyre, Henry, & Co. 512

F
Fabergé 547, 674
Façon de Venise 90, 202, 209,
   213, 226
Faenza 72–3
faience 48, 51, 55, 72–3
Fairyland Lustre 104
famille rose,
   bowls 173–7
   cup stands 201
   cups 177
   dishes 87, 174, 183, 186
   figures 86
   garden seats 88
   garnitures 194, 200
   ice pails 201
   jardinières 189
   plates 86, 184–5, 187
   pots 201
   tureens 87–8, 192
   vases 84, 88, 194–5, 199
famille verte,
   dishes 80, 181, 183, 188
   ewers 86
   figures 86
   plates 180
   teapots 551
   vases 88, 193–4, 197
   wine ewers 86
fans 643–5
Farrell, Edward 518, 552
fauteuils 297
Faux, John 529
Fawdery, William 549
Federzeichnung 226
fenders 332, 411–12
Ferguson 501
Ferner, F.J. 536
Field, Daniel 446
figures,
   animal 614
   Art Deco 594–5, 615
   Art Nouveau 574, 576
   bronze 560–5, 574–5, 595,
      615, 701–7
   ivory 481, 595, 615
   marble 481–2

metal 594
oriental 178–9, 706
people 594–5, 614–15
porcelain 71–8, 86, 115–31
pottery 33–44, 69–71, 97,
   99, 614, 706
terracotta 704
film ephemera 731–3
Finch, John 444
Finlayson, J. 494
fire grates 332
fire irons 332, 412–13
fireplaces 408–12
firescreens 306, 365–6
firing glasses 222–3
Fischer 662
fishing 680–3
flagons 477
Flamand 629
Flammarien, Camille 497
flasks 100, 180
flatware 78–80, 132–9, 180–9
Flavell, Ray 623
Fleetwood, Willm 434
Flemish 640
Flight & Barr 112, 151, 155
Flight, Barr & Barr 79, 137,
   139–40, 151, 155, 685
Folch and Sons 72
folio cabinets 293
folio stands 310, 373
football 683
footstools 312
Ford, E. Onslow 563
Fornasetti 600
Forster, Jacob 314
Fortnum and Mason 678
Fossey, John 520
Foullet, P.A. 325
four-poster beds 288
Fox, Charles Thomas 552
Fox, George 552
Franchini 227–8
Frankenthal 77, 123, 129
Fray, James 516, 537
Friend 464
Fritsch, Elizabeth 633
Frodsham & Keen 486
Frodsham, Charles 431
Froget 501
fruitwood 540, 543
Fukagawa 200
Fulda 77
furniture 231–407, 413–17,
   624–7
   architects' tables 313
   armchairs 234–5, 274–81,
      294–7
   Art Deco 595–6, 624–7
   Art Nouveau 573–4
   beds 231, 252–3, 288, 624
   bonheurs du jour 253–4,
      292
   bookcases 289–91, 330
   breakfast tables 318, 377–9
   breakfront bookcases 254–
      5, 289
   buckets 259–60
   bureau bookcases 251–7,
      286, 290
   bureau cabinets 265–6, 290
   bureaux 231–2, 260–4, 286,
      291–2, 302
   cabinets 232, 265–72, 292–
      3, 624
   cabinets on stands 232,
      269, 292–3, 709
   canterburies 272–4
   card tables 313–14, 379–82
   centre tables 246, 315–16,
      325, 383–5
   chairs 232–8, 281–4, 286,
      295–8, 333–6, 625
   chests 238–40, 286, 299–
      300, 709
   chests on chests 341–2
   chests of drawers 238, 299,
      302, 330, 337–41
   chests on stands 343–4
   coffers 238–40, 251, 286, 709
   commode chests 345–7
   commodes 300–1, 344–5
   console tables 311–18, 385–
      6
   corner cupboards 348–9
   cupboards 240–2, 328, 330,

348–51, 626
davenports 302, 351–2
desks 302, 326, 353–8
dining chairs 232, 237,
   282–4, 298, 333–5, 625
dining tables 246, 250, 318,
   381–8
display cabinets 261–9,
   289, 291, 330
display tables 389
drawleaf tables 246
dressers 242–5, 287, 328
dressing tables 389–90
dropleaf tables 390
drum tables 318–19
dumb waiters 310, 358
dwarf bookcases 257
games tables 319, 390–1
hall chairs 298, 336
lamp tables 402
library bookcases 254–5,
   257–9
library tables 318–19, 391–
   2
linen presses 349–50
lowboys 248–50, 287
mirrors & frames 303–5,
   359–65, 626
miscellaneous 251, 407
nests of tables 392
occasional tables 319, 393
oriental 694–5, 709–10
pedestal tables 320, 393–4
Pembroke tables 320, 394–5
reading tables 320
screens 306, 365–6, 709
secretaire bookcases 255,
   259, 289
serving tables 320, 395–6
settees 308–9, 361–70
settles 237–8
shelves 325, 370
side cabinets 269–72, 291,
   293, 624
side chairs 336
side tables 247–50, 287,
   321–2, 391–8
sideboards 244, 307, 326,
   328, 370–3, 626
sofa tables 322–3, 398–9
sofas 308–9
stands 310, 373–4, 710
steps 374
stools 245, 311–12, 374–7
Sutherland tables 400
tables 245–51, 287, 313–25,
   377–405, 626
tallboys 299
tea tables 313, 323, 400–1
teapoys 327
toilet tables 401
tripod tables 249–50, 323,
   402
wardrobes 326, 328, 350–1,
   626
washstands 310, 406
Wellington chests 344
whatnots 310, 401–7
wine tables 402
work tables 323, 403
writing tables 324–5, 404–5
Fürstenberg 105, 114, 140,
   227

G
Gallé 572, 576, 614, 617–18
games 661–7
games boxes 671
games tables 319, 390–1
garden lanterns 88
garden seats 74, 88, 413–17
garden statuary 417–25
Gardiner, J. 558
Gardner 444
garnitures 194, 200, 440
Garrard, James 522
Garrard, Robert 478, 506,
   514, 518, 524, 542
Garrard, Sebastian 514
Garrat 446
gateleg tables 245–7, 318
Gebrüder Heubach 648–9
gentleman's presses 350
Gerrard, J. 461
Gibson and Co. Ltd. 509

Gillois, Pierre 539–40
girandoles 303, 305, 362–3
glass 89–92, 202–30, 611–18,
   620–3
   Art Deco 229, 591–7
   Art Nouveau 571–7
   beakers 202, 223
   bottles 89, 202–3
   bowls 203
   candelabra 686
   chandeliers 617
   decanters 89, 204–8, 597
   drinking glasses 208–23
   inkwells 226
   jugs 89, 223–4
   lamps 611–17, 620–1
   miscellaneous 221–7
   oriental 695
   paperweights 224–5
   scent bottles 91–2, 227–30
   tankards 227
   tea caddies 541–7
   vases 225–6, 611–18, 620–3
goblets 90, 211–15, 576
Godfrey, Elizabeth 477
gold 558, 707
Goldscheider 571, 594, 614
Goldsmiths and Silversmiths
   Company 479, 507, 513, 523
golf 683
Goodwin, Charles 507
Gordon, Hugh 548
Goss china 162–9
Gossin, Louis 563
Gouda 572
Gough, William 474, 519
Gould, Chr. 430
Gount, S. Garie 502
Grace, William 430
grand pianos 721
Grandi, Giuseppe 564
grandmother clocks pointer
   446
grape scissors 530
Green, John 434
Gregson 469
Gretton, Cha. 461
grotto chairs 297
grotto mirrors 304
Grue, Niccolo Tommaso 72
Grundy, William 475
gueridon tables 319–20, 323
Guild of Handicraft 579–80
guns 717
Gunthermann 663–4
Gurley, W. & L.E. 498
Gurney and Cooke 521
Guy, Samuel 464
Guydamour 458

H
Hadley 155
Haggart, Donald Campbell
   602
hall chairs 298, 336
hall lanterns 681–7
Hall, Martin 446, 513, 527
Hall-in-Tyrol 90
Hancock & Sons 614
Háncock, C.F. 519
hanging lamps 478, 714–15
hanging presses 241
Hannam, Thomas 527
Harckell 487
Harper, John, & Co. 662
Harper, Robert 506
Harrison & Howson 514
Hausmaler 183, 536
Hawksworth, Eyre Ltd. 511
Heal, Ambrose 569
helmets 608, 704, 758
Henderson, Robert 431
Hennell, David 522
Hennell, R. & H. 507
Hennell, Robert 514, 521–2,
   549
Hennell, Samuel 507, 527,
   544
Hepplewhite 276, 284, 334,
   345, 371
Herbert, Cornelius 447
Herbert, Samuel, & Co. 542
Heriz 718, 720
Hertel, O. 563
Heweston, Christopher 481

Heymann, Ludw. Jul. 497
Hicks & Meigh 51
Hicks, Meigh & Johnson 65
Higgs, Jas 486
high chairs 237
Hispano-Flemish 605
Hispano-Moresque 48, 50, 72
Hoeting, J.A. 507
Holland, Thomas 542
Holst, H.E. 459
honey pots 476
Hope, Thomas 480
Hornby 666
Houles & Co. 522
Howard, E. 489
Howell & James 462
Howse, Charles 431
Hoyt 658
HS Ltd. 516
Huggins 454
Hughes, William 518
Hunt & Roskell 478, 535
Hunt, John S. 475, 523
Hunter, Thomas 502
hunters 469

I
ice pails 201
Imari,
  basins 84
  beakers 177
  bowls 84, 170, 176
  dishes 87, 181–2, 187–8
  ewers 178
  figures 179
  jardinieres 189
  jars 87, 191
  spittoons 201
  tankards 177
  tureens 83, 88
  vases 88, 193–5, 197–9
Indo-Persian 721–7
Ingersoll 490
inkstands 98, 476, 480, 518
inkwells 84, 140, 226
International Watch
  Company 490
Invar 469
ironstone 47
Islamic art 725–7
Islington Glass Co. 224
ivory 601–2, 691–7
  boxes 671
  busts 602
  figures 481, 595, 615
  tea caddies 548

J
Jackson, John 549
Jacobite 219, 222
Jacobite glasses pointer 218
Jacobs, John 525, 550
Jacot, Henri 438, 462
Jacqumar 469
jade 697, 701–7
Jaeger LeCoultre 470, 490
Janesich, L. 512
Japy & Fils 458, 467
Japy Freres 437, 458–9
jardinieres 49, 73, 140, 189
jars,
  oriental 189–91
  porcelain 87, 161
  pottery 49–51, 706
Jay, Henry 520
jelly glasses 226
jelly moulds 558
Jensen, Georg 536, 597–9,
  627–9
jewel boxes 671–2
jewellery 577–8, 597, 622,
  731–7
Johnson, Joseph 432
Johnston, W. & A.K., Ltd.
  496
Jones, George 49, 64
Jones, Henry 464
Jones, John 515
Jones, Robert 525
Jones, W. & S. 496
jugs,
  glass 89, 223–4
  porcelain 75, 79–80, 141–3
  silver 518–19

Jumeau 649–51, 703
Junyao 175

K
K.P.M. 113
Kaga 176
Kakiemon,
  bowls 75, 84, 171
  dishes 86, 182–3, 185
  snuff boxes 76
  tea caddies 547
  tureens 87
Kammer & Reinhart 653–4,
  703
Kanjiro Kawai 633
Karabagh Kelleh 720
Karussell 469
Kashan 719–20
Kestner, J.D. 651, 703
Kevitt, Richard 488
Kinkozan 199
Kipling, William 446
Kirk, Thomas 644
Kirkby, Waterhouse &
  Hodgson 478
Kirman 719
Kit Kat 215
Kitchen & Lloyd 446
kitchenalia 751–3
Kloss, Johann Georg 548
Kloster Veilsdorf 77–8
kneehole desks 302, 353–8
Knibb, Joseph 461
knife boxes 670–2
Knox, Archibald 579–80
Ko-Imari 84
Koch, Rasmus 498
Kodak 504
Kogo 707
Korean 88
koro 710
Koryo 171, 174
Kraak porselein 86
Kray 159
Kruse, Kathe 656
Kutani 191, 199–200
Kyo-Satsuma 199

L
lace 639–41
Lacour 457
lacquer 546, 671
Ladd, W., & Co. 500
ladles 160
Lalique glass 228–9, 587–9,
  620–1, 678
Lalique pointer 587
Lambeth 41–7, 50, 584
lambing chairs 235
Lamerie, Paul de 471–7, 542
lamp bases 687
lamp stands 688
lamp tables 402
lamps 578–9, 611–17, 620–1,
  715
Langford, J. 544
Langlands, John 519–21
lantern clocks 441
lanterns 478
lap desks 407
Lapini, C. 603
larder cupboards 330
latticini 90, 226
Lavergne 565
Lawson, William 448
Le Roy 451–7, 468
Le Sage, Augustin 517
Le Sage, John Hugh 517
Leach, Bernard 633
lead soldiers and figures 661–
  2
leather 678–9
LeCoultre 469–70
Lee & Son 434
Leeds 51, 62, 533
Leitz, E. 504–5
Leleu 596, 624
Lenci 614, 651, 703
Leoni, Antonio 481
Lepke, Ferdinand 420
Lesieur 467
Lesney 663
letter racks 95
letterboxes 327

Levasseur, E. 479
lever watches 470
Levy, Charles 560
Liberty 572–3, 577–81, 598–9,
  622, 625–7, 630
library bookcases 254–5, 257–
  9
library desks 302
library tables 318–19, 391–2
Liger, Isaac 476
lighting 685–9
Limbach 125
Limoges 146, 591
Linemar 663
linen presses 349–50
Linthorpe 571, 614
lits en bateau 288
lits à la polonaise 288
Liverpool,
  bowls 104
  coffee pots 533
  cups 33
  dishes 137
  figures 77
  jugs 52, 142–3
  mugs 143–4
  plates 47, 138
  sauceboats 147
  tiles 64
  vases 65
Liverpool Penningtons 104
livery cupboards 242
Llanelly 46
Lloyd, John 517
Lochmann 669
Lock, Nathaniel 510
Lodi 72
Lofthouse, Seth 521
Logie, Robert 447
London 29, 33, 45–6, 50–1, 64,
  69
longcase clocks 442–53, 464,
  466
longcase clocks pointer 450
Longton Hall 75, 78, 123, 128,
  147–8
Lorenzl 594–5
Love, George 529
low dressers 245
lowboys 248–50, 287
Lowestoft, dishes 139, 148
Lowndes, J. 461
Lowndes, Thomas 524
Ludwigsburg 78
luggage 678–9
Lugkin Rule Co. 500
Lumpkin, Thomas 447
Lupton, Edith 584
Lurcat, Jean 600
Lycett, Edward 524
Lynn 219

M
McMaster 446
majolica,
  bowls 30
  dishes 48–9
  ewers 33
  jardinières 73
  jugs 52, 54
  teapots 74, 568
  tureens 65
Majolica, Louis 624, 626
Makepeace, Robert 475
Makepeace, Thomas 475
Malpass, L. 158
mantel clocks 454–60, 467–8
Mappin & Webb 518, 521–7
marble 481–2, 602–4, 607
  busts 481, 602–3, 704
  figures 481–2
Marcolini 82, 105, 114
Mardi, J. 563
Marioton, Eugene 564
Marklin 665–6, 701
marquises 308
marriage chests 407
Marriott 432
Marseille, Armand 652
Marseilles 140
Marshall & Sons 528
Martin & Co. 454
Martin, B. 500
Martin Bros. 570
Mason, Humphrey 448

Masonic 87
Mason's Ironstone,
  dishes 47
  jugs 52–3
  letter racks 95
  mugs 60, 70
  plates 72
  punch bowls 69
  services 62
  tureens 64
  vases 65–6
massagers 707
match strikers 98
Maurice, E., & Co. 437
measures 558
meat dishes 475
Meccano 664, 701
Mechlin 640
medical instruments 501–3
medicine chests 330
Meissen,
  bottles 75
  bowls 105
  boxes 106, 483
  candelabra 711
  centrepieces 107
  clocks 84, 107
  coffee pots 150–1
  cups 76, 114
  dishes 80
  ecuelles 83
  figures 78, 115–18, 123–31
  inkstands 140
  jugs 80
  mugs 144
  needlecases 610
  plaques 81, 145–6
  plates 79, 134, 131–7
  scent bottles 230
  services 82, 150–1, 531–7
  snuff boxes 76
  tea caddies 541–7
  teapots 81, 551
  tureens 82, 152
  vases 83, 154, 158
Melas 719
Mene, Pierre-Jules 560, 562
Mennecy 106
Mercier Frères 624
Merry, John 513
metalware 558–67, 607–8
  Art Deco 594–5, 598–9
  Art Nouveau 579–81
  brass 558–9
  bronze 480, 559–65
  copper 566, 623
  firemarks 566
  iron 561–7
  oriental 698–9
  ormolu 479–80, 567
  pewter 558
Methuen, George 516
Mettayer, Lewis 476
Meyer, Charles 489
microscopes 473, 500
millefiori 91, 225
Milles, Ruth 562
Millis, Joseph 447
Mills, Nathaniel 510–11
Milner, Thos 448
Ming,
  bowls 174
  dishes 86, 180, 181–7
  jardinières 189
  jars 189
  vases 88, 192, 195
miniature bureaux 262–3
Minton,
  ewers 33
  jardinières 49, 572
  jugs 52, 54–5
  services 148–9
  teapots 568
  tureens 65
  vases 66, 74, 154
mirrors & frames 303–5, 359–
  65, 626
models 665–6
Moigniez, Jules 560–1, 564
Moireau, Augte. 486
monarch chronology pointer
  231
money banks 662
monteiths 176
moon flasks 708
Moorcroft 583–4

Moore, John 508
Moreau, François Hippolyte 564
Moreau, L. 480
Morgan, William de 568
Morgan, Wm 432
Morris, William 630
Morris & Co. 573, 576, 630
Mortimer, John 523
Moulson, William 526
muffin dishes 627
mugs,
  porcelain 143–4
  pottery 60–1, 70, 100
  silver 519–22
mule chests 330
Muller Frères 621, 629
music cabinets 268
musical 668–70
  gramophones 670
  musical boxes 669–70
  musical instruments 668–9, 721

N

Nailsea 223
Naire & Blunt 472, 493
Nantgarw 152
napkin rings 629
Naples 82
natsume 708
Neale & Co. 57
necessaires 407, 675
necklaces 622
needlework panels 638–9
needlework pictures 638–9, 723
nests of tables 392
netsuke 697, 700, 708
netting tools 610
Neuchâtel 483
New Hall 535, 614
Newcastle 213
Newman and Guardia 504
Newport 33
Newton & Berry 496
Nicklin 449
Nicole Frères 669
Norrie, D. 448
Nottingham 60
nursing chairs 236, 336
Nymphenburg 78, 80, 130

O

oak & country furniture 231–51
  beds 231
  bureaux 231–2
  cabinets 232
  chairs 232–8
  chests 238–40
  cupboards 240–2
  dressers 242–5
  miscellaneous 251
  stools 245
  tables 245–51
occasional chairs 336
occasional tables 319, 393
Odiot, J.B.C. 517
Ohr, George 633
oil lamps 688–9
okimono 696
Omega 491
orders 716
oriental 692–700, 701–10
  cloisonné 692–3
  costume 693–4
  enamel 692–3
  furniture 694–5, 709–10
  glass 695
  ivory 691–7
  jade 697
  metal 698–9
  netsuke 700
  snuff bottles 700
oriental pottery and porcelain 170–201
  bottles 170
  bowls 170–7
  cups 177
  ewers 178
  figures 178–9, 706
  flasks 180
  flatware 180–9

jardinières 189
jars 189–91
  miscellaneous 201
  tureens 191–2
  vases 192–200
ormolu 711–15
  candelabra 686, 711–12
  candlesticks 479, 712
  centrepieces 479
  chandeliers 688–9, 713–14
  inkstands 84
  plaques 479
  vases 479
  wall lights 713
orreries 473
Ottoman 725–6
Ottway, W., and Son Ltd. 499
overmantels 303–4, 360, 362–3

P

padouk bureau 263
Pain, David 448
Paisley 612
panels, wood 482
Panton 486
paperweights 224–5
papier mâché 647–8, 736
Paraud, P. 474
Pardoe, Thomas 162
parian ware 31
Paris 81, 137–8, 158
Parker, John 476
Parkes, J., & Co. 515
Parr 447
Partington, W.L.M. 454
partners' desks 302, 354–8
pastille burners 32, 76, 108
Pastorelli, J. 495
patina pointer 247
Pattison 448
Payne, Humphrey 476
Payne, John 520–1
pearlware,
  busts 31
  cow creamers 32
  figures 33–4, 31–42, 69
  jugs 30, 52, 54–7
  services 63
  tureens 153
Peavy, William 506
pedestal breakfast tables 378
pedestal cabinets 272
pedestal card tables 382
pedestal desks 302, 326, 353–7
pedestal sideboards 307, 372–3
pedestal tables 320, 393–4
pedestals 310
Peignat 468
Pellegrino, F. 494
Pellet, I.P. 475
pelmets 639
Pembroke tables 320, 394–5
pen holders 33–4
Pennell, Ronald 623
pens 479
Pepfenhauser, Johann 510
Perigal & Duterrau 432
Perregaux, Girard 471
pewter 675
Philip, George, & Son Ltd 472, 496
Philippe, Patek 469, 471, 489
Philippe, Paul 594–5
Phipps & Robinson 529
Physick, Edward Gustavus 481
Piaget 492
pianos 721
Piatto di Pompa 72
Picasso, Pablo 634
Picault, Emile 564
pier mirrors 360–1, 365
pier tables 316
Piguet, Audemars 470
Piguet, Isaac Daniel 469
Pilkington 571, 590–1
pin trays 99
Pina, Alfredo 480
Pinas, J. 503
Pinder, William 506
pine furniture 328, 330, 738–50

beds 738
bookcases 330, 738
chairs 738
chests 330, 738–42
clocks 742
commodes 742
cupboards 328, 330, 742–4
desks 744
dressers 745
dressing tables 746
miscellaneous 750
sideboards 328
stools 746
tables 741–8
wardrobes 328, 748–9
washstands 750
Pinxton 112, 141
pipes 95
Pirkenhammer 158
pistols 760–1
plank coffers 251
plant stands 373
plaques 61, 81, 145–6, 707
plates,
  pottery 44–8, 72, 91–100
  silver 627
plinths 479
Plummer, William 506
Plymouth 104, 122, 144
pocket watches 469
Podio, Joseph Felix 507
Poertzel, Otto 614
polescreens 365–6
Polti-Exon 494
Pontremoli 719
Poole 571
pop ephemera 728–31
porcelain 101–69
  baskets 78, 101–3
  beakers 76, 80
  bottles 75, 103
  bowls 75, 84, 103–5, 635–6
  boxes 76, 105–6
  busts 76
  butter tubs 152
  caskets 106
  centrepieces 101–7
  clocks 107–8
  coffee pots 81
  cottages 108
  crested china 162–9
  cups 76, 109–14
  dishes 81–7, 132
  ewers 84, 86, 115
  figures,
    animal 71–7, 86, 115–18
    people 71–8, 118–31
  flatware 78–80, 132–9
  Goss china 162–9
  inkwells 84, 140
  jardinières 140
  jars 87, 161
  jugs 75, 79–80, 141–3
  miscellaneous 160–1
  mugs 143–4
  oriental 170–201
  pastille burners 76, 108
  plaques 81, 145–6
  pots 141–7
  sauceboats 147–8
  services 82, 148–52
  snuff boxes 76
  tankards 152
  tea and coffee pots 81
  tea services 82
  tureens 83–4, 87–8, 152–3
  vases 83, 88, 153–60
Porquier, Adolphe 99
port glasses 223
post-war design 600
posters 733
  tea and coffee 534–5
pot board dressers 243, 287
pot lids 62, 100
pots 61–2, 100, 141–7
Potschapel, Carl Thieme 107
pottery 29–74, 93–100, 608, 632–4
  bottles 29, 69
  bowls 29–30, 98, 100
  boxes 30
  busts 31
  butter tubs 65
  candlesticks 69
  chargers 45
  coffee pots 74, 533–4

commemorative 30–1
cottages 32
cow creamers 32
cups 33
dishes 100
ewers 33
figures,
  animal 33–7, 69–71, 614
  people 38–44, 97, 99, 614, 706
flatware 44–9, 72
garden seats 74
jardinières 49, 73
jars 49–51, 706
jugs 30–1, 51–60, 73–4, 100
miscellaneous 94–5
mugs 60–1, 70, 100
oriental 170–201
pastille burners 32
plaques 01
plates 44–8, 72, 91–100
pot lids 62, 100
pots 61–2, 100
Quimper 91–100
sauceboats 62
services 62–3
Staffordshire figures 43–4
teapots 97
tiles 64
Toby jugs 55–60, 73–4
tureens 64–5
vases 65–7, 74, 98–100, 614
Wemyss 67–8, 93–4
pottery and porcelain pointer 173
Powell, James, & Sons 600
Pradier, L. 564
Pratt ware,
  figures 34
  jugs 56, 58–9, 74
  pipes 95
  plaques 61
  sauceboats 62
prayer rugs 719
prayer seats 297
Preiss, F. 576, 595, 599, 614
presentation caskets 479
Price, Jno. 449
processional lanterns 478
pub tables 417
Puiforcat 627–8
punch bowls 69, 474, 579
Punc'hong ware 88
puppets 657
Purdey, J. 717
purses 638
puzzle goblets 90

Q

qajar 725–7
qilin 710
quartetto tables 392
Quimper 91–100

R

Raby, E.J. 158
radios 676
Ramsden, Omar 509
Ray, Wm 432, 455
Reading, Robert 489
reading tables 320
reels 680–2
refectory tables 247
Regency Axminster 720
regulator clocks 468, 485
Reiley & Storer 551
reliquaries 482
repeating watches 469
revolvers 717
Reynolds, Thos. 490
Rhead, Charlotte 590
Richards, George 524, 550
Richardson's 'Waterlily' 212
Ridgway, A.W., & Co. 54
Ridgway, John 148
Rie, Lucie 635–6
Righetti, Guido 565
ring dials 473
Robert 457
Roberts, F.B. 451
Robertson, James 466
Robins, Thomas 478, 551
Robinson and Leadbetter 38
Rockingham 101, 151

Rodrigues, A. 327
Roe, Ebenezer 539
roemers 90
Rogers, John, & Son 65
Rogers, John Randolph 603
rogin boxes 708
Rolex 471, 490–2
roll top desks 358
Rollin 458
Romer, Emick 475
Roode, Alexander 520
Rooker, Richard 449
Rookwood 572
Rosenthal 664
Rotherhams 489
Roullet and Decamps 658
Roussel, Alexandre 460
Rowell 436
Royal Crown Derby 148–9, 160
Royal Derby 149
Royal Doulton 584–6
Royal Dux 106, 122, 124–5, 129–31, 572
Royal Worcester,
    bowls 105
    candle snuffers 161
    cups 113
    ewers 115
    figures 116, 121–4, 127
    jardinières 140
    jars 161
    lamp bases 687
    plates 136
    services 151
    vases 155–9
Roycrofters 623
Rudolstadt-Volkstedt 107
rugs 718–19
rummers 213–16
Rundell, Bridge & Rundell 511
Rundell, Philip 528
Rushton, Raymond 157
Ruslen, John 516
Russell, Gordon 624, 626
Rysbrack, Michael 604
Ryss, François-Joseph 508

S
S.F.B.J. 652–3
Safavid 725, 727
St Cloud 161
St Louis 91
salon cabinets 269
salt spoons 160
saltglaze,
    butter tubs 65
    candlesticks 69
    coffee pots 534
    cups 69
    figures 70
    jugs 54, 73
    teapots 74
salts 75, 161, 522–3
salvers 523–5
samplers 642
Samson 117, 128–31
Sancai 170, 192, 706
Sanders, Joseph 525
Sandiford, James 451
Sang, Jacob 212–13
Satsuma 179, 188–90, 191–9
sauce bottles 203
sauce tureens 478
sauceboats 62, 147–8, 525
saucers 177
Savill 498
Savona 50, 71
Savonnerie 719
Savory, Albert 523
Savory, Joseph 523
Scandrett 435
scent bottles 91–2, 227–30
Schiaparelli 611
Schofield, Paul 527
Schonberger, M. 485
Schreibmayr, Johan 434
Schrettegger, Johan 496
Schwinger, Herman 212
scientific instruments 472–3, 491–505
    barometers 472–3, 493–5
    cameras 504–5
    dental 503

dials 472–3, 496
globes 472–3, 491–7
medical 501–3
microscopes 473, 500
surveying 498–9
telescopes 472–3, 499
viewers 505
Scofield, John 525
Scott, William 449, 466
screens 306, 365–6, 709
sculptures 710
seals 708
seats 237
Sebille, J. 544
secretaire bookcases 255, 259, 289
secretaire cabinets 290
secretaire chests 339
secretaire tallboys 299, 341
secretaires à abattant 289–90
Seddon, John 450
Senneh Hamadan 719
services,
    porcelain 82, 148–52
    pottery 62–3
    silver 477, 521–7
serving tables 320, 395–6
settees 308–9, 361–70
settles 237–8
Sèvres,
    bowls 105
    caskets 674
    centrepieces 101–7
    clocks 108, 468
    cups 535
    ewers 115
    figures 126
    jardinières 140
    plates 132, 136
    services 82, 535
    trays 137–8
    vases 84, 158–60
sewing 609–10
sewing cases 609
sewing machines 610
Sharp, Robert 548
shaving bowls 474
Shelley 590
shelves 325, 370
Shepherd Hardware Co. 662
Sheraton 262–3, 276, 381, 395, 399, 672
Sherratt, Obadiah 37
shibuichi boxes 707–8
shoes 99, 723
Shuttleworth 449
Sibley, R. 517
Sidaway, John 541
side cabinets 269–72, 291, 293, 624
side chairs 234, 336
side tables 247–50, 287, 321–2, 391–8
sideboards, pine 328
silver 474–8, 501–30, 627–9, 711
    baskets 474, 501–7
    beakers 508
    bowls 474, 508–9
    boxes 510–11, 708
    candelabra 474–5, 511–12, 629, 711
    candlesticks 474, 512–13, 711
    casters 513
    centrepieces 474–5, 514
    chocolate pots 476
    coffee pots 476, 533–4
    coffee services 477, 535–8, 628
    cups 514–15
    cutlery 515–16, 627
    dishes 475, 511–18
    epergnes 475
    inkstands 476, 518
    jugs 518–19
    miscellaneous 528–30
    mugs 519–22
    plates 518
    salts 522–3
    salvers 523–5
    sauceboats 525
    services 477, 521–7
    tankards 477, 519–22
    tea caddies 477–8, 538–48
    tea kettles 549–50

tea services 477, 535–8, 628
teapots 476, 550–2
trays 527–8, 627
tureens 478, 527, 628
vases 628
wine coolers 478
silver plate 530–1, 689
Sim, Alexander 450
Simms 498
Simon & Halbig 653–4
Sinding, Stephan 480
Sissons, W. and G. 519
Sitzendorf 131
skeleton clocks 486
Skiner, John 445
Sleath, Gabriel 474
sleighs 407
slipware 30, 73
Smith & Sons 485
Smith, Benjamin 477, 549
Smith, Daniel 548
Smith, George 516
Smith, James 450
Smith, Stephen 515
Smith, Wm. 432
smoking 753
snooker tables 388
snuff bottles 700
snuff boxes 76, 483, 558, 673
snuff flasks 99
snufftaking 753
sofa tables 322–3, 398–9
sofas 308–9
Soldani-Benzi, Massimiliano 559
Solnhofer 472
Sorley, R. and W. 507, 537
soup plates 78
soup tureens 478
Southwark 71
spelter 688
Spence, Alexander 527
spill holders 37
spill vases 34–6, 98
spirit bottles 89, 202–3
spirit decanters 204–8
Splitgerber, David 477
Spode 48, 63, 104, 154
spoon trays 137
sports 680–4
    cricket 680
    fishing 680–3
    football 683
    golf 683
    miscellaneous 683–4
Staffordshire,
    bottles 29
    bowls 29
    coffee pots 533–4
    cow creamers 32
    cups 33, 69, 114
    dishes 47, 49
    figures 33–4, 43–4, 69–71, 128
    garden seats 74
    inkwells 140
    jugs 31, 52, 54–8
    money boxes 32
    mugs 60–1, 683
    pastille burners 76
    penholders 71
    pots 62, 73
    sauceboats 62
    services 63, 150–1, 536
    snuff boxes 673
    tea urns 548
    tureens 64–5
    vases 154
    Victorian figures 43–4
    watch holders 70
stands 310, 373–4, 710
Stankard, Paul 224
statues 482
Steiff 658–61, 665, 703
Steiner, Jules 654
steps 374
Stevens, Sam. 449
Steward, J.H. 493–4
Stickley, Gustav 623–6
Stinton, Harry 151–9, 535
Stinton, John 156
stirrup cups 114
Stollwerck 664
stoneware 632–6
stools 245, 311–12, 374–7, 746
Storr, Mortimer & Hunt 535

Storr, Paul 475–8, 514, 517–19, 534, 543, 549, 551
Stourbridge 226
Stradivari 721
Strasbourg 78
Street, R.W., & Co. 499
striking watches 469
sugar boxes 477, 539, 541, 545
supper tables 320
surveying 498–9
Sutherland tables 400
suzuribako 708
sweetmeat glasses 226
Swift, J., & Son 500
Swift, John 508
swords 760
Syng, Philip 477

T
table lamps 687–8
tables 245–51, 287, 313–25, 377–405, 626
    architects' 313
    breakfast 318
    card 313–14
    centre 246, 315–16, 385
    console 311–18
    counter 246
    cricket 250
    dining 246, 250, 318
    drawleaf 246
    drum 318–19
    games 319
    gateleg 245–7, 318
    library 318–19
    oak & country 245–51
    occasional 319
    pedestal 320
    pier 316
    pine 741–8
    pub 417
    refectory 247
    serving 320
    side 247–50, 321–2
    sofa 322–3
    supper 320
    tea 313, 323
    tripod 249–50, 323
    work 323
    writing 324
tables à écrire 325
tablesticks 474
tabourets 312
Tadolini, Scipione 482
tallboys 299, 341–4
tambour cylinder bureaux 264
tambour desks 302
tankards 152, 227, 477, 519–22
tapestries 642–3, 722
Tarra, N. 494
Taylor, Peter 545
Taylor, Samuel 538, 540
Taylor, William 549
tazzas 90, 203–4
tea caddies 538–48
    glass 541–7
    ivory 548
    paperwork 484
    silver 477–8, 538–48
    tortoiseshell 542–5, 547
    wood 540, 542–4, 541–7
tea and coffee pots 81
tea cosies 553
tea kettles 549–50
tea kettles pointer 549
tea services,
    porcelain 82
    silver 477, 535–8, 628
    silver plated 547
tea strainers 553
tea tables 313, 323, 400–1
tea urns 548–9
teacups and saucers 177
teapots 97, 476, 550–2
teapoys 327
teddy bears 658–61, 703
telephones 671–7
telescopes 472–3, 499
terracotta 482, 604, 632–4
    busts 482, 600, 604, 704
    figures 704
Terratti, A. 495
Terrey, John Edward 544

Terry, I.E. 550
tester beds 231, 252, 288
Tetard, E.D. 476
Tetard Frères 477, 628
textiles 611–12, 637–43, 722–3
 costume 611–12, 637–8
 embroidery 638–9
 lace 639–41
 miscellaneous 643
 samplers 642
 tapestries 642–3, 722
theatre ephemera 731–3
Theobalds, William 530
thermometers 473
Thibault 468
thimbles 610
Thompson, Robert 596
Thorne, Samuel 539
Tiffany 458–9, 474, 525, 572, 621
tiles 64, 75
Timbroll, Robert 533
tinplate 662–4, 701
Tipp & Co. 662–3
tobacco jars 673
Toby jugs 55–60, 73–4
toilet mirrors 305, 360–2, 364
toilet tables 401
Tokkuri 193
Tondino 72
Tookey, Thomas 515
tools 753
torchères 310, 713–14
tortoiseshell 542–5, 547, 670, 673, 675
Tourneau 471
toys 658–67, 701
 automata 658, 701
 lead soldiers and figures 661–2
 miscellaneous 664–5
 money banks 662
 teddy bears 658–61, 703
 tinplate 662–4, 701
Transitional 88, 171, 190, 192
Transitional wares pointer 183
transport 677–8
tray top tables 321
trays 478, 710
 silver 527–8, 627
treen 753
tribal art 690–2
tripod tables 249–50, 323, 402
trivets 567
Troby, John 528
Troubetskoy, Prince Paul
Troughton & Simms 472
tsuitate 709
tub chairs 296
Tudman, James 461
Tudric 579–80
Tuite, William 540
tumblers 222–3
Tunbridge ware 674–5, 755–7
tureens,
 oriental 191–2
 porcelain 83–4, 87–8, 152–3

pottery 64–5
silver 478, 527, 628
silver plate 531
turner's chairs 237
Twentyman, William Henry 548
tygs 29

U
uniforms 761
Universal 471
universal ring dials 473
Upjohn, Thomas 448
Upjohn, Will. 450
Urbino 72
urn stands 310, 373
urns 421–5, 482, 484, 548–9

V
Vacheron & Constantin 469, 471, 491–2
Van Erp, Dirk 623
vases 710
 glass 225–6, 611–18, 620–3
 oriental 192–200
 porcelain 83, 88, 153–60
 pottery 65–7, 74, 98–100, 614
 silver 628
vegetable dishes 475
vehicles 677
Velasco, Juan A. Sanz de 510
Venetian,
 bowls 90, 203–4
 furniture 265, 362–3, 398
 goblets 214
 scent bottles 227–8
 vases 225
Venice 81
Venini 622
Verberckt, Jan Baptist 476
verge watches 469
vestas 674
Vienna 135, 137–8, 146, 159–60
Vienna regulator pointer 485
viewers 505
vinaigrette flasks 230
vinaigrettes 92
Vincennes 78, 715
Vincent, William 541
Viner, Edward 523
violins 721
violoncellos 721
vitrine tables 389
vitrines 267–9
Vonham, Frederick 477
Vuitton, Louis 678–9
Vulliamy, Benjamin 451, 454, 467–8

W
W.M.F. 579–81, 599, 627–8
W.M.F. pointer 581

Wadere, H. 475
wainscot chairs 236
Wakelin, Edward 476, 478, 544
Wakelin, John 506, 524, 549
Walker 450–2
Walker & Hall 524, 526
Walker, John 452, 455, 512
walking sticks 754
wall appliqués 688–9
wall brackets 327
wall clocks 468, 481–7
wall lights 715
wall mirrors 305, 363–4
Waltershausen 656
Walton 56
wardrobes 326, 328, 350–1, 626
 breakfront 326
 pine 328, 748–9
washstands 310, 406, 750
watches 469–71, 488–92
water glasses 222
Watson, Henry 451
Watson, W., & Sons 504
wax dolls 641–7
weathervanes 567
Webb 204
Wedgwood 48–9, 54, 62–3, 74
Wedgwood & Bentley 30, 61
Weiss 502
Welch, John 441
Wellington 209
Wellington chests 344
Wemyss 67–8, 93–4
Westclox 487
whatnots 310, 401–7
Wheeler and Cronin 511
Whieldon 55, 60, 69–72, 74
Whipham & Wright 520, 548
Whipman, Thomas 548
White, E. 454
White, Fuller 534
White, John 534
Whiting, John James 515
Widenham 455
Wilkinson 57
Wilkinson, Henry, & Co. Ltd. 510
Wilkinson, Thomas 466
Willaume, David 517
Williamson, Timy 469
Winchester 717
Winder, William 450
Windmills, Joseph 452, 461, 466
Windsor chairs 234–6, 286
Windsor, Robert 452
wine antiques 554–7
wine coasters 555–6
wine coolers 325, 327, 478, 554–5
wine coolers pointer 555
wine cups 177
wine ewers 86
wine flutes 209
wine funnels 556
wine glasses 89–90, 209, 214–

23, 571–7
wine tables 402
Winkler, F.E. 703
Winterhalter, Franz Xaver 562
Wisden 680
Wise, J. 466
Withers, William 452
Wolfsohn, Helena 159
Wood, Enoch 59
Wood, Ralph 31, 35, 38–9, 41–2, 55, 58–9
Wood, Samuel 513
woodcarvings 482, 604–6
Woodward, Horace 514
Worcester,
 asparagus servers 160
 baskets 102
 bottles 75, 103
 bowls 75, 104–5
 butter tubs 152
 candlesticks 685
 cups 76, 109–14, 535
 dishes 133–7, 139
 figures 122
 inkwells 140
 jardinières 140
 jugs 75, 79, 141–3
 mugs 144
 plates 79, 132, 134, 138
 pots 141–7
 sauceboats 147
 saucers 76
 services 150–1, 535
 spittoons 160
 spoons 161
 tankards 152
 tea caddies 539
 teapots 81, 550
 tureens 83, 153
 vases 83, 155–7
work tables 323, 403
Worth 228–9
Wrangham, John 526
Wright, Charles 520, 548
Wright, Frank Lloyd 625–6, 630
Wright, William 435
wristwatches 470–1, 490–2
writing slopes 484
writing tables 324–5, 404–5
Wucai 84, 173, 189–90

Y
Yeadon, William 452
Yeates, Andrew 496
Yixing 200
Yorkshire 58–9
Younge, S.C. and Co. 530

Z
Zeiss, Carl 500, 504
Zincke, Christian Friedrich 483

LAKESIDE
l i m i t e d

LAKESIDES FURNITURE FEATURES STRONG, CLASSIC DESIGNS
WHETHER FOR THE AMERICAN OR EUROPEAN MARKET.
USING ONLY OLD OR WELL SEASONED MATERIALS, THE HIGHEST
QUALITY IS ASSURED

OUR SKILLED CRAFTSMAN MAKE EACH PIECE INDIVIDUALLY TO
EXACT STANDARDS THEREFORE WE CAN TAILOR TO SPECIFIC NEEDS.
WE CAN ALSO MANUFACTURE CUSTOMISED DESIGNS IN A
VARIETY OF MATERIALS.